Notes from the
Grooming Table

An All-Breed Grooming Guide for the Professional Pet Stylist

by Melissa Verplank, CMG

with Illustrations by Lisa VanSweden

Published by White Dog Enterprises, Inc.

WHITE DOG ENTERPRISES, Inc.
16060 Peach Ridge Avenue
Kent City Michigan 49330

~ To My Father ~

*For his constant support as
I have followed
my passions and my dreams.*

White Dog Enterprises educational materials may be purchased
in bulk for educational, business or sales promotional use.
For information, please write:

White Dog Enterprises, Inc.
16060 Peach Ridge Avenue
Kent City, Michigan 49330

www.whitedogenterpriscs.com

Published by WHITE DOG ENTERPRISES, Inc.
16060 Peach Ridge Avenue Kent City Michigan 49330

A subsidiary of The Paragon School of Pet Grooming, Inc.
110 Chicago Drive Jenison Michigan 49428

While the purpose of this book is for the enhanced grooming practices for
professional pet groomers and stylists, every effort has been made to showcase
exceptional representation of all the breeds, based on the written breed standard
per the American Kennel Club, Inc. Many different references and observations
were chosen and combined to illustrate each dog individually and perchance it
may represent any one person's pet, property or work is purely coincidental.

ISBN Number : 978-0-692-65807-9

Printed in the United States

Acknowledgements

I want to thank everyone who made the dream of creating this book a reality, especially Lisa VanSweden, whose unbelievable talent was totally unleashed with the hundreds of realistic images she created for this book. I am so grateful for her complete dedication and commitment to me and to this project.

Professional pet grooming is ever-changing. New tools are developed. Products are created to help us do our jobs better. New breeds are introduced to the American Kennel Club. Grooming styles and trends evolve over the years. I feel fortunate to continue my grooming education through the talent of all my *Learn2GroomDogs.com* training partners. The knowledge these top stylists possess is immense. With every video we film and produce, I learn something. To date there are over 500 educational pet grooming videos in the on-line library. As I revised this edition of *Notes From the Grooming Table*, I have been able to incorporate much of their knowledge within its pages.

Special thanks go out to a few exceptionally talented stylists whose enthusiasm and critical review was extremely helpful. Kendra Otto for her help and guidance with the rustic coated dogs. Lisa Leady in providing wonderful reference material for the Smooth Fox Terrier. Irina "Pina" Pinkusevich for her help searching out grooming directions for the Berger Picard and the Belgian Laekenois.

I'm grateful to all of my entire team of incredible key staff members. They have allowed me to grow multiple companies beyond what I ever imagined. Their commitment to each business—and to me—is unwavering. They have allowed me to continually focus on enhancing our educational product lines. Special thanks go out to: Teresa Dreese, Joelle Asmondy, Ryan Walsh, Leslie Sowers, and Sue Hess.

Sue Bakkila has done an amazing job reformatting the entire book. Her eye for detail and thoroughness during the entire book revising project has been nothing short of brilliant. Barry Heydenberk has done a fabulous job organizing the entire publishing process while keeping us on task and focused!

I am eternally grateful to all the talented stylists, handlers, judges, competitors, students and professionals who shared their knowledge with me throughout my career. Without your generosity, *Notes* would yet remain a dream. Their interest and encouragement have been the driving force to the completion of this book. Thank you.

Heartfelt gratitude also must go to my best friend and extremely talented canine stylist, Marc LaFleur. I could not have done this without his assistance, patience, professional criticism, commitment, and love. He is my biggest supporter and cheerleader.

Notes From The Grooming Table ©2016

Table of Contents: Volume One

Table of Contents: Volume One

Table of Contents: Volume One

THE WORKING GROUP

For the second half of the book, please see:
Notes from the Grooming Table, Volume Two.

Table of Contents: Volume Two

Table of Contents: Volume Two

Table of Contents: Volume Two

14

Introduction

All of us who entered this profession did so because we followed a dream, a passion—
we simply love dogs. So much so, we have opted to make them our career. Not all
careers or job opportunities start this way. Those of us who have chosen this path
are truly fortunate to be able to follow our dreams.

Notes from the Grooming Table is designed as a basic educational resource for the
professional pet groomer. The illustrations work hand-in-hand with the text to make
Notes easy to understand and follow, whether you are learning how to groom all
breeds or just need a quick refresher on a more unusual breed. It was designed to
put solid foundation skills at your fingertips in a single source.

I recognize there are multiple styling options for the pet dog. Many dogs that
are traditionally hand-stripped or shown in a natural full coat are clipper-cut in
the pet world. Although I always encourage pet stylists to closely adhere to breed
standards, that sometimes isn't feasible for the pet, the owner or the stylist. Learning
to understand and interpret the correct breed standard for all purebreds is critical
to capturing the proper essence of the breed. Whether the dog is a champion
conformation winner or simply a beloved family pet, a well balanced, stylish and
impeccable finish will always reflect positively on any grooming salon.

Introduction

It is important to remember that owners have pets for different reasons. Not all owners want a "show dog" look. They may simply want a handsome family pet that is clean and well groomed. It's our job to assist the owner in that pet care responsibility. There are hundreds of styling options that will be appropriate to the animal based on the lifestyle of the pet and the owner's wishes. Our role is to select the styling option that will make the owner and the pet happy. It also may be necessary to educate the owner on proper pet hygiene, or to teach the owner to brush between professional groomings. No matter what the owner requests, we, as professionals, should never put the dog at risk of injury or loss of dignity. Always practice the golden rule for all professional pet groomers and stylists—humanity before vanity.

Notes from the Grooming Table is a wonderful collection of information gleaned from a career that has spanned more than 30 years. I am a self-taught stylist. Over the years, I have worked with thousands of dogs, testing ideas and perfecting skills. My classroom was on-the-job training and learning through hundreds of lectures, seminars and workshops across the country. I learned and perfected my craft in the contest arena and in my mobile grooming van with everyday client pets. I listened to top stylists, judges, handlers and breeders who graciously took the time to share their knowledge with me. Conformational dog shows, breed books and the study of canine structure and movement all are indispensable tools when learning the finer details of professional pet styling. This all-breed grooming guide is a collection of information gathered through years of personal study and the knowledge shared by true professionals.

Introduction

Notes From the Grooming Table is not designed to be the culmination of your educational pursuit, but a stepping stone in what I hope is a long and fulfilling career. Learning is a continual process and as your own methods and skills develop, you will discover more specialized information on how to enhance a particular breed or individual dog. Knowing this, I have left plenty of room for your own "notes." I encourage you to constantly learn and strive to be the best you can be, in every aspect of your career as a professional pet groomer and stylist. The excitement of learning new things, the satisfaction on an owner's face and a happy, well groomed animal are among the many reasons that make this such a rewarding career.

Enjoy the quest of being the best you can be and keeping both your two-legged and four-legged clients happy.

Happy Trimming!

19

Canine Anatomy

Whether a Yorkshire Terrier, a Great Dane, a Bulldog or a Dachshund—all dogs possess identical bone and muscle structure. Fundamentally, they all are the same. The domestic dog is a human-made creature developed from generations of carefully controlled breeding practices. We have created dogs to assist us in many daily functions.

Many breeds still excel at their original functions or jobs, such as herding, hunting or tracking. As times changed, some were no longer required to perform their initial roles, even though the breed itself remains with us today. Other breeds have evolved a proficiency in other activities that allow them to continue to assist people.

For every purebred dog, there is a written standard developed by parent breed organizations that outlines what the "ideal" dog of that breed should look like. That "look" is a key part of maintaining a dog in a condition to perform its original job with the highest degree of proficiency. In other words, to help it be all it can be.

Being able to decipher the official breed standard can be challenging at first. Speaking the "language" is a key component to understanding how to work professionally with the canine species.

In order to safely handle a dog for grooming or to style the dog to accentuate its best features, you need to understand basic anatomy and individual breed standards.

- What are the key components that make up a structurally sound and balanced animal, purebred or mixed breed?

- How do you measure or select reference points?

- How do you apply those points in the trimming process?

- How can you handle or manipulate the dog to create a harmonious relationship?

On dogs with definite trim styles, a pet stylist can accentuate proper structure while minimizing conformational faults. To the untrained eye, accentuating or detracting the conformation of the pet will be subtle, but will make a large difference in the overall quality of the haircut.

Your familiarity with its natural limitation of movement can make grooming much more comfortable for the pet. When the pet is comfortable, it is much more willing to cooperate.

Understanding key pressure points and holds allows both the pet and the stylist the greatest degree of safety through the entire grooming process.

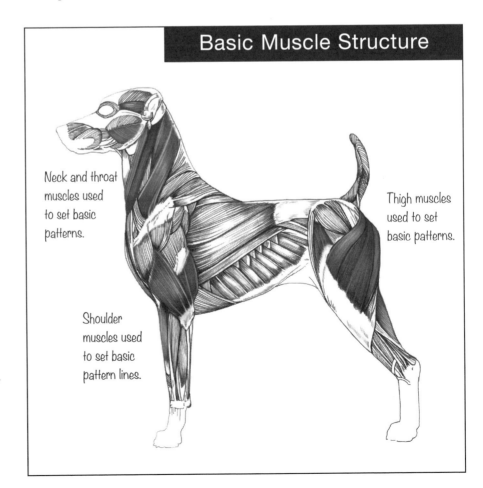

Basic Muscle Structure

Neck and throat muscles used to set basic patterns.

Thigh muscles used to set basic patterns.

Shoulder muscles used to set basic pattern lines.

Canine Anatomy

Topographical Anatomy

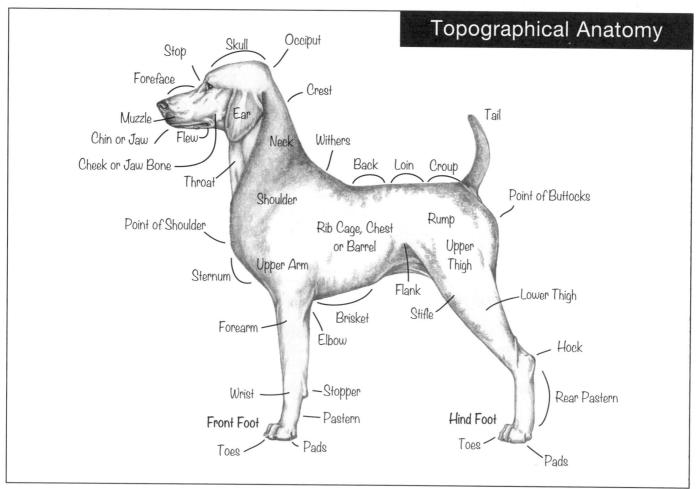

Stop
Skull
Occiput
Foreface
Crest
Muzzle
Ear
Tail
Chin or Jaw
Flew
Neck
Withers
Cheek or Jaw Bone
Back
Loin
Croup
Throat
Point of Buttocks
Shoulder
Rump
Point of Shoulder
Rib Cage, Chest or Barrel
Upper Thigh
Upper Arm
Sternum
Lower Thigh
Flank
Forearm
Brisket
Stifle
Elbow
Hock
Wrist
Stopper
Rear Pastern
Front Foot
Pastern
Hind Foot
Toes
Pads
Toes
Pads

Bone Structure

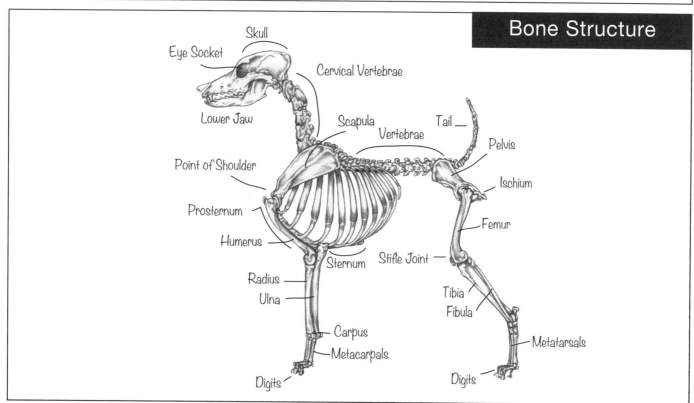

Skull
Eye Socket
Cervical Vertebrae
Lower Jaw
Scapula
Tail
Vertebrae
Pelvis
Point of Shoulder
Ischium
Prosternum
Femur
Humerus
Stifle Joint
Sternum
Radius
Ulna
Tibia
Fibula
Carpus
Metatarsals
Metacarpals
Digits
Digits

Notes From The Grooming Table ©2016

Canine Anatomy

STRUCTURE OF A DOG— FRONT AND REAR ASSEMBLIES

Front Assembly

This area makes up the shoulder and front legs. It consists of bones, muscles and tendons. The angles of the bones, combined with their length, dictate how efficiently the dog will move. The shoulder blade is held in place by muscles and tendons that allow for good forward and back movement, but limited movement side to side. Some dogs are more limber than others. When lifting a foot or leg, never extend it beyond the point of mild resistance when the dog is relaxed.

Rear Assembly

These are the bones, muscles and tendons that make up the hips and rear legs. The angles of the bones, combined with their length, dictate how efficiently the dog will move. The pelvic and femur bones are held in place by a ball and socket that form the hip joint. The ball and socket offers a greater degree of rotation through the hip joint than in the front assembly. However, older dogs or dogs with joint discomfort will not be as flexible as a pet that is pain free. When lifting a foot or leg, never extend it beyond the point of mild resistance when the dog is relaxed.

MEASURING OUT A DOG — KEY LANDMARKS

Finding the Outline of a Dog

The overall length of a dog is measured from the point of shoulder to the point of rump and from withers to ground. The distance between the withers and the top of the elbow and the distance between the elbow and the ground will dictate the overall balance and proportion of a dog. Most breed standards refer to the body proportion as being square or rectangular.

Measuring the Head

Skull types come in a wide variety of shapes and sizes. The overall length refers to the points from the occiput to the tip of the nose. The stop area is frequently used as a key measuring point of the relationship between the length of the top of the skull and the muzzle.

Pattern Setting

All patterns are set in relationship to the bones and muscles on the dog. There are a few key areas about the neck, chest, shoulders, ribs and thighs that allow stylists to set body patterns on the dog that are well balanced and symmetrical. On the head, the key pattern-setting points are the stop area, eye socket rims, ears, cheeks and the back corners of the mouth, and the occiput.

On trimmed pets, pattern placement is critical to creating a stylish haircut that accentuates the dog's features in a positive light. Balance, style and flair all are seen at their best when a trim is founded on a sound basic knowledge of overall canine anatomy. Like anything else, the more knowledge one has on a topic, the easier it is to apply. And, with time, correct application will become second nature.

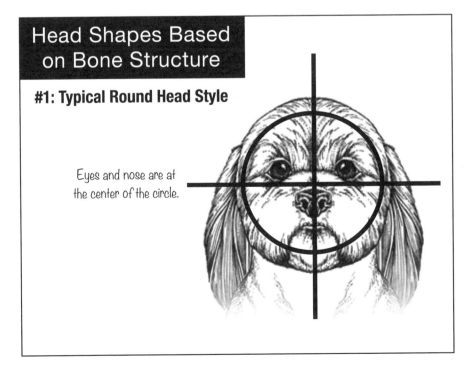

Head Shapes Based on Bone Structure

#1: Typical Round Head Style

Eyes and nose are at the center of the circle.

Head Shapes Based on Bone Structure

#2: Typical Poodle Topknot

Topknot flare follows the planes of the cheek bones. Lay a comb along side face to check the line. Hair falling outside the line is removed, hair inside the line stays.

Height of topknot is roughly the same distance as between outside corners of the eyes.

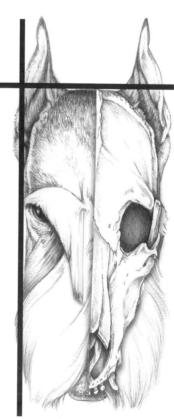

Head Shapes Based on Bone Structure

#3: Typical Rectangular Head Style

Hair inside the line stays; remove if outside the line.

Straight line along the side of the skull. Use a greyhound comb to double check your work.

Eye socket ridge creates the arched line for the brows.

Notes From The Grooming Table ©2016

Canine Anatomy

Common Measuring Points Used in Breed Standard Descriptions in Reference to Canine Grooming

Squarely-Built Body Outline

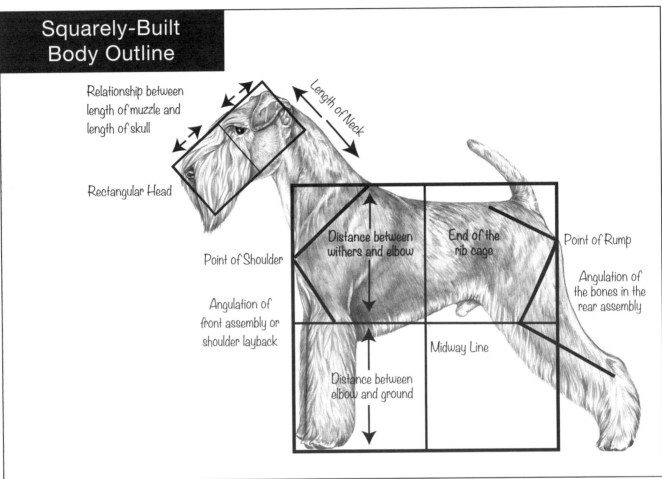

Relationship between length of muzzle and length of skull

Length of Neck

Rectangular Head

Point of Shoulder

Distance between withers and elbow

End of the rib cage

Point of Rump

Angulation of front assembly or shoulder layback

Angulation of the bones in the rear assembly

Midway Line

Distance between elbow and ground

Rectangular Body Outline

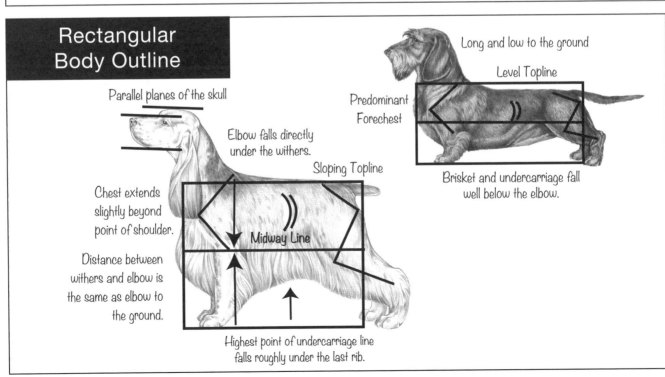

Parallel planes of the skull

Long and low to the ground

Level Topline

Elbow falls directly under the withers.

Predominant Forechest

Sloping Topline

Chest extends slightly beyond point of shoulder.

Midway Line

Brisket and undercarriage fall well below the elbow.

Distance between withers and elbow is the same as elbow to the ground.

Highest point of undercarriage line falls roughly under the last rib.

Canine Anatomy

Common Physical Landmarks Used in Pattern Setting

Patterns are Set Based on Bone and Muscle Structure

Topknot is set at the bony ridge that separates the top skull from the cheek and jowl areas.

Top of the tail pom-pom should be almost level with the skull.

The end ⅔ of the tail is covered with fur creating the rounded pom-pom of a poodle tail.

The neck line runs along the muscle at the sides of the throat that runs from the base of the ear to just above the breast bone. On many dogs, a cowlick seam parallels this muscle too.

Angulation of the rear assembly is set by following the muscles of the thigh. The angulation of the rear leg accentuates the point where the muscles and tendons converge.

Shoulder and legs are separated by the turn of the shoulder muscle where it meets the top of the leg at the elbow.

Pattern lines and undercarriage lines are set at the center line of the dog. The last two ribs normally mark this point on the body.

The digits of the foot are clipped to a point where the bones of the feet meet the metatarsal bones or the bones of the pasterns. There is a slight bump on the sides of the foot where these bones join.

Notes From The Grooming Table ©2016

Tools and Equipment

There is a wide variety of equipment and supplies available to the professional pet care specialist. The proper selection and care of this equipment, as well as the proper selection of all grooming supplies, is essential to efficient grooming.

The professional must have a thorough knowledge of this subject in order to understand advances made by equipment and supply manufacturers and to distinguish high quality from inferior tools. High quality equipment can last many years and facilitate the art of grooming.

Variety is important, too. Try different types of equipment and tools. With practice, you will be able to match the dog's needs to your skills and the right equipment. Having the right tool handy for the right job will contribute to your overall efficiency.

Professional Clipper

Professional clippers with detachable blades are the first choice of most professional groomers. In addition to the standard electric corded clipper, rechargeable cordless clippers are available in the full sized models.

Smaller, lightweight clippers and trimmers are also available. These smaller clippers typically have a single blade that adjusts to multiple lengths. Simply by pushing a small lever, the cutting range of the blade varies between a #30 to a #9 blade length. These clippers come with a selection of guard combs that fit over the blade for longer cutting options.

To work properly, clippers must be maintained and kept clean. Don't neglect routine maintenance. Hair should be regularly removed from the external moving parts with a small brush. On certain clippers, the cap on the bottom can be removed to grease the gears. Oil should only be added about once a year, or when a clipper begins to squeal. Read the owner's manual for individual maintenance requirements for each model.

Blades

Clipper blades are an extremely important part of the professional groomer's equipment list. Blades must be properly maintained for optimum performance. New blades may be coated with a protective substance that must be removed with a cleaner, such as a blade wash, before they can be used. Make sure the blade is dry before using it on a pet. Most blades consist of several pieces and are assembled with proper tension and alignment. With constant use, the tension on these blades can vary, causing a blade to "drag." Blade drag also can occur from hair stuck between the blade parts, generally caused when the clipper is pulled too quickly through a coat. Dropping a blade is a sure way to render it useless. Routinely inspect blades for broken or chipped teeth. If damaged, consider replacing the blade to avoid injury to the pet. Regular cleaning of blades will keep them in optimal operating condition. Quick cleaning can be accomplished with one of the many "cooling-lubricant" sprays available on the market. For a more thorough cleaning, separate the blades and clean them with a blade wash, spray or oil. Blade chatter occurs when blades are not aligned properly. In many cases, a groomer can realign these blades with pliers or a screwdriver. If a clipper does not cut after these adjustments, it should be sent to a carefully selected professional blade sharpener. During use, it is important to keep the blade from heating due to friction. A hot blade can burn a pet. Blades can be cooled by several methods, such as using a spray coolant during use or simply switching to a different blade while allowing the first to cool.

Guard Combs /Snap-On Combs or Attach-On Combs

The terminology for this item is interchangeable. Guard combs, snap-on combs, or attach-on combs—they all do basically the same thing. They act as an extension of metal blades by snapping over the top of them to allow for longer trimming. They come in either plastic or metal. Some are held in place with a spring attachment. Others simply glide into place. Others are held onto the main blade magnetically.

There are a wide variety of guard combs fluctuating greatly in size. The size range will leave coats from under ¼ inch long to over a full 1 inch with the mega combs—and everything in between. The most commonly used guard combs leave the coat between ½ inch to a little over ¾ inch. With each brand and coat type, there will be slight variances as to how each comb cuts through a coat. Experiment with your guard comb set of choice.

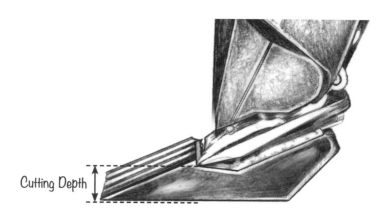

Cutting Depth

Term Used In This Book

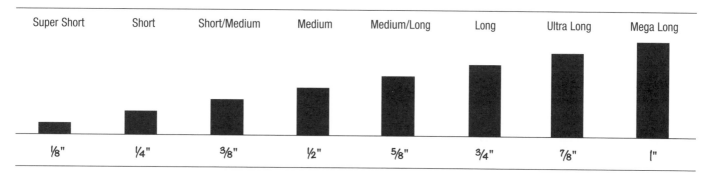

Super Short	Short	Short/Medium	Medium	Medium/Long	Long	Ultra Long	Mega Long
⅛"	¼"	⅜"	½"	⅝"	¾"	⅞"	1"

Estimated Length of Remaining Coat

Tools and Equipment

Scissors and Shears

TOOLS & EQUIPMENT

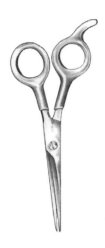

Straight scissors are the all-purpose scissoring tool of the groomer and are used for cutting straight planes, general body scissoring and scissor finishing. Heavier scissors are better suited to cut through thicker, dense coats.

Thinning Shears & Blenders

They are available in various sizes and tooth configurations. They are used for bulk thinning and blending the coat. The most preferred thinners are made with one straight blade and one toothed blade. Double-sided thinners are available but not generally used by professionals. The amount of fur that a shear will cut is dictated by the amount of hair trapped at the top of the teeth when the blades are closed. The smaller the teeth, the finer the blend. Usually, a coarser shear with fewer teeth is preferred when bulk thinning a thick coat, a finer toothed thinner is favored for top thinning and blending.

Scissors/Shears

There are many types of scissors, but a select few are particularly useful in grooming. Keep in mind that high quality shears hold an edge longer that inexpensive ones. Scissor maintenance is simple but important. Keep the scissor blades clean, oiled and dry to ensure long life. Any scissors that are dropped will, in most cases, need to be sent out for sharpening. Be selective when choosing a scissor sharpener. Scissors are produced in various metals, such as carbon steel, stainless steel and cobalt. They are made in three basic types: straight, curved, and thinning.

The shear style is represented by varying degrees of shear weight, blade widths and shank lengths. The wide assortment of styles allows for a comfortable fit for all hand sizes. Straight scissors range in size, weight and style, from more than 10 inches to less than 5 inches. A general rule is the larger the dog, the longer the scissors used.

Curved scissors also come in a variety of sizes and degree of curve. These scissors are best on curved areas of the dog such as topknots, to set angulation on the rear legs and to round the feet. A longer scissor with a less dramatic curve should be used on the larger breeds and a shorter more dramatic curve should be used on the smaller breed.

Chunkers /Super Blenders

Chunkers or super blenders are a welcome addition to a serious pet stylist's tool kit. They have much coarser teeth than a typical thinning shear. They come in standard and longer lengths designed for adding texture and volume to a coat. They are a huge time saver when it comes to removing coat, softening lines, smoothing out rough areas, blending, and feathering shorter coat into longer areas on almost any dog or coat type.

Brushes and Combs

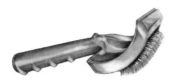

Pin Brush
The pin brush preserves long coats by minimizing hair breakage. Pin brushes are available in many different sizes and styles. The long polished pins have rounded tips to minimize scratching and skin irritation. Pin brushes are most often used for breeds with long flowing coats in good condition or on dogs with long show coats.

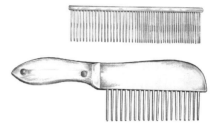

Brushes
Brushes come in various types and sizes for specific purposes. Common ones include slicker brushes, pin brushes and a rubber curry brush. The slicker brush is the favorite of most professional groomers. It comes in various sizes, both flat and curved, and has close-set, bent wire teeth that are either firm or soft. The heavier slicker is ideal for dense coats that are curly, wavy or straight. It is also used for removing undercoat on double-coated breeds, such as the Arctic and shepherd breeds. The softer slicker is designed for delicate skin commonly found on puppies or small dogs with fine fur. The slicker is considered an all-purpose brush and can be used for all but the short, fine-coated breeds such as the Boxer and Dalmatian. It is important to note that an improperly used slicker can severely injure a pet by scraping the skin and causing brush burn.

Rubber Brushes
Rubber brushes come in various sizes and teeth configurations. They are excellent for fine coated or shorthaired dogs. In the tub, it is a highly efficient tool as a shampoo brush for many large breeds of all coat types. Other types of brushes available to the professional groomer are the terrier palm pad, bristle brush, hound glove and palm brush.

Combs
Combs are produced in various styles, widths and lengths, with handles and without. The comb generally is used in conjunction with the brush to untangle a coat when preparing the pet for a bath. The comb also is used in combination with scissors in finish grooming. The best combs are made of chrome or Teflon-plated brass and have strong tempered teeth with rounded tips to prevent scratching and skin irritation. Most professional groomers prefer the "greyhound" comb—a combination of fine/medium or medium/coarse comb without a handle. Also popular is the wide-toothed comb used for longer, dense coats. The wide-toothed comb, however, can miss small tangles, so it is best used simultaneously with a greyhound comb.

General Tools

Nail Clippers
Nail clippers are available in two basic types—the guillotine and scissor. It is all a matter of personal preference as to which nail trimmer is used. However, the scissor type can be more adaptable to multiple nail situations. Some of the scissor type nail trimmers are spring-loaded with a safety stop that limits the amount of nail trimmed. Electric nail grinders also are available. Extreme caution should be exercised when using this tool because the grinder will file the nail very quickly and also has the tendency to catch the longer hair around the foot, which will then wrap around the grinder. Metal or large coarse nail files can be used to smooth the nail after clipping.

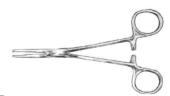

Hemostats
Hemostats are used to remove hair from inside the ears of certain breeds, for applying bows, and removing ticks. Styles available include different lengths, curved or straight, locking or non-locking. It is all a matter of personal preference.

Tools and Equipment

Shedding, Undercoat, Stripping and Dematting Tools

Shedding Tools

Shedding tools are used for removing loose coat. There are many styles, shapes and sizes. The shedding blade, for example, has a long, flexible metal blade with leather handles on each end and both a smooth and a serrated edge. The blade can be held in two hands or bent into a teardrop shape and held with one hand. With proper use it becomes an excellent tool for removing loose undercoat from double-coated breeds.

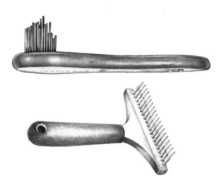

Rakes

Dog grooming rakes are used on thick double coats, heavy coats or rustic coat types. They have teeth designed to remove the dead coat while leaving the top outer coat undisturbed. Typically, these rakes are designed in a "T" shape or with pins at one end of the handle. They have single or double rounded pins that sink into the coat, gliding through thick coats with relative ease.

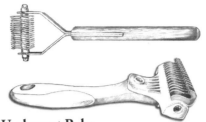

Undercoat Rake

Undercoat rakes have many small, curved blades set close together that remove undercoat. They are available in a variety of tooth widths making this tool suitable for a wide range of breeds. On shedding breeds, they can remove dead, fuzzy undercoat in minutes yet leave the top coat shiny and healthy. On harsh coated dogs, they mimic the hand-stripped look quickly and easily. Undercoat rakes can be used on a wet or a dry coat.

Pumice Stone

This is a light, porous piece of stone-like material that is dark gray in color. The abrasive surface makes it an ideal tool to pull soft undercoat from a dog's coat. It can be used either by dragging the stone over the top of the coat or by working a seam line, much in the same manner as line combing and line brushing.

Stripping Knives

Stripping knives have several purposes and are available in many different styles. Most professional groomers have a collection of strippers to deal with a wide array of coat types. They are single blades with varying degrees of serrated edges or detailing sticks. Some are used to strip out loose topcoat of the terrier type, or harsh-coated breeds. Others are used to "card" the undercoat and can be used on a variety of breeds including silky or shedding breeds. Others can even be used on shorthaired cats. The only way to know which tool is best for a particular job is to try it or talk with seasoned stylists who specialize in this grooming technique.

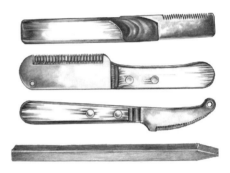

Dematting Tools

De-matting tools come in many types. They are used in conjunction with brushes and combs to remove mats from a coat by cutting through the mat and breaking it into smaller pieces. As dematting tools are very sharp, the procedure requires the utmost attention and care to prevent injury to the pet.

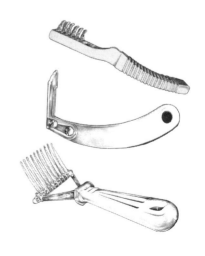

Drying Tools

High-Velocity Dryer
High-velocity dryers are used in all stages of grooming and drying. The high air velocity blows water off the coat, straightens the hair shaft, adds volume to the coat, aids in dematting and de-shedding, is highly adaptable to many coat types and is extremely safe to use on most pets.

Stand Dryers
Hair dryers are made as either heat element dryers or high-velocity dryers or a combination of both. Choosing the proper dryer will greatly facilitate grooming. Proper care and maintenance of dryers will result in years of reliable service. The key to maintaining a dryer is to keep it free of hair, which tends to accumulate on the intake screen. Routine external cleaning of this area will extend the life of the dryer. Heat-element dryers have a motor and a fan that blows air past a heating element. Different models offer varying fan speeds and adjustable heat controls. These dryers are generally used during the final phase of drying. Proper drying technique with a brush and warm stand dryer will result in the desired straight coat, ready for finishing.

Kennel Dryers
A kennel dryer is an enclosed space that holds a pet while passing a gentle air stream over the animal. This is considered an inactive drying tool and is designed as an aid in the final drying of certain pets. It is not meant to be the only drying tool in a salon. Combined with active drying methods, a kennel dryer can efficiently speed up the process. **Pets need to be constantly monitored while in a kennel dryer.** *For the safety of the pet, very little or no heat should be used in a kennel dryer.*

Grooming Stations, Kennel Units, Safety and Convenience Items

Grooming Stations
Grooming stations are available in different configurations and with such options as one-piece modular units with built-in mirrors, drawers, cabinets, electrical outlets, etc. Stations are chosen by personal preference.

Kennel Units
Kennel units are available in wire, plastic, solid fiberglass, Formica and stainless steel. Stainless steel will last the longest and is generally the most expensive. Formica kennels are the next most expensive, followed by fiberglass. Personal preference usually determines the choice. Least expensive is the wire and plastic kennel, which makes it a popular choice when budget is a concern.

Clipper Vacuuming System
The clipper vacuuming system is an excellent hygienic choice and a great supplement to the clipper. It is based on a central vacuum type system and attaches to the clipper with a hose. The clipper vacuum sucks up clipped hair and prevents tiny hairs from floating in the air. But more than a benefit to the environment and to good health, the system also produces a smooth finish.

Grooming Loops
Grooming loops are made of different materials. The most common is the flat nylon type with a metal clip. The grooming loop is the pet's safety loop —and yours. Always adjust it so the dog can stand comfortably but has very little slack in the tension.

Muzzles
Muzzles are an important part of the groomer's tool kit and can help prevent dogs from biting you. There are many varieties, including metal basket, plastic basket, nylon, Velcro and leather.

Elizabethan Collars
These collars may be used to prevent injury to the groomer from a biting dog or cat. They look like a large plastic cone that fits snugly around the neck but leaves the head and face open. The stylist must keep his hands behind the collar to remain safe.

Grooming Aprons & Smocks
Grooming apparel promotes a professional appearance and is necessary to keep a stylist clean and free of hair. There are many styles and colors. Most are made of fabrics that will repel water, hair and soil.

Detailing Items

Bathing Systems

For years, hand washing pets was considered standard practice and it is still common practice. However, today we are seeing an assortment of bathing systems bolstering standard hand washing practices. Hydrobathing is powerful recirculating washing method. These systems use a limited amount of water and shampoo combined with powerful water flow to cleanse the dog. Other systems premix the shampoo with the water.

Saving time is one of the largest benefits to these bathing systems. Plus, many conserve water and shampoo as well.

Bathing Aids

Bathing aids facilitate getting the pet's coat cleaner than by simply using your hands and fingers. By using a bathing aid, or a combination of aids, you will be able to penetrate the coat better, allowing dirt and debris to be swiftly lifted away. May groomers find it beneficial to use any of the following on different coat types to get their pets clean in the least amount of time: bathing mitts, rubber curries, scrub brushes, toothbrushes around the eye area, washcloths, natural loofahs or bathing scrubbies. It is important to match the best bathing aids to the coat type and skin sensitivity with each pet for their safety and comfort.

Bows & Bandanas

These are an optional decorative finish to a groomed pet. Bows are commonly applied to the ears or in a tied-up topknot but other areas of the pet's body can be used as well. Some stylists prefer to attach a bow to a collar or add a colorful bandana to the pet's wardrobe.

Perfumes & Colognes

The finale of most professional grooms is a small spritz of perfume or cologne on a freshly groomed dog. A light fragrance is intended to enhance the grooming experience for the pet owner. However, remember that some people are highly sensitive to different smells or may be allergic to fragrances altogether. Always ask the owner before applying a perfume or cologne to a dog before they go home.

Products & Sprays

There is an extensive assortment of products and sprays to enhance coats, making them more manageable for the grooming process. Manufacturers are constantly developing new shampoos, conditioners, antistatic sprays, demating formulas, coat color and texture enhancers, hairsprays, coat polish, and coat volumizers, plus chalks and powders. The best way to learn about all these different pet products is to actively talk with other pet professionals, attend industry trade shows and stay current with industry catalogs and publications.

In Closing

The professional groomer must remember that equipment designs continually change. Be aware of new products and test them for possible use in your grooming operation. Many groomers are innovative and substitute equipment and tools to achieve a desired result. Many tools are interchangeable and some can be used for applications other than their intended design. Don't be afraid to experiment, but always keep in mind that the welfare of the pet is your primary concern.

Notes:

Notes:

Pre-Work

When a professional stylist talks "pre-work," he or she is normally referring to a series of steps that are elementary to all professional grooming procedures:

- Appraising the overall condition of the pet
- Bathing
- Drying
- Trimming nails
- Trimming pads

- Cleaning ears
- Clearing the sanitary areas of some breeds
- Checking anal glands
- Evaluation process

No matter the dog, the first step in grooming is to appraise the pet's overall condition.

- Do the skin and coat appear healthy?
- Does the pet have a foul odor?
- Does the skin appear red or inflamed?
- Does the pet scratch or itch?
- Are parasites present?

- Is the coat filmy, oily, dry or limp?
- Is this an active, outdoor dog or a pampered princess?
- Is the pet bathed weekly or is this visit to you its first in six months?

The conditions that you find will help you communicate to the owner what you can or cannot do for their pet on that day.

Bathing
Bathing is the foundation of good grooming. Getting a pet really clean is the only way to produce a top quality trim. Bathing also helps you match the right products to the skin and coat conditions for the best end result—a clean pet whose coat is properly prepared for grooming and styling.

Drying
Getting a pet dry can be accomplished by a combination of methods. These include:
- Towel drying
- Blanket drying
- High-velocity drying
- Kennel drying
- Natural air drying
- Hand-fluff or Stretch-drying techniques

The method or combination of methods chosen is based on producing the optimum result for the finished style, coupled with speed and efficiency.

Nail Care

Long nails are more than unsightly, they also present a potential health problem. Unattended nails may grow long enough to cause the entire tendon and bone structure of the foot and pastern to break down. From an aesthetic standpoint, nails that are too long make it all but impossible to trim a perfectly styled foot shape because the long nails disfigure the rounded line of the foot.

Trimming the Pads

Most dogs, other than the really fine, short-coated pets, grow an excessive amount of fur between the pads of the feet. Clipping the coat short in this area can minimize the amount of dirt a pet tracks into the house. If there is long coat present between the foot pads in climates where snow and ice is present, ice balls cling to the foot pads and cause great discomfort to an active pet. From a professional standpoint, untrimmed foot pads indicate an unfinished groom job and a stylist who ignores the finer points of the craft.

Ear Cleaning

All dogs need to have their ears inspected and gently cleaned. On some breeds, hair grows down inside the ear canal. That coat should be removed so air can circulate. Other dogs have smooth ear canals without any visual sign of hair growth. Some breeds, such as those with heavy, long ears, are more prone to ear problems than others.

Sanitary Trimming

In pet grooming, the sanitary areas are generally considered to be the areas between the eyes, in front of the ear canal on pets with drop ears, the groin area and under the tail. These areas are prone to collect natural discharge from the pet. Some dogs need to have the sanitary area trimmed, others do not. Typical candidates for bath and brush type work—such as Labrador Retrievers, Golden Retrievers, Collies and other, similarly coated dogs—have very little need for artificial trimming in these areas, especially about the head and facial regions. These breeds are normally left in their natural state unless there is a condition that requires trimming or the owner requests differently. If the pet is normally a candidate for full body styling, then the sanitary regions are clipped closely with a very light hand.

Anal Glands

These glands, or sacs, are located under the tail on either side of the rectum and contain a foul-smelling substance that most dogs pass naturally when they have a bowel movement. Sometimes these sacs need to be expressed. A question arises as to whether they should be expressed during the grooming process or whether the job be left for a veterinarian. At the very least, it is important for the professional stylist to check the glands for any signs of abnormality. Anything unusual should be brought to the attention of the pet owner and explained in a professional manner. If you do decide to express these glands, during bathing is the best time as any substance expressed can be quickly and easily washed down the drain. For instruction on how to express anal glands, talk to your local veterinarian.

Foundation Skills

These skills are the foundation of all grooming. Every caring pet owner faces a choice when it comes to grooming: Use a professional service, do the job themselves or not have the pet groomed at all. Grooming a pet correctly is not something anyone can just "pick up." It is a skill carefully mastered after many hours of practice and experience. Never underestimate the value of strong foundation skills. These are the basis of your career and your professional worth to the caring pet owner. They form the building blocks of a long and successful career as a professional pet stylist. Master these skills to a fault.

Notes:

How often should toenails be trimmed? That depends on the dog and its lifestyle, but most pets benefit from having their nails trimmed every four to six weeks.

A dog that is "well up on his pasterns" and that constantly walks on hard surfaces will naturally wear down his nails. This dog may never require nail trimming. Professional pet stylists, however, work mostly on house pets that are rarely exposed to an environment that will naturally wear down the nail.

Long nails are more than unsightly—they present a potential health problem. The nail of a dog is very strong and has a tendency to grow in a slight downward curve. Unattended nails may grow long enough to cause the entire tendon and bone structure of the foot and pastern to weaken.

Over time, the continued striking of long nails on the ground places excessive pressure on bones and tendons and may cause discomfort to the pet. This pressure, coupled with the weight of the pet, will weaken the natural foot structure. As an active dog plays, these longer nails will break off to expose the soft and sensitive underlying flesh, or quick, which is quite painful. On smaller pets, the nail tends to grow in a circle, and, if left unattended, back into the foot pad.

Unattended dew claws, too, will curve back into the pad, causing a puncture wound that is painful and prone to infection.

Trimming the Nail

The nails should be trimmed back as far as possible without causing excessive bleeding. If the nails are only "tipped," the quick will continue to grow farther and farther out into the nail, eventually making it impossible to obtain a healthy, short nail.

Trimming a white nail is fairly easy, for the pink of the quick can be easily seen. Place your nail trimmer at the point where the pink stops. Commit to the spot and quickly make your cut. Black nails are a bit more challenging, because the quick cannot be viewed from the outside. Start by taking the hook off the nail. Now look at the end of the nail. There will be a darker black circle in the middle of the nail bed. This is the blood vessel, but not the part that bleeds. Continue to cut off small sections until that darker circle covers most of the nail bed. Once you have gotten to a small white dot at the center, that is as far as you can trim without cutting into the quick. Once a length is established for one nail, use that as a guide for trimming the remaining nails. On many dogs, the rear nails are shorter than the front because the rear foot is the point of power and drive—they push off with their rear legs, digging into the ground and naturally wear down the rear nails.

Handling the Pet for Nail Trimming

Some dogs are totally indifferent to having their nails trimmed, other dogs dislike it with a passion, others will fall somewhere in between. Always use a grooming loop as a safety precaution.

The correct tension on the loop should have enough slack so the pet can breathe easily and stand comfortably in a natural position, but does not give free movement about the grooming table. If you are unfamiliar with a pet, start on a rear foot, and make sure there is no excessive play in the grooming loop. Watch for a reaction after trimming one of the rear nails. If there is no reaction, continue trimming the rest of the nails. If a mildly adverse reaction is noted, continue with caution in a calm but authoritative manner, using the grooming loop to its full advantage. Work quickly and low to the table. If the pet reacts strongly, stop and muzzle it. Continue in a calm manner.

Make sure that once you grasp a foot you maintain control. If a pet jerks away, it learns bad habits—it "wins"—so hold on. Brace your hand against the table to help maintain control. This technique will keep the pet's foot low and relieve unnecessary strain on its shoulders and hips.

Whenever possible, learn to stand in one general spot while trimming nails. This technique is highly efficient for small to medium size pets. On larger pets, there may be no other choice but to move around the dog. Working swiftly and smoothly is the key to getting the job accomplished while putting the least stress on the pet and the groomer.

Filing Nails

This can either be done with a coarse, heavy duty emery board or with a rotary tool. Working with an emery board is a quick way to remove the sharp edges of a freshly trimmed toenail. Working with a rotary tool is a great alternative to trimming toenails by hand. Many dogs also tolerate filing much better than trimming nails by hand.

To start the filing process, support the toe and nail in one hand. This lessens the vibration of the filing procedure while stabilizing the toe, making it more comfortable for the pet. Gently push up on the digit to expose the nail.

If you are working with an emery board, run the file over the freshly trimmed edges of each nail. It should only take a pass or two to remove the sharp edge.

If you are working with a multi speed rotary tool, make sure any longer hair is totally out of the way of the rotating drum. Hold the toe and nail steady. With the tool running at a speed you and the pet are comfortable with, lightly touch the end of the untrimmed nail to the rotating filing drum. Let the power of the tool do the work, applying only light pressure for just a few seconds at time. Repeat with

each toe using caution not to file into the quick. You never want to go any shorter than when you start to see the little white dot in the center of the tip of a dark nail or get to close to the vein on a light colored nail.

If hair accidentally gets caught in the rotary tool, immediately turn off the tool. Untangle the hair from the head. Pay attention to long ears, beards, tails and your own hair if it is long. To keep long hair and fur out of the way, use an old nylon stocking. Push each nail through the fabric and proceed as directed above.

Trimming the Nail Too Close

Every so often the quick needs to be slightly cut. This will cause it to draw back into the nail bed and make a closer trim possible in the future. There are products on the market that stop bleeding. To use them, apply the product to your finger and then to the end of the nail. Apply steady, firm pressure for a minimum of 30 seconds. Occasionally, a full minute of pressure is needed to stop the blood flow. It is possible for a freshly-cut nail to break open and bleed should the pet come in contact with an abrasive surface, such as concrete or asphalt.

It is generally accepted that nails should be trimmed prior to the bath,

during the pre-work stage of the groom. Then, if a nail is "quicked," the bleeding can be stopped without having to re-wash a pet because of blood or styptic powder in its coat. If the bleeding is not adequately controlled, there is a chance it may start again when the foot gets wet. If this happens, reassess the bleeding and reapply the product using more pressure to the nail. In some cases, simply running cold water over the foot will constrict the blood flow and stop the bleeding. Recheck the nail when the pet is out of the bath and again before returning it to the owner.

If the bleeding is very difficult to control, inform the owner and advise her to keep an eye on it. Send the owner home with a small amount of styptic powder and application directions, in the event the nail again breaks open. Also advise that hydrogen peroxide will safely and effectively remove blood from any fabric or natural fiber, such as fur. That can eliminate the need to re-bathe a pet, prevent clothing stains and/or avoid the expense of professional carpet or upholstery cleaning. If the nail breaks open at home and you have not supplied the client with styptic powder, advise them that corn starch or flour applied to the end of the bleeding nail also will help stop the bleeding.

Nail Structure

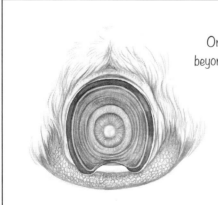

On a black nail, do not trim beyond the small white dot at the center of the nail bed.

Trim the nail as short as possible without cutting into the vein.

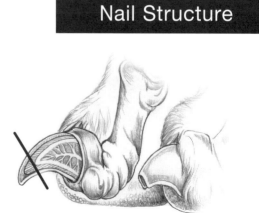

37

Cleaning the ears of a pet is considered a standard pre-work item for all professional pet groomers and stylists. A healthy ear will look clean with pink, shiny skin in the canal area.

Healthy ears do not emit an unpleasant odor and have very little dirt or debris trapped in the ear canal. Many dogs have smooth, hair-free ear canals and require only a mild swabbing with ear cleanser. Other pets have hair that grows down inside the ear canal. This extra hair may need to be gently removed, allowing air to circulate and to minimize the risk of ear problems later.

Ear problems may take the form of odor, excessive discharge, red inflammation of the canal or sensitivity from the pet. Check for mats on those dogs where long hair covers the ear leathers. If one ear is matted and the other ear is not, be suspicious of a problem in the tangled ear.

Excessive moisture in the ear causes problems. When bathing a pet, avoid getting any water in the ear while working around the head. Either protect the ear canal by holding it shut, or apply cotton balls to block the canal. Make sure the cotton is inserted firmly enough not to be easily dislodged should the dog shake itself. Cotton in the ears will not only minimize the risk of water in the ear, but will muffle sounds that can upset a fearful pet, especially during the drying process. If you do insert cotton for bathing and grooming, always remember to remove it before the pet goes home.

Pricked-eared dogs rarely have problems associated with the ear canal, primarily because such ears have excellent air circulation; thus, minimal risk of infections. The job of the groomer is simply to swab the ears with an antiseptic cleanser. While cleaning, the stylist should carefully check the canal to confirm its health and ensure no problems are present.

Dropped or folded ears are more prone to problems. Moisture can get trapped in ears that fold over the canal opening. When ear leather covers the canal opening, a warm moist breeding ground for bacteria is created. The heavier the ear, the more likely this could be a problem for a pet. There are a number of things a groomer can do to help the owner and the pet with this situation. First, remove the hair at the front edge of the ear canal opening, with clippers or thinning shears.

Second, if the inside of the ear leather is heavily coated, remove some of the fur with a very close cutting blade. Start at the perimeter of the ear canal opening and work out onto the leather. Remove as much coat as necessary based on the heaviness of the ear and the severity of the problem. Both of these actions promote better air circulation and improved access for cleaning.

Many dogs that require full-body haircuts or dogs that have long and flowing coats will have hair that grows deep into the ear canal. This can impede healthy airflow and trap discharge deep in the canal where ear problems can begin. Hair should be plucked from within the ear canal only as necessary for healthy ear management. If the ear appears healthy and the amount of hair is minimal, trim only the longest hair from the canal and clean the ear with a liquid cleaner. Plucking the fur from this type of ear may cause more harm than good.

However, if the ear is full of hair and debris, the ear should be carefully plucked and cleaned. Use a small amount of ear powder designed for this purpose. The ear powder will improve the grip on the hair, reduce the odor and help dry out the ear canal. Lightly sprinkle the powder into the opening and massage the ear to work the powder into the canal. Once the powder is worked in, begin to gently remove small amounts of fur at a time with either your fingers or hemostats, whichever is safest based on the demeanor of the dog.

If, after plucking, natural discharge remains in the canal, or if the ear looks at all irritated, follow up by swabbing with a non-irritating liquid ear cleanser and recommend a visit to the veterinarian to seek proper treatment.

Some pets have extremely oily ears, either naturally or from medical treatment. Removing that oil can be difficult. If the inside of the ear is heavily coated, start by clipping the inside of the ear leather. Once the excessive coat is removed, generously apply ear powder, corn starch or baby powder to the fur, working it in well. Let it sit for 15 minutes or more prior to bathing. The powder will absorb the oil, making it easier to remove with shampoo. Use a dirt and grease cutting shampoo to help remove oily film from the coat.

Dogs with severely matted ears are likely candidates for hematoma type swellings once the ear is shaved clean. (A hematoma is a localized swelling filled with blood resulting from a break in a blood vessel.) Most prone to this condition are those ears that have become fully encased in a solid, hard mat. Such mats are sometimes so tight around the skin that circulation to the leather has been restricted. Once the mat is shaved off, the circulation rapidly returns, often creating a swelling inside the ear leather. Pets accustomed to heavy ear matting normally find the removal of this thick coat unusual and will commonly shake their heads or scratch their ears. These behaviors aid in the development of hematomas. Although a pet shows no signs of being sick, an ear hematoma is a medical condition that should be treated by a veterinarian.

A pet care specialist is a trained observer, not a medical doctor. Any time you probe farther than you can see, you are entering veterinarian territory that is totally off limits to a professional groomer or stylist. Never diagnose any problem or potential problem you may find on a pet. Whenever you notice anything abnormal in an ear, certainly bring it to the attention of the owner. It is the owner's responsibility, and his decision, to seek further treatment for his pet.

Ear Structure

When cleaning an ear, never probe farther than you can see. If the canal is hair free, softly swab the ear with a liquid ear cleanser on a cotton ball, removing any debris. If the canal is filled with hair, apply ear powder and gently remove the hair with your fingertips, hemostat, or by trimming—whichever is safest based on the dog's demeanor. Only remove enough hair for healthy ear management.

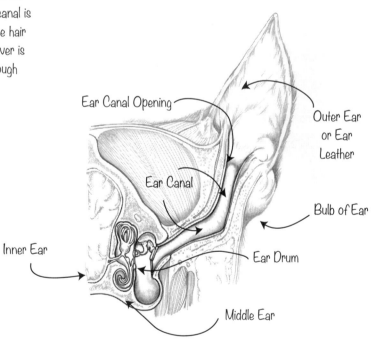

Ear Canal Opening

Outer Ear or Ear Leather

Ear Canal

Bulb of Ear

Inner Ear

Ear Drum

Middle Ear

Notes From The Grooming Table ©2016

Bathing

Place the pet in the tub and secure it so its head cannot hang over the edge of the tub. A rubber mat on the bottom of the tub will help make the pet feel more comfortable and prevent its feet from sliding.

The water temperature should be warm and comfortable to the touch.

Wet the coat, beginning at the back of the neck, then down the spine toward the tail. Keep the water nozzle very close to the skin to allow the water to fully penetrate the coat. Bring the water back to the shoulder area and work one side of the pet, including the legs. Repeat the process on the opposite side. If the pet has a heavy coat, be sure it is thoroughly saturated. Return the sprayer to the head area and wet the head. Take care not to get water into the ears or up the pet's nose. If the pet resists, lower the water pressure and place your hand between the eyes and the nose to create a shield that will prevent the water from getting into the nose. If the pet has any type of debris caught in the fur around its eyes, in the furnishings of the ears or under the tail, saturate those areas with warm water. Allow these areas to soak while wetting the rest of the body. Keep the spray hose as close to the pet's body as possible to work efficiently. Check the pet's glands and express them, if necessary. Rinse any debris off the pet and down the drain.

Usually, more than one shampooing is needed in order to get a pet really clean. The first application breaks up the dirt and oils, allowing for better saturation of product during the next shampoo. This is especially true of thick coats. The first shampoo can be quick; thorough rinsing is not necessary at this point. The second product application will produce more lather, and should easily lift all traces of dirt and debris loosened by the first shampooing. Rinse thoroughly after the second shampoo application.

For a normal groom, apply the standard shampoo, unless the situation dictates otherwise. Follow the same pattern to apply the shampoo as wetting the pet down. Some shampoos are designed to be low sudsing, so the first application will not produce many suds.

Massage shampoo into the dog's skin with your fingers.

If the coat is very long, avoid scrubbing in a back and forth motion, as this will cause it to tangle. If the coat is very dense and/or very dirty, use a rubber curry or a scrub brush to help lift the dirt out. Rinse using the same method as noted earlier. The first rinse does not have to be extremely thorough, just enough to wash away the bulk of the dirt.

Apply a second lather and wash as outlined above. The second application will produce more lather. Pay close attention to the feet, under the tail, the ears, around the mouth and eyes as these are areas where dirt and debris can accumulate.

Rinse as before.

Keep the sprayer very close to the pet's body to force the shampoo away from the skin and coat. To work most efficiently, use one hand to force the water from the coat as fresh water is applied.

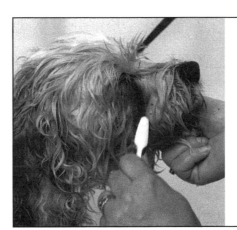

Pay close attention to the feet, under the tail, the ears, around the mouth and eyes as these are areas where dirt and debris can accumulate.

Occasionally, a third shampooing will be necessary for an extremely dirty or oily pet. Usually, just rewashing the dirty area will suffice. Whatever the case, the dog is not clean until the coat feels "squeaky."

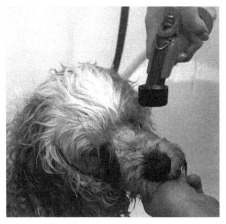

Let a gentle stream of water run over the pet's eyes to flush out any traces of shampoo caught there.

When rinsing the eyes on short muzzled pets, use extreme caution not to let any water get into the nasal cavity and into the lungs of the dog. During the final rinse, be sure all traces of shampoo are removed. Listen for the "squeak" as in "squeaky clean." Shampoo residue left in the coat is the primary reason for skin irritation after bathing. Any shampoo residue that remains will cause the coat to look and feel oily to the touch.

Once all traces of shampoo are removed, apply a light application of skin and coat conditioner. Apply the conditioner to the entire pet, following the same procedure as for wetting the pet and applying shampoo.

Massage into the pet's skin. Some conditioning products are designed to be left in the coat while others need to be thoroughly rinsed out. Read the directions concerning the product being used. If the pet has a heavy coat or if it has some loose tangles still in the coat, use more conditioner. This will aid in removing any loose coat and make tangles easier to blow out or brush out later. Many harsh coated terrier types coats do not benefit from an application of coat conditioner since this would soften the hair shaft.

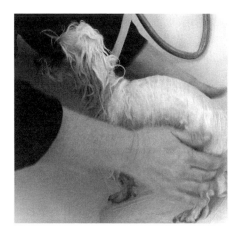

Squeegee as much water as possible from the pet's body using your hands, the back of a slicker brush or the back of a shedding blade. Towel dry the pet before moving on to the drying method best suited for the pet's coat type.

Special Notes
- The dark warm environment of the ear canal is a perfect breeding ground for bacteria, which is a primary cause of ear problems. Take care not to get water in the ears, which can cause mild irritation to the pet and/or lead to an ear infection.
- On small pets, as little as a few teaspoons of inhaled water can cause a severe reaction in their ability to breath and may possibly drown the animal. It is extremely important to avoid getting water into the nasal cavity of a small dog or cat.

Notes:

Drying

Drying Techniques

There are five basic drying techniques that professionals use on pets. They are based on size, coat condition, coat type and personality of the pet. The coat type often will dictate which technique is used to produce the highest quality result. The different drying methods are:

1. Towel Drying   2. High-Velocity Drying   3. Stretch Drying   4. Kennel Drying   5. Blanket Drying

---

Towel Drying

This method is used on almost every pet we see. The most effective way to towel dry is to squeegee as much water off the pet by using your hands, the back of a brush or a scraper. Once all the excess is off, use a moisture magnet or a thick towel and gently, but firmly, blot the pet. Wring out the magnet and repeat until there is very little moisture left in the coat. (Moisture magnets work best when moist.) Once the magnet or initial towel is no longer effective, switch to a fresh cotton towel. Wrap the pet in the towel and rub all over its body to remove any moisture. Again, be firm but gentle. Pay particular attention to the legs and ears.

With the moist towel, examine the eye area for any remaining debris and wipe it out. For those pets with an abundance of coat, place the damp towel on the drying table under the pet to catch any drips or moisture that will be blown off with the high-velocity dryer. This may not be necessary for small pets without heavy coats.

If a moisture magnet is not used, use two towels, the first to remove the bulk of the moisture, the second to finish with and use under the pet. A very large pet with a lot of coat many require up to four towels.

High-Velocity Drying

This drying method produces the fastest results with the highest quality if used correctly on any given coat type.

High-Velocity Drying Pros:
- a quick dry time
- a very flexible procedure
- adaptability to many different coat types
- ability to remove loose coat on shedding pets
- ability to do a large percentage of dematting on many coat types
- a clear view of the skin
- a safe procedure for all skin types

High-Velocity Drying Cons:
- some pets object to the noise and force of air
- it can tangle a long coat
- it will produce a mess on heavily shedding pets.

As you can see, the positive points far outweigh the negative. Almost all of the negative points can be overcome through proper pet/dryer handling and correct technique.

Many professional stylists who regularly use this drying method will protect themselves by wearing facemasks, goggles and earplugs. These simple items minimize the amount of pet fur and dander that reaches the eyes and lungs, and helps deaden the noise to protect ears from long-term exposure.

Using the High-Velocity Dryer

This method should be introduced slowly with any new pet or a puppy. Have the pet listen to the sound before the air is introduced. Help build its confidence. Once the pet seems calm, slowly and from a distance bring the air up around its feet or rear. Do this on a single speed, with no condenser cone. Once the pet accepts that, slowly bring the air in closer and move it up the body. Try not to let the air pass over the pet's face or in its ears. As the pet grows more accepting, try adding the condenser cone, or, boost the dryer up to a second speed and then add the cone. If at any point the pet objects or becomes difficult to handle, back down to the previous step that produced a positive result. If the pet severely objects to having its face dried, try placing cotton balls in the ears to reduce the air flow into the ears as well as the sound. Just don't forget to remove the cotton balls. Always remember, the pet takes its cue from you. Your confidence will communicate to the pet. Work gently, but firmly, using a minimal amount of verbal positive or negative reinforcement. Let your hands and eyes do the speaking for you.

The process outlined above may take just a few minutes or several, based upon the individual pet and your handling techniques. On occasion, a pet just will not accept high-velocity drying and another method will be necessary.

Once you have the pet's cooperation, you can focus on the most effective way of using the high-velocity dryer on that pet's individual coat type.

With most drop coated, double coated, wavy coated or curly coated breeds to build body and fluff the coat, begin at the base of the tail and blow the air forward, working against the grain of the coat growth, using a condenser cone. With other coats like the short, silky and wiry coated breeds, you'll want the coat to lay flat against the body. On those pets, start at the back of the neck, blowing the air in the direction of the coat growth, the same order listed below only working from the neck to the tail working with the direction of coat growth.

Move as rapidly as possible and work forward over the entire pet, excluding the head, watching for spray coming off the coat (the moisture you missed with the towel). When there is no visible spray coming off any portion of the pet, begin again at the rump area. Focus on getting the pet dry and the coat straightened.

Hold the dryer as close as possible to the skin without curling the coat onto itself, causing tangles. Rapidly move the air around in a small, confined space. Watch the area constantly.

When you first start on a section, the coat will appear slightly clumped together. As the hair dries, it will separate and become very fine. This is your signal to move to another area.

Work from the rump up over the bulk of the body, keeping the air flowing forward as long as the pet will allow it.

Return to the rear legs and proceed to the front. Leave the head, tail and ears until last. If the pet objects to having air blown around its face, change the direction of the air so that it does not blow over the face and ears.

If the pet shows only mild objection, then hold its head for more control. If the problem continues, remove the cone to handle the neck and chest area. If the coat is slightly matted or the pet is shedding heavily, you will notice the matted hair form a kind of spidery web as the coat begins to dry. Guide the air just behind the webbed section to work it out.

Use the condenser cone with as much air force as the pet will allow. You must watch this process constantly to be effective.

If the pet will not allow a condenser cone, or if you have worked the loose coat or mat as far as it will go with the air, give the coat a "boost" with a brush and mild air flow. Normally, this will remove the rest of the loose coat with the least amount of wear and tear on you and the pet.

Now that the pet is dry, primarily from the condenser cone work, remove the cone and hold the base of the hose right next to the skin. High-velocity dryers do not have a heating element, but once they have run for a few minutes, the air they produce will be a little warmer.

Removing the condenser cone and placing the dryer hose right against the skin takes advantage of the optimum power of a high-velocity dryer to "set the coat." Setting the coat means straightening each hair shaft. Plus, holding the warm air right next to the skin will remove any remaining dampness. Work over the entire dog using the same method as previously outlined, but now work very close to the skin.

Finish the entire drying process at the head and ears. Work from the base of the skull—the occiput—forward.

If the pet is fidgety, grasp the ear at the base. This firm grip offers the most control and covers the ear canal. In most cases, a fidgety pet is objecting to the air going down into the ear canal. Don't use a condenser cone for the head and face, but do keep the base of the hose right next to the skin for optimum speed and coat straightening.

Pets pre-clipped shorter than a #7 blade length before the bath will not need a high-velocity drying in the short areas. These areas will dry naturally as other coated areas are dried. Normally, a #7 blade length or shorter does not need straightening to yield the best results in the finish work.

Drying

Stretch Drying

Stretch drying uses mild, warm air with rapid, light brushing only where the air is striking the coat. It's like the reverse of using a human curling iron, where you want to hold the hair around the iron for long time to get a tight curl. To get a quality finish on most clipper and scissor-trims, the coat needs to be as straight as possible. There should be between one and four brush strokes per second depending upon the length of the hair. The brushing technique together with the warm air sets the coat straight and gives the fluffy appearance. The better the stretch dry, the faster and easier it will be to finish the trim. A well-executed stretch dry is the only way to get a beautiful finish on a hand-scissored coat.

Dryers used in stretch or fluff drying will have a heating element that creates air temperatures from warm to very hot. Always be aware of the air temperature out of the dryer. Air that is too hot could be uncomfortable for the pet and, at worst, may burn its skin.

There are stand dryers designed for this process or a small, hand-held human hair dryer with side air vents can be used. The small, hand hair dryers normally are attached to the stylist's waist or held in a bracket that hangs from the neck to place the dryer at chest level. Brush selection is based on the coat texture of the pet and the length of the fur.

On most pets, a heavy slicker brush used with light strokes is preferred. If the pet has extremely delicate skin and/or a short fine coat, a soft slicker will be the brush of choice.

Start with the shortest coat on the body, if it needs attention, moving forward over the body of the dog towards the head. Next, work on fluffing the rear legs. Proceed to the

front legs and finish with the head, ears and tail. *Work only in the area where the air is striking.* Make your brush strokes light and rapid, one to four strokes per second based on coat length. When dealing with a heavily coated pet, line brush the area where the air strikes. Remember, the goal is to straighten the coat. Don't move to the next area until the coat is as straight as possible and is bone dry. Straightening some coats will prove more challenging than others.

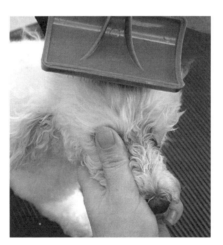

When working on the head, always cover the eye with a finger to protect it from an accidental scratch from the brush. There are cases of pets receiving eye scratches from stylists who were careless with the slicker brush. This is obviously painful to the pet, and in the worst case, can lead to blindness.

Where light matting is still left in the coat, the coat can be de-matted and stretch dried at the same time. If for some reason the mat cannot be removed, make a mental note to return to that area and remove it after finishing the drying, but before the finish clipping and scissoring.

On many coats, a pet hair spray or styling mousse will hold the coat straight, just as it does for people, and allows for more effective clipping and scissoring. Apply the spray as a final step in stretch drying. Lightly spray the section. Set the spray with the warm air as you quickly brush it in. Make sure all mats are removed before applying the hair spray.

Kennel Drying

A kennel dryer is a holding area where the pet sits under gentle air flow. Some dryers are designed just for this purpose. However, any confined space can be turned into a kennel dryer. Some stylists attach the high-velocity hose, with the dryer turned low, to a kennel door or place a simple box fan in front of pet in a confined space.

Kennel drying is reserved mainly for straight-coated pets, for very close overall body trim styles or for extremely heavy coated pets. It also can be used for those pets that will not accept the high-velocity dryer. A kennel dryer can be a great help in a busy salon, however, used alone it rarely produces top quality results. Any non-active drying method will allow the coat to dry in its natural state, wavy or curly. Once waves or curls become set in, the only way to remove them is to re-wet the pet.

Kennel drying should only be used as a time saver on certain pets and always in conjunction with other drying processes that produce far superior results.

It should be noted that kennel drying can be very dangerous if used with any type of heat. Pets never should be left unattended while in a drying kennel with any type of heat involved. Pets can easily and quickly become overheated, possibly enough to suffer "heat stroke," a potentially deadly condition. Short-nosed pets are even more susceptible to this problem than dogs with longer muzzles.

Blanket Drying
There are two primary ways to work with this method;
• Wrap a towel snuggly around a pet
• Sack the coat

Wrapping a pet in a towel takes place after most of the moisture has been removed by towel drying. Simply wrap the pet in a towel and allow it to sit for a few minutes while the towel absorbs excess moisture. It's the same method people use to dry their long hair after washing. Within a short time, the towel has drawn most of the moisture from the fur. This method works on all pet coat types and coat lengths. It is very effective for busy stylists who want to maximize their time by working a number of pets in the same stage of grooming.

Care must be taken to not let the pet sit too long, however, because the natural body heat of the pet, along with the towel, will dry a pet very quickly, setting in a curl or wave. The number of towels used and how heavily the pet should be wrapped depends on how much coat it has and how dry it needs to be.

The basic procedure for wrapping a dog is to use a medium to large dry towel. Stand behind the dog and drape a towel over its back, letting the longer sections of the towel hang over the dog's sides. Draw one section under the dog's neck, around the chest, and bring the end of the towel up to the withers. Draw the opposite end of the towel under the dog's belly and up toward the withers where the two ends can be fastened with a clip. Let the pet sit in a safe, confined space for a short time before proceeding to an active drying method.

How to Wrap a Pet

Lay the towel across the pet's back.

With the towel draped over the dog, pull one end around the chest, push the other end under the dog.

Pull one of the towel ends across the chest, the other end is pulled under the dog's body.

Clip towel snugly around the dog.

Sacking
Sacking is a preferred method of drying for pets in show trims where the "jacket" of the dog is to lie close to the skin. This includes such sporting breeds as setters and spaniels, and hand-stripped terriers. In most pet grooming salons, these trims have been modified and shortened to a closely clipped body trim.

To "sack a coat," begin with a vigorous towel drying. Brush the jacket coat into the correct position for the finished groom. Use a thick towel that is large enough to be drawn up around the dog's chest and wrap around its body. With the coat brushed into place, gently lay the towel over the pet. Pin the towel into place at the throat. If the coat has become ruffled, brush it back into place and pull the towel snuggly along the back of the dog. Pin the towel tightly at the tuck-up area. Place the pet in a confined area or begin to stretch dry the longer furnishings while the jacket of the pet dries. When removing the towel, slide it off the pet from the rear so you do not disturb the coat.

As with kennel drying, sacking normally should be used in conjunction with another drying method to produce superior results.

It is important to master drying skills. There are several drying methods and combinations to choose from, based on coat type, trim and pet tolerance.

Incorrect techniques or careless attention to drying will waste more of a professional groomer's time than almost anything else. An active form of drying always will yield the best results. Having a beautifully clean and dried coat also will lessen the amount of time it takes to execute the final grooming procedures on a pet.

Clippers: Handling & Dexterity Skills

The best professional stylists are those who have developed a confident degree of dexterity with the clippers. Moreover, good scissor work is rarely found on a badly clipped dog. The two just do not go together.

Holding the Clipper

For maximum freedom of movement and improved efficiency, hold the clipper like a large pencil, between the thumb and fingers. "Palming" the clipper makes for clumsy, awkward clipper handling and puts the pet at risk for cuts, nicks and irritation. Concentrate on positioning yourself so that the clipper is pulled toward you and held comfortably like a pencil. There are rare times when holding the clippers in your palm will improve dexterity, but this applies to very few moves.

To create the least amount of stress on your fingers and wrist, grasp the clipper at the "balance point" so the weight is equally distributed between each end. Hold the clipper in the correct position, then rotate it between your thumb and fingers.

This positioning keeps your wrist firm but flexible, yet allows for almost unlimited wrist movement. This hold offers access to the most difficult corners of the pet with minimum effort. Concentrate on minimizing your wrist action.

Allow the weight of the clippers to do the work. Your hand and wrist are simply its guide. As you move from the top of the pet to make downward strokes, simulate the same amount of pressure that gravity provided on the top.

Your hand and wrist will act as a shock absorber during clipping, leveling out the bumps and dents in order to obtain a satin-smooth finish. No matter what blade you use, it is important to maintain a consistent degree of "tip" to the blade, also known as "keeping the blade up on

its cutting edge." Imagine a pencil being held right under the blade as you guide it over the body. The closer the pencil is to the teeth, the higher the tip angle; the farther back you keep the imaginary pencil, the lesser the degree of tip. Generally speaking, the closer the blade cuts, the higher you need to tip the blade for it to be effective.

A Clean Pet

Every top quality stylist knows the importance of a clean pet. It is impossible to obtain a satin-smooth finish on a pet that has a dirty or filmy coat. On most pets, two baths with the correct shampoo is normally considered adequate to produce a squeaky clean coat. Rinsing the pet thoroughly is critical to avoid shampoo residue that looks oily on a dry coat and produces a film you can feel on your hands.

Degree of Tip Scale

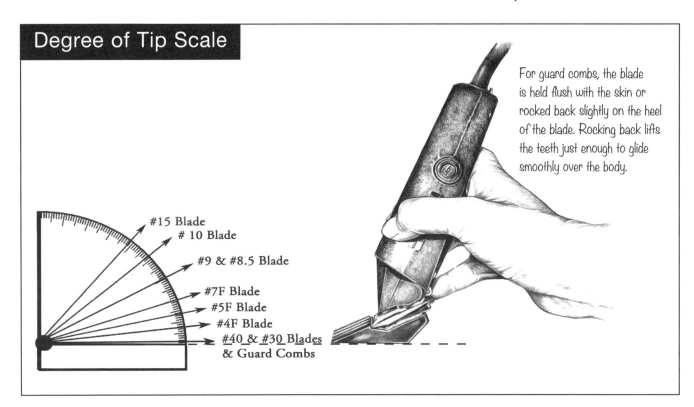

For guard combs, the blade is held flush with the skin or rocked back slightly on the heel of the blade. Rocking back lifts the teeth just enough to glide smoothly over the body.

#15 Blade
10 Blade
#9 & #8.5 Blade
#7F Blade
#5F Blade
#4F Blade
#40 & #30 Blades & Guard Combs

Degree of Tip Scale

The degree of tip on close cutting blades is greater than their longer cutting cousins.

Only the teeth come in contact with the skin, while the heel of the blade is raised off the skin.

#15 Blade
10 Blade

#9 & #8.5 Blade

#7F Blade
#5F Blade
#4F Blade
#40 & #30 Blades
& Guard Combs

Setting the Coat Up

"Setting the coat up" is important to produce the finest clipper work.

This is achieved in a couple of steps:

#1: The Drying Process

The goal is to dry the coat so there is absolutely no curl or wave left in it. The natural coat of the pet— whether curly, wavy or straight—will determine which drying process will achieve the desired result. Correct use of a high-velocity dryer can effectively produce a straight coat. Heat will "set" the coat straight. In some cases, the heat of the high-velocity dryer, without the condensing cone, held against the skin in the final stages of drying will produce the desired effect.

With very curly coats, hand stretch drying or hand fluff drying the coat using a stand type or hand held dryer is necessary. Curly coats need to be as straight as possible in order to achieve a smooth, high quality finish. With a higher level of heat from the drying source, it is important to keep the air moving within a small section, while brushing in very rapid, light strokes, up to one to four strokes per second, just where the air is blowing. This will straighten the coat, just as a curling iron would curl a strand of human hair.

#2: Back Brushing

Back brushing is done with a slicker brush while brushing the coat against the grain. The pressure on the brush should be very light and the entire pad of the brush should make contact with the skin and coat. Keep the pressure light on the brush so the skin is not scraped, causing a potential "brush burn." Back brush the entire coat once and make a clipper pass over the pet using effective techniques. When the bulk of the coat is gone, repeat the process a second time to get a smoother finish.

On the third back brush pass, look only for high spots or uneven areas. Minimize the number of passes with the clipper, otherwise the set up coat will be crushed.

#3: Body Roll

On drop-coated breeds, when a medium to longer guard is used to clip the pet, a "body roll" is normally more effective than back brushing. The body roll simulates the natural shake of a dog, setting up the coat in its most natural position. Ideally, the pet will shake when it is placed on the table. Take advantage of this and make the first full pass with the clipper.

If the pet does not shake when it is first set on the table, sometimes simply blowing lightly in its ear will encourage a natural shake. A body roll can be mimicked by standing behind the dog and grasping a small amount of coat, low on either side of the rib cage. Tug one side and then the other, making the skin and coat rock back and forth as it would in a natural shake. Most pets do not find this move uncomfortable as long as it is done quickly and gently.

On the third pass, lightly back brush the area or use thinning shears to smooth out the uneven areas.

Final Thoughts

Clipper work is not complete until no more coat is being clipped off and the coat is properly set up. If the clipper has been used effectively, there should be a minimum of thinner and shear work remaining to make the pet appear smooth and polished.

Areas that may need a bit more detail are around the outside edges of the feet, the ears, around the tail, under the front legs and the face.

Blending, also called "feathering" or "skimming," to create a smooth transition between the shorter clipped coat and the longer scissored coat may also be necessary.

The ideal number of passes over a pet to get a satin smooth finish should be three or less. The first pass removes the bulk, the second pass is to add smoothness while the third pass removes the last of the rough spots.

The finished pet should have a nice, clean outline when viewed from all angles at a slight distance. Upon closer inspection, the coat should be of a consistent length without any clipper marks. If these steps are followed and the coat is properly set up, the stylist will produce a high quality hair cut.

The degree of tip working with a #5F blade on a pet poodle.

#3	Skip-Toothed Blade	Leaves hair ½" long.	Good for harsh coated terrier type coats to mimic a hand-stripped look.
#3F	Full-Toothed Blade	Leaves hair ½" long.	Overall clipping on a wide variety of dogs.
#4	Skipped-Tooth Blade	Leaves hair ⁵⁄₁₆" to ⅜" long.	Good for harsh coated terrier type coats to mimic a hand-stripped look.
#4F	Full-Toothed Blade	Leaves hair ⁵⁄₁₆" to ⅜" long.	Excellent for overall clipping on a wide variety of dogs.
#5	Skip-Toothed Blade	Leaves hair about ¼" long.	Good overall clipping and rough-in work on matted pets.
#5F	Full-Toothed Blade	Leaves hair about ¼" long.	Good for matted pets.
#7	Skip-Toothed Blade	Leaves hair about ⅛" long.	
#7F	Full-Toothed Blade	Leaves hair about ⅛" long.	Excellent for all-over clipping on a wide variety of dogs. One of the most popular blades for terrier and sporting dog patterns. The "workhorse" blade for matted pets.
#8.5	Close Cutting Length	Leaves hair about ³⁄₁₆" long.	
#9	Close Cutting Length	Leaves hair about ⁵⁄₆₄" long.	
#10	Close Cutting Length	Leaves hair about ¹⁄₁₆" long. Natural coat color will still show through when used with the grain.	For general clipping on dogs in warm climates. Excellent blade for shaving cats. Used extensively on close clipper work of pets around the face and sanitary areas.
#15	Close Cutting Length	Leaves hair about ³⁄₆₄" long. Shows more skin than #10.	Use on the feet of most pet poodles and on ears where the ear leather is clipped.
#30	Very Close Cutting	Leaves hair about ¹⁄₅₀" long. Mostly used for show clipping.	Works well under metal guard combs.
#40	Extra-Fine Cutting	Leaves hair about ¹⁄₁₀₀" long. Surgical length.	Use for show clips and for cleaning surgical areas. Used widely on pads, insides of ears and under plastic guard combs.
#50	Ultra-Fine Cutting	Leaves hair about ¹⁄₁₂₅" long. Surgical length.	Good for hard-to-get spots, toy dogs and setting intricate patterns on poodles.
#5/8	Close Cutting	Leaves hair about ¹⁄₃₂" length. Blade is ⅝" wide; smaller than standard.	Good for hard-to-get spots on small dogs and setting intricate patterns in the coat.

Brushing

There are many types of combs and brushes on the market. They have different design elements and are used for different coat types. Combs come in different sizes, tooth length and with variously spaced teeth. Some combs have handles, some do not. Some are designed for heavy work; others are designed for more delicate jobs. With brushes, there are pin brushes, natural bristled brushes, rubber brushes and wire slicker brushes. They are both small and large. They can be rounded, rectangular or triangular in shape, flat or with curved backs. The two tools primarily used for pet grooming are the greyhound comb and the slicker brush.

The **greyhound comb** is about 8–9 inches long. Normally, there are two types of teeth; a fine section with close spacing and a coarser section where the teeth are farther apart. The teeth are from 1–1.5 inches long. This style of comb has no handle.

The **slicker brush** has a large number of small, curved wire pins, set in a rubber pad for flexibility. Some slicker brushes are made for pets with fine, soft coats or that have delicate skin. Others are firmer and

designed for thicker, fuller coats. Still others are extremely tough and designed to take on the thickest coats, full of mats, tangles or undercoat. The slicker brush comes in a variety of shapes, sizes and density levels for special uses. The all-purpose model is rectangular in shape, smaller and has firm bristles.

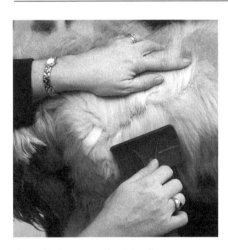

A technique used with almost all longer haired pets is "line brushing." This is a systematic way to effectively work the coat, right down to the skin.

This is done by working evenly over the pet, holding or pushing up the coat with one hand. It can be done with either a comb or a brush, but in most cases the comb is reserved for double checking the work of the brush. With the slicker brush, work

the seam line, pulling down a small amount of fur with each stroke. Do not move to the next section until the brush stroke glides smoothly and the skin at the seam line is seen.

The motion used for line brushing is a "pat and pull." Softly pat the coat with the full pad of the brush and pull out and away from the skin with each stroke. The wrist remains in a neutral, or straight, position. Flicking the wrist can puncture or brush burn the dog's skin. The motion of the brush comes from the shoulder and is a round, sweeping motion. After the technique is mastered, the momentum from each stroke carries naturally into the next.

Line brushing is very gentle and easy on the pet's skin when done correctly. It is also stylist-friendly because of the soft nature of the strokes with the wrist in a locked and neutral position.

Hold the brush lightly at the balance point—normally where the pad and the handle meet. A couple of the most efficient holds are to grip the handle or hold it between your fingers, letting the pad of the brush rest on the back side of your hand or fingers. Whatever the hold, it should move very lightly and smoothly over the dog's body without scraping the skin. If scraping is heard or the brushing is too firm, skin irritation is likely to follow.

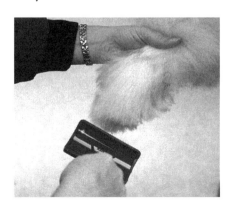

Line brushing requires skill and finesse versus power and muscle. Practice the stroke on your own bare forearm.

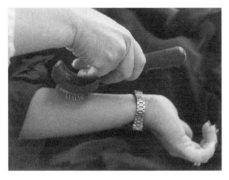

Hold your arm out in front of you and lightly set the full pad of the wire bristles on your arm. Next, lightly draw the brush across your arm and notice how it feels. Experiment with the amount of pressure you apply to the brush.

Note how it feels when you flick your wrist, sending the top row of teeth into a downward motion as you lift the brush off your arm. Try brushing your arm firmly until red lines appear.

Now, try a softer stroke using the heel of the wire bristles. Learn what it feels like when only brushing with the top row of teeth on the brush head.

Pay attention to the movements you make with the brush and to how those movements feel on your skin. The pet will feel the same thing. The correct movement is: pat the coat gently and then pull away.

Few pets will object to being brushed after this technique is mastered. Even the most difficult mats and tangles can be removed without creating discomfort to the pet or injuring its skin. Take the time to work systematically over the dog to ensure all parts of the body are brushed thoroughly.

Start at the lowest sections and work your way up. For example, on a leg, start at the toes and work up the leg.

On long coats, start at the outer edges of the fur and work up towards the skin. In time, your hands alone will be able to tell which areas of the pet need work and which areas can be handled another way. At this point, you will have become very efficient at brushing.

Notes:

Notes From The Grooming Table ©2016

Scissoring

Scissoring is slowly becoming the "lost art" of the professional pet stylist. It is a skill that requires practice and a trained eye. With beautiful hand-scissoring, the groomer becomes an artist or "stylist." Not only must a stylist learn to have full control over their shears, they must master the art of safe scissoring to avoid injuring any pet while trimming it. For those who become proficient at this skill, the final product can be exquisite. When you watch a top stylist at work, you quickly realize you are watching an artist and begin to understand the skill required of a true master. Top stylists are three-dimensional sculptors and their medium is fur. Balance, style, grace and flair all become working components of a pet with fur that has been sculpted to show off its most positive aspects.

So how do you learn to become a master of the hand-scissor? First, you need to learn to run your shear smoothly and proficiently. A beginner can learn to do this through a series of exercises to be practiced without a real pet present. This is the easy part—the mechanics of scissoring. One becomes a highly skilled stylist through learning, understanding and interpreting the dynamics of breed anatomy and proper breed standards. This is the greater challenge as it takes time, patience and application of sound mechanics. In this section we will focus on the mechanics of scissoring.

Shear Terminology
Shears come in many styles, shapes and weights. The size of your hand and the type of coat on which you are working will determine the shear best suited for the job. One pet may require three or four different shears to obtain the desired trim, all depending on what part of the dog you are working. For example, one shear will be needed to bulk out mass amounts of coat on the body and quite another for detailing a tiny area around the eyes.

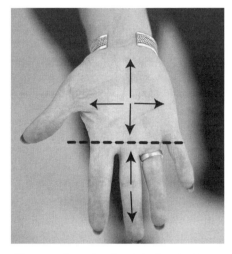

The size of your hand and the length of your fingers will make a difference in the size, style and weight of the shears that will be the most comfortable and efficient for you to operate.

Anatomy of Shears

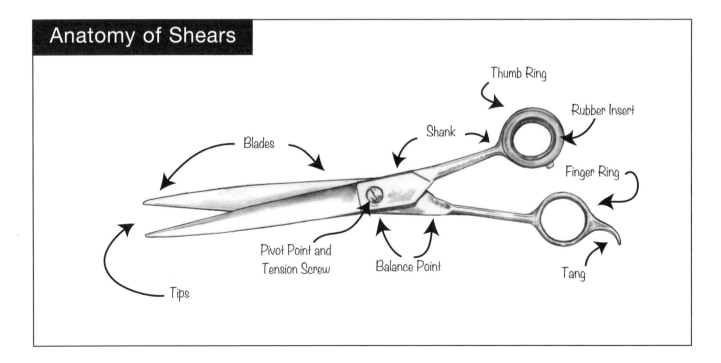

Thumb Ring

Rubber Insert

Shank

Blades

Finger Ring

Pivot Point and Tension Screw

Balance Point

Tang

Tips

The Balance Game

Lay the shear across your scissor hand. With the shear lying across, find the balance point where it will stay level, neither tipping forward through the tip of the shear, nor back toward the handles, like a see-saw in perfect balance. This balance point normally will be somewhere close to the "pivot point" (screw head) of the shear.

Leave your index finger at that balance point, rotate the shear up on its side and insert your thumb into the thumb hole. Do not let your thumb slide into this ring any farther than your first knuckle.

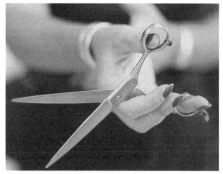

Gently slide your ring finger into the lower ring of the handles. Keep your index finger stretched to the pivot point with your second finger acting as an added stabilizer.

The shear should now be in proper position and balanced at right angles to your arm and hand when the wrist is in a neutral, unbent position.

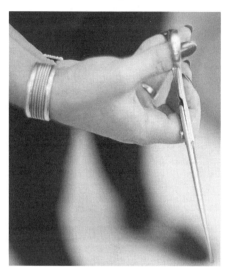

With shears in proper position, you are ready to begin the exercises. You must maintain proper positioning at all times in order for these exercises to be effective.

The Exercises

Running The Shear

With the shears in your hand, drop your hand to your side. The shears should be parallel to the floor, creating a right angle to your hand when they are in position. Maintain the hold and begin to open and close the blades using only your thumb. It is critical that the shears remain parallel to the floor. As you begin to get comfortable with this exercise, begin to lift your arm up and out.

Continue to maintain the proper position in relationship to the shears and your hand. If you begin to lose the position, drop your hand back to your side and realign yourself.

Scissoring

Stabilizing Operations

With shears positioned properly, cup your other hand under the heel of your scissor hand. Begin to open and close the blades of the shears by allowing only your thumb to move up and down. Stabilize the rest of your fingers with the help of your other hand. **Do not** let your thumb slide through the ring. **Make sure** you maintain the stretch of your index finger to the pivot point.

If you have trouble maintaining the correct position, decrease the distance you are attempting to open the blades and take smaller snips. Once you can maintain the position, open the blades farther and farther. Remember, *only* the thumb should move. Repeat this exercise until it becomes totally natural without the aid of the supporting hand.

You can simulate the same exercise by simply resting the heel of your hand on a steady surface. It's best to find a place where the blades of the shears can hang over the edge, like the arm of a sofa or a table. Gently press weight through the heel of your hand and open and close the shears, using only your thumb to run the blade movement. This is an excellent exercise to perform while sitting in front of a TV or while talking on the phone.

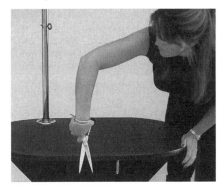

Losing the Bounce

Divots in the coat? Try this exercise. Divots are caused when the shear blade is slightly cocked one way or another as you glide over the surface of a coat. While holding the shears correctly lay them against any smooth edge—straight or curved—and begin the proper scissor motion. Slide the shears across these surfaces. This exercise will teach your hand to adjust and maintain a level position when gliding across any surface, whether a flat plateau or a curved line.

Scissoring with Your Body

Another key point about scissoring is that the entire motion stems more from your feet, knees, hips and waist rather than the pulling and pushing of your arm to and from your upper body. Let the motion originate from these areas as you cover a surface. Think of your entire body as a single, fluid, operating unit with your thumb opening and closing the blades in rapid succession. Though your upper body is somewhat locked into position, the movement over an area stems from your lower joints. Maintain a fluid feel as you glide the scissors over the pet.

Move from the waist.

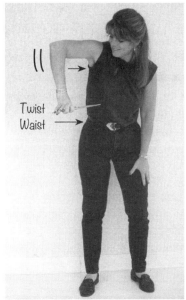

Twist Waist

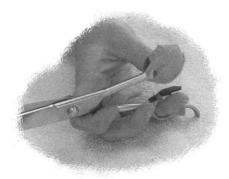

Fitting the Shear with "Training Wheels"

If you have difficulty keeping your fingers in position, there are "training wheels" that can help. Insert finger and thumb guards into the rings of the shears. Make sure the guard creates enough "fill" to prevent your thumb

from sliding through. If finger guards are not readily available, there are other items you can use to make the finger ring smaller. Try vet wrap, medical tape… even Band-Aids will work in a pinch. Next, lay a piece of tape over the back side of the thumb ring to stop your thumb from sliding through.

Sliced lengthwise, triangular eraser-type pencil guards create a great support on the shank of the shear. This aid allows one to maintain the proper "stretch" to the pivot point.

Slight modifications are needed to the ends of these guards to allow the different shear types to close properly. *(This is not hard to do as they are easy to cut.)*

Fitting your shears with these aids will keep your hand in the correct position for optimum control and minimize how much thought goes into learning how to move with your shears. With time, holding the shears correctly will become second nature, as will operating the shears while trimming a pet.

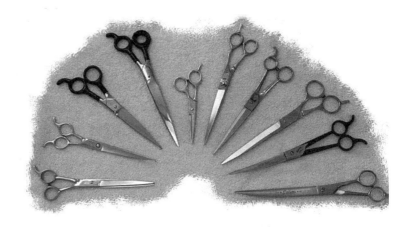

A working sample of the many different shear types.

Carding & Hand-Stripping

Hand-stripping, carding and plucking are ancient grooming practices used to maintain the proper coat texture of many harsh, broken coated or flat coated breeds. This correct texture helps protect the dog's skin as they do the jobs they were bred to do. Stripping tools are used to literally pull out the dead or blown coat from the roots. As a result of this grooming method, the hair grows back in a tight fitting "jacket" that lays flat against the dog's body. The hair will be harder than a clipped coat and brilliant in color. A stripped coat will take between six to twelve weeks to grow back in based on the dog and the type of coat it has. Many lighter coat breeds are easy to maintain with simple carding and plucking/hand-stripping techniques. Other dogs, such as those with a "broken coat" like an Airedale or Wire Fox Terrier, the hand-stripping process can be lengthy requiring time and experience to do it properly.

Carding

Carding is a natural technique in which the soft, downy undercoat is pulled from the dog's body. Typical tools used with this technique are: a pumice stone; a fine-toothed stripping knife, which is pulled through the coat; or a fine blade, such as a #40, held between the fingers and pulled through the coat.

Carding can be done before or after bathing and drying. Removal of the soft undercoat allows the topcoat to lie closer to the natural outline of the dog, accentuating the dog's structure. It also promotes a profuse harsh outer coat with a rich color and protects the skin.

There are two methods of carding. With the first approach, you simply pull the carding tool over the top of the coat. The second method is known as "line carding." It is a very systematic way to work over the dog.

With line carding, the fur is pushed up and out of the way, creating a seam line in the hair. With each stroke of the carding tool, a small section of fur is pulled down, much like with line combing and brushing. The amount of pressure applied while using carding tools will vary based on coat density, sensitivity of the skin and how highly detailed the area needs to be that is being worked. There should be enough pressure applied to pull out the downy undercoat but not so much so as to injure the skin. Caution should be exercised when carding. Repeatedly going over the same area with these types of tools can create an open wound much like scraping your knees on pavement.

Working with a Pumice Stone
The pumice stone is a light, porous piece of stone-like material that is dark gray in color. The abrasive surface makes it an ideal tool to pull soft undercoat from a dog's coat. It can be used either by dragging the stone over the top of the coat or by working a seam line, much in the same manner as line combing and line brushing.

The stone should fit comfortably in your hand. Many stylists prefer to use this tool prior to bathing due to its mildly offensive odor and granular residue the stone will leave behind as it is used. When not in use, it is advisable to store the stone in a closed container due to the odor and abrasive nature.

Carding with a #40 Blade
A dull #40 blade works as a wonderful carding tool. Hold the blade between your fingers, with your thumb nestled in the groove area on the back of the blade. Top card or line card the coat by dragging the fine teeth of the blade through the coat. Angle the blade slightly towards you as you pull. Adjust the pressure on the blade based on the coat density and amount of coat being removed. A fine-tooth stripping knife may be used in the same manor.

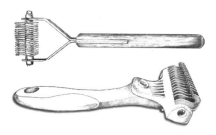

Undercoat Rake
Undercoat rakes have many small, sharp, curved blades set close together that remove undercoat. They are available in a variety of tooth

widths making this tool suitable for a wide range of breeds. On shedding breeds, rakes can remove dead, fuzzy undercoat in minutes yet leave the top coat shiny and healthy. On harsh coated dogs, they mimic the hand-stripped look quickly and easily.

Undercoat rakes can be used on a wet or a dry coat. Pull the rake in the direction of the coat growth. Always start with wider toothed rake to start. Work down to narrower teeth as the tool pulls through easily, removing less and less coat.

Undercoat rakes normally work better when used prior to bathing or in the tub on a wet coat. Use caution working with this tool. On some coat types or heavy coated dogs, they will cut the top coat while removing the undercoat.

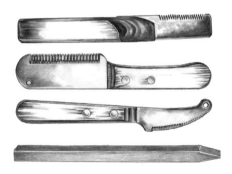

Hand-Stripping the Body Pattern

Hand-stripping is a technique in which the outer guard coat is plucked from the dog's skin. This procedure helps promote the proper coat texture and rich color of the breed. In most cases, the preferred time to hand-strip a dog is before the bath. During certain times of the year, the coat is easier to pull out. When the coat comes out easily, it is called a "blowing coat" or "blown coat."

Ideally, hand-stripping should correspond with the dog's natural cycle, based on its environment and hormonal levels. Using your fingers, a carding tool, stripping knife, stripping stone, or stripping stick, pull out a few hairs at a time to shape the coat and accentuate the dog's natural outline. Work methodically, pulling small amounts of coat at a time, always working in the direction of the coat growth.

Proper hand-stripping employs a gentle momentum and rhythm to remove hair, not brute force, which is uncomfortable for both the groomer and the pet. Keep your wrist locked in a neutral position and allow the rhythmic movement to stem from your shoulder, not your wrist or elbow. In general, the main body coat is easily removed and most pets do not mind the plucking process.

The cheeks, throat and private areas may be more sensitive, requiring the use of thinning shears or clippers. The length of coat to be left varies from under an inch to a little more than an inch and depends on the body section you are working. The coat should always appear very natural, never clipped or heavily trimmed. On many coats, a light application of chalk or powder before the bath allows a better grip on the coat and makes plucking and stripping much easier.

Finger Plucking

A number of harsh coated breeds are easy to hand-strip by simply finger plucking the longer guard hair. Grasp a few hairs at a time and pull in the direction of the coat growth. If the hair comes out easily, continue to pull out only the longer hairs that distract from the outline of the dog.

Most of these breed types should look very natural and an overly groomed look is frowned upon. On some coats, a light application of chalk or powder before the bath allows a better grip on the coat and makes plucking and stripping much easier.

In Closing

On many breeds, both carding and hand-stripping methods of grooming will be employed, especially with harsh coated breed types. When first learning how to hand-strip a coat, start with carding and finger plucking grooming techniques. The difference in coat texture between clipping and hand-stripping can be amazing and beautiful.

REASONS FOR TRIMMING THE PADS OF THE FEET

Health of Pet
Mats can cause discomfort between the toes and pads. Mats and excessive coat between the pads traps moisture, causing skin irritation. In winter climates, excessive coat causes ice and salt buildup between the pads and toes. Excessive coat hides burrs, thorns, tar, gum and a wide range of items that can be uncomfortable to the pet.

Cleanliness
A clean foot pad does not track as much dirt and mud into an owner's home.

Visual
Each breed standard will call for a certain type of foot. Trimming accentuates the proper foot type. It presents a "finished picture" of a well groomed pet.

The blades needed on most pets will range from a #15 to a #40, all used with a light touch. Hold the clipper like a pencil, unless unusual circumstances warrant differently. Always start with a rear foot. It's a safe distance that will allow you to note any adverse reaction from the pet to the handling of its feet. For safety reasons, we highly encourage using a clipper instead of scissors to clear the pad of long hair minimizing the risk of injury to the dog.

Lift the foot only high enough to get the job done. There is no reason to make the pet uncomfortable while you work. Keep the foot as low to the table as you can and still be able to clip freely—generally only an inch or two off the tabletop. This will ensure both the pet's comfort and safety, and yours, should the pet become unruly or try to bite.

Slide your hand down the pet's leg, with your thumb and first finger closest to the table. As you approach the foot, gently lift and let your thumb and first finger rest flush with the pet's foot pad. Holding the foot in this manner gives you the most control over the pet and reduces the risk of trimming up into the side coat of the foot. It also allows you to use your fingers as a brace to remove stubborn excessive coat from around the foot.

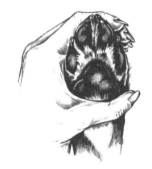

Keeping the clipper blade flush with the foot pad, lightly start clipping at the nail bed of the center two digits. Make a pass over the entire pad of the foot while barely making contact with the pads.

The second pass should focus on the outside digits and then repeat the process on the opposite outside digits. At this point, all the excessive coat should be removed from the foot

pad. (The outside of many foot pads can be "edged" at the same time.) Finish the procedure by clipping between the large heel pad and the digit pads.

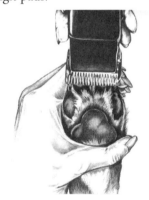

Spread the foot slightly with one hand and make two soft bouncing motions into the crevice area. On the second bounce, follow through and gently scoop the excessive hair out of the way. Repeat on the other side of the foot pad. Rotate clippers and repeat the soft bounce and follow-through action from the opposite direction.

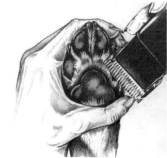

Creating a Natural Foot

Breeds that are candidates for feet trimming normally have short, silky or double-coated coats. The coat on their legs ranges from short, like the Labrador Retriever, to a combination of short and smooth coat with longer furnishings off the rear side of the legs, like a Golden Retriever. Their feet may look almost perfect with only a few sprigs popping up between their toes, or their feet may be fully covered by long, unkempt fur that hides the entire shape of the foot. In either case, the finished foot should show off the natural bone structure. It should look natural, without any scissor marks, and hold together long after the professional grooming is finished. There is nothing worse than seeing a foot three days after grooming with large hairs sticking out between the toes.

Do not dig into the crevice if the fur does not come out easily. Gently spread the crevice apart and work at the difficult area with a light touch. (This is normally a very large mat that will have skin irritations under the matting.) Clipping the pads should take between 10 and 30 seconds per foot depending on the size and attitude of the pet.

On smaller pets, you basically will remain in one spot as you move from one foot to another on the pet. Start with one back foot, then move to the opposite back foot, proceed to the front foot nearest you and finally reach over the pet and trim the opposite front foot. On a larger pet, you will need to move around the pet but still try to maintain your position while working from foot to foot. Follow the same procedure for the smaller pet, except you will reach under the pet rather than over the top of the body.

The foot pads may be trimmed before or after the bath. Trimming before, saves the time it takes to wash and dry the surrounding coat. However, you will have likely clipped through a very dirty coat that will act like sand paper on your blade. Waiting until after the bath allows you to work on a clean coat, which makes clipping easier and prolongs the life of your blade. In either case, the finish work can not be started, nor the job properly completed, until the pads are trimmed and clean.

Learn How Much Pressure to Apply
To learn how to apply the proper pressure to the blade while learning how to effectively clip the pads, practice on your own hand. Feel how much pressure is comfortable to you. With the clipper turned off, rotate and move it over your own fingers to learn how to manipulate it in difficult areas. If it's comfortable on your skin, it will be comfortable to the pet. When clipping a pet, always monitor the heat of the blade for safety and comfort.

Notes:

Notes From The Grooming Table ©2016

Trimming a Natural Foot with Bath and Brush-Style Pet

   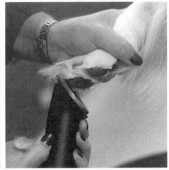

Trim the pads starting at the center two digits.

Remove the long fur at the edges of the foot while clipping the pads with a very close blade and a gentle touch.

Make sure to keep the blade flush with the pad while clipping.

While working flush with the pads, come right up under the nail bed.

Feet Types

The shape of the foot will be oval, cat-like or hare-footed, based on the original purpose of the dog. Breed standards for most dogs call for a well-arched toe. In general, the cat foot is found on breeds in which endurance is needed. The hare foot is found on breeds that need great speed and excel at jumping great distances. The oval foot is a combination of the cat and the hare foot, typical for breeds in which both endurance and speed are important. Large feet were developed for traveling in snow or sand or for swimming. Small feet were developed for dogs that had to travel rough and rocky terrain. When trimming the feet, not only is it important to create a neat outline of the foot but also to show off the proper shape of the foot for the breed.

Clipping the Pads

Start with a clean and dry coat. Trim the pads with a very close blade, ranging between a #40 and a #15 blade length. When trimming the long hair from between the pads, edge the outside of the foot pads by gently gliding over the perimeter of the digits. Make sure to stay flush with the pad of the foot. Do not cut up into the sides of the foot with this very short blade.

Trimming by Hand

Trimming the pads after the dog has been bathed will extend the life of your blades. Cutting through dirty hair on the pads is like cutting through sandpaper. Plus, you'll save time because the coat has already been fully prepared for finish work, so the pads will only need to be handled once.

Feet

Once the pads are clean, move to the top of the foot. Hold the foot in your hand and back brush with a slicker brush, starting at the nail bed of the toes. Repeat the back brushing stroke three or four times to pull the long fur up from between the toes. Use the full pad of a firm slicker brush.

Once the coat is standing away from the foot, begin trimming with either thinning shears or small scissors. Hold the shears at right angles to the foot and cut straight up. Trimming in this manner will ensure a "well-arched toe."

Once the long fur is removed, lift your elbow so the shear runs parallel to the dog's leg. Lifting your elbow minimizes the risk of taking too much coat off the top of the knuckles, flattening out the foot. Trim the long fur on the foot to the same length as the natural shorter coat found further up the leg, in the saddled area When you finish, the foot should look very neat and natural, as if it naturally grew that way. Thinning shears are a great help in achieving a very natural finish on any coat type.

Do some light detailing around the nail bed of the foot with small detailing shears to get a really neat look. Double-check the trimming work one last time by back brushing each foot. Correct anything found on the final brush up.

Creating a Natural Foot

Hocks

Some breeds can grow excessive coat on the hocks. Most coated breeds have a fair amount of bone, and this should be shown off when trimming the hock. Very agile dogs will be lighter boned. Athletic dogs should be moderately boned and drover type animals will be the heaviest boned.

Brush the coat out and away from the hock bone at right angles with a firm slicker brush.

With thinning shears or shears, trim off the excessive coat with the tips of the shears pointed toward the tabletop. If using regular shears, finish with thinning shears to enhance the natural look of the coat and remove any scissor marks. As with the feet, double-check the trimming work by brushing the coat out and away from the hock. Make sure the entire area is smooth and even.

Clipper-Trimming

Feet: Advanced Shortcut

With some dogs that are light or medium coated, the tops of the feet can be trimmed with a clipper using a longer blade, such as a #4F. When using this procedure, work against the lay of the coat. A #4F blade, used in reverse will provide roughly the length of a #7F, or two blade lengths shorter than working with the grain. When using a blade on the top of the foot, the fur does not need to be back brushed at the beginning of the procedure.

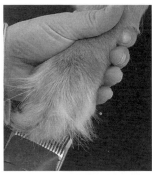

Lift the dog's foot and begin clipping at the nail beds, working first over the middle two digits. Lift the heel of the blade slightly to help the coat feed into the blade. Use a soft touch with a small, bouncing motion.

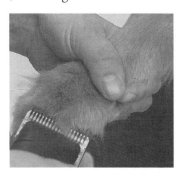

Once the top of the center two digits is clear, move to an outside digit and repeat the process, starting at the nail bed and working up into the foot. Repeat on the opposite side.

Next, spread the center digits slightly and with *only the edge of the blade*, lightly ride the side of each toe, much like doing a poodle foot but not as extreme. Never dig deeply between the toes with a longer clipper blade. You could easily catch the webbing between the toes with the blade and cut the dog. Back brush your work to check it. Remove any stray hairs with thinning shears or small detailing shears. Trim around the nail bed if necessary.

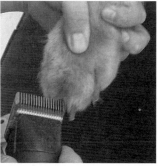

Hocks: Advanced Shortcut

The hocks on dogs that are light or medium coated can be trimmed with a longer blade like the one used for the advanced shortcut on the feet. Keep in mind that whenever a blade is used in reverse, it shortens the coat by clipping approximately two blade lengths more than clipping with the grain. Thus, if you reverse a #4F, you get roughly the length of a #7F used with the grain of the coat.

Again, there is no need to brush the coat out to clipper-cut the hocks. Start at the heel of the foot and run the blade smoothly and lightly up the hock. If there are long strays peeking out, quickly remove them by turning the blade around and going down on the hock, working with the lay of the coat. If the area continues to stick out, quickly remove the hairs with thinning shears as you detail the entire hock for the final finish.

Closing Thoughts

Whatever your chosen technique, the finished product should look very natural. The feet are neat and tidy without any clipper or scissor marks. The toes are well arched. The transition area between the natural saddled out areas found on the legs should blend seamlessly into the trimmed area of the foot.

Structure of a Mat

A mat is a tangled mass of hair, held together by interwoven fibers. There are many types of mats, some easier to remove than others based on the coat type of the pet.

Some coat types get matted and tangled easier than others because their hair shafts have more spurs. Fine-coated breeds such as Bichons, Poodles, Cockers and Schnauzers can get tangles in their coats that can be very difficult to brush out. Drop-coated breeds such as Shih Tzus, Lhasas and Malteses have similar problems with their fur. Dogs with combination coats such as Goldens, Australian Shepherds or Border Collies have target areas subject to tight tangles in the longer areas around the rump and behind the ears. Breeds that shed heavily will have dead coat packed into the guard coat that can, in most cases, easily be removed during the shedding season with the correct products and tools.

When seen under a microscope, a single hair shaft looks much like a single sprig from a briar bush with little thorns. Some hair types have lots of barbs on the hair shaft while others are much smoother. As a general rule, the guard coat has the most barbs per centimeter. The typical mat consists of numerous coarse guard hairs, crisscrossing one another. These guard hairs often end up catching and holding loose hairs from the finer undercoat. In other cases, the finer undercoat is still firmly attached to the skin. One of the reasons mats become so dense is that undercoat grows at a faster pace than the guard coat. Once tangles start to occur in the guard coat, the undercoat quickly packs up very tightly.

Other factors that cause matting are dirt, static, moisture, friction or compression. Dirt, dander and other debris that get caught up in the fur will literally hold the hair shafts together. If detected early enough, this type of tangling can easily be removed with the correct product and tools. Static can cause coats to tangle more easily. Adding a topical conditioner to the hair will help this dry weather problem as well as adding humidity to the pet's living environment.

Too much moisture is another dreaded culprit in pet hair matting. If a pet is not thoroughly brushed on a regular basis, any type of moisture—bathing, dew in the grass, a romp in the snow or swimming—can make mats impossible to remove with some coat types. Once a slightly tangled coat is wet and allowed to dry without brushing or blow-drying, the hair acts much like a wool sweater washed in warm water or dried in a dryer—the fibers shrink and become extremely tight.

Combing out this type of mat is extremely hard on the pet if a tangle is too tight. The only alternative is to shave if off and let the coat grow out again.

Areas that rub together on a pet are likely places for mats to form. These friction areas can vary depending on the lifestyle and body makeup of the pet, but typical areas are behind the ears, the legs and the rear section, especially the front legs and the inner thigh area. Other regions are tails, ears and collar areas. Compression mats are common in pets that are inactive and spend the majority of their time lounging. Most pets are right or left sided, just like people, so it's common to find one hip or side of the pet more tangled that the other.

Removing Mats and Tangles
In all but the most severe cases, washing and drying the dog before a full brush out is one of the most effective means of mat removal.

Remember, many mats are tangles held together by dirt and static. In most cases, it is better to wash the pet prior to any dematting work. The general rule is—if water and soap can penetrate the tangle, bathe the pet first.

The shampoo will have much the same effect on the tangle that soap does in getting a tight ring to slide off a finger. The same principle applies in the bath, where water and shampoo can work their magic. Once the coat is clean, use a high-velocity dryer to push the tangle apart.

With severe tangles, the high-velocity dryer can even be used in the tub after a second application of shampoo. With the lather still thick and foamy on the dog, blow the majority of shampoo and mats from the coat. Complete the bathing and continue dematting as you dry the coat.

Both these techniques are highly effective and humane. Both remove a high percentage of tangles, yet are extremely gentle on the animal's skin.

Should bathing and high velocity drying fail to remove a stubborn tangle, the best alternatives are good old-fashioned elbow grease by thoroughly line brushing the area or shaving the mat out.

Whatever method you choose for mat and tangle removal, make sure the procedure is kind and humane. Each animal has its own pain tolerance level. Most pets will react to pain in similar fashion as a two-year-old child. Most owners want the best for their pet and would never want to hurt their family friend.

Educate them on proper "at home" maintenance between groomings. If they are reluctant to take on simple "at home" maintenance, they have two choices—bring the pet in more frequently or learn to appreciate the pet in a short, low maintenance hair cut.

No matter what the owner says, your first concern is for the pet. Always put humanity before vanity.

Notes:

Bathing & Drying Directions Per Coat Type

Notes From The Grooming Table ©2016

Smooth Coated

Sporting Group
- German Shorthaired Pointer
- Pointer
- Vizsla
- Weimaraner

Hound Group
- Basenji
- Cirneco dell'Etna
- Dachshund (Smooth)
- Greyhound
- Ibizan Hound (Smooth)
- Pharaoh Hound
- Plott
- Redbone Coonhound
- Rhodesian Ridgeback
- Whippet

Working Group
- Boxer
- Cane Corso
- Dogue de Bordeaux
- Doberman Pinscher
- German Pinscher
- Great Dane

Terrier Group
- American Staffordshire Terrier
- Bull Terrier
- Manchester Terrier (Standard)
- Miniature Bull Terrier
- Staffordshire Bull Terrier

Toy Group
- Chihuahua (Short Haired)
- Italian Greyhound
- Manchester Terrier
- Miniature Pinscher
- Toy Fox Terrier

Non-Sporting Group
- Boston Terrier
- Bulldog
- Dalmatian
- French Bulldog

Miscellaneous Group
- Azawakh
- Sloughi
- Dogo Argentino

Coat & Skin Characteristics
- Coat short, close to body.
- Generally clean with few odor problems.
- Not well suited for extended exposure to weather without coats or jackets, especially colder climates.
- Biting insects can be a problem in warmer climates.
- Skin soft, sensitive to harsh products, tools and/or equipment, especially when used improperly.
- Fine coat sheds, has tendency to weave into fabrics.

Frequency
Bathe once a week to once every 12 weeks.

Pre-Work
Trim or grind nails at least every four to six weeks to maintain a healthy foot structure. Swab the ears clean with a mild ear cleaning solution. Prior to bathing, quickly go over the entire body with a high-velocity dryer to help lift dirt and dander away from the skin and loosen any shedding coat.

Bathing
Use a regular, all-purpose shampoo followed by a skin conditioner, unless another type of product is indicated. Massage the lather into all parts of the body to ensure cleanliness. On an exceptionally dirty pet, a soft natural scrub brush can be used. Use a gentle touch and follow the natural direction of coat growth to quickly clean the dog.

Drying
A number of drying methods can be used on this coat type. Start with hand towel drying. Follow with high-velocity drying to remove excess moisture and to blow out any loose fur, using the most powerful setting the dog will tolerate. Always keep one hand on the pet to help stabilize it during high-velocity drying.

Some Toy dogs cannot tolerate this drying method due to their size and sensitivity. If the high-velocity dryer is tolerated, dry until no moisture is being sprayed from the fur and/or no loose coat is being blown out. Finish with a different drying method. Some stylists remove the condenser cone and continue with the high-velocity dryer, holding the end of the nozzle right against the skin. Work in one area, with the coat growth, until the coat in that area is dry to the touch. Or, switch to natural air drying or kennel drying using a low temperature setting. Whatever process or combination of processes is used, drying is not finished until the coat is completely cool and dry to the touch.

Coat & Skin Characteristics
• Coat is short, close to the body and harsh.
• A wide range of weather conditions, both warm and cool, are tolerated.
• Tendency to produce natural body oil that creates "doggie odor" in some dogs.
• A film can be felt if dog is dirty
• Harsh coat sheds during typical shedding periods in cooler climates; can be profuse.
• Guard coat clings and weaves into fabrics, and can be difficult to remove.

Frequency
Bathe once a week to once every 12 weeks.

Pre-Work
Trim or grind nails at least every four to six weeks to maintain a healthy foot structure. Swab the ears clean with a mild ear cleaning solution. Prior to bathing, quickly go over the entire body with a high-velocity dryer to help lift dirt and dander away from the skin and loosen any shedding coat.

Bathing
Use a regular, all-purpose shampoo followed by a skin conditioner, unless another type of product is indicated. Sink your fingers deeply into the coat while scrubbing to be thorough. A rubber curry with cone-type teeth also does an excellent job of working the shampoo to the skin and lifting dirt and debris to the surface where it can easily be rinsed away. A natural bristle scrub brush works very well on the coat, especially around the feet and legs. With either a rubber curry or a scrub brush, scrub in the direction of the coat growth.

Drying
A number of drying methods can be used on this coat type. Start with a vigorous hand towel drying. Follow with high-velocity drying to remove excess moisture and to blow out the bulk of the loose fur, using the most powerful setting the dog will tolerate. When no moisture is being sprayed from the fur and/or no loose coat is being blown out, another drying method may be used. Many stylists remove the condenser cone and continue with the high-velocity dryer, holding the end of the nozzle right against the skin and blowing in the direction of the natural lay of the coat. Work the air in a small circular fashion with the lay of the coat until the coat in that area is dry. Drying may be continued with natural air-drying or kennel drying using a low temperature setting. Or, finish drying by hand using a heat-stand dryer while brushing the coat with a pliable brush. Whatever process or combination of processes is used, drying is not complete until the coat is completely cool and dry to the touch.

Sporting Group
• Chesapeake Bay Retriever
• Curly-Coated Retriever
• Labrador Retriever

Hound Group
• American English Coonhound
• American Foxhound
• Basset Hound
• Beagle
• Black and Tan Coonhound
• Bloodhound
• Bluetick Coonhound
• English Foxhound
• Harrier
• Portuguese Podengo Pequeno (Smooth)
• Treeing Walker Coonhound

Working Group
• Boerboel
• Bullmastiff
• Greater Swiss Mountain Dog
• Mastiff
• Neapolitan Mastiff
• Rottweiler

Terrier Group
• Fox Terrier (Smooth)
• Parson Russell Terrier (Smooth)
• Rat Terrier
• Russell Terrier (Smooth)

Toy Group
• Pug

Non-Sporting Group
• Chinese Shar-Pei
• Norwegian Lundehund

Herding Group
• Australian Cattle Dog
• Belgian Malinois
• Beauceron
• Canaan Dog
• Collie (Smooth)
• Entlebucher Mountain Dog

Miscellaneous Group
• Portuguese Podengo (Smooth)

Notes From The Grooming Table ©2016

Combination Coated

BATHING & DRYING

Sporting Group
- American Water Spaniel
- Flat-Coated Retriever
- Golden Retriever
- Nova Scotia Duck Tolling Retriever

Hound Group
- Borzoi
- Dachshund (Long Haired)
- Saluki

Working Group
- Kuvasz

Toy Group
- Cavalier King Charles Spaniel
- Chihuahua (Long Haired)
- English Toy Spaniel
- Japanese Chin
- Papillon

Non-Sporting Group
- Tibetan Spaniel

Herding Group
- Miniature American Shepherd
- Australian Shepherd
- Belgian Sheepdog
- Belgian Tervuren
- Border Collie

Coat & Skin Characteristics
- Combination of long, silky coat and short smooth coat. Very short, tight coat about face and front sides of legs, shorter coat on body and longer furnishings on undercarriage, rear sides of legs and tail
- Longer coat has tendency to form mats and tangles if not brushed often enough (from daily to weekly)
- Coat between feet and pads is long and has tendency to mat and collect dirt and debris
- Seasonal shedding pattern depends on climate
- During shedding, loose coat collects everywhere and clings to everything
- Wide range of temperatures can be tolerated, both warm and cool

Frequency
Bathe once a week to once every 12 weeks.

Pre-Work
Trim/grind nails at least every four to six weeks to maintain a healthy foot structure. Swab ears with a mild ear cleaning solution. Prior to bathing, quickly go over entire body with a high-velocity dryer to lift dirt and dander away from the skin and loosen any shedding coat.

Bathing
Use a regular, all-purpose shampoo followed by a skin conditioner unless otherwise indicated. Sink your fingers deeply into the coat while scrubbing to do a thorough job. A rubber curry with cone-type teeth does an excellent job helping shampoo penetrate the longer coat. A natural bristle scrub brush works very well on the shorter coat, especially around the feet and legs. A scrub brush works well on longer fur when used with the growth of the coat, such the rear of the dog where fecal matter can cling to the fur.

Drying
A variety of drying methods can be used, starting with vigorous hand towel drying. Follow with high velocity drying in the direction of the coat growth to remove excess moisture and blow out the bulk of loose fur; use the most powerful setting the dog will tolerate. Be sure the high-pressure airflow does not fold the coat onto itself, causing "whip knots," that are almost impossible to remove. To avoid whip knots and use the high-velocity dryer effectively, keep the airflow as close to the skin as possible but far enough away so the coat does not totally fold over onto itself. Dryer distance from coat changes with the coat length—closer for shorter fur, further away for longer fur. This process is tricky so pay attention to technique. When no moisture is being sprayed from the fur and/or no loose coat is being blown out, another drying method may be used. Some stylists continue with the high-velocity dryer, removing the condenser cone. If using the high-velocity dryer, hold the end of the nozzle, minus the condenser cone, right against the skin, blowing in the direction of the natural lay of the coat. Work the air in a small circular fashion until the coat is dry in that area. Or, switch to natural-air drying or kennel drying using a low temperature setting. Another option is to finish drying with a heat stand dryer while brushing the coat. Whatever process, or combination of processes used, drying is not finished until the coat is completely cool and dry to the touch. This coat type needs some sort of active drying method, either high velocity drying or heat stretch drying during the final stage, to produce a high-quality grooming. When using airflow, work in the direction the coat grows to allow the coat to lie close to the skin.

Coat & Skin Characteristics
• Coat is a combination of straight and short to moderate length. Outer guard coat is harsh to touch, while abundant soft down undercoat is thick and dense to protect dog in extreme weather conditions
• A wide range of weather conditions can be tolerated, both warm and extremely cold.
• Tendency to produce a natural body oil creating "doggie odor" in some dogs.
• A film can be felt if dog is dirty.
• Harsh coat sheds during typical shedding periods in cooler climates.
• Shedding can be profuse in areas that have seasonal climate changes.
• Coat clings and weaves into fabrics and can be very difficult to remove.

Frequency
Bathe once a week to once every 12 weeks.

Pre-Work
Trim/grind nails at least every four to six weeks to maintain a healthy foot structure. Swab ears with a mild ear cleaning solution. Prior to bathing, quickly go over entire body with a high-velocity dryer to lift dirt and dander away from the skin and loosen any shedding coat.

Bathing
Use a regular, all-purpose shampoo followed by a skin conditioner, unless otherwise indicated. Sink your fingers deeply into the coat while scrubbing to do a thorough job. A rubber curry with cone-type teeth does an excellent job of helping shampoo to penetrate the longer coat. A natural bristle scrub brush works very well on the shorter coat, especially around the feet and legs. A scrub brush works well on longer fur used with the growth of coat, such as on the rear of the dog where fecal matter may cling to the fur.

Drying
A variety of drying methods can be used starting with a vigorous hand towel drying. Follow with high velocity drying to remove excess moisture and to blow out the bulk of the loose fur, using the most powerful setting the dog will tolerate. Be sure the high-pressure airflow does not fold the coat onto itself, causing "whip knots" that are almost impossible to remove later. To avoid "whip knots" and use the high-velocity dryer effectively, keep the airflow as close to the skin as possible but far enough away so the coat does not totally fold over onto itself. The distance of the dryer from the coat changes with the length of the coat, i.e., closer for shorter fur, further away for longer fur. This process is tricky so pay attention to technique. When no moisture is being sprayed from the fur and/ or no loose coat is being blown out, another drying method may be used. Some stylists continue with the high-velocity dryer, removing the condenser cone. In that case, hold the end of the nozzle right against the skin. Work the air in a small circular fashion until the coat is dry in that area. Or, switch to natural-air drying or kennel drying using a low temperature setting. You also may finish drying with a heat stand dryer while brushing. Whatever process or combination of processes is used, drying is not finished until the coat is completely cool and dry to the touch. This coat type needs to have some sort of active drying method in the final stage, either high velocity or heat stretch, to produce a high quality groom job.

Hound Group
• Norwegian Elkhound

Working Group
• Akita
• Alaskan Malamute
• Anatolian Shepherd Dog
• Chinook
• Siberian Husky

Non-Sporting Group
• Finnish Spitz
• Norwegian Lundehund
• Schipperke
• Shiba Inu

Herding Group
• German Shepherd Dog
• Norwegian Buhund
• Swedish Vallhund
• Welsh Corgi (Cardigan)
• Welsh Corgi (Pembroke)

Miscellaneous Group
• Norrbottenspets

Heavy Coated

BATHING & DRYING

Working Group
- Bernese Mountain Dog
- Great Pyrenees
- Leonberger
- Newfoundland
- Saint Bernard
- Samoyed
- Tibetan Mastiff

Toy Group
- Pekingese
- Pomeranian

Non-Sporting Group
- American Eskimo Dog
- Chow Chow
- Keeshond

Herding Group
- Collie (Rough)
- Finnish Lapphund
- Icelandic Sheepdog
- Shetland Sheepdog

Coat & Skin Characteristics
- A combination of long, thick, silky coat and limited amount of short, smooth coat.
- Longer coat has tendency to form severe mats and tangles if not brushed regularly (from daily to weekly). If not cared for, skin may become inflamed and/or infected due to lack of air circulation.
- Coat between feet and pads is long and has tendency to mat and collect dirt and debris.
- Seasonal shedding pattern depends on climate.
- During shedding, loose coat collects everywhere and clings to everything.
- Coat clings and weaves into fabrics and can be very difficult to remove.

Frequency
Bathe once a week to once every 12 weeks.

Pre-Work
Trim/grind nails at least every four to six weeks to maintain a healthy foot structure. Swab ears with a mild ear cleaning solution. Prior to bathing, quickly go over entire body with a high-velocity dryer to lift dirt and dander away from the skin and loosen any shedding coat.

Bathing
Use a regular, all-purpose shampoo followed by a skin conditioner unless otherwise indicated. Sink your fingers deeply into the coat while scrubbing to do a thorough job. A rubber curry with cone-type teeth does an excellent job helping shampoo penetrate the longer coat. A natural bristle scrub brush works very well on the shorter coat, especially around the feet and legs. A scrub brush works well on longer fur when used with the growth of the coat, such the rear of the dog where fecal matter can cling to the fur.

Drying
A variety of drying methods can be used, starting with vigorous hand towel drying. Follow with high velocity drying in the direction of the coat growth to remove excess moisture and blow out the bulk of the loose fur; use the most powerful setting the dog will tolerate. Be sure the high-pressure airflow does not fold the coat onto itself, causing "whip knots" that are almost impossible to remove. To avoid whip knots and use the high-velocity dryer effectively, keep the airflow as close to the skin as possible but far enough away so the coat does not totally fold over onto itself. The distance of the dryer from the coat changes with the coat length—closer for shorter fur, further away for longer fur. This process is tricky so pay attention to technique. When no moisture is being sprayed from the fur and/or no loose coat is being blown out, another drying method may be used. Some stylists continue with the high-velocity dryer, removing the condenser cone. If using the high-velocity dryer, hold the end of the nozzle, minus the condenser cone, right against the skin, blowing in the direction of the natural lay of the coat. Work the air in a small circular fashion until the coat is dry in that area. Or, switch to natural-air drying or kennel drying using a low temperature setting. Another option is to finish drying with a heat stand dryer while brushing the coat. Whatever process or combination of processes is used, drying is not finished until the coat is completely cool and dry to the touch. This coat type needs some sort of active drying method, either high velocity drying or heat stretch drying during the final stage, to produce a high-quality groom job.

Coat & Skin Characteristics

- These animals have a combination of long, silky coat as well as short, smooth coat on some parts of their bodies.
- They have very short, tight coat about the face and on areas of the front sides of the legs, a shorter coat on the body and longer furnishings on the undercarriage and rear sides of the legs and tail.
- The longer coat has a tendency to form mats and tangles depending on how often the dog is brushed (from daily to weekly).
- This coat type will have a seasonal shedding pattern depending on the climate in which the dog lives.
- Coat between the feet and pads will be long and have a tendency to mat and collect dirt and debris.
- When shedding, the loose coat collects everywhere and clings to everything.

Sporting Group
- Boykin Spaniel
- Brittany Spaniel
- Cocker Spaniel
- Clumber Spaniel
- English Cocker Spaniel
- English Setter
- English Springer Spaniel
- Field Spaniel
- Gordon Setter
- Irish Red and White Setter
- Irish Setter
- Sussex Spaniel
- Welsh Springer Spaniel

Terrier Group
- Cesky Terrier

Frequency

Bathe once a week to once every 12 weeks.

Pre-Work

Trim/grind nails at least every four to six weeks to maintain a healthy foot structure. Swab ears with a mild ear cleaning solution. Prior to bathing, quickly go over entire body with a high-velocity dryer to lift dirt and dander away from the skin and loosen any shedding coat.

Bathing

Use a regular, all-purpose shampoo followed by a skin conditioner unless otherwise indicated. Sink your fingers deeply into the coat while scrubbing to do a thorough job. A rubber curry with cone-type teeth does an excellent job helping shampoo penetrate the longer coat. A natural bristle scrub brush works very well on the shorter coat, especially around the feet and legs. A scrub brush works well on longer fur when used with the growth of the coat, such the rear of the dog where fecal matter can cling to the fur.

Drying

A variety of drying methods can be used, starting with vigorous hand towel drying. Follow with high velocity drying in the direction of the coat growth to remove excess moisture and blow out the bulk of the loose fur; use the most powerful setting the dog will tolerate. Be sure the high-pressure airflow does not fold the coat onto itself, causing "whip knots," that are almost impossible to remove. To avoid whip knots and use the high-velocity dryer effectively, keep the airflow as close to the skin as possible but far enough away so the coat does not totally fold over onto itself. The distance of the dryer from the coat changes with the length of the coat—closer for shorter fur, further away for longer fur. This process is tricky so pay attention to technique. When no moisture is being sprayed from the fur and/or no loose coat is being blown out, another drying method may be used. Some stylists continue with the high-velocity dryer, removing the condenser cone. If using the high-velocity dryer, hold the end of the nozzle, without the condenser cone, right against the skin, blowing in the direction of the natural lay of the coat. Work the air in a small circular fashion until the coat is dry in that area. Another method is to blanket the dog's body, while still wet, in a large towel, fastening the towel so it fits snugly around the body. Before placing the towel, comb or brush the moist coat in the direction you want it to lay in the finished trim. Then drape the towel over the pet and fasten it at the throat and belly to hold it in place. Once the "blanket" is in place, proceed with either natural-air drying, kennel drying using a low temperature setting, or continuing to hand blow dry the longer furnishings with mild heat (which will yield the best quality finish for the final trim). Whatever process or combination of processes is used, drying is not finished until the coat is completely cool and dry to the touch. This coat type needs to have some sort of active drying method, either high velocity drying or heat stretch drying during the final stage, to produce a high quality groom job. When using airflow, work in the direction the coat grows to allow the coat to lie close to the skin.

Natural Long Haired

BATHING & DRYING

Hound Group
- Afghan Hound 🐾

Terrier Group
- Skye Terrier 🐾

Toy Group
- Chinese Crested (Powderpuff) 🐾
- Havanese 🐾
- Maltese 🐾
- Shih Tzu 🐾
- Silky Terrier 🐾
- Yorkshire Terrier 🐾

Non-Sporting Group
- Coton de Tulear
- Lhasa Apso 🐾
- Löwchen 🐾
- Tibetan Terrier 🐾

Herding Group
- Bearded Collie
- Berger Picard
- Briard
- Old English Sheepdog 🐾
- Polish Lowland Sheepdog
- Pyrenean Shepherd

🐾 *When maintaining pet trims with coats less than 3" long, use Curly and Wavy Coated bathing and drying directions.*

Coat & Skin Characteristics
- Long coat over entire body, drop-coat type, considered non-shedding
- Groomed-to-breed standard, long coats are left in natural state, with very little trimming. Pet owners often choose shorter, lower maintenance trims. *(See "Classic Pet Poodles and Drop Coat Styles" section)*
- Coat has tendency to form mats and tangles if not brushed regularly —at least three times weekly—unless the dog is kept in low maintenance trim style. If not properly cared for, mats and tangles may make shaving the coat and starting over the only humane alternative.
- If left unattended, skin can become inflamed and/or infected due to poor air circulation.
- Coat between feet and pads is long and has tendency to mat and collect dirt and debris
- Ear and eye problems due to excessive coat
- Wide range of weather conditions can be tolerated, both warm & cool

Frequency
Bathe once a week to once every 12 weeks.

Pre-Work
Trim or grind nails every four to six weeks to maintain a healthy foot structure. Clean the ears by swabbing with a mild ear cleaning solution. Hair should be plucked from within the ear canal only as necessary for healthy ear management. Use a small amount of ear powder designed for this purpose. Once the powder is worked in, begin to gently remove small amounts of fur at a time with either your fingers or hemostats, whichever is safest based on the demeanor of the dog.

Prior to bathing, quickly go over the entire body and remove any serious mats or tangles. If the tangle can be penetrated with water, leave it and remove when the dog is clean. If the pet has not been in for professional grooming for six weeks or more, remove the excessive body coat and set the pattern before bathing, if setting a pet clipper-trim.

Bathing
Use a regular, all-purpose type shampoo followed by a skin and coat conditioner, unless otherwise indicated. Sink your fingers deeply into the coat while massaging the shampoo to do a thorough job. A rubber curry with cone-type teeth also does an excellent job of helping shampoo penetrate the longer coat. A natural bristle scrub brush works very well when used in long strokes with the lay of the coat.

Tip #1: Many mats and tangles are locked into place by dirt and debris. If the tangles are not severe, removing them is much easier when the dog is clean.

Tip # 2: Removing tough tangles from a coat is very similar to using a lubricating agent to remove a ring that is too tight on a finger. After the first shampoo and most of the dirt has been removed, apply a second lather. With the shampoo worked into the coat, hold a section of fur between your fingers and begin brushing from the tips of the coat in towards the root. Always use your own hand as a buffer between the pet's skin and the brush while working the tangle from the coat.

Wet dog skin, just like our own, is more susceptible to injury, but the lubricant from the shampoo will allow you to work even the most stubborn mats from the coat.

Tip #3: Apply a heavy conditioner to the pet's clean coat after bathing. With the conditioner still in the coat, place the pet in a warm, confined space, wrapped in a towel for 15–20 minutes. Rinse as usual. In the drying process, let the high-velocity dryer blow most of the tangles free.

Drying

In order to get a quality result in the final groom, an active drying method must be used to add body to the coat. Start by firmly blotting the coat with a thick towel. Change to a fresh one when the towel is saturated. Continue with this process until the dog is almost dry. Follow with high velocity drying to remove excess moisture. Use the highest power setting the dog will tolerate, keeping one hand on the pet at all times to help stabilize it. Be sure the high-pressure airflow is not folding the coat onto itself, causing "whip knots," that are almost impossible to remove later. During the initial high velocity drying, look for tangles in the coat and work them out with the high volume airflow instead of totally removing them with a brush or comb.

Work over the entire body, starting at the rump and working forward. Concentrate on the body first, and then move on to the legs, finishing with the head and ears. When no moisture is being sprayed from the fur and as many tangles as possible have been removed with the dryer, another drying method may be used. Some stylists remove the condenser cone and continue with the high-velocity dryer. If using the high-velocity dryer, hold the end of the nozzle, without the condenser cone, as close to the skin as possible without folding the coat onto itself, to avoid whip tangles. With your free hand—and using a firm brush—lightly brush the area of the coat on which the air is blowing. Work in light, quick strokes (1 to 2 strokes per second depending on the length of fur) not moving to another section until the brush flows freely. When the pet is almost dry, switch to natural-air drying or kennel drying using a low temperature setting for the final drying process. Or, finish drying with a heat stand dryer while brushing the coat. This will bring the warm air right down to the skin, allowing the coat to be straightened and dried from the inside out.

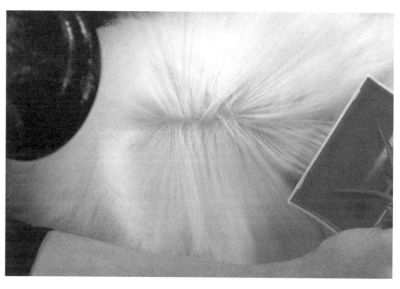

To get a quality finish on long coated breeds, the coat needs to be as straight as possible. There should be between one and four brush strokes per second depending upon the length of the hair. The light brushing technique together with the warm air sets the coat straight and gives the fluffy appearance. Brush only where the air is striking the coat.

Where light matting is still left in the coat, the coat can be de-matted and stretch dried at the same time.

Curly & Wavy Coated

Sporting Group
- Irish Water Spaniel

Hound Group
- Afghan Hound 🐾

Working Group
- Black Russian Terrier
- Portuguese Water Dog

Terrier
- Bedlington Terrier
- Kerry Blue Terrier
- Skye Terrier 🐾
- Soft Coated Wheaten Terrier

Toy Group
- Chinese Crested (Powderpuff) 🐾
- Havanese 🐾
- Maltese 🐾
- Shih Tzu 🐾
- Silky Terrier 🐾
- Yorkshire Terrier 🐾

Non-Sporting Group
- Bichon Frise
- Lhasa Apso 🐾
- Löwchen 🐾
- Poodle
- Tibetan Terrier 🐾

Herding Group
- Bouvier des Flandres
- Old English Sheepdog 🐾

🐾 *When maintaining pet trims with coats longer than 3" long, use Natural Long Haired bathing and drying directions.*

Coat & Skin Characteristics
- Soft, curly or wavy coat, considered non-shedding coat type.
- Coat has tendency to form mats and tangles if not brushed regularly—at least three times weekly, unless the dog is kept in low maintenance trim style.
- Regular bathing and trimming required for coat to remain healthy and manageable.
- A wide range of weather conditions can be tolerated, both warm and cool.

Frequency
Bathe once a week to once every 12 weeks. Trim every four to six weeks to maintain a stylized fashion.

Pre-Work
Trim or grind nails at least every four to six weeks to maintain a healthy foot structure. Clean the ears by swabbing with a mild ear cleaning solution. Hair should be plucked from within the ear canal only as necessary for healthy ear management. Prior to bathing, quickly go over the entire body and remove any serious mats or tangles. *If the tangle can be penetrated with water, leave it and remove when the dog is clean.* If the pet has not been in for professional grooming for six weeks or more, remove the excessive body coat and set the pattern before bathing.

Bathing
Use a regular, all-purpose shampoo followed by a skin conditioner unless otherwise indicated. Sink your fingers deeply into the coat while scrubbing to do a thorough job. A rubber curry with cone-type teeth does an excellent job of helping shampoo to penetrate the longer coat. A natural bristle scrub brush works very well on the shorter coat, especially around the feet and legs.

Drying
In order to get a quality result in the final trim, an active drying method must be used to add body to the coat. A few breeds have coats that are supposed to be wavy or curly. These do not require the same degree of effort as the curly type with a coat that needs to be fully fluffed and straightened, but both require active drying methods. Start with a vigorous hand towel drying. Follow with high velocity drying to remove excessive moisture, using the highest power setting the dog will tolerate. Be sure the airflow does not fold the coat onto itself, causing "whip knots" that are almost impossible to remove later. During the initial high velocity drying, look for tangles in the coat and work them out with the high volume airflow instead of removing them totally with a brush or comb. Work over the entire dog, starting at the rump and working forward. Concentrate on the shorter coat of the body first and then start on the legs. Any fur trimmed shorter than a #7 blade length needs very little active drying attention. When no moisture is sprayed from the fur, another drying method may be used. With a curly-coated dog, it is important to straighten all the kinks in the coat so you can get a really smooth finish on the final trim.

Continue with the high-velocity dryer. Whether or not you use the condenser cone depends on the density and curl factor of the coat. If working without the condenser cone, hold the end of the nozzle right against the skin. Work the air in a small circular fashion until the coat is almost dry in that area. Once the pet is cool/damp, finish drying by "stretch drying" or "fluff drying" with a heated stand dryer while brushing the coat by hand. Focus the warm air right in the area you are brushing, allowing the coat to be straightened and dried in the most efficient manner. Work in small sections with rapid, light brush strokes—2–3 strokes per second—until the coat is dry.

When dealing with a breed that requires the coat to be wavy or curly, leave it slightly damp and move to an inactive drying method to finish up. This will leave the desired texture in the coat. Switch to natural air-drying or kennel drying using a low temperature setting.

Whatever process or combination of processes is used, drying is not complete until the coat is completely cool and dry to the touch.

Brushing
Prior to the haircut, the dog must be completely tangle-free. Use a firm slicker brush or a wide-toothed comb to methodically work over the entire body in a line brush fashion. If the pet has very fine fur or delicate skin, use a soft slicker brush instead. Pay close attention to the friction points where mats and tangles typically hide: behind the ears, around the ruff, in the armpits, the thigh area, the undercarriage and the tail. Be careful when using any tool with metal teeth or bristles. A heavy hand or too much repetition in an area can cause cuts and/or brush burns.

Breeds that require a curly or wavy coat when the grooming is finished:
- *Irish Water Spaniel*
- *Portuguese Water Dog (wavy coated)*
- *Kerry Blue Terrier (back coat only)*

See individual Grooming and Trimming Instructions on specific breeds for further instructions.

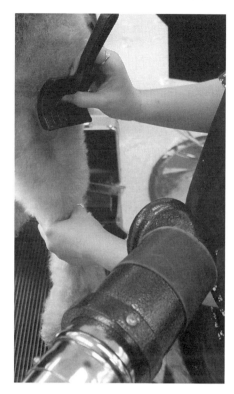

Work only in the area where the air is striking. Make your brush strokes light and rapid, one to four strokes per second based on coat length.

Focus on getting the pet dry and the coat straightened. Hold the dryer as close as possible to the skin without curling the coat onto itself, causing tangles. Watch the area constantly. When you first start on a section, the coat will appear slightly clumped together. As the hair dries, it will separate and become very fine. This is your signal to move to another area.

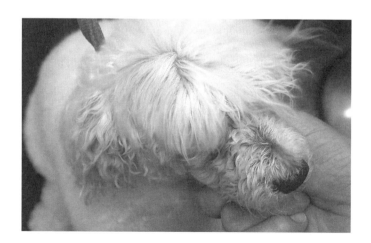

Finish the entire drying process at the head and ears. Work from the base of the skull—the occiput—forward. Don't use a condenser cone for the head and face, but do keep the base of the nozzle very close to the skin for optimum speed and coat straightening.

Notes From The Grooming Table ©2016

Wire Coated

Sporting Group
- German Wirehaired Pointer
- Spinone Italiano
- Wirehaired Pointing Griffon
- Wirehaired Vizsla

Hound Group
- Dachshund (Wire Haired)
- Ibizan Hound (Wire Haired)
- Irish Wolfhound
- Otterhound
- Petit Basset Griffon Vendéen
- Portuguese Podengo Pequeno (Wire Haired)
- Scottish Deerhound

Working Group
- Giant Schnauzer
- Standard Schnauzer

Terrier Group
- Airedale Terrier
- Australian Terrier
- Border Terrier
- Cairn Terrier
- Dandie Dinmont Terrier
- Fox Terrier (Wire Haired)
- Glen of Imaal Terrier
- Irish Terrier
- Lakeland Terrier
- Miniature Schnauzer
- Norfolk Terrier
- Norwich Terrier
- Parson Russell Terrier (Rough)
- Russell Terrier (Broken or Rough)
- Scottish Terrier
- Sealyham Terrier
- Welsh Terrier
- West Highland White Terrier

Toy Group
- Affenpinscher
- Brussels Griffon

Miscellaneous Group
- Grand Basset Griffon Vendéen
- Portuguese Podengo (Wire Haired)

Coat & Skin Characteristics
- Combination of soft, dense undercoat over bulk of body.
- Wiry guard hair grows over entire body: face, ears, body, legs and tail.
- Longer guard coat has tendency to form mats and tangles if bathing, brushing, hand-plucking or hand-stripping is not done regularly, every four to eight weeks.
- Able to tolerate a wide range of weather conditions, both warm and cool. (During natural shedding seasons in cooler climates, soft undercoat will shed out.
- Coat between feet and pads is long and has tendency to mat and collect dirt and debris.

Frequency
Bathe once a week to once every 12 weeks. Trim every four to six weeks to maintain a stylized fashion.

Pre-Work
Card and hand-strip dog prior to bathing and drying.

Bathing
Use a regular, all-purpose shampoo. If the skin is exceptionally dry, apply a light skin conditioner, otherwise, bypass this step because the conditioner will soften the coat. That is undesirable for this coat type. To be thorough, sink your fingers deeply into the coat while scrubbing. A rubber curry with cone-type teeth also does an excellent job of working the shampoo right to the skin and lifting dirt and debris to the surface where it can easily be rinsed away. A natural bristle scrub brush works very well on the shorter coat, especially around the feet and legs. With either a rubber curry or a scrub brush, scrub in the direction of the coat growth.

Drying
A number of drying methods can be used on this coat type. Start with a vigorous hand towel drying. Follow with high-velocity drying in the direction of the coat growth to remove excess moisture and to blow out the bulk of the loose fur, using the most powerful setting the dog will tolerate. When no moisture is being sprayed from the fur and/or no loose coat is being blown out, another drying method may be used. Many stylists remove the condenser cone and continue with the high-velocity dryer, holding the end of the nozzle close to the skin. (On pets that have been clipper-cut, areas that were trimmed with blades shorter than a #7F need no special drying attention.) Work the air in a small circular fashion, with the natural lay of the coat, until the coat is dry in that area. Drying may be continued with natural air-drying or kennel drying using a low temperature setting. Or, finish drying with a heat-stand dryer while brushing the coat. Blanket drying also works well with this coat type if the coat is being hand-stripped. Once the bulk of the moisture is removed, use a fine brush or comb to brush the coat in the direction you want the hair to lie. Drape a large towel over the body of the dog. Pin the towel snugly around the neck area and under the belly to flatten the coat. This drying technique will ensure the coat conforms to the natural outline of the dog. Whatever process or combination of processes is used, drying is not finished until the coat is completely cool and dry to the touch.

Coat & Skin Characteristics

- Cords vary slightly in shape and density but are about the size of a high-lighter pen on most breeds, with the exception of the Bergamasco which has thicker cords.
- Cords are made up of strong top coat entwining itself around soft, wooly undercoat to form each cord. Referred to as a "controlled mat."
- A well cared for coat has cords that grow nearly to the ground.
- Cord coats are difficult to make as the coat transitions from puppy to adult.
- Fingers are the primary tool for maintaining a corded coat.
- Cords can be split apart with shears should the cord get too thick.
- Frequent bathing is not recommended. Shampoo is difficult to rinse out completely, and it is extremely difficult to get the dog thoroughly dry.
- A properly cared for coat takes about three years to attain full length. This means weekly maintenance.
- Skin problems and fleas must be avoided.

Working Group
- Komondor

Toy Group
- Havanese

Non-Sporting Group
- Poodle

Herding Group
- Bergamasco
- Puli
- Spanish Water Dog

Frequency

Bathe every 12 weeks or when needed. Work the cords once a week to once every four weeks, without a full bath.

Pre-Work

Trim or grind nails at least every four to six weeks to maintain a healthy foot structure. Clean the ears every four to six weeks. If hair forms inside the ear canal, apply an ear powder and gently pluck the hair from inside the canal. Use care not to pull any coat from outside the canal opening. Clean ears by swabbing with a mild ear cleaning solution.

Bathing

Bathe the dog with a heavily diluted, very gentle shampoo. Squeeze the shampoo solution through the coat, never rub or scrub. Rinse while squeezing the water through the cords. Do not stop until the water runs clear.

Drying

Wrap the dog in towels and blot the cords dry. Apply gentle pressure to handfuls of cords. Get the coat as dry as possible using this method. Use as many towels as necessary to do a thorough job or the dog may never dry totally. Air dry in a kennel enclosure where it is warm and comfortable. Use box fans to keep air circulating around the dog. Total drying time with a corded coat can take anywhere from 3–12 hours, or more. Much depends on how much moisture is present in the coat, the air flow around the dog and the humidity in the drying area. Because of the extended drying time, care must be taken to maintain a low heat temperature in the circulating air, or the dog will be at risk for heat stroke. For the same reason, it is important to have water available for the dog. If the coat has not been thoroughly dried, in a few days bacteria will form inside the cords, creating a foul odor. If this happens, the entire bathing process has to be repeated or you risk losing the cords.

Cords

The base of a cord is about 1–2 inches square. Very often the cords will start to form by themselves, with little assistance. Prior to bathing, gently pull the strands away from one another to keep the cord as a separate strand. If the coat is shorter and feels "spongy" to the touch, it may not be forming natural cords. Mist the area with water or a light skin conditioner to help see the natural cord separation. Separate the area with your fingers into ½–1 inch square sections, starting at the base of each cord. If a cord is too thick, it can be split in two by working it with your fingers or by carefully cutting the cord with shears. Try to follow the natural separation as it splits.

Toy
- Chinese Crested (Hairless)

Non-Sporting Group
- Xoloitzcuintli

Miscellaneous
- American Hairless Terrier
- Peruvian Inca Orchid

Coat & Skin Characteristics
- Some breeds will have a few sprigs of hair on select parts of their body or even be lightly coated on areas that are traditionally hairless. The exception is the Chinese Crested which has plumes and feathers on select areas of their body.
- Prone to acne and blackheads especially when the dogs are young.
- Can have a doggie odor due to the oils produced in their skin.
- Prone to dry skin problems.
- Some hairless dogs have an adverse reaction to lanolin commonly found in moisturizers and occasionally in shampoo products.
- In some cases, a hairless dog takes more care than a coated breed due to the exposure of their skin.
- Many hairless dogs are susceptible to problems associated with excessive sun exposure, especially dogs with lighter colored skin.
- Let them air dry or use a dryer on a very LOW setting to keep their skin from drying out.

Frequency
Wipe down daily with a moist cloth. Wash weekly with a gentle cleanser. Address oily or dry skin based on climate and/or skin condition with appropriate products.

Pre-Work
Bathe every 1 to 2 weeks or when needed. Wipe down with a warm washcloth on a daily basis in between shampoos to remove daily dirt and debris.

Bathing
Bathe the dog with a very gentle shampoo. Use a loofah pad, bath puff, or bath gloves to apply shampoo and wash the dog. This will aid in removing the dead skin cells. Use very mild pressure to ensure you do not irritate the skin. If the dog is prone to dry skin apply a conditioner to the skin as a final step prior to drying. If the dog is prone to acne and blackheads, many breeders suggest utilizing an exfoliating product during the bathing process.

Drying
Wrap the dog in towels and blot dry. Let the dog air dry if you are in a warm area. If you opt to use a blow dryer, make sure it is on a very LOW heat setting while gently rubbing the skin with your hands. If the dog has furnishings, such as a Chinese Crested, gently brush through the furnishings while drying.

Moisturizing Treatments
Some hairless breeds need added moisture applied to their skin based on skin type, genetics and climate. After the bath and drying process is the best time to apply a moisture enhancing product. There are many moisturizers and natural oil treatments that are safe and effective to use on most pets.

Rustic Coated

Coat & Skin Characteristics
- The finished look of this coat type is rustic, tousled, and unkempt looking.
- With most rustic coated breeds, the first year, as the coat goes from puppy to adult, it can be a challenge to keep the coat from matting.
- Weekly combing and raking are primary tools for maintaining a rustic coat. Encourage owners to comb and rake their dogs using a wide tooth comb and/or rake. They can also monitor the coat by spreading their fingers apart and sink them all the way to the skin as they pet their dog keeping the curls and ringlets separated.
- Always use a wide-toothed comb or rake on their coats. Comb or rake them out prior to the bath or while they are still wet.
- To maintain the natural look, rustic coated dogs should never be brushed or blown dry. Towel and air dry only.
- Let them air dry or use a dryer on a very LOW temperature and speed setting so as not to straighten the hair shaft. You want to encourage the coat to curl, thus achieving the natural, or rustic look.

Sporting Group
- Lagotto Romagnolo

Herding Group
- Spanish Water Dog

Miscellaneous Group
- Belgian Laekenois
- Pumi

Frequency
Bathe every 3 to 12 weeks or when needed. Rake through the coat every 2–3 weeks with or without a bath, to keep matting under control. Lighter colored dogs with ringlets may need more frequent combing and raking as their coats tends to mat more easily than darker colored dogs

Pre-Work
Rake out the coat prior to bathing to keep the coat from becoming a solid pelted mass. This will remove the undercoat "lint," preventing matting in the future. Trim or grind nails at least every four to six weeks to maintain a healthy foot structure. Clean the ears every four to six weeks. Optional: If hair forms inside the ear canal, apply an ear powder and gently pluck the hair from inside the canal. Use care not to pull any coat from outside the canal opening. Finish by cleaning ears by swabbing with a mild ear cleaning solution.

Bathing
Bathe the dog with a very mild shampoo. With coats over 3 inches, squeeze the shampoo solution through the coat, never rub or scrub. Rinse while squeezing the water through the coat if it is longer. Do not stop until the water runs clear. On dogs with ringlets, a conditioner may be applied to aid in making future, weekly comb-outs easier.

Drying
Wrap the dog in towels and blot dry. Apply gentle pressure. Get the coat as dry as possible using this method. Air dry in a kennel enclosure where it is comfortable and safe for the dog. Use box fans to keep air circulating around the dog. Total drying time with a rustic coat can take quite a bit of time. How long depends on how much moisture is present in the coat, the air flow around the dog and the humidity in the drying area. Maintaining the curl or tousled look to the coat is important for the correct "look" for the rustic breeds. An inactive drying method is the best choice. Let them totally air dry naturally or place them where gentle airflow will circulate around the dog. Care must be taken to maintain a LOW heat setting in the circulating air, or the dog will be at risk for heat stroke. For the same reason, it is important to have water available for the dog and monitor their drying progress carefully.

79

Notes From The Grooming Table ©2016

80

Breeds in the Sporting Group are active and alert. The invention of the gun led to the development of the sporting, or "gun" dogs, to assist in hunting upland game birds and waterfowl, performing at the direction of the hunter. While some breeds perform more than one task, different breeds have been developed to point, flush and retrieve game. These dogs are eager to please and are happiest when they get plenty of exercise.

American Water Spaniel

Breed Facts & Characteristics

Country of Origin: United States

Height at Shoulder: 15"–18"

Coat Length/Type: Wavy/Thick Combination

Color: The coat comes in all shades of brown and liver tones.

Correct grooming procedure:
Brush Out/Minor Trimming

Common pet grooming practices:
Bathe & Brush/Clipper-Trim

~The Goal ~
The coat should be fresh smelling, clean and shiny. The body coat is wavy. No mats or shedding hair.

The top of the head and muzzle should be smooth and free of long hair. If the top of the head or muzzle is not naturally smooth, clip with a #7F used with the grain. If there is a small amount of longer, fine fur in this area, finger pluck or use thinning shears to smooth the coat out.

Brush with a pliable rubber curry brush, a shedding blade or a de-shedding tool designed for short to medium coated dogs. This breed may be lightly trimmed to present a neat and clean outline.

Tail is moderately feathered.

The ears may be shaved or left natural.

Shave pads. Trim the feet to appear neat and natural with thinning shears or a longer clipper blade such as a #4F used in reverse.

Neaten hocks.

Trim nails as short as possible or grind.

Grooming Procedures & Recommendations

See page 68 for
Bathing & Drying Instructions

Frequency
Bathe once a week to once every 12 weeks.

Pre-Work
Trim or grind nails every four to six weeks to maintain a healthy foot structure. Clean the ears by swabbing with a mild ear cleaning solution. Use a rubber curry, shedding blade, undercoat rake, pumice stone, carding tool, fine stripping knife or natural bristle brush to loosen skin dander and remove loose coat. Use a high-velocity dryer over the coat to quickly and effectively lift dirt and debris away from the skin and loosen coat. Brush out or remove any matting found in the long-coated areas. If the tangles are loose enough so water can fully penetrate the area, remove them after bathing and drying. If water cannot penetrate, remove the mat or tangle prior to bathing.

Brushing
Line brush, working in sections until the dog is entirely tangle-free and all loose coat is removed. When finished, there should be little, if any, fur still being removed with a firm slicker brush. Double-check the work with a comb and your hands. Go over the entire body, feeling for any inconsistencies in the density levels of the coat. If an area seems moist to the touch or fuller than the rest of the coat, rework the area with the appropriate tool. Mats, tangles and excessive coat are easily trapped in the following areas: behind the ears, around the ruff, the thigh area, the undercarriage and the tail. Give extra attention to these areas before finishing the groom.

Carding
If a dog has an abundance of loose undercoat, line card the shorter areas with a carding tool. Common tools can be a fine stripping knife, undercoat rake, a pumice stone, or a #40 blade held between your fingers. Any carding tool should be pulled over the body, working in the direction of the coat growth. This will remove the soft, downy undercoat, allowing the guard coat to conform more closely to the natural outline of the body. It will also aid in the removal of loose, shedding coat, a seasonal problem for many pet owners.

Feet & Hocks
Trim the pads with a close blade ranging from a #15 to a #40. Use a very light touch to clean the pads of long hair. If there is long fur between the toes, back brush the fur so it stands up on top of and away from the foot. With thinning shears, trim the excess to create a neat and very natural looking foot. Tidy the outside edge of the foot, if needed, with small detailing shears. If the hocks have longer coat, trim lightly with thinning shears to show a neat, clean area. A #4F blade, used carefully in reverse, works well for trimming the tops of the feet and the hocks on some dogs.

Detail Finish
Edge the ears lightly with thinning shears to neaten and keep a natural look. Hand pluck any long wispy, flyaway hair from around the ears. Removal of whiskers on the muzzle is optional based on client preference. Finish with a fine mist of coat polish on the body coat for added shine. Application of bows and mild cologne is optional.

Suggested Tools & Equipment

- Nail Trimmers
- Styptic Powder
- Ear Cleaning Solution
- Cotton Balls
- Clippers
- #40 and #15 Blades for Pads
- #4F for Feet & Hocks (optional)
- Slicker Brush
- Greyhound Comb
- Rubber Curry
- Carding Tool
- De-Shedding Tools
- Small Detailing Shears
- Thinning Shears

Notes:

Notes From The Grooming Table ©2016

Boykin Spaniel

Breed Facts & Characteristics

Country of Origin: United States

Height at Shoulder: 14"–18"

Coat Length/Type: Combination/Silky

Color: All shades of solid browns. Small amount of white on chest and toes allowed.

Correct grooming procedure:

Card/Hand-Strip/Minor Trimming

Common pet grooming practices:

Card/Hand-Strip/Minor Trimming

-The Goal-
The coat should be fresh smelling, light and shiny. The natural body jacket should lay tight to the body. No loose hair or tangles left in the coat.

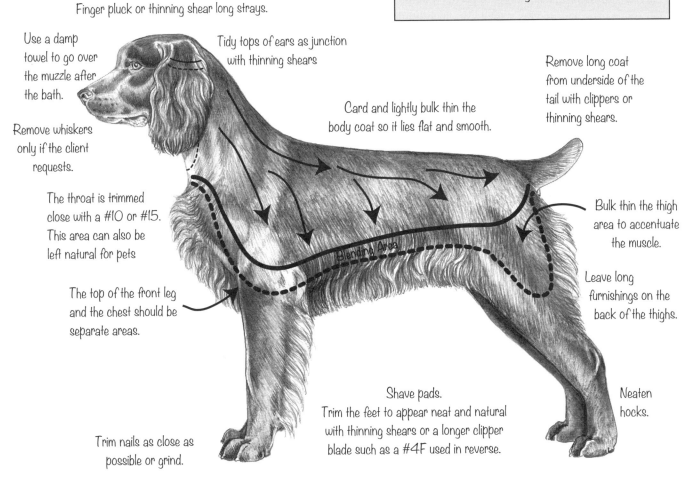

Coat on top of the head lies smoothly. Finger pluck or thinning shear long strays.

Tidy tops of ears as junction with thinning shears

Use a damp towel to go over the muzzle after the bath.

Remove whiskers only if the client requests.

The throat is trimmed close with a #10 or #15. This area can also be left natural for pets

The top of the front leg and the chest should be separate areas.

Trim nails as close as possible or grind.

Card and lightly bulk thin the body coat so it lies flat and smooth.

Remove long coat from underside of the tail with clippers or thinning shears.

Bulk thin the thigh area to accentuate the muscle.

Leave long furnishings on the back of the thighs.

Neaten hocks.

Blending Area

Shave pads. Trim the feet to appear neat and natural with thinning shears or a longer clipper blade such as a #4F used in reverse.

Grooming Procedures & Recommendations

See page 68 for
Bathing & Drying Instructions

Frequency
Bathe once a week to once every 12 weeks.

Pre-Work
Trim or grind nails every four to six weeks to maintain a healthy foot structure. Clean the ears by swabbing with a mild ear cleaning solution. Use a rubber curry, shedding blade, undercoat rake, pumice stone, carding tool, fine stripping knife or natural bristle brush to loosen skin dander and remove loose coat. Use a high-velocity dryer over the coat to quickly and effectively lift dirt and debris away from the skin and loosen coat. Brush out or remove any matting found in the long-coated areas. If the tangles are loose enough so water can fully penetrate the area, remove them after bathing and drying. If water cannot penetrate, remove the mat or tangle prior to bathing.

Brushing
Line brush, working in sections until the dog is entirely tangle-free and all loose coat is removed. When finished, there should be little, if any, fur still being removed with a firm slicker brush. Double-check the work with a comb and your hands. Go over the entire body, feeling for any inconsistencies in the density levels of the coat. If an area seems moist to the touch or fuller than the rest of the coat, rework the area with the appropriate tool. Mats, tangles and excessive coat are easily trapped in the following areas: behind the ears, around the ruff, the thigh area, the undercarriage and the tail. Give extra attention to these areas before finishing the groom.

Carding
If a dog has an abundance of loose undercoat, line card the shorter areas

with a carding tool. Common tools can be a fine stripping knife, undercoat rake, a pumice stone, or a #40 blade held between your fingers. Any carding tool should be pulled over the body, working in the direction of the coat growth. This will remove the soft, downy undercoat, allowing the guard coat to conform more closely to the natural outline of the body. It will also aid in the removal of loose, shedding coat, a seasonal problem for many pet owners.

Feet & Hocks
Trim the pads with a close blade ranging from a #15 to a #40. Use a very light touch to clean the pads of long hair. If there is long fur between the toes, back brush the fur so it stands up on top of and away from the foot. With thinning shears, trim the excess to create a neat and very natural looking foot. Tidy the outside edge of the foot, if needed, with small detailing shears. If the hocks have longer coat, trim lightly with thinning shears to show a neat, clean area. A #4F blade, used carefully in reverse, works well for trimming the tops of the feet and the hocks on some dogs.

Detail Finish
With thinning shears, tidy the junction where the ear leather meets the skull so it smoothly joins the two areas. Hand pluck any long wispy, flyaway hair from around the ears. Removal of whiskers on the muzzle is optional based on client preference. Finish with a fine mist of coat polish on the body coat for added shine. Application of bows and mild cologne is optional.

For Show
It is common to clip the throat area very close with a #10 or #15 blade, creating a soft "V" shape. Blend the cheeks into the clipped area with thinning shears. The pattern line follows the natural cowlick lines or "seam" down the side of the throat. After clipping, blend with thinning shears to make the seam invisible.

Suggested Tools & Equipment

- Nail Trimmers
- Styptic Powder
- Ear Cleaning Solution
- Cotton Balls
- Clippers
- #40 and #15 Blades for Pads
- #4F for Feet & Hocks (optional)
- Slicker Brush
- Greyhound Comb
- Rubber Curry
- Carding Tool
- De-Shedding Tools
- Small Detailing Shears
- Thinning Shears

Special Note
In most cases, the body coat of these breeds lays tight enough to the body that owners do not want their pets clipper-cut. It is not recommended, but should a client request a clipper-cut for a pet, follow the general pattern guidelines found on most Sporting Dogs according to breed similarity.

Notes:

Notes From The Grooming Table ©2016

Brittany

Breed Facts & Characteristics

Country of Origin: France

Height at Shoulder: 17½"–20½"

Coat Length/Type: Combination/Silky

Color: Orange and white or liver and white patches or a tricolor pattern of orange, liver and white. Color may be clear, ticked or roaned.

Correct grooming procedure:

Hand-Strip/Minor Trimming

Common pet grooming practices:

Bathe & Brush/Clipper-Trim

-The Goal-
The coat should be fresh smelling, light and shiny.
The natural body jacket should lay tight to the body.
No loose hair or tangles left in the coat.

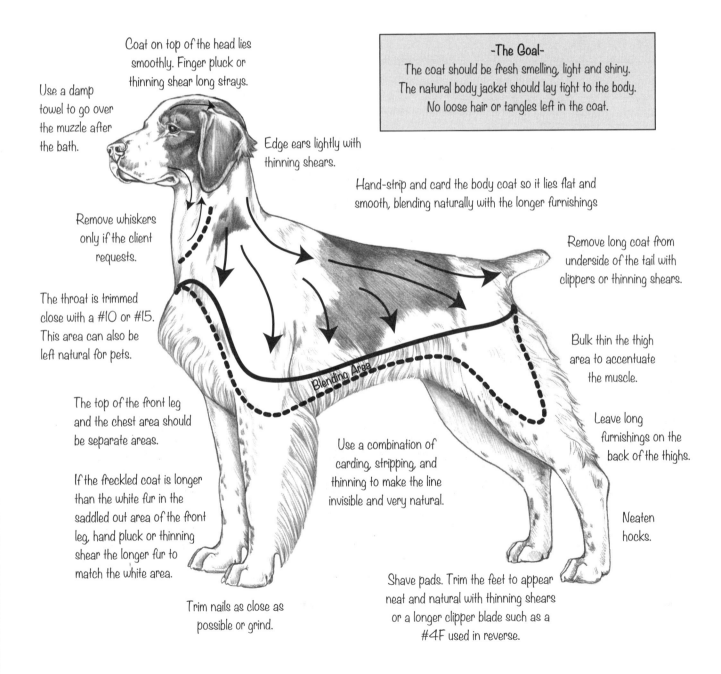

Coat on top of the head lies smoothly. Finger pluck or thinning shear long strays.

Use a damp towel to go over the muzzle after the bath.

Edge ears lightly with thinning shears.

Hand-strip and card the body coat so it lies flat and smooth, blending naturally with the longer furnishings

Remove whiskers only if the client requests.

Remove long coat from underside of the tail with clippers or thinning shears.

The throat is trimmed close with a #10 or #15. This area can also be left natural for pets.

Bulk thin the thigh area to accentuate the muscle.

Blending Area

Leave long furnishings on the back of the thighs.

The top of the front leg and the chest area should be separate areas.

Use a combination of carding, stripping, and thinning to make the line invisible and very natural.

Neaten hocks.

If the freckled coat is longer than the white fur in the saddled out area of the front leg, hand pluck or thinning shear the longer fur to match the white area.

Shave pads. Trim the feet to appear neat and natural with thinning shears or a longer clipper blade such as a #4F used in reverse.

Trim nails as close as possible or grind.

Grooming Procedures & Recommendations

See page 71 for Bathing & Drying Instructions

Frequency
Bathe once a week to once every 12 weeks.

Pre-Work
Trim or grind nails every four to six weeks to maintain a healthy foot structure. Clean the ears by swabbing with a mild ear cleaning solution. Use a rubber curry, shedding blade, undercoat rake, pumice stone, carding tool, fine stripping knife or natural bristle brush to loosen skin dander and remove loose coat. Use a high-velocity dryer over the coat to quickly and effectively lift dirt and debris away from the skin and loosen coat. Brush out or remove any matting found in the long-coated areas. If the tangles are loose enough so water can fully penetrate the area, remove them after bathing and drying. If water cannot penetrate, remove the mat or tangle prior to bathing.

Brushing
Line brush, working in sections until the dog is entirely tangle-free and all loose coat is removed. When finished, there should be little, if any, fur still being removed with a firm slicker brush. Double-check the work with a comb and your hands. Go over the entire body, feeling for any inconsistencies in the density levels of the coat. If an area seems moist to the touch or fuller than the rest of the coat, rework the area with the appropriate tool. Mats, tangles and excessive coat are easily trapped in the following areas: behind the ears, around the ruff, the thigh area, the undercarriage and the tail. Give extra attention to these areas before finishing the groom.

Carding
If a dog has an abundance of loose undercoat, line card the shorter areas with a carding tool. Common tools can be a fine stripping knife, undercoat rake, a pumice stone, or a #40 blade held between your fingers. Any carding tool should be pulled over the body, working in the direction of the coat growth. This will remove the soft, downy undercoat, allowing the guard coat to conform more closely to the natural outline of the body. It will also aid in the removal of loose, shedding coat, a seasonal problem for many pet owners.

Feet & Hocks
Trim the pads with a close blade ranging from a #15 to a #40. Use a very light touch to clean the pads of long hair. If there is long fur between the toes, back brush the fur so it stands up on top of and away from the foot. With thinning shears, trim the excess to create a neat and very natural looking foot. Tidy the outside edge of the foot, if needed, with small detailing shears. If the hocks have longer coat, trim lightly with thinning shears to show a neat, clean area. A #4F blade, used carefully in reverse, works well for trimming the tops of the feet and the hocks on some dogs.

Detail Finish
Edge the ears lightly with thinning shears to neaten and keep a natural look. Hand pluck any long wispy, flyaway hair from around the ears. Removal of whiskers on the muzzle is optional based on client preference. Finish with a fine mist of coat polish on the body coat for added shine. Application of bows and mild cologne is optional.

For Show
It is common to clip the throat area very close with a #10 or #15 blade, creating a soft "V" shape. Blend the cheeks into the clipped area with thinning shears. The pattern line follows the natural cowlick lines or "seam" down the side of the throat. After clipping, blend with thinning shears to make the seam invisible.

Suggested Tools & Equipment

- Nail Trimmers
- Styptic Powder
- Ear Cleaning Solution
- Cotton Balls
- Clippers
- #40 and #15 Blades for Pads
- #4F for Feet & Hocks (optional)
- Slicker Brush
- Greyhound Comb
- Rubber Curry
- Carding Tool
- De-Shedding Tools
- Small Detailing Shears
- Thinning Shears

Special Note
In most cases, the body coat of these breeds lays tight enough to the body that owners do not want their pets clipper-cut. It is not recommended, but should a client request a clipper-cut for a pet, follow the general pattern guidelines found on most Sporting Dogs according to breed similarity.

Notes:

Notes From The Grooming Table ©2016

Chesapeake Bay Retriever

Breed Facts & Characteristics

Country of Origin: United States

Height at Shoulder: 21"–26"

Coat Length/Type: Short/Dense

Color: All shades of brown and tan.

Correct grooming procedure:
Bathe & Brush Out

Common pet grooming practices:
Bathe & Brush Out

Use a damp towel to go over the muzzle after the bath.

High-velocity dryers work great to remove excessive loose hair with shedding.

-The Goal-
The coat should be fresh smelling, light and stand off the body. No loose hair.

Rubber curry brush all over body to remove loose fur.

Remove whiskers only if the client requests.

Apply a light coat polish to bring up the shine of the coat when finished.

Neaten hocks if needed.

Neaten pads & feet if needed.

Trim nails as short as possible or grind.

See page 67 for Bathing & Drying Instructions	Suggested Tools & Equipment	
• Nail Trimmers	• Clippers	• Carding Tool
• Styptic Powder	• #40 or #15 Blade	• De-Shedding Tools
• Ear Cleaning Solution	• Slicker Brush	• Small Detailing Shears
• Cotton Balls	• Rubber Curry	• Thinning Shears

Notes *from your* Grooming Table

Clumber Spaniel   SPORTING   SILKY COATED

Breed Facts & Characteristics

Country of Origin: England

Height at Shoulder: 17"–20"

Coat Length/Type: Combination/Silky

Color: Predominatly white in color with lemon or tan patches.

Correct grooming procedure:
Card & Hand-Strip

Common pet grooming practices:
Card & Hand-Strip or Clipper-Trim

General Description

The Clumber is a low set, heavy dog with massive bone. He works at a slow and methodical pace in the field. The chest is deep and broad, reaching to the elbows. The topline is level, blending smoothly into a docked tail set. The head is noble with a very deep and pronounced stop, hefty brow and pendulous lips. The coat of a Clumber Spaniel is soft and silky. The base color is white with a limited number of red or tan markings. The jacket coat should lay smoothly over the head, throat, neck, shoulders, back, down the sides of the dog and the thighs. There are longer furnishings on the ears, chest, undercarriage, belly, the back of the legs and the tail.

-The Goal-
The coat should be fresh smelling, light and shiny. The natural body jacket should lay tight to the body. If clipping, no clipper marks. No loose hair or tangles left in the coat.

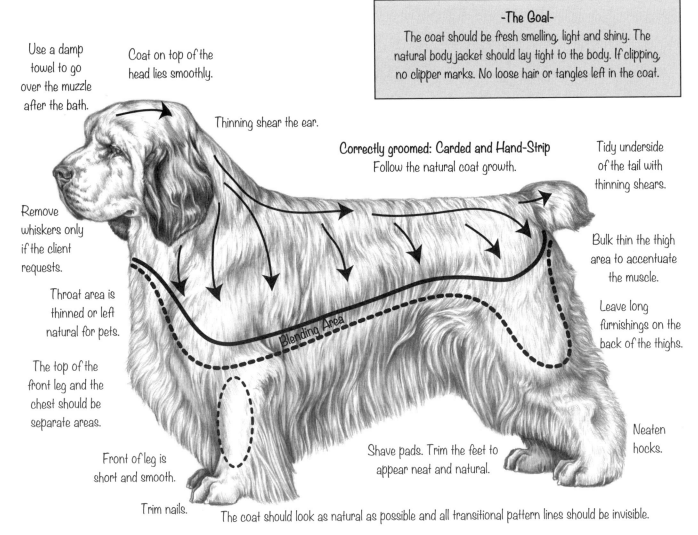

Use a damp towel to go over the muzzle after the bath.

Coat on top of the head lies smoothly.

Thinning shear the ear.

Correctly groomed: Carded and Hand-Strip
Follow the natural coat growth.

Tidy underside of the tail with thinning shears.

Remove whiskers only if the client requests.

Throat area is thinned or left natural for pets.

The top of the front leg and the chest should be separate areas.

Blending Area

Bulk thin the thigh area to accentuate the muscle.

Leave long furnishings on the back of the thighs.

Neaten hocks.

Front of leg is short and smooth.

Shave pads. Trim the feet to appear neat and natural.

Trim nails.

The coat should look as natural as possible and all transitional pattern lines should be invisible.

Optional: Typical blades used on the body for pet grooming; #7F, #5F, #4F, #2 guard comb or a combination of those blades. Card coat after clipping.

Grooming Procedures & Recommendations

See page 71 for
Bathing & Drying Instructions

Frequency
Bathe once a week to once every 12 weeks.

Pre-Work
Trim or grind nails every four to six weeks to maintain a healthy foot structure. Clean the ears by swabbing with a mild ear cleaning solution. Use a rubber curry, shedding blade, undercoat rake, pumice stone, carding tool, fine stripping knife or natural bristle brush to loosen skin dander and remove loose coat. Use a high-velocity dryer over the coat to quickly and effectively lift dirt and debris away from the skin and loosen coat. Brush out or remove any matting found in the long-coated areas. If the tangles are loose enough so water can fully penetrate the area, remove them after bathing and drying. If water cannot penetrate, remove the mat or tangle prior to bathing.

Brushing
Line brush, working in sections until the dog is entirely tangle-free and all loose coat is removed. When finished, there should be little, if any, fur still being removed with a firm slicker brush. Double-check the work with a comb and your hands. Go over the entire body, feeling for any inconsistencies in the density levels of the coat. If an area seems moist to the touch or fuller than the rest of the coat, rework the area with the appropriate tool. Mats, tangles and excessive coat are easily trapped in the following areas: behind the ears, around the ruff, the thigh area, the undercarriage and the tail. Give extra attention to these areas before finishing the groom.

Hand-Stripping & Thinning the Body Pattern
Ideally, the coat should be worked with hand-stripping techniques, carding and thinning shears to retain the proper coat texture, brilliant color and natural look. Sporting dogs are extremely athletic. When trimming them, this trait is emphasized by working with their natural bone structure and muscle tone. Start shaping the coat by carding and hand-stripping. If there is still an abundance of coat, trim the coat with a moderately toothed, single-sided thinning shear. This style of shear will minimize how much coat is removed with each cut. Slide the smooth blade of the shear up under the coat. With the smooth blade against the skin, cock the shear slightly, making it impossible to accidentally pinch the skin when closing the blades. Make one cut, then extract the shear and repeat right next to the preceding cut. Work in a methodical manner, handling one area at a time. Once four to six cuts have been made in one area, stop and brush the cut coat out with a heavy slicker brush. Continue to bulk thin the area until the coat lies smoothly, but not so thin that the long guard coat is totally removed. Always slide the shears up under the coat in keeping the blade parallel with the natural growth of the hair. Cutting "cross grain" will create holes in the coat that are almost impossible to correct.

Clipper-Trimming the Body Pattern
Blades ranging from a #10 to a #4F, along with guard combs, are commonly used to set the pattern on the body as an alternative to proper pet grooming techniques. They can be used with the grain or against the grain with longer blades. Keep in mind, the shorter the trim on the body pattern the more difficult it is to blend the pattern later into the longer furnishings, for these lines should be invisible. A longer cut also allows you to mold the coat a

The groom should leave the dog looking as natural as possible. The head is free of long hair. The entire ear leather is thinned. The fur on the front of the front legs is smooth and short. Dog is well feathered. Hocks are neatened. Feet are trimmed to look natural.

Coat on the head lies smoothly. Finger pluck or thinning shear long strays if light coated. Follow with carding and thinning. For heavier coated dogs, clip the cheeks and top of the head with blades ranging from a #7F to a #4F, used with or against the grain.

Remove whiskers only if the client requests or the muzzle needs to be clipped.

The ears are lightly covered with hair that is about a half inch to one inch in length. The edges are trimmed with thinning shears to show off a natural outline.

Lightly thinning shear the throat area to neaten slightly.

bit and apply carding techniques to retain some of the proper coat texture. Longer cutting blades are preferred over shorter ones. At the front of the dog, the pattern starts just above the breast bone and drops on a diagonal line to the point where the chest meets the top of the front leg. The entire front of the front leg should be free of long fur, blending into the naturally short coat on the front of the leg. Moving down the side of the dog, the pattern is set at the lower bulge of the shoulder muscle, just above the elbow. It continues behind the elbow and on a slight angle up into the flank area. The pattern line rises over the flank, dropping in a "U" shape to expose the upper thigh muscle. The "U" shape rises back up to just below the base of the tail, leaving the long feathers at the back of the thigh. When blending the pattern, the transitional areas will be

½ inch to 2 inches in width depending on the area and the conformation of the dog. At the blending areas, bulk thin or top thin with thinning shears so the main body area blends invisibly with the longer furnishings.

Carding

If a dog has an abundance of loose undercoat, line card the areas with a carding tool. Common tools can be a fine stripping knife, an undercoat rake, a pumice stone, or a #40 blade held between your fingers. Any carding tool should be pulled over the body and worked in the direction of the coat growth. This will remove the soft, downy undercoat, allowing the guard coat to conform closer to the natural outline of the body. It will also aid in the removal of loose, shedding coat which is a seasonal problem for many pet owners.

Furnishings

The back of the front legs and the rear section of the thighs and undercarriage should be well feathered. The feathering is left natural, but with extremely heavy coats the leg hair may be trimmed slightly to neaten and balance the outline. On the front of the front legs, the coat should be saddled out short, smooth and fine. If the leg is covered with long coat, the front legs will need to be trimmed to simulate this natural short-coated look. At the rump, the long coat falls off the rear side of the thighs. There is a clean separation between the tail and the long feathers.

Head & Throat

The head is covered with fine, short hair that conforms to the shape of the skull. Some dogs come by this trait more naturally than others.

With light-coated dogs, the longer hair may be finger plucked, carded or stripped out by hand, retaining a neat and natural look. For those dogs with longer coat covering sections of their head and muzzle, the coat is removed with thinning shears or by clipping. If the coat is extremely heavy, clip the area using blades ranging from a #15 to a #7F on the muzzle. A longer blade can be used for the top skull. Work with or against the coat growth based on how smooth and close the area needs to be and the dog's skin sensitivity. The throat is thinned lightly.

Ears
The ears are covered with hair that is about a half inch long in length. Finger pluck or use thinning shears to establish the coat length for a natural look. Edge the ears with thinning shears to softly show off the outline of the ear leather. If the coat is profuse, heavy or if there is a strong odor coming from the ear canal, clip the inside of the ear with a very close blade ranging from a #40 to a #10. Use a light touch and clear the upper section inside the ear leather to assist with the sanitation and overall health of the ear.

Tail
The tail is handled in the same trimming style as the body coat. Continue your work right out onto the tail, leaving a small flag. Detail the underside of the tail with thinning shears. The tail should be an extension of the spine and the coat is short, neat and clean.

Feet & Hocks
Trim the pads with a close cutting blade ranging from a #15 to a #40. Use a very light touch to clean the pads of long hair. If there is long fur between the toes, back brush the fur so it stands up on top of and away from the foot. With thinning shears, trim off the excess creating a neat and very natural looking foot. Tidy the outside edge of the foot, if needed, with small detailing shears. If the hocks have longer coat, trim lightly with thinning shears to show a neat, clean area. A #4F blade used in reverse works well for trimming the tops of the feet and the hocks on some dogs.

Detail Finish
Removal of whiskers on the muzzle is optional, based on client preference or the amount of fur on the muzzle. Finish with a fine mist of coat polish on the body coat for added shine. Application of bows and mild cologne is optional.

Suggested Tools & Equipment

- Nail Trimmers
- Styptic Powder
- Ear Cleaning Solution
- Cotton Balls
- Clippers
- Slicker Brush
- Greyhound Comb
- Pin Brush
- Rubber Curry
- Pumice Stone
- Carding Tools
- Stripping Knives
- Straight Shears
- Curved Shears
- Small Detailing Shears
- Thinning Shears
- Dematting Tools

Common Blade Options:
- #40, #15, #10
- #7F, #5F, #4F
- Variety of Guard Combs

Notes:

Cocker Spaniel

Breed Facts & Characteristics

Country of Origin: England

Height at Shoulder: 14"–15"

Coat Length/Type: Soft/Thick

Color: Wide variety of colors. Reds, creams, browns, black, black and tan, parti colored with white, and tricolored. For multi-colored dogs, the color should be clear and crisp with roaning and flecking allowable on dogs with white making up their base color patterns.

Correct grooming procedure:

Card & Hand-Strip

Common pet grooming practices:

Clipper-Trim

General Description

The American Cocker Spaniel is the smallest of the gun dogs. It is a well-balanced, compact and firmly built dog with great speed and endurance. The chest is deep, reaching to the elbows. The topline is level or slightly sloping. The docked tail is an extension of the topline. The head is well balanced with a rounded skull, pronounced stop and full lips. The ears are long and the expression soft, kind and intelligent. The coat of an American Cocker Spaniel is soft and silky, and found in a number of color combinations. The coat should lie smoothly over the head, throat, neck, shoulders, back, down the sides of the dog and the thighs. There is much longer and profuse feathering on the ears, chest, undercarriage, belly and legs.

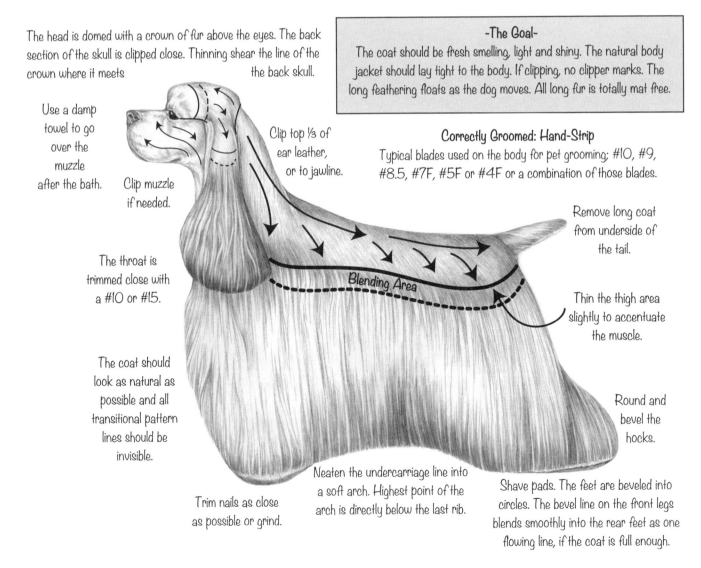

The head is domed with a crown of fur above the eyes. The back section of the skull is clipped close. Thinning shear the line of the crown where it meets the back skull.

-The Goal-
The coat should be fresh smelling, light and shiny. The natural body jacket should lay tight to the body. If clipping, no clipper marks. The long feathering floats as the dog moves. All long fur is totally mat free.

Use a damp towel to go over the muzzle after the bath.

Clip muzzle if needed.

Clip top ⅓ of ear leather, or to jawline.

Correctly Groomed: Hand-Strip
Typical blades used on the body for pet grooming; #10, #9, #8.5, #7F, #5F or #4F or a combination of those blades.

Remove long coat from underside of the tail.

The throat is trimmed close with a #10 or #15.

Blending Area

Thin the thigh area slightly to accentuate the muscle.

The coat should look as natural as possible and all transitional pattern lines should be invisible.

Round and bevel the hocks.

Trim nails as close as possible or grind.

Neaten the undercarriage line into a soft arch. Highest point of the arch is directly below the last rib.

Shave pads. The feet are beveled into circles. The bevel line on the front legs blends smoothly into the rear feet as one flowing line, if the coat is full enough.

Grooming Procedures & Recommendations

See page 71 for
Bathing & Drying Instructions

Full Coated Trim

Frequency
Bathe once a week to once every 12 weeks.

Pre-Work
Trim or grind nails every four to six weeks to maintain a healthy foot structure. Clean the ears by swabbing with a mild ear cleaning solution. Use a rubber curry, shedding blade, undercoat rake, pumice stone, carding tool, fine stripping knife or natural bristle brush to loosen skin dander and remove loose coat. Use a high-velocity dryer over the coat to quickly and effectively lift dirt and debris away from the skin and loosen coat. Brush out or remove any matting found in the long-coated areas. If the tangles are loose enough so water can fully penetrate the area, remove them after bathing and drying. If water cannot penetrate, remove the mat or tangle prior to bathing.

Brushing
Line brush, working in sections until the dog is entirely tangle-free and all loose coat is removed. When finished, there should be little, if any, fur still being removed with a firm slicker brush. Double-check the work with a comb and your hands. Go over the entire body, feeling for any inconsistencies in the density levels of the coat. If an area seems moist to the touch or fuller than the rest of the coat, rework the area with the appropriate tool. Mats, tangles and excessive coat are easily trapped in the following areas: behind the ears, around the ruff, the thigh area, the undercarriage and the tail. Give extra attention to these areas before finishing the groom.

Hand-Stripping & Thinning the Body Pattern
Ideally, the coat should be worked with hand-stripping techniques, carding and thinning shears to retain the proper coat texture, brilliant color and natural look. Sporting dogs are extremely athletic. When trimming them, this trait is emphasized by working with their natural bone structure and muscle tone. Start shaping the coat by carding and hand-stripping. If there is still an abundance of coat, trim the coat with a moderately toothed, single-sided thinning shear. This style of shear will minimize how much coat is removed with each cut. Slide the smooth blade of the shear up under the coat. With the smooth blade against the skin, cock the shear slightly, making it impossible to accidentally pinch the skin when closing the blades. Make one cut, then extract the shear and repeat right next to the preceding cut. Work in a methodical manner, handling one area at a time. Once four to six cuts have been made in one area, stop and brush the cut coat out with a heavy slicker brush. Continue to bulk thin the area until the coat lies smoothly, but not so thin that the long guard coat is totally removed. Always slide the shears up under the coat in keeping the blade parallel with the natural growth of the hair. Cutting "cross grain" will create holes in the coat that are almost impossible to correct.

Clipper-Trimming the Body Pattern
Blades ranging from a #10 to a #4F are commonly used to set the pattern on the body as an alternative to proper grooming techniques for pets. They can be used with the grain or against the grain with longer blades. Keep in mind, the shorter the trim on the body pattern the more difficult it is to blend the pattern later into the longer furnishings, for these lines should be invisible. A longer cut also allows you

The Cocker has higher pattern lines than many breeds. The blending areas start midway up on the shoulder. Actual placement of the pattern lines can vary based on client preference and how much coat the dog has naturally. Furnishings are left long and natural. Bevels are neatly flared. The line of the bevel can vary but they should be even on all four feet.

Notes From The Grooming Table ©2016

The Cocker has a rounded skull, a deep stop and a soft, kind expression. To accentuate these traits, there is a crown of fur above the eyes to about half way back on the skull. The back section of the skull is clipped close with a #10 or #15 with the grain or a #7F in reverse, following the ridge where the head and neck meet. With thinning shears blend the line of the crown and the short fur of the back skull. The line is well blended when done and the crown looks very natural.

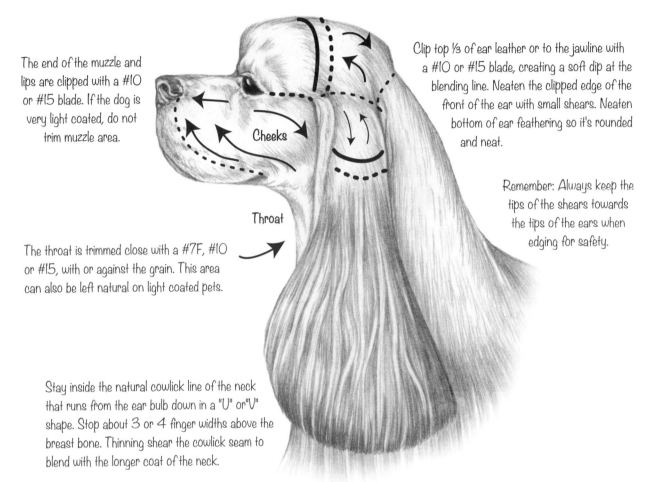

The end of the muzzle and lips are clipped with a #10 or #15 blade. If the dog is very light coated, do not trim muzzle area.

Cheeks

Clip top ⅓ of ear leather or to the jawline with a #10 or #15 blade, creating a soft dip at the blending line. Neaten the clipped edge of the front of the ear with small shears. Neaten bottom of ear feathering so it's rounded and neat.

Remember: Always keep the tips of the shears towards the tips of the ears when edging for safety.

Throat

The throat is trimmed close with a #7F, #10 or #15, with or against the grain. This area can also be left natural on light coated pets.

Stay inside the natural cowlick line of the neck that runs from the ear bulb down in a "U" or "V" shape. Stop about 3 or 4 finger widths above the breast bone. Thinning shear the cowlick seam to blend with the longer coat of the neck.

to mold the coat a bit and apply carding techniques to retain some of the proper coat texture. Longer cutting blades are preferred over shorter ones. At the front of the dog, the pattern starts just above the breastbone and drops on a diagonal line to the top of the shoulder muscle or at almost the same level as the shoulder joint. The pattern line travels down the side of the dog towards the flank where it may rise slightly. As it rises over the flank, it then drops into a very shallow

"U" shape to expose the upper thigh muscle. The "U" shape rises back up to just below the base of the tail, leaving the long feathers at the back of the thigh. When blending the pattern, the transitional areas will be ½ inch to 2 inches in width depending on the area and the conformation of the dog. At the blending areas, bulk thin or top thin with thinning shears so the main body area blends invisibly with the longer furnishings.

Feet

Trim the pads with a close cutting blade ranging from a #15 to a #40. Use a very light touch to clean the pads of long hair. Thoroughly line comb and brush every section of the feathering. Once the coat is free of mats and tangles, you can shape the feet into round, beveled circles. With the dog standing squarely on the table, comb all the fur straight down over the foot. Begin trimming a foot by forming a box around it with long

Grooming Procedures & Recommendations

straight shears. Bevel the shears so there will be an upward curve from the foot to the outer line of the coat. Once you have a box, re-comb the fur and with long, curved shears, begin forming the round, beveled foot. Once all four feet are done, comb all the hair down on the sides of the dog and neaten the undercarriage line. The line will be a soft, flowing arch with the highest point falling directly under the last rib. This sweeping line will connect the front of the dog with the rear, making the entire dog blend together.

Head

The majority of the head is covered with fine, short hair. A crown of longer fur is left above the eyes to accentuate the roundness of the skull, the eyebrows and a deep stop. If the dog is light-coated, use thinning shears to remove any of the longer fur. If the coat is long or thick, clip the muzzle, cheeks, throat and back of the skull using blades ranging from a #15 to a #7F. Work with or against the coat growth based on how smooth and close the area needs to be, coupled with the sensitivity of the dog's skin. Leave longer hair over the eye area to shape with thinning shears once all the other long hair is removed. You can easily find the pattern line for the crown by placing your thumb and first fingers at the back corner of each eye. Coat behind this line is removed with clippers to the occiput. Ahead of the line, leave the fur to trim by hand with thinning shears, creating the classical domed skull of the American Cocker Spaniel. Clip the throat area from the base of the ear bulbs in a "V" shape, following the cowlick line at the sides of the neck with a #15 or #10 blade. The lowest point of the "V" will be three to four finger widths above the breastbone. Finish by blending the cowlick line seam to be invisible between the neck and the throat.

Ears

The tops of the ears are trimmed close to the skin using thinning shears or clippers. Trim the top ⅓ of the outer ear leather or, if the ear is very long, set the line to the jaw. On the outside of the leather, the blending line will be a soft "U" shape. Keep this line above the widest section of the ear. If clipping, use a #10 or #15 blade, either with or against the coat growth based on coat density and skin sensitivity. If the coat is profuse, heavy or there is a strong odor coming from the ear canal, clip the inside of the ear with a very close blade ranging from a #40 to a #10. Use a light touch and clear the upper section inside the ear leather to assist with the sanitation and overall health of the ear. If both sides of the ear leather have been clipped, edge the top front section of the ear leather with detailing shears, keeping the tips of the shears towards the tips of the ears. Lightly round the long feathering at the bottom of the ears with shears for a neat look.

Tail

The tail is handled in the same trimming style as the body coat. Continue your work right out onto the tail. Detail the underside of the tail with thinning shears or clippers. The tail should be an extension of the spine and the coat is short, neat and clean.

Detail Finish

Removal of whiskers on the muzzle is optional, based on the amount of fur on the muzzle. Finish with a fine mist of coat polish on the body coat for added shine. Application of bows and mild cologne is optional.

Suggested Tools & Equipment

- Nail Trimmers
- Styptic Powder
- Ear Cleaning Solution
- Cotton Balls
- Clippers
- Slicker Brush
- Greyhound Comb
- Pin Brush
- Rubber Curry
- Pumice Stone
- Carding Tools
- Stripping Knives
- Straight Shears
- Curved Shears
- Small Detailing Shears
- Thinning Shears
- Dematting Tools

Common Blade Options:

- #40, #15, #10
- #7F, #5F, #4F
- Variety of Guard Combs

Notes:

The Fool

Modified Show Trim

-The Goal-
The coat should be fresh smelling, light and shiny. Clipper and scissor work is smooth and even. All longer fur is totally mat free.

The coat should look as natural as possible and all transitional pattern lines should be invisible.

On furnishings, hand-scissor the coat to a consistent length between 2-4 inches. Keep the tips of the shears pointed towards the table top to minimize scissor marks. Blend with thinning shears to finish.

Correctly Groomed: Hand-Strip
Typical blades used on the body for pet grooming; #10, #9, #8.5, #7F, #5F or #4F or a combination of those blades.

Blending Area

Bulk thin the thigh area slightly to accentuate the muscle.

Shave pads.
The feet are beveled into circles. Box the foot in first, then round neatly with shears. Double check work multiple times.

Legs are hand-scissored very full. They fall in straight columns or can flair slightly out to large neatly beveled feet. Bulk thin at the pattern line so it blends seamlessly into the longer furnishings.

Modified Show Trim In General

This trim mimics the full show trim style in an easier-to-care-for version. Some owners go a step further and have a large section of the underbelly clipped short as well. This allows the longer furnishings to drape over and conceal the clipped section while the pet is standing.

Furnishings

The longest coat on the furnishings can range from 2 to 4 inches. The front and back legs drop straight down from the body or flair slightly towards the beveled feet. The pattern lines on the head and body are identical to the show style cocker trim. The coat at the body pattern lines will be short and taper into the longer leg furnishings. Most stylists prefer to shape the legs by hand, with shears ranging from 8.5 inches to 10 inches in length. Keeping the tips of the shears pointed downward minimizes cut marks in the coat. Another method of blending off at the top of the leg includes using one of the large attachment combs, followed by hand-scissoring and blending with thinning shears or large blenders ("chunkers"). When the trim is complete, all four legs form columns that drop into full, round, beveled feet. All four legs should be well balanced and equal in size. While the front legs should be straight, the back legs will accentuate the angles of the rear assembly.

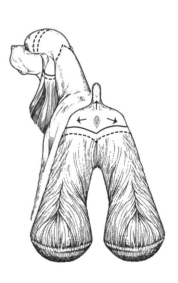

-The Goal-
The coat should be fresh smelling, light and shiny. Clipper and scissor work is smooth and even. All longer fur is totally mat free.

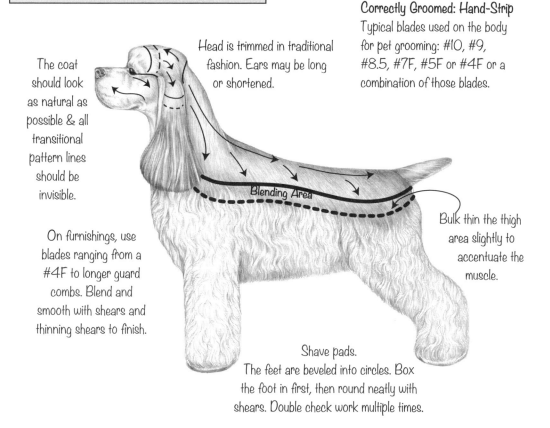

The coat should look as natural as possible & all transitional pattern lines should be invisible.

Head is trimmed in traditional fashion. Ears may be long or shortened.

Correctly Groomed: Hand-Strip
Typical blades used on the body for pet grooming: #10, #9, #8.5, #7F, #5F or #4F or a combination of those blades.

On furnishings, use blades ranging from a #4F to longer guard combs. Blend and smooth with shears and thinning shears to finish.

Blending Area

Bulk thin the thigh area slightly to accentuate the muscle.

Shave pads.
The feet are beveled into circles. Box the foot in first, then round neatly with shears. Double check work multiple times.

The Cocker has higher pattern lines than many breeds. The blending areas start midway up on the shoulder. Actual placement of the pattern lines can vary based on client preference and how much coat the dog has naturally. Legs fall in straight columns to neatly beveled feet.

Pet Trim In General

This trim is a low maintenance version that captures the essence of the breed. On the furnishings for very active pets whose coats easily form mats, opt for the shorter blades ranging from the #4F blade to shorter to medium guard comb to create the trim. For owners willing to brush between grooming appointments, longer guard combs work well for this trim style.

Furnishings

The longest coat on the furnishings can range from 1⁄4 inch to 2 inches based on client preference. The front and back legs drop straight down from the body toward the beveled feet. The pattern lines on the head and body are identical to the show style cocker trim. The coat at the body pattern lines will be short, and taper into the longer leg furnishings. Using a longer "F" blade, or a guard comb attachment, trim the bulk of the furnishings. Follow

by hand-scissoring and blending with thinning shears to smooth the coat and remove clipper marks. When the trim is complete, all four legs should form columns that drop into beveled feet. All four legs should be well balanced and equal in size. While the front legs will be straight, the back legs will accentuate the angles of the rear assembly.

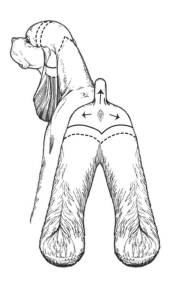

Curly-Coated Retriever

SPORTING   SHORT COATED

Breed Facts & Characteristics

Country of Origin: England

Height at Shoulder: 23"–27"

Coat Length/Type: Short/Curly

Color: Black or Liver

Correct grooming procedure:
Bathe & Brush Out

Common pet grooming practices:
Bathe & Brush Out

-The Goal-
The coat should be fresh smelling, light and stand off the body. No loose hair.

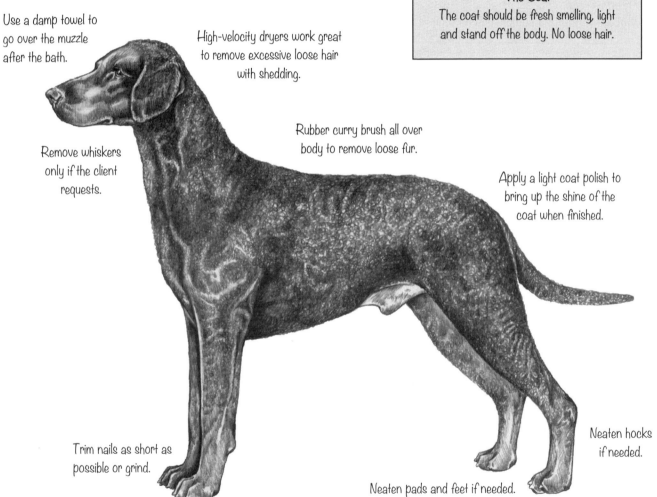

Use a damp towel to go over the muzzle after the bath.

High-velocity dryers work great to remove excessive loose hair with shedding.

Remove whiskers only if the client requests.

Rubber curry brush all over body to remove loose fur.

Apply a light coat polish to bring up the shine of the coat when finished.

Trim nails as short as possible or grind.

Neaten pads and feet if needed.

Neaten hocks if needed.

See page 67 for
Bathing & Drying Instructions

Suggested Tools & Equipment

- Nail Trimmers
- Styptic Powder
- Ear Cleaning Solution
- Cotton Balls

- Clippers
- #40 or #15 Blade
- Slicker Brush
- Rubber Curry

- Carding Tool
- De-Shedding Tools
- Small Detailing Shears
- Thinning Shears

Notes *from your*
Grooming Table

English Cocker Spaniel   SPORTING   SILKY COATED

Breed Facts & Characteristics

Country of Origin: England

Height at Shoulder: 15"–17"

Coat Length/Type: Combination/Silky

Color: The most common coat color is white and liver or white and black. Other acceptable colors, but not nearly as common, are tricolored with black and white or liver and white with tan points and blue or liver roans.

Correct grooming procedure:
Card & Hand-Strip

Common pet grooming practices:
Clipper-Trim/Hand-Strip

General Description

The English Cocker Spaniel is a highly energetic, enthusiastic gun dog of classic good looks. It is a well balanced, firmly built dog with great endurance. The chest is deep, reaching to the elbows. The topline is level or slightly sloping. The docked tail is an extension of the topline. The head is well balanced and fine, blending smoothly between areas. The ears are long and the expression soft, kind and intelligent. The coat of an English Cocker Spaniel is soft and silky. They come in a number of color combinations. The jacket coat should lay smoothly over the head, throat, neck, shoulders, back, down the sides of the dog and the thighs. There is longer feathering on the ears, chest, undercarriage, belly and the back of the legs.

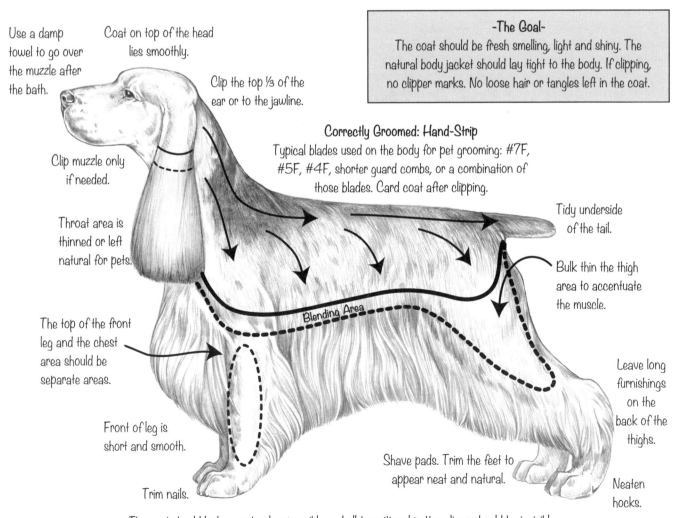

Use a damp towel to go over the muzzle after the bath.

Coat on top of the head lies smoothly.

Clip the top ⅓ of the ear or to the jawline.

Clip muzzle only if needed.

Throat area is thinned or left natural for pets.

The top of the front leg and the chest area should be separate areas.

Front of leg is short and smooth.

Trim nails.

-The Goal-
The coat should be fresh smelling, light and shiny. The natural body jacket should lay tight to the body. If clipping, no clipper marks. No loose hair or tangles left in the coat.

Correctly Groomed: Hand-Strip
Typical blades used on the body for pet grooming: #7F, #5F, #4F, shorter guard combs, or a combination of those blades. Card coat after clipping.

Blending Area

Tidy underside of the tail.

Bulk thin the thigh area to accentuate the muscle.

Leave long furnishings on the back of the thighs.

Neaten hocks.

Shave pads. Trim the feet to appear neat and natural.

The coat should look as natural as possible and all transitional pattern lines should be invisible.

Grooming Procedures & Recommendations

See page 71 for
Bathing & Drying Instructions

Frequency
Bathe once a week to once every 12 weeks.

Pre-Work
Trim or grind nails every four to six weeks to maintain a healthy foot structure. Clean the ears by swabbing with a mild ear cleaning solution. Use a rubber curry, shedding blade, undercoat rake, pumice stone, carding tool, fine stripping knife or natural bristle brush to loosen skin dander and remove loose coat. Use a high-velocity dryer over the coat to quickly and effectively lift dirt and debris away from the skin and loosen coat. Brush out or remove any matting found in the long-coated areas. If the tangles are loose enough so water can fully penetrate the area, remove them after bathing and drying. If water cannot penetrate, remove the mat or tangle prior to bathing.

Brushing
Line brush, working in sections until the dog is entirely tangle-free and all loose coat is removed. When finished, there should be little, if any, fur still being removed with a firm slicker brush. Double-check the work with a wide-toothed comb and your hands. Go over the entire body, feeling for any inconsistencies in the density levels of the coat. If an area seems moist to the touch or fuller than the rest of the coat, rework the area with the appropriate tool. Mats, tangles and excessive coat are easily trapped in the following areas: behind the ears, around the ruff, the thigh area, the undercarriage and the tail. Give extra attention to these areas before finishing the groom.

Hand-Stripping & Thinning the Body Pattern
Ideally, the coat should be worked with hand-stripping techniques, carding and thinning shears to retain the proper coat texture, brilliant color and natural look. Sporting dogs are extremely athletic. When trimming them, this trait is emphasized by working with their natural bone structure and muscle tone. Start shaping the coat by carding and hand-stripping. If there is still an abundance of coat, trim the coat with a moderately toothed, single-sided thinning shear. This style of shear will minimize how much coat is removed with each cut. Slide the smooth blade of the shear up under the coat. With the smooth blade against the skin, cock the shear slightly, making it impossible to accidentally pinch the skin when closing the blades. Make one cut, then extract the shear and repeat right next to the preceding cut. Work in a methodical manner, handling one area at a time. Once four to six cuts have been made in one area, stop and brush the cut coat out with a heavy slicker brush. Continue to bulk thin the area until the coat lies smoothly, but not so thin that the long guard coat is totally removed. Always slide the shears up under the coat in keeping the blade parallel with the natural growth of the hair. Cutting "cross grain" will create holes in the coat that are almost impossible to correct.

Clipper-Trimming the Body Pattern
Blades ranging from a #10 to a #4F, or shorter guard combs, are commonly used to set the pattern on the body as an alternative to proper grooming techniques for pets. They can be used with the grain or against the grain with longer blades. Keep in mind, the shorter the trim on the body pattern, the more difficult it is to blend the pattern later into the longer furnishings, for these lines should be invisible. A longer cut also allows you to mold the coat a bit and apply carding techniques to retain some of the proper coat texture. Longer cutting blades are preferred over shorter ones. At the front of the dog, the pattern starts just above the breast bone and drops on a diagonal line to the point where the chest meets the top of the front leg. The entire front of the front leg should be free of long fur, blending

The groom should leave the dog looking as natural as possible. The head is free of long hair. Top ⅓ of the ear leather or to the jawline is clipped. The fur on the front of the front legs is smooth and short. Dog is well feathered. Hocks are trimmed. Feet are natural.

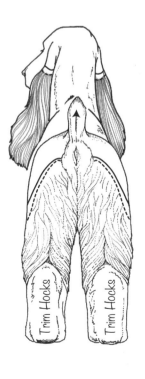

Trim Hocks   Trim Hocks

Notes From The Grooming Table ©2016

Coat on the head lies smoothly. Finger pluck or thinning shear long strays if light coated. For heavier coated dogs, clip the cheeks and top of the head with blades ranging from a #7F to a #4F, used with or against the grain.

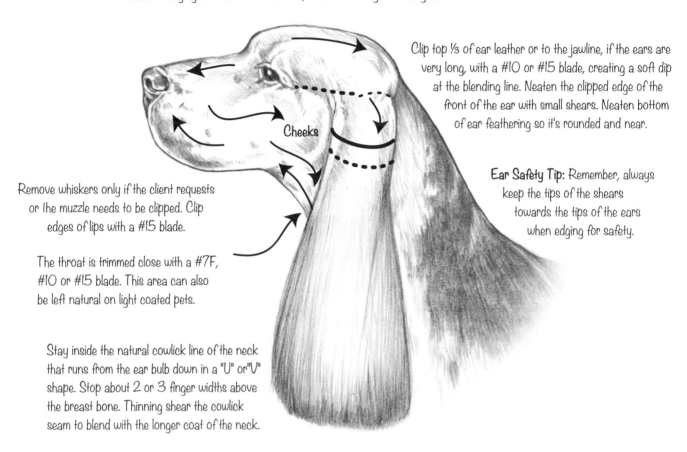

Clip top ⅓ of ear leather or to the jawline, if the ears are very long, with a #10 or #15 blade, creating a soft dip at the blending line. Neaten the clipped edge of the front of the ear with small shears. Neaten bottom of ear feathering so it's rounded and near.

Cheeks

Remove whiskers only if the client requests or the muzzle needs to be clipped. Clip edges of lips with a #15 blade.

The throat is trimmed close with a #7F, #10 or #15 blade. This area can also be left natural on light coated pets.

Ear Safety Tip: Remember, always keep the tips of the shears towards the tips of the ears when edging for safety.

Stay inside the natural cowlick line of the neck that runs from the ear bulb down in a "U" or "V" shape. Stop about 2 or 3 finger widths above the breast bone. Thinning shear the cowlick seam to blend with the longer coat of the neck.

into the naturally short coat on the front of the leg. Moving down the side of the dog, the pattern is set at the lower bulge of the shoulder muscle, just above the elbow. It continues behind the elbow and on a slight angle up into the flank area. The pattern line rises over the flank, dropping in a "U" shape to expose the upper thigh muscle. The "U" shape rises back up to just below the base of the tail, leaving the long feathers at the back of the thigh. When blending the pattern, the transitional areas will be ½ inch to 2 inches in width depending on the area and the conformation of the dog. At the blending areas, bulk thin or top thin with thinning shears so the main body area blends invisibly with the longer furnishings.

Carding

If a dog has an abundance of loose undercoat, card the areas with a carding tool. Common tools can be a fine stripping knife, an undercoat rake, a pumice stone, or a #40 blade held between your fingers. Any carding tool should be pulled over the body and worked in the direction of the coat growth. This will remove the soft, downy undercoat, allowing the guard coat to conform closer to the natural outline of the body. It will also aid in the removal of loose, shedding coat, which is a seasonal problem for many pet owners.

Furnishings

The back of the front legs and the rear section of the thighs and undercarriage should be well feathered. The feathering is left natural. With extremely heavy coats the leg hair may be trimmed slightly to neaten and balance the outline. On the front of the front legs, the coat should be saddled out short, smooth and fine. If the leg is covered with long coat, the front legs will need to be trimmed to simulate this natural short-coated look. At the rump, the long coat falls off the rear side of the thighs. There is a clean separation between the tail and the long feathers.

Grooming Procedures & Recommendations

Head

The head is covered with fine, short hair that conforms to the shape of the skull. Some dogs come by this trait more naturally than others. With light-coated dogs, the longer hair may be finger plucked, carded or stripped out by hand, retaining a neat and natural look. For those dogs with longer coat covering sections of their head and muzzle, the coat is removed with thinning shears or by clipping. If the coat is extremely heavy, clip the area using blades ranging from a #15 to a #7F on the muzzle. A longer blade can be used for the top skull. Work with or against the coat growth based on how smooth and close the area needs to be and the dog's skin sensitivity. Clip the throat area from the base of the ear bulbs in a "V" shape, following the cowlick line at the sides of the neck with a #15 or #10 blade. The lowest point of the "V" will be three to four finger widths above the breastbone. Finish by blending the cowlick line seam so it is invisible between the neck and the throat.

Ears

The tops of the ears are trimmed close to the skin using thinning shears or clippers. Trim the top ⅓ of the outer ear leather or, if the ear is very long, set the line to the jaw. On the outside of the leather, the blending line will be a soft "U" shape. Keep this line above the widest section of the ear. If clipping, use a #10 or #15 blade, either with or against the coat growth based on coat density and skin sensitivity. If the coat is profuse, heavy or there is a strong odor coming from the ear canal, clip the inside of the ear with a very close blade ranging from a #40 to a #10. Use a light touch and clear the upper section inside the ear leather to assist with the sanitation and overall health of the ear. If both sides of the ear leather have been clipped, edge the top front section of the ear leather with detailing shears, keeping the tips of the shears towards the tips of the ears. Lightly round the long feathering at the bottom of the ears with shears for a neat look.

Tail

The tail is handled in the same trimming style as the body coat. Continue your work right out onto the tail. Detail the underside of the tail with thinning shears or clippers. The tail should be an extension of the spine and the coat is short, neat and clean.

Feet & Hocks

Trim the pads with a close cutting blade ranging from a #15 to a #40. Use a very light touch to clean the pads of long hair. If there is long fur between the toes, back brush the fur so it stands up on top of and away from the foot. With thinning shears, trim off the excess, creating a neat and very natural looking foot. Tidy the outside edge of the foot, if needed, with small detailing shears. If the hocks have longer coat, trim lightly with thinning shears to show a neat, clean area. A #4F blade used in reverse works well for trimming the tops of the feet and the hocks on some dogs.

Detail Finish

Removal of whiskers on the muzzle is optional, based on client preference or the amount of fur on the muzzle. Finish with a fine mist of coat polish on the body coat for added shine. Application of bows and mild cologne is optional.

Suggested Tools & Equipment

- Nail Trimmers
- Styptic Powder
- Ear Cleaning Solution
- Cotton Balls
- Clippers
- Slicker Brush
- Greyhound Comb
- Pin Brush
- Rubber Curry
- Pumice Stone
- Carding Tools
- Stripping Knives
- Straight Shears
- Curved Shears
- Small Detailing Shears
- Thinning Shears
- Dematting Tools

Common Blade Options:
- #40, #15, #10
- #7F, #5F, #4F
- Variety of Guard Combs

Notes:

Notes From The Grooming Table ©2016

Breed Facts & Characteristics

Country of Origin: England

Height at Shoulder: 24"–25"

Coat Length/Type: Combination/Silky

Color: Background color always white with black, blue, red, liver or spots and flecking. Tricolors also acceptable.

Correct grooming procedure:

Card & Hand-Strip

Common pet grooming practices:

Clipper-Trim/Hand-Strip

General Description

The English Setter is a gun dog of great style and beauty. It is well balanced, moderate in size. The chest is deep, reaching to the elbows. The topline is level or slightly sloping. The tail is an extension of the topline, with no dip or break at the junction point. The tail is shaped like a flag and reaches to the hock when the dog is relaxed. The head is long and slender. The coat of an English Setter is soft, silky and speckled in color. The base color is always white with flecking, or roaning, in varying shades. The jacket coat should lay smoothly over the head, throat, neck, shoulders, back, down the sides of the dog and the thighs. There are longer furnishings on the ears, chest, undercarriage, belly, the back of the legs and the tail.

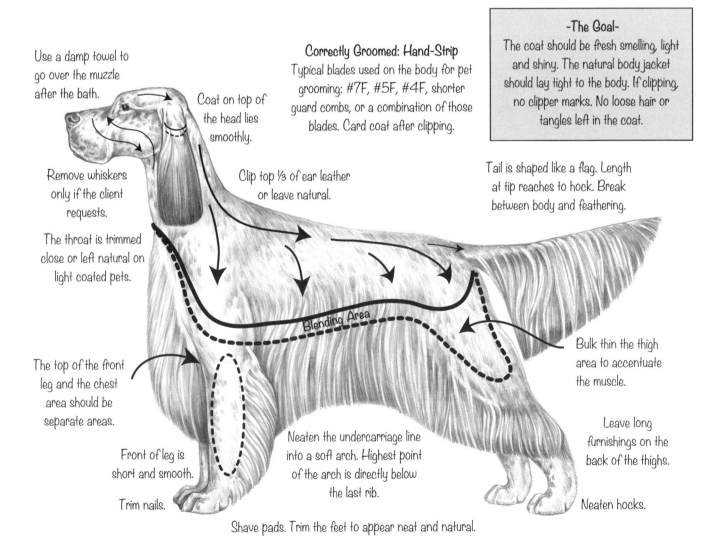

-The Goal-
The coat should be fresh smelling, light and shiny. The natural body jacket should lay tight to the body. If clipping, no clipper marks. No loose hair or tangles left in the coat.

Use a damp towel to go over the muzzle after the bath.

Coat on top of the head lies smoothly.

Correctly Groomed: Hand-Strip
Typical blades used on the body for pet grooming: #7F, #5F, #4F, shorter guard combs, or a combination of those blades. Card coat after clipping.

Remove whiskers only if the client requests.

The throat is trimmed close or left natural on light coated pets.

Clip top ⅓ of ear leather or leave natural.

Tail is shaped like a flag. Length at tip reaches to hock. Break between body and feathering.

Blending Area

The top of the front leg and the chest area should be separate areas.

Front of leg is short and smooth.

Trim nails.

Neaten the undercarriage line into a soft arch. Highest point of the arch is directly below the last rib.

Bulk thin the thigh area to accentuate the muscle.

Leave long furnishings on the back of the thighs.

Neaten hocks.

Shave pads. Trim the feet to appear neat and natural.

The coat should look as natural as possible and all transitional pattern lines should be invisible.

See page 71 for Bathing & Drying Instructions

Frequency
Bathe once a week to once every 12 weeks.

Pre-Work
Trim or grind nails every four to six weeks to maintain a healthy foot structure. Clean the ears by swabbing with a mild ear cleaning solution. Use a rubber curry, shedding blade, undercoat rake, pumice stone, carding tool, fine stripping knife or natural bristle brush to loosen skin dander and remove loose coat. Use a high-velocity dryer over the coat to quickly and effectively lift dirt and debris away from the skin and loosen coat. Brush out or remove any matting found in the long-coated areas. If the tangles are loose enough so water can fully penetrate the area, remove them after bathing and drying. If water cannot penetrate, remove the mat or tangle prior to bathing.

Brushing
Line brush, working in sections until the dog is entirely tangle-free and all loose coat is removed. When finished, there should be little, if any, fur still being removed with a firm slicker brush. Double-check the work with a comb and your hands. Go over the entire body, feeling for any inconsistencies in the density levels of the coat. If an area seems moist to the touch or fuller than the rest of the coat, rework the area with the appropriate tool. Mats, tangles and excessive coat are easily trapped in the following areas: behind the ears, around the ruff, the thigh area, the undercarriage and the tail. Give extra attention to these areas before finishing the groom.

Hand-Stripping & Thinning the Body Pattern
Ideally, the coat should be worked with hand-stripping techniques, carding and thinning shears to retain the proper coat texture, brilliant color and natural look. Sporting dogs are extremely athletic. When trimming them, this trait is emphasized by working with their natural bone structure and muscle tone. Start shaping the coat by carding and hand-stripping. If there is still an abundance of coat, trim the coat with a moderately toothed, single-sided thinning shear. This style of shear will minimize how much coat is removed with each cut. Slide the smooth blade of the shear up under the coat. With the smooth blade against the skin, cock the shear slightly, making it impossible to accidentally pinch the skin when closing the blades. Make one cut, then extract the shear and repeat right next to the preceding cut. Work in a methodical manner, handling one area at a time. Once four to six cuts have been made in one area, stop and brush the cut coat out with a heavy slicker brush. Continue to bulk thin the area until the coat lies smoothly, but not so thin that the long guard coat is totally removed. Always slide the shears up under the coat in keeping the blade parallel with the natural growth of the hair. Cutting "cross grain" will create holes in the coat that are almost impossible to correct.

Clipper-Trimming the Body Pattern
Blades ranging from a #10 to a #4F, or shorter guards, are commonly used to set the pattern on the body as an alternative to proper grooming techniques for pets. They can be used with the grain or against the grain with longer blades. Keep in mind, the shorter the trim on the body pattern, the more difficult it is to blend the pattern later into the longer furnishings, for these lines should be invisible. A longer cut also allows you to mold the coat a bit and apply carding techniques to retain some of the proper coat texture. Longer cutting blades are preferred over shorter ones. At the front of the dog, the pattern starts just above the breast bone and drops on a diagonal line to the point where the chest meets the top of the front leg. The entire front of the front leg should be free of long fur, blending into the naturally

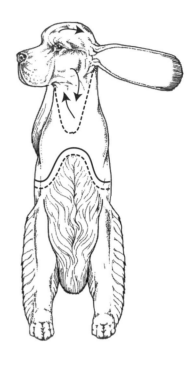

The groom should leave the dog looking as natural as possible. The head is free of long hair. Top ⅓ of the ear leather is clipped. The fur on the front of the front legs is smooth and short. Dog is well feathered. Tail is flag shaped and reaches to the hock. Hocks are trimmed. Feet are natural.

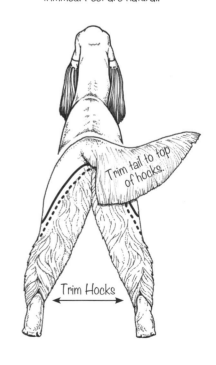

Trim tail to top of hocks.

Trim Hocks

Coat on the head lies smoothly. Finger pluck or thinning shear long strays if light coated. Follow with carding and thinning. For heavier coated dogs, clip the cheeks and top of the head with blades ranging from a #7F to a #4F, used with or against the grain.

Clip top ⅓ of the ear leather with a #10 or #15 blade, creating a soft dip at the blending line. Or, thinning shear the top of the ear if the dog is very light coated. Neaten bottom of ear feathering so it's rounded and neat. Do not clip inside the ear leather. Leave the top, front edge untrimmed, helping to create a soft expression.

Remove whiskers only if the client requests or the muzzle needs to be clipped.

Cheeks

Throat

The throat is trimmed close with a #10 or #15. This area can also be left natural on light coated pets. Cheeks are left as natural as possible, to still give a smooth appearance.

Stay inside the natural cowlick line of the neck that runs from the ear bulb down in a "U" or "V" shape. Stop about 3 or 4 finger widths above the breast bone. Thinning shear the cowlick seam to blend with the longer coat of the neck.

short coat on the front of the leg. Moving down the side of the dog, the pattern is set at the lower bulge of the shoulder muscle, just above the elbow. It continues behind the elbow and on a slight angle up into the flank area. The pattern line rises over the flank, dropping in a "U" shape to expose the upper thigh muscle. The "U" shape rises back up to just below the base of the tail, leaving the long feathers at the back of the thigh. When blending the pattern, the transitional areas will be ½ inch to 2 inches in width depending on the area and the conformation of the dog. At the blending areas, bulk thin or top thin with thinning shears so the main body area blends invisibly with the longer furnishings.

Carding
If a dog has an abundance of loose undercoat, line card the areas with a carding tool. Common tools can be a fine stripping knife, an undercoat rake, a pumice stone, or a #40 blade held between your fingers. Any carding tool should be pulled over the body and worked in the direction of the coat growth. This will remove the soft, downy undercoat, allowing the guard coat to conform closer to the natural outline of the body. It will also aid in the removal of loose, shedding coat which is a seasonal problem for many pet owners.

Furnishings
The back of the front legs and the rear section of the thighs and undercarriage should be well feathered. The feathering is left natural. With extremely heavy coats the leg hair may be trimmed slightly to neaten and balance the outline. On the front of the front legs, the coat should be saddled out short, smooth and fine. If the leg is covered with long coat, the front legs will need to be trimmed to simulate this natural short-coated look. At the rump, the long coat falls off the rear side of the thighs. There is a clean separation between the tail and the long feathers.

Grooming Procedures & Recommendations

Head
The head is covered with fine, short hair that conforms to the shape of the skull. Some dogs come by this trait more naturally than others. With light-coated dogs, the longer hair may be finger plucked, carded or stripped out by hand, retaining a neat and natural look. For those dogs with longer coat covering sections of their head and muzzle, the coat is removed with thinning shears or by clipping. If the coat is extremely heavy, clip the area using blades ranging from a #15 to a #7F on the muzzle. A longer blade can be used for the top skull. Work with or against the coat growth based on how smooth and close the area needs to be and the dog's skin sensitivity. Clip the throat area from the base of the ear bulbs in a "V" shape, following the cowlick line at the sides of the neck with a #15 or #10 blade. The lowest point of the "V" will be three to four finger widths above the breastbone. Finish by blending the cowlick line seam so it is invisible between the neck and the throat.

Ears
The tops of the ears are trimmed close to the skin using thinning shears or clippers. Trim the top to ⅓ of the ear leather on the outside of the ear. On the outside of the leather, the blending line will be a soft "U" shape. Keep this line above the widest section of the ear. If clipping, use a #10 or #15 blade, either with or against the coat growth based on coat density and skin sensitivity. Lightly round the long feathering at the bottom of the ears with shears for a neat look.

Tail
The tail is in the shape of a triangular flag. The pointed tip should reach to the top of the hock. The top of the tail is covered with short, smooth, harsh coat while the long silky feathers fall from the underside. At the root base, there is a break in the fur, separating the tail from the body. Shape the tail to look very natural with thinning shears or shears.

Feet & Hocks
Trim the pads with a close cutting blade ranging from a #15 to a #40. Use a very light touch to clean the pads of long hair. If there is long fur between the toes, back brush the fur so it stands up on top of and away from the foot. With thinning shears, trim off the excess creating a neat and very natural looking foot. Tidy the outside edge of the foot, if needed, with small detailing shears. If the hocks have longer coat, trim lightly with thinning shears to show a neat, clean area. A #4F blade used in reverse works well for trimming the tops of the feet and the hocks on some dogs.

Detail Finish
Removal of whiskers on the muzzle is optional, based on client preference or the amount of fur on the muzzle. Finish with a fine mist of coat polish on the body coat for added shine. Application of bows and mild cologne is optional.

Suggested Tools & Equipment
- Nail Trimmers
- Styptic Powder
- Ear Cleaning Solution
- Cotton Balls
- Clippers
- Slicker Brush
- Greyhound Comb
- Pin Brush
- Rubber Curry
- Pumice Stone
- Carding Tools
- Stripping Knives
- Straight Shears
- Curved Shears
- Small Detailing Shears
- Thinning Shears
- Dematting Tools

Common Blade Options:
- #40, #15, #10
- #7F, #5F, #4F
- Variety of Guard Combs

Notes:

Breed Facts & Characteristics

Country of Origin: England

Height at Shoulder: 19"–20"

Coat Length/Type: Combination/Silky

Color: The most common coat color is white and liver or white and black. Other acceptable colors, but not nearly as common are tricolored with black and white or liver and white with tan points and blue or liver roans.

Correct grooming procedure:

Card & Hand-Strip

Common pet grooming practices:

Clipper-Trim & Hand-Strip

General Description

The English Springer Spaniel is a gun dog of classic good looks and versatility. It is well balanced, medium in size. The chest is deep, reaching to the elbows. The topline is level or slightly sloping. The docked tail is an extension of the topline. The head is well balanced. The ears are long and the expression soft and trusting. The coat of an English Springer Spaniel is soft and silky. They come in a number of color combinations but the most common is liver and white or black and white. The jacket coat should lay smoothly over the head, throat, neck, shoulders, back, down the sides of the dog and the thighs. There is longer feathering on the ears, chest, undercarriage, belly and the back of all the legs.

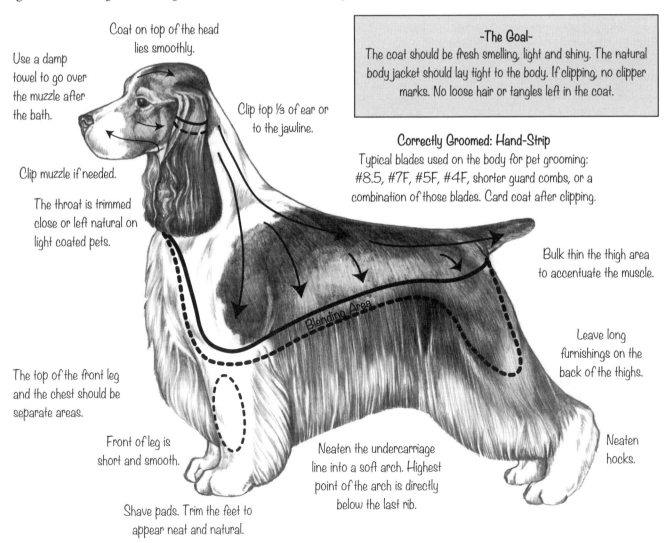

Coat on top of the head lies smoothly.

Use a damp towel to go over the muzzle after the bath.

Clip muzzle if needed.

The throat is trimmed close or left natural on light coated pets.

Clip top ⅓ of ear or to the jawline.

-The Goal-
The coat should be fresh smelling, light and shiny. The natural body jacket should lay tight to the body. If clipping, no clipper marks. No loose hair or tangles left in the coat.

Correctly Groomed: Hand-Strip
Typical blades used on the body for pet grooming: #8.5, #7F, #5F, #4F, shorter guard combs, or a combination of those blades. Card coat after clipping.

Bulk thin the thigh area to accentuate the muscle.

Leave long furnishings on the back of the thighs.

Blending Area

The top of the front leg and the chest should be separate areas.

Front of leg is short and smooth.

Neaten hocks.

Neaten the undercarriage line into a soft arch. Highest point of the arch is directly below the last rib.

Shave pads. Trim the feet to appear neat and natural.

The coat should look as natural as possible and all transitional pattern lines should be invisible.

See page 71 for
Bathing & Drying Instructions

Frequency
Bathe once a week to once every
12 weeks.

Pre-Work
Trim or grind nails every four to
six weeks to maintain a healthy foot
structure. Clean the ears by swabbing
with a mild ear cleaning solution. Use a
rubber curry, shedding blade, undercoat
rake, pumice stone, carding tool, fine
stripping knife or natural bristle brush
to loosen skin dander and remove loose
coat. Use a high-velocity dryer over
the coat to quickly and effectively lift
dirt and debris away from the skin and
loosen coat. Brush out or remove any
matting found in the long-coated areas.
If the tangles are loose enough so water
can fully penetrate the area, remove
them after bathing and drying. If water
cannot penetrate, remove the mat or
tangle prior to bathing.

Brushing
Line brush, working in sections until
the dog is entirely tangle-free and all
loose coat is removed. When finished,
there should be little, if any, fur still
being removed with a firm slicker brush.
Double-check the work with a comb
and your hands. Go over the entire
body, feeling for any inconsistencies in
the density levels of the coat. If an area
seems moist to the touch or fuller than
the rest of the coat, rework the area
with the appropriate tool. Mats, tangles
and excessive coat are easily trapped in
the following areas: behind the ears,
around the ruff, the thigh area, the
undercarriage and the tail. Give extra
attention to these areas before finishing
the groom.

Hand-Stripping &
Thinning the Body Pattern
Ideally, the coat should be worked with
hand-stripping techniques, carding and
thinning shears to retain the proper
coat texture, brilliant color and natural
look. Sporting dogs are extremely
athletic. When trimming them, this
trait is emphasized by working with
their natural bone structure and muscle
tone. Start shaping the coat by carding
and hand-stripping. If there is still an
abundance of coat, trim the coat with
a moderately toothed, single-sided
thinning shear. This style of shear will
minimize how much coat is removed
with each cut. Slide the smooth blade of
the shear up under the coat. With the
smooth blade against the skin, cock the
shear slightly, making it impossible to
accidentally pinch the skin when closing
the blades. Make one cut, then extract
the shear and repeat right next to the
preceding cut. Work in a methodical
manner, handling one area at a time.
Once four to six cuts have been made
in one area, stop and brush the cut
coat out with a heavy slicker brush.
Continue to bulk thin the area until the
coat lies smoothly, but not so thin that
the long guard coat is totally removed.
Always slide the shears up under the
coat in keeping the blade parallel with
the natural growth of the hair. Cutting
"cross grain" will create holes in the coat
that are almost impossible to correct.

Clipper-Trimming the Body Pattern
Blades ranging from a #10 to a #4F,
or shorter guard combs, are commonly
used to set the pattern on the body
as an alternative to proper grooming
techniques for pets. They can be used
with the grain or against the grain with
longer blades. Keep in mind, the shorter
the trim on the body pattern the more
difficult it is to blend the pattern later
into the longer furnishings, for these
lines should be invisible. A longer cut
also allows you to mold the coat a

The groom should leave the dog looking
as natural as possible. The head is free
of long hair. Top ⅓ of the ear leather
or to the jawline is clipped. The fur on
the front of the front legs is smooth and
short. Dog is well feathered. Hocks are
trimmed. Feet are natural.

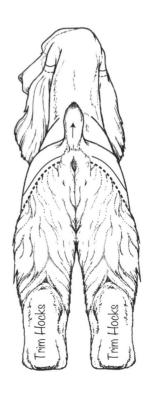

111

Coat on the head lies smoothly. Finger pluck or thinning shear long strays if light coated. For heavier coated dogs, clip the cheeks and top of the head with blades ranging from a #7F to a #4F, used with or against the grain.

Clip top ⅓ of ear leather or to the jawline if the ears are very long with a #10 or #15 blade, creating a soft dip at the blending line. Neaten the clipped edge of the front of the ear with small shears. Neaten bottom of ear feathering so it's rounded and neat.

Remove whiskers only if the client requests or the muzzle needs to be clipped.

Cheeks

Blend

Ear Safety Tip: Remember, always keep the tips of the shears towards the tips of the ears when edging for safety.

Cheeks are left as natural as possible to give a smooth appearance.

The throat is trimmed close with a #7F, #10 or #15 blade. This area can also be left natural on light coated pets.

Stay inside the natural cowlick line of the neck that runs from the ear bulb down in a "U" or"V" shape. Stop about 3 or 4 finger widths above the breast bone. Thinning shear the cowlick seam to blend with the longer coat of the neck.

bit and apply carding techniques to retain some of the proper coat texture. Longer cutting blades are preferred over shorter ones. At the front of the dog, the pattern starts just above the breast bone and drops on a diagonal line to the point where the chest meets the top of the front leg. The entire front of the front leg should be free of long fur, blending into the naturally short coat on the front of the leg. Moving down the side of the dog, the pattern is set at the lower bulge of the shoulder muscle, just above the elbow. It continues behind the elbow and on a slight angle up into the flank area. The pattern line rises over the flank, dropping in a "U" shape

to expose the upper thigh muscle. The "U" shape rises back up to just below the base of the tail, leaving the long feathers at the back of the thigh. When blending the pattern, the transitional areas will be ½ inch to 2 inches in width depending on the area and the conformation of the dog. At the blending areas, bulk thin or top thin with thinning shears so the main body area blends invisibly with the longer furnishings.

Carding
If a dog has an abundance of loose undercoat, line card the areas with a carding tool. Common tools can be a fine stripping knife, an undercoat rake, a pumice stone, or a #40 blade

held between your fingers. Any carding tool should be pulled over the body and worked in the direction of the coat growth. This will remove the soft, downy undercoat, allowing the guard coat to conform closer to the natural outline of the body. It will also aid in the removal of loose, shedding coat which is a seasonal problem for many pet owners.

Furnishings
The back of the front legs and the rear section of the thighs and undercarriage should be well feathered. The feathering is left natural. With extremely heavy coats the leg hair may be trimmed slightly to neaten and balance the outline.

On the front of the front legs, the coat should be saddled out short, smooth and fine. If the leg is covered with long coat, the front legs will need to be trimmed to simulate this natural short-coated look. At the rump, the long coat falls off the rear side of the thighs. There is a clean separation between the tail and the long feathers.

Head

The head is covered with fine, short hair that conforms to the shape of the skull. Some dogs come by this trait more naturally than others. With light-coated dogs, the longer hair may be finger plucked, carded or stripped out by hand, retaining a neat and natural look. For those dogs with longer coat covering sections of their head and muzzle, the coat is removed with thinning shears or by clipping. If the coat is extremely heavy, clip the area using blades ranging from a #15 to a #7F on the muzzle. A longer blade can be used for the top skull. Work with or against the coat growth based on how smooth and close the area needs to be and the dog's skin sensitivity. Clip the throat area from the base of the ear bulbs in a "V" shape, following the cowlick line at the sides of the neck with a #15 or #10 blade. The lowest point of the "V" will be three to four finger widths above the breastbone. Finish by blending the cowlick line seam so it is invisible between the neck and the throat.

Ears

The tops of the ears are trimmed close to the skin using thinning shears or clippers. Trim the top ⅓ of the outer ear leather or, if the ear is very long, set the line to the jaw. On the outside of the leather, the blending line will be a soft "U" shape. Keep this line above the widest section of the ear. If clipping, use a #10 or #15 blade, either with or against the coat growth based on coat density and skin sensitivity. If the coat

is profuse, heavy or there is a strong odor coming from the ear canal, clip the inside of the ear with a very close blade ranging from a #40 to a #10. Use a light touch and clear the upper section inside the ear leather to assist with the sanitation and overall health of the ear. If both sides of the ear leather have been clipped, edge the top front section of the ear leather with detailing shears, keeping the tips of the shears towards the tips of the ears. Lightly round the long feathering at the bottom of the ears with shears for a neat look.

Tail

The tail is handled in the same trimming style as the body coat. Continue your work right out onto the tail. Detail the underside of the tail with thinning shears or clippers. The tail should be an extension of the spine and the coat is short, neat and clean.

Feet & Hocks

Trim the pads with a close cutting blade ranging from a #15 to a #40. Use a very light touch to clean the pads of long hair. If there is long fur between the toes, back brush the fur so it stands up on top of and away from the foot. With thinning shears, trim off the excess creating a neat and very natural looking foot. Tidy the outside edge of the foot, if needed, with small detailing shears. If the hocks have longer coat, trim lightly with thinning shears to show a neat, clean area. A #4F blade used in reverse works well for trimming the tops of the feet and the hocks on some dogs.

Detail Finish

Removal of whiskers on the muzzle is optional, based on client preference or the amount of fur on the muzzle. Finish with a fine mist of coat polish on the body coat for added shine. Application of bows and mild cologne is optional.

Suggested Tools & Equipment

- Nail Trimmers
- Styptic Powder
- Ear Cleaning Solution
- Cotton Balls
- Clippers
- Slicker Brush
- Greyhound Comb
- Pin Brush
- Rubber Curry
- Pumice Stone
- Carding Tools
- Stripping Knives
- Straight Shears
- Curved Shears
- Small Detailing Shears
- Thinning Shears
- Dematting Tools

Common Blade Options:

- #40, #15, #10
- #7F, #5F, #4F
- Variety of Guard Combs

Notes:

Notes From The Grooming Table ©2016

Breed Facts & Characteristics

Country of Origin: England

Height at Shoulder: 17"–18"

Coat Length/Type: Combination/Silky

Color: Acceptable colors are liver, black or roan, or any one of these with tan markings.

Correct grooming procedure:
Card & Hand-Strip

Common pet grooming practices:
Card or Clipper-Trim

-The Goal-
The coat should be fresh smelling, light and shiny. The natural body jacket should lay tight to the body. No loose hair or tangles left in the coat.

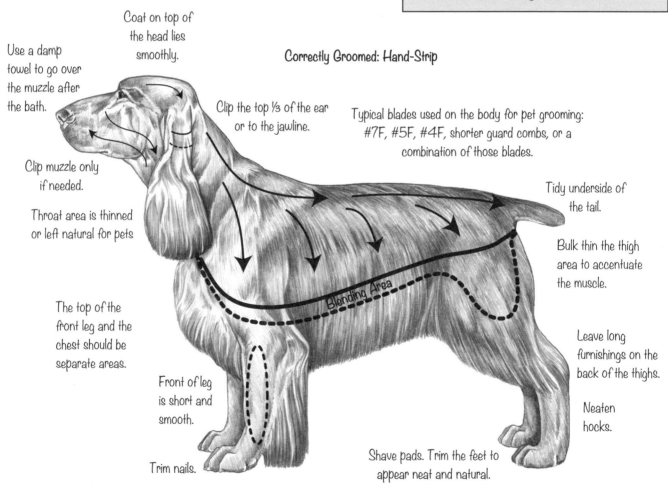

Coat on top of the head lies smoothly.

Use a damp towel to go over the muzzle after the bath.

Correctly Groomed: Hand-Strip

Clip the top ⅓ of the ear or to the jawline.

Typical blades used on the body for pet grooming: #7F, #5F, #4F, shorter guard combs, or a combination of those blades.

Clip muzzle only if needed.

Throat area is thinned or left natural for pets

Tidy underside of the tail.

Bulk thin the thigh area to accentuate the muscle.

The top of the front leg and the chest should be separate areas.

Blending Area

Leave long furnishings on the back of the thighs.

Front of leg is short and smooth.

Neaten hocks.

Trim nails.

Shave pads. Trim the feet to appear neat and natural.

The coat should look as natural as possible and all transitional pattern lines should be invisible.

Grooming Procedures & Recommendations

See page 71 for
Bathing & Drying Instructions

Frequency
Bathe once a week to once every 12 weeks.

Pre-Work
Trim or grind nails every four to six weeks to maintain a healthy foot structure. Clean the ears by swabbing with a mild ear cleaning solution. Use a rubber curry, shedding blade, undercoat rake, pumice stone, carding tool, fine stripping knife or natural bristle brush to loosen skin dander and remove loose coat. Use a high-velocity dryer over the coat to quickly and effectively lift dirt and debris away from the skin and loosen coat. Brush out or remove any matting found in the long-coated areas. If the tangles are loose enough so water can fully penetrate the area, remove them after bathing and drying. If water cannot penetrate, remove the mat or tangle prior to bathing.

Brushing
Line brush, working in sections until the dog is entirely tangle-free and all loose coat is removed. When finished, there should be little, if any, fur still being removed with a firm slicker brush. Double-check the work with a comb and your hands. Go over the entire body, feeling for any inconsistencies in the density levels of the coat. If an area seems moist to the touch or fuller than the rest of the coat, rework the area with the appropriate tool. Mats, tangles and excessive coat are easily trapped in the following areas: behind the ears, around the ruff, the thigh area, the undercarriage and the tail. Give extra attention to these areas before finishing the groom.

Carding
If a dog has an abundance of loose undercoat, line card the areas with a carding tool. Common tools can be a fine stripping knife, undercoat rake, a pumice stone, or a #40 blade held between your fingers. Any carding tool should be pulled over the body, working in the direction of the coat growth. This will remove the soft, downy undercoat, allowing the guard coat to conform more closely to the natural outline of the body. It will also aid in the removal of loose, shedding coat, a seasonal problem for many pet owners.

Feet & Hocks
Trim the pads with a close blade ranging from a #15 to a #40. Use a very light touch to clean the pads of long hair. If there is long fur between the toes, back brush the fur so it stands up on top of and away from the foot. With thinning shears, trim the excess to create a neat and very natural looking foot. Tidy the outside edge of the foot, if needed, with small detailing shears. If the hocks have longer coat, trim lightly with thinning shears to show a neat, clean area. A #4F blade, used carefully in reverse, works well for trimming the tops of the feet and the hocks on some dogs.

Ears
The tops of the ears are trimmed close to the skin using thinning shears or clippers. Trim the top to ⅓ of the ear leather or to the jawline if the hair is long on the outside of the ear. On the outside of the leather, the blending line will be a soft "U" shape. Keep this line above the widest section of the ear. If clipping, use a #10 or #15 blade, either with or against the coat growth based on coat density and skin sensitivity. If the coat is profuse, heavy or there is a strong odor coming from the ear canal, clip the inside of the ear with a very close blade ranging from a #40 to a #10. Use a light touch and clear the upper section inside the ear leather to assist with the sanitation and overall health of the ear. If both sides of the ear leather have been clipped, edge the top front section of the ear leather with detailing shears, keeping the tips of the shears towards the tips of the ears. Lightly round the long feathering at the bottom of the ears with shears for a neat look.

Suggested Tools & Equipment
- Nail Trimmers
- Styptic Powder
- Ear Cleaning Solution
- Cotton Balls
- Clippers
- Slicker Brush
- Greyhound Comb
- Pin Brush
- Rubber Curry
- Pumice Stone
- Carding Tools
- Stripping Knives
- Straight Shears
- Curved Shears
- Small Detailing Shears
- Thinning Shears
- Dematting Tools

Common Blade Options:
- #40, #15, #10
- #7F, #5F, #4F
- Variety of Guard Combs

Detail Finish
Edge the ears lightly with thinning shears to neaten and keep a natural look. Hand pluck any long wispy, flyaway hair from around the ears. Removal of whiskers on the muzzle is optional based on client preference. Finish with a fine mist of coat polish on the body coat for added shine. Application of bows and mild cologne is optional.

Special Note
In most cases, the body coat of these breeds lays tight enough to the body that owners do not want their pets clipper-cut. It is not recommended, but should a client request a clipper-cut for a pet, follow the general pattern guidelines found on most Sporting Dogs according to breed similarity.

Breed Facts & Characteristics

Country of Origin: England

Height at Shoulder: 22"–24½"

Coat Length/Type: Combination/Silky

Color: Black or Liver

Correct grooming procedure:

Bathe & Brush Out/Minor Trimming

Common pet grooming practices:

Bathe & Brush Out/Minor Trimming

-The Goal-
The coat should be fresh smelling, light and stand off the body. No loose hair.

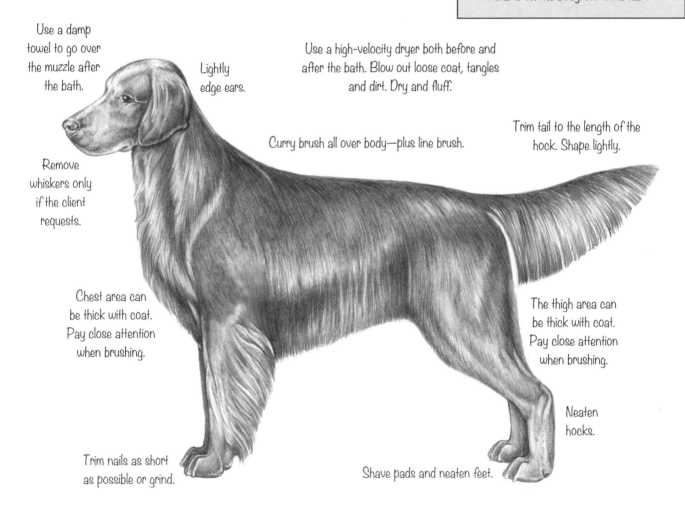

Use a damp towel to go over the muzzle after the bath.

Lightly edge ears.

Use a high-velocity dryer both before and after the bath. Blow out loose coat, tangles and dirt. Dry and fluff.

Curry brush all over body—plus line brush.

Trim tail to the length of the hock. Shape lightly.

Remove whiskers only if the client requests.

Chest area can be thick with coat. Pay close attention when brushing.

The thigh area can be thick with coat. Pay close attention when brushing.

Neaten hocks.

Trim nails as short as possible or grind.

Shave pads and neaten feet.

Grooming Procedures & Recommendations

See page 68 for Bathing & Drying Instructions

Frequency
Bathe once a week to once every 12 weeks.

Pre-Work
Trim or grind nails every four to six weeks to maintain a healthy foot structure. Clean the ears by swabbing with a mild ear cleaning solution. Use a rubber curry, shedding blade, undercoat rake, pumice stone, carding tool, fine stripping knife or natural bristle brush to loosen skin dander and remove loose coat. Use a high-velocity dryer over the coat to quickly and effectively lift dirt and debris away from the skin and loosen coat. Brush out or remove any matting found in the long-coated areas. If the tangles are loose enough so water can fully penetrate the area, remove them after bathing and drying. If water cannot penetrate, remove the mat or tangle prior to bathing.

Brushing
Line brush, working in sections until the dog is entirely tangle-free and all loose coat is removed. When finished, there should be little, if any, fur still being removed with a firm slicker brush. Double-check the work with a wide-toothed comb and your hands. Go over the entire body, feeling for any inconsistencies in the density levels of the coat. If an area seems moist to the touch or fuller than the rest of the coat, rework the area with the appropriate tool. Mats, tangles and excessive coat are easily trapped in the following areas: behind the ears, around the ruff, the thigh area, the undercarriage and the tail. Give extra attention to these areas before finishing the groom.

Carding
If a dog has an abundance of loose undercoat, line card the shorter areas with a carding tool. Common tools can be a fine stripping knife, undercoat rake, a pumice stone, or a #40 blade held between your fingers. Any carding tool should be pulled over the body, working in the direction of the coat growth. This will remove the soft, downy undercoat, allowing the guard coat to conform more closely to the natural outline of the body. It will also aid in the removal of loose, shedding coat, a seasonal problem for many pet owners.

Feet & Hocks
Trim the pads with a close blade ranging from a #15 to a #40. Use a very light touch to clean the pads of long hair. If there is long fur between the toes, back brush the fur so it stands up on top of and away from the foot. With thinning shears, trim the excess to create a neat and very natural looking foot. Tidy the outside edge of the foot, if needed, with small detailing shears. If the hocks have longer coat, trim lightly with thinning shears to show a neat, clean area. A #4F blade, used carefully in reverse, works well for trimming the tops of the feet and the hocks on some dogs.

Detail Finish
Edge the ears lightly with thinning shears to neaten and keep a natural look. Hand pluck any long wispy, flyaway hair from around the ears. Removal of whiskers on the muzzle is optional based on client preference. Finish with a fine mist of coat polish on the body coat for added shine. Application of bows and mild cologne is optional.

Suggested Tools & Equipment

- Nail Trimmers
- Styptic Powder
- Ear Cleaning Solution
- Cotton Balls
- Clippers
- #40 and #15 Blades for Pads
- #4F for Feet & Hocks (optional)
- Slicker Brush
- Greyhound Comb
- Rubber Curry
- Carding Tool
- De-Shedding Tools
- Small Detailing Shears
- Thinning Shears

Notes:

German Shorthaired Pointer SPORTING SMOOTH COATED

Breed Facts & Characteristics

Country of Origin: Germany

Height at Shoulder: 21"–25"

Coat Length/Type: Short/Smooth

Color: Can be solid liver or any combination of liver with white or roaning patterns.

Correct grooming procedure:

Bathe & Curry Brush

Common pet grooming practices:

Bathe & Curry Brush

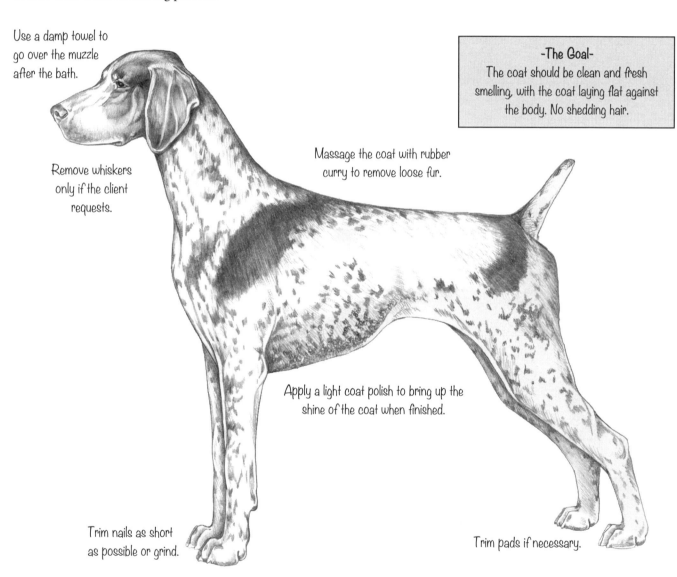

Use a damp towel to go over the muzzle after the bath.

-The Goal-
The coat should be clean and fresh smelling, with the coat laying flat against the body. No shedding hair.

Remove whiskers only if the client requests.

Massage the coat with rubber curry to remove loose fur.

Apply a light coat polish to bring up the shine of the coat when finished.

Trim nails as short as possible or grind.

Trim pads if necessary.

See page 66 for
Bathing & Drying Instructions

Suggested Tools & Equipment

- Nail Trimmers
- Styptic Powder
- Ear Cleaning Solution
- Cotton Balls
- Clippers
- #40 or #15 Blade
- Rubber Curry
- Carding Tool
- Small Detailing Shears
- Thinning Shears

Notes *from your*
Grooming Table

German Wirehaired Pointer   SPORTING   WIRE COATED

Breed Facts & Characteristics

Country of Origin: Germany

Height at Shoulder: 22"–26"

Coat Length/Type: Moderate/Wiry

Color: Can be solid liver or any combination of liver with white or roaning patterns.

Correct grooming procedure:
Bathe & Brush Out/Hand-Strip

Common pet grooming practices:
Bathe & Brush Out/Hand-Strip

General Description

The German Wirehaired Pointer is a tough, all-purpose hunting dog developed in Germany. The breed is slightly stockier than other pointers, yet still extremely agile with great stamina. The distinctive coat is made up of a wiry and tight-fitting outer coat with a thick under coat that is heavier in the winter and almost non-existent in the summer. The harsh, outer guard coat normally is between 1 and 2 inches in length, long enough to protect the dog, but not so long as to hide the true silhouette of the animal. The extended "eyebrows" and the typical beard give the German Wirehaired Pointer his characteristic appearance. The breed is seen in a variety of patterns all based on its two primary colors—liver with white.

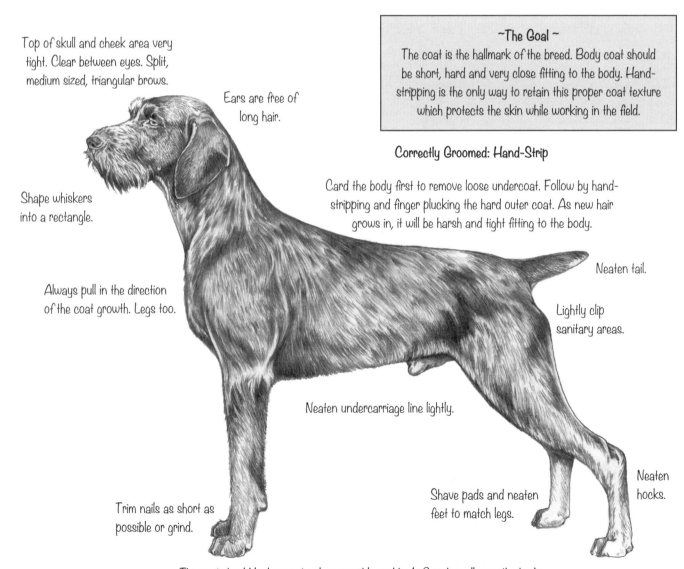

~The Goal ~
The coat is the hallmark of the breed. Body coat should be short, hard and very close fitting to the body. Hand-stripping is the only way to retain this proper coat texture which protects the skin while working in the field.

Correctly Groomed: Hand-Strip

Top of skull and cheek area very tight. Clear between eyes. Split, medium sized, triangular brows.

Ears are free of long hair.

Card the body first to remove loose undercoat. Follow by hand-stripping and finger plucking the hard outer coat. As new hair grows in, it will be harsh and tight fitting to the body.

Shape whiskers into a rectangle.

Neaten tail.

Always pull in the direction of the coat growth. Legs too.

Lightly clip sanitary areas.

Neaten undercarriage line lightly.

Neaten hocks.

Trim nails as short as possible or grind.

Shave pads and neaten feet to match legs.

The coat should look as natural as possible and be 1–2 inches all over the body.

Grooming Procedures & Recommendations

See page 76 for
Bathing & Drying Instructions

Frequency
Bathe once a week to once every 12 weeks.

Pre-Work
Trim or grind nails at least every four to six weeks to maintain a healthy foot structure. Swab the ears clean with a mild ear cleaning solution. Prior to bathing, quickly go over the entire body with a high-velocity dryer to help lift dirt and dander away from the skin and to loosen any shedding coat. *Normally, card and hand-strip dog prior to bathing and drying.*

Brushing
Use a rubber curry, shedding blade, undercoat rake, pumice stone, carding tool, fine stripping knife, slicker brush or natural bristled brush to remove any remaining loose coat or tangles. Be careful when using any tool with metal teeth or bristles. A heavy hand or too much repetition in an area can cause cuts and/or brush burns. Brushing is not finished until all loose fur is removed, or when it becomes difficult to remove more than a half a brush full after repeated brushing.

Carding
Carding is a natural technique in which the soft, downy undercoat is pulled from the dog's body. Typical tools used with this technique are: a pumice stone; a fine-toothed stripping knife that is pulled through the coat; an undercoat rake; or a fine blade, such as a #40, held between the fingers and pulled through the coat. Carding can be done before or after bathing and drying. Removal of the soft undercoat allows the topcoat to lie closer to the natural outline of the dog and accentuate the dog's structure. It also promotes profuse harsh outer coat, creates a rich coat color and protects the skin.

Hand-Stripping
Hand-stripping is a technique in which the outer guard coat is plucked from the dog's skin. This procedure helps retain the proper coat texture and rich color of the breed. During certain times of the year, the coat is easier to pull out. When the coat easily comes out, it is called a "blowing coat" or "blown coat." Ideally, hand-stripping should correspond with the dog's natural cycle, based on the environment and its hormonal levels.

Using your fingers, a carding tool or a stripping knife, pull out a few hairs at a time to shape the coat, accentuating the natural outline of the dog. Work methodically, pulling small amounts of coat at a time, always working in the direction of the coat growth. Proper hand-stripping removes hair with a gentle momentum and rhythm, not brute force, which is uncomfortable for both groomer and pet. The wrist stays locked in a neutral position while the rhythmic movement stems from the shoulder, not the wrist or elbow.

In general, the main body coat is easy to remove. Most pets do not mind the plucking process. The cheeks, throat and private areas may be more sensitive, requiring thinning shears or clippers.

Leave enough coat to be between 1 to 2 inches long. The coat should always appear very natural, never clipped or heavily trimmed. On some coats, a light application of chalk or powder before the bath will allow a better grip and make plucking and stripping much easier.

Head
Leave the coat longer on the muzzle. Hand-strip or pluck the top skull, throat and cheeks. Leave small triangles of coat above each eye to form the moderate eyebrows that accentuate the eye area. Ears are stripped of longer hair. If the coat on the ear leather does not strip/pluck out easily, clipper with blades ranging from a #10 to a #15 on the outside of the ear leather. Clipper the inside of the ear using blades ranging from a #40 to a #10. Finish by edging the ear with detailing shears, keeping the tips of the shears toward the tip of the ear.

Suggested Tools & Equipment

- Nail Trimmers
- Styptic Powder
- Ear Powder
- Ear Cleaning Solution
- Cotton Balls
- Hemostat
- Clippers
- Slicker Brush
- Greyhound Comb
- Pumice Stone
- Carding Tools
- Stripping Knives
- Straight Shears
- Curved Shears
- Small Detailing Shears
- Thinning Shears
- Dematting Tools

Common Blade Options:
- #40, #15, #10

Feet & Hocks
Trim the pads with a close cutting blade ranging from a #15 to a #40. Use a very light touch to clean the pads of long hair. Tidy the outside edge of the foot, if needed, with small detailing shears. If the hocks have longer coat, trim lightly with thinning shears to show a neat, clean area.

Detail Finish
Application of bows and mild cologne is optional.

Special Note
Clipping a wired-coated dog will result in a dramatic change in the texture and color of the coat. The correct harsh wire coat needs to be encouraged by plucking the blown coat when it is ready to be removed. This process stimulates hair follicles to produce new guard coat. Without hand-stripping, the guard coat is not stimulated and will not grow in properly. It will loose its brilliant color and texture. If only the undercoat grows, the guard coat color becomes that of the lighter, soft undercoat.

Golden Retriever

Breed Facts & Characteristics

Country of Origin: England

Height at Shoulder: 21½"–24"

Coat Length/Type: Combination/Silky

Color: Deep rich red-gold to light cream. Lighter on the under parts.

Correct grooming procedure:
Bathe & Brush Out/Minor Trimming

Common pet grooming practices:
Bathe & Brush Out/Minor Trimming

-The Goal-
The coat should be fresh smelling, light and stand off the body. No loose hair.

Use a damp towel to go over the muzzle after the bath.

Lightly edge ears.

Use a high-velocity dryer both before and after the bath blow out loose coat, tangles, dirt. Dry and fluff.

Curry brush all over body—plus line brush.

Remove whiskers only if the client requests.

Chest area can be thick with coat. Pay close attention when brushing.

Trim tail to the length of the hock. Shape lightly.

Thigh area can be thick with coat. Pay close attention when brushing.

Neaten hocks.

Trim nails as short as possible or grind.

Shave pads and neaten feet.

Grooming Procedures & Recommendations

**See page 68 for
Bathing & Drying Instructions**

Frequency
Bathe once a week to once every 12 weeks.

Pre-Work
Trim or grind nails every four to six weeks to maintain a healthy foot structure. Clean the ears by swabbing with a mild ear cleaning solution. Use a rubber curry, shedding blade, undercoat rake, pumice stone, carding tool, fine stripping knife or natural bristle brush to loosen skin dander and remove loose coat. Use a high-velocity dryer over the coat to quickly and effectively lift dirt and debris away from the skin and loosen coat. Brush out or remove any matting found in the long-coated areas. If the tangles are loose enough so water can fully penetrate the area, remove them after bathing and drying. If water cannot penetrate, remove the mat or tangle prior to bathing.

Brushing
Line brush, working in sections until the dog is entirely tangle-free and all loose coat is removed. When finished, there should be little, if any, fur still being removed with a firm slicker brush. Double-check the work with a wide-toothed comb and your hands. Go over the entire body, feeling for any inconsistencies in the density levels of the coat. If an area seems moist to the touch or fuller than the rest of the coat, rework the area with the appropriate tool. Mats, tangles and excessive coat are easily trapped in the following areas: behind the ears, around the ruff, the thigh area, the undercarriage and the tail. Give extra attention to these areas before finishing the groom.

Carding
If a dog has an abundance of loose undercoat, line card the shorter areas with a carding tool. Common tools can be a fine stripping knife, undercoat rake, a pumice stone, or a #40 blade held between your fingers. Any carding tool should be pulled over the body, working in the direction of the coat growth. This will remove the soft, downy undercoat, allowing the guard coat to conform more closely to the natural outline of the body. It will also aid in the removal of loose, shedding coat, a seasonal problem for many pet owners.

Feet & Hocks
Trim the pads with a close blade ranging from a #15 to a #40. Use a very light touch to clean the pads of long hair. If there is long fur between the toes, back brush the fur so it stands up on top of and away from the foot. With thinning shears, trim the excess to create a neat and very natural looking foot. Tidy the outside edge of the foot, if needed, with small detailing shears. If the hocks have longer coat, trim lightly with thinning shears to show a neat, clean area. A #4F blade, used carefully in reverse, works well for trimming the tops of the feet and the hocks on some dogs.

Detail Finish
Edge the ears lightly with thinning shears to neaten and keep a natural look. Hand pluck any long wispy, flyaway hair from around the ears. Removal of whiskers on the muzzle is optional based on client preference. Finish with a fine mist of coat polish on the body coat for added shine. Application of bows and mild cologne is optional.

Suggested Tools & Equipment

- Nail Trimmers
- Styptic Powder
- Ear Cleaning Solution
- Cotton Balls
- Clippers
- #40 and #15 Blades for Pads
- #4F for Feet & Hocks (optional)
- Slicker Brush
- Greyhound Comb
- Rubber Curry
- Carding Tool
- De-Shedding Tools
- Small Detailing Shears
- Thinning Shears

Notes:

Notes From The Grooming Table ©2016

Gordon Setter

Breed Facts & Characteristics

Country of Origin: Scotland

Height at Shoulder: 23"–27"

Coat Length/Type: Combination/Silky

Color: Black with tan or mahogany points.

Correct grooming procedure:
Card & Hand-Strip

Common pet grooming practices:
Clipper-Trim/Card & Hand-Strip

General Description

The Gordon Setter is a gun dog of great style and stamina. It is well balanced with excellent muscle tone and substantial bone. The chest is deep, reaching to the elbows. The topline is level or slightly sloping. The tail is an extension of the topline, with no dip or break at the junction point. The tail is shaped like a flag and reaches to the hock when the dog is relaxed. The head is deep and noble. The coat of a Gordon Setter is black and tan in color. The texture is soft and silky. The jacket coat should lay smoothly over the head, throat, neck, shoulders, back, down the sides of the dog and the thighs. There are longer furnishings on the ears, chest, undercarriage, belly, the back of the legs and the tail.

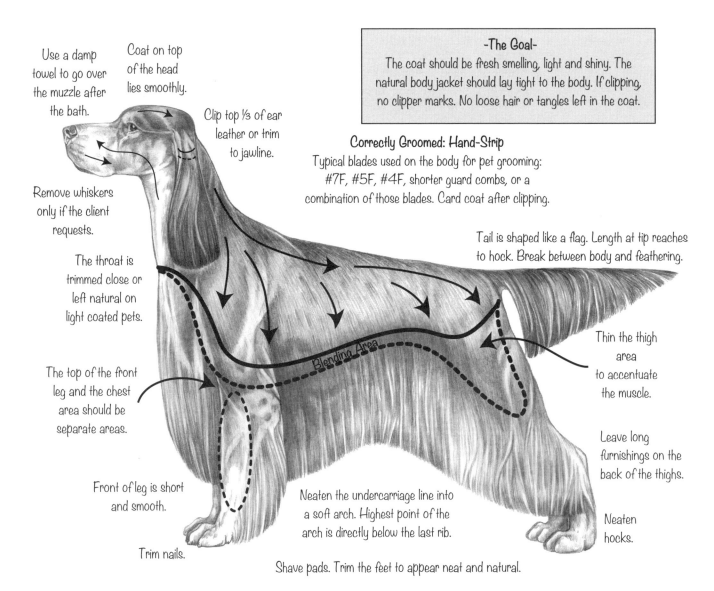

Use a damp towel to go over the muzzle after the bath.

Coat on top of the head lies smoothly.

Clip top ⅓ of ear leather or trim to jawline.

Remove whiskers only if the client requests.

The throat is trimmed close or left natural on light coated pets.

The top of the front leg and the chest area should be separate areas.

Front of leg is short and smooth.

Trim nails.

Blending Area

Neaten the undercarriage line into a soft arch. Highest point of the arch is directly below the last rib.

Shave pads. Trim the feet to appear neat and natural.

Tail is shaped like a flag. Length at tip reaches to hock. Break between body and feathering.

Thin the thigh area to accentuate the muscle.

Leave long furnishings on the back of the thighs.

Neaten hocks.

-The Goal-
The coat should be fresh smelling, light and shiny. The natural body jacket should lay tight to the body. If clipping, no clipper marks. No loose hair or tangles left in the coat.

Correctly Groomed: Hand-Strip
Typical blades used on the body for pet grooming:
#7F, #5F, #4F, shorter guard combs, or a combination of those blades. Card coat after clipping.

The coat should look as natural as possible and all transitional pattern lines should be invisible.

See page 71 for
Bathing & Drying Instructions

Frequency
Bathe once a week to once every
12 weeks.

Pre-Work
Trim or grind nails every four to
six weeks to maintain a healthy foot
structure. Clean the ears by swabbing
with a mild ear cleaning solution. Use a
rubber curry, shedding blade, undercoat
rake, pumice stone, carding tool, fine
stripping knife or natural bristle brush
to loosen skin dander and remove loose
coat. Use a high-velocity dryer over
the coat to quickly and effectively lift
dirt and debris away from the skin and
loosen coat. Brush out or remove any
matting found in the long-coated areas.
If the tangles are loose enough so water
can fully penetrate the area, remove
them after bathing and drying. If water
cannot penetrate, remove the mat or
tangle prior to bathing.

Brushing
Line brush, working in sections until
the dog is entirely tangle-free and all
loose coat is removed. When finished,
there should be little, if any, fur still
being removed with a firm slicker brush.
Double-check the work with a comb
and your hands. Go over the entire
body, feeling for any inconsistencies in
the density levels of the coat. If an area
seems moist to the touch or fuller than
the rest of the coat, rework the area
with the appropriate tool. Mats, tangles
and excessive coat are easily trapped in
the following areas: behind the ears,
around the ruff, the thigh area, the
undercarriage and the tail. Give extra
attention to these areas before finishing
the groom.

Hand-Stripping & Thinning the Body Pattern
Ideally, the coat should be worked with
hand-stripping techniques, carding and
thinning shears to retain the proper
coat texture, brilliant color and natural
look. Sporting dogs are extremely
athletic. When trimming them, this
trait is emphasized by working with
their natural bone structure and muscle
tone. Start shaping the coat by carding
and hand-stripping. If there is still an
abundance of coat, trim the coat with
a moderately toothed, single-sided
thinning shear. This style of shear will
minimize how much coat is removed
with each cut. Slide the smooth blade of
the shear up under the coat. With the
smooth blade against the skin, cock the
shear slightly, making it impossible to
accidentally pinch the skin when closing
the blades. Make one cut, then extract
the shear and repeat right next to the
preceding cut. Work in a methodical
manner, handling one area at a time.
Once four to six cuts have been made
in one area, stop and brush the cut
coat out with a heavy slicker brush.
Continue to bulk thin the area until the
coat lies smoothly, but not so thin that
the long guard coat is totally removed.
Always slide the shears up under the
coat in keeping the blade parallel with
the natural growth of the hair. Cutting
"cross grain" will create holes in the coat
that are almost impossible to correct.

Clipper-Trimming the Body Pattern
Blades ranging from a #10 to a #4F,
or shorter guard combs, are commonly
used to set the pattern on the body
as an alternative to proper grooming
techniques for pets. They can be used
with the grain or against the grain with
longer blades. Keep in mind, the shorter
the trim on the body pattern the more
difficult it is to blend the pattern later
into the longer furnishings, for these
lines should be invisible. A longer cut
also allows you to mold the coat a

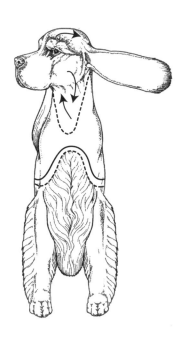

The groom should leave the dog looking
as natural as possible. The head is free of
long hair. Tops of the ears are short. The
fur on the front of the front legs is smooth
and short. Dog is well feathered. Tail is flag
shaped and reaches to the hock. Hocks are
trimmed. Feet are natural.

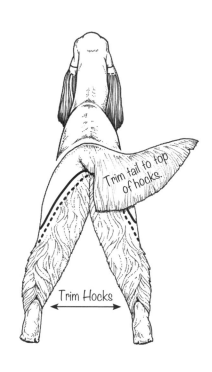

Trim tail to top of hocks

Trim Hocks

SPORTING

Coat on the head lies smoothly. Finger pluck or thinning shear long strays if light coated. For heavier coated dogs, clip the cheeks and top of the head with blades ranging from a #7F to a #4F, used with or against the grain.

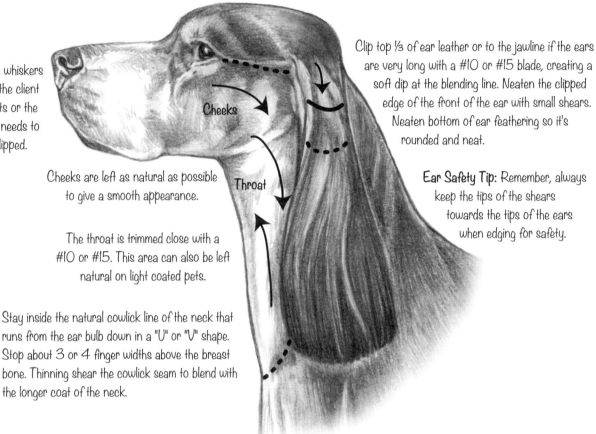

Remove whiskers only if the client requests or the muzzle needs to be clipped.

Cheeks

Cheeks are left as natural as possible to give a smooth appearance.

The throat is trimmed close with a #10 or #15. This area can also be left natural on light coated pets.

Throat

Stay inside the natural cowlick line of the neck that runs from the ear bulb down in a "U" or "V" shape. Stop about 3 or 4 finger widths above the breast bone. Thinning shear the cowlick seam to blend with the longer coat of the neck.

Clip top ⅓ of ear leather or to the jawline if the ears are very long with a #10 or #15 blade, creating a soft dip at the blending line. Neaten the clipped edge of the front of the ear with small shears. Neaten bottom of ear feathering so it's rounded and neat.

Ear Safety Tip: Remember, always keep the tips of the shears towards the tips of the ears when edging for safety.

bit and apply carding techniques to retain some of the proper coat texture. Longer cutting blades are preferred over shorter ones. At the front of the dog, the pattern starts just above the breast bone and drops on a diagonal line to the point where the chest meets the top of the front leg. The entire front of the front leg should be free of long fur, blending into the naturally short coat on the front of the leg. Moving down the side of the dog, the pattern is set at the lower bulge of the shoulder muscle, just above the elbow. It continues behind the elbow and on a slight angle up into the flank area. The pattern line rises over

the flank, dropping in a "U" shape to expose the upper thigh muscle. The "U" shape rises back up to just below the base of the tail, leaving the long feathers at the back of the thigh. When blending the pattern, the transitional areas will be ½ inch to 2 inches in width depending on the area and the conformation of the dog. At the blending areas, bulk thin or top thin with thinning shears so the main body area blends invisibly with the longer furnishings.

Carding
If a dog has an abundance of loose undercoat, line card the areas with a carding tool. Common tools can be

a fine stripping knife, an undercoat rake, a pumice stone, or a #40 blade held between your fingers. Any carding tool should be pulled over the body and worked in the direction of the coat growth. This will remove the soft, downy undercoat, allowing the guard coat to conform closer to the natural outline of the body. It will also aid in the removal of loose, shedding coat which is a seasonal problem for many pet owners.

Furnishings
The back of the front legs and the rear section of the thighs and undercarriage should be well feathered. The feathering is left natural. With

extremely heavy coats the leg hair may be trimmed slightly to neaten and balance the outline. On the front of the front legs, the coat should be saddled out short, smooth and fine. If the leg is covered with long coat, the front legs will need to be trimmed to simulate this natural short-coated look. At the rump, the long coat falls off the rear side of the thighs. There is a clean separation between the tail and the long feathers.

Head

The head is covered with fine, short hair that conforms to the shape of the skull. Some dogs come by this trait more naturally than others. With light-coated dogs, the longer hair may be finger plucked, carded or stripped out by hand, retaining a neat and natural look. For those dogs with longer coat covering sections of their head and muzzle, the coat is removed with thinning shears or by clipping. If the coat is extremely heavy, clip the area using blades ranging from a #15 to a #7F on the muzzle. A longer blade can be used for the top skull. Work with or against the coat growth based on how smooth and close the area needs to be and the dog's skin sensitivity. Clip the throat area from the base of the ear bulbs in a "V" shape, following the cowlick line at the sides of the neck with a #15 or #10 blade. The lowest point of the "V" will be three to four finger widths above the breastbone. Finish by blending the cowlick line seam so it is invisible between the neck and the throat.

Ears

The tops of the ears are trimmed close to the skin using thinning shears or clippers. Trim the top ⅓ of the outer ear leather or, if the ear is very long, set the line to the jaw. On the outside of the leather, the blending line will be a soft "U" shape. Keep this line above the widest section of the ear. If clipping, use a #10 or #15 blade, either with or against the coat growth based on coat density and skin

sensitivity. If the coat is profuse, heavy or there is a strong odor coming from the ear canal, clip the inside of the ear with a very close blade ranging from a #40 to a #10. Use a light touch and clear the upper section inside the ear leather to assist with the sanitation and overall health of the ear. If both sides of the ear leather have been clipped, edge the top front section of the ear leather with detailing shears, keeping the tips of the shears towards the tips of the ears. Lightly round the long feathering at the bottom of the ears with shears for a neat look.

Tail

The tail is in the shape of a triangular flag. The pointed tip should reach to the top of the hock. The top of the tail is covered with short, smooth, harsh coat while the long silky feathers fall from the underside. At the root base, there is a break in the fur, separating the tail from the body. Shape the tail to look very natural with thinning shears or shears.

Feet & Hocks

Trim the pads with a close cutting blade ranging from a #15 to a #40. Use a very light touch to clean the pads of long hair. If there is long fur between the toes, back brush the fur so it stands up on top of and away from the foot. With thinning shears, trim off the excess creating a neat and very natural looking foot. Tidy the outside edge of the foot, if needed, with small detailing shears. If the hocks have longer coat, trim lightly with thinning shears to show a neat, clean area. A #4F blade used in reverse works well for trimming the tops of the feet and the hocks on some dogs.

Detail Finish

Removal of whiskers on the muzzle is optional, based on client preference or the amount of fur on the muzzle. Finish with a fine mist of coat polish on the body coat for added shine. Application of bows and mild cologne is optional.

Suggested Tools & Equipment

- Nail Trimmers
- Styptic Powder
- Ear Cleaning Solution
- Cotton Balls
- Clippers
- Slicker Brush
- Greyhound Comb
- Pin Brush
- Rubber Curry
- Pumice Stone
- Carding Tools
- Stripping Knives
- Straight Shears
- Curved Shears
- Small Detailing Shears
- Thinning Shears
- Dematting Tools

Common Blade Options:

- #40, #15, #10
- #7F, #5F, #4F
- Variety of Guard Combs

Notes:

Irish Red and White Setter   SPORTING   SILKY

Breed Facts & Characteristics

Country of Origin: Ireland

Height at Shoulder: 22½"–26"

Coat Length/Type: Combination/Silky

Color: Base color white with clear patches of reds.

Correct grooming procedure:

Card/Hand-Strip/Minor Trimming

Common pet grooming practices:

Card/Hand-Strip/Minor Trimming

General Description

The Irish Red and White Setter is primarily an athletic field dog with great style. It is well balanced and medium in size. The chest is deep, reaching to the elbow. The neck and back are strong. The topline from the withers to the croup is level. The croup is well rounded, sloping slightly downward to the tail. The tail is shaped like a flag and reaches to the hock. The coat should lay smoothly over the head, throat, neck, shoulders, back, down the sides of the dog and the thighs. The longer furnishings on the ears, chest, undercarriage, belly and the back of the thighs and tail are all moderate in length and density.

> **-The Goal-**
> The coat should be fresh smelling, light and shiny.
> The natural body jacket should lay tight to the body.
> No loose hair or tangles left in the coat.

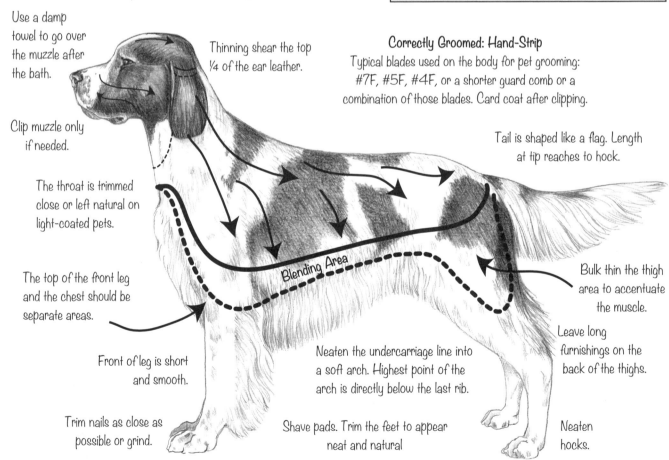

Coat on top of the head lies smoothly.

Use a damp towel to go over the muzzle after the bath.

Thinning shear the top ¼ of the ear leather.

Clip muzzle only if needed.

Correctly Groomed: Hand-Strip
Typical blades used on the body for pet grooming: #7F, #5F, #4F, or a shorter guard comb or a combination of those blades. Card coat after clipping.

Tail is shaped like a flag. Length at tip reaches to hock.

The throat is trimmed close or left natural on light-coated pets.

The top of the front leg and the chest should be separate areas.

Blending Area

Bulk thin the thigh area to accentuate the muscle.

Leave long furnishings on the back of the thighs.

Front of leg is short and smooth.

Neaten the undercarriage line into a soft arch. Highest point of the arch is directly below the last rib.

Trim nails as close as possible or grind.

Shave pads. Trim the feet to appear neat and natural

Neaten hocks.

The coat should look as natural as possible and all transitional pattern lines should be invisible.
Carding or raking out the loose body coat following the pattern outline for a natural look is perfered over clipping.

See page 71 for
Bathing & Drying Instructions

Frequency
Bathe once a week to once every
12 weeks.

Pre-Work
Trim or grind nails at least every four
to six weeks to maintain a healthy foot
structure. Clean the ears by swabbing
with a mild ear cleaning solution. Use a
rubber curry, shedding blade, undercoat
rake, pumice stone, carding tool, fine
stripping knife or natural bristle brush
to loosen skin dander and remove loose
coat. Quickly blow out the dog with
a high velocity dryer to effectively lift
dirt and debris away from the skin and
loosen coat. Brush out or remove any
matting found in the longer coated
areas. If the tangles are loose enough to
be fully penetrated by water, remove
them after bathing and drying. If water
cannot penetrate, remove the mat or
tangle prior to bathing.

Brushing
Line brush, working in sections until the
dog is entirely tangle-free. Double check
the work with a comb and your hands.
Go over the entire body, feeling for any
inconsistencies in the density levels of
the coat. If an area seems moist to the
touch or fuller than the rest of the coat,
rework the area with the appropriate
tool. Mats, tangles and excessive coat
are easily trapped in the following areas:
behind the ears, around the ruff, the
thigh area, the undercarriage and the
tail. Give extra attention to these areas
before finishing the groom.

Hand-Stripping &
Thinning the Body Pattern
Ideally, the coat should be worked with
hand-stripping techniques, carding and
thinning shears to retain the proper

coat texture, brilliant color and natural
look. Sporting dogs are extremely
athletic. When trimming them, this
trait is emphasized by working with
their natural bone structure and muscle
tone. Start shaping the coat by carding
and hand-stripping. If there is still an
abundance of coat, trim the coat with
a moderately toothed, single-sided
thinning shear. This style of shear will
minimize how much coat is removed
with each cut. Slide the smooth blade
of the shear up under the coat. With
the smooth blade against the skin, cock
the shear slightly, making it nearly
impossible to accidentally pinch the skin
when closing the blades. Make one cut,
then extract the shear and repeat right
next to the preceding cut. Work in a
methodical manner, handling one area at
a time. Once four to six cuts have been
made in one area, stop and brush the
cut coat out with a heavy slicker brush.
Continue to bulk thin the area until the
coat lies smoothly, but not so thin that
the long guard coat is totally removed.
Always slide the shears up under the
coat in keeping the blade parallel with
the natural growth of the hair. Cutting
"cross grain" will create holes in the coat
that are almost impossible to correct.

Clipper-Cut Body Pattern
Blades ranging from a #7F to a #4F
or shorter guard combs are commonly
used to set the pattern on the body as an
alternative to proper grooming techniques
for pets. They can be used with the grain
or against the grain with longer blades.
Keep in mind, the shorter the trim on
the body pattern the more difficult it is
to blend the pattern later into the longer
furnishings, for these lines should be
invisible. A longer cut also allows you to
mold the coat a bit and apply carding
techniques to retain some of the proper
coat texture. Longer cutting blades are
preferred over shorter ones.

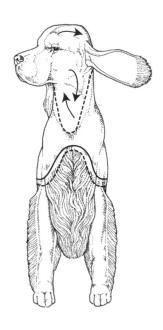

The groom should leave the dog looking
as natural as possible. The head is
free of long hair. Tops of the ears
are short. The fur on the front of the
front legs is smooth and short. Dog
is well feathered. Tail is flag shaped
and reaches to the hock. Hocks are
trimmed. Feet are natural.

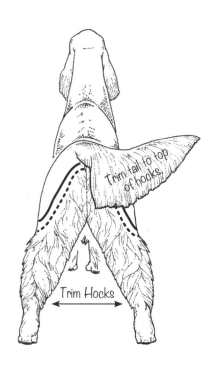

Trim tail to top of hocks

Trim Hocks

Coat on the head lies smoothly. Finger pluck or thinning shear long strays if light coated. Follow with carding and thinning. For heavier coated dogs, clip the cheeks and top of the head with blades ranging from a #7F to a #4F, used with or against the grain.

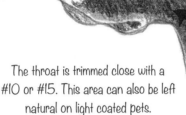

Remove whiskers only if the client requests or the muzzle needs to be clipped.

Thinning shear or clip the top ⅓ of the ear with a #10 or #15 blade. Neaten bottom of ear so it's rounded and neat. Do not clip the inside of ear leather. Leave the top, front edge untrimmed, helping to create a soft expression.

Ear Safety Tip: Remember, always keep the tips of the shears towards the tips of the ears when edging for safety.

The throat is trimmed close with a #10 or #15. This area can also be left natural on light coated pets.

Stay inside the natural cowlick line of the neck that runs from the ear bulb down in a "U" or "V" shape. Stop about 3 or 4 finger widths above the breast bone. Thinning shear the cowlick seam to blend with the longer coat of the neck.

At the front of the dog, the pattern starts just above the breast bone and drops on a diagonal line to the point where the forearm meets the upper arm. The front of the forearm should be free of long fur, blending into the naturally short coat on the front of the leg. Moving down the side of the dog, the pattern is set at the lower bulge of the shoulder muscle, just above the elbow. It continues behind the elbow and on a slight angle up into the flank area. The pattern line rises over the flank, dropping in a "U" shape to expose the upper thigh muscle. The "U" shape rises back up to just below the base of the tail, leaving the long feathers at the back of the thigh. At the blending areas, bulk thin or top thin with thinning shears so the main body area blends invisibly with the longer furnishings.

Carding

If a dog has an abundance of loose undercoat, card the areas with a carding tool. Common tools can be a fine stripping knife, undercoat rake a pumice stone or a #40 blade held between your fingers. Any carding tool should be pulled over the body and worked in the direction of the coat growth. This will remove the soft, downy undercoat, allowing the guard coat to conform closer to the natural outline of the body. It will also aid in the removal of loose, shedding coat, which is a seasonal problem for many pet owners.

Furnishings

The back of the front legs and the rear section of the thighs and undercarriage should be well feathered. The feathering is left natural. With extremely heavy coats the leg hair may be trimmed slightly to neaten and balance the outline. On the front of the front legs, the coat should be saddled out short, smooth and fine. If the leg is covered with long coat, the front legs will need to be trimmed to simulate this natural short-coated look. At the rump, the long coat falls off the rear side of the thighs. There is a clean separation between the tail and the long feathers.

Head

The head is covered with fine, short hair that conforms to the shape of the skull. Some dogs come by this trait more naturally than others. With light-coated dogs, the longer hair may be finger plucked, carded or stripped out by hand, retaining a neat and natural look. For those dogs with longer coat covering sections of their head and muzzle, the coat is removed with thinning shears or by clipping. If the coat is extremely heavy, clip the area using blades ranging from a #15 to a #7F on the muzzle. A longer blade can be used for the top skull. Work with or against the coat growth based on how smooth and close the area needs to be and the dog's skin sensitivity.

Clip the throat area from the base of the ear bulbs in a "V" shape, following the cowlick line at the sides of the neck with a #15 or #10 blade. The lowest point of the "V" will be three to four finger widths above the breastbone. Finish by blending the cowlick line seam so it is invisible between the neck and the throat.

Ears

The tops of the ears are trimmed using thinning shears. Lightly trim this area only to remove any excessive coat that hides a clean junction between the skull and the top of the ear. If the coat is profuse, heavy or there is a strong odor coming from the ear canal, clip the inside of the ear with a very close blade ranging from a #40 to a #10. Use a light touch and clear the upper section inside the ear leather to assist with the sanitation and overall health of the ear. If needed, lightly round the feathering at the bottom of the ears with shears or thinners for a neat look.

Tail

The tail is in the shape of a triangular flag. The pointed tip should reach to the top of the hock. The top of the tail is covered with short, smooth, harsh coat while the long silky feathers fall from the underside. At the root base, there is a break in the fur, separating the tail from the body. Shape the tail to look very natural with thinning shears or scissors.

Feet & Hocks

Trim the pads with a close cutting blade ranging from a #15 to a #40. Use a very light touch to clean the pads of long hair. If there is long fur between the toes, back brush the fur so it stands up on top of and away from the foot. With thinning shears, trim off the excess creating a neat and very natural looking foot. Tidy the outside edge of the foot, if needed, with small detailing shears. If the hocks have longer coat, trim lightly with thinning shears to show a neat, clean area. A #4F blade used in reverse works well for trimming the tops of the feet and the hocks on some dogs.

Detail Finish

Removal of whiskers on the muzzle is optional, based on client preference or the amount of fur on the muzzle. Finish with a fine mist of coat polish on the body coat for added shine. Application of bows and mild cologne is optional.

Suggested Tools & Equipment

- Nail Trimmers
- Styptic Powder
- Ear Cleaning Solution
- Cotton Balls
- Clippers
- Slicker Brush
- Greyhound Comb
- Pin Brush
- Rubber Curry
- Pumice Stone
- Carding Tools
- Stripping Knives
- Straight Shears
- Curved Shears
- Small Detailing Shears
- Thinning Shears
- Dematting Tools

Common Blade Options:

- #40, #15, #10
- #7F, #5F, #4F
- Variety of Guard Combs

Notes:

Irish Setter

Breed Facts & Characteristics

Country of Origin: Ireland

Height at Shoulder: 25"–27"

Coat Length/Type: Combination/Silky

Color: Deep, rich chestnut red or brown.

Correct grooming procedure:
Card & Hand-Strip

Common pet grooming practices:
Clipper-Trim/Card & Hand-Strip

General Description

The Irish Setter is a gun dog of great style and beauty. It is well balanced, medium in size. The chest is deep, reaching to the elbows. The topline is level or slightly sloping. The tail is an extension of the topline, with no dip or break at the junction point. The tail is shaped like a flag and reaches to the hock when the dog is relaxed. The head is long and slender. The coat of an Irish Setter is soft, silky and brilliant red in color. The jacket coat should lay smoothly over the head, throat, neck, shoulders, back, down the sides of the dog and the thighs. There are longer furnishings on the ears, chest, undercarriage, belly, the back of all the legs and the tail.

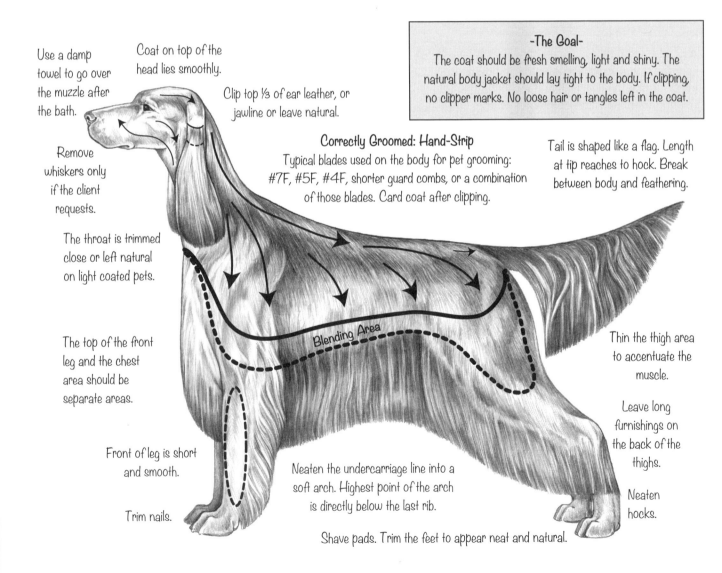

Use a damp towel to go over the muzzle after the bath.

Coat on top of the head lies smoothly.

Clip top ⅓ of ear leather, or jawline or leave natural.

-The Goal-
The coat should be fresh smelling, light and shiny. The natural body jacket should lay tight to the body. If clipping, no clipper marks. No loose hair or tangles left in the coat.

Remove whiskers only if the client requests.

Correctly Groomed: Hand-Strip
Typical blades used on the body for pet grooming: #7F, #5F, #4F, shorter guard combs, or a combination of those blades. Card coat after clipping.

Tail is shaped like a flag. Length at tip reaches to hock. Break between body and feathering.

The throat is trimmed close or left natural on light coated pets.

Blending Area

The top of the front leg and the chest area should be separate areas.

Thin the thigh area to accentuate the muscle.

Leave long furnishings on the back of the thighs.

Front of leg is short and smooth.

Trim nails.

Neaten the undercarriage line into a soft arch. Highest point of the arch is directly below the last rib.

Neaten hocks.

Shave pads. Trim the feet to appear neat and natural.

The coat should look as natural as possible and all transitional pattern lines should be invisible.

See page 71 for
Bathing & Drying Instructions

Frequency
Bathe once a week to once every
12 weeks.

Pre-Work
Trim or grind nails every four to
six weeks to maintain a healthy foot
structure. Clean the ears by swabbing
with a mild ear cleaning solution. Use a
rubber curry, shedding blade, undercoat
rake, pumice stone, carding tool, fine
stripping knife or natural bristle brush
to loosen skin dander and remove loose
coat. Use a high-velocity dryer over
the coat to quickly and effectively lift
dirt and debris away from the skin and
loosen coat. Brush out or remove any
matting found in the long-coated areas.
If the tangles are loose enough so water
can fully penetrate the area, remove
them after bathing and drying. If water
cannot penetrate, remove the mat or
tangle prior to bathing.

Brushing
Line brush, working in sections until
the dog is entirely tangle-free and all
loose coat is removed. When finished,
there should be little, if any, fur still
being removed with a firm slicker brush.
Double-check the work with a comb
and your hands. Go over the entire
body, feeling for any inconsistencies in
the density levels of the coat. If an area
seems moist to the touch or fuller than
the rest of the coat, rework the area
with the appropriate tool. Mats, tangles
and excessive coat are easily trapped in
the following areas: behind the ears,
around the ruff, the thigh area, the
undercarriage and the tail. Give extra
attention to these areas before finishing
the groom.

Hand-Stripping & Thinning the Body Pattern
Ideally, the coat should be worked with
hand-stripping techniques, carding and
thinning shears to retain the proper
coat texture, brilliant color and natural
look. Sporting dogs are extremely
athletic. When trimming them, this
trait is emphasized by working with
their natural bone structure and muscle
tone. Start shaping the coat by carding
and hand-stripping. If there is still an
abundance of coat, trim the coat with
a moderately toothed, single-sided
thinning shear. This style of shear will
minimize how much coat is removed
with each cut. Slide the smooth blade of
the shear up under the coat. With the
smooth blade against the skin, cock the
shear slightly, making it impossible to
accidentally pinch the skin when closing
the blades. Make one cut, then extract
the shear and repeat right next to the
preceding cut. Work in a methodical
manner, handling one area at a time.
Once four to six cuts have been made
in one area, stop and brush the cut
coat out with a heavy slicker brush.
Continue to bulk thin the area until the
coat lies smoothly, but not so thin that
the long guard coat is totally removed.
Always slide the shears up under the
coat in keeping the blade parallel with
the natural growth of the hair. Cutting
"cross grain" will create holes in the coat
that are almost impossible to correct.

Clipper-Trimming the Body Pattern
Blades ranging from a #10 to a #4F,
or shorter guard combs, are commonly
used to set the pattern on the body
as an alternative to proper grooming
techniques for pets. They can be used
with the grain or against the grain with
longer blades. Keep in mind, the shorter
the trim on the body pattern the more
difficult it is to blend the pattern later
into the longer furnishings, for these
lines should be invisible. A longer cut
also allows you to mold the coat a

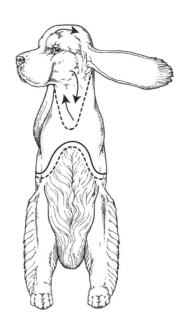

The groom should leave the dog looking as
natural as possible. The head is free of long
hair. Tops of the ears are short. The fur on
the front of the front legs is smooth and
short. Dog is well feathered. Tail is flag shaped
and reaches to the top of the hock. Hocks are
trimmed. Feet are natural.

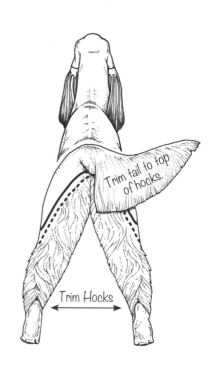

Trim tail to top of hocks.

Trim Hocks

Coat on the head lies smoothly. Finger pluck or thinning shear long strays if light coated. Follow with carding and thinning. The coat can change colors so dramatically on the Irish Setter, it is not recommended to clip the top of the head, even on pets. If clipping the body, then follow thorough with clipping the top of the head as well with a #7F, working with the lay of the coat.

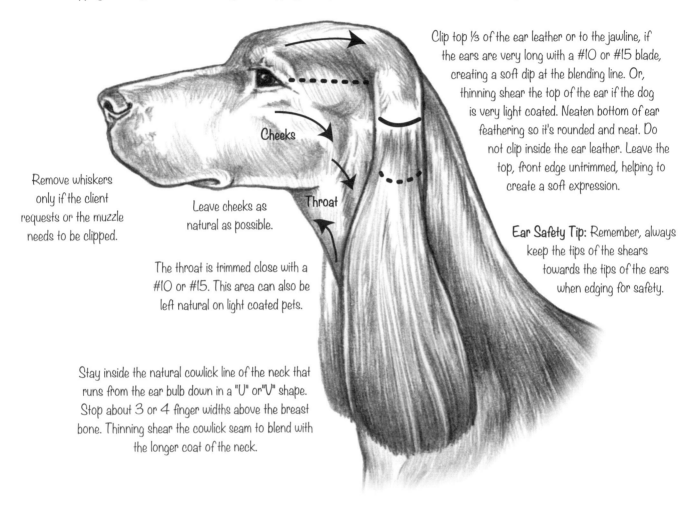

Clip top ⅓ of the ear leather or to the jawline, if the ears are very long with a #10 or #15 blade, creating a soft dip at the blending line. Or, thinning shear the top of the ear if the dog is very light coated. Neaten bottom of ear feathering so it's rounded and neat. Do not clip inside the ear leather. Leave the top, front edge untrimmed, helping to create a soft expression.

Ear Safety Tip: Remember, always keep the tips of the shears towards the tips of the ears when edging for safety.

Cheeks

Throat

Remove whiskers only if the client requests or the muzzle needs to be clipped.

Leave cheeks as natural as possible.

The throat is trimmed close with a #10 or #15. This area can also be left natural on light coated pets.

Stay inside the natural cowlick line of the neck that runs from the ear bulb down in a "U" or "V" shape. Stop about 3 or 4 finger widths above the breast bone. Thinning shear the cowlick seam to blend with the longer coat of the neck.

bit and apply carding techniques to retain some of the proper coat texture. Longer cutting blades are preferred over shorter ones. At the front of the dog, the pattern starts just above the breast bone and drops on a diagonal line to the point where the chest meets the top of the front leg. The entire front of the front leg should be free of long fur, blending into the naturally short coat on the front of the leg. Moving down the side of the dog, the pattern is set at the lower bulge of the shoulder muscle, just above the elbow. It continues behind the elbow and

on a slight angle up into the flank area. The pattern line rises over the flank, dropping in a "U" shape to expose the upper thigh muscle. The "U" shape rises back up to just below the base of the tail, leaving the long feathers at the back of the thigh. When blending the pattern, the transitional areas will be ½ inch to 2 inches in width depending on the area and the conformation of the dog. At the blending areas, bulk thin or top thin with thinning shears so the main body area blends invisibly with the longer furnishings.

Carding
If a dog has an abundance of loose undercoat, line card the areas with a carding tool. Common tools can be a fine stripping knife, an undercoat rake, a pumice stone, or a #40 blade held between your fingers. Any carding tool should be pulled over the body and worked in the direction of the coat growth. This will remove the soft, downy undercoat, allowing the guard coat to conform closer to the natural outline of the body. It will also aid in the removal of loose, shedding coat which is a seasonal problem for many pet owners.

Grooming Procedures & Recommendations

Furnishings

The back of the front legs and the rear section of the thighs and undercarriage should be well feathered. The feathering is left natural. With extremely heavy coats the leg hair may be trimmed slightly to neaten and balance the outline. On the front of the front legs, the coat should be saddled out short, smooth and fine. If the leg is covered with long coat, the front legs will need to be trimmed to simulate this natural short-coated look. At the rump, the long coat falls off the rear side of the thighs. There is a clean separation between the tail and the long feathers.

Head

The head is covered with fine, short hair that conforms to the shape of the skull. Some dogs come by this trait more naturally than others. With light-coated dogs, the longer hair may be finger plucked, carded or stripped out by hand, retaining a neat and natural look. For those dogs with longer coat covering sections of their head and muzzle, the coat is removed with thinning shears or by clipping. If the coat is extremely heavy, clip the area using blades ranging from a #15 to a #7F on the muzzle. A longer blade can be used for the top skull. Work with or against the coat growth based on how smooth and close the area needs to be and the dog's skin sensitivity. Clip the throat area from the base of the ear bulbs in a "V" shape, following the cowlick line at the sides of the neck with a #15 or #10 blade. The lowest point of the "V" will be 2 to 3 finger widths above the breastbone. Finish by blending the cowlick line seam so it is invisible between the neck and the throat.

Ears

The tops of the ears are trimmed close to the skin using thinning shears or clippers. Trim the top ⅓ of the outer ear leather or, if the ear is very long, set the line to the jaw. On the outside of the leather, the blending line will be a soft "U" shape. Keep this line above the widest section of the ear. If clipping, use a #10 or #15 blade, either with or against the coat growth based on coat density and skin sensitivity. If the coat is profuse, heavy or there is a strong odor coming from the ear canal, clip the inside of the ear with a very close blade ranging from a #40 to a #10. Use a light touch and clear the upper section inside the ear leather to assist with the sanitation and overall health of the ear. If both sides of the ear leather have been clipped, edge the top front section of the ear leather with detailing shears, keeping the tips of the shears towards the tips of the ears. Lightly round the long feathering at the bottom of the ears with shears for a neat look.

Tail

The tail is in the shape of a triangular flag. The pointed tip should reach to the top of the hock. The top of the tail is covered with short, smooth harsh coat while the long silky feathers fall from the underside. At the root base, there is a break in the fur, separating the tail from the body. Shape the tail to look very natural with thinning shears or shears.

Feet & Hocks

Trim the pads with a close cutting blade ranging from a #15 to a #40. Use a very light touch to clean the pads of long hair. If there is long fur between the toes, back brush the fur so it stands up on top of and away from the foot. With thinning shears, trim off the excess creating a neat and very natural looking foot. Tidy the outside edge of the foot, if needed, with small detailing shears. If the hocks have longer coat, trim lightly with thinning shears to show a neat, clean area. A #4F blade used in reverse works well for trimming the tops of the feet and the hocks on some dogs.

Suggested Tools & Equipment

- Nail Trimmers
- Styptic Powder
- Ear Cleaning Solution
- Cotton Balls
- Clippers
- Slicker Brush
- Greyhound Comb
- Pin Brush
- Rubber Curry
- Pumice Stone
- Carding Tools
- Stripping Knives
- Straight Shears
- Curved Shears
- Small Detailing Shears
- Thinning Shears
- Dematting Tools

Common Blade Options:

- #40, #15, #10
- #7F, #5F, #4F
- Variety of Guard Combs

Detail Finish

Removal of whiskers on the muzzle is optional, based on client preference or the amount of fur on the muzzle. Finish with a fine mist of coat polish on the body coat for added shine. Application of bows and mild cologne is optional.

Notes:

Irish Water Spaniel

Breed Facts & Characteristics

Country of Origin: Ireland

Height at Shoulder: 21"–24"

Coat Length/Type: Curly/Thick

Color: Solid liver color.

Correct grooming procedure:
Hand-Scissor

Common pet grooming practices:
Clipper-Trim

General Description

The Irish Water Spaniel is a breed that was developed to be a tough and rugged water dog. He is the largest of the spaniel breeds. His coat and overall look are unique with a thick curly brown coat, long ears, clean face and rat tail.

-The Goal-
This breed has a coat that is highly distinguishable by the thick, curly brown coat. This feature is highly desirable when trimming. When finished, the coat should be fresh smelling, full of body and curly. No mats or tangles.

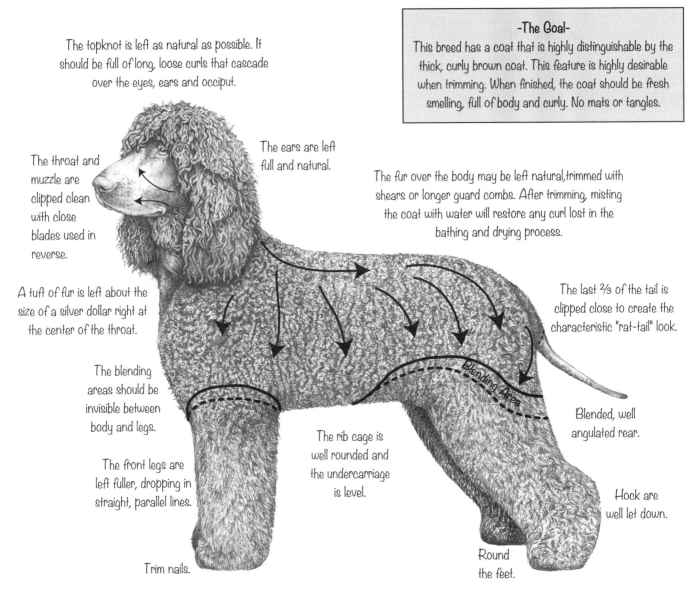

The topknot is left as natural as possible. It should be full of long, loose curls that cascade over the eyes, ears and occiput.

The throat and muzzle are clipped clean with close blades used in reverse.

The ears are left full and natural.

The fur over the body may be left natural, trimmed with shears or longer guard combs. After trimming, misting the coat with water will restore any curl lost in the bathing and drying process.

A tuft of fur is left about the size of a silver dollar right at the center of the throat.

The last ⅔ of the tail is clipped close to create the characteristic "rat-tail" look.

The blending areas should be invisible between body and legs.

Blending Area

Blended, well angulated rear.

The front legs are left fuller, dropping in straight, parallel lines.

The rib cage is well rounded and the undercarriage is level.

Hock are well let down.

Trim nails.

Round the feet.

This coat can easily be modified into a shorter trim version for a lower maintenance haircut while still retaining the essence of the proper breed profile.

See page 74 for
Bathing & Drying Instructions

Frequency
Bathe once a week to once every 12 weeks. Trim every four to six weeks to maintain a stylized fashion.

Pre-Work
Trim or grind nails at least every four to six weeks to maintain a healthy foot structure. Clean the ears by swabbing with a mild ear cleaning solution. Hair should be plucked from within the ear canal only as necessary for healthy ear management. Prior to bathing, quickly go over the entire body and remove any serious mats or tangles. If the tangle can be penetrated with water, leave it and remove when the dog is clean. If the pet has not been in for professional grooming for six weeks or more, remove the excessive body coat and set the pattern before bathing. Before starting the final haircut, make sure the dog's coat is throughly brushed out and tangle free.

Pattern Lines In General
The Irish Water Spaniel can be left in full coat or trimmed. If trimmed, there should be enough fur left so that the texture and curl of the coat is clearly visible. Commonly, the body is taken shorter while the legs are left full and long. There are no broken lines anywhere on the main body of the dog. The muzzle and the tail are clipped very close. For low maintenance pet trims, this haircut style may be modified into shorter versions.

Body
The body can be left natural, hand-scissored or clipper-cut with a longer guard comb. If trimming, leave the coat between 1 and 2 inches long over the entire body. Follow the contour of the body. The finish should be even without any scissor or clipper marks.

Hindquarters
Hand-scissor or clipper-cut with a longer guard comb to leave the legs fuller than the body. Follow the contour of the dog. The tail is set on low to the body and gives a rounded appearance to the rump when viewed in profile. The finish should be smooth and even without any scissor or clipper marks, while letting the texture and curls of the coat show through.

Front Legs
Shape the legs in parallel columns, falling straight down from the widest point of the shoulder. The leg coat should be left fuller than the body. The finish should be smooth and even without any scissor or clipper marks while letting the texture and curls of the coat show through. The front and the rear legs should be well balanced.

Feet
Round the feet with shears to blend with the legs. Box the foot in first with straight shears to create a square. Finish by using curved shears, rounding and beveling the edges of the foot.

Tail
One of the unique characteristics about this breed is its "rat tail." The end two-thirds is clippered close with a #10 or #15 blade used with, or against, the grain. The tail closest to the body is hand-scissored short to blend from the rump and taper into the clipped area. The tail should have the shape of a long carrot, thicker at the base, tapering to a point.

Head in General
The top of the head is to be covered with long curls. This mass of curls is a hallmark of the breed. They cascade over the occiput and the top of the ears, falling in loose ringlets.

At transition points on the body, blend the lines so they are invisible. Legs should be left fuller and fall into straight columns, from the body to the feet on both the front and rear legs. The face is clean. A tuft of hair is left at the juncture of the jaw and throat. Topknot is a mass of curls that cascade over the head. Ears are long and natural. Coat is curly. Rat tail.

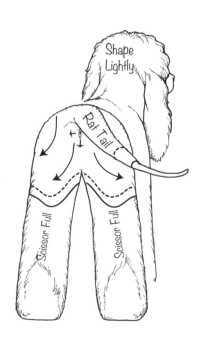

The lines for clipping the face start at the opening of the ear canal, in a straight line riding the bone to the back corner of the eye. Proceed under the eye, down the muzzle and clearing the stop area.

The topknot is left as natural as possible. It should be full of long, loose curls that cascade over the eyes, ears and occiput. Shape lightly with shears or thinning shears. After topknot is fully brushed out and shaped, spritz with water and scrunch the fur to bring the curls back into the hair.

The ears are left full and natural.

The throat and muzzle are clipped clean with close blades used in reverse. Typical blades are a #7F, #10 or a #15 blade.

Traditionally, a tuft of fur is left at the base of the jaw just before it meets the throat. The goatee should hang from the jaw line. It is important that it not come from the throat area. This tuft protects the area while retrieving ducks while hunting.

The throat will be "U" shaped starting at the base of the ears. The lowest point will be about 4 finger widths above the breast bone.

A unique feature of the Irish Water Spaniel is a tuft of fur left on the lower jaw. This tuft of fur is located on the jaw just ahead of the junction of the throat. It is a narrow tuft of fur hanging from the jaw but never comes beyond the back corners of the mouth. It is left long and natural, never hanging below the ears. It is there to protect the throat while working in the field.

Muzzle & Throat

The muzzle, jaw, cheeks and throat are trimmed close using a #10 or #15 blade, with or against the coat growth, based on skin sensitivity. The lines of the clipped area of the face are from the ear canal opening forward to the back corner of the eye, under the eye and down the muzzle towards the nose. A small inverted "V" is clipped in at the stop area. The jaw and throat will drop down in a soft "V" or "U" to about four fingers above the breast bone.

A unique feature of the Irish Water Spaniel is a tuft of fur left on the lower jaw. This tuft of fur is located on the jaw *just ahead* of the junction of the throat. It is a narrow tuft of fur hanging from the jaw but never comes beyond the back corners of the mouth. It is left long and natural, never hanging below the ears, to protect the throat.

Ears

The coat on the ears is left long and natural. Lightly trim the bottom to neaten the furnishings.

Finish Detail

If the coat has been straightened during the finishing process, lightly mist the coat with water or a light coat conditioner. Scrunch the moist fur between your fingers to re-form the curls and ringlets. Application of mild cologne and collar bows is optional.

Breed Note:

The coat is a hallmark of the Irish Water Spaniel. The breed standard requires the dog's coat to be curly and fall in ringlets. After you have air blown most of the moisture from the coat, change to an inactive drying method to help set the curls. If the coat gets too dry and is not curly, lightly mist the area with water from a spray bottle. Work the light moisture back into the coat with your fingers to re-establish the natural curl in the coat. Let the dog air dry either naturally or with very mild air flow. Whatever process or combination of processes is used, drying is not complete until the coat is completely cool and dry to the touch.

Suggested Tools & Equipment

- Nail Trimmers
- Styptic Powder
- Ear Powder
- Ear Cleaning Solution
- Cotton Balls
- Hemostat
- Clippers
- Slicker Brush
- Greyhound Comb
- Straight Shears
- Curved Shears
- Small Detailing Shears
- Thinning Shears
- Dematting Tools
- High-Velocity Dryer

Common Blade Options:

- #40, #15, #10
- #7F, #5F, #4F
- Variety of Guard Combs

Notes:

Labrador Retriever   SPORTING   SHORT COATED

Breed Facts & Characteristics

Country of Origin: Newfoundland, Canada

Height at Shoulder: 21½"–24½"

Coat Length/Type: Short/Dense

Color: Solid black, yellow or chocolate.

Correct grooming procedure:
Bathe & Brush Out

Common pet grooming practices:
Bathe & Brush Out

-The Goal-
The coat should be clean and fresh smelling, with the coat laying flat against the body. No shedding hair.

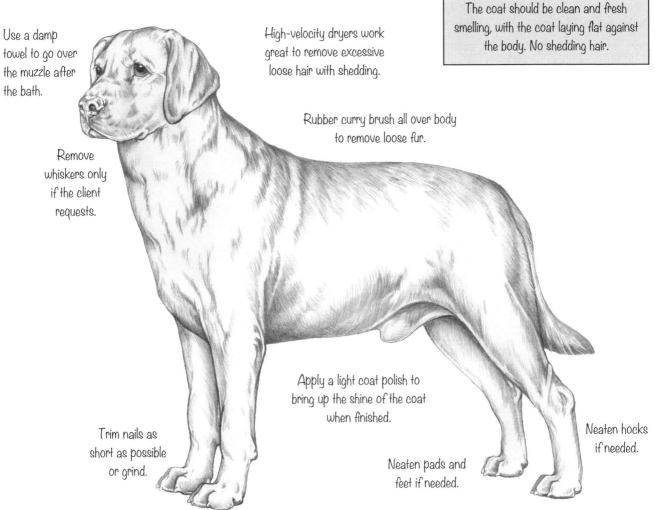

Use a damp towel to go over the muzzle after the bath.

High-velocity dryers work great to remove excessive loose hair with shedding.

Rubber curry brush all over body to remove loose fur.

Remove whiskers only if the client requests.

Apply a light coat polish to bring up the shine of the coat when finished.

Trim nails as short as possible or grind.

Neaten pads and feet if needed.

Neaten hocks if needed.

See page 67 for Bathing & Drying Instructions

Suggested Tools & Equipment

- Nail Trimmers
- Styptic Powder
- Ear Cleaning Solution
- Cotton Balls

- Clippers
- #40 or #15 Blade
- Slicker Brush
- Rubber Curry

- Carding Tool
- De-Shedding Tools
- Small Detailing Shears
- Thinning Shears

Notes *from your*
Grooming Table

Lagotto Romagnolo   SPORTING   RUSTIC COATED

Breed Facts & Characteristics

Country of Origin: Italy

Height at Shoulder: 15½"–19½"

Coat Length/Type: Rustic/Curly

Color: Off white, orange or browns solid colors or off white with brown or orange spots. Roaning and/or limited white allowed.

Correct grooming procedure:
Rake & Hand-Scissor

Common pet grooming practices:
Rake & Hand-Scissor

General Description

The Lagotto is an active, medium sized dog with great eagerness for life. It was originally bred as a water dog but with its keen sense of smell, and strong ability for searching, it earned the job as a truffle hunter. It is a well-proportioned, squarely built dog with a round head and a long, carrot shaped tail. Rustic coated dogs **never** appear fluffy, polished or well groomed. Their coats are always air dried to maintain the springy curls characteristic of the breed.

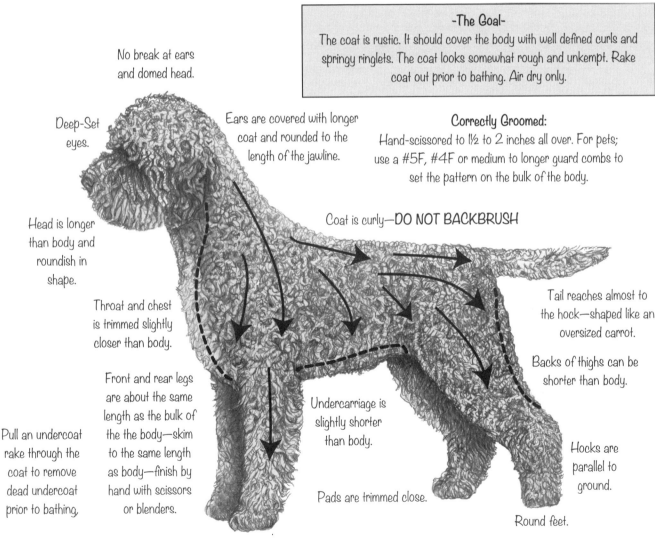

-The Goal-
The coat is rustic. It should cover the body with well defined curls and springy ringlets. The coat looks somewhat rough and unkempt. Rake coat out prior to bathing. Air dry only.

No break at ears and domed head.

Deep-Set eyes.

Ears are covered with longer coat and rounded to the length of the jawline.

Correctly Groomed:
Hand-scissored to 1½ to 2 inches all over. For pets; use a #5F, #4F or medium to longer guard combs to set the pattern on the bulk of the body.

Head is longer than body and roundish in shape.

Coat is curly—DO NOT BACKBRUSH

Throat and chest is trimmed slightly closer than body.

Tail reaches almost to the hock—shaped like an oversized carrot.

Front and rear legs are about the same length as the bulk of the the body—skim to the same length as body—finish by hand with scissors or blenders.

Backs of thighs can be shorter than body.

Pull an undercoat rake through the coat to remove dead undercoat prior to bathing.

Undercarriage is slightly shorter than body.

Hocks are parallel to ground.

Pads are trimmed close.

Round feet.

Feet are rounded and face straight forward.

Either hand-scissor the entire dog or clipper-trim to set the basic pattern. Pet dogs can be modified into shorter trim styles using the same basic pattern. Blenders and thinners work great on this coat type.

Grooming Procedures & Recommendations

See page 79 for
Bathing & Drying Instructions

Frequency
Bathe every 3 to 12 weeks or when needed. Rake through the coat every 1–3 weeks with, or without a bath, to keep matting under control. Trim every 4 to 6 weeks. Lighter colored dogs with ringlets may need more frequent combing and raking as their coats tends to mat more easily than darker colored dogs.

Pre-Work
Thoroughly rake out the coat prior to bathing to keep the coat from becoming a solid pelted mass. This will remove the undercoat "lint," preventing matting in the future. Trim or grind nails at least every four to six weeks to maintain a healthy foot structure. Clean the ears by swabbing with a mild ear cleaning solution. Hair should be plucked from within the ear canal only as necessary for healthy ear management. Rustic coated breeds are **never** blown or fluffed dried. They are always naturally air dried to maintain the curly, unkempt and tousled looking coat.

General Pattern Lines
The breed standard calls for the wavy and curly coat to be no longer than 1½ to 2 inches long all over. The actual coat length may vary slightly to accentuate or lessen key conformation points of the dog. There are no broken lines anywhere, and the coat outlines the natural contour of the body.

Body
The body can be either hand-scissored or clipper-cut with a longer guard comb. Start at the withers and work back over the body towards the tail. Use caution if working with guard combs as they can get stuck in the coat. Leave coat about 1 to 1½ inches long over the entire body. Follow the contour of the body. Do not back brush. The goal is a dog whose coat is somewhat rough and messy looking. If the coat needs to be fluffed, fluff with a coarse or wide-toothed comb. Many pet owners opt for less than 1 inch of coat for easier home maintenance trim styling.

Undercarriage
The highest point of the tuck up falls just below the last rib. From that point forward, the undercarriage angles slightly down towards the elbow. The undercarriage line should not fall below the elbow between the front legs.

Tail
The tail is shaped like an oversized blunt carrot. If working with a blade or a guard comb on the body, come up the back and front sides of the tail with the same blade or guard. Leave the sides of the tail to shape with scissors or blending shears. The tail will be slightly wider at the base, tapering to a blunt tip. When the tail is hanging down, it should almost reach the hock.

Feet
Both the front and rear feet are compact with arched toes. To show off these traits, the feet are trimmed very close to the edge of the foot, beveling out into the fuller leg coat. The feet should point straight ahead, toeing neither in nor out. Begin by gently picking up the leg and with a wide-toothed comb, comb the coat over the foot. Slide your hand down the leg to the foot. Scissor off the coat that hangs below the level of the foot pad with shears. Work around the outer perimeter of the foot with detailing shears to minimize the risk of injury —never cross over the foot pad with scissors. Set the foot on the table and neaten the foot with shears or blending shears beveled out into the longer coat on the leg. An alternative for quickly rounding the feet is to do it when the

There are only slight variations in coat length over the entire dog. The eyes and nose are at the center of the round head piece. Eyes are barely visible under a heavy brow. Ears blend with domed head and are level with the jaw. At transition points between the body and the legs, blend the lines so they are invisible. The legs are only a little longer in length than the body. They should fall into straight columns, to the rounded feet, when view from the front or rear. There are no breaks in the pattern anywhere on the dog. Tail shaped like a long carrot.

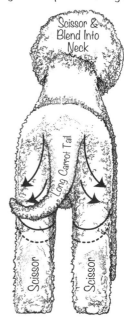

Notes From The Grooming Table ©2016

Head is round and domed shape, slightly longer than the coat on the body.

Trim ears to the leather on the outside and lower edge—a bit longer next to the cheek so it blends seamlessly with the headpiece.

Use thinners, framing the eyes creating a beveled edge and a heavy brow.

No break in ears at skull junction.

Layer length of coat on ears to blend with headpiece.

Clear the inside corners of the eyes with thinners but leave coat on bridge of nose.

Trim off excessive coat that extends beyond the end of the muzzle.

Jaw rounded and to the length of the ear when dog is relaxed.

Blend head onto neck.

pads are trimmed. If a very close cutting blade is used to trim the pads, use a wide tooth comb to pull the longer hair over the outer edges of the pad and trim that hair at the same time the pads are clipped clean.

Front Legs

The longest coat on the legs can range from 1 to 2 inches depending on the amount of bone and coat density. Ideally it should be basically the same length as the body coat. The front legs drop straight down from the body. When viewed in profile, the front legs fall directly below the withers. Blend off at the top of the leg using scissors or the same blade

or guard comb that was used on the body. Follow with blending with shears to finish shaping the leg and to tidy it slightly. After the final trim, the legs should form two parallel columns descending from the shoulder into tight, round feet. The coat at the back of the elbow may be very short, falling straight down off the back of the leg toward the ground; angling in slightly at the pasterns.

Hindquarters

The hindquarters are powerful with muscular thighs. If trimming over this area with clippers, clip over the thigh muscle and the rear with the same blade used on the body to set

in the angles of the rear assembly. Start to feather off where the muscle starts to turn under on a diagonal line from the flank region to about three or four fingers above the hock. The blending should be invisible when the trim is finished. If using a medium to longer guard comb, you can continue to clip down the outside and inside areas of the rear leg to help establish the length of coat to be left. Fluff the coat with a wide tooth comb, retaining the rustic look and maintaining the curls of the coat. The stifle area should have just enough coat left to give the legs substance and angulation. Shape this area by hand with shears after the clipper work is complete. When viewed from the rear, the legs should form two parallel lines to the ground. The hocks are well let down and perpendicular to the ground. There should be adequate coat on the hock area to accentuate the angles of the rear assembly.

Head

The head is moderately broad and round in shape. The topskull is slightly longer than the muzzle. The majority of the head will have slightly longer coat than the body. Use shears, thinners or a longer guard comb to create the arched shape over the top of the head. There is no break in the domed shape where the ears join the head. Come over the sides of the face and under the ears maintaining the same length of coat. Feather off into slightly longer muzzle coat. Shape the muzzle by hand, starting at the end of the muzzle. Comb the coat forward and trim off the excess that extends beyond the nose at a diagonal. Next comb the coat down over the muzzle, trimming it level with the ears following the jawline. Soften the edge of the jawline with thinners to round out the edge. The muzzle coat on males is styled slightly longer than on females.

Eyes

The eyes are deep set. Coat is left between the eyes and in the stop area to protect the eyes as the dog searches the ground for scents. The inside corner of the eyes can be cleared slightly if there is an overabundance of coat in this area. At the brow area, comb the hair forward over the eyes. With thinning shears create a deep-set arch over the

eyes to frame them. Do not cut into the cheek coat. While trimming, bevel the shear out and away from the eye, creating a heavy brow. Use fine thinners to frame the eye exposing them slightly. Leave the coat in the stop area.

Ears

The ears are triangular. Edge the ears to show the natural shape of the leather. To achieve the correct length, carefully skim the leather, both inside and outside the leather, with a medium length guard comb or layer the coat by hand with scissors or thinning shears. There should be no break between the top of the skull and the top of the ear. When viewed from the front, the domed top skull and the ears blend together in one continuous line, while the lowest point of the ear does not fall below the line of the jaw.

Neck

The back of the neck starts from the occiput to the withers area. Leave this area to the last to trim, pulling together the head, neck and body. Fluff softly with a wide tooth comb. Scissor off long sections between the top of the head and the body. Blend the sides of the neck down to show off a moderate length, well-muscled neck with a slight arch.

Detail Finish

Lightly re-fluff all your work, checking for stray hairs. The coat should not look polished and smooth. The goal is a dog that is mat- and tangle-free that looks reasonably tidy but unkempt, curly and messy at the same time. Application of mild cologne and bows is optional.

Suggested Tools & Equipment

- Nail Trimmers
- Styptic Powder
- Ear Powder
- Cleaning Solution
- Cotton Balls
- Hemostat
- Clippers
- Undercoat Rake
- Greyhound Comb
- Wide-Toothed Comb
- Straight Shears
- Curved Shears
- Small Detailing Shears
- Thinning Shears
- Dematting Tools

Common Blade Options:

- #40, #15, #10
- #7F, #5F, #4F
- Medium to Long Guard Combs

Notes:

Notes From The Grooming Table ©2016

Nova Scotia Duck Tolling Retriever SPORTING COMBINATION

Breed Facts & Characteristics

Country of Origin: Canada

Height at Shoulder: 17"–21"

Coat Length/Type: Combination/Thick

Color: All shades of red and deep golden. Limited amounts of white in the form of a blaze on the head, chest, and/or tips of tail or toes.

Correct grooming procedure:

Bathe & Brush Out

Common pet grooming practices:

Bathe & Brush Out

-The Goal-
The coat should be fresh smelling, light and stand off the body. No loose hair.

Lightly finger pluck dead coat and edge ears with thinners.

Use a damp towel to go over the muzzle after the bath.

Use a high-velocity dryer both before and after the bath. Blow out loose coat, tangles and dirt. Dry and fluff.

Curry brush all over body—plus line brush.

Remove whiskers only if the client requests.

Trim tail to the length of the hock. Shape lightly.

Chest area can be thick with coat. Pay close attention when brushing.

The thigh area can be thick with coat. Pay close attention when brushing.

Neaten hocks.

Trim nails as short as possible or grind.

Shave pads and neaten feet.

Grooming Procedures & Recommendations

See page 68 for
Bathing & Drying Instructions

Frequency
Bathe once a week to once every 12 weeks.

Pre-Work
Trim or grind nails every four to six weeks to maintain a healthy foot structure. Clean the ears by swabbing with a mild ear cleaning solution. Use a rubber curry, shedding blade, undercoat rake, pumice stone, carding tool, fine stripping knife or natural bristle brush to loosen skin dander and remove loose coat. Use a high-velocity dryer over the coat to quickly and effectively lift dirt and debris away from the skin and loosen coat. Brush out or remove any matting found in the long-coated areas. If the tangles are loose enough so water can fully penetrate the area, remove them after bathing and drying. If water cannot penetrate, remove the mat or tangle prior to bathing.

Brushing
Line brush, working in sections until the dog is entirely tangle-free and all loose coat is removed. When finished, there should be little, if any, fur still being removed with a firm slicker brush. Double-check the work with a comb and your hands. Go over the entire body, feeling for any inconsistencies in the density levels of the coat. If an area seems moist to the touch or fuller than the rest of the coat, rework the area with the appropriate tool. Mats, tangles and excessive coat are easily trapped in the following areas: behind the ears, around the ruff, the thigh area, the undercarriage and the tail. Give extra attention to these areas before finishing the groom.

Carding
If a dog has an abundance of loose undercoat, line card the shorter areas with a carding tool. Common tools can be a fine stripping knife, undercoat rake, a pumice stone, or a #40 blade held between your fingers. Any carding tool should be pulled over the body, working in the direction of the coat growth. This will remove the soft, downy undercoat, allowing the guard coat to conform more closely to the natural outline of the body. It will also aid in the removal of loose, shedding coat, a seasonal problem for many pet owners.

Feet & Hocks
Trim the pads with a close blade ranging from a #15 to a #40. Use a very light touch to clean the pads of long hair. If there is long fur between the toes, back brush the fur so it stands up on top of and away from the foot. With thinning shears, trim the excess to create a neat and very natural looking foot. Tidy the outside edge of the foot, if needed, with small detailing shears. If the hocks have longer coat, trim lightly with thinning shears to show a neat, clean area. A #4F blade, used carefully in reverse, works well for trimming the tops of the feet and the hocks on some dogs.

Detail Finish
Edge the ears lightly with thinning shears to neaten and keep a natural look. Hand pluck any long wispy, flyaway hair from around the ears. Removal of whiskers on the muzzle is optional based on client preference. Finish with a fine mist of coat polish on the body coat for added shine. Application of bows and mild cologne is optional.

Suggested Tools & Equipment

- Nail Trimmers
- Styptic Powder
- Ear Cleaning Solution
- Cotton Balls
- Clippers
- #40 and #15 Blades for Pads
- #4F for Feet & Hocks (optional)
- Slicker Brush
- Greyhound Comb
- Rubber Curry
- Carding Tool
- De-Shedding Tools
- Small Detailing Shears
- Thinning Shears

Notes:

Pointer

Breed Facts & Characteristics

Country of Origin: Spain

Height at Shoulder: 23"–28"

Coat Length/Type: Short/Smooth

Color: Acceptable colors are liver, black, lemon and orange. Any of these colors can stand alone be combined with white. Usually, the darker dogs have a black or brown nose. The lighter breeds have a lighter colored or even a flesh tone colored nose.

Correct grooming procedure:

Bathe & Curry Brush

Common pet grooming practices:

Bathe & Curry Brush

-The Goal-
The coat should be clean and fresh smelling, with the coat laying flat against the body. No shedding hair.

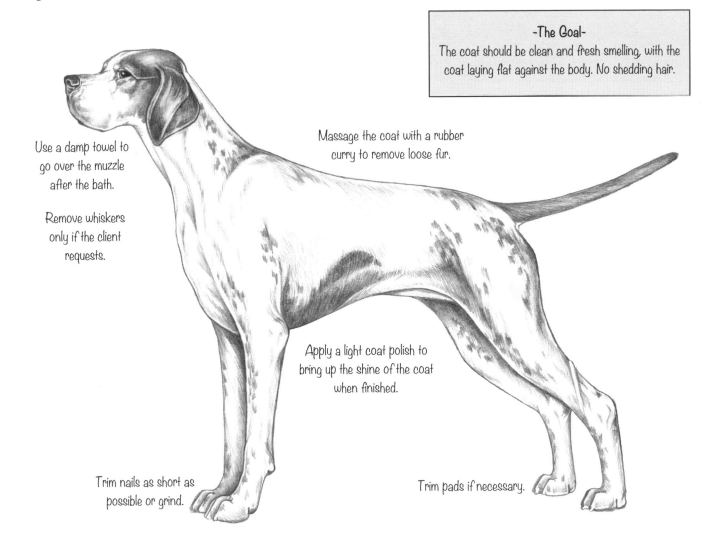

Use a damp towel to go over the muzzle after the bath.

Remove whiskers only if the client requests.

Massage the coat with a rubber curry to remove loose fur.

Apply a light coat polish to bring up the shine of the coat when finished.

Trim nails as short as possible or grind.

Trim pads if necessary.

See page 66 for Bathing & Drying Instructions

Suggested Tools & Equipment

- Nail Trimmers
- Styptic Powder
- Ear Cleaning Solution
- Cotton Balls
- Clippers
- #40 or #15 Blade
- Rubber Curry
- Carding Tool
- Small Detailing Shears
- Thinning Shears

Notes *from your*
Grooming Table

Spinone Italiano

Breed Facts & Characteristics

Country of Origin: Italy

Height at Shoulder: 22"–27"

Coat Length/Type: Hard/Wiry

Color: All white or white with tan, rust or brown areas.

Correct grooming procedure:
Card & Hand-Strip

Common pet grooming practices:
Hand-Strip

General Description

Spinone Italiano is a tough, all-purpose hunting dog of moderate size. He is a slow, methodical, yet efficient hunter. The head is somewhat rectangular and accentuated by a harsh-coated beard. The eyes are set off by shaggy eyebrows. The coat is made up of a wiry, harsh outer coat with a thick under coat that is heavier in the winter and almost non-existent in the summer. The harsh outer coat is normally short and rough. Ideally the dog is covered with coat ranging between 1 and 3 inches.

~ The Goal ~

This breed looks more like a hound than a pointer. The coat should be hard, a bit rough and wiry. Hand-stripping is the only way to retain this proper coat texture, which protects the skin while working in the field.

Top of skull and cheek area very tight. Clear between eyes. Split, medium sized, triangular brows.

Correctly Groomed: Hand-Strip

Card the body first to remove loose undercoat. Follow by hand-stripping and finger plucking the hard outer coat. As new hair grows in, it will be harsh and tight fitting to the body.

Shape whiskers into a rectangle.

Ears are coated.

Neaten tail.

Lightly clip sanitary areas.

Neaten undercarriage line lightly.

Always pull in the direction of the coat growth. Legs too.

Trim nails as short as possible or grind.

Shave pads and neaten feet to match legs.

Neaten hocks.

The coat should look as natural as possible and be 1–2 inches all over the body.

Grooming Procedures & Recommendations

See page 76 for
Bathing & Drying Instructions

Frequency
Bathe once a week to once every
12 weeks.

Pre-Work
Trim or grind nails at least every four
to six weeks to maintain a healthy foot
structure. Swab the ears clean with a
mild ear cleaning solution. Prior to
bathing, quickly go over the entire
body with a high-velocity dryer to help
lift dirt and dander away from the skin
and to loosen any shedding coat. *Card
and hand-strip dog prior to bathing
and drying.*

Brushing
Use a rubber curry, shedding blade,
undercoat rake, pumice stone, carding
tool, fine stripping knife, slicker brush
or natural bristled brush to remove
any remaining loose coat or tangles. Be
careful when using any tool with metal
teeth or bristles. A heavy hand or too
much repetition in an area can cause
cuts and/or brush burns. Brushing is not
finished until all loose fur is removed,
or when it becomes difficult to remove
more than a half a brush full after
repeated brushing.

Carding
Carding is a natural technique in which
the soft, downy undercoat is pulled
from the dog's body. Typical tools used
with this technique are: a pumice stone;
a fine-toothed stripping knife that is
pulled through the coat; an undercoat
rake; or a fine blade, such as a #40, held
between the fingers and pulled through
the coat. Carding can be done before or
after bathing and drying. Removal of the
soft undercoat allows the topcoat to lie
closer to the natural outline of the dog
and accentuate the dog's structure. It also
promotes profuse harsh outer coat, creates
a rich coat color and protects the skin.

Hand-Stripping
Hand-stripping is a technique in which
the outer guard coat is plucked from the
dog's skin. This procedure helps retain
the proper coat texture and rich color of
the breed. During certain times of the
year, the coat is easier to pull out. When
the coat easily comes out, it is called a
"blowing coat" or "blown coat." Ideally,
hand-stripping should correspond with
the dog's natural cycle, based on the
environment and its hormonal levels.
Using your fingers, a carding tool or a
stripping knife, pull out a few hairs at
a time to shape the coat, accentuating
the natural outline of the dog. Work
methodically, pulling small amounts of
coat at a time, always working in the
direction of the coat growth. Proper
hand-stripping removes hair with a
gentle momentum and rhythm, not
brute force, which is uncomfortable
for both groomer and pet. The wrist
stays locked in a neutral position while
the rhythmic movement stems from
the shoulder, not the wrist or elbow.
In general, the main body coat is easy
to remove. Most pets do not mind the
plucking process. The cheeks, throat
and private areas may be more sensitive,
requiring thinning shears or clippers.
Leave enough coat to be between 1 to
2 inches long. The coat should always
appear very natural, never clipped or
heavily trimmed. On some coats, a light
application of chalk or powder before the
bath will allow a better grip and make
plucking and stripping much easier.

Head
Leave the coat longer on the muzzle.
Hand-strip or pluck the top skull, throat
and cheeks. Leave triangles of coat above
each eye to form the moderate bushy
eyebrows that accentuate the eye area.
Ears are left long and natural

Feet & Hocks
Trim the pads with a close cutting blade
ranging from a #15 to a #40. Use a very
light touch to clean the pads of long hair.
Tidy the outside edge of the foot, if

Suggested
Tools & Equipment

- Nail Trimmers
- Styptic Powder
- Ear Powder
- Ear Cleaning Solution
- Cotton Balls
- Hemostat
- Clippers
- Slicker Brush
- Greyhound Comb
- Pumice Stone
- Carding Tools
- Stripping Knives
- Straight Shears
- Curved Shears
- Small Detailing Shears
- Thinning Shears
- Dematting Tools

Common Blade Options:
- #40, #15, #10

needed, with small detailing shears. If the
hocks have longer coat, trim lightly with
thinning shears to show a neat, clean area.

Detail Finish
For added shine, finish with a fine mist
of coat polish on the body. Application
of bows and mild cologne is optional.

Special Note
Clipping a wired-coated dog will result
in a dramatic change in the texture and
color of the coat. The correct harsh wire
coat needs to be encouraged by plucking
the blown coat when it is ready to be
removed. This process stimulates hair
follicles to produce new guard coat.
Without hand-stripping, the guard coat
is not stimulated and will not grow in
properly. It will lose its brilliant color
and texture. If only the undercoat
grows, the guard coat color becomes
that of the lighter, soft undercoat.

Notes From The Grooming Table ©2016

Sussex Spaniel

Breed Facts & Characteristics

Country of Origin: England

Height at Shoulder: 13"–15"

Coat Length/Type: Combination/Silky

Color: Rich golden liver is the only acceptable color but they will become sun bleached if spending a lot of time outdoors. A small amount of white is allowed on the chest but not desirable.

Correct grooming procedure:
Card & Hand-Strip

Common pet grooming practices:
Bathe & Brush Out, Card & Hand-Strip

-The Goal-
The coat should be fresh smelling, light and shiny. The natural body jacket should lay tight to the body. If clipping, no clipper marks. No loose hair or tangles left in the coat.

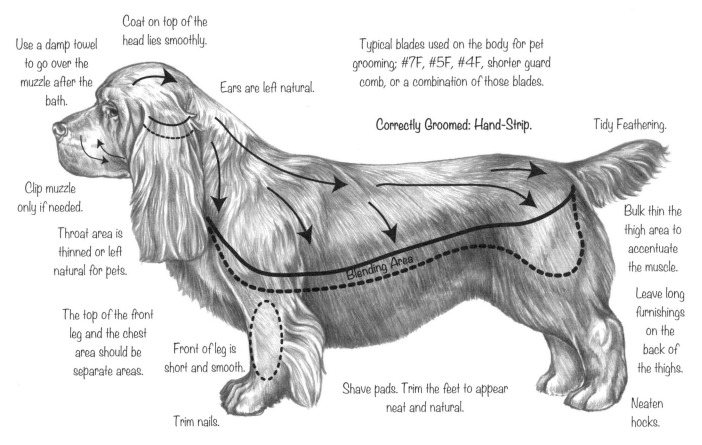

Coat on top of the head lies smoothly.

Use a damp towel to go over the muzzle after the bath.

Ears are left natural.

Typical blades used on the body for pet grooming; #7F, #5F, #4F, shorter guard comb, or a combination of those blades.

Correctly Groomed: Hand-Strip.

Tidy Feathering.

Clip muzzle only if needed.

Throat area is thinned or left natural for pets.

The top of the front leg and the chest area should be separate areas.

Front of leg is short and smooth.

Blending Area

Bulk thin the thigh area to accentuate the muscle.

Leave long furnishings on the back of the thighs.

Neaten hocks.

Trim nails.

Shave pads. Trim the feet to appear neat and natural.

The coat should look as natural as possible and all transitional pattern lines should be invisible.

Grooming Procedures & Recommendations

See page 71 for
Bathing & Drying Instructions

Frequency
Bathe once a week to once every 12 weeks.

Pre-Work
Trim or grind nails every four to six weeks to maintain a healthy foot structure. Clean the ears by swabbing with a mild ear cleaning solution. Use a rubber curry, shedding blade, undercoat rake, pumice stone, carding tool, fine stripping knife or natural bristle brush to loosen skin dander and remove loose coat. Use a high-velocity dryer over the coat to quickly and effectively lift dirt and debris away from the skin and loosen coat. Brush out or remove any matting found in the long-coated areas. If the tangles are loose enough so water can fully penetrate the area, remove them after bathing and drying. If water cannot penetrate, remove the mat or tangle prior to bathing.

Brushing
Line brush, working in sections until the dog is entirely tangle-free and all loose coat is removed. When finished, there should be little, if any, fur still being removed with a firm slicker brush. Double-check the work with a comb and your hands. Go over the entire body, feeling for any inconsistencies in the density levels of the coat. If an area seems moist to the touch or fuller than the rest of the coat, rework the area with the appropriate tool. Mats, tangles and excessive coat are easily trapped in the following areas: behind the ears, around the ruff, the thigh area, the undercarriage and the tail. Give extra attention to these areas before finishing the groom.

Carding
If a dog has an abundance of loose undercoat, line card the shorter areas with a carding tool. Common tools can be a fine stripping knife, undercoat rake, a pumice stone, or a #40 blade held between your fingers. Any carding tool should be pulled over the body, working in the direction of the coat growth. This will remove the soft, downy undercoat, allowing the guard coat to conform more closely to the natural outline of the body. It will also aid in the removal of loose, shedding coat, a seasonal problem for many pet owners.

Feet & Hocks
Trim the pads with a close blade ranging from a #15 to a #40. Use a very light touch to clean the pads of long hair. If there is long fur between the toes, back brush the fur so it stands up on top of and away from the foot. With thinning shears, trim the excess to create a neat and very natural looking foot. Tidy the outside edge of the foot, if needed, with small detailing shears. If the hocks have longer coat, trim lightly with thinning shears to show a neat, clean area. A #4F blade, used carefully in reverse, works well for trimming the tops of the feet and the hocks on some dogs.

Detail Finish
Edge the ears lightly with thinning shears to neaten and keep a natural look. Hand pluck any long wispy, flyaway hair from around the ears. Removal of whiskers on the muzzle is optional based on client preference. Finish with a fine mist of coat polish on the body coat for added shine. Application of bows and mild cologne is optional.

Special Note
In most cases, the body coat of these breeds lays tight enough to the body that owners do not want their pets clipper-cut. It is not recommended, but should a client request a clipper-cut, follow the general pattern guidelines found on most Sporting Dogs according to breed similarity.

Suggested Tools & Equipment
- Nail Trimmers
- Styptic Powder
- Ear Cleaning Solution
- Cotton Balls
- Clippers
- Slicker Brush
- Greyhound Comb
- Pin Brush
- Rubber Curry
- Pumice Stone
- Carding Tools
- Stripping Knives
- Straight Shears
- Curved Shears
- Small Detailing Shears
- Thinning Shears
- Dematting Tools

Common Blade Options:
- #40, #15, #10
- #7F, #5F, #4F
- Variety of Guard Combs

Notes:

Vizsla

Breed Facts & Characteristics

Country of Origin: Hungary

Height at Shoulder: 21"–24"

Coat Length/Type: Short/Smooth

Color: They were developed with a short, golden-rust coat to aid in the camouflage on the dead grassy plains of their native land.

Correct grooming procedure:

Bathe & Curry Brush

Common pet grooming practices:

Bathe & Curry Brush

-The Goal-
The coat should be clean and fresh smelling, with the coat laying flat against the body. No shedding hair.

Use a damp towel to go over the muzzle after the bath.

Remove whiskers only if the client requests.

Massage the coat with a rubber curry to remove loose fur.

Apply a light coat polish to bring up the shine of the coat when finished.

Trim nails as short as possible or grind.

Trim pads if necessary.

See page 66 for Bathing & Drying Instructions

Suggested Tools & Equipment

- Nail Trimmers
- Styptic Powder
- Ear Cleaning Solution
- Cotton Balls

- Clippers
- #40 or #15 Blade
- Rubber Curry
- Carding Tool

- Small Detailing Shears
- Thinning Shears

Weimaraner

Breed Facts & Characteristics

Country of Origin: Germany

Height at Shoulder: 23"–27"

Coat Length/Type: Short/Smooth

Color: The only allowable color is gray.

Correct grooming procedure:
Bathe & Curry Brush

Common pet grooming practices:
Bathe & Curry Brush

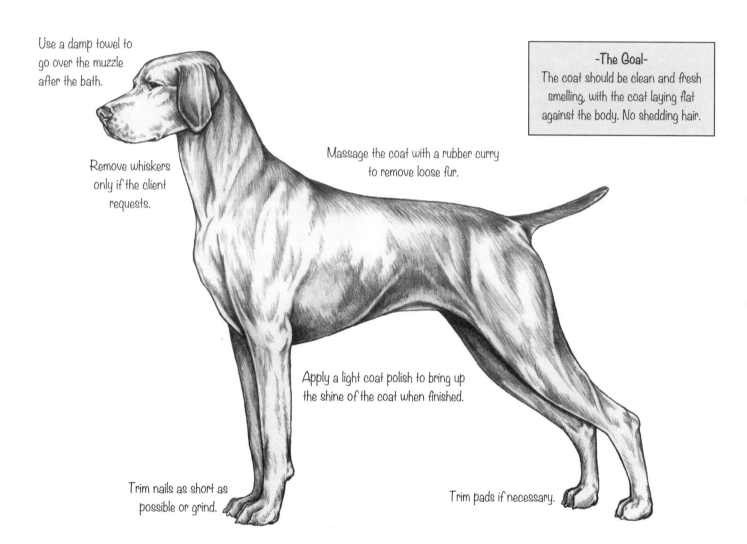

Use a damp towel to go over the muzzle after the bath.

Remove whiskers only if the client requests.

Massage the coat with a rubber curry to remove loose fur.

-The Goal-
The coat should be clean and fresh smelling, with the coat laying flat against the body. No shedding hair.

Apply a light coat polish to bring up the shine of the coat when finished.

Trim nails as short as possible or grind.

Trim pads if necessary.

See page 66 for Bathing & Drying Instructions

Suggested Tools & Equipment

- Nail Trimmers
- Styptic Powder
- Ear Cleaning Solution
- Cotton Balls

- Clippers
- #40 or #15 Blade
- Rubber Curry
- Carding Tool

- Small Detailing Shears
- Thinning Shears

Welsh Springer Spaniel   SPORTING   SILKY COATED

Breed Facts & Characteristics

Country of Origin: England

Height at Shoulder: 17"–19"

Coat Length/Type: Combination/Silky

Color: Red and white with red flecking in the white areas.

Correct grooming procedure:
Card & Hand-Strip

Common pet grooming practices:
Bathe & Brush/Card or Clipper-Trim

-The Goal-
The coat should be fresh smelling, light and shiny. The natural body jacket should lay tight to the body. No loose hair or tangles left in the coat.

Correctly Groomed: Hand-Strip

Typical blades used on the body for pet grooming: #7F, #5F, #4F, short guard comb or a combination of those blades.

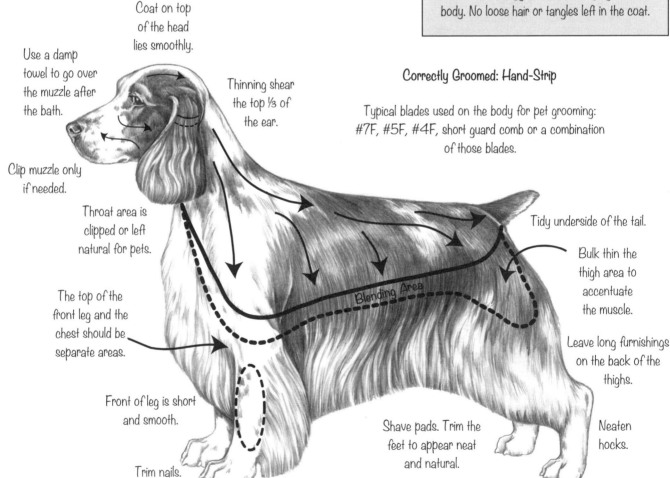

Coat on top of the head lies smoothly.

Use a damp towel to go over the muzzle after the bath.

Thinning shear the top ⅓ of the ear.

Clip muzzle only if needed.

Throat area is clipped or left natural for pets.

The top of the front leg and the chest should be separate areas.

Blending Area

Tidy underside of the tail.

Bulk thin the thigh area to accentuate the muscle.

Leave long furnishings on the back of the thighs.

Front of leg is short and smooth.

Trim nails.

Shave pads. Trim the feet to appear neat and natural.

Neaten hocks.

The coat should look as natural as possible and all transitional pattern lines should be invisible.

Grooming Procedures & Recommendations

See page 71 for
Bathing & Drying Instructions

Frequency
Bathe once a week to once every 12 weeks.

Pre-Work
Trim or grind nails every four to six weeks to maintain a healthy foot structure. Clean the ears by swabbing with a mild ear cleaning solution. Use a rubber curry, shedding blade, undercoat rake, pumice stone, carding tool, fine stripping knife or natural bristle brush to loosen skin dander and remove loose coat. Use a high-velocity dryer over the coat to quickly and effectively lift dirt and debris away from the skin and loosen coat. Brush out or remove any matting found in the long-coated areas. If the tangles are loose enough so water can fully penetrate the area, remove them after bathing and drying. If water cannot penetrate, remove the mat or tangle prior to bathing.

Brushing
Line brush, working in sections until the dog is entirely tangle-free and all loose coat is removed. When finished, there should be little, if any, fur still being removed with a firm slicker brush. Double-check the work with a comb and your hands. Go over the entire body, feeling for any inconsistencies in the density levels of the coat. If an area seems moist to the touch or fuller than the rest of the coat, rework the area with the appropriate tool. Mats, tangles and excessive coat are easily trapped in the following areas: behind the ears, around the ruff, the thigh area, the undercarriage and the tail. Give extra attention to these areas before finishing the groom.

Carding
If a dog has an abundance of loose undercoat, line card the shorter areas with a carding tool. Common tools can be a fine stripping knife, undercoat rake, a pumice stone, or a #40 blade held between your fingers. Any carding tool should be pulled over the body, working in the direction of the coat growth. This will remove the soft, downy undercoat, allowing the guard coat to conform more closely to the natural outline of the body. It will also aid in the removal of loose, shedding coat, a seasonal problem for many pet owners.

Feet & Hocks
Trim the pads with a close blade ranging from a #15 to a #40. Use a very light touch to clean the pads of long hair. If there is long fur between the toes, back brush the fur so it stands up on top of and away from the foot. With thinning shears, trim the excess to create a neat and very natural looking foot. Tidy the outside edge of the foot, if needed, with small detailing shears. If the hocks have longer coat, trim lightly with thinning shears to show a neat, clean area. A #4F blade, used carefully in reverse, works well for trimming the tops of the feet and the hocks on some dogs.

Detail Finish
Edge the ears lightly with thinning shears to neaten and keep a natural look. Hand pluck any long wispy, flyaway hair from around the ears. Removal of whiskers on the muzzle is optional based on client preference. Finish with a fine mist of coat polish on the body coat for added shine. Application of bows and mild cologne is optional.

Special Note
In most cases, the body coat of these breeds lays tight enough to the body that owners do not want their pets clipper-cut. It is not recommended, but should a client request a clipper-cut, follow the general pattern guidelines found on most Sporting Dogs according to breed similarity.

Suggested Tools & Equipment

- Nail Trimmers
- Styptic Powder
- Ear Cleaning Solution
- Cotton Balls
- Clippers
- Slicker Brush
- Greyhound Comb
- Pin Brush
- Rubber Curry
- Pumice Stone
- Carding Tools
- Stripping Knives
- Straight Shears
- Curved Shears
- Small Detailing Shears
- Thinning Shears
- Dematting Tools

Common Blade Options:

- #40, #15, #10
- #7F, #5F, #4F
- Variety of Guard Combs

Notes:

Notes From The Grooming Table ©2016

Wirehaired Pointing Griffon   SPORTING   WIRE COATED

Breed Facts & Characteristics

Country of Origin: Holland

Height at Shoulder: 20"–24"

Coat Length/Type: Moderate/Wiry

Color: Their base color is grizzled gray with strong liver color tones coming through the coat.

Correct grooming procedure:
Hand-Strip

Common pet grooming practices:
Hand-Strip, Bathe & Brush Out

General Description

The Wirehaired Pointing Griffon is a tough, all-purpose hunting dog of moderate size. The breed has great stamina and excels in wet, swampy terrain. The distinctive coat is made up of a wiry, harsh outer coat with a thick under coat that is heavier in the winter and almost non-existent in the summer. The harsh, outer guard coat is normally between 1 and 2 inches in length and never trimmed, giving the breed a shaggy, rough appearance. The extended "eyebrows" and the typical beard give the Wirehaired Pointing Griffon his characteristic appearance.

-The Goal-
The coat is a hallmark of the breed. It is a double coat; the topcoat is harsh wiry, medium length and straight. The undercoat is thick and dense. The dog should appear somewhat rough and untidy but clean.

Lightly hand-strip the top of the head, the ears and the cheeks.

Eyebrows are full and triangular in shape.

Brush with a firm slicker brush to remove dead coat and tangles. Finger pluck harsh outer jacket to neaten slightly.

Neaten tail to match body.

Lightly clip sanitary areas: Under tail and tummy if needed with a #10.

If shedding, card coat to remove loose undercoat.

Typically, the legs are covered with shorter and softer coat than found on the body.

Neaten undercarriage line lightly.

Neaten hocks.

Shave pads and neaten feet to match legs.

Trim nails as short as possible or grind.

Grooming Procedures & Recommendations

**See page 76 for
Bathing & Drying Instructions**

Frequency

Bathe once a week to once every 12 weeks.

Pre-Work

Trim or grind nails at least every four to six weeks to maintain a healthy foot structure. Swab the ears clean with a mild ear cleaning solution. Prior to bathing, quickly go over the entire body with a high-velocity dryer to help lift dirt and dander away from the skin and to loosen any shedding coat. ***Card and hand-strip dog prior to bathing and drying.***

Carding

Carding is a natural technique in which the soft, downy undercoat is pulled from the dog's body. Typical tools used with this technique are: a pumice stone; a fine-toothed stripping knife that is pulled through the coat; an undercoat rake; or a fine blade, such as a #40, held between the fingers and pulled through the coat. Carding can be done before or after bathing and drying. Removal of the soft undercoat allows the topcoat to lie closer to the natural outline of the dog and accentuate the dog's structure. It also promotes profuse harsh outer coat, creates a rich coat color and protects the skin.

Hand-Stripping

Hand-stripping is a technique in which the outer guard coat is plucked from the dog's skin. This procedure helps retain the proper coat texture and rich color of the breed. During certain times of the year, the coat is easier to pull out. When the coat easily comes out, it is called a "blowing coat" or "blown coat." Ideally, hand-stripping should correspond with the dog's natural cycle, based on the environment and its hormonal levels. Using your fingers, a carding tool or a stripping knife, pull out a few hairs at a time to shape the coat,

accentuating the natural outline of the dog. Work methodically, pulling small amounts of coat at a time, always working in the direction of the coat growth. Proper hand-stripping removes hair with a gentle momentum and rhythm, not brute force, which is uncomfortable for both groomer and pet. The wrist stays locked in a neutral position while the rhythmic movement stems from the shoulder, not the wrist or elbow. In general, the main body coat is easy to remove. Most pets do not mind the plucking process. The cheeks, throat and private areas may be more sensitive, requiring thinning shears or clippers. Leave enough coat to be between 1 to 2 inches long. The coat should always appear very natural, never clipped or heavily trimmed. On some coats, a light application of chalk or powder before the bath will allow a better grip and make plucking and stripping much easier.

Brushing

Use a rubber curry, shedding blade, undercoat rake, pumice stone, carding tool, fine stripping knife, slicker brush or natural bristled brush to remove any remaining loose coat or tangles. Be careful when using any tool with metal teeth or bristles. A heavy hand or too much repetition in an area can cause cuts and/ or brush burns. Brushing is not finished until all loose fur is removed, or when it becomes difficult to remove more than a half a brush full after repeated brushing.

Head

Leave the coat longer on the muzzle. Lightly hand-strip or pluck the top skull, throat and cheeks. Leave triangles of coat above each eye to form the long, arched eyebrows that accentuate the eye area. Trim the brows short at the back corner of the eye with curved shears used in reverse extending out to almost the half way point between the stop and the nose. Ears are stripped of only the longest hair.

Feet & Hocks

Trim the pads with a close cutting blade ranging from a #15 to a #40. Use a very

light touch to clean the pads of long hair. Tidy the outside edge of the foot, if needed, with small detailing shears. If the hocks have longer coat, trim lightly with thinning shears to show a neat, clean area.

Detail Finish

Application of bows and mild cologne is optional.

Special Note

Clipping a wired-coated dog will result in a dramatic change in the texture and color of the coat. The correct harsh wire coat needs to be encouraged by plucking the blown coat when it is ready to be removed. This process stimulates hair follicles to produce new guard coat. Without hand-stripping, the guard coat is not stimulated and will not grow in properly. It will loose its brilliant color and texture. If only the undercoat grows, the guard coat color becomes that of the lighter, soft undercoat.

Breed Facts & Characteristics

Country of Origin: Hungary

Height at Shoulder: 21"–25"

Coat Length/Type: Hard/Wiry

Color: All shades of red and deep golden.

Correct grooming procedure:
Hand-Strip

Common pet grooming practices:
Hand-Strip

-The Goal-
The reddish color and coat texture are hallmarks of the breed. Body coat should be short, hard and very close fitting. Hand-stripping is the only way to retain this proper coat texture, which protects the skin while working in the field.

Top of skull and cheek area very tight.

Clear between eyes. Split, small sized, triangular brows.

Ears are free of long hair.

Correctly Groomed: Hand-Strip

Card the body first to remove loose undercoat. Follow by hand-stripping and finger plucking the longer hard outer coat. As new hair grows in, it will be harsh and tight fitting to the body.

Shape whiskers into a bushy rectangle.

Neaten tail.

Lightly clip sanitary areas.

Always pull in the direction of the coat growth. Legs too.

Neaten undercarriage line lightly.

Neaten hocks.

Trim nails as short as possible or grind.

Shave pads and neaten feet to match legs.

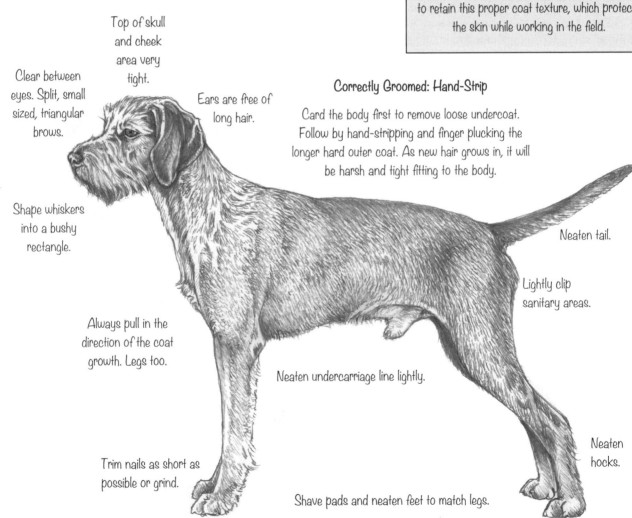

The coat should look as natural as possible and be about 1 inch all over the body.

Grooming Procedures & Recommendations

See page 76 for
Bathing & Drying Instructions

Frequency
Bathe once a week to once every 12 weeks.

Pre-Work
Trim or grind nails at least every four to six weeks to maintain a healthy foot structure. Swab the ears clean with a mild ear cleaning solution. Prior to bathing, quickly go over the entire body with a high-velocity dryer to help lift dirt and dander away from the skin and to loosen any shedding coat. *Normally, card and hand-strip dog prior to bathing and drying.*

Brushing
Use a rubber curry, shedding blade, undercoat rake, pumice stone, carding tool, fine stripping knife, slicker brush or natural bristled brush to remove any remaining loose coat or tangles. Be careful when using any tool with metal teeth or bristles. A heavy hand or too much repetition in an area can cause cuts and/or brush burns. Brushing is not finished until all loose fur is removed, or when it becomes difficult to remove more than a half a brush full after repeated brushing.

Carding
Carding is a natural technique in which the soft, downy undercoat is pulled from the dog's body. Typical tools used with this technique are: a pumice stone; a fine-toothed stripping knife that is pulled through the coat; an undercoat rake; or a fine blade, such as a #40, held between the fingers and pulled through the coat. Carding can be done before or after bathing and drying. Removal of the soft undercoat allows the topcoat to lie closer to the natural outline of the dog and accentuate the dog's structure. It also promotes profuse harsh outer coat, creates a rich coat color and protects the skin.

Hand-Stripping
Hand-stripping is a technique in which the outer guard coat is plucked from the dog's skin. This procedure helps retain the proper coat texture and rich color of the breed. During certain times of the year, the coat is easier to pull out. When the coat easily comes out, it is called a "blowing coat" or "blown coat." Ideally, hand-stripping should correspond with the dog's natural cycle, based on the environment and its hormonal levels.

Using your fingers, a carding tool or a stripping knife, pull out a few hairs at a time to shape the coat, accentuating the natural outline of the dog. Work methodically, pulling small amounts of coat at a time, always working in the direction of the coat growth. Proper hand-stripping removes hair with a gentle momentum and rhythm, not brute force, which is uncomfortable for both groomer and pet. The wrist stays locked in a neutral position while the rhythmic movement stems from the shoulder, not the wrist or elbow.

In general, the main body coat is easy to remove. Most pets do not mind the plucking process. The cheeks, throat and private areas may be more sensitive, requiring thinning shears or clippers.

Leave enough coat to be between 1 to 2 inches long. The coat should always appear very natural, never clipped or heavily trimmed. On some coats, a light application of chalk or powder before the bath will allow a better grip and make plucking and stripping much easier.

Head
Leave the coat longer on the muzzle. Hand-strip or pluck the top skull, throat and cheeks. Leave small triangles of coat above each eye to form the moderate eyebrows that accentuate the eye area. Ears are stripped of longer hair. If the coat on the ear leather does not strip/pluck out easily, clipper with blades ranging from a #10 to a #15 on the outside of the ear leather. Clipper the inside of the ear using blades ranging from a #40 to a #10. Finish by edging the ear with detailing shears, keeping the tips of the shears toward the tip of the ear.

Suggested Tools & Equipment

- Nail Trimmers
- Styptic Powder
- Ear Powder
- Ear Cleaning Solution
- Cotton Balls
- Hemostat
- Clippers
- Slicker Brush
- Greyhound Comb
- Pumice Stone
- Carding Tools
- Stripping Knives
- Straight Shears
- Curved Shears
- Small Detailing Shears
- Thinning Shears
- Dematting Tools

Common Blade Options:
- #40, #15, #10

Feet & Hocks
Trim the pads with a close cutting blade ranging from a #15 to a #40. Use a very light touch to clean the pads of long hair. Tidy the outside edge of the foot, if needed, with small detailing shears. If the hocks have longer coat, trim lightly with thinning shears to show a neat, clean area.

Detail Finish
Application of bows and mild cologne is optional.

Special Note
Clipping a wired-coated dog will result in a dramatic change in the texture and color of the coat. The correct harsh wire coat needs to be encouraged by plucking the blown coat when it is ready to be removed. This process stimulates hair follicles to produce new guard coat. Without hand-stripping, the guard coat is not stimulated and will not grow in properly. It will loose its brilliant color and texture. If only the undercoat grows, the guard coat color becomes that of the lighter, soft undercoat.

162

Most of the breeds in the Hound Group were created to hunt by sight or scent. They were developed to act somewhat independently for their humans. They have been used by hunters to track down prey, as well as by law enforcement agencies to track fugitives or sniff out contraband. They vary in size and speed but all have an acute sense of sight or smell that makes them valuable in the field.

HOUNDS

Breed Facts & Characteristics

Country of Origin: Afghanistan

Height at Shoulder: 24"–"28"

Coat Length/Type: Long/Flowing

Color: All colors are allowed. White markings, especially about the head area are very undesirable.

Correct grooming procedure:

Brush Out/Minor Trimming

Common pet grooming practices:

Clipper-Cut/Bathe & Brush Out

Face can be short or have a goatee. Always consult with the owner as to how they want the muzzle area finished before removing any hair.

Line comb and brush **every** inch of this dog, right down to the skin.

Leave ears long.

-The Goal-
Coat should be mat- and tangle-free. The fur should be light and airy, moving freely with the dog as it moves.

If the dog has a "natural saddle" accentuate by hand-stripping out any soft, fuzzy undercoat. Some dogs have this, some don't.

Tidy tail in a flag shape narrowing at the tip.

Lightly trim sanitary areas—both under tail and tummy.

Watch friction areas:
• Collar Area
• Arm Pits
• Behind Ears
• Legs & Thighs

Shave pads and scissor feet round. Neaten undercarriage line.

🐾 Bathing and Drying Directions:
• For coats longer than 3", use Natural Long Haired
• For coats shorter than 3", use Curly and Wavy Coated.

Grooming Procedures & Recommendations

See page 72 for
Bathing & Drying Instructions

See page 602 for
Dop Coat Styling Options

Frequency
Bathe once a week to once every 12 weeks.

Pre-Work
Trim or grind nails every four to six weeks to maintain a healthy foot structure. Clean the ears by swabbing with a mild ear cleaning solution. Pluck any long hair inside the ear canal using an ear powder and your fingers or hemostat. Prior to bathing, quickly go over the entire body and remove any serious mats or tangles. If the tangle can be penetrated with water, leave it and remove when the dog is clean. If the pet has not been in for professional grooming for six weeks or more, remove the excessive body coat and set the pattern before bathing.

Brushing
Systematically line brush the entire coat, right down to the skin. With a slicker brush, the motion used for line brushing is a "pat and pull." Softly pat the coat with the full pad of the brush and pull out and away from the skin with each stroke. The wrist remains in a neutral, or straight, position. The motion should be light and gentle. Start on the lower rear legs and work upwards towards the thigh. Repeat on every leg then proceed to the body, neck, head ears and tail. Work evenly over the pet, holding or pushing up the coat with one hand. It can be done with either a comb or a brush, but in most cases the comb is reserved for double checking the work of the brush. With the slicker brush, work the seam line, pulling down a small amount of fur with each stroke. Do not move to the next section until

the brush stroke glides smoothly and the skin at the seam line is seen. Pay close attention to the legs, under the front legs, collar area, ears, and tail. Let your hands feel for coat density levels. If an area feels heavier or thicker, it will need special attention with a brush or a comb. If static electricity is a problem while brushing, lightly mist the coat with an anti-static product or water while brushing. When finished, each strand of hair should float freely about as the dog moves.

Head
The face may be covered with a smooth, short, tight fitting coat or it may have longer fur on the muzzle and lower jaw that forms a beard and/or goatee. Based on client request, you can leave this area natural or remove the longer hair with a clipper blade to create a smooth clean face. If clipping, use blades ranging from a #10 to a #7F, used either with the grain or against the coat growth based on client preference.

Back Saddle Area
Some Afghans have a natural saddle along the spine that is made up of short, soft hair. This area often needs to be lightly neatened by pulling out any long fuzzy hair with a carding tool or by simply finger plucking the wispy coat. This shorter coat may extend all the way to the tail.

Tail
The underside of the tail should be nicely feathered with long fur. The top of the tail bone may be saddled out or may be covered with the same type of fur as the body. If the tail is naturally saddled out, clean up the smooth area, if necessary, by finger plucking or carding out any long, wispy hairs.

Suggested Tools & Equipment

- Nail Trimmers
- Styptic Powder
- Ear Powder
- Ear Cleaning Solution
- Hemostat
- Cotton Balls
- Clippers
- #40 and #15 Blades for Pads
- Slicker Brush
- Greyhound Comb
- Pin Brush
- Dematting Tools
- Straight Shears
- Curved Shears
- Small Detailing Shears
- Thinning Shears

Feet & Hocks
Trim the pads with a close cutting action blade ranging from a #15 to a #40. Use a very light touch to clean the pads of long hair. To create a very rounded foot, first block in the foot to form a square. This will help create a full circular shape with the toes pointing directly forward. Finish detailing and rounding the outline of the foot by using long, curved shears.

Detail Finish
Lightly neaten the entire outline of the dog, removing long, shaggy stray hairs that interrupt a smooth flow. The finished appearance is very natural. This can be done with thinning shears or shears as long as the look remains natural. Finish with a fine mist of coat polish on the body coat for added shine.

American English Coonhound HOUND SHORT COATED

Breed Facts & Characteristics

Country of Origin: United States

Height at Shoulder: 23"–26"

Coat Length/Type: Short/Smooth

Color: Black or blue ticked with white, red and white ticked or tri-colored ticked with white.

Correct grooming procedure:
Bathe & Curry Brush

Common pet grooming practices:
Bathe & Curry Brush

-The Goal-
The coat should be clean and fresh smelling, with the coat laying flat against the body. No shedding hair.

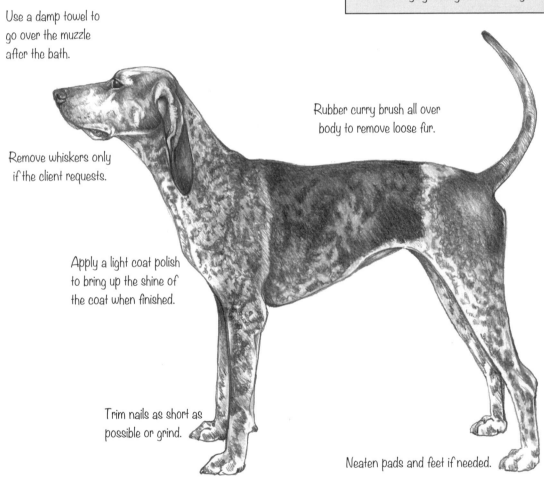

Use a damp towel to go over the muzzle after the bath.

Remove whiskers only if the client requests.

Apply a light coat polish to bring up the shine of the coat when finished.

Trim nails as short as possible or grind.

Rubber curry brush all over body to remove loose fur.

Neaten pads and feet if needed.

See page 67 for Bathing & Drying Instructions

Suggested Tools & Equipment

- Nail Trimmers
- Styptic Powder
- Ear Cleaning Solution
- Cotton Balls
- Clippers
- #40 or #15 Blade
- Rubber Curry
- Carding Tool
- Small Detailing Shears
- Thinning Shears

Breed Facts & Characteristics

Country of Origin: Africa

Height at Shoulder: 16"–17"

Coat Length/Type: Short/Smooth

Color: Deep reds, black or brindle as a base color on body with white points on chest, feet and end of tail, or tricolors. White legs, facial blaze and collar are permitted.

Correct grooming procedure:
Bathe & Curry Brush

Common pet grooming practices:
Bathe & Curry Brush

-The Goal-
The coat should be clean and fresh smelling, with the coat laying flat against the body. No shedding hair.

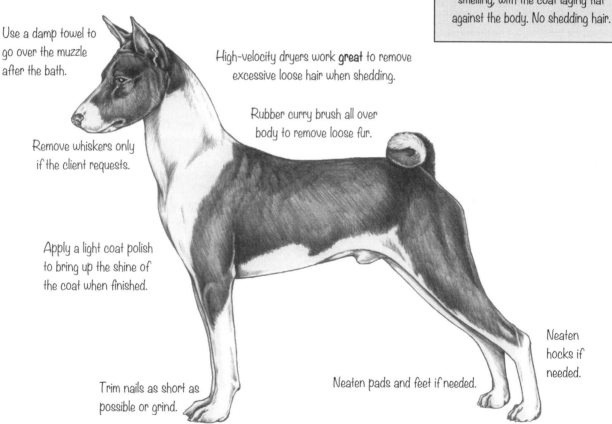

Use a damp towel to go over the muzzle after the bath.

High-velocity dryers work **great** to remove excessive loose hair when shedding.

Rubber curry brush all over body to remove loose fur.

Remove whiskers only if the client requests.

Apply a light coat polish to bring up the shine of the coat when finished.

Neaten hocks if needed.

Trim nails as short as possible or grind.

Neaten pads and feet if needed.

See page 66 for Bathing & Drying Instructions

Suggested Tools & Equipment

- Nail Trimmers
- Styptic Powder
- Ear Cleaning Solution
- Cotton Balls
- Clippers
- #40 or #15 Blade
- Rubber Curry
- Carding Tool
- Small Detailing Shears
- Thinning Shears

Basset Hound

Breed Facts & Characteristics

Country of Origin: France

Height at Shoulder: 13"–14"

Coat Length/Type: Short/Smooth

Color: Base color is white with a mixture of tans, reds and/or black with flecking.

Correct grooming procedure:

Bathe & Curry Brush

Common pet grooming practices:

Bathe & Curry Brush

-The Goal-
The coat should be clean and fresh
smelling, with the coat laying flat against
the body. No shedding hair.

Use a damp towel to go over the muzzle after the bath.

High-velocity dryers work **great** to remove excessive loose hair when shedding.

Rubber curry brush all over body to remove loose fur.

Remove whiskers only if the client requests.

Apply a light coat polish to bring up the shine of the coat when finished.

Trim nails as short as possible or grind.

Neaten hocks if needed.

Neaten pads and feet if needed.

See page 67 for Bathing & Drying Instructions	Suggested Tools & Equipment

- Nail Trimmers
- Styptic Powder
- Ear Cleaning Solution
- Cotton Balls

- Clippers
- #40 or #15 Blade
- Slicker Brush
- Rubber Curry

- Carding Tool
- De-Shedding Tools
- Small Detailing Shears
- Thinning Shears

Breed Facts & Characteristics

Country of Origin: England (modern)

Height at Shoulder: 12"–15"

Coat Length/Type: Short/Smooth

Color: Base color is white with a mixture of tans and/or black with gray color combinations.

Correct grooming procedure:
Bathe & Curry Brush

Common pet grooming practices:
Bathe & Curry Brush

-The Goal-
The coat should be clean and fresh smelling, with the coat laying flat against the body. No shedding hair.

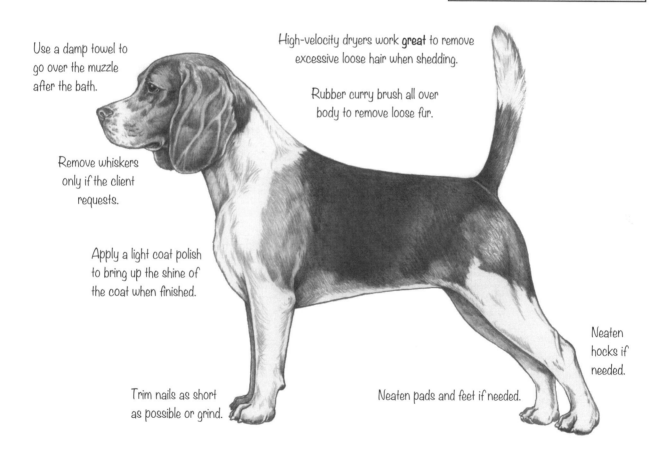

Use a damp towel to go over the muzzle after the bath.

High-velocity dryers work **great** to remove excessive loose hair when shedding.

Rubber curry brush all over body to remove loose fur.

Remove whiskers only if the client requests.

Apply a light coat polish to bring up the shine of the coat when finished.

Neaten hocks if needed.

Trim nails as short as possible or grind.

Neaten pads and feet if needed.

See page 67 for Bathing & Drying Instructions

Suggested Tools & Equipment

- Nail Trimmers
- Styptic Powder
- Ear Cleaning Solution
- Cotton Balls
- Clippers
- #40 or #15 Blade
- Slicker Brush
- Rubber Curry
- Carding Tool
- De-Shedding Tools
- Small Detailing Shears
- Thinning Shears

Notes From The Grooming Table ©2016

Black and Tan Coonhound   HOUNDS   SHORT COATED

Breed Facts & Characteristics

Country of Origin: United States

Height at Shoulder: 23"–27"

Coat Length/Type: Short/Smooth

Color: Black and tan.

Correct grooming procedure:
Bathe & Curry Brush

Common pet grooming practices:
Bathe & Curry Brush

-The Goal-
The coat should be clean and fresh smelling, with the coat laying flat against the body. No shedding hair.

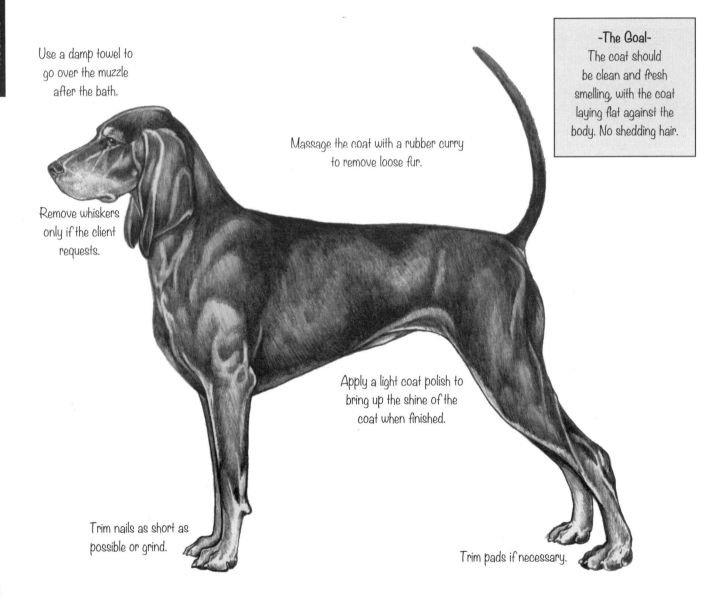

Use a damp towel to go over the muzzle after the bath.

Remove whiskers only if the client requests.

Massage the coat with a rubber curry to remove loose fur.

Apply a light coat polish to bring up the shine of the coat when finished.

Trim nails as short as possible or grind.

Trim pads if necessary.

See page 67 for
Bathing & Drying Instructions

Suggested Tools & Equipment

- Nail Trimmers
- Styptic Powder
- Ear Cleaning Solution
- Cotton Balls
- Clippers
- #40 or #15 Blade
- Slicker Brush
- Rubber Curry
- Carding Tool
- De-Shedding Tools
- Small Detailing Shears
- Thinning Shears

Breed Facts & Characteristics

Country of Origin: Europe

Height at Shoulder: 23"–27"

Coat Length/Type: Short/Smooth

Color: Black and tan, brown and tan or red. The darker colors will commonly be found in a saddle pattern of the back of the dog and/or in a facial mask.

Correct grooming procedure:
Bathe & Curry Brush

Common pet grooming practices:
Bathe & Curry Brush

-The Goal-
The coat should be fresh smelling, light and stand off the body. No loose hair.

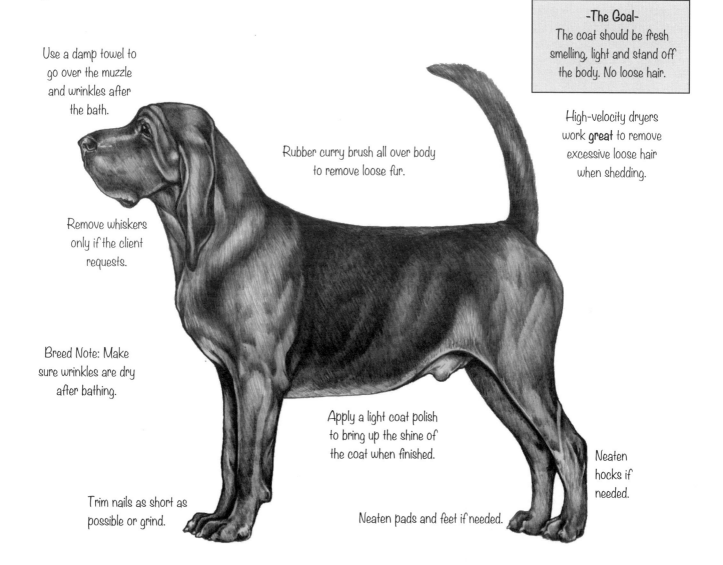

Use a damp towel to go over the muzzle and wrinkles after the bath.

Remove whiskers only if the client requests.

Breed Note: Make sure wrinkles are dry after bathing.

Trim nails as short as possible or grind.

Rubber curry brush all over body to remove loose fur.

High-velocity dryers work **great** to remove excessive loose hair when shedding.

Apply a light coat polish to bring up the shine of the coat when finished.

Neaten pads and feet if needed.

Neaten hocks if needed.

See page 67 for Bathing & Drying Instructions	Suggested Tools & Equipment

- Nail Trimmers
- Styptic Powder
- Ear Cleaning Solution
- Cotton Balls

- Clippers
- #40 or #15 Blade
- Slicker Brush
- Rubber Curry

- Carding Tool
- De-Shedding Tools
- Small Detailing Shears
- Thinning Shears

Bluetick Coonhound

Breed Facts & Characteristics

Country of Origin: United States

Height at Shoulder: 21"–27"

Coat Length/Type: Short/Smooth

Color: Dark blue thickly speckled body combined with blue or black solid spots and patches. Head and ears are mostly black combined with tan markings. Tan can also be found in the chest and lower areas of the body. Red ticking common on the lower legs and feet.

Correct grooming procedure:

Bathe & Curry Brush

Common pet grooming practices:

Bathe & Curry Brush

-The Goal-
The coat should be clean and fresh smelling, with the coat laying flat against the body. No shedding hair.

Use a damp towel to go over the muzzle and wrinkles after the bath.

Rubber curry brush all over body to remove loose fur.

Remove whiskers only if the client requests.

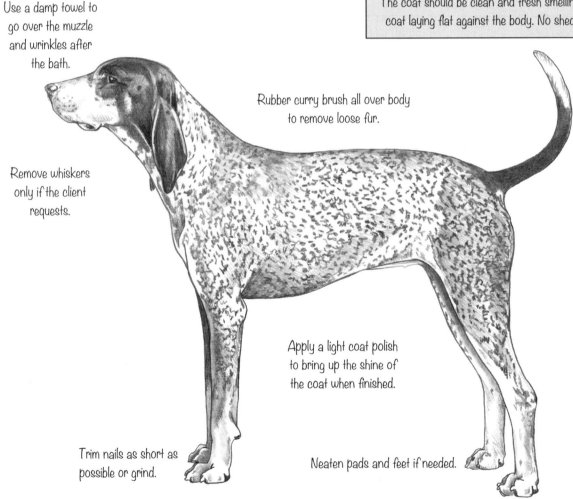

Apply a light coat polish to bring up the shine of the coat when finished.

Trim nails as short as possible or grind.

Neaten pads and feet if needed.

See page 67 for Bathing & Drying Instructions

Suggested Tools & Equipment

- Nail Trimmers
- Styptic Powder
- Ear Cleaning Solution
- Cotton Balls

- Clippers
- #40 or #15 Blade
- Slicker Brush
- Rubber Curry

- Carding Tool
- De-Shedding Tools
- Small Detailing Shears
- Thinning Shears

Notes *from your*
Grooming Table

Breed Facts & Characteristics

Country of Origin: Russia

Height at Shoulder: 26"–29"

Coat Length/Type: Combination/Silky

Color: All colors or color combinations are acceptable.

Correct grooming procedure:
Bathe & Brush Out

Common pet grooming practices:
Bathe & Brush Out

-The Goal-
Coat should be mat free, shiny, light and airy. As the dog moves, the coat should bounce and float with the dog.

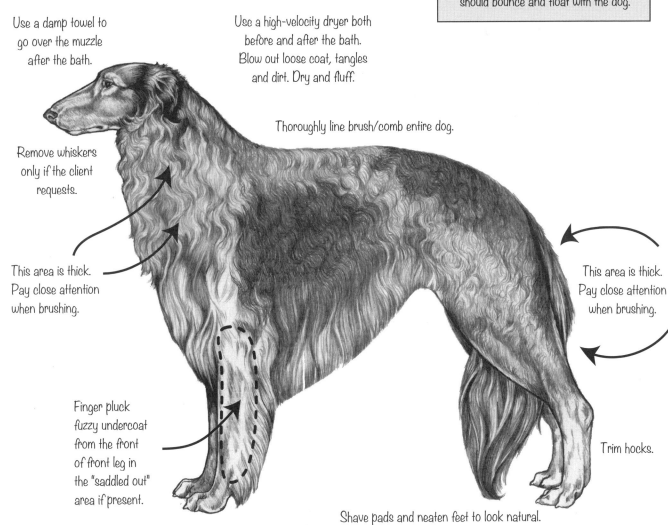

Use a damp towel to go over the muzzle after the bath.

Use a high-velocity dryer both before and after the bath. Blow out loose coat, tangles and dirt. Dry and fluff.

Thoroughly line brush/comb entire dog.

Remove whiskers only if the client requests.

This area is thick. Pay close attention when brushing.

This area is thick. Pay close attention when brushing.

Finger pluck fuzzy undercoat from the front of front leg in the "saddled out" area if present.

Trim hocks.

Shave pads and neaten feet to look natural.

Grooming Procedures & Recommendations

See page 68 for
Bathing & Drying Instructions

Frequency
Bathe once a week to once every 12 weeks.

Pre-Work
Trim or grind nails every four to six weeks to maintain a healthy foot structure. Clean the ears by swabbing with a mild ear cleaning solution. Use a rubber curry, shedding blade, undercoat rake, pumice stone, carding tool, fine stripping knife or natural bristle brush to loosen skin dander and remove loose coat. Use a high-velocity dryer over the coat to quickly and effectively lift dirt and debris away from the skin and loosen coat. Brush out or remove any matting found in the long-coated areas. If the tangles are loose enough so water can fully penetrate the area, remove them after bathing and drying. If water cannot penetrate, remove the mat or tangle prior to bathing.

Brushing
Line brush, working in sections until the dog is entirely tangle-free and all loose coat is removed. When finished, there should be little, if any, fur still being removed with a firm slicker brush. Double-check the work with a comb and your hands. Go over the entire body, feeling for any inconsistencies in the density levels of the coat. If an area seems moist to the touch or fuller than the rest of the coat, rework the area with the appropriate tool. Mats, tangles and excessive coat are easily trapped in the following areas: behind the ears, around the ruff, the thigh area, the undercarriage and the tail. Give extra attention to these areas before finishing the groom.

Carding
If a dog has an abundance of loose undercoat, card the shorter areas with a carding tool. Common tools can be a fine stripping knife, undercoat rake, a pumice stone, or a #40 blade held between your fingers. Any carding tool should be pulled over the body, working in the direction of the coat growth. This will remove the soft, downy undercoat, allowing the guard coat to conform more closely to the natural outline of the body. It will also aid in the removal of loose, shedding coat, a seasonal problem for many pet owners.

Feet & Hocks
Trim the pads with a close blade ranging from a #15 to a #40. Use a very light touch to clean the pads of long hair. If there is long fur between the toes, back brush the fur so it stands up on top of and away from the foot. With thinning shears, trim the excess to create a neat and very natural looking foot. Tidy the outside edge of the foot, if needed, with small detailing shears. If the hocks have longer coat, trim lightly with thinning shears to show a neat, clean area. A #4F blade, used carefully in reverse, works well for trimming the tops of the feet and the hocks on some dogs.

Detail Finish
Edge the ears lightly with thinning shears to neaten and keep a natural look. Hand pluck any long wispy, flyaway hair from around the ears. Removal of whiskers on the muzzle is optional based on client preference. Finish with a fine mist of coat polish on the body coat for added shine. Application of bows and mild cologne is optional.

Suggested Tools & Equipment

- Nail Trimmers
- Styptic Powder
- Ear Cleaning Solution
- Cotton Balls
- Clippers
- #40 and #15 Blades for Pads
- #4F for Feet & Hocks (optional)
- Slicker Brush
- Greyhound Comb
- Rubber Curry
- Carding Tool
- De-Shedding Tools
- Small Detailing Shears
- Thinning Shears

Notes:

Notes From The Grooming Table ©2016

Cirneco dell'Etna

Breed Facts & Characteristics

Country of Origin: Italy

Height at Shoulder: 16"–21½"

Coat Length/Type: Short/Smooth

Color: All shades of tan to chestnut with limited amount of white accepted but not encouraged.

Correct grooming procedure:
Bathe & Curry Brush

Common pet grooming practices:
Bathe & Curry Brush

-The Goal-
The coat should be clean & fresh smelling, with the coat laying flat against the body No shedding hair.

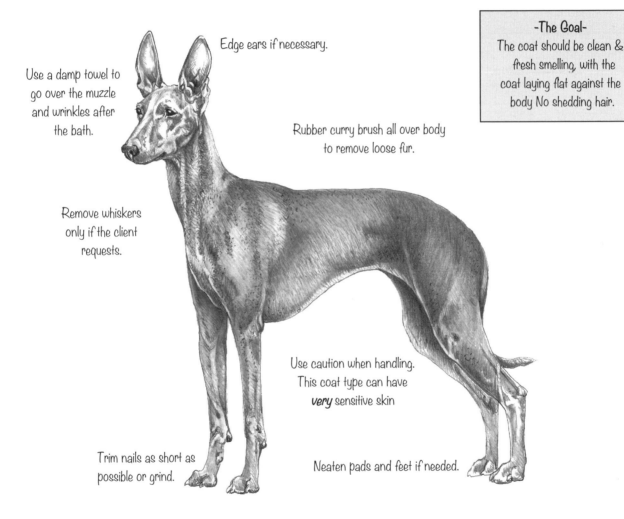

Edge ears if necessary.

Use a damp towel to go over the muzzle and wrinkles after the bath.

Rubber curry brush all over body to remove loose fur.

Remove whiskers only if the client requests.

Use caution when handling. This coat type can have **very** sensitive skin

Trim nails as short as possible or grind.

Neaten pads and feet if needed.

See page 66 for Bathing & Drying Instructions	Suggested Tools & Equipment

- Nail Trimmers
- Styptic Powder
- Ear Cleaning Solution
- Cotton Balls

- Clippers
- #40 or #15 Blade
- Rubber Curry
- Carding Tool

- Small Detailing Shears
- Thinning Shears

Notes *from your* Grooming Table

Dachshund (Long Haired)

Breed Facts & Characteristics

Country of Origin: Europe

Height at Shoulder: 7"–11"

Coat Length/Type: Combination/Silky

Color: Common colors are red or black and tan. Other colors are acceptable including: brown, fawn, gray, all with tan points; a mixture of black, brown and gray hair known as wild boar; all shades of red or blue dapples, as well as brindled.

Correct grooming procedure:
Brush Out/Minor Trimming

Common pet grooming practices:
Brush Out/Minor Trimming

-The Goal-
Coat should be mat free, shiny, with the body coat laying tight against the skin. As the dog moves, the longer feathering should bounce and float with the dog.

Top of skull is smooth.

Use a damp towel to go over the muzzle after the bath.

Ears are long/natural.

Use a high-velocity dryer both before and after the bath. Blow out loose coat, tangles and dirt. Dry and fluff.

Thoroughly line brush/comb all the feathering.

Shape tail into a flag with pointed tip.

Remove whiskers only if the client requests.

This area is thick. Pay close attention when brushing.

This area is thick. Pay close attention when brushing.

Finger pluck fuzzy undercoat from the front of front leg in the "saddled out" area if present.

Shave pads and neaten feet to look natural.

Neaten hocks.

Grooming Procedures & Recommendations

See page 68 for Bathing & Drying Instructions

Frequency
Bathe once a week to once every 12 weeks.

Pre-Work
Trim or grind nails every four to six weeks to maintain a healthy foot structure. Clean the ears by swabbing with a mild ear cleaning solution. Use a rubber curry, shedding blade, undercoat rake, pumice stone, carding tool, fine stripping knife or natural bristle brush to loosen skin dander and remove loose coat. Use a high-velocity dryer over the coat to quickly and effectively lift dirt and debris away from the skin and loosen coat. Brush out or remove any matting found in the long-coated areas. If the tangles are loose enough so water can fully penetrate the area, remove them after bathing and drying. If water cannot penetrate, remove the mat or tangle prior to bathing.

Brushing
Line brush, working in sections until the dog is entirely tangle-free and all loose coat is removed. When finished, there should be little, if any, fur still being removed with a firm slicker brush. Double-check the work with a comb and your hands. Go over the entire body, feeling for any inconsistencies in the density levels of the coat. If an area seems moist to the touch or fuller than the rest of the coat, rework the area with the appropriate tool. Mats, tangles and excessive coat are easily trapped in the following areas: behind the ears, around the ruff, the thigh area, the undercarriage and the tail. Give extra attention to these areas before finishing the groom.

Carding
If a dog has an abundance of loose undercoat, card the shorter areas with a carding tool. Common tools can be a fine stripping knife, undercoat rake, a pumice stone, or a #40 blade held between your fingers. Any carding tool should be pulled over the body, working in the direction of the coat growth. This will remove the soft, downy undercoat, allowing the guard coat to conform more closely to the natural outline of the body. It will also aid in the removal of loose, shedding coat, a seasonal problem for many pet owners.

Feet & Hocks
Trim the pads with a close blade ranging from a #15 to a #40. Use a very light touch to clean the pads of long hair. If there is long fur between the toes, back brush the fur so it stands up on top of and away from the foot. With thinning shears, trim the excess to create a neat and very natural looking foot. Tidy the outside edge of the foot, if needed, with small detailing shears. If the hocks have longer coat, trim lightly with thinning shears to show a neat, clean area. A #4F blade, used carefully in reverse, works well for trimming the tops of the feet and the hocks on some dogs.

Detail Finish
Edge the ears lightly with thinning shears to neaten and keep a natural look. Hand pluck any long wispy, flyaway hair from around the ears. Removal of whiskers on the muzzle is optional based on client preference. Finish with a fine mist of coat polish on the body coat for added shine. Application of bows and mild cologne is optional.

Suggested Tools & Equipment

- Nail Trimmers
- Styptic Powder
- Ear Cleaning Solution
- Cotton Balls
- Clippers
- #40 and #15 Blades for Pads
- #4F for Feet & Hocks (optional)
- Slicker Brush
- Greyhound Comb
- Rubber Curry
- Carding Tool
- De-Shedding Tools
- Small Detailing Shears
- Thinning Shears

Notes:

Notes From The Grooming Table ©2016

Breed Facts & Characteristics

Country of Origin: Europe

Height at Shoulder: 7"–11"

Coat Length/Type: Combination/Wiry

Color: Common colors are red or black and tan. Other colors are acceptable including: brown, fawn, gray, all with tan points; a mixture of black, brown and gray hair known as wild boar; all shades of red or blue dapples, as well as brindled.

Correct grooming procedure:
Hand-Strip

Common pet grooming practices:
Clipper-Trim or Hand-Strip

General Description

Except for its head, the wire-coated Dachshund would almost look like the smooth variety. On the head, the eyes are framed by eyebrows and the muzzle is covered with a rectangular beard. The ears are almost smooth and void of any long hair. The body, tail and legs are covered with a thick, tight-fitting jacket of harsh coat.

-The Goal-
From a distance, this variety should resemble its smooth hair cousin with the exception of the distinctive brows and beard. The body coat, including the tail, should be short, hard and very close fitting to the body. Hand-stripping is the only way to retain this proper coat texture.

Top of the skull should be hand-stripped very short. Leave two tufts of fur over the eyes to form the divided, triangular eyebrows. Shape brows with shears.

Ears are smooth.

Card the body first to remove the bulk of the loose undercoat. Follow by hand-stripping the hard outer coat. As new hair grows in, it will be harsh and tight fitting to the body. Always pull in the direction of the coat growth. Legs too.

Beard is full and rectangular in shape. Cheeks and throat are very short. If clipping, use a #10 or #15 blade against the grain with a light touch.

Tail is covered with short, hard hair.

Lightly clip sanitary areas: Under tail and tummy with #10.

Neaten hocks.

Shave pads and neaten edges of feet.

**See page 76 for
Bathing & Drying Instructions**

Frequency

Bathe once a week to once every
12 weeks.

Pre-Work

Trim or grind nails at least every four
to six weeks to maintain a healthy foot
structure. Swab the ears clean with a
mild ear cleaning solution. Prior to
bathing, quickly go over the entire
body with a high-velocity dryer to help
lift dirt and dander away from the skin
and to loosen any shedding coat. ***Card
and hand-strip dog prior to bathing
and drying.***

Brushing

Use a rubber curry, shedding blade,
undercoat rake, pumice stone, carding
tool, fine stripping knife, slicker brush
or natural bristled brush to remove any
remaining loose coat or tangles. Be careful
when using any tool with metal teeth
or bristles. A heavy hand or too much
repetition in an area can cause cuts and/
or brush burns. Brushing is not finished
until all loose fur is removed, or when it
becomes difficult to remove more than a
half a brush full after repeated brushing.

Carding

Carding is a natural technique in which
the soft, downy undercoat is pulled
from the dog's body. Typical tools used
with this technique are: a pumice stone;
a fine-toothed stripping knife that is
pulled through the coat; an undercoat
rake; or a fine blade, such as a #40, held
between the fingers and pulled through
the coat. Carding can be done before or
after bathing and drying. Removal of the
soft undercoat allows the topcoat to lie
closer to the natural outline of the dog
and accentuate the dog's structure. It also
promotes profuse harsh outer coat, creates
a rich coat color and protects the skin.

Hand-Stripping

Hand-stripping is a technique in which
the outer guard coat is plucked from the
dog's skin. This procedure helps retain
the proper coat texture and rich color of
the breed. During certain times of the
year, the coat is easier to pull out. When
the coat easily comes out, it is called a
"blowing coat" or "blown coat." Ideally,
hand-stripping should correspond with
the dog's natural cycle, based on the
environment and its hormonal levels.
Using your fingers, a carding tool or a
stripping knife, pull out a few hairs at
a time to shape the coat, accentuating
the natural outline of the dog. Work
methodically, pulling small amounts of
coat at a time, always working in the
direction of the coat growth. Proper
hand-stripping removes hair with a
gentle momentum and rhythm, not
brute force, which is uncomfortable
for both groomer and pet. The wrist
stays locked in a neutral position while
the rhythmic movement stems from
the shoulder, not the wrist or elbow.
In general, the main body coat is easy
to remove. Most pets do not mind the
plucking process. The cheeks, throat
and private areas may be more sensitive,
requiring thinning shears or clippers.
Leave enough coat to be between ¼ to
1 inch long. The coat should always
appear very natural, never clipped. On
some coats, a light application of chalk
or powder before the bath will allow
a better grip and make plucking and
stripping much easier.

Head

Leave the coat longer on the muzzle.
Hand-strip or pluck the top skull, throat
and cheeks. Leave triangles of coat above
each eye to form the moderate eyebrows
that accentuate the eye area. Ears are
stripped of longer hair. If the coat on
the ear leather does not strip/pluck out
easily, clipper with blades ranging from
a #10 to a #15 on the outside of the
ear leather. Clipper the inside of the ear

Notes:

Notes From The Grooming Table ©2016

HOUNDS

Shape the arched eyebrows by following the eye socket ridge. Brows are split at the stop area. Use curved shears in reverse to help set the brow. The coat is very short at the back of the eye and gets longer towards the nose.

Or clipper the top skull very close. If clipping, use blades ranging from a #10 used with the grain a #4F used against the grain depending on the coat density.

The occiput is the dividing line between the head and the neck.

The ears should be smooth and fine. Remove long hair by hand-stripping or clipping with blades ranging from a #10 or #15 on the outside and a #40 on the inside. Finish by edging the ears with small detailing shears.

The beard and mustache form a rectangular head style. When viewed from straight on, the cheeks and the beard should form one continuous line.

The cheeks and throat are smooth and clean. Blades ranging from a #10 to a #15, used with or against the grain, are common in pet styling. The line runs from the back corner of the eye to the cheek whisker nodule, to the chin nodule, up to the opposite cheek whisker nodule and opposite eye. Use the zygomatic arch to set the line from the back corner of the eye to the ear canal. The natural cowlick line assists with setting the throat area. Create a soft "V" or "U" shape coming about 2 finger widths above the breast bone.

using blades ranging from a #40 to a #10. Finish by edging the ear with detailing shears, keeping the tips of the shears toward the tip of the ear.

Feet & Hocks
Trim the pads with a close cutting blade ranging from a #15 to a #40. Use a very light touch to clean the pads of long hair. Tidy the outside edge of the foot, if needed, with small detailing shears. If the hocks have longer coat, trim lightly with thinning shears to show a neat, clean area.

Detail Finish
Application of bows and mild cologne is optional.

Special Note
Clipping a wired-coated dog will result in a dramatic change in the texture and color of the coat. The correct harsh wire coat needs to be encouraged by plucking the blown coat when it is ready to be removed. This process stimulates hair follicles to produce new guard coat. Without hand-stripping, the

guard coat is not stimulated and will not grow in properly. It will loose its brilliant color and texture. If only the undercoat grows, the guard coat color becomes that of the lighter, soft undercoat.

Notes *from your*
Grooming Table

HOUNDS

Breed Facts & Characteristics

Country of Origin: Europe

Height at Shoulder: 7"–11"

Coat Length/Type: Short/Smooth

Color: Common colors are red or black and tan. Other colors are acceptable including: brown, fawn, gray, all with tan points; a mixture of black, brown and gray hair known as wild boar; all shades of red or blue dapples, as well as brindled.

Correct grooming procedure:
Bathe & Curry Brush

Common pet grooming practices:
Bathe & Curry Brush

-The Goal-
The coat should be clean and fresh smelling, with the coat laying flat against the body. No shedding hair.

Use a damp towel to go over the muzzle after the bath.

Remove whiskers only if the client requests.

Massage the coat with a rubber curry to remove loose fur.

Apply a light coat polish to bring up the shine of the coat when finished.

Trim nails as short as possible or grind.

Trim pads if necessary.

See page 66 for Bathing & Drying Instructions	Suggested Tools & Equipment

- Nail Trimmers
- Styptic Powder
- Ear Cleaning Solution
- Cotton Balls

- Clippers
- #40 or #15 Blade
- Rubber Curry
- Carding Tool

- Small Detailing Shears
- Thinning Shears

Breed Facts & Characteristics

Country of Origin: United States

Height at Shoulder: 21"–25"

Coat Length/Type: Short/Smooth

Color: Any color, but typical hound colors where the base color is white with a mixture of tans and/or black with gray color combinations are common.

Correct grooming procedure:
Bathe & Curry Brush

Common pet grooming practices:
Bathe & Curry Brush

-The Goal-
The coat should be clean and fresh smelling, with the coat laying flat against the body. No shedding hair.

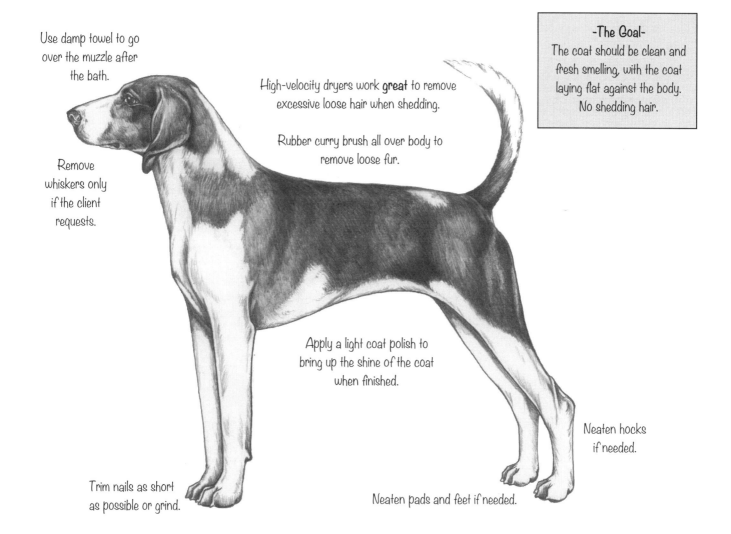

Use damp towel to go over the muzzle after the bath.

High-velocity dryers work **great** to remove excessive loose hair when shedding.

Rubber curry brush all over body to remove loose fur.

Remove whiskers only if the client requests.

Apply a light coat polish to bring up the shine of the coat when finished.

Neaten hocks if needed.

Trim nails as short as possible or grind.

Neaten pads and feet if needed.

See page 67 for Bathing & Drying Instructions

Suggested Tools & Equipment

- Nail Trimmers
- Styptic Powder
- Ear Cleaning Solution
- Cotton Balls

- Clippers
- #40 or #15 Blade
- Slicker Brush
- Rubber Curry

- Carding Tool
- De-Shedding Tools
- Small Detailing Shears
- Thinning Shears

Breed Facts & Characteristics

Country of Origin: England

Height at Shoulder: 23"–25"

Coat Length/Type: Short/Smooth

Color: Any color, but typical hound colors where the base color is white with a mixture of tans and/or black with gray color combinations are common.

Correct grooming procedure:

Bathe & Curry Brush

Common pet grooming practices:

Bathe & Curry Brush

-The Goal-
The coat should be clean and fresh smelling, with the coat laying flat against the body. No shedding hair.

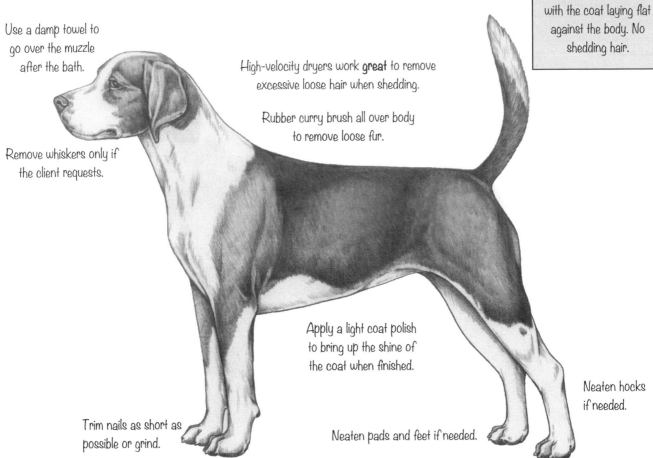

Use a damp towel to go over the muzzle after the bath.

High-velocity dryers work **great** to remove excessive loose hair when shedding.

Rubber curry brush all over body to remove loose fur.

Remove whiskers only if the client requests.

Apply a light coat polish to bring up the shine of the coat when finished.

Neaten hocks if needed.

Trim nails as short as possible or grind.

Neaten pads and feet if needed.

See page 67 for Bathing & Drying Instructions

Suggested Tools & Equipment

- Nail Trimmers
- Styptic Powder
- Ear Cleaning Solution
- Cotton Balls
- Clippers
- #40 or #15 Blade
- Slicker Brush
- Rubber Curry
- Carding Tool
- De-Shedding Tools
- Small Detailing Shears
- Thinning Shears

HOUNDS

Greyhound

Breed Facts & Characteristics

Country of Origin: Egypt

Height at Shoulder: 27"–30"

Coat Length/Type: Short/Smooth

Color: Any color.

Correct grooming procedure:
Bathe & Curry Brush

Common pet grooming practices:
Bathe & Curry Brush

Use a damp towel to go over the muzzle after the bath.

-The Goal-
The coat should be clean and fresh smelling, with the coat laying flat against the body. No shedding hair.

Remove whiskers only if the client requests.

Massage the coat with a rubber curry to remove loose fur.

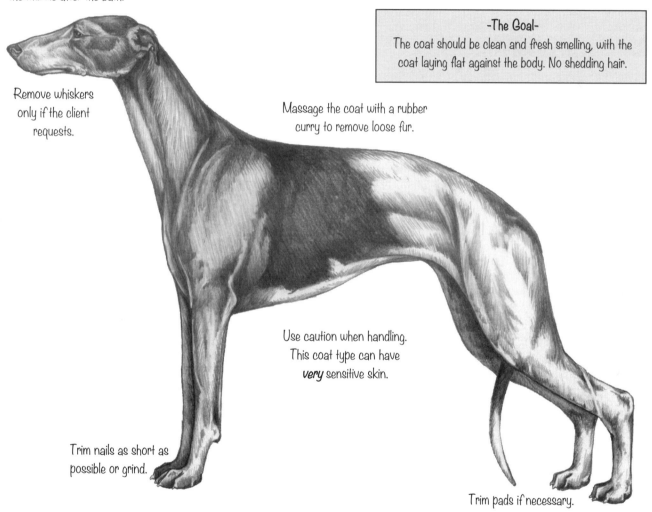

Use caution when handling. This coat type can have *very* sensitive skin.

Trim nails as short as possible or grind.

Trim pads if necessary.

See page 66 for Bathing & Drying Instructions

Suggested Tools & Equipment

- Nail Trimmers
- Styptic Powder
- Ear Cleaning Solution
- Cotton Balls
- Clippers
- #40 or #15 Blade
- Rubber Curry
- Carding Tool
- Small Detailing Shears
- Thinning Shears

Harrier

Breed Facts & Characteristics

Country of Origin: England

Height at Shoulder: 19"–21"

Coat Length/Type: Short/Smooth

Color: Any color, but typical hound colors where the base color is white with a mixture of tans and/or black with gray color combinations are common.

Correct grooming procedure:

Bathe & Curry Brush

Common pet grooming practices:

Bathe & Curry Brush

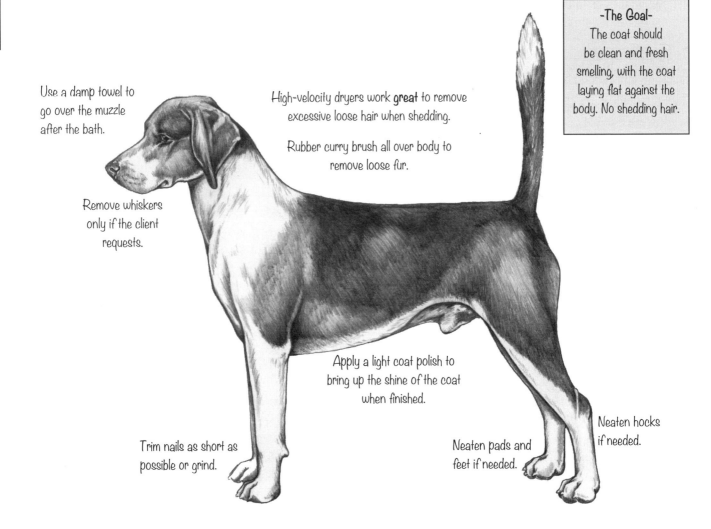

-The Goal-
The coat should be clean and fresh smelling, with the coat laying flat against the body. No shedding hair.

Use a damp towel to go over the muzzle after the bath.

High-velocity dryers work **great** to remove excessive loose hair when shedding.

Rubber curry brush all over body to remove loose fur.

Remove whiskers only if the client requests.

Apply a light coat polish to bring up the shine of the coat when finished.

Neaten hocks if needed.

Trim nails as short as possible or grind.

Neaten pads and feet if needed.

See page 67 for Bathing & Drying Instructions

Suggested Tools & Equipment

- Nail Trimmers
- Styptic Powder
- Ear Cleaning Solution
- Cotton Balls

- Clippers
- #40 or #15 Blade
- Slicker Brush
- Rubber Curry

- Carding Tool
- De-Shedding Tools
- Small Detailing Shears
- Thinning Shears

Breed Facts & Characteristics

Country of Origin: Egypt

Height at Shoulder: 22½"–27½"

Coat Length/Type: Short/Smooth

Color: Red or white or any combination of those two colors.

Correct grooming procedure:
Bathe & Curry Brush

Common pet grooming practices:
Bathe & Curry Brush

-The Goal-
The coat should be clean and fresh smelling, with the coat laying flat against the body. No shedding hair.

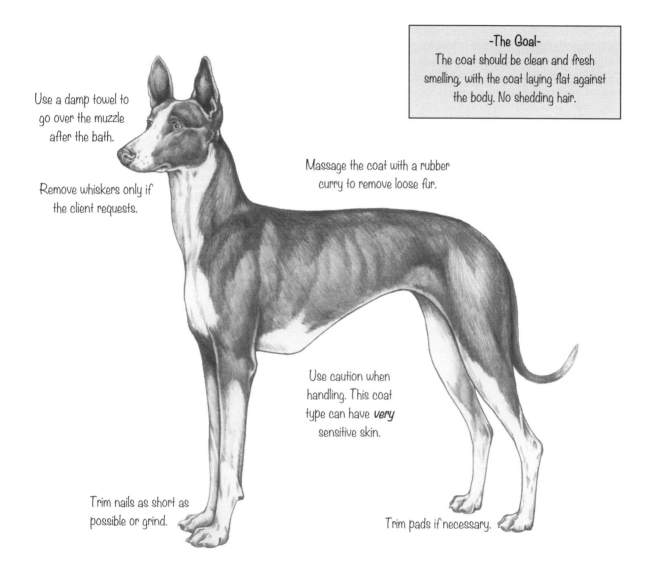

Use a damp towel to go over the muzzle after the bath.

Remove whiskers only if the client requests.

Massage the coat with a rubber curry to remove loose fur.

Use caution when handling. This coat type can have **very** sensitive skin.

Trim nails as short as possible or grind.

Trim pads if necessary.

See page 66 for Bathing & Drying Instructions	Suggested Tools & Equipment

- Nail Trimmers
- Styptic Powder
- Ear Cleaning Solution
- Cotton Balls

- Clippers
- #40 or #15 Blade
- Rubber Curry
- Carding Tool

- Small Detailing Shears
- Thinning Shears

Notes From The Grooming Table ©2016

Breed Facts & Characteristics

Country of Origin: Egypt

Height at Shoulder: 22½"–27½"

Coat Length/Type: Moderate/Wiry

Color: Red or white or any combination of those two colors.

Correct grooming procedure:
Card & Hand-Strip

Common pet grooming practices:
Card & Hand-Strip

General Description

The wire-coated Ibizan will be covered with between 1 and 3 inches of long, wiry coat. The eyes are accentuated by bushy eyebrows. The muzzle can be covered with long harsh coat that makes up the beard. The longer fur will be located on the back, on the back of the legs and on the underside of the tail. Other than the coat type, the two varieties are identical in structure.

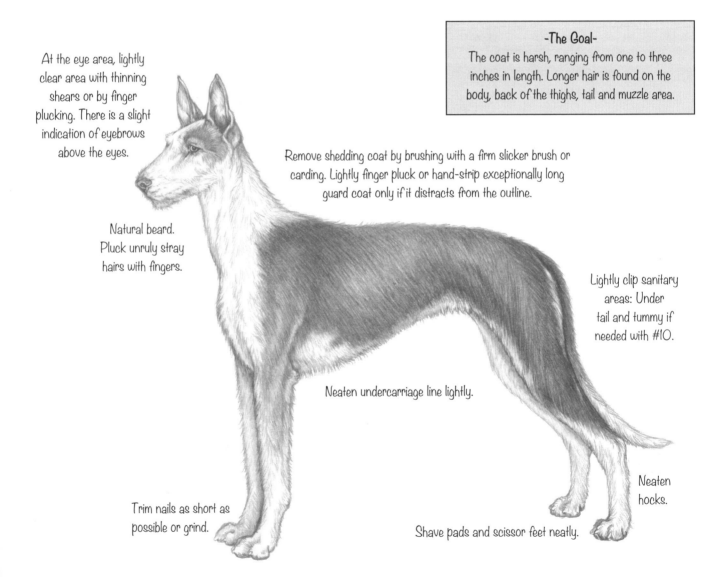

-The Goal-
The coat is harsh, ranging from one to three inches in length. Longer hair is found on the body, back of the thighs, tail and muzzle area.

At the eye area, lightly clear area with thinning shears or by finger plucking. There is a slight indication of eyebrows above the eyes.

Remove shedding coat by brushing with a firm slicker brush or carding. Lightly finger pluck or hand-strip exceptionally long guard coat only if it distracts from the outline.

Natural beard. Pluck unruly stray hairs with fingers.

Lightly clip sanitary areas: Under tail and tummy if needed with #10.

Neaten undercarriage line lightly.

Neaten hocks.

Trim nails as short as possible or grind.

Shave pads and scissor feet neatly.

Grooming Procedures & Recommendations

See page 76 for Bathing & Drying Instructions

Frequency
Bathe once a week to once every 12 weeks.

Pre-Work
Trim or grind nails at least every four to six weeks to maintain a healthy foot structure. Swab the ears clean with a mild ear cleaning solution. Prior to bathing, quickly go over the entire body with a high-velocity dryer to help lift dirt and dander away from the skin and to loosen any shedding coat. *Card and hand-strip dog prior to bathing and drying.*

Brushing
Use a rubber curry, shedding blade, undercoat rake, pumice stone, carding tool, fine stripping knife, slicker brush or natural bristled brush to remove any remaining loose coat or tangles. Be careful when using any tool with metal teeth or bristles. A heavy hand or too much repetition in an area can cause cuts and/or brush burns. Brushing is not finished until all loose fur is removed, or when it becomes difficult to remove more than a half a brush full after repeated brushing.

Carding
Carding is a natural technique in which the soft, downy undercoat is pulled from the dog's body. Typical tools used with this technique are: a pumice stone; a fine-toothed stripping knife that is pulled through the coat; an undercoat rake; or a fine blade, such as a #40, held between the fingers and pulled through the coat. Carding can be done before or after bathing and drying. Removal of the soft undercoat allows the topcoat to lie closer to the natural outline of the dog and accentuate the dog's structure. It also promotes profuse harsh outer coat, creates a rich coat color and protects the skin.

Hand-Stripping
Hand-stripping is a technique in which the outer guard coat is plucked from the dog's skin. This procedure helps retain the proper coat texture and rich color of the breed. During certain times of the year, the coat is easier to pull out. When the coat easily comes out, it is called a "blowing coat" or "blown coat." Ideally, hand-stripping should correspond with the dog's natural cycle, based on the environment and its hormonal levels. Using your fingers, a carding tool or a stripping knife, pull out a few hairs at a time to shape the coat, accentuating the natural outline of the dog. Work methodically, pulling small amounts of coat at a time, always working in the direction of the coat growth. Proper hand-stripping removes hair with a gentle momentum and rhythm, not brute force, which is uncomfortable for both groomer and pet. The wrist stays locked in a neutral position while the rhythmic movement stems from the shoulder, not the wrist or elbow. In general, the main body coat is easy to remove. Most pets do not mind the plucking process. The cheeks, throat and private areas may be more sensitive, requiring thinning shears or clippers. Leave enough coat to be between 1 to 3 inches. The coat should always appear very natural, never clipped or heavily trimmed. On some coats, a light application of chalk or powder before the bath will allow a better grip and make plucking and stripping much easier.

Head
Leave the coat longer on the muzzle. Hand-strip or pluck the top skull, throat and cheeks. Leave triangles of coat above each eye to form the small eyebrows that accentuate the eye area. Ears are stripped of longer hair. If the coat on the ear leather does not strip/pluck out easily, clipper with blades ranging from a #10 to a #15 on the outside of the ear leather. Clipper the inside of the ear using blades ranging from a #40 to a #10. Finish by edging the ear with detailing shears, keeping the tips of the shears toward the tip of the ear.

Feet & Hocks
Trim the pads with a close cutting blade ranging from a #15 to a #40. Use a very light touch to clean the pads of long hair. Tidy the outside edge of the foot, if needed, with small detailing shears. If the hocks have longer coat, trim lightly with thinning shears to show a neat, clean area.

Detail Finish
Application of bows and mild cologne is optional.

Special Note
Clipping a wired-coated dog will result in a dramatic change in the texture and color of the coat. The correct harsh wire coat needs to be encouraged by plucking the blown coat when it is ready to be removed. This process stimulates hair follicles to produce new guard coat. Without hand-stripping, the guard coat is not stimulated and will not grow in properly. It will loose its brilliant color and texture. If only the undercoat grows, the guard coat color becomes that of the lighter, soft undercoat.

Suggested Tools & Equipment

- Nail Trimmers
- Styptic Powder
- Ear Powder
- Ear Cleaning Solution
- Cotton Balls
- Hemostat
- Clippers
- Slicker Brush
- Greyhound Comb
- Pumice Stone
- Carding Tools
- Stripping Knives
- Straight Shears
- Curved Shears
- Small Detailing Shears
- Thinning Shears
- Dematting Tools

Common Blade Options:
- #40, #15, #10

Notes From The Grooming Table ©2016

Irish Wolfhound

Breed Facts & Characteristics

Country of Origin: Ireland

Height at Shoulder: 30"–32"

Coat Length/Type: Moderate/Wiry

Color: Tans, gray, red, black, cream, white , black and brindled.

Correct grooming procedure:
Card & Hand-Strip

Common pet grooming practices:
Card & Hand-Strip

General Description

This is a giant dog covered with a harsh, wiry coat. The hair is fuller over the eyes and on the muzzle, making the head look rectangular in shape.

-The Goal-
This is a large, rugged looking dog with a harsh, rough coat that is to be left in a totally natural state with only minor neatening to accentuate the dog's form

At eye area, lightly clear with thinning shears or by finger plucking. There is a slight indication of eyebrows above the eyes.

Remove shedding coat by brushing with a firm slicker brush or carding. Lightly finger pluck or hand-strip exceptionally long guard coat only if it distracts from the outline.

Full beard. Head is left natural. Pluck unruly stray hairs with fingers.

Lightly clip sanitary areas: Under tail and tummy if needed with #10.

Pull an undercoat rake through the coat to remove blown coat prior to bathing.

Neaten undercarriage line lightly.

Trim nails as short as possible or grind.

Neaten hocks.

Shave pads and scissor feet round.

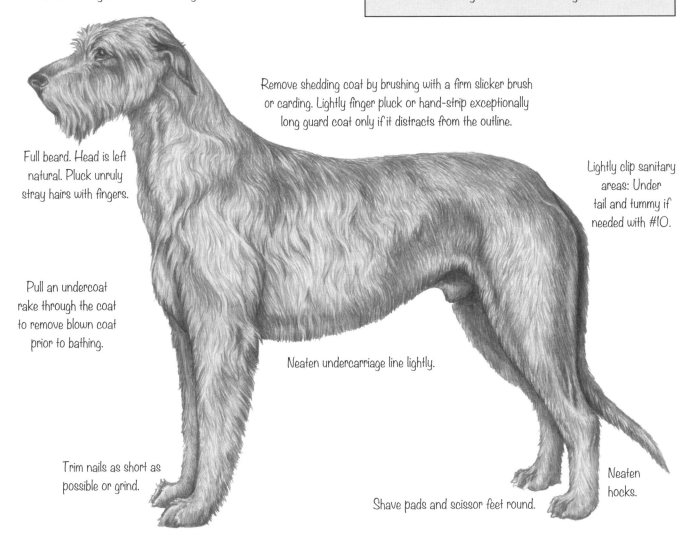

See page 76 for Bathing & Drying Instructions

Frequency
Bathe once a week to once every 12 weeks.

Pre-Work
Trim or grind nails at least every four to six weeks to maintain a healthy foot structure. Swab the ears clean with a mild ear cleaning solution. Prior to bathing, quickly go over the entire body with a high-velocity dryer to help lift dirt and dander away from the skin and to loosen any shedding coat. *Card and hand-strip dog prior to bathing and drying*

Brushing
Use a rubber curry, shedding blade, undercoat rake, pumice stone, carding tool, fine stripping knife, slicker brush or natural bristled brush to remove any remaining loose coat or tangles. Be careful when using any tool with metal teeth or bristles. A heavy hand or too much repetition in an area can cause cuts and/or brush burns. Brushing is not finished until all loose fur is removed, or when it becomes difficult to remove more than a half a brush full after repeated brushing.

Carding
Carding is a natural technique in which the soft, downy undercoat is pulled from the dog's body. Typical tools used with this technique are: a pumice stone; a fine-toothed stripping knife that is pulled through the coat; an undercoat rake; or a fine blade, such as a #40, held between the fingers and pulled through the coat. Carding can be done before or after bathing and drying. Removal of the soft undercoat allows the topcoat to lie closer to the natural outline of the dog and accentuate the dog's structure. It also promotes profuse harsh outer coat, creates a rich coat color and protects the skin.

Hand-Stripping
Hand-stripping is a technique in which the outer guard coat is plucked from the dog's skin. This procedure helps retain the proper coat texture and rich color of the breed. During certain times of the year, the coat is easier to pull out. When the coat easily comes out, it is called a "blowing coat" or "blown coat." Ideally, hand-stripping should correspond with the dog's natural cycle, based on the environment and its hormonal levels. Using your fingers, a carding tool or a stripping knife, pull out a few hairs at a time to shape the coat, accentuating the natural outline of the dog. Work methodically, pulling small amounts of coat at a time, always working in the direction of the coat growth. Proper hand-stripping removes hair with a gentle momentum and rhythm, not brute force, which is uncomfortable for both groomer and pet. The wrist stays locked in a neutral position while the rhythmic movement stems from the shoulder, not the wrist or elbow. In general, the main body coat is easy to remove. Most pets do not mind the plucking process. The cheeks, throat and private areas may be more sensitive, requiring thinning shears or clippers. Leave enough coat to be between 1 to 3 inches long. The coats always should appear very natural, never clipped or heavily trimmed. On some coats, a light application of chalk or powder before the bath will allow a better grip and make plucking and stripping much easier.

Head
Leave the coat longer on the muzzle. Lightly hand-strip or pluck the top skull, throat and cheeks. Leave triangles of coat above each eye to form the moderate eyebrows that accentuate the eye area. Ears are stripped of longer hair. If the coat on the ear leather does not strip/pluck out easily, clipper with blades ranging from a #10 to a #15 on the outside of the ear leather. Clipper the inside of the ear using blades ranging from a #40 to a #10. Finish by edging the ear with detailing shears, keeping the tips of the shears toward the tip of the ear.

Feet & Hocks
Trim the pads with a close cutting blade ranging from a #15 to a #40. Use a very light touch to clean the pads of long hair. Tidy the outside edge of the foot, if needed, with small detailing shears. If the hocks have longer coat, trim lightly with thinning shears to show a neat, clean area.

Detail Finish
Application of bows and mild cologne is optional.

Special Note
Clipping a wired-coated dog will result in a dramatic change in the texture and color of the coat. The correct harsh wire coat needs to be encouraged by plucking the blown coat when it is ready to be removed. This process stimulates hair follicles to produce new guard coat. Without hand-stripping, the guard coat is not stimulated and will not grow in properly. It will loose its brilliant color and texture. If only the undercoat grows, the guard coat color becomes that of the lighter, soft undercoat.

Suggested Tools & Equipment

- Nail Trimmers
- Styptic Powder
- Ear Powder
- Ear Cleaning Solution
- Cotton Balls
- Hemostat
- Clippers
- Slicker Brush
- Greyhound Comb
- Pumice Stone
- Carding Tools
- Stripping Knives
- Straight Shears
- Curved Shears
- Small Detailing Shears
- Thinning Shears
- Dematting Tools

Common Blade Options:
- #40, #15, #10

Breed Facts & Characteristics

Country of Origin: Norway

Height at Shoulder: 19½"–20½"

Coat Length/Type: Double Coated

Color: Deep blue/gray, blacks, tans, and brindles. Dark masks and ears are typical on the lighter colored dogs.

Correct grooming procedure:
Bathe & Brush Out

Common pet grooming practices:
Bathe & Brush Out

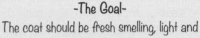

-The Goal-
The coat should be fresh smelling, light and stand off the body. No loose hair.

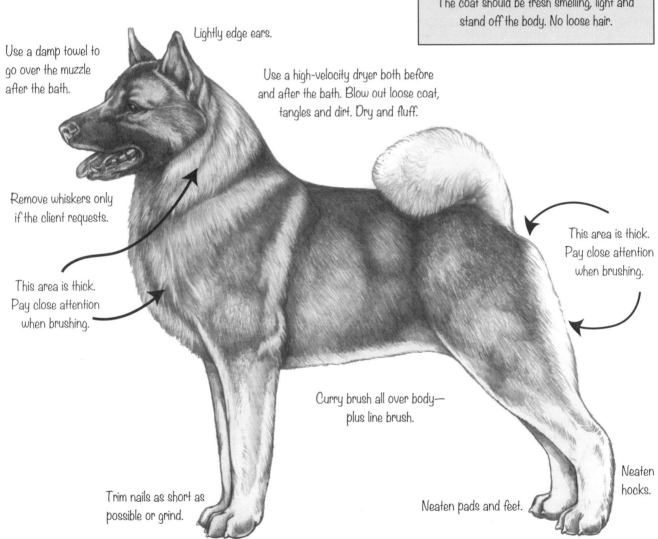

Lightly edge ears.

Use a damp towel to go over the muzzle after the bath.

Use a high-velocity dryer both before and after the bath. Blow out loose coat, tangles and dirt. Dry and fluff.

Remove whiskers only if the client requests.

This area is thick. Pay close attention when brushing.

This area is thick. Pay close attention when brushing.

Curry brush all over body— plus line brush.

Neaten hocks.

Trim nails as short as possible or grind.

Neaten pads and feet.

Grooming Procedures & Recommendations

**See page 69 for
Bathing & Drying Instructions**

Frequency
Bathe once a week to once every
12 weeks.

Pre-Work
Trim or grind nails at least every four
to six weeks to maintain a healthy foot
structure. Clean the ears by swabbing
with a mild ear cleaning solution. Prior
to bathing, quickly go over the entire
body with a high-velocity dryer to help
lift dirt and dander away from the skin
and loosen any shedding coat.

Brushing
Use a slicker brush, rubber curry,
shedding blade, dematting tool or
undercoat rake to loosen skin dander
and remove loose coat. Be careful
when using any tool with metal teeth
or bristles. A heavy hand or too much
repetition in an area can cause cuts and/
or brush burns. Brushing and combing
is not finished until all loose fur is
removed, or it has become difficult to
remove more than a half a brush full
after repeated brushing.

Feet & Hocks
Trim the pads with a close cutting
action blade, ranging from a #15 to a
#40. Use a very light touch to clean the
pads of long hair. If there is long fur
between the toes, back brush the fur so
it stands up and away from the foot.
With thinning shears, trim off the excess
creating a neat and very natural looking
foot with well arched toes. Tidy the
outside edge of the foot, if needed, with
small detailing shears. If the hocks have
longer coat on them, trim lightly with
thinning shears showing a neat, clean
area. A #4F blade used in reverse works
well for trimming the tops of the feet
and the hocks on some dogs.

Detail Finish
Removal of whiskers on the muzzle is
optional, based on client preference.
Finish with a fine mist of coat polish on
the body for added shine. Application of
bows and mild cologne is optional.

Grooming Tip
Let your hands guide you. Learn to feel
for differences in coat density levels.
Areas that feel heavier or denser than
other areas need special attention when
bathing, brushing and drying.

Suggested Tools & Equipment
- Nail Trimmers
- Styptic Powder
- Ear Cleaning Solution
- Cotton Balls
- Clippers
- #40 and #15 Blades for Pads
- #4F for Feet & Hocks (optional)
- Slicker Brush
- Greyhound Comb
- Rubber Curry
- Carding Tool
- De-Shedding Tools
- Small Detailing Shears
- Thinning Shears
- High-Velocity Dryer

Notes:

Notes From The Grooming Table ©2016

Breed Facts & Characteristics

Country of Origin: England

Height at Shoulder: 24"–27"

Coat Length/Type: Moderate/Wiry

Color: All colors and combinations of colors are acceptable.

Correct grooming procedure:
Hand-Strip

Common pet grooming practices:
Card/Hand-Strip

General Description
The rough and wiry coat of an Otterhound should never be clipper-trimmed and only moderately shaped with hand-stripping techniques. Overall, this breed should look rough and unkempt with up to 2 to 4 inches of coat over its main body. The head, ears and tail have longer furnishings.

-The Goal-
This is a large, rugged looking dog with a harsh, rough coat that is to be left in a natural state with only minor neatening to accentuate the dog's form

At eye area, lightly clear area with thinning shears or by finger plucking.

Remove shedding coat by brushing with a firm slicker brush or carding. Lightly finger pluck or hand-strip exceptionally long guard coat only if it distracts from the outline.

Lightly clip sanitary areas: Under tail and tummy with #10.

Head is left natural. Pluck unruly stray hairs with fingers.

Tail to length of hocks.

Pull an undercoat rake through the coat to remove blown coat prior to bathing.

Neaten undercarriage line lightly.

Neaten hocks.

Trim nails as short as possible or grind.

Shave pads and scissor feet round.

Grooming Procedures & Recommendations

See page 76 for
Bathing & Drying Instructions

Frequency
Bathe once a week to once every 12 weeks.

Pre-Work
Trim or grind nails at least every four to six weeks to maintain a healthy foot structure. Swab the ears clean with a mild ear cleaning solution. Prior to bathing, quickly go over the entire body with a high-velocity dryer to help lift dirt and dander away from the skin and to loosen any shedding coat. ***Card and hand-strip dog prior to bathing and drying.***

Brushing
Use a rubber curry, shedding blade, undercoat rake, pumice stone, carding tool, fine stripping knife, slicker brush or natural bristled brush to remove any remaining loose coat or tangles. Be careful when using any tool with metal teeth or bristles. A heavy hand or too much repetition in an area can cause cuts and/or brush burns. Brushing is not finished until all loose fur is removed, or when it becomes difficult to remove more than a half a brush full after repeated brushing.

Carding
Carding is a natural technique in which the soft, downy undercoat is pulled from the dog's body. Typical tools used with this technique are: a pumice stone; a fine-toothed stripping knife that is pulled through the coat; an undercoat rake; or a fine blade, such as a #40, held between the fingers and pulled through the coat. Carding can be done before or after bathing and drying. Removal of the soft undercoat allows the topcoat to lie closer to the natural outline of the dog and accentuate the dog's structure. It also promotes profuse harsh outer coat, creates a rich coat color and protects the skin.

Hand-Stripping
Hand-stripping is a technique in which the outer guard coat is plucked from the dog's skin. This procedure helps retain the proper coat texture and rich color of the breed. During certain times of the year, the coat is easier to pull out. When the coat easily comes out, it is called a "blowing coat" or "blown coat." Ideally, hand-stripping should correspond with the dog's natural cycle, based on the environment and its hormonal levels. Using your fingers, a carding tool or a stripping knife, pull out a few hairs at a time to shape the coat, accentuating the natural outline of the dog. Work methodically, pulling small amounts of coat at a time, always working in the direction of the coat growth. Proper hand-stripping removes hair with a gentle momentum and rhythm, not brute force, which is uncomfortable for both groomer and pet. The wrist stays locked in a neutral position while the rhythmic movement stems from the shoulder, not the wrist or elbow. In general, the main body coat is easy to remove. Most pets do not mind the plucking process. The cheeks, throat and private areas may be more sensitive, requiring thinning shears or clippers. Leave enough coat to be between 2 to 4 inches long. The coat should always appear very natural, never clipped or heavily trimmed. On some coats, a light application of chalk or powder before the bath will allow a better grip and make plucking and stripping much easier.

Head
Leave the coat longer on the muzzle. Lightly hand-strip or pluck the top skull, throat and cheeks. Leave triangles of coat above each eye to form the moderate eyebrows that accentuate the eye area. Ears are left long and natural.

Feet & Hocks
Trim the pads with a close cutting blade ranging from a #15 to a #40. Use a very light touch to clean the pads of long

hair. Tidy the outside edge of the foot, if needed, with small detailing shears. If the hocks have longer coat, trim lightly with thinning shears to show a neat, clean area.

Detail Finish
Application of bows and mild cologne is optional.

Special Note
Clipping a wired-coated dog will result in a dramatic change in the texture and color of the coat. The correct harsh wire coat needs to be encouraged by plucking the blown coat when it is ready to be removed. This process stimulates hair follicles to produce new guard coat. Without hand-stripping, the guard coat is not stimulated and will not grow in properly. It will lose its brilliant color and texture. If only the undercoat grows, the guard coat color becomes that of the lighter, soft undercoat.

Notes From The Grooming Table ©2016

Petit Basset Griffon Vendéen

Breed Facts & Characteristics

Country of Origin: France

Height at Shoulder: 13"–15"

Coat Length/Type: Moderate/Wiry

Color: The coat is mostly white, with patches of black, orange, or grizzle.

Correct grooming procedure:

Hand-Strip

Common pet grooming practices:

Card/Hand-Strip

General Description

The coat is made up of a wiry outer coat with a thick under coat. The harsh, outer guard coat is normally between 1 and 2 inches in length. The extended "eyebrows" and the typical beard give the PBGV his characteristic tousled appearance.

-The Goal-
Make this a casual looking dog with a "tousled" look. The outer coat is crisp and harsh. The undercoat is thick and short. The overall appearance of the dog is to be totally natural with only minor neatening to accentuate the dog's form.

Slight indication of triangular brows over eyes but the eye is not fully covered by the eyebrow.

Pull an undercoat rake through the coat to remove blown coat prior to bathing.

Remove shedding coat by brushing with a firm slicker brush or carding. Lightly finger pluck or hand-strip exceptionally long guard coat only if it distracts from the outline.

Pluck long hairs from the tail to balance with body.

Full Beard.

Head is left natural with long ears. Pluck unruly stray hairs with fingers.

Lightly clip sanitary areas: Under tail and tummy with #10.

Neaten hocks.

Neaten undercarriage line lightly.

Trim nails as short as possible or grind.

Shave pads and scissor feet round.

Grooming Procedures & Recommendations

See page 76 for
Bathing & Drying Instructions

Frequency
Bathe once a week to once every 12 weeks.

Pre-Work
Trim or grind nails at least every four to six weeks to maintain a healthy foot structure. Swab the ears clean with a mild ear cleaning solution. Prior to bathing, quickly go over the entire body with a high-velocity dryer to help lift dirt and dander away from the skin and to loosen any shedding coat. ***Card and hand-strip dog prior to bathing and drying.***

Brushing
Use a rubber curry, shedding blade, undercoat rake, pumice stone, carding tool, fine stripping knife, slicker brush or natural bristled brush to remove any remaining loose coat or tangles. Be careful when using any tool with metal teeth or bristles. A heavy hand or too much repetition in an area can cause cuts and/or brush burns. Brushing is not finished until all loose fur is removed, or when it becomes difficult to remove more than a half a brush full after repeated brushing.

Carding
Carding is a natural technique in which the soft, downy undercoat is pulled from the dog's body. Typical tools used with this technique are: a pumice stone; a fine-toothed stripping knife that is pulled through the coat; an undercoat rake; or a fine blade, such as a #40, held between the fingers and pulled through the coat. Carding can be done before or after bathing and drying. Removal of the soft undercoat allows the topcoat to lie closer to the natural outline of the dog and accentuate the dog's structure. It also promotes profuse harsh outer coat, creates a rich coat color and protects the skin.

Hand-Stripping
Hand-stripping is a technique in which the outer guard coat is plucked from the dog's skin. This procedure helps retain the proper coat texture and rich color of the breed. During certain times of the year, the coat is easier to pull out. When the coat easily comes out, it is called a "blowing coat" or "blown coat." Ideally, hand-stripping should correspond with the dog's natural cycle, based on the environment and its hormonal levels. Using your fingers, a carding tool or a stripping knife, pull out a few hairs at a time to shape the coat, accentuating the natural outline of the dog. Work methodically, pulling small amounts of coat at a time, always working in the direction of the coat growth. Proper hand-stripping removes hair with a gentle momentum and rhythm, not brute force, which is uncomfortable for both groomer and pet. The wrist stays locked in a neutral position while the rhythmic movement stems from the shoulder, not the wrist or elbow. In general, the main body coat is easy to remove. Most pets do not mind the plucking process. The cheeks, throat and private areas may be more sensitive, requiring thinning shears or clippers. Leave enough coat to be between 1 to 2 inches long. The coat should always appear very natural, never clipped or heavily trimmed. On some coats, a light application of chalk or powder before the bath will allow a better grip and make plucking and stripping much easier.

Head
Leave the coat longer on the muzzle. Lightly hand-strip or pluck the top skull, throat and cheeks. Leave triangles of coat above each eye to form the moderate eyebrows that accentuate the eye area. Ears are left long and natural.

Feet & Hocks
Trim the pads with a close cutting blade ranging from a #15 to a #40. Use a very light touch to clean the pads of long hair. Tidy the outside edge of the foot, if needed, with small detailing shears. If the hocks have longer coat, trim lightly with thinning shears to show a neat, clean area.

Detail Finish
Application of bows and mild cologne is optional.

Special Note
Clipping a wired-coated dog will result in a dramatic change in the texture and color of the coat. The correct harsh wire coat needs to be encouraged by plucking the blown coat when it is ready to be removed. This process stimulates hair follicles to produce new guard coat. Without hand-stripping, the guard coat is not stimulated and will not grow in properly. It will lose its brilliant color and texture. If only the undercoat grows, the guard coat color becomes that of the lighter, soft undercoat.

Suggested Tools & Equipment

- Nail Trimmers
- Styptic Powder
- Ear Powder
- Ear Cleaning Solution
- Cotton Balls
- Hemostat
- Clippers
- Slicker Brush
- Greyhound Comb
- Pumice Stone
- Carding Tools
- Stripping Knives
- Straight Shears
- Curved Shears
- Small Detailing Shears
- Thinning Shears
- Dematting Tools

Common Blade Options:
- #40, #15, #10

Notes From The Grooming Table ©2016

Pharaoh Hound

HOUNDS   SMOOTH COATED

HOUNDS

Breed Facts & Characteristics

Country of Origin: Egypt

Height at Shoulder: 21"–25"

Coat Length/Type: Short/Smooth

Color: The coat ranges from rich tan to chestnut and may have white markings and the amber-colored eyes are one of this breed's most distinctive characteristics.

Correct grooming procedure:
Bathe & Curry Brush

Common pet grooming practices:
Bathe & Curry Brush

-The Goal-
The coat should be clean and fresh smelling, with the coat laying flat against the body. No shedding hair.

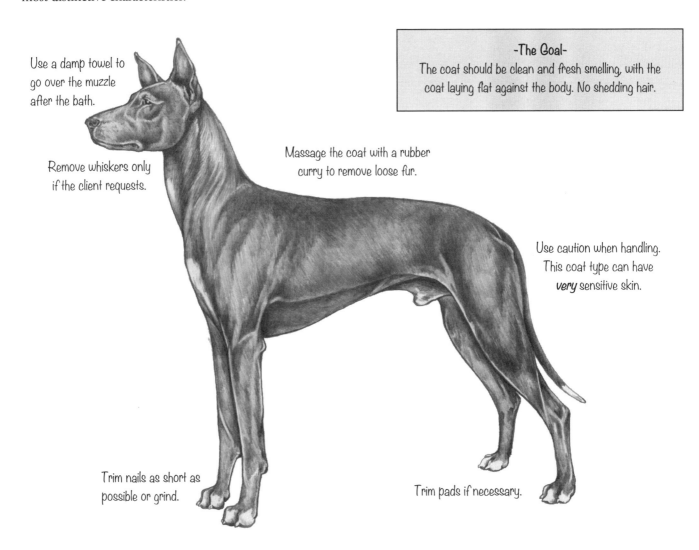

Use a damp towel to go over the muzzle after the bath.

Remove whiskers only if the client requests.

Massage the coat with a rubber curry to remove loose fur.

Use caution when handling. This coat type can have *very* sensitive skin.

Trim nails as short as possible or grind.

Trim pads if necessary.

See page 66 for Bathing & Drying Instructions	Suggested Tools & Equipment

- Nail Trimmers
- Styptic Powder
- Ear Cleaning Solution
- Cotton Balls
- Clippers
- #40 or #15 Blade
- Rubber Curry
- Carding Tool
- Small Detailing Shears
- Thinning Shears

Notes From The Grooming Table ©2016

200

Breed Facts & Characteristics

Country of Origin: United States

Height at Shoulder: 20"–25"

Coat Length/Type: Short/Smooth

Color: Most commonly seen in all shades of brindle, solid black or black with brindle. Small amount of white allowed on chest and toes.

Correct grooming procedure:
Bathe & Curry Brush

Common pet grooming practices:
Bathe & Curry Brush

-The Goal-
The coat should be clean and fresh smelling, with the coat laying flat against the body. No shedding hair.

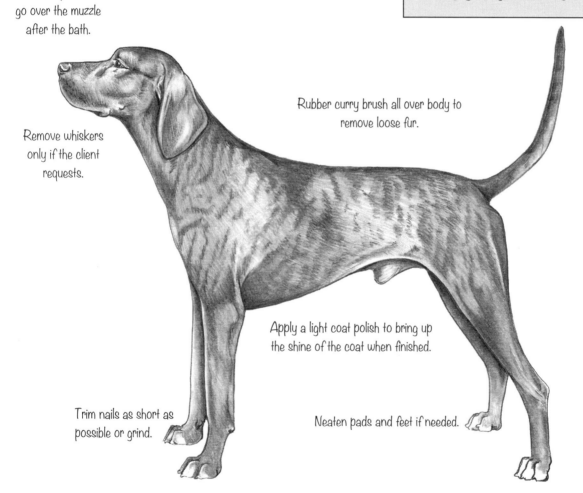

Use a damp towel to go over the muzzle after the bath.

Remove whiskers only if the client requests.

Rubber curry brush all over body to remove loose fur.

Apply a light coat polish to bring up the shine of the coat when finished.

Trim nails as short as possible or grind.

Neaten pads and feet if needed.

See page 66 for Bathing & Drying Instructions

Suggested Tools & Equipment

- Nail Trimmers
- Styptic Powder
- Ear Cleaning Solution
- Cotton Balls

- Clippers
- #40 or #15 Blade
- Rubber Curry
- Carding Tool

- Small Detailing Shears
- Thinning Shears

Portuguese Podengo Pequeno (Smooth) SHORT COATED

Breed Facts & Characteristics

Country of Origin: Portugal

Height at Shoulder: 8"–12"

Coat Length/Type: Short/Smooth

Color: Most commonly seen in all shades of tan, either solid or combined with white markings.

Correct grooming procedure:
Bathe & Curry Brush

Common pet grooming practices:
Bathe & Curry Brush

-The Goal-
The coat should be clean and fresh smelling, with the coat laying flat against the body. No shedding hair.

If necessary, edge ears with small shears...keep the tips of the shears toward tips of the ears.

Use a damp towel to go over the muzzle after the bath.

Rubber curry brush all over body to remove loose fur.

Remove whiskers only if the client requests.

Apply a light coat polish to bring up the shine of the coat when finished.

Trim nails as short as possible or grind.

Neaten pads and feet if needed.

See page 67 for Bathing & Drying Instructions

Suggested Tools & Equipment

- Nail Trimmers
- Styptic Powder
- Ear Cleaning Solution
- Cotton Balls
- Clippers
- #40 or #15 Blade
- Rubber Curry
- Carding Tool
- Small Detailing Shears
- Thinning Shears

Notes from your Grooming Table

Portuguese Podengo Pequeno (Wire Haired) WIRE HAIRED

HOUNDS

Breed Facts & Characteristics

Country of Origin: Portugal

Height at Shoulder: 8"–12"

Coat Length/Type: Hard/Wiry (no undercoat)

Color: Most commonly seen in all shades of tan either solid or combined with white markings.

Correct grooming procedure:
Card & Hand-Strip

Common pet grooming practices:
Card & Hand-Strip

General Description

The Podengo is a hunting dog developed in a variety of sizes based on the type of quarry he was after. The muzzle has a distinctive beard. The longer fur will be located on the back, on the back of the legs, and on the underside of the tail. Other than the coat type, the two varieties are identical in structure.

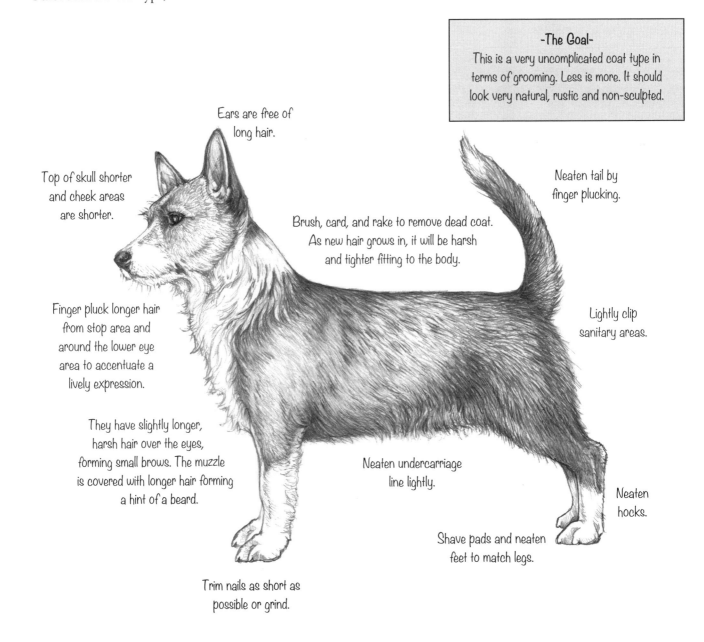

-The Goal-
This is a very uncomplicated coat type in terms of grooming. Less is more. It should look very natural, rustic and non-sculpted.

Ears are free of long hair.

Top of skull shorter and cheek areas are shorter.

Brush, card, and rake to remove dead coat. As new hair grows in, it will be harsh and tighter fitting to the body.

Neaten tail by finger plucking.

Finger pluck longer hair from stop area and around the lower eye area to accentuate a lively expression.

Lightly clip sanitary areas.

They have slightly longer, harsh hair over the eyes, forming small brows. The muzzle is covered with longer hair forming a hint of a beard.

Neaten undercarriage line lightly.

Neaten hocks.

Shave pads and neaten feet to match legs.

Trim nails as short as possible or grind.

**See page 76 for
Bathing & Drying Instructions**

Frequency
Bathe once a week to once every 12 weeks.

Pre-Work
Trim or grind nails at least every four to six weeks to maintain a healthy foot structure. Swab the ears clean with a mild ear cleaning solution. Prior to bathing, quickly go over the entire body with a high-velocity dryer to help lift dirt and dander away from the skin and to loosen any shedding coat. *Card and hand-strip dog prior to bathing and drying.*

Brushing
Use a rubber curry, shedding blade, undercoat rake, pumice stone, carding tool, fine stripping knife, slicker brush or natural bristled brush to remove any remaining loose coat or tangles. Be careful when using any tool with metal teeth or bristles. A heavy hand or too much repetition in an area can cause cuts and/or brush burns. Brushing is not finished until all loose fur is removed, or when it becomes difficult to remove more than a half a brush full after repeated brushing.

Carding
Carding is a natural technique in which the soft, downy undercoat is pulled from the dog's body. Typical tools used with this technique are: a pumice stone; a fine-toothed stripping knife that is pulled through the coat; an undercoat rake; or a fine blade, such as a #40, held between the fingers and pulled through the coat. Carding can be done before or after bathing and drying. Removal of the soft undercoat allows the topcoat to lie closer to the natural outline of the dog and accentuate the dog's structure. It also promotes profuse harsh outer coat, creates a rich coat color and protects the skin.

Hand-Stripping
Hand-stripping is a technique in which the outer guard coat is plucked from the dog's skin. This procedure helps retain the proper coat texture and rich color of the breed. During certain times of the year, the coat is easier to pull out. When the coat easily comes out, it is called a "blowing coat" or "blown coat." Ideally, hand-stripping should correspond with the dog's natural cycle, based on the environment and its hormonal levels. Using your fingers, a carding tool or a stripping knife, pull out a few hairs at a time to shape the coat, accentuating the natural outline of the dog. Work methodically, pulling small amounts of coat at a time, always working in the direction of the coat growth. Proper hand-stripping removes hair with a gentle momentum and rhythm, not brute force, which is uncomfortable for both groomer and pet. The wrist stays locked in a neutral position while the rhythmic movement stems from the shoulder, not the wrist or elbow. In general, the main body coat is easy to remove. Most pets do not mind the plucking process. The cheeks, throat and private areas may be more sensitive, requiring thinning shears or clippers. Leave enough coat to be between 1 to 2 inches long. The coat should always appear very natural, never clipped or heavily trimmed. On some coats, a light application of chalk or powder before the bath will allow a better grip and make plucking and stripping much easier.

Head
Leave the coat longer on the muzzle. Hand-strip or pluck the top skull, throat and cheeks. Leave triangles of coat above each eye to form the moderate bushy eyebrows that accentuate the eye area. Remove any longer hair from the ears that distract from their natural outline.

Feet & Hocks
Trim the pads with a close cutting blade ranging from a #15 to a #40. Use a very light touch to clean the pads of long hair. Tidy the outside edge of the foot,

Suggested Tools & Equipment

- Nail Trimmers
- Styptic Powder
- Ear Powder
- Ear Cleaning Solution
- Cotton Balls
- Hemostat
- Clippers
- Slicker Brush
- Greyhound Comb
- Pumice Stone
- Carding Tools
- Stripping Knives
- Straight Shears
- Curved Shears
- Small Detailing Shears
- Thinning Shears
- Dematting Tools

Common Blade Options:
- #40, #15, #10

if needed, with small detailing shears. If the hocks have longer coat, trim lightly with thinning shears to show a neat, clean area.

Detail Finish
For added shine, finish with a fine mist of coat polish on the body. Application of bows and mild cologne is optional.

Special Note
Clipping a wired-coated dog will result in a dramatic change in the texture and color of the coat. The correct harsh wire coat needs to be encouraged by plucking the blown coat when it is ready to be removed. This process stimulates hair follicles to produce new guard coat. Without hand-stripping, the guard coat is not stimulated and will not grow in properly. It will lose its brilliant color and texture. If only the undercoat grows, the guard coat color becomes that of the lighter, soft undercoat.

Redbone Coonhound   HOUND   SMOOTH COATED

Breed Facts & Characteristics

Country of Origin: United States

Height at Shoulder: 21"–27"

Coat Length/Type: Short/Smooth

Color: Solid red. Darker muzzle and a very limited amount of white is tolerated on the chest and toes.

Correct grooming procedure:
Bathe & Curry Brush

Common pet grooming practices:
Bathe & Curry Brush

-The Goal-
The coat should be clean and fresh smelling, with the coat laying flat against the body. No shedding hair.

Use a damp towel to go over the muzzle after the bath.

Remove whiskers only if the client requests.

Rubber curry brush all over body to remove loose fur.

Apply a light coat polish to bring up the shine of the coat when finished.

Trim nails as short as possible or grind.

Neaten pads and feet if needed.

See page 66 for Bathing & Drying Instructions

Suggested Tools & Equipment

- Nail Trimmers
- Styptic Powder
- Ear Cleaning Solution
- Cotton Balls
- Clippers
- #40 or #15 Blade
- Rubber Curry
- Carding Tool
- Small Detailing Shears
- Thinning Shears

Breed Facts & Characteristics

Country of Origin: South Africa

Height at Shoulder: 24"–27"

Coat Length/Type: Short/Smooth

Color: A solid colored dog of tan or red tones.

Correct grooming procedure:
Bathe & Curry Brush

Common pet grooming practices:
Bathe & Curry Brush

-The Goal-
The coat should be clean and fresh smelling, with the coat laying flat against the body. No shedding hair.

Use a damp towel to go over the muzzle after the bath.

Remove whiskers only if the client requests.

High-velocity dryers work **great** to remove excessive loose hair when shedding.

Rubber curry brush all over body to remove loose fur.

Apply a light coat polish to bring up the shine of the coat when finished.

Trim nails as short as possible or grind.

Neaten hocks if needed.

Neaten pads and feet if needed.

See page 66 for Bathing & Drying Instructions

Suggested Tools & Equipment

- Nail Trimmers
- Styptic Powder
- Ear Cleaning Solution
- Cotton Balls

- Clippers
- #40 or #15 Blade
- Rubber Curry
- Carding Tool

- Small Detailing Shears
- Thinning Shears

HOUNDS

Breed Facts & Characteristics

Country of Origin: Egypt

Height at Shoulder: 23"–28"

Coat Length/Type: Silky/Smooth

Color: They come in a wide range of coat colors including, white, cream, tan, golden, chestnut, grizzle and tan; black and tan as well as tricolored with white, tan and black.

Correct grooming procedure:

Bathe & Brush Out/Minor Trimming

Common pet grooming practices:

Bathe & Brush Out/Minor Trimming

-The Goal-
This is a graceful dog of typical sight hound build. When finished, the dog is clean, shiny and mat free. The feathers should float as the dog moves and all shedding coat is removed.

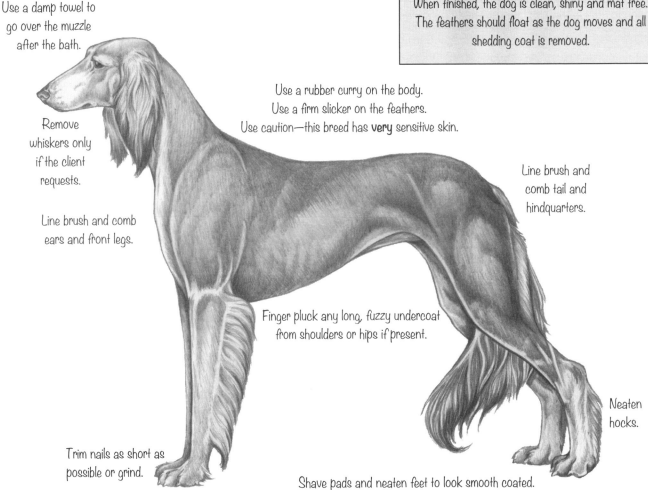

Use a damp towel to go over the muzzle after the bath.

Remove whiskers only if the client requests.

Line brush and comb ears and front legs.

Use a rubber curry on the body.
Use a firm slicker on the feathers.
Use caution—this breed has **very** sensitive skin.

Line brush and comb tail and hindquarters.

Finger pluck any long, fuzzy undercoat from shoulders or hips if present.

Neaten hocks.

Trim nails as short as possible or grind.

Shave pads and neaten feet to look smooth coated.

Grooming Procedures & Recommendations

See page 68 for
Bathing & Drying Instructions

Frequency
Bathe once a week to once every
12 weeks.

Pre-Work
Trim or grind nails every four to
six weeks to maintain a healthy foot
structure. Clean the ears by swabbing
with a mild ear cleaning solution. Use a
rubber curry, shedding blade, undercoat
rake, pumice stone, carding tool, fine
stripping knife or natural bristle brush
to loosen skin dander and remove loose
coat. Use a high-velocity dryer over
the coat to quickly and effectively lift
dirt and debris away from the skin and
loosen coat. Brush out or remove any
matting found in the long-coated areas.
If the tangles are loose enough so water
can fully penetrate the area, remove
them after bathing and drying. If water
cannot penetrate, remove the mat or
tangle prior to bathing.

Brushing
Line brush, working in sections until
the dog is entirely tangle-free and all
loose coat is removed. When finished,
there should be little, if any, fur still
being removed with a firm slicker brush.
Double-check the work with a comb
and your hands. Go over the entire
body, feeling for any inconsistencies in
the density levels of the coat. If an area
seems moist to the touch or fuller than
the rest of the coat, rework the area
with the appropriate tool. Mats, tangles
and excessive coat are easily trapped in
the following areas: behind the ears,
the thigh area, and the tail. Give extra
attention to these areas before finishing
the groom.

Carding
If a dog has an abundance of loose
undercoat, card the shorter areas with
a carding tool. Common tools can be
a fine stripping knife, undercoat rake,
a pumice stone, or a #40 blade held
between your fingers. Any carding tool
should be pulled over the body, working
in the direction of the coat growth. This
will remove the soft, downy undercoat,
allowing the guard coat to conform
more closely to the natural outline of
the body. It will also aid in the removal
of loose, shedding coat, a seasonal
problem for many pet owners.

Feet & Hocks
Trim the pads with a close blade ranging
from a #15 to a #40. Use a very light
touch to clean the pads of long hair. If
there is long fur between the toes, back
brush the fur so it stands up on top of
and away from the foot. With thinning
shears, trim the excess to create a neat
and very natural looking foot. Tidy the
outside edge of the foot, if needed, with
small detailing shears. If the hocks have
longer coat, trim lightly with thinning
shears to show a neat, clean area. A #4F
blade, used carefully in reverse, works
well for trimming the tops of the feet
and the hocks on some dogs.

Detail Finish
Edge the ears lightly with thinning
shears to neaten and keep a natural look.
Hand pluck any long wispy, flyaway
hair from around the ears. Removal of
whiskers on the muzzle is optional based
on client preference. Finish with a fine
mist of coat polish on the body coat for
added shine. Application of bows and
mild cologne is optional.

Suggested Tools & Equipment

- Nail Trimmers
- Styptic Powder
- Ear Cleaning Solution
- Cotton Balls
- Clippers
- #40 and #15 Blades for Pads
- #4F for Feet & Hocks (optional)
- Slicker Brush
- Greyhound Comb
- Rubber Curry
- Carding Tool
- De-Shedding Tools
- Small Detailing Shears
- Thinning Shears

Notes:

Notes From The Grooming Table ©2016

Scottish Deerhound

HOUNDS   **WIRE COATED**

HOUNDS

Breed Facts & Characteristics

Country of Origin: Europe

Height at Shoulder: 28"–32"

Coat Length/Type: Moderate/Wiry

Color: Deep blue/gray, blacks, tans, and brindles. Dark masks and ears are typical on the lighter colored dogs.

Correct grooming procedure:
Card & Hand-Strip

Common pet grooming practices:
Card & Hand-Strip

General Description

The entire dog is covered with a harsh wiry coat. The hair can be between 3 and 4 inches in length, slightly longer over the eyes and on the muzzle. The ears are normally smooth and free of long hair.

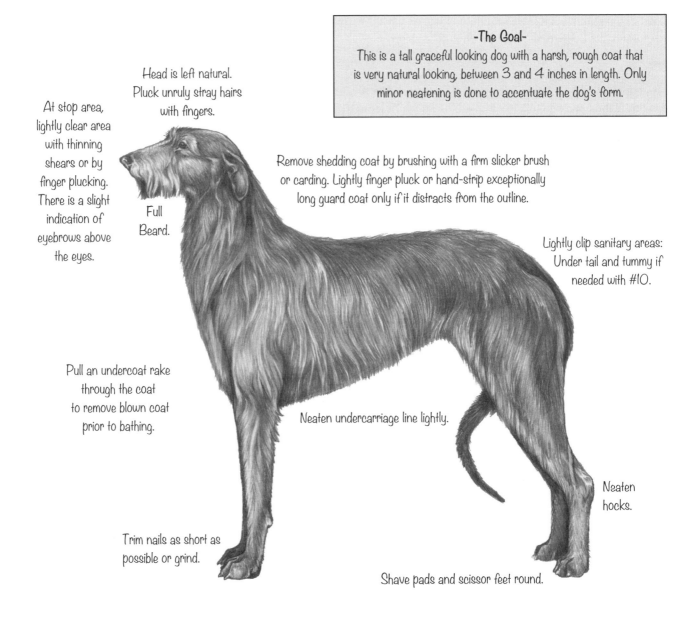

-The Goal-
This is a tall graceful looking dog with a harsh, rough coat that is very natural looking, between 3 and 4 inches in length. Only minor neatening is done to accentuate the dog's form.

Head is left natural. Pluck unruly stray hairs with fingers.

At stop area, lightly clear area with thinning shears or by finger plucking. There is a slight indication of eyebrows above the eyes.

Full Beard.

Remove shedding coat by brushing with a firm slicker brush or carding. Lightly finger pluck or hand-strip exceptionally long guard coat only if it distracts from the outline.

Lightly clip sanitary areas: Under tail and tummy if needed with #10.

Pull an undercoat rake through the coat to remove blown coat prior to bathing.

Neaten undercarriage line lightly.

Neaten hocks.

Trim nails as short as possible or grind.

Shave pads and scissor feet round.

See page 76 for Bathing & Drying Instructions

Frequency

Bathe once a week to once every 12 weeks.

Pre-Work

Trim or grind nails at least every four to six weeks to maintain a healthy foot structure. Swab the ears clean with a mild ear cleaning solution. Prior to bathing, quickly go over the entire body with a high-velocity dryer to help lift dirt and dander away from the skin and to loosen any shedding coat. ***Card and hand-strip dog prior to bathing and drying.***

Brushing

Use a rubber curry, shedding blade, undercoat rake, pumice stone, carding tool, fine stripping knife, slicker brush or natural bristled brush to remove any remaining loose coat or tangles. Be careful when using any tool with metal teeth or bristles. A heavy hand or too much repetition in an area can cause cuts and/or brush burns. Brushing is not finished until all loose fur is removed, or when it becomes difficult to remove more than a half a brush full after repeated brushing.

Carding

Carding is a natural technique in which the soft, downy undercoat is pulled from the dog's body. Typical tools used with this technique are: a pumice stone; a fine-toothed stripping knife that is pulled through the coat; an undercoat rake; or a fine blade, such as a #40, held between the fingers and pulled through the coat. Carding can be done before or after bathing and drying. Removal of the soft undercoat allows the topcoat to lie closer to the natural outline of the dog and accentuate the dog's structure. It also promotes profuse harsh outer coat, creates a rich coat color and protects the skin.

Hand-Stripping

Hand-stripping is a technique in which the outer guard coat is plucked from the dog's skin. This procedure helps retain the proper coat texture and rich color of the breed. During certain times of the year, the coat is easier to pull out. When the coat easily comes out, it is called a "blowing coat" or "blown coat." Ideally, hand-stripping should correspond with the dog's natural cycle, based on the environment and its hormonal levels. Using your fingers, a carding tool or a stripping knife, pull out a few hairs at a time to shape the coat, accentuating the natural outline of the dog. Work methodically, pulling small amounts of coat at a time, always working in the direction of the coat growth. Proper hand-stripping removes hair with a gentle momentum and rhythm, not brute force, which is uncomfortable for both groomer and pet. The wrist stays locked in a neutral position while the rhythmic movement stems from the shoulder, not the wrist or elbow. In general, the main body coat is easy to remove. Most pets do not mind the plucking process. The cheeks, throat and private areas may be more sensitive, requiring thinning shears or clippers. Leave enough coat to be between 3 to 4 inches long. The coat should always appear very natural, never clipped or heavily trimmed. On some coats, a light application of chalk or powder before the bath will allow a better grip and make plucking and stripping much easier.

Head

Leave the coat longer on the muzzle. Lightly hand-strip or pluck the top skull, throat and cheeks. Leave triangles of coat above each eye to form the moderate eyebrows that accentuate the eye area. Ears are stripped of longer hair. If the coat on the ear leather does not strip/pluck out easily, clipper with blades ranging from a #10 to a #15 on the outside of the ear leather. Clipper the inside of the ear using blades ranging from a #40 to a #10. Finish by edging the ear with detailing shears, keeping the tips of the shears toward the tip of the ear.

Feet & Hocks

Trim the pads with a close cutting blade ranging from a #15 to a #40. Use a very light touch to clean the pads of long hair. Tidy the outside edge of the foot, if needed, with small detailing shears. If the hocks have longer coat, trim lightly with thinning shears to show a neat, clean area.

Detail Finish

Application of bows and mild cologne is optional.

Special Note

Clipping a wired-coated dog will result in a dramatic change in the texture and color of the coat. The correct harsh wire coat needs to be encouraged by plucking the blown coat when it is ready to be removed. This process stimulates hair follicles to produce new guard coat. Without hand-stripping, the guard coat is not stimulated and will not grow in properly. It will lose its brilliant color and texture. If only the undercoat grows, the guard coat color becomes that of the lighter, soft undercoat.

Suggested Tools & Equipment

- Nail Trimmers
- Styptic Powder
- Ear Powder
- Ear Cleaning Solution
- Cotton Balls
- Hemostat
- Clippers
- Slicker Brush
- Greyhound Comb
- Pumice Stone
- Carding Tools
- Stripping Knives
- Straight Shears
- Curved Shears
- Small Detailing Shears
- Thinning Shears
- Dematting Tools

Common Blade Options:

- #40, #15, #10

HOUNDS

Breed Facts & Characteristics

Country of Origin: United States

Height at Shoulder: 20"–27"

Coat Length/Type: Short/Smooth

Color: Tri-colored in typical hound patterns of black, white and chestnut.

Correct grooming procedure:

Bathe & Curry Brush

Common pet grooming practices:

Bathe & Curry Brush

-The Goal-
The coat should be clean and fresh smelling, with the coat laying flat against the body. No shedding hair.

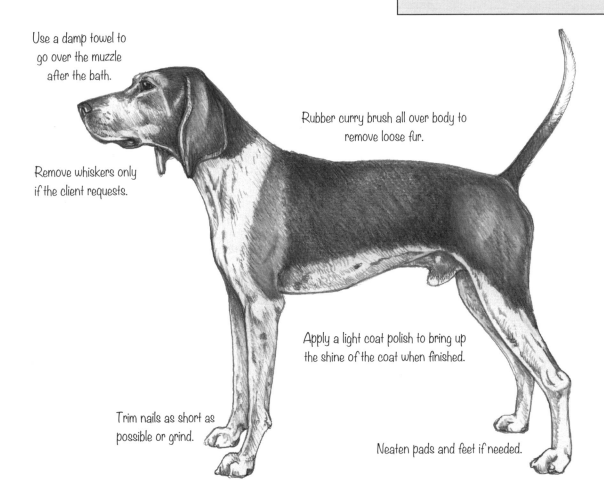

Use a damp towel to go over the muzzle after the bath.

Remove whiskers only if the client requests.

Rubber curry brush all over body to remove loose fur.

Apply a light coat polish to bring up the shine of the coat when finished.

Trim nails as short as possible or grind.

Neaten pads and feet if needed.

See page 67 for Bathing & Drying Instructions

Suggested Tools & Equipment

- Nail Trimmers
- Styptic Powder
- Ear Cleaning Solution
- Cotton Balls

- Clippers
- #40 or #15 Blade
- Rubber Curry
- Carding Tool

- Small Detailing Shears
- Thinning Shears

Breed Facts & Characteristics

Country of Origin: England

Height at Shoulder: 18"–22"

Coat Length/Type: Short/Smooth

Color: They come in a wide variety of colors.

Correct grooming procedure:
Bathe & Curry Brush

Common pet grooming practices:
Bathe & Curry Brush

-The Goal-
The coat should be clean and fresh smelling, with the coat laying flat against the body. No shedding hair.

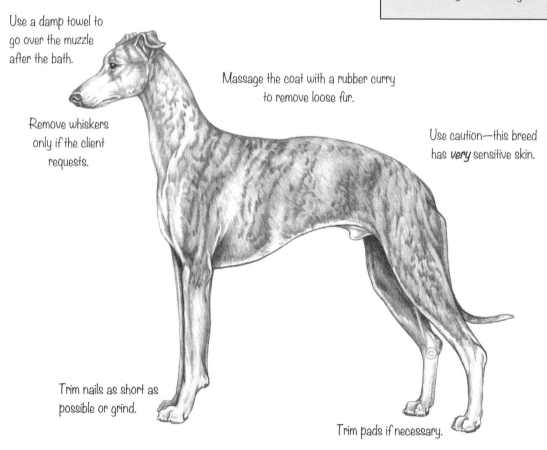

Use a damp towel to go over the muzzle after the bath.

Remove whiskers only if the client requests.

Massage the coat with a rubber curry to remove loose fur.

Use caution—this breed has **very** sensitive skin.

Trim nails as short as possible or grind.

Trim pads if necessary.

See page 66 for Bathing & Drying Instructions

Suggested Tools & Equipment

- Nail Trimmers
- Styptic Powder
- Ear Cleaning Solution
- Cotton Balls
- Clippers
- #40 or #15 Blade
- Rubber Curry
- Carding Tool
- Small Detailing Shears
- Thinning Shears

Notes From The Grooming Table ©2016

The Working Group

The Working Group was bred to work alongside humans to assist as guardians and to perform various tasks. Most are powerfully built and intelligent. Many breeds in this group are working farm and draft dogs. Others guard homes and livestock, serve courageously as police and military dogs, security dogs, or guide and service dogs.

Breed Facts & Characteristics

Country of Origin: Japan

Height at Shoulder: 24"–28"

Coat Length/Type: Double Coated/Harsh

Color: All colors including brindles and pintos. Colors should be clear, well balanced and bold. Dark masks and white blazes are allowed on all colors except white dogs.

Correct grooming procedure:
Bathe & Brush Out

Common pet grooming practices:
Bathe & Brush Out

-The Goal-
The coat should be harsh and stand off the dog. As the dog moves, the coat should bounce and shimmer with the dog. You should be able to sink a wide-toothed comb to the skin and pull it freely out to the end of the hair shaft.

~Seasonal Shedding~
In Colder Climates

When shedding—the more work you can do with a powerful high-velocity dryer, the less "elbow grease" you will have to apply.

Let a powerful high-velocity dryer help in all aspects of grooming this type of coat, before and after the bath. Blow out loose coat, tangles and dirt. Dry and fluff.

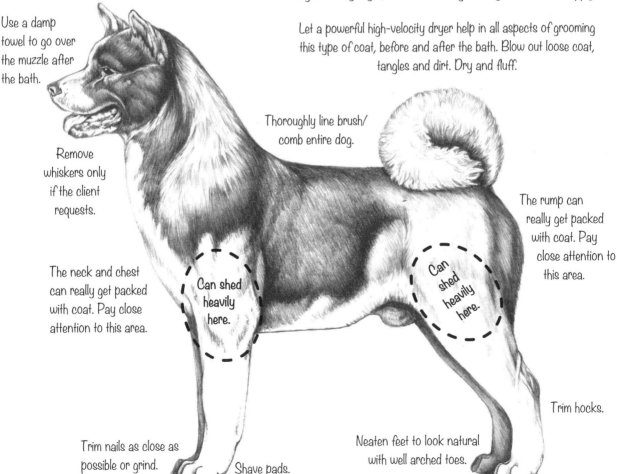

Edge ears with thinning shears to make very natural and neat.

Use a damp towel to go over the muzzle after the bath.

Remove whiskers only if the client requests.

The neck and chest can really get packed with coat. Pay close attention to this area.

Can shed heavily here.

Thoroughly line brush/comb entire dog.

Can shed heavily here.

The rump can really get packed with coat. Pay close attention to this area.

Trim nails as close as possible or grind.

Shave pads.

Neaten feet to look natural with well arched toes.

Trim hocks.

Grooming Procedures & Recommendations

See page 69 for
Bathing & Drying Instructions

Frequency
Bathe once a week to once every 12 weeks.

Pre-Work
Trim or grind nails at least every four to six weeks to maintain a healthy foot structure. Clean the ears by swabbing with a mild ear cleaning solution. Prior to bathing, quickly go over the entire body with a high-velocity dryer to help lift dirt and dander away from the skin and loosen any shedding coat.

Brushing
Use a slicker brush, rubber curry, shedding blade, dematting tool or undercoat rake to loosen skin dander and remove loose coat. Be careful when using any tool with metal teeth or bristles. A heavy hand or too much repetition in an area can cause cuts and/or brush burns. Brushing and combing is not finished until all loose fur is removed, or it has become difficult to remove more than a half a brush full after repeated brushing.

Sanitary Area
If the dog has a sanitation problem under the tail, lightly trim this area with thinning shears. Only clear enough coat to accomplish the goal and keep it looking very natural. Trimming of the groin area is not recommended unless there is a sanitary problem. If the groin needs to be trimmed, do so very lightly and try to leave the fur long enough so that the harsh coat does not prickle the skin, causing the dog to lick at the irritation.

Feet & Hocks
Trim the pads with a close cutting action blade, ranging from a #15 to a #40. Use a very light touch to clean the pads of long hair. If there is long fur between the toes, back brush the fur so it stands up and away from the foot. With thinning shears, trim off the excess creating a neat and very natural looking foot with well arched toes. Tidy the outside edge of the foot, if needed, with small detailing shears. If the hocks have longer coat on them, trim lightly with thinning shears showing a neat, clean area. A #4F blade used in reverse works well for trimming the tops of the feet and the hocks on some dogs.

Detail Finish
Removal of whiskers on the muzzle is optional, based on client preference. Finish with a fine mist of coat polish on the body for added shine. Application of bows and mild cologne is optional.

Grooming Tip
Let your hands guide you. Learn to feel for differences in coat density levels. Areas that feel heavier or more dense than other areas need special attention when bathing, brushing and drying.

Suggested Tools & Equipment

- Nail Trimmers
- Styptic Powder
- Ear Cleaning Solution
- Cotton Balls
- Clippers
- #40 and #15 Blades for Pads
- #4F for Feet & Hocks (optional)
- Slicker Brush
- Greyhound Comb
- Rubber Curry
- Carding Tool
- De-Shedding Tools
- Small Detailing Shears
- Thinning Shears
- High-Velocity Dryer

Notes:

Notes From The Grooming Table ©2016

Alaskan Malamute

Breed Facts & Characteristics

Country of Origin: United States

Height at Shoulder: 23"–25"

Coat Length/Type: Double Coated/Harsh

Color: The undercoat color is always white. The guard hair can be varying shades of black, red, tan or sable. One of these colors shines through the undercoat and accentuates key points on the dog.

Correct grooming procedure:

Bathe & Brush Out

Common pet grooming practices:

Bathe & Brush Out

> **-The Goal-**
> The coat should be harsh and stand off the dog. As the dog moves, the coat should bounce and shimmer with the dog. You should be able to sink a wide-toothed comb to the skin and pull it freely out to the end of the hair shaft.

~Seasonal Shedding~
In Colder Climates

When shedding—the more work you can do with a powerful high-velocity dryer, the less "elbow grease" you will have to apply.

Let a powerful high-velocity dryer help in all aspects of grooming this type of coat, before and after the bath. Blow out loose coat, tangles and dirt. Dry and fluff.

Edge ears with thinning shears to make very natural and neat.

Use a damp towel to go over the muzzle after the bath.

Remove whiskers only if the client requests.

The neck and chest can really get packed with coat. Pay close attention to this area.

Thoroughly line brush/comb entire dog.

The rump can really get packed with coat. Pay close attention to this area.

Can shed heavily here.

Can shed heavily here.

Neaten the back of the pattern to the stopper pad.

Trim nails as close as possible or grind.

Shave pads.

Neaten feet to look natural with well arched toes.

Trim hocks.

**See page 69 for
Bathing & Drying Instructions**

Frequency
Bathe once a week to once every 12 weeks.

Pre-Work
Trim or grind nails at least every four to six weeks to maintain a healthy foot structure. Clean the ears by swabbing with a mild ear cleaning solution. Prior to bathing, quickly go over the entire body with a high-velocity dryer to help lift dirt and dander away from the skin and loosen any shedding coat.

Brushing
Use a slicker brush, rubber curry, shedding blade, dematting tool or undercoat rake to loosen skin dander and remove loose coat. Be careful when using any tool with metal teeth or bristles. A heavy hand or too much repetition in an area can cause cuts and/or brush burns. Brushing and combing is not finished until all loose fur is removed, or it has become difficult to remove more than a half a brush full after repeated brushing.

Sanitary Area
If the dog has a sanitation problem under the tail, lightly trim this area with thinning shears. Only clear enough coat to accomplish the goal and keep it looking very natural. Trimming of the groin area is not recommended unless there is a sanitary problem. If the groin needs to be trimmed, do so very lightly and try to leave the fur long enough so that the harsh coat does not prickle the skin, causing the dog to lick at the irritation.

Feet & Hocks
Trim the pads with a close cutting action blade, ranging from a #15 to a #40. Use a very light touch to clean the pads of long hair. If there is long fur between the toes, back brush the fur so it stands up and away from the foot. With thinning shears, trim off the excess creating a neat and very natural looking foot with well arched toes. Tidy the outside edge of the foot, if needed, with small detailing shears. If the hocks have longer coat on them, trim lightly with thinning shears showing a neat, clean area. A #4F blade used in reverse works well for trimming the tops of the feet and the hocks on some dogs.

Detail Finish
Removal of whiskers on the muzzle is optional, based on client preference. Finish with a fine mist of coat polish on the body for added shine. Application of bows and mild cologne is optional.

Grooming Tip
Let your hands guide you. Learn to feel for differences in coat density levels. Areas that feel heavier or more dense than other areas need special attention when bathing, brushing and drying.

Suggested Tools & Equipment

- Nail Trimmers
- Styptic Powder
- Ear Cleaning Solution
- Cotton Balls
- Clippers
- #40 and #15 Blades for Pads
- #4F for Feet & Hocks (optional)
- Slicker Brush
- Greyhound Comb
- Rubber Curry
- Carding Tool
- De-Shedding Tools
- Small Detailing Shears
- Thinning Shears
- High-Velocity Dryer

Notes:

Notes From The Grooming Table ©2016

Anatolian Shepherd Dog   WORKING   DOUBLE COATED

Breed Facts & Characteristics

Country of Origin: Turkey

Height at Shoulder: 27"–29"

Coat Length/Type: Double Coated/Harsh

Color: All color patterns are accepted, but fawn with black masks and black points is commonly seen

Correct grooming procedure:
Bathe & Brush Out

Common pet grooming practices:
Bathe & Brush Out

-The Goal-
The coat should be fresh smelling, shiny and full of body. No loose or shedding hair.

~Seasonal Shedding~
In Colder Climates

When shedding—the more work you can do with a powerful high-velocity dryer, the less "elbow grease" you will have to apply.

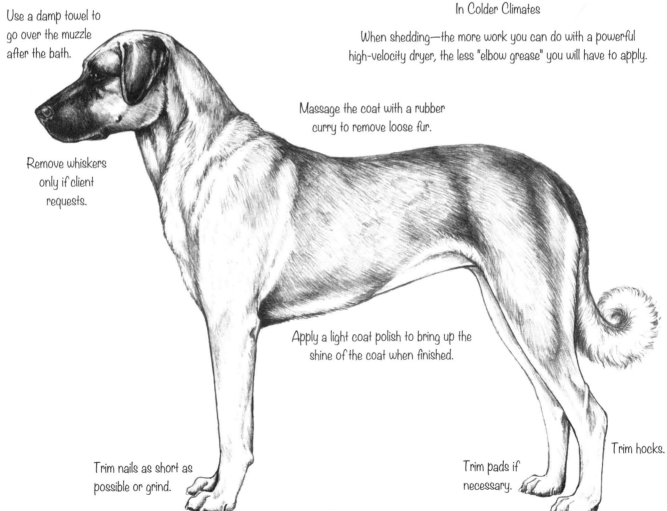

Use a damp towel to go over the muzzle after the bath.

Remove whiskers only if client requests.

Massage the coat with a rubber curry to remove loose fur.

Apply a light coat polish to bring up the shine of the coat when finished.

Trim nails as short as possible or grind.

Trim pads if necessary.

Trim hocks.

Grooming Procedures & Recommendations

See page 69 for Bathing & Drying Instructions

Frequency
Bathe once a week to once every 12 weeks.

Pre-Work
Trim or grind nails at least every four to six weeks to maintain a healthy foot structure. Clean the ears by swabbing with a mild ear cleaning solution. Prior to bathing, quickly go over the entire body with a high-velocity dryer to help lift dirt and dander away from the skin and loosen any shedding coat.

Brushing
Use a slicker brush, rubber curry, shedding blade, dematting tool or undercoat rake to loosen skin dander and remove loose coat. Be careful when using any tool with metal teeth or bristles. A heavy hand or too much repetition in an area can cause cuts and/or brush burns. Brushing and combing is not finished until all loose fur is removed, or it has become difficult to remove more than a half a brush full after repeated brushing.

Sanitary Area
If the dog has a sanitation problem under the tail, lightly trim this area with thinning shears. Only clear enough coat to accomplish the goal and keep it looking very natural. Trimming of the groin area is not recommended unless there is a sanitary problem. If the groin needs to be trimmed, do so very lightly and try to leave the fur long enough so that the harsh coat does not prickle the skin, causing the dog to lick at the irritation.

Feet & Hocks
Trim the pads with a close cutting action blade, ranging from a #15 to a #40. Use a very light touch to clean the pads of long hair. If there is long fur between the toes, back brush the fur so it stands up and away from the foot. With thinning shears, trim off the excess creating a neat and very natural looking foot with well arched toes. Tidy the outside edge of the foot, if needed, with small detailing shears. If the hocks have longer coat on them, trim lightly with thinning shears showing a neat, clean area. A #4F blade used in reverse works well for trimming the tops of the feet and the hocks on some dogs.

Detail Finish
Removal of whiskers on the muzzle is optional, based on client preference. Finish with a fine mist of coat polish on the body for added shine. Application of bows and mild cologne is optional.

Grooming Tip
Let your hands guide you. Learn to feel for differences in coat density levels. Areas that feel heavier or more dense than other areas need special attention when bathing, brushing and drying.

Suggested Tools & Equipment

- Nail Trimmers
- Styptic Powder
- Ear Cleaning Solution
- Cotton Balls
- Clippers
- #40 and #15 Blades for Pads
- #4F for Feet & Hocks (optional)
- Slicker Brush
- Greyhound Comb
- Rubber Curry
- Carding Tool
- De-shedding Tool
- Small Detailing Shears
- Thinning Shears
- High-Velocity Dryer

Notes:

Bernese Mountain Dog WORKING   HEAVY COATED

Breed Facts & Characteristics

Country of Origin: Switzerland

Height at Shoulder: 23"–27½"

Coat Length/Type: Combination/Heavy

Color: Deep, rich tricolors in black, chestnut and white.

Correct grooming procedure:
Bathe & Brush Out

Common pet grooming practices:
Bathe & Brush Out

-The Goal-
The coat should be shiny, light and airy. As the dog moves, the coat should bounce and float with the dog.

Hand pluck any soft, downy fuzz that may be on the top of the head.

Use a damp towel to go over the muzzle after the bath.

Let a powerful high-velocity dryer help in all aspects of grooming this type of coat, before and after the bath. Blow out loose coat, tangles and dirt. Dry and fluff.

Thoroughly line brush/comb entire dog.

Remove whiskers only if the client requests.

The rump can really get packed with coat. Pay close attention to this area.

The neck and chest can really get packed with coat. Pay close attention to this area.

Tail should reach to the hocks.

Neaten feet to look natural with well arched toes.

Trim hocks.

Trim nails as short as possible or grind.

Shave pads.

See page 70 for
Bathing & Drying Instructions

Frequency
Bathe once a week to once every 12 weeks.

Pre-Work
Trim or grind nails at least every four to six weeks to maintain a healthy foot structure. Clean the ears by swabbing with a mild ear cleaning solution. Use a rubber curry, shedding blade, undercoat rake, pumice stone, carding tool, fine stripping knife or natural bristled brush to loosen skin dander and remove loose coat. Quickly blowing out the dog with a high-velocity dryer can effectively lift dirt and debris away from the skin and loosen coat. Brush out or remove any matting found in the longer coated areas. If the tangles are loose enough so water can fully penetrate the area, remove after the bathing and drying stages. If water cannot penetrate, remove the mat or tangle prior to bathing.

Brushing
Line brush, working in sections until the dog is entirely tangle-free. When finished, there should be little, if any, fur still being removed with a firm slicker brush. Double-check the work with a wide-toothed comb and your hands. Go over the entire body, feeling for any inconsistencies in the density levels of the coat. If an area seems moist to the touch or fuller than the rest of the coat, rework the area with the appropriate tool. Mats, tangles and excessive coat are easily trapped in the following areas: behind the ears, around the ruff, the thigh area, the undercarriage and the tail. Give extra attention to these areas before finishing the groom.

Sanitary Area
If the dog has a sanitation problem under the tail, lightly trim this area with thinning shears. Only clear enough coat to accomplish the goal and keep it looking very natural. Trimming of the groin area is not recommended unless there is a sanitary problem. If the groin needs to be trimmed, do so very lightly and try to leave the fur long enough so that the harsh coat does not prickle the skin, causing the dog to lick at the irritation.

Feet & Hocks
Trim the pads with a close cutting action blade ranging from a #15 to a #40. Use a very light touch to clean the pads of long hair. If there is long fur between the toes, back brush the fur so it stands up and away from the foot. With thinning shears, trim off the excess creating a neat and very natural looking foot with well arched toes. Tidy the outside edge of the foot, if needed, with small detailing shears. If the hocks have longer coat, trim lightly with thinning shears showing a neat, clean area. A #4F blade used in reverse works well for trimming the tops of the feet and the hocks on some dogs.

Detail Finish
Edge the ears lightly with thinning shears to neaten but look natural. Hand-pluck any long wispy, flyaway hair from around the ears. Removal of whiskers on the muzzle is optional based on client preference. Finish with a fine mist of coat polish on the body coat for added shine. Application of bows and mild cologne are optional.

Grooming Tip
Let your hands guide you. Learn to feel for differences in coat density levels. Areas that feel heavier or denser than other areas need special attention when bathing, brushing and drying.

Suggested Tools & Equipment

- Nail Trimmers
- Styptic Powder
- Ear Cleaning Solution
- Cotton Balls
- Clippers
- #40 and #15 Blades for Pads
- #4F for Feet & Hocks (optional)
- Slicker Brush
- Wide-Toothed Comb
- Rubber Curry
- Undercoat Rake
- Dematting Tools
- High-Velocity Dryer
- Small Detailing Shears
- Curved Shears
- Thinning Shears

Notes:

Black Russian Terrier

Breed Facts & Characteristics

Country of Origin: Russia

Height at Shoulder: 26"–30"

Coat Length/Type: Longer/Wavy

Color: Black

Correct grooming procedure:
Card/Clip/Scissor

Common pet grooming practices:
Card/Clip/Scissor

General Description

The Black Russian Terrier is very powerful with great courage and endurance. Everything about this breed is immense. Their outline is almost square with a massive head that is in proportion to the size of the body and approximately the same length as the neck. The chest reaches to the elbows. Withers are high yet the back is level. The tail may be natural or docked. The coat is "tousled" with a combination of harsh guard coat and soft undercoat. It is trimmed and styled to 1–4 inches in length over much of the body and legs. The head is blocky with flat top skull and an untrimmed veil of hair covering the eyes and muzzle. The ears are natural and triangular in shape..

-The Goal-
This breed is large and powerful. It is slightly longer than tall. The "tousled" double coat should be a combination of harsh and soft textures. The coat should be clean and mat-free. Head is full and rectangular with a heavy fall over the eyes.

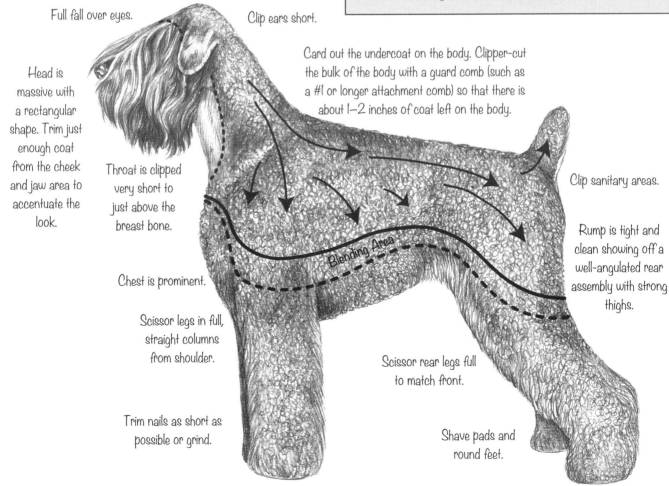

Trim a square right at the center of the skull to start the rectangular shape of the head with a #10 or #7 blade.

Full fall over eyes.

Clip ears short.

Card out the undercoat on the body. Clipper-cut the bulk of the body with a guard comb (such as a #1 or longer attachment comb) so that there is about 1–2 inches of coat left on the body.

Head is massive with a rectangular shape. Trim just enough coat from the cheek and jaw area to accentuate the look.

Throat is clipped very short to just above the breast bone.

Clip sanitary areas.

Rump is tight and clean showing off a well-angulated rear assembly with strong thighs.

Blending Area

Chest is prominent.

Scissor legs in full, straight columns from shoulder.

Scissor rear legs full to match front.

Trim nails as short as possible or grind.

Shave pads and round feet.

Grooming Procedures & Recommendations

See page 74 for
Bathing & Drying Instructions

Frequency
Bathe once a week to once every
12 weeks.

Pre-Work
Trim or grind nails at least every four
to six weeks to maintain a healthy foot
structure. Clean the ears by swabbing
with a mild ear cleaning solution. Hair
should be plucked from within the
ear canal only as necessary for healthy
ear management. Prior to bathing,
quickly go over the entire body with
an undercoat rake and remove any
serious mats or tangles. If the tangle
can be penetrated with water, leave it
and remove when the dog is clean. If
the pet has not been in for professional
grooming for six weeks or more,
remove the excessive body coat and
set the pattern before bathing. Before
starting the final haircut, make sure
the dog's coat is throughly brushed out
and tangle free.

General Pattern Lines
The pattern is based on the bone and
muscle structure of the dog. After the
final trim, all pattern lines are to be
invisible. The longer the blade choice
for the body, the easier it is to blend
the pattern into the longer furnishings
of the legs and undercarriage. At the
transition points, feather off with the
clippers in a smooth, steady fashion.
If the pattern line is still visible after
clipping, use thinning shears to blend
the line. On the head, the pattern lines
are crisp and clean.

Body
The breed standard states the body coat
will vary from 1½ to 4 inches in length
on the body. Many pet owners choose a
shorter trim for manageability. Typical
blades used in pet grooming range from

a #4F to a long guard comb attachment
blade used over a close-cutting blade, or
a combination of blades that make up
the bulk of the body work. The pattern
lines start at the turn of the shoulder to
just above the elbow. From that point,
blend off just under the turn of ribs
back to the flank on a diagonal and
then drop into the thigh region.

Throat
Blades ranging from #10 to #7F,
with or against the grain, based on
the sensitivity of the dog's skin, are
common in the throat area. Follow the
natural cowlick line that runs in a "V"
shape from the base of the ears towards
the base of the neck. Clip only the
throat—do not clip into the cheeks.

Chest
The chest blends off from the throat
and neck area working with the same
length as used on the bulk of the body.
The blending point begins about three
or four fingers above the breast bone
blending into a pronounced forechest.

Front Legs
The longest coat on the legs can range
from 1½ to 4 inches depending on
the amount of bone and coat density.
The front legs drop straight down
from the body and have ample bone
and muscle to show off an extremely
powerful and sturdy animal. The
pattern line beginning at the shoulder
is about three or four fingers above the
top of the elbow, at the point where
the muscle begins to turn under.
The coat at the transition line will be
shorter, and taper into the longer leg
furnishings. This is accomplished by
feathering off at the blending point
with the same blade used on the body.
To do this effectively, you need a
steady hand and a dog that stands still.
Most stylists prefer to shape the legs
by hand, with shears ranging from 8.5
inches to 10 inches in length. Other

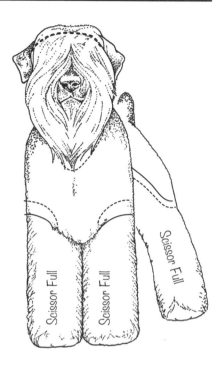

On the head, the fall is full and natural without
any trimming. The throat line is crisp and clean.
At transition points on the body, blend the lines
so they are invisible. Legs should be left fuller
and fall into straight columns, from the body to
the feet, on both the front and rear legs. The
chest is full, rounded in shape.

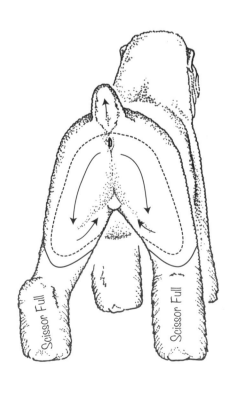

The fall is created by leaving all the coat covering the eyes. Use the eye socket ridge as your guide for the start of the fall. This will create a full fall of hair over the eyes and stop area. Do NOT split the brows nor trim the outer edges of the fall near the eyes.

The head is well balanced to the body of the dog and should give the impression or power and strength.

Clip ears very close with a #10 or #15 on the outside and as close as a #40 on the inside, used with a very light touch. Edge ears with small detailing shears to finish.

Leave fall natural.

The beard and mustache are left full and natural to highlight the impressive scale of the head piece.

Trim the jowl area on and angle to accentuate a rectangular head.

The throat is clipped very close with a #10 or #15 in reverse. Start just under the ear bulb, trimming in a "U" shape to 2 to 3 fingers above the breast bone.

Slightly longer coat is left on the back of the neck to create a "mane" down to the withers.

The top of the skull is flat. Accentuate this by clipping a square shape just behind the eyes with a #7F or a #5F, creating "platform." Blend the short coat into the longer coat on the top of the head at the outer edges of the box so the lines are invisible but leave the fall area long and natural.

methods of blending off at the top of the leg include using one of the giant attachment combs, followed by hand-scissoring and thinning shears. When the trim is complete, the legs form two parallel columns dropping from the elbow into round feet. The coat at the back of the elbow is very short and falls straight down off the back of the leg toward the ground.

Hindquarters
The hindquarters should be strong and powerful. To accentuate a well angulated rear on the very back side of the rear legs, trim the back of the thighs with a close blade ranging from a #10 to a #7F blade length. When clipping over the hips and outer thighs, use the same blade that

was used on the body. Feather off at the top of the thigh muscle, blending the coat naturally into the longer leg furnishings. The pattern line starts to turn diagonally from the flank region to about the halfway point between the tail and the hock. The blending should be invisible when the trim is finished. Blend with thinning shears if necessary. The stifle area should have enough furnishing left to give the legs substance and angulation. The longest coat on the legs can range from 1½ to 4 inches depending on the amount of bone and the coat density. Shape this area by hand with shears and thinners after the clipper work is complete. When viewed from the rear, the legs should form two parallel lines to the

ground. The hocks are well let down. There should be adequate coat on the hock area to accentuate the angles of the rear assembly.

Feet
Both the front and rear feet are compact with well arched toes. To emphasize this, the feet are trimmed very close to the edge of the foot and some nail is routinely exposed. The feet should point straight ahead, toeing neither in nor out. Trim the feet round by first boxing them in the shape of a square, while the dog is standing in a natural, square position. With the dog's feet firmly planted on the table, remove the square corners of the box and round the feet facing straight forward, beveling the coat into

the longer leg fur. If detailing the feet with the foot off the tabletop, always use a small pair of detailing shears to minimize the risk of accidentally cutting the pads. If a very close cutting blade is used to trim the pads, use a firm slicker brush to brush the longer leg coat over the outer edges of the pad and trim that hair at the same time the pads are clipped clean.

Undercarriage
The groin is normally trimmed close with a #10 or #15 blade to a point near the navel. From this point forward toward the brisket, the coat is longer, creating the illusion of depth of chest. There is not a lot of coat remaining in the finished trim. Most Black Russians have a well-developed chest and only a small amount of coat is needed to create the proper look for this area. Trim with shears or thinning shears depending on the amount of coat so that the coat does not fall below the line of the elbow.

Tail
The top of the tail is trimmed with the same blade as the body. The underside of the tail is clipped close, with blades ranging from #15 to a #7F, used with or against the grain, based on the dog's skin sensitivity. Continue with the same blade around the rectum. If the dog has a long tail, shape the coat to about 1½ to 3 inches long so that it balances with the rest of the dog and blends with the body coat.

The Head in General
The head is rectangular and well balanced to the body of the dog. It should give the impression of power and great strength.

Ears
Ears are clipped with a close blade. It is common to see a #10 or #15 blade used on the outside of the ear leather while a #40 blade is used on the inside. When working with close blades in this delicate area, always work from the base or center of the ear out toward the edge. Gently brace the ear with your fingers to clip over it. To finish, use small finishing shears to trim around the outside edge of the ear leather, keeping the tips of the shears toward the tip of the ears.

Top Skull
The top of the skull is flat. To accentuate this, clip a square shape on the top of the head starting just behind the eyes with a #10 or #15 blade creating a platform. Carefully blend this short area into the longer areas near the fall, into the ears and over the occiput area.

Fall
The coat over and between the eyes is left long and full to create a fall. It is left long and natural, fully covering the eyes.

Cheeks
The cheeks are tapered into the long and natural beard and fall area. Use a medium to longer guard comb to blend this area or use shears or thinning shears to enhance the massive rectangular head.

Beard
The coat on the entire muzzle, including the jaw area, is left full and natural. This gives the head a substantial rectangular appearance, highlighting the impressive scale of the headpiece.

Detail Finish
Remove any scissor marks or clipper tracks with thinning shears. Application of mild cologne and collar bows is optional.

Suggested Tools & Equipment
- Nail Trimmers
- Styptic Powder
- Ear Powder
- Ear Cleaning Solution
- Cotton Balls
- Hemostat
- Clippers
- Slicker Brush
- Greyhound Comb
- Pumice Stone
- Carding Tools
- Stripping Knives
- Straight Shears
- Curved Shears
- Small Detailing Shears
- Thinning Shears
- Dematting Tools

Common Blade Options:
- #40, #15, #10
- #7F
- Variety of Guard Combs

Notes:

Boerboel

Breed Facts & Characteristics

Country of Origin: Africa

Height at Shoulder: 22"–27"

Coat Length/Type: Short/Smooth

Color: All shades of tans, browns and brindles—with or without a dark mask. Limited amount of clear white on their chest and feet is acceptable.

Correct grooming procedure:
Bathe & Curry Brush

Common pet grooming practices:
Bathe & Curry Brush

~ The Goal~
The coat should be clean and fresh smelling, with the coat laying flat against the body. No shedding hair.

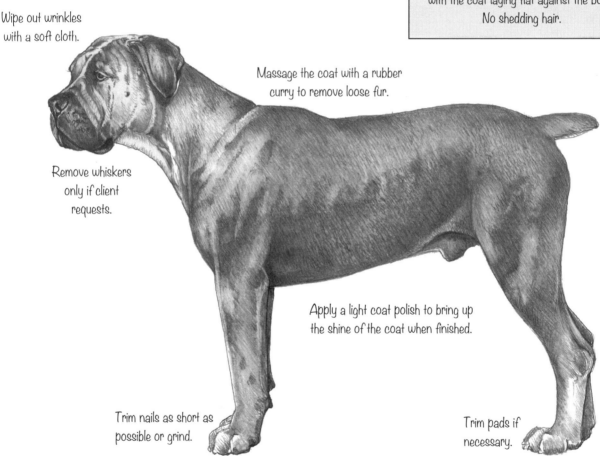

Wipe out wrinkles with a soft cloth.

Massage the coat with a rubber curry to remove loose fur.

Remove whiskers only if client requests.

Apply a light coat polish to bring up the shine of the coat when finished.

Trim nails as short as possible or grind.

Trim pads if necessary.

See page 67 for Bathing & Drying Instructions

Suggested Tools & Equipment

- Nail Trimmers
- Styptic Powder
- Ear Cleaning Solution
- Cotton Balls
- Clippers
- #40 or #15 Blade
- Rubber Curry
- Carding Tool
- Small Detailing Shears
- Thinning Shears

Boxer

WORKING SMOOTH COATED

Breed Facts & Characteristics

Country of Origin: Germany

Height at Shoulder: 21.5"–25"

Coat Length/Type: Short/Smooth

Color: Tan and brindled with a limited amount of white and a black mask about the face.

Correct grooming procedure:
Bathe & Curry Brush

Common pet grooming practices:
Bathe & Curry Brush

~ The Goal~
The coat should be clean and fresh smelling, with the coat laying flat against the body. No shedding hair.

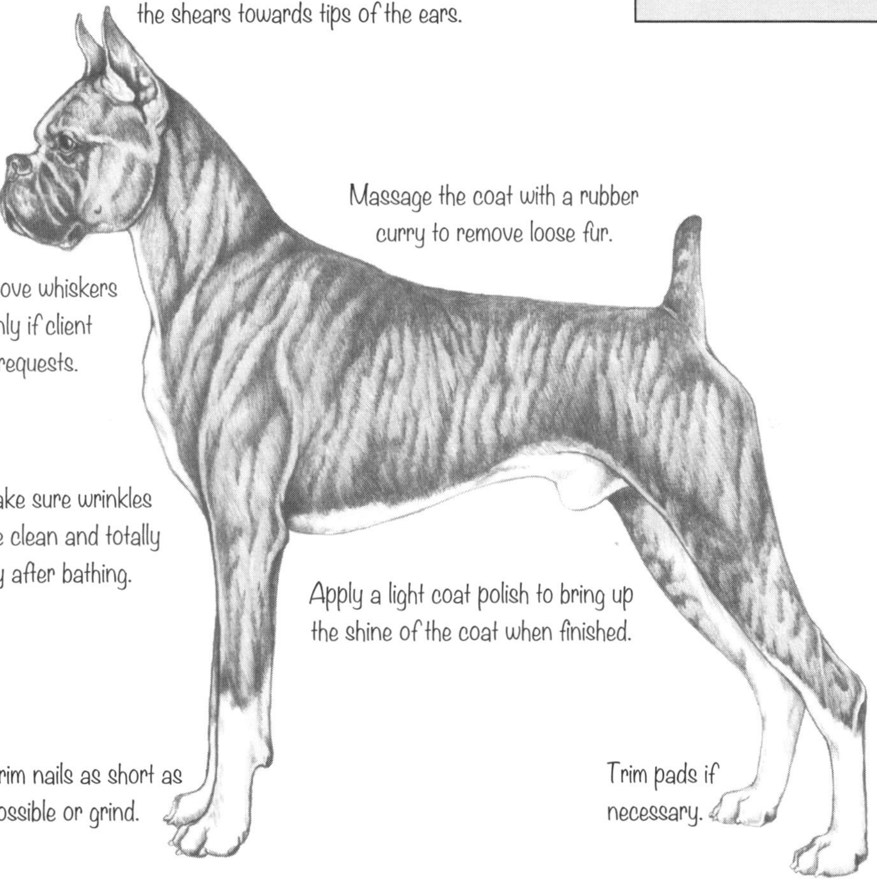

Clip inside of ear with blades ranging from a #15 to #40. Edge ears with small shears. Keep the tips of the shears towards tips of the ears.
Massage the coat with a rubber curry to remove loose fur.
Remove whiskers only if client requests.
Make sure wrinkles are clean and totally dry after bathing.
Apply a light coat polish to bring up the shine of the coat when finished.
Trim nails as short as possible or grind.
Trim pads if necessary.

See page 66 for Bathing & Drying Instructions

Suggested Tools & Equipment

- Nail Trimmers
- Styptic Powder
- Ear Cleaning Solution
- Cotton Balls
- Clippers
- #40 or #15 Blade
- Slicker Brush
- Rubber Curry
- Carding Tool
- De-Shedding Tools
- Small Detailing Shears
- Thinning Shears

Bullmastiff

Breed Facts & Characteristics

Country of Origin: England

Height at Shoulder: 24"–27"

Coat Length/Type: Short/Smooth

Color: Tan, red and brindled. A black mask about the face is common.

Correct grooming procedure:
Bathe & Curry Brush

Common pet grooming practices:
Bathe & Curry Brush

-The Goal-
The coat should be clean and fresh smelling, with the coat laying flat against the body. No shedding hair.

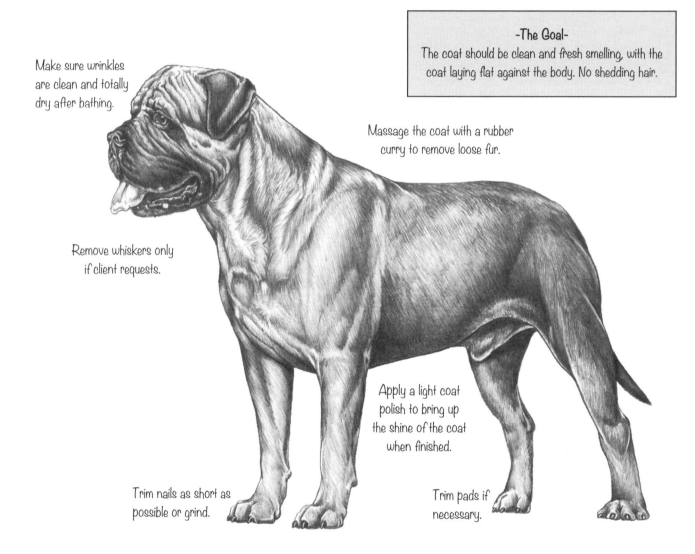

Make sure wrinkles are clean and totally dry after bathing.

Massage the coat with a rubber curry to remove loose fur.

Remove whiskers only if client requests.

Apply a light coat polish to bring up the shine of the coat when finished.

Trim nails as short as possible or grind.

Trim pads if necessary.

See page 67 for Bathing & Drying Instructions

Suggested Tools & Equipment

- Nail Trimmers
- Styptic Powder
- Ear Cleaning Solution
- Cotton Balls
- Clippers
- #40 or #15 Blade
- Rubber Curry
- Carding Tool
- Small Detailing Shears
- Thinning Shears

WORKING

Breed Facts & Characteristics

Country of Origin: Italy

Height at Shoulder: 23½"–27½"

Coat Length/Type: Short/Smooth

Color: Shades of tan or gray, red, black or brindle. Tan and red dogs have a black or gray mask. Limited amount of white on chest, throat, pasterns and toes.

Correct grooming procedure:
Bathe & Curry Brush

Common pet grooming practices:
Bathe & Curry Brush

-The Goal-
The coat should be clean and fresh smelling, with the coat laying flat against the body. No shedding hair.

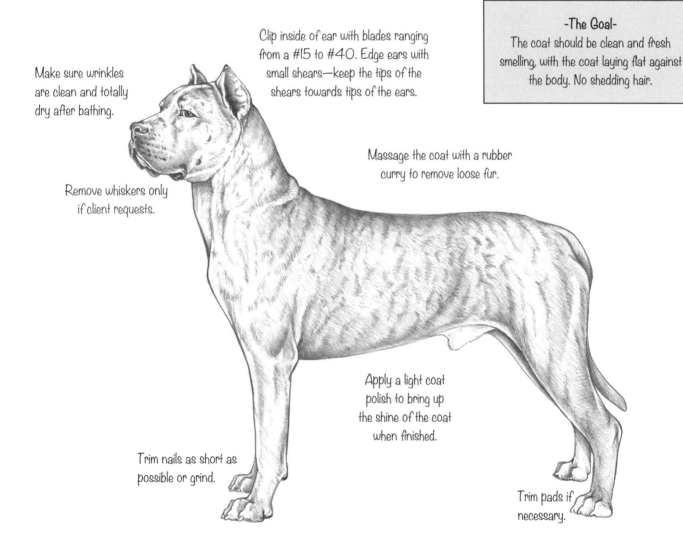

Make sure wrinkles are clean and totally dry after bathing.

Clip inside of ear with blades ranging from a #15 to #40. Edge ears with small shears—keep the tips of the shears towards tips of the ears.

Massage the coat with a rubber curry to remove loose fur.

Remove whiskers only if client requests.

Apply a light coat polish to bring up the shine of the coat when finished.

Trim nails as short as possible or grind.

Trim pads if necessary.

See page 66 for Bathing & Drying Instructions	Suggested Tools & Equipment	
• Nail Trimmers • Styptic Powder • Ear Cleaning Solution • Cotton Balls	• Clippers • #40 or #15 Blade • Slicker Brush • Rubber Curry	• Carding Tool • De-Shedding Tools • Small Detailing Shears • Thinning Shears

Notes From The Grooming Table ©2016

Chinook

Breed Facts & Characteristics

Country of Origin: United States

Height at Shoulder: 22"–26"

Coat Length/Type: Double Coated

Color: Tan to reddish gold with or without dark muzzle and ears. Symmetrical lighter color is acceptable on the sides of the cheeks, throat, chest, and undersides.

Correct grooming procedure:
Bathe & Brush Out

Common pet grooming practices:
Bathe & Brush Out

-The Goal-
The coat should light and stand off the dog. The coat should bounce and shimmer with the dog it moves.

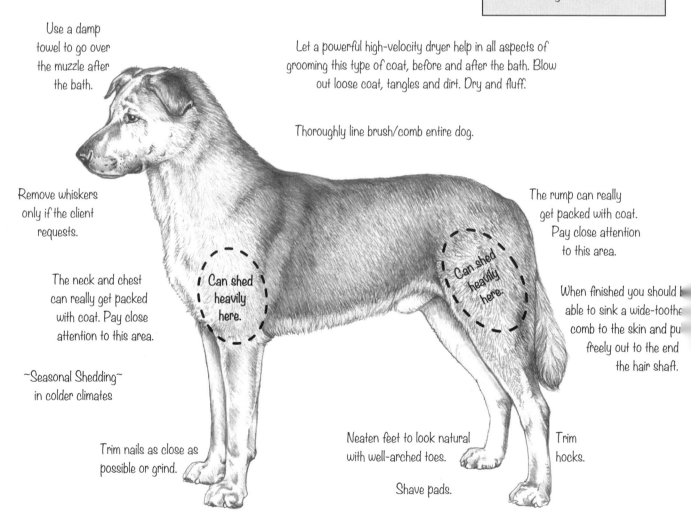

Use a damp towel to go over the muzzle after the bath.

Let a powerful high-velocity dryer help in all aspects of grooming this type of coat, before and after the bath. Blow out loose coat, tangles and dirt. Dry and fluff.

Thoroughly line brush/comb entire dog.

Remove whiskers only if the client requests.

The rump can really get packed with coat. Pay close attention to this area.

The neck and chest can really get packed with coat. Pay close attention to this area.

Can shed heavily here.

Can shed heavily here.

When finished you should be able to sink a wide-toothed comb to the skin and pull freely out to the end the hair shaft.

~Seasonal Shedding~ in colder climates

Trim nails as close as possible or grind.

Neaten feet to look natural with well-arched toes.

Trim hocks.

Shave pads.

When shedding—the more work you can do with a powerful high velocity dryer, the less "elbow grease" you will have to exert.

Notes From The Grooming Table ©2016   232

Grooming Procedures & Recommendations

See page 69 for
Bathing & Drying Instructions

Frequency
Bathe once a week to once every 12 weeks.

Pre-Work
Trim or grind nails at least every four to six weeks to maintain a healthy foot structure. Clean the ears by swabbing with a mild ear cleaning solution. Prior to bathing, quickly go over the entire body with a high-velocity dryer to help lift dirt and dander away from the skin and loosen any shedding coat.

Brushing
Use a slicker brush, rubber curry, shedding blade, dematting tool or undercoat rake to loosen skin dander and remove loose coat. Be careful when using any tool with metal teeth or bristles. A heavy hand or too much repetition in an area can cause cuts and/or brush burns. Brushing and combing is not finished until all loose fur is removed, or it has become difficult to remove more than a half a brush full after repeated brushing.

Feet & Hocks
Trim the pads with a close cutting action blade, ranging from a #15 to a #40. Use a very light touch to clean the pads of long hair. If there is long fur between the toes, back brush the fur so it stands up and away from the foot. With thinning shears, trim off the excess creating a neat and very natural looking foot with well arched toes. Tidy the outside edge of the foot, if needed, with small detailing shears. If the hocks have longer coat on them, trim lightly with thinning shears showing a neat, clean area. A #4F blade used in reverse works well for trimming the tops of the feet and the hocks on some dogs.

Detail Finish
Removal of whiskers on the muzzle is optional, based on client preference. Finish with a fine mist of coat polish on the body for added shine. Application of bows and mild cologne is optional.

Grooming Tip
Let your hands guide you. Learn to feel for differences in coat density levels. Areas that feel heavier or denser than other areas need special attention when bathing, brushing and drying.

Suggested Tools & Equipment

- Nail Trimmers
- Styptic Powder
- Ear Cleaning Solution
- Cotton Balls
- Clippers
- #40 and #15 Blades for Pads
- #4F for Feet & Hocks (optional)
- Slicker Brush
- Greyhound Comb
- Rubber Curry
- Carding Tool
- De-Shedding Tools
- Small Detailing Shears
- Thinning Shears
- High-Velocity Dryer

Notes:

Notes From The Grooming Table ©2016

Doberman Pinscher

Breed Facts & Characteristics

Country of Origin: Germany

Height at Shoulder: 24"–28"

Coat Length/Type: Short/Smooth

Color: Black and tan, red and tan, blue and tan, and fawn and tan.

Correct grooming procedure:
Bathe & Curry Brush

Common pet grooming practices:
Bathe & Curry Brush

-The Goal-
The coat should be clean and fresh smelling, with the coat laying flat against the body. No shedding hair.

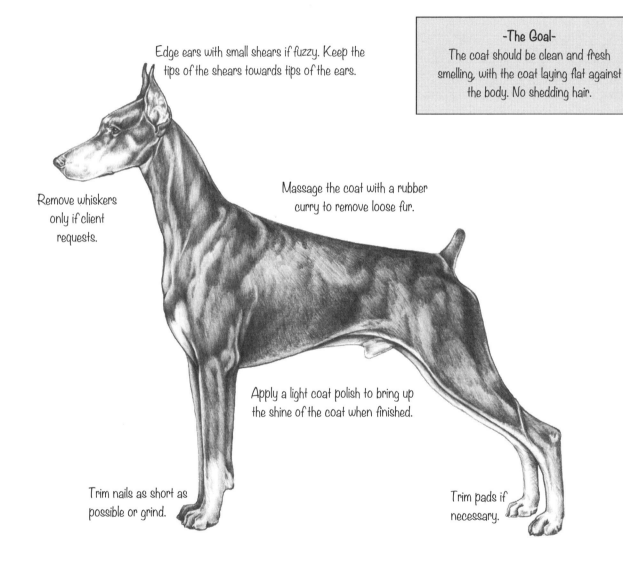

Edge ears with small shears if fuzzy. Keep the tips of the shears towards tips of the ears.

Remove whiskers only if client requests.

Massage the coat with a rubber curry to remove loose fur.

Apply a light coat polish to bring up the shine of the coat when finished.

Trim nails as short as possible or grind.

Trim pads if necessary.

See page 66 for Bathing & Drying Instructions

Suggested Tools & Equipment

- Nail Trimmers
- Styptic Powder
- Ear Cleaning Solution
- Cotton Balls

- Clippers
- #40 or #15 Blade
- Slicker Brush
- Rubber Curry

- Carding Tool
- De-Shedding Tools
- Small Detailing Shears
- Thinning Shears

WORKING

Dogue de Bordeaux

WORKING   SMOOTH COATED

Breed Facts & Characteristics

Country of Origin: France

Height at Shoulder: 23"–27"

Coat Length/Type: Short/Smooth

Color: All shades of fawn from dark to light. Darker mask in either black or brown are typical. Limited amount of white on the chest and toes is accepted.

Correct grooming procedure:

Bathe & Curry Brush

Common pet grooming practices:

Bathe & Curry Brush

-The Goal-
The coat should be clean and fresh smelling, with the coat laying flat against the body. No shedding hair.

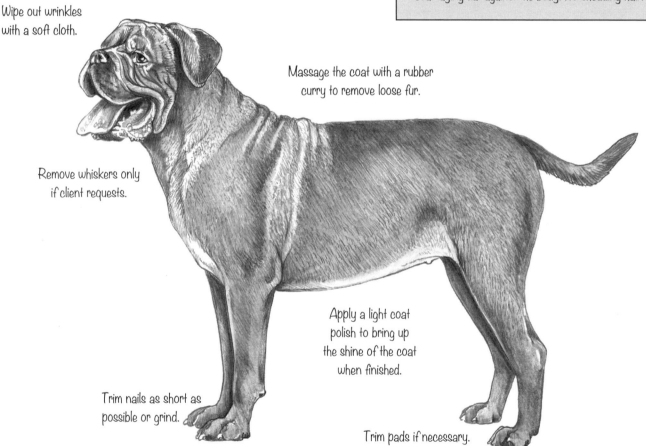

Wipe out wrinkles with a soft cloth.

Massage the coat with a rubber curry to remove loose fur.

Remove whiskers only if client requests.

Apply a light coat polish to bring up the shine of the coat when finished.

Trim nails as short as possible or grind.

Trim pads if necessary.

See page 66 for Bathing & Drying Instructions	Suggested Tools & Equipment

- Nail Trimmers
- Styptic Powder
- Ear Cleaning Solution
- Cotton Balls

- Clippers
- #40 or #15 Blade
- Rubber Curry
- Carding Tool

- Small Detailing Shears
- Thinning Shears

235   *Notes From The Grooming Table* ©2016

German Pinscher

Breed Facts & Characteristics

Country of Origin: Germany

Height at Shoulder: 17"–20"

Coat Length/Type: Short/Smooth

Color: All shades of fawns and reds, black and tan, black and blues with tan markings or reds with tan markings.

Correct grooming procedure:
Bathe & Curry Brush

Common pet grooming practices:
Bathe & Curry Brush

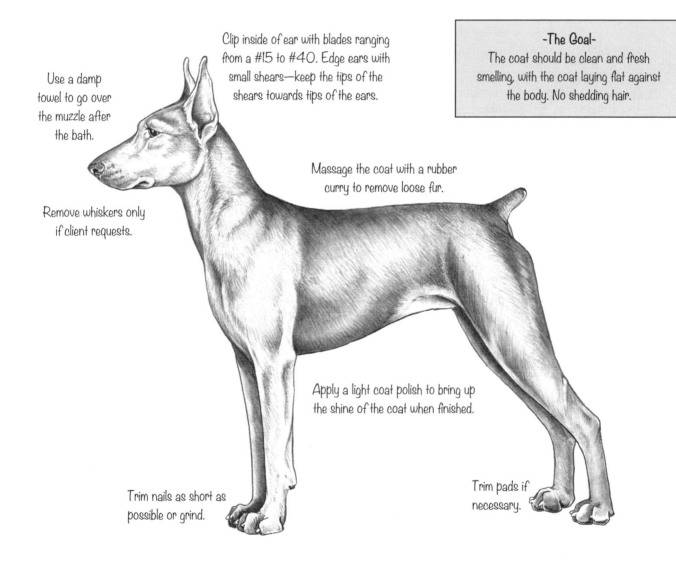

Clip inside of ear with blades ranging from a #15 to #40. Edge ears with small shears—keep the tips of the shears towards tips of the ears.

Use a damp towel to go over the muzzle after the bath.

-The Goal-
The coat should be clean and fresh smelling, with the coat laying flat against the body. No shedding hair.

Remove whiskers only if client requests.

Massage the coat with a rubber curry to remove loose fur.

Apply a light coat polish to bring up the shine of the coat when finished.

Trim nails as short as possible or grind.

Trim pads if necessary.

WORKING

See page 66 for Bathing & Drying Instructions	Suggested Tools & Equipment		
• Nail Trimmers	• Clippers	• Small Detailing Shears
• Styptic Powder	• #40 or #15 Blade	• Thinning Shears
• Ear Cleaning Solution	• Rubber Curry	
• Cotton Balls	• Carding Tool	

Notes *from your* Grooming Table

Giant Schnauzer

Breed Facts & Characteristics

Country of Origin: Germany

Height at Shoulder: 23"–27"

Coat Length/Type: Hard/Wiry

Color: Salt and pepper or black.

Correct grooming procedure:

Hand-Strip

Common pet grooming practices:

Clipper-Trim

General Description

The Giant Schnauzer is a powerful, muscular and squarely built dog of high energy and great intelligence. Its tail is docked short. It may have cropped or uncropped ears. When grooming a Schnauzer, remember there is nothing soft or fluffy about the breed. In the finished groom, there is very little coat hiding the contours of its body. The leg coat and muzzle coat are slightly longer. The hallmark of the breed is its rectangular head, arched eyebrows and full mustache and beard.

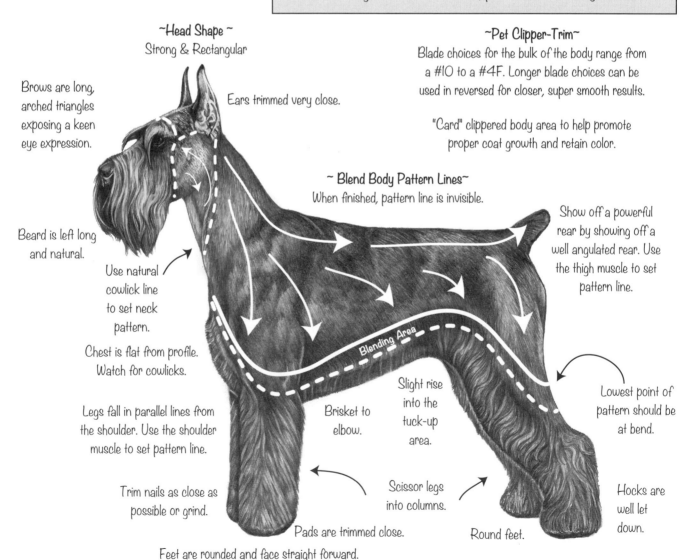

-The Goal-
This is a tight and very tailored looking dog. The body is almost square in build with a rectangular head. When finished, pattern line on the body is invisible.

~Head Shape~
Strong & Rectangular

Brows are long, arched triangles exposing a keen eye expression.

Ears trimmed very close.

~Pet Clipper-Trim~
Blade choices for the bulk of the body range from a #10 to a #4F. Longer blade choices can be used in reversed for closer, super smooth results.

"Card" clippered body area to help promote proper coat growth and retain color.

~ Blend Body Pattern Lines~
When finished, pattern line is invisible.

Beard is left long and natural.

Use natural cowlick line to set neck pattern.

Chest is flat from profile. Watch for cowlicks.

Legs fall in parallel lines from the shoulder. Use the shoulder muscle to set pattern line.

Trim nails as close as possible or grind.

Blending Area

Brisket to elbow.

Slight rise into the tuck-up area.

Scissor legs into columns.

Pads are trimmed close.

Feet are rounded and face straight forward.

Show off a powerful rear by showing off a well angulated rear. Use the thigh muscle to set pattern line.

Lowest point of pattern should be at bend.

Round feet.

Hocks are well let down.

**See page 76 for
Bathing & Drying Instructions**

Frequency

Bathe once a week to once every 12 weeks. Trim every four to six weeks to maintain a stylized fashion.

Pre-Work

Trim or grind nails at least every four to six weeks to maintain a healthy foot structure. Clean the ears by swabbing with a mild ear cleaning solution. Hair should be plucked from within the ear canal only as necessary for healthy ear management. Prior to bathing, quickly go over the entire body and remove any serious mats or tangles. If the tangle can be penetrated with water, leave it and remove when the dog is clean. If the pet has not been in for professional grooming for six weeks or more, remove the excessive body coat and set the pattern before bathing.

Brushing

Prior to the haircut, the dog must be completely tangle-free. Use a firm slicker brush or a wide-toothed comb to methodically work over the entire body in a line brush fashion. Pay close attention to the friction points where mats and tangles typically hide: behind the ears, around the ruff, in the armpits, the thigh area, the undercarriage and the tail. Be careful when using any tool with metal teeth or bristles. A heavy hand or too much repetition in an area can cause cuts and/or brush burns.

Pattern Lines in General

The pattern is based on the bone and muscle structure of the dog. After the final trim, all pattern lines on the body should be invisible. At the transition points, feather off with the clippers in a smooth and steady fashion. If the pattern line is still visible after clipping, use thinning shears to blend the line. On the head, the pattern lines are crisp and clean.

Body

For either hand-stripped or clipper-cut dogs, the general pattern is the same. Typical blades used in pet grooming range from a #10 to a #7F, or a combination of those blades for the bulk of the body work. Some stylists find reversing a slightly longer blade very effective in achieving an extremely smooth finish on the body. Reversing a blade will shorten the cutting action by about two blade lengths as the same blade used with the grain of the coat. Choose one of the methods and follow the direction of the natural coat growth of the fur. After clipping, card the coat to help promote proper coat growth while retaining some of the rich color and harsh coat texture. Carding also will assist in the removal of any minor tracking left in the coat from clipping. The pattern lines start at the turn of the shoulder and continue to just above the elbow, back to the flank on a diagonal and then drop into the thigh region.

Undercarriage

Right around the navel area, the coat will be very short and start to get longer as the line moves forward towards the brisket, creating the illusion of a deep chest. When viewed in profile, the distance from the elbow to the bottom of the foot is equal to the distance between the withers and the brisket. There is only enough fur left on the undercarriage to accentuate depth of chest and an athletic build. The pattern line is well blended and invisible.

Tail & Rear

The top side of the tail is trimmed with the same blade as the body. The underside of the tail is clipped close, with blades ranging from #15 to a #7F, used with or against the grain based on the sensitivity of the dog's skin. Continue with the same blade around the rectum and on the inner side of the cowlick lines going down the back side of the thighs.

At transition points on the body, blend the lines so they are invisible. Legs should be left fuller and fall into straight columns, from the body to the feet, on both the front and rear legs. The chest should be flat, but use caution not to bald out this area due to cowlicks found where the front legs meet the chest, on both the front and rear legs.

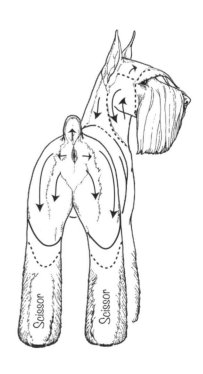

WORKING

Shape the arched eyebrows by following the eye socket ridge. The stop area is clear, creating split brows. Use curved shears in reverse to help shape the eyebrows. The coat is very short at the back of the eye and gets longer towards the nose. Brow tips reach to the halfway point of the muzzle.

Hand-strip or clipper the top skull very close. If clipping, use blades ranging from a #10 used with the grain to a #4F used against the grain, depending on the coat density.

The ears may be cropped or natural. Either type is clipper-trimmed very close with blades ranging from a #10 or #15 on the outside and a #40 on the inside. Finish by edging the ears with small detailing shears.

The beard and mustache form a rectangular head style. When viewed straight on, the cheeks and the beard should form one continuous line.

The occiput is the dividing line between the head and the neck.

The cheeks and throat are smooth and clean. Blades ranging from a #10 to a #15, used with or against the grain, are common in pet styling. The line runs from the back corner of the eye to the cheek whisker nodule, to the chin nodule, up to the opposite cheek whisker nodule and opposite eye. Use the zygomatic arch to set the line from the back corner of the eye to the ear canal. The natural cowlick line assists with setting the throat area. Create a soft "V" or "U" shape coming about 3–4 finger widths above the breast bone.

Hindquarters

The hindquarters should be strong and powerful. When clipping this area, expose the thigh muscle with the same blade used on the body. Start to feather off with the blade where the muscle starts to turn under on a diagonal line from the flank region to about three or four fingers above the hock. Using a short to medium guard comb can facilitate feathering in the blending line. The pattern line should be invisible when the trim is finished. Blend with thinning shears if necessary. The stifle area should have enough furnishing left to give the legs substance and angulation. The longest coat on the legs can range from 1 to 3.5 inches depending on the amount of bone and coat density. Shape this area by hand with shears after the clipper work is complete. When viewed from the rear, the legs should form two parallel lines to the ground. The hocks are well let down. There should be adequate coat on the hock area to accentuate the angles of the rear assembly.

Front Legs

The coat on the legs can range from 1/16 of an inch to 3 inches in length depending on the amount of bone, the size of the dog and coat density. The front legs drop straight down from the body and have ample bone and muscle to show off a powerful and sturdy animal. The pattern line at the shoulder is about 1 or 2 fingers above the top of the elbow, at the point where the muscle begins to turn under. The coat at the transition line will be very short, and taper into the longer leg furnishings. This can be accomplished by feathering off at the blending point with the same blade used on the body. Other methods of blending off at the top of the leg include using an attachment comb followed by hand-scissoring and blending with thinning shears. Most stylists prefer to leave the legs to shape by hand with shears. After the final trim, the legs need to form two parallel columns going down from the elbow into tight, round feet. The coat at the back of the elbow is very short and falls straight down off the back of the leg toward the ground.

Feet

The feet are small for the size of the dog. Both the front and rear feet are compact with well arched toes. To show off these traits, the feet are trimmed very close to the edge of the foot and some nail is routinely exposed. The feet should point straight ahead, toeing neither in nor out. Trim the feet round by first boxing them in the shape of a square while the dog is standing in a natural, square position. Then remove the sharp corners of the box and round the feet facing straight forward. If detailing the feet with the foot off the tabletop, always use a small pair of shears to minimize the risk of accidentally cutting the pads.

Throat & Chest

Blades ranging from #10 to #7F, with or against the grain, based on the sensitivity of the dog's skin, are common in the throat area. Follow the natural cowlick line that runs in a "V" shape from the base of the ears towards the base of the neck. The blending point begins about 3 or 4 fingers above the breast bone and drops to just below the turn of the muscle at the elbow/ shoulder, creating a "W" shape when viewed straight on. When viewed in profile, the neck into the chest should be straight without a predominant forechest. When blending the chest, be aware of the heavy cowlicks in the area.

Many stylists prefer to leave the chest area to blend by hand with thinning shears or shears. When finished in this area, double check your work to be sure the neck, chest and front legs drop down in a straight line when viewed in profile.

The Head in General: Top Skull

The top of the head can be clipped as close as a #10 used with the grain; to a #7F or #5F, used with the grain or against depending on the dog's sensitivity and density of the coat.

Ears

Both cropped and uncropped ears are clipped with a close blade. It is common to see a #10 or #15 blade used on the outside of the ear leather while a #40 blade is used on the inside. When working with close blades in this delicate area, always work from the base or center of the ear out toward the edge. Gently brace the ear with your fingers to clip over it. To finish, use small finishing shears to trim around the outside edge of the ear leather, keeping the tips of the shears toward the tip of the ears.

Brows

To form the arched, triangular eyebrows follow the eye socket rim, working with or against the grain of the coat. Schnauzers have a slight stop between the eyes that acts as a natural split for the brows. Either lightly clip this area when clipping the top skull or leave it to do by hand with thinning shears. Shape the brows into long arched triangles that accentuate the typically keen look. They will be very short at the back corner of the eye and longer at the tips, coming almost halfway down the bridge of the nose. When viewed in profile, the brows should barely break the line of the top skull as they arch out over the nose. Use curved shears in reverse to set the brow. Line the tip of the shear up with a

point on the nose. Repeat on the other brow. By using the nose as a set point, the length and angle of both eyebrows remain the same. Bevel the blades of the shears away from the pet's skin to avoid accidentally cutting the dog at the back corner of the eye when you close the shear to cut the brow.

Throat & Cheeks

The throat and cheek areas are clipped using blades ranging from a #10 to a #7F, used either with or against the grain. Use the natural cowlick line of the neck to be the guide to create the "U" or "V" shape of the throat. The lowest point will be about 3 fingers above the breast bone. The line that breaks the top skull and the cheeks is from the back corner of the eye straight back to the ear canal.

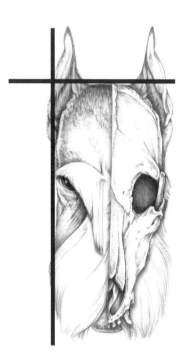

Any hair falling outside the line of the cheek bone needs to leave. Any hair remaining inside the line needs to stay, creating the correct "rectangular" head style for the breed.

WORKING

Beard & Goatee

The fur on the muzzle is a natural length as it forms the beard. The basic transition line between the cheek and the beard runs on an imaginary line from just behind the back corner of the eyes to the whisker nodule on the cheeks. The line continues under the jaw to the single center whisker nodule. The line should be very crisp and clean, just clearing the outside corner of the mouth so when the dog pants, you can see the separation between the top and the bottom jaw. The coat under the eye area is never clipped as this hair forms one of the critical lines of the classic rectangular head style. The line on the dog's face should be straight, from the flat cheek down into the beard area. Double check this line by laying a greyhound comb along side the head. Any fur that sticks out beyond the comb should be removed. Any hair inside this line needs to remain and to be blended to create the rectangular shape.

Detail Finish

Application of bows and mild cologne is optional.

Grooming Tips

A light setting gel, mousse or texturing shampoo can add body to the leg coat, making it easier to scissor. Try spritzing unruly eyebrows while they are still damp with a styling spray. Work the product into the damp brows. Brush or comb the brows into place or dry them into the position you want them in the final trim.

Special Note

Harsh-coated terriers have a coat that will normally brush out quite easily, especially after they are clean.

Suggested Tools & Equipment

- Nail Trimmers
- Styptic Powder
- Ear Powder
- Ear Cleaning Solution
- Cotton Balls
- Hemostat
- Clippers
- Slicker Brush
- Greyhound Comb
- Pumice Stone
- Carding Tools
- Stripping Knives
- Straight Shears
- Curved Shears
- Small Detailing Shears
- Thinning Shears
- Dematting Tools

Common Blade Options:

- #40, #15, #10
- #7F, #5F, #4F
- Variety of Guard Combs

Notes:

Notes *from your* Grooming Table

Great Dane

Breed Facts & Characteristics

Country of Origin: Germany

Height at Shoulder: 28"–34"

Coat Length/Type: Short/Smooth

Color: Tan with a black mask, brindle, steel gray, black and harlequin.

Correct grooming procedure:
Bathe & Curry Brush

Common pet grooming practices:
Bathe & Curry Brush

-The Goal-
The coat should be clean and fresh smelling, with the coat laying flat against the body. No shedding hair.

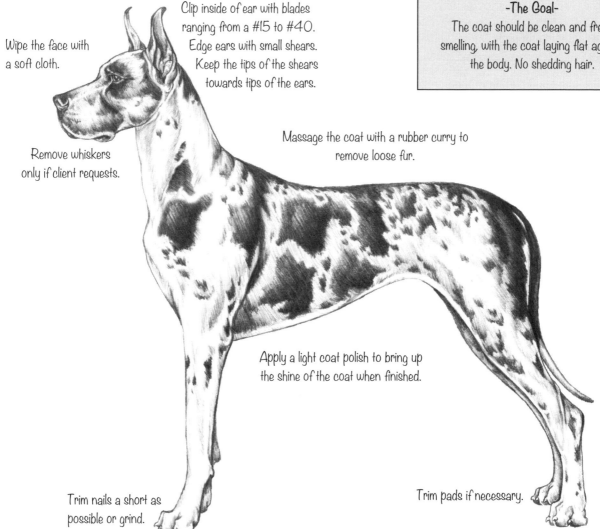

Wipe the face with a soft cloth.

Clip inside of ear with blades ranging from a #15 to #40. Edge ears with small shears. Keep the tips of the shears towards tips of the ears.

Remove whiskers only if client requests.

Massage the coat with a rubber curry to remove loose fur.

Apply a light coat polish to bring up the shine of the coat when finished.

Trim nails a short as possible or grind.

Trim pads if necessary.

See page 66 for Bathing & Drying Instructions

Suggested Tools & Equipment

- Nail Trimmers
- Styptic Powder
- Ear Cleaning Solution
- Cotton Balls

- Clippers
- #40 or #15 Blade
- Rubber Curry
- Carding Tool

- Small Detailing Shears
- Thinning Shears

Notes *from your* Grooming Table

Great Pyrenees

Breed Facts & Characteristics

Country of Origin: France

Height at Shoulder: 25"–32"

Coat Length/Type: Soft/Thick

Color: Primary white in color, may have grey or tan badger type markings on the head. A few patches of light color may appear on the body or tail.

Correct grooming procedure:
Bathe & Brush Out/Minor Trimming

Common pet grooming practices:
Bathe & Brush Out

-The Goal-
The coat should be shiny, light and airy. The coat should bounce and float with the dog as it moves. You should be able to sink a wide-toothed comb to the skin and pull it freely out to the end of the hair shaft.

Let a powerful high-velocity dryer help in all aspects of grooming this type of coat, before and after the bath. Blow out loose coat, tangles and dirt. Dry and fluff.

Thoroughly line brush/comb entire dog.

Use a damp towel to go over the muzzle after the bath.

Remove whiskers only if the client requests.

The neck and chest can really get packed with coat. Pay close attention to this area.

The rump can really get packed with coat. Pay close attention to this area.

Friction points:
• Armpits
• Inside Thighs

Trim nails as close as possible or grind.

Shave pads.

Neaten feet to look natural.

Trim hocks.

Look for double dew claws on the rear legs.

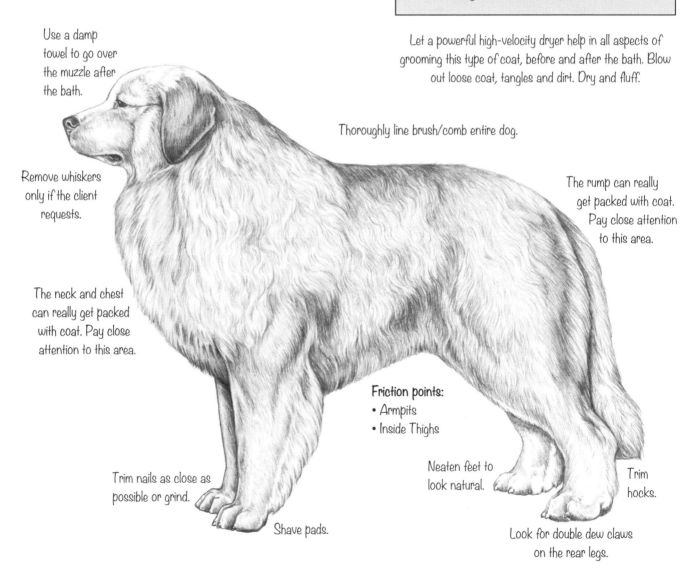

See page 70 for Bathing & Drying Instructions

Frequency

Bathe once a week to once every 12 weeks.

Pre-Work

Trim or grind nails at least every four to six weeks to maintain a healthy foot structure. Clean the ears by swabbing with a mild ear cleaning solution. Use a rubber curry, shedding blade, undercoat rake, pumice stone, carding tool, fine stripping knife or natural bristled brush to loosen skin dander and remove loose coat. Quickly blowing out the dog with a high-velocity dryer can effectively lift dirt and debris away from the skin and loosen coat. Brush out or remove any matting found in the longer coated areas. If the tangles are loose enough so water can fully penetrate the area, remove after the bathing and drying stages. If water cannot penetrate, remove the mat or tangle prior to bathing.

Brushing

Line brush, working in sections until the dog is entirely tangle-free. When finished, there should be little, if any, fur still being removed with a firm slicker brush. Double-check the work with a wide-toohed comb and your hands. Go over the entire body, feeling for any inconsistencies in the density levels of the coat. If an area seems moist to the touch or fuller than the rest of the coat, rework the area with the appropriate tool. Mats, tangles and excessive coat are easily trapped in the following areas: behind the ears, around the ruff, the thigh area, the undercarriage and the tail. Give extra attention to these areas before finishing the groom.

Sanitary Area

If the dog has a sanitation problem under the tail, lightly trim this area with thinning shears. Only clear enough coat to accomplish the goal and keep it looking very natural. Trimming of the groin area is not recommended unless there is a sanitary problem. If the groin needs to be trimmed, do so very lightly and try to leave the fur long enough so that the harsh coat does not prickle the skin, causing the dog to lick at the irritation.

Feet & Hocks

Trim the pads with a close cutting action blade ranging from a #15 to a #40. Use a very light touch to clean the pads of long hair. If there is long fur between the toes, back brush the fur so it stands up and away from the foot. With thinning shears, trim off the excess creating a neat and very natural looking foot with well arched toes. Tidy the outside edge of the foot, if needed, with small detailing shears. If the hocks have longer coat, trim lightly with thinning shears showing a neat, clean area. A #4F blade used in reverse works well for trimming the tops of the feet and the hocks on some dogs.

Detail Finish

Edge the ears lightly with thinning shears to neaten but look natural. Hand-pluck any long wispy, flyaway hair from around the ears. Removal of whiskers on the muzzle is optional based on client preference. Finish with a fine mist of coat polish on the body coat for added shine. Application of bows and mild cologne are optional.

Grooming Tip

Let your hands guide you. Learn to feel for differences in coat density levels. Areas that feel heavier or denser than other areas need special attention when bathing, brushing and drying.

Suggested Tools & Equipment

- Nail Trimmers
- Styptic Powder
- Ear Cleaning Solution
- Cotton Balls
- Clippers
- #40 and #15 Blades for Pads
- #4F for Feet &Hocks (optional)
- Slicker Brush
- Wide-Toothed Comb
- Rubber Curry
- Undercoat Rake
- Dematting Tools
- High-Velocity Dryer
- Small Detailing Shears
- Curved Shears
- Thinning Shears

Notes:

Notes From The Grooming Table ©2016

Greater Swiss Mountain Dog   WORKING   SHORT COATED

Breed Facts & Characteristics

Country of Origin: Switzerland

Height at Shoulder: 23½"–28½"

Coat Length/Type: Harsh/Coarse

Color: Deep, rich tricolors in black, chestnut and white.

Correct grooming procedure:
Bathe & Curry Brush

Common pet grooming practices:
Bathe & Curry Brush

-The Goal-
The coat should be clean and fresh smelling, with the coat laying flat against the body. No shedding hair.

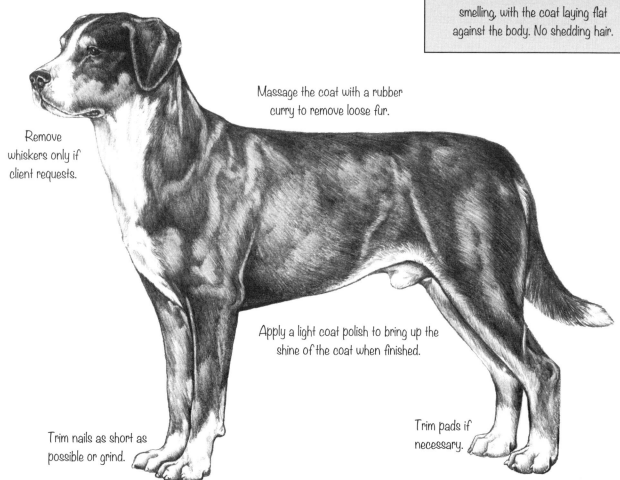

Massage the coat with a rubber curry to remove loose fur.

Remove whiskers only if client requests.

Apply a light coat polish to bring up the shine of the coat when finished.

Trim nails as short as possible or grind.

Trim pads if necessary.

See page 67 for Bathing & Drying Instructions

Suggested Tools & Equipment

- Nail Trimmers
- Styptic Powder
- Ear Cleaning Solution
- Cotton Balls

- Clippers
- #40 or #15 Blade
- Slicker Brush
- Rubber Curry

- Carding Tool
- De-Shedding Tools
- Small Detailing Shears
- Thinning Shears

Notes *from your* Grooming Table

Breed Facts & Characteristics

Country of Origin: Hungary

Height at Shoulder: 25½"–29½"

Coat Length/Type: Corded/Long

Color: White

Correct grooming procedure:
Corded

Common pet grooming practices:
Clipper-Trim

-The Goal-
Getting the dog clean and totally dry. The cords should be uniform in thickness and fully separated to the skin.

Separate cords by gently pulling them apart down to the skin. The base of each cord should be about ½ inch to 1½ inch in diameter.

This coat type can take 12 to 24 hours to totally dry.

When shampooing, squeeze shampoo solution through the cords. Never scrub.

Trim nails as close as possible or grind.

The cords should be about the size of a high-lighter pen, getting broader and flatter at the ends.

Grooming Procedures & Recommendations

See page 77 for
Bathing & Drying Instructions

Frequency

Bathe every 12 weeks or when needed. Work the cords once a week to once every four weeks, without a full bath.

Pre-Work

Trim or grind nails at least every four to six weeks to maintain a healthy foot structure. Clean the ears ever four to six weeks. If hair forms inside the ear canal, apply an ear powder and gently pluck the hair from inside the canal. Use care not to pull any coat from outside the canal opening. Clean ears by swabbing with a mild ear cleaning solution

Cords

The base of a cord is about ½ to 1½ inches square. Very often the cords will start to form by themselves, with little assistance. Prior to bathing, gently pull the strands away from one another to keep the cord as a separate strand. If the coat is shorter and feels "spongy" to the touch, it may not be forming natural cords. Mist the area with water or a light skin conditioner to help see the natural cord separation. Separate the area with your fingers into ½ to 1½ inch sections, starting at the base of each cord. If a cord is too thick, the cord can be split in two by working it with your fingers or by carefully cutting the cord with shears. Try to follow the natural separation as it splits.

Feet

Trim the pads with a close cutting blade, ranging from a #15 to a #40. Use a very light touch to clean the pads of long hair. With shears, round the foot slightly to create an oval shape with toes facing forward.

Detail Finish

When the dog is dry, continue to divide and separate the cords. Pay close attention to the friction areas: ears, under the front legs, the rump and under the tail. These are the areas where the skin is the most sensitive and is prone to injury. Use extreme caution when splitting the coat in these areas. Trimming the cords to a few inches all over enables the pet dog to maintain look of the breed yet makes care easier than for the full coat.

Pet Dogs

Some pet owners choose to keep their pets brushed out or trimmed close, not dealing with the corded coat at all.

Grooming Tips & Trends

This is a coat type that requires a fair amount of attention, especially in the initial cording phases. Once the cords have formed, keeping them up requires only the use of your fingers. Pet owners can do this during idle time, like watching TV. With practice, their fingers will gravitate to the areas of greatest density, and they will be able to work the area without even looking at it.

Suggested Tools & Equipment

- Nail Trimmers
- Styptic Powder
- Ear Cleaning Solution
- Cotton Balls
- Clippers
- #40 and #15 Blades for Pads
- Straight Shear
- Strong Fingers

Notes:

Notes From The Grooming Table ©2016

Kuvasz

Breed Facts & Characteristics

Country of Origin: Hungary

Height at Shoulder: 26"–30"

Coat Length/Type: Combination/Dense

Color: White

Correct grooming procedure:
Bathe & Brush Out/Minor Trimming

Common pet grooming practices:
Bathe & Brush Out/Minor Trimming

-The Goal-
The coat should be shiny light and airy.
As the dog moves, the coat should
bounce and float with the dog.

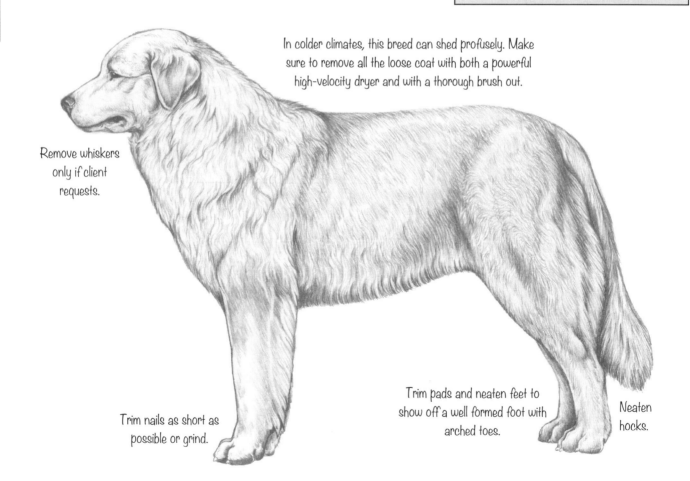

In colder climates, this breed can shed profusely. Make
sure to remove all the loose coat with both a powerful
high-velocity dryer and with a thorough brush out.

Remove whiskers
only if client
requests.

Trim nails as short as
possible or grind.

Trim pads and neaten feet to
show off a well formed foot with
arched toes.

Neaten
hocks.

Grooming Procedures & Recommendations

See page 68 for
Bathing & Drying Instructions

Frequency
Bathe once a week to once every
12 weeks.

Pre-Work
Trim or grind nails at least every four
to six weeks to maintain a healthy foot
structure. Clean the ears by swabbing
with a mild ear cleaning solution. Use a
rubber curry, shedding blade, undercoat
rake, pumice stone, carding tool, fine
stripping knife or natural bristled brush
to loosen skin dander and remove loose
coat. Quickly blowing out the dog with
a high-velocity dryer can effectively lift
dirt and debris away from the skin and
loosen coat. Brush out or remove any
matting found in the longer coated
areas. If the tangles are loose enough
so water can fully penetrate the area,
remove after the bathing and drying
stages. If water cannot penetrate, remove
the mat or tangle prior to bathing.

Brushing
Line brush, working in sections until
the dog is entirely tangle-free. When
finished, there should be little, if any,
fur still being removed with a firm
slicker brush. Double-check the work
with a comb and your hands. Go
over the entire body, feeling for any
inconsistencies in the density levels of
the coat. If an area seems moist to the
touch or fuller than the rest of the coat,
rework the area with the appropriate
tool. Mats, tangles and excessive coat
are easily trapped in the following areas:
behind the ears, around the ruff, the
thigh area, the undercarriage and the
tail. Give extra attention to these areas
before finishing the groom.

Carding
If a dog has an abundance of loose
undercoat, card the shorter areas with
a carding tool. Common tools can be
a fine stripping knife, undercoat rake,
a pumice stone, or a #40 blade held
between your fingers. Any carding tool
should be pulled over the body, working
in the direction of the coat growth. This
will remove the soft, downy undercoat,
allowing the guard coat to conform
more closely to the natural outline of
the body. It will also aid in the removal
of loose, shedding coat, a seasonal
problem for many pet owners.

Sanitary Area
If the dog has a sanitation problem
under the tail, lightly trim this area with
thinning shears. Only clear enough
coat to accomplish the goal and keep it
looking very natural. Trimming of the
groin area is not recommended unless
there is a sanitary problem. If the groin
needs to be trimmed, do so very lightly
and try to leave the fur long enough
so that the harsh coat does not prickle
the skin, causing the dog to lick at the
irritation.

Feet & Hocks
Trim the pads with a close cutting
action blade ranging from a #15 to a
#40. Use a very light touch to clean the
pads of long hair. If there is long fur
between the toes, back brush the fur so
it stands up and away from the foot.
With thinning shears, trim off the excess
creating a neat and very natural looking
foot with well arched toes. Tidy the
outside edge of the foot, if needed, with
small detailing shears. If the hocks have
longer coat, trim lightly with thinning
shears showing a neat, clean area. A
#4F blade used in reverse works well for
trimming the tops of the feet and the
hocks on some dogs.

Suggested Tools & Equipment

- Nail Trimmers
- Styptic Powder
- Ear Cleaning Solution
- Cotton Balls
- Clippers
- #40 and #15 Blades for Pads
- #4F for Feet & Hocks (optional)
- Slicker Brush
- Greyhound Comb
- Rubber Curry
- Carding Tool
- De-Shedding Tools
- Small Detailing Shears
- Thinning Shears

Detail Finish
Edge the ears lightly with thinning
shears to neaten but look natural.
Hand-pluck any long wispy, flyaway
hair from around the ears. Removal
of whiskers on the muzzle is optional
based on client preference. Finish with
a fine mist of coat polish on the body
coat for added shine. Application of
bows and mild cologne are optional.

Breed Facts & Characteristics

Country of Origin: Germany

Height at Shoulder: 25"–31½"

Coat Length/Type: Combination/Heavy

Color: Sable in all shades of rich brown with black masks. Tiny amount of white on the chest and toes is tolerated.

Correct grooming procedure:

Bathe & Brush Out

Common pet grooming practices:

Bathe & Brush Out

-The Goal-
The coat should be shiny, light and airy. The coat should bounce and float with the dog as it moves. You should be able to sink a wide-toothed comb to the skin and pull it freely out to the end of the hair shaft.

Use a damp towel to go over the muzzle after the bath.

Let a powerful high-velocity dryer help in all aspects of grooming this type of coat, before and after the bath. Blow out loose coat, tangles and dirt. Dry and fluff.

Thoroughly line brush/comb entire dog.

The rump can really get packed with coat. Pay close attention to this area.

Remove whiskers only if the client requests.

The neck and chest can really get packed with coat. Pay close attention to this area.

Friction points:
• Armpits
• Inside Thighs

Trim nails as close as possible or grind.

Neaten feet to look natural.

Trim hocks.

Shave pads.

Look for double dew claws on the rear legs.

Grooming Procedures & Recommendations

See page 70 for
Bathing & Drying Instructions

Frequency
Bathe once a week to once every 12 weeks.

Pre-Work
Trim or grind nails at least every four to six weeks to maintain a healthy foot structure. Swab the ears clean with a mild ear cleaning solution. Quickly blow out the dog's coat with a high-velocity dryer to effectively lift dirt and debris away from the skin and loosen coat. Brush out or remove any matting found in the longer coated areas. If the tangles are loose enough so that water can fully penetrate them, remove them after bathing and drying. If water cannot penetrate, remove the mat or tangle prior to bathing.

Brushing
Line brush, working in sections, until the dog is entirely tangle-free. When finished, there should be little, if any, fur still being removed with a firm slicker brush. Double-check the work with a wide-toothed comb and your hands. Go over the entire body, feeling for any inconsistencies in the density levels of the coat. If an area seems moist to the touch or fuller than the rest of the coat, rework the area with the appropriate tool. Mats, tangles and excessive coat are easily trapped in the following areas: behind the ears, around the ruff, the thigh area, the undercarriage and the tail. Give extra attention to these areas before finishing the groom.

Feet & Hocks
Trim the pads with blades ranging from a #15 to a #40. Use a very light touch to clean the pads of long hair. If there is long fur between the toes, brush it back so the fur stands up and away from the foot. With thinning shears, trim off the excess to create a neat and very natural looking foot with well-arched toes. Tidy the outside edge of the foot, if needed, with small detailing shears. If the hocks have longer coat, trim lightly with thinning shears to show a neat, clean area. A #4F blade used in reverse works well for trimming the tops of the feet and the hocks on small to larger dogs that are light to moderately coated. With very heavy-coated or giant dogs, handle the top of the feet and hocks using hand-trimming techniques instead of a clipper.

Sanitary Area
If the dog has a sanitation problem under the tail, lightly trim this area with thinning shears. Only clear enough coat to accomplish the goal and keep it looking very natural. Trimming of the groin area is not recommended unless there is a sanitary problem. If the groin needs to be trimmed, do so very lightly and try to leave the fur long enough so that the harsh coat does not prickle the skin, causing the dog to lick at the irritation.

Detail Finish
Removal of muzzle whiskers is optional, based on client preference. For added shine, finish with a fine mist of coat polish on the body coat. Application of bows and mild cologne is optional.

Suggested Tools & Equipment

- Nail Trimmers
- Styptic Powder
- Ear Cleaning Solution
- Cotton Balls
- Clippers
- #40 and #15 Blades for Pads
- #4F for Feet & Hocks (optional)
- Slicker Brush
- Wide-Toothed Comb
- Rubber Curry
- Undercoat Rake
- Dematting Tools
- High-Velocity Dryer
- Small Detailing Shears
- Curved Shears
- Thinning Shears

Notes:

Mastiff

Breed Facts & Characteristics

Country of Origin: England

Height at Shoulder: 27½"–32"

Coat Length/Type: Short/Harsh

Color: All shades of tan or tan brindled with a dark mask on the face and ears.

Correct grooming procedure:

Bathe & Curry Brush

Common pet grooming practices:

Bathe & Curry Brush

-The Goal-
The coat should be clean and fresh smelling, with the coat laying flat against the body. No shedding hair.

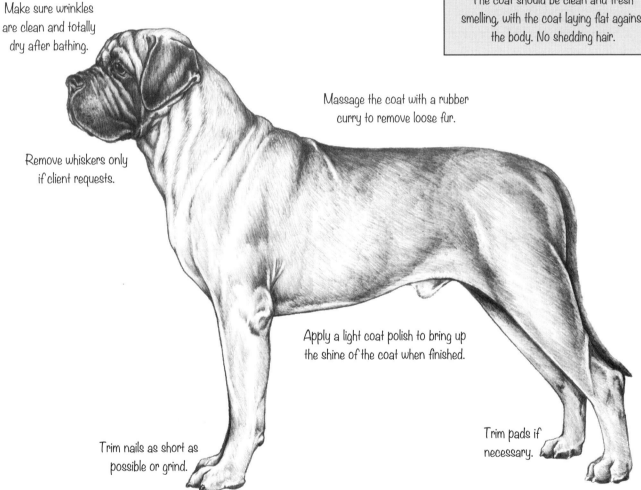

Make sure wrinkles are clean and totally dry after bathing.

Massage the coat with a rubber curry to remove loose fur.

Remove whiskers only if client requests.

Apply a light coat polish to bring up the shine of the coat when finished.

Trim nails as short as possible or grind.

Trim pads if necessary.

See page 67 for Bathing & Drying Instructions	Suggested Tools & Equipment

- Nail Trimmers
- Styptic Powder
- Ear Cleaning Solution
- Cotton Balls

- Clippers
- #40 or #15 Blade
- Slicker Brush
- Rubber Curry

- Carding Tool
- De-Shedding Tools
- Small Detailing Shears
- Thinning Shears

Breed Facts & Characteristics

Country of Origin: Italy

Height at Shoulder: 24"–31"

Coat Length/Type: Short/Smooth

Color: Solid shades of tawny, gray, black. Some degree of brindling allowed. Very limited amount of white accepted on chest, throat, underside of body, backs of pasterns and toes.

Correct grooming procedure:
Bathe & Curry Brush

Common pet grooming practices:
Bathe & Curry Brush

-The Goal-
The coat should be clean and fresh smelling, with the coat laying flat against the body. No shedding hair.

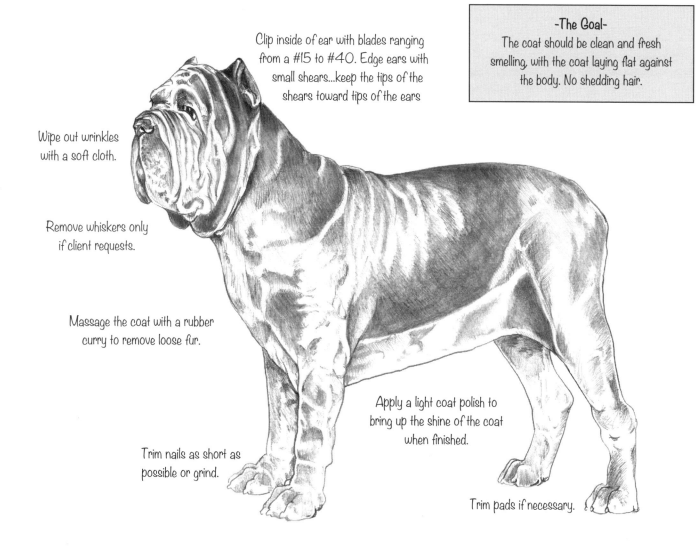

Clip inside of ear with blades ranging from a #15 to #40. Edge ears with small shears...keep the tips of the shears toward tips of the ears

Wipe out wrinkles with a soft cloth.

Remove whiskers only if client requests.

Massage the coat with a rubber curry to remove loose fur.

Trim nails as short as possible or grind.

Apply a light coat polish to bring up the shine of the coat when finished.

Trim pads if necessary.

See page 67 for
Bathing & Drying Instructions

Suggested Tools & Equipment

- Nail Trimmers
- Styptic Powder
- Ear Cleaning Solution
- Cotton Balls
- Clippers
- #40 or #15 Blade
- Slicker Brush
- Rubber Curry
- Carding Tool
- De-Shedding Tools
- Small Detailing Shears
- Thinning Shears

Breed Facts & Characteristics

Country of Origin: Newfoundland, Canada

Height at Shoulder: 26"–28"

Coat Length/Type: Combination/Heavy

Color: Black, brown and gray solid colors. The "Landseer" is a black and white dog with sharp, crisp, large markings.

Correct grooming procedure:
Bathe & Brush Out/Minor Trimming

Common pet grooming practices:
Bathe & Brush Out/Minor Trimming

-The Goal-
The coat should be shiny, light and airy. The coat should bounce and float with the dog as it moves.

Use a damp towel to go over the muzzle after the bath.

Remove whiskers only if the client requests.

The neck and chest can really get packed with coat. Pay close attention to this area.

Trim nails as close as possible or grind.

Let a powerful high-velocity dryer help in all aspects of grooming this type of coat, before and after the bath. Blow out loose coat, tangles and dirt. Dry and fluff.

Thoroughly line brush/comb entire dog.

The rump can really get packed with coat. Pay close attention to this area.

Friction points:
• Armpits
• Inside Thighs

Trim hocks.

Shave pads.

Neaten feet to look natural.

See page 70 for
Bathing & Drying Instructions

Frequency
Bathe once a week to once every 12 weeks.

Pre-Work
Trim or grind nails at least every four to six weeks to maintain a healthy foot structure. Clean the ears by swabbing with a mild ear cleaning solution. Use a rubber curry, shedding blade, undercoat rake, pumice stone, carding tool, fine stripping knife or natural bristled brush to loosen skin dander and remove loose coat. Quickly blowing out the dog with a high-velocity dryer can effectively lift dirt and debris away from the skin and loosen coat. Brush out or remove any matting found in the longer coated areas. If the tangles are loose enough so water can fully penetrate the area, remove after the bathing and drying stages. If water cannot penetrate, remove the mat or tangle prior to bathing.

Brushing
Line brush, working in sections until the dog is entirely tangle-free. When finished, there should be little, if any, fur still being removed with a firm slicker brush. Double-check the work with a wide-toothed comb and your hands. Go over the entire body, feeling for any inconsistencies in the density levels of the coat. If an area seems moist to the touch or fuller than the rest of the coat, rework the area with the appropriate tool. Mats, tangles and excessive coat are easily trapped in the following areas: behind the ears, around the ruff, the thigh area, the undercarriage and the tail. Give extra attention to these areas before finishing the groom.

Sanitary Area
If the dog has a sanitation problem under the tail, lightly trim this area with thinning shears. Only clear enough coat to accomplish the goal and keep it looking very natural. Trimming of the groin area is not recommended unless there is a sanitary problem. If the groin needs to be trimmed, do so very lightly and try to leave the fur long enough so that the harsh coat does not prickle the skin, causing the dog to lick at the irritation.

Feet & Hocks
Trim the pads with a close cutting action blade ranging from a #15 to a #40. Use a very light touch to clean the pads of long hair. If there is long fur between the toes, back brush the fur so it stands up and away from the foot. With thinning shears, trim off the excess creating a neat and very natural looking foot with well arched toes. Tidy the outside edge of the foot, if needed, with small detailing shears. If the hocks have longer coat, trim lightly with thinning shears showing a neat, clean area. A #4F blade used in reverse works well for trimming the tops of the feet and the hocks on some dogs.

Detail Finish
Edge the ears lightly with thinning shears to neaten but look natural. Hand-pluck any long wispy, flyaway hair from around the ears. Removal of whiskers on the muzzle is optional based on client preference. Finish with a fine mist of coat polish on the body coat for added shine. Application of bows and mild cologne are optional.

Grooming Tip
Let your hands guide you. Learn to feel for differences in coat density levels. Areas that feel heavier or denser than other areas need special attention when bathing, brushing and drying.

Suggested Tools & Equipment

- Nail Trimmers
- Styptic Powder
- Ear Cleaning Solution
- Cotton Balls
- Clippers
- #40 and #15 Blades for Pads
- #4F for Feet & Hocks (optional)
- Slicker Brush
- Wide-Toothed Comb
- Rubber Curry
- Undercoat Rake
- Dematting Tools
- High-Velocity Dryer
- Small Detailing Shears
- Curved Shears
- Thinning Shears

Notes:

WORKING

Breed Facts & Characteristics

Country of Origin: Portugal

Height at Shoulder: 17"–23"

Coat Length/Type: Curly/Thick or Wavy/Long

Color: Black, white and all shades of brown. The black or browns can be combined with white for a two color dog.

Correct grooming procedure:
Hand-Scissor

Common pet grooming practices:
Clipper-Trim

General Description

The Portuguese Water Dog is an active, robust water dog. It was developed to assist fishermen off the shores of Portugal. It is tough and highly intelligent. It is a medium-sized working dog, slightly longer than it is tall at the withers. The head is broad, the ears heart-shaped, the neck short and the feet webbed. It has good substance with a muscular body.

~Wavy Coated Variety~
Same Trim Pattern

-The Goal-
The coat is full of body and perfectly fluffed out. Well balanced. Totally mat free. No scissor marks in coat.

Either hand-scissor the entire dog or use a guard comb to set the basic pattern. Pet dogs can be modified into shorter trim styles using the same basic pattern.

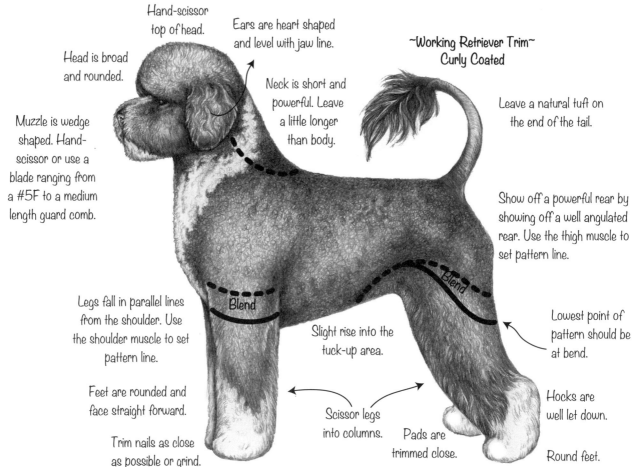

Hand-scissor top of head.

Head is broad and rounded.

Ears are heart shaped and level with jaw line.

Neck is short and powerful. Leave a little longer than body.

~Working Retriever Trim~
Curly Coated

Leave a natural tuft on the end of the tail.

Muzzle is wedge shaped. Hand-scissor or use a blade ranging from a #5F to a medium length guard comb.

Show off a powerful rear by showing off a well angulated rear. Use the thigh muscle to set pattern line.

Legs fall in parallel lines from the shoulder. Use the shoulder muscle to set pattern line.

Blend

Blend

Lowest point of pattern should be at bend.

Slight rise into the tuck-up area.

Feet are rounded and face straight forward.

Hocks are well let down.

Scissor legs into columns.

Pads are trimmed close.

Round feet.

Trim nails as close as possible or grind.

Grooming Procedures & Recommendations

Coat Types & Acceptable Trims

This breed is unique, with two equally accepted coat types and two approved trim styles. The two trims are the Lion Clip and the Working Retriever Clip. The coat types are a wavy and a tight curly coat.

See page 74 for Bathing & Drying Instructions

Frequency
Bathe once a week to once every 12 weeks. Trim every four to six weeks to maintain a stylized fashion.

Pre-Work
Trim or grind nails at least every four to six weeks to maintain a healthy foot structure. Clean the ears by swabbing with a mild ear cleaning solution. Hair should be plucked from within the ear canal only as necessary for healthy ear management. Prior to bathing, quickly go over the entire body and remove any serious mats or tangles. If the tangle can be penetrated with water, leave it and remove when the dog is clean. If the pet has not been in for professional grooming for six weeks or more, remove the excessive body coat and set the pattern before bathing.

Brushing
Prior to the haircut, the dog must be completely tangle-free. Use a firm slicker brush or a wide-toothed comb to methodically work over the entire body in a line brush fashion. Pay close attention to the friction points where mats and tangles typically hide: behind the ears, around the ruff, in the armpits, the thigh area, the undercarriage and the tail. Be careful when using any tool with metal teeth or bristles. A heavy hand or too much repetition in an area can cause cuts and/or brush burns.

Feet & Hocks
Trim the pads with a close cutting action blade ranging from a #15 to a #40. Use a very light touch to clean the pads of long hair. Tidy the outside edge of the foot, if needed, with small detailing shears.

Working Retriever Trim

Pattern Lines
This pattern calls for the coat to be approximately one inch long all over. There are no broken lines anywhere, and it outlines the natural contour of the body. A long tuft is left at the end of the tail.

Body
The body can be either hand-scissored or clipper-cut with a longer guard comb. Leave coat about one inch long over the entire body. Follow the contour of the body. The finish should be smooth and even without any scissor or clipper marks.

Chest & Neck
Hand-scissor or clipper-cut with a longer guard comb to approximately one inch in length. Follow the contour of the dog. The finish should be smooth and even without any scissor or clipper marks.

Tail
Hand-scissor or clipper-cut the base of the tail with a longer guard comb leaving approximately one inch in length cover the tail bone. A long natural tuft of fur, or plume, will be left on the end of the tailbone, covering the last third to half of the end of the tail.

Hindquarters
Hand-scissor or clipper-cut with a longer guard comb to approximately one inch in length. Follow the contour of the dog. The finish should be smooth and even without any scissor or clipper marks.

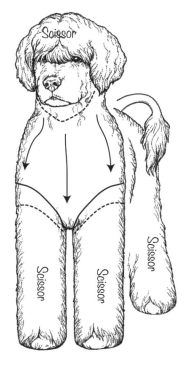

At transition points between the body and the legs, blend the lines so they are invisible. The legs should fall into straight columns, from the body to the rounded feet, when viewed from the front or rear.

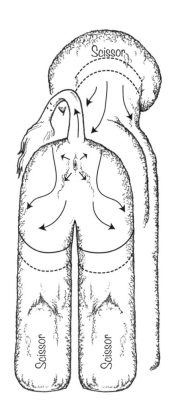

Notes From The Grooming Table ©2016

WORKING

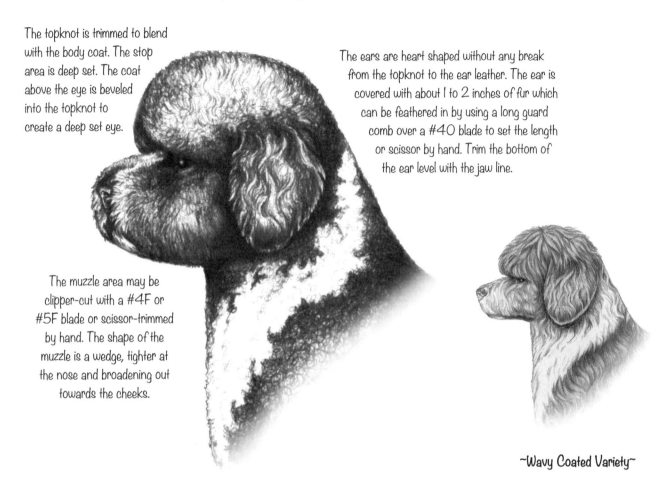

~Curly Coated Variety~

The topknot is trimmed to blend with the body coat. The stop area is deep set. The coat above the eye is beveled into the topknot to create a deep set eye.

The ears are heart shaped without any break from the topknot to the ear leather. The ear is covered with about 1 to 2 inches of fur which can be feathered in by using a long guard comb over a #40 blade to set the length or scissor by hand. Trim the bottom of the ear level with the jaw line.

The muzzle area may be clipper-cut with a #4F or #5F blade or scissor-trimmed by hand. The shape of the muzzle is a wedge, tighter at the nose and broadening out towards the cheeks.

~Wavy Coated Variety~

Front Legs
Shape the legs in parallel columns, falling straight down from the widest point of the shoulder. The coat should be approximately the same length as on the body, about 1 inch.

Feet
Round the feet with shears to blend with the legs. Box the foot in first with straight shears and then round the edges.

Head
The head is large for the size of the dog with a broad, domed skull. The eyes are round in shape and set off by a well-defined stop. Trim the stop area just enough to expose the eye, either with thinning shears or a moderately close blade such as a #10. Create a deep set eye by clearing the fur over the eye area at an angle, closer right above the eyelids and getting longer as it goes away from the eye, in a slight wedge or visor. The top of the head should be shaped either by hand with shears or with a long guard comb to blend the head with the neck and body and create a soft domed shape. There are no breaks in the coat either over the ears or at the back of the head where the head joins the body. It should balance with the overall dog.

Muzzle
The muzzle is not as long as the top skull and is wedged-shaped in structure, narrower at the nose and broadening out as it merges with the cheek and jaw area. The entire muzzle area can be hand-scissored or clipper-cut shorter than the body. If using a clipper blade, use a #5F or #4F to set the length of the pattern. Clip the entire nose/muzzle area up to the back corner of the eye, down the cheek and under the jaw, creating a soft "U" shape. Fur is left in front of the ear and on the throat to blend with the neck and chest.

Lion Trim

Pattern Lines

With the Lion Clip, the long coat is removed from the hindquarters with blades ranging from a #10 to a #4F, based on client preference. The front half of the dog is covered with longer fur, approximately three inches in length, following the natural conformation. The longer coat is either hand-scissored or the length is set using a long guard comb over a clipper blade. The muzzle and throat are clipped short, with blades ranging from a #10 to a #4F. Fur is left long and natural at the end of the tail creating a tuft. The front feet are rounded while the back feet are clipped short.

Body

The pattern line splitting the body is set at the halfway point between the fore chest, or prosternum, and the point of rump, or ischium. Another good point of reference for setting the pattern line is at approximately the second to last rib. Clip the rear with blades ranging from a #10 to a #4F, used either with or against the natural coat growth. The blade length will be based on the sensitivity of the pet's skin, the local weather conditions and client preference. Once the pattern line is set, the dog appears well balanced from front to rear, and the pattern line is clean and symmetrical from side to side.

~Curly Coated Variety~
Same Trim Pattern

-The Goal-
The pattern lines are crisp and clean. The coat is wavy and full of body. The coat floats with the dog as it moves.

Thinning shears work great with this coat type to soften and blend the coat. They are erasers for any sharp marks in the coat left from scissors or clippers.

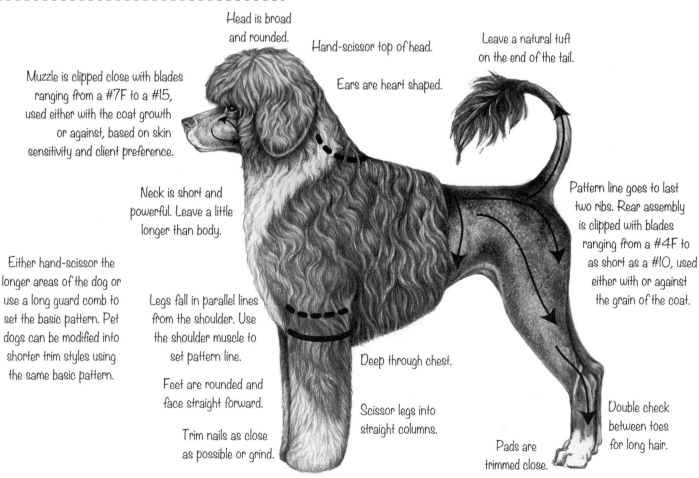

Head is broad and rounded.

Hand-scissor top of head.

Leave a natural tuft on the end of the tail.

Ears are heart shaped.

Muzzle is clipped close with blades ranging from a #7F to a #15, used either with the coat growth or against, based on skin sensitivity and client preference.

Neck is short and powerful. Leave a little longer than body.

Pattern line goes to last two ribs. Rear assembly is clipped with blades ranging from a #4F to as short as a #10, used either with or against the grain of the coat.

Either hand-scissor the longer areas of the dog or use a long guard comb to set the basic pattern. Pet dogs can be modified into shorter trim styles using the same basic pattern.

Legs fall in parallel lines from the shoulder. Use the shoulder muscle to set pattern line.

Feet are rounded and face straight forward.

Trim nails as close as possible or grind.

Deep through chest.

Scissor legs into straight columns.

Pads are trimmed close.

Double check between toes for long hair.

WORKING

The topknot is trimmed to blend with the body coat. The stop area is deep set. The coat above the eye is beveled into the topknot to create a deep set eye.

The ears are heart shaped without any break from the topknot to the ear leather. The ear is covered with about 1 to 2 inches of fur which can be feathered in by using a long guard comb over a #40 blade to set the length, or scissor by hand. Trim the bottom of the ear level with the jaw line.

The muzzle area is clipper-cut with blades ranging from a #4 to a #10 blade. Clip the entire muzzle and jaw. Do not clip back to the ear canal or down throat.

~Wavy Coated Variety~

Curly Coated Variety

Chest & Neck
Hand-scissor or use a long guard comb to follow the contour of the dog's structure. The Lion Trim calls for approximately three inches of coat left over the front section of the dog.

Tail
Clip the tail using the same blade as used on the rear section of the dog. A long natural tuft of fur, or plume, will be left on the end of the tailbone, covering the last third to half of the end of the tail.

Hindquarters
Clip the hindquarters with blades ranging from a #10 to a #4F, either with or against the grain of the coat.

The finish should be smooth and even over the entire rear section.

Front Legs
Shape the legs in parallel columns, falling straight down from the widest point of the shoulder. The coat should be approximately the same length as on the body, about 3 inches in length.

Feet
Round the feet with shears to blend with the legs.

Head
The head is large for the size of the dog with a broad, domed skull. The eyes are round in shape and set off by a well-defined stop. Trim the stop area just enough to expose the eye, either with thinning shears or a moderately close blade such as a #10. Create a deep set eye by clearing the fur over the eye area at an angle, closer right above the eyelids and getting longer going away from the eye, in a slight wedge or visor. The top of the head should be shaped either by hand with shears or with a long guard comb to blend the head with the neck and body and create the soft domed shape. There are no breaks in the coat either over the ears or at the back of the head where the head joins the body.

Grooming Procedures & Recommendations

Muzzle

The muzzle is not as long as the top skull and is wedged-shaped in structure, narrower at the nose and broadening out as it merges with the cheek and jaw area. The entire muzzle area is clipped with blades ranging from a #10 to a #4F, used either with or against the coat growth. The pattern lines are set by clipping the muzzle up to the back corner of the eye, down the cheek and under the jaw, creating a soft "U" shape. Fur is left in front of the ear and on the throat to blend with the neck and chest.

Ears

The ears are heart-shaped and trimmed to show the natural shape of the leather. The correct length can be achieved by carefully skimming the leather with a #4F blade or a short guard comb. Finish the ear by outlining the natural shape with shears or thinning shears. There should be no break between the top of the skull and the top of the ear. When viewed from the front, the domed top skull and the ears blend together in one continuous line, while the lowest point of the ear does not fall below the line of the jaw.

Special Note

The goal with the curly coat is a velvety smooth finish, similar to that of a well-groomed Poodle or Bichon. The wavy variety is similar to a cock-a-poo type dog with good coat texture. By using thinning shears in the final finish, a beautiful, smooth finish can be obtained without clipper or scissor marks on the wavy coat. The current trend for grooming the Portuguese Water Dog is to not overly stylize it when trimming, either for pet or show. To remain current with national grooming trends, attend or watch the top-winning dogs at AKC sanctioned dog shows or talk with award winning pet stylists at pet grooming shows.

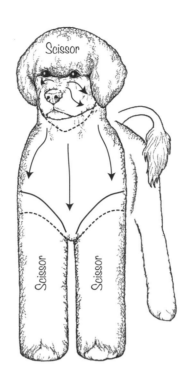

At transition points between the body and the legs, blend the lines so they are invisible. The legs should fall into straight columns, from the body to the rounded feet, when viewed from the front or rear.

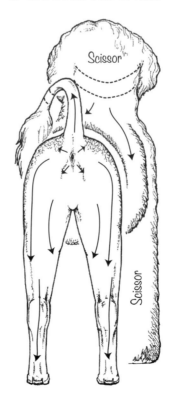

Suggested Tools & Equipment

- Nail Trimmers
- Styptic Powder
- Ear Powder
- Ear Cleaning Solution
- Cotton Balls
- Hemostat
- Clippers
- Slicker Brush
- Greyhound Comb
- Straight Shears
- Curved Shears
- Small Detailing Shears
- Thinning Shears
- Dematting Tools
- High-Velocity Dryer

Common Blade Options:

- #40, #15, #10
- #7F, #5F, #4F
- Variety of Guard Combs

Notes:

Notes From The Grooming Table ©2016

Rottweiler

Breed Facts & Characteristics

Country of Origin: Ancient Rome

Height at Shoulder: 22"–27"

Coat Length/Type: Short/Harsh

Color: The main body is always deep black with rich chestnut brown markings.

Correct grooming procedure:
Bathe & Curry Brush

Common pet grooming practices:
Bathe & Curry Brush

-The Goal-
The coat should be clean and fresh smelling, with the coat laying flat against the body. No shedding hair.

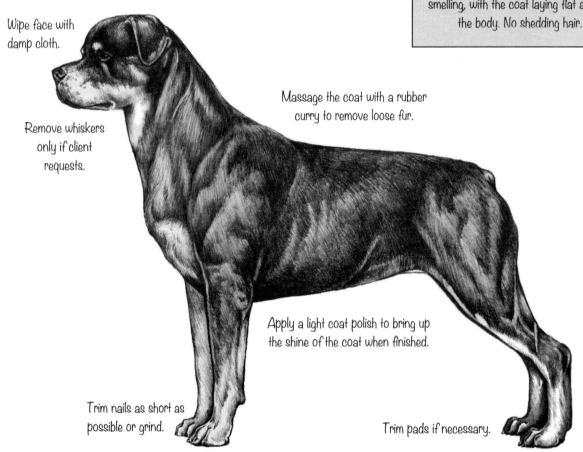

Wipe face with damp cloth.

Remove whiskers only if client requests.

Massage the coat with a rubber curry to remove loose fur.

Apply a light coat polish to bring up the shine of the coat when finished.

Trim nails as short as possible or grind.

Trim pads if necessary.

See page 67 for Bathing & Drying Instructions

Suggested Tools & Equipment

- Nail Trimmers
- Styptic Powder
- Ear Cleaning Solution
- Cotton Balls

- Clippers
- #40 or #15 Blade
- Slicker Brush
- Rubber Curry

- Carding Tool
- De-Shedding Tools
- Small Detailing Shears
- Thinning Shears

Notes *from your*
Grooming Table

Saint Bernard

WORKING   HEAVY COATED

Breed Facts & Characteristics

Country of Origin: Switzerland

Height at Shoulder: 25½"–28½"

Coat Length/Type: Combination/Heavy

Color: All shades of red combined with white. The colors should be clear patches. Black mask and ears common and desirable.

Correct grooming procedure:
Bathe & Brush Out/Minor Trimming

Common pet grooming practices:
Bathe & Brush Out/Minor Trimming

-The Goal-
The coat should be shiny, light and airy. The coat should bounce and float with the dog as it moves.

Use a damp towel to go over the muzzle after the bath.

Let a powerful high-velocity dryer help in all aspects of grooming this type of coat, before and after the bath. Blow out loose coat, tangles and dirt. Dry and fluff.

Thoroughly line brush/comb entire dog.

Remove whiskers only if the client requests.

The rump can really get packed with coat. Pay close attention to this area.

The neck and chest can really get packed with coat. Pay close attention to this area.

Friction points:
• Armpits
• Inside Thighs

Trim nails as close as possible or grind.

Trim hocks.

Neaten feet to look natural.

Shave pads.

Notes From The Grooming Table ©2016

Grooming Procedures & Recommendations

See page 70 for Bathing & Drying Instructions

Frequency
Bathe once a week to once every 12 weeks.

Pre-Work
Trim or grind nails at least every four to six weeks to maintain a healthy foot structure. Clean the ears by swabbing with a mild ear cleaning solution. Use a rubber curry, shedding blade, undercoat rake, pumice stone, carding tool, fine stripping knife or natural bristled brush to loosen skin dander and remove loose coat. Quickly blowing out the dog with a high-velocity dryer can effectively lift dirt and debris away from the skin and loosen coat. Brush out or remove any matting found in the longer coated areas. If the tangles are loose enough so water can fully penetrate the area, remove after the bathing and drying stages. If water cannot penetrate, remove the mat or tangle prior to bathing.

Brushing
Line brush, working in sections until the dog is entirely tangle-free. When finished, there should be little, if any, fur still being removed with a firm slicker brush. Double-check the work with a wide-toothed comb and your hands. Go over the entire body, feeling for any inconsistencies in the density levels of the coat. If an area seems moist to the touch or fuller than the rest of the coat, rework the area with the appropriate tool. Mats, tangles and excessive coat are easily trapped in the following areas: behind the ears, around the ruff, the thigh area, the undercarriage and the tail. Give extra attention to these areas before finishing the groom.

Sanitary Area
If the dog has a sanitation problem under the tail, lightly trim this area with thinning shears. Only clear enough coat to accomplish the goal and keep it looking very natural. Trimming of the groin area is not recommended unless there is a sanitary problem. If the groin needs to be trimmed, do so very lightly and try to leave the fur long enough so that the harsh coat does not prickle the skin, causing the dog to lick at the irritation.

Feet & Hocks
Trim the pads with a close cutting action blade ranging from a #15 to a #40. Use a very light touch to clean the pads of long hair. If there is long fur between the toes, back brush the fur so it stands up and away from the foot. With thinning shears, trim off the excess creating a neat and very natural looking foot with well arched toes. Tidy the outside edge of the foot, if needed, with small detailing shears. If the hocks have longer coat, trim lightly with thinning shears showing a neat, clean area. A #4F blade used in reverse works well for trimming the tops of the feet and the hocks on some dogs.

Detail Finish
Edge the ears lightly with thinning shears to neaten but look natural. Hand-pluck any long wispy, flyaway hair from around the ears. Removal of whiskers on the muzzle is optional based on client preference. Finish with a fine mist of coat polish on the body coat for added shine. Application of bows and mild cologne are optional.

Grooming Tip
Let your hands guide you. Learn to feel for differences in coat density levels. Areas that feel heavier or denser than other areas need special attention when bathing, brushing and drying.

Suggested Tools & Equipment
- Nail Trimmers
- Styptic Powder
- Ear Cleaning Solution
- Cotton Balls
- Clippers
- #40 and #15 Blades for Pads
- #4F for Feet & Hocks (optional)
- Slicker Brush
- Wide-Toothed Comb
- Rubber Curry
- Undercoat Rake
- Dematting Tools
- High-Velocity Dryer
- Small Detailing Shears
- Curved Shears
- Thinning Shears

Notes:

Notes From The Grooming Table ©2016

Breed Facts & Characteristics

Country of Origin: Siberia

Height at Shoulder: 19"–23½"

Coat Length/Type: Combination/Thick

Color: White. Cream patches or biscuit patches allowed.

Correct grooming procedure:
Bathe & Brush Out/Minor Trimming

Common pet grooming practices:
Bathe & Brush Out/Minor Trimming

Let a powerful high-velocity dryer help in all aspects of grooming this type of coat, before and after the bath. Blow out loose coat, tangles and dirt. Dry and fluff.

-The Goal-
The coat should be shiny, light and airy. The coat should bounce and float with the dog as it moves.

Edge ears with thinning shears to make very natural and neat.

Watch for mats.

~Seasonal Shedding~
In Colder Climates.

Use a damp towel to go over the muzzle after the bath.

Thoroughly line brush/comb entire dog.

The rump can really get packed with coat. Pay close attention to this area.

Remove whiskers only if client requests.

When finished you should be able to sink a wide-toothed comb to the skin and pull it freely out to the end of the hair shaft.

The neck and chest can really get packed with coat. Pay close attention to this area.

Can shed heavily here.

Can shed heavily here.

Trim nails as close as possible or grind.

Trim hocks.

Shave pads and neaten feet to look natural with well arched toes.

Grooming Procedures & Recommendations

See page 70 for
Bathing & Drying Instructions

Frequency
Bathe once a week to once every 12 weeks.

Pre-Work
Trim or grind nails at least every four to six weeks to maintain a healthy foot structure. Clean the ears by swabbing with a mild ear cleaning solution. Use a rubber curry, shedding blade, undercoat rake, pumice stone, carding tool, fine stripping knife or natural bristled brush to loosen skin dander and remove loose coat. Quickly blowing out the dog with a high-velocity dryer can effectively lift dirt and debris away from the skin and loosen coat. Brush out or remove any matting found in the longer coated areas. If the tangles are loose enough so water can fully penetrate the area, remove after the bathing and drying stages. If water cannot penetrate, remove the mat or tangle prior to bathing.

Brushing
Line brush, working in sections until the dog is entirely tangle-free. When finished, there should be little, if any, fur still being removed with a firm slicker brush. Double-check the work with a wide-toothed comb and your hands. Go over the entire body, feeling for any inconsistencies in the density levels of the coat. If an area seems moist to the touch or fuller than the rest of the coat, rework the area with the appropriate tool. Mats, tangles and excessive coat are easily trapped in the following areas: behind the ears, around the ruff, the thigh area, the undercarriage and the tail. Give extra attention to these areas before finishing the groom.

Sanitary Area
If the dog has a sanitation problem under the tail, lightly trim this area with thinning shears. Only clear enough coat to accomplish the goal and keep it looking very natural. Trimming of the groin area is not recommended unless there is a sanitary problem. If the groin needs to be trimmed, do so very lightly and try to leave the fur long enough so that the harsh coat does not prickle the skin, causing the dog to lick at the irritation.

Feet & Hocks
Trim the pads with a close cutting action blade ranging from a #15 to a #40. Use a very light touch to clean the pads of long hair. If there is long fur between the toes, back brush the fur so it stands up and away from the foot. With thinning shears, trim off the excess creating a neat and very natural looking foot with well arched toes. Tidy the outside edge of the foot, if needed, with small detailing shears. If the hocks have longer coat, trim lightly with thinning shears showing a neat, clean area. A #4F blade used in reverse works well for trimming the tops of the feet and the hocks on some dogs.

Detail Finish
Edge the ears lightly with thinning shears to neaten but look natural. Hand-pluck any long wispy, flyaway hair from around the ears. Removal of whiskers on the muzzle is optional based on client preference. Finish with a fine mist of coat polish on the body coat for added shine. Application of bows and mild cologne are optional.

Grooming Tip
Let your hands guide you. Learn to feel for differences in coat density levels. Areas that feel heavier or denser than other areas need special attention when bathing, brushing and drying.

Suggested Tools & Equipment

- Nail Trimmers
- Styptic Powder
- Ear Cleaning Solution
- Cotton Balls
- Clippers
- #40 and #15 Blades for Pads
- #4F for Feet & Hocks (optional)
- Slicker Brush
- Wide-Toothed Comb
- Rubber Curry
- Undercoat Rake
- Dematting Tools
- High-Velocity Dryer
- Small Detailing Shears
- Curved Shears
- Thinning Shears

Notes:

Siberian Husky

Breed Facts & Characteristics

Country of Origin: Siberia

Height at Shoulder: 20"–23½"

Coat Length/Type: Double Coated/Dense

Color: All colors are allowed. Undercoat is typically light in color.

Correct grooming procedure:
Bathe & Brush Out

Common pet grooming practices:
Bathe & Brush Out

-The Goal-
The coat should be light and stand off the dog. The coat should bounce and shimmer with the dog as it moves. You should be able to sink a wide-toothed comb to the skin and pull it freely out to the end of the hair shaft.

~Seasonal Shedding~
In Colder Climates.

When shedding—the more work you can do with a powerful high-velocity dryer, the less "elbow grease" you will have to apply.

Let a powerful high-velocity dryer help in all aspects of grooming this type of coat, before and after the bath. Blow out loose coat, tangles and dirt. Dry and fluff.

Edge ears with thinning shears to make very natural and neat.

Use a damp towel to go over the muzzle after the bath.

Thoroughly line brush/comb entire dog.

The rump can really get packed with coat. Pay close attention to this area.

Remove whiskers only if the client requests.

The neck and chest can really get packed with coat. Pay close attention to this area.

Can shed heavily here.

Can shed heavily here.

Neaten the back of the pastern to the stopper pad.

Trim nails.

Trim hocks.

Shave pads.

Neaten feet to look natural with well arched toes.

Grooming Procedures & Recommendations

See page 69 for
Bathing & Drying Instructions

Frequency
Bathe once a week to once every
12 weeks.

Pre-Work
Trim or grind nails at least every four
to six weeks to maintain a healthy foot
structure. Clean the ears by swabbing
with a mild ear cleaning solution. Prior
to bathing, quickly go over the entire
body with a high-velocity dryer to help
lift dirt and dander away from the skin
and loosen any shedding coat.

Brushing
Use a slicker brush, rubber curry,
shedding blade, dematting tool or
undercoat rake to loosen skin dander
and remove loose coat. Be careful
when using any tool with metal teeth
or bristles. A heavy hand or too much
repetition in an area can cause cuts and/
or brush burns. Brushing and combing
is not finished until all loose fur is
removed, or it has become difficult to
remove more than a half a brush full
after repeated brushing.

Sanitary Area
If the dog has a sanitation problem
under the tail, lightly trim this area
with thinning shears. Only clear
enough coat to accomplish the goal
and keep it looking very natural.
Trimming of the groin area is not
recommended unless there is a sanitary
problem. If the groin needs to be
trimmed, do so very lightly and try to
leave the fur long enough so that the
harsh coat does not prickle the skin,
causing the dog to lick at the irritation.

Feet & Hocks
Trim the pads with a close cutting
action blade, ranging from a #15 to a
#40. Use a very light touch to clean the
pads of long hair. If there is long fur
between the toes, back brush the fur so
it stands up and away from the foot.
With thinning shears, trim off the excess
creating a neat and very natural looking
foot with well arched toes. Tidy the
outside edge of the foot, if needed, with
small detailing shears. If the hocks have
longer coat on them, trim lightly with
thinning shears showing a neat, clean
area. A #4F blade used in reverse works
well for trimming the tops of the feet
and the hocks on some dogs.

Detail Finish
Removal of whiskers on the muzzle is
optional, based on client preference.
Finish with a fine mist of coat polish on
the body for added shine. Application of
bows and mild cologne is optional.

Grooming Tip
Let your hands guide you. Learn to feel
for differences in coat density levels.
Areas that feel heavier or denser than
other areas need special attention when
bathing, brushing and drying.

Suggested Tools & Equipment

- Nail Trimmers
- Styptic Powder
- Ear Cleaning Solution
- Cotton Balls
- Clippers
- #40 and #15 Blades for Pads
- #4F for Feet & Hocks (optional)
- Slicker Brush
- Greyhound Comb
- Rubber Curry
- Carding Tool
- De-Shedding Tools
- Small Detailing Shears
- Thinning Shears
- High-Velocity Dryer

Notes:

Standard Schnauzer   WORKING   WIRE COATED

Breed Facts & Characteristics

Country of Origin: Germany

Height at Shoulder: 17½"–19½"

Coat Length/Type: Hard/Wiry

Color: Salt and pepper or black.

Correct grooming procedure:
Hand-Strip

Common pet grooming practices:
Clipper-Trim

General Description

The Standard Schnauzer is a powerful, muscular and squarely built dog of high energy and great intelligence. Its tail is docked short. It may have cropped or uncropped ears. When grooming a Schnauzer, remember there is nothing soft or fluffy about the breed. In the finished groom, there is very little coat hiding the contours of its body. The leg coat and muzzle coat are slightly longer. The hallmark of the breed is its rectangular head, arched eyebrows and full mustache and beard.

-The Goal-
This is a tight and very tailored-looking dog. The body is almost square in build with a rectangular head. When finished, pattern line on the body is invisible.

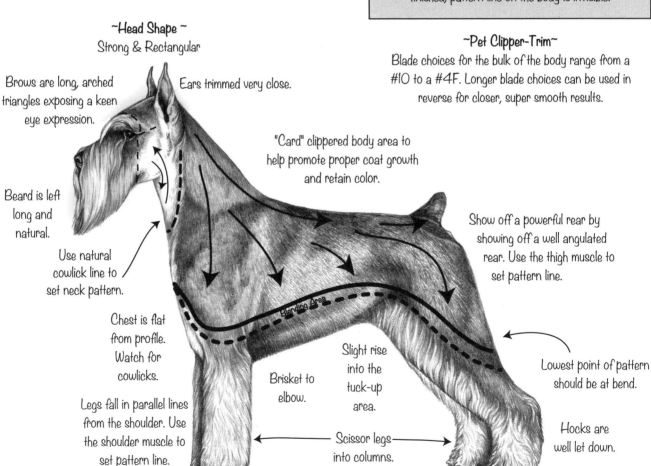

~Head Shape~
Strong & Rectangular

Brows are long, arched triangles exposing a keen eye expression.

Ears trimmed very close.

~Pet Clipper-Trim~
Blade choices for the bulk of the body range from a #10 to a #4F. Longer blade choices can be used in reverse for closer, super smooth results.

"Card" clippered body area to help promote proper coat growth and retain color.

Beard is left long and natural.

Use natural cowlick line to set neck pattern.

Show off a powerful rear by showing off a well angulated rear. Use the thigh muscle to set pattern line.

Chest is flat from profile. Watch for cowlicks.

Blending Area

Slight rise into the tuck-up area.

Brisket to elbow.

Lowest point of pattern should be at bend.

Legs fall in parallel lines from the shoulder. Use the shoulder muscle to set pattern line.

Scissor legs into columns.

Hocks are well let down.

Feet are rounded and face straight forward.

Pads are trimmed close.   Round feet.

Grooming Procedures & Recommendations

See page 76 for
Bathing & Drying Instructions

Frequency
Bathe once a week to once every 12 weeks. Trim every four to six weeks to maintain a stylized fashion.

Pre-Work
Trim or grind nails at least every four to six weeks to maintain a healthy foot structure. Clean the ears by swabbing with a mild ear cleaning solution. Hair should be plucked from within the ear canal only as necessary for healthy ear management. Prior to bathing, quickly go over the entire body and remove any serious mats or tangles. If the tangle can be penetrated with water, leave it and remove when the dog is clean. If the pet has not been in for professional grooming for six weeks or more, remove the excessive body coat and set the pattern before bathing.

Brushing
Prior to the haircut, the dog must be completely tangle-free. Use a firm slicker brush or a wide-toothed comb to methodically work over the entire body in a line brush fashion. Pay close attention to the friction points where mats and tangles typically hide: behind the ears, around the ruff, in the armpits, the thigh area, the undercarriage and the tail. Be careful when using any tool with metal teeth or bristles. A heavy hand or too much repetition in an area can cause cuts and/or brush burns.

Pattern Lines in General
The pattern is based on the bone and muscle structure of the dog. After the final trim, all pattern lines on the body should be invisible. At the transition points, feather off with the clippers in a smooth and steady fashion. If the pattern line is still visible after clipping, use thinning shears to blend the line. On the head, the pattern lines are crisp and clean.

Body
For either hand-stripped or clipper-cut dogs, the general pattern is the same. Typical blades used in pet grooming range from a #10 to a #7F, or a combination of those blades for the bulk of the body work. Some stylists find reversing a slightly longer blade very effective in achieving an extremely smooth finish on the body. Reversing a blade will shorten the cutting action by about two blade lengths as the same blade used with the grain of the coat. Choose one of the methods and follow the direction of the natural coat growth of the fur. After clipping, card the coat to help promote proper coat growth while retaining some of the rich color and harsh coat texture. Carding also will assist in the removal of any minor tracking left in the coat from clipping. The pattern lines start at the turn of the shoulder and continue to just above the elbow, back to the flank on a diagonal and then drop into the thigh region.

Undercarriage
Right around the navel area, the coat will be very short and start to get longer as the line moves forward towards the brisket, creating the illusion of a deep chest. When viewed in profile, the distance from the elbow to the bottom of the foot is equal to the distance between the withers and the brisket. There is only enough fur left on the undercarriage to accentuate depth of chest and an athletic build. The pattern line is well blended and invisible.

Tail & Rear
The top side of the tail is trimmed with the same blade as the body. The underside of the tail is clipped close, with blades ranging from #15 to a #7F, used with or against the grain based on the sensitivity of the dog's skin. Continue with the same blade around the rectum and on the inner side of the cowlick lines going down the back side of the thighs.

At transition points on the body, blend the lines so they are invisible. Legs should be left fuller and fall into straight columns, from the body to the feet, on both the front and rear legs. The chest should be flat but use caution not to bald out this area due to cowlicks found where the front legs meet the chest.

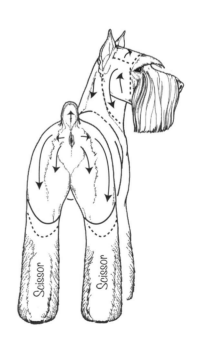

Shape the arched eyebrows by following the eye socket ridge. The stop area is clear, creating split brows. Use curved shears in reverse to help shape the eyebrows. The coat is very short at the back of the eye and gets longer towards the nose. Brows tips reach to the halfway point of the muzzle.

Hand-strip or clipper the top skull very close. If clipping, use blades ranging from a #10 used with the grain to a #4F used against the grain, depending on the coat density.

The ears may be cropped or natural. Either type is clipper-trimmed very close with blades ranging from a #10 or #15 on the outside and a #40 on the inside. Finish by edging the ears with small detailing shears.

The beard and mustache form a rectangular head style. When viewed straight on, the cheeks and the beard should form one continuous line.

The occiput is the dividing line between the head and the neck.

The cheeks and throat are smooth and clean. Blades ranging from a #10 to a #15, used with or against the grain, are common in pet styling. The line runs from the back corner of the eye to the cheek whisker nodule, to the chin nodule, up to the opposite cheek whisker nodule and opposite eye. Use the zygomatic arch to set the line from the back corner of the eye to the ear canal. The natural cowlick line assists with setting the throat area. Create a soft "V" or "U" shape coming about 3–4 finger widths above the breast bone.

Hindquarters

The hindquarters should be strong and powerful. When clipping this area, expose the thigh muscle with the same blade used on the body. Start to feather off with the blade where the muscle starts to turn under on a diagonal line from the flank region to about three or four fingers above the hock. Using a short to medium guard comb can facilitate feathering in the blending line. The pattern line should be invisible when the trim is finished. Blend with thinning shears if necessary. The stifle area should have enough furnishing left to give the legs substance and angulation. The longest

coat on the legs can range from 1 to 3.5 inches depending on the amount of bone and coat density. Shape this area by hand with shears after the clipper work is complete. When viewed from the rear, the legs should form two parallel lines to the ground. The hocks are well let down. There should be adequate coat on the hock area to accentuate the angles of the rear assembly.

Front Legs

The coat on the legs can range from ⅟₁₆ of an inch to 3 inches in length depending on the amount of bone, the size of the dog and coat density.

The front legs drop straight down from the body and have ample bone and muscle to show off a powerful and sturdy animal. The pattern line at the shoulder is about 1 or 2 fingers above the top of the elbow, at the point where the muscle begins to turn under. The coat at the transition line will be very short, and taper into the longer leg furnishings. This can be accomplished by feathering off at the blending point with the same blade used on the body. Other methods of blending off at the top of the leg include using an attachment comb followed by hand-scissoring and blending with thinning shears. Most stylists prefer to leave the legs to shape by hand with shears. After the final trim, the legs need to form two parallel columns going down from the elbow into tight, round feet. The coat at the back of the elbow is very short and falls straight down off the back of the leg toward the ground.

Feet

The feet are small for the size of the dog. Both the front and rear feet are compact with well arched toes. To show off these traits, the feet are trimmed very close to the edge of the foot and some nail is routinely exposed. The feet should point straight ahead, toeing neither in nor out. Trim the feet round by first boxing them in the shape of a square while the dog is standing in a natural, square position. Then remove the sharp corners of the box and round the feet facing straight forward. If detailing the feet with the foot off the tabletop, always use a small pair of shears to minimize the risk of accidentally cutting the pads.

Throat & Chest

Blades ranging from #10 to #7F, with or against the grain, based on the sensitivity of the dog's skin, are common in the throat area. Follow the natural cowlick line that runs in a "V" shape from the base of the ears towards the base of the neck. The blending point begins about 3 or 4 fingers above the breast bone and drops to just below the turn of the muscle at the elbow/shoulder, creating a "W" shape when viewed straight on. When viewed in profile, the neck into the chest should be straight without a predominant forechest. When blending the chest, be aware of the heavy cowlicks in the area. Many stylists prefer to leave the chest area to blend by hand with thinning shears or shears. When finished in this area, double check your work to be sure the neck, chest and front legs drop down in a straight line when viewed in profile.

The Head in General: Top Skull

The top of the head can be clipped as close as a #10 used with the grain; to a #7F or #5F, used with the grain or against depending on the dog's sensitivity and density of the coat.

Ears

Both cropped and uncropped ears are clipped with a close blade. It is common to see a #10 or #15 blade used on the outside of the ear leather while a #40 blade is used on the inside. When working with close blades in this delicate area, always work from the base or center of the ear out toward the edge. Gently brace the ear with your fingers to clip over it. To finish, use small finishing shears to trim around the outside edge of the ear leather, keeping the tips of the shears toward the tip of the ears.

Brows

To form the arched, triangular eyebrows follow the eye socket rim, working with or against the grain of the coat. Schnauzers have a slight stop between the eyes that acts as a natural split for the brows. Either lightly clip this area when clipping the top skull or leave it to do by hand with thinning shears. Shape the brows into long arched triangles that accentuate the typically keen look. They will be very short at the back corner of the eye and longer at the tips, coming almost halfway down the bridge of the nose. When viewed in profile, the brows should barely break the line of the top skull as they arch out over the nose. Use curved shears in reverse to set the brow. Line the tip of the shear up with a point on the nose. Repeat on the other brow. By using the nose as a set point, the length and angle of both eyebrows remain the same. Bevel the blades of the shears away from the pet's skin to avoid accidentally cutting the dog at the back corner of the eye when you close the shear to cut the brow.

Throat & Cheeks

The throat and cheek areas are clipped using blades ranging from a #10 to a #7F, used either with or against the grain. Use the natural cowlick line of the neck to be the guide to create the "U" or "V" shape of the throat. The lowest point will be about 3 fingers above the breast bone. The line that breaks the top skull and the cheeks is from the back corner of the eye straight back to the ear canal.

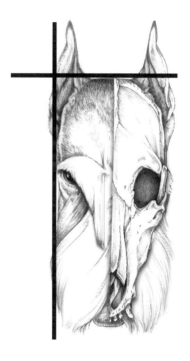

Any hair falling outside the line of the cheek bone needs to leave. Any hair remaining inside the line needs to stay, creating the correct "rectangular" head style for the breed.

Notes:

WORKING

Beard & Goatee

The fur on the muzzle is a natural length as it forms the beard. The basic transition line between the cheek and the beard runs on an imaginary line from just behind the back corner of the eyes to the whisker nodule on the cheeks. The line continues under the jaw to the single center whisker nodule. The line should be very crisp and clean, just clearing the outside corner of the mouth so when the dog pants, you can see the separation between the top and the bottom jaw. The coat under the eye area is never clipped as this hair forms one of the critical lines of the classic rectangular head style. The line on the dog's face should be straight, from the flat cheek down into the beard area. Double check this line by laying a greyhound comb along side the head. Any fur that sticks out beyond the comb should be removed. Any hair inside this line needs to remain and to be blended to create the rectangular shape.

Detail Finish

Application of bows and mild cologne is optional.

Grooming Tips

A light setting gel, mousse or texturing shampoo can add body to the leg coat, making it easier to scissor. Try spritzing unruly eyebrows while they are still damp with a styling spray. Work the product into the damp brows. Brush or comb the brows into place or dry them into the position you want them in the final trim.

Special Note

Harsh-coated terriers have a coat that will normally brush out quite easily, especially after they are clean.

Suggested Tools & Equipment

- Nail Trimmers
- Styptic Powder
- Ear Powder
- Ear Cleaning Solution
- Cotton Balls
- Hemostat
- Clippers
- Slicker Brush
- Greyhound Comb
- Pumice Stone
- Carding Tools
- Stripping Knives
- Straight Shears
- Curved Shears
- Small Detailing Shears
- Thinning Shears
- Dematting Tools

Common Blade Options:

- #40, #15, #10
- #7F, #5F, #4F
- Variety of Guard Combs

Notes:

Notes *from your*
Grooming Table

Notes From The Grooming Table ©2016

Breed Facts & Characteristics

Country of Origin: Tibet

Height at Shoulder: 24"–29"

Coat Length/Type: Combination/Heavy

Color: Lighter phantom markings on all shades of black, brown, gray main colored coats. Limited amount of white accepted on the chest and toes.

Correct grooming procedure:
Bathe & Brush Out

Common pet grooming practices:
Bathe & Brush Out

-The Goal-
Coat should be mat free, shiny, light and airy. The coat should bounce and float with the dog as it moves. No loose coat.

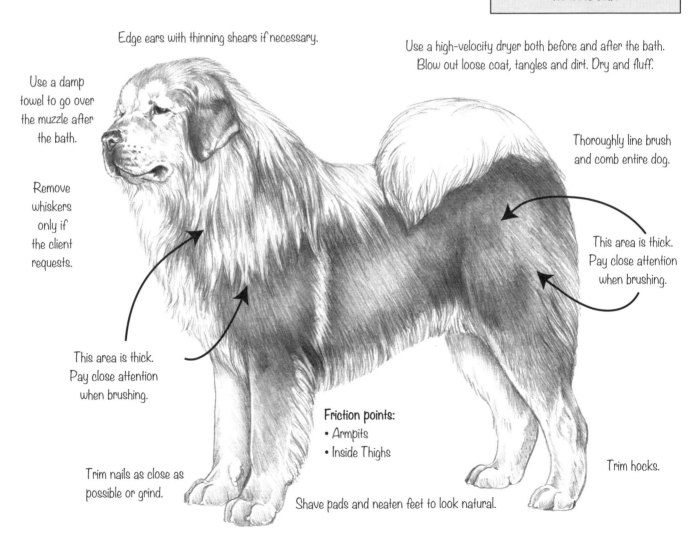

Edge ears with thinning shears if necessary.

Use a high-velocity dryer both before and after the bath. Blow out loose coat, tangles and dirt. Dry and fluff.

Use a damp towel to go over the muzzle after the bath.

Remove whiskers only if the client requests.

Thoroughly line brush and comb entire dog.

This area is thick. Pay close attention when brushing.

This area is thick. Pay close attention when brushing.

Friction points:
• Armpits
• Inside Thighs

Trim nails as close as possible or grind.

Shave pads and neaten feet to look natural.

Trim hocks.

See page 70 for
Bathing & Drying Instructions

Frequency
Bathe once a week to once every 12 weeks.

Pre-Work
Trim or grind nails at least every four to six weeks to maintain a healthy foot structure. Swab the ears clean with a mild ear cleaning solution. Quickly blow out the dog's coat with a high-velocity dryer to effectively lift dirt and debris away from the skin and loosen coat. Brush out or remove any matting found in the longer coated areas. If the tangles are loose enough so that water can fully penetrate them, remove them after bathing and drying. If water cannot penetrate, remove the mat or tangle prior to bathing.

Brushing
Line brush, working in sections, until the dog is entirely tangle-free. When finished, there should be little, if any, fur still being removed with a firm slicker brush. Double-check the work with a wide-toothed comb and your hands. Go over the entire body, feeling for any inconsistencies in the density levels of the coat. If an area seems moist to the touch or fuller than the rest of the coat, rework the area with the appropriate tool. Mats, tangles and excessive coat are easily trapped in the following areas: behind the ears, around the ruff, the thigh area, the undercarriage and the tail. Give extra attention to these areas before finishing the groom.

Feet & Hocks
Trim the pads with blades ranging from a #15 to a #40. Use a very light touch to clean the pads of long hair. If there is long fur between the toes, brush it back so the fur stands up and away from the foot. With thinning shears, trim off the excess to create a neat and very natural looking foot with well-arched toes. Tidy the outside edge of the foot, if needed, with small detailing shears. If the hocks have longer coat, trim lightly with thinning shears to show a neat, clean area. A #4F blade used in reverse works well for trimming the tops of the feet and the hocks on small to larger dogs that are light to moderately coated. With very heavy-coated or giant dogs, handle the top of the feet and hocks using hand-trimming techniques instead of a clipper.

Sanitary Area
If the dog has a sanitation problem under the tail, lightly trim this area with thinning shears. Only clear enough coat to accomplish the goal and keep it looking very natural. Trimming of the groin area is not recommended unless there is a sanitary problem. If the groin needs to be trimmed, do so very lightly and try to leave the fur long enough so that the harsh coat does not prickle the skin, causing the dog to lick at the irritation.

Detail Finish
Removal of muzzle whiskers is optional, based on client preference. For added shine, finish with a fine mist of coat polish on the body coat. Application of bows and mild cologne is optional.

Suggested Tools & Equipment

- Nail Trimmers
- Styptic Powder
- Ear Cleaning Solution
- Cotton Balls
- Clippers
- #40 and #15 Blades for Pads
- #4F for Feet & Hocks (optional)
- Slicker Brush
- Wide-Toothed Comb
- Rubber Curry
- Undercoat Rake
- Dematting Tools
- High-Velocity Dryer
- Small Detailing Shears
- Curved Shears
- Thinning Shears

Notes:

For the first half of the book, please see:
Notes from the Grooming Table, Volume One.

Table of Contents: Volume Two

Table of Contents: Volume Two

Table of Contents: Volume Two

The Terrier Group

Dogs in the Terrier Group were bred to locate and capture vermin. Commonly described as "feisty," dogs in this group typically don't do well with other dogs. Breeds in this category show great determination, courage and self-confidence, with a great willingness to go to ground in search of their quarry. This is a very energetic group of dogs with fun personalities as long as things are going the way they want them to go.

Airedale

Breed Facts & Characteristics

Country of Origin: England

Height at Shoulder: 22"–23"

Coat Length/Type: Hard/Wiry

Color: Black & Tan: black saddle, tan flatwork and furnishings.

Correct grooming procedure:

Hand-Strip

Common pet grooming practices:

Clipper-Trim

General Description

Everything about the Airedale is tight and tailored. This is a dog of great strength, power and agility. They are known as the "King of Terriers." When grooming an Airedale, remember there is nothing soft or fluffy about the breed. In the finished groom, there is very little coat hiding the contours of its body. The leg coat is slightly longer. The head is rectangular in shape with a piercing expression, moderate muzzle coat and small brows.

Correctly Groomed: Hand-Stripped

Typical blades used on the body for pet grooming: #10, #8.5, #7F, #5F, #4F or shorter guard comb or a combination of those blades. Card coat after clipping to help maintain correct coat texture and color.

-The Goal-

Everything about this breed is tight and tailored. The well-toned body is accentuated by the groom. The head is rectangular in shape. All pattern lines are invisible.

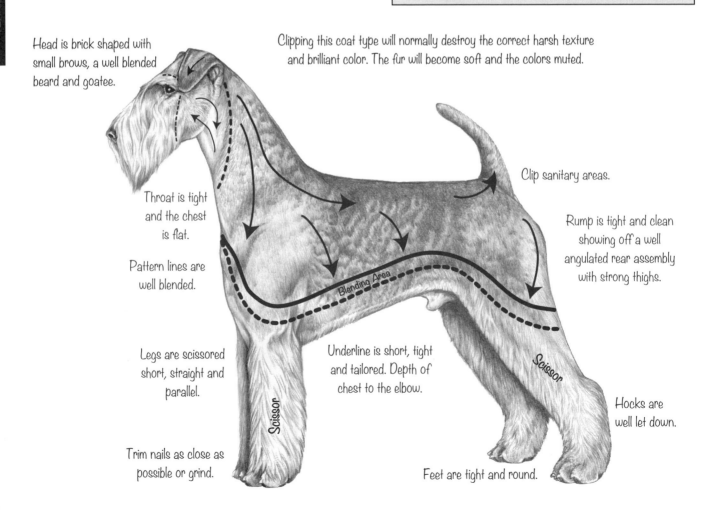

Head is brick shaped with small brows, a well blended beard and goatee.

Clipping this coat type will normally destroy the correct harsh texture and brilliant color. The fur will become soft and the colors muted.

Throat is tight and the chest is flat.

Pattern lines are well blended.

Legs are scissored short, straight and parallel.

Trim nails as close as possible or grind.

Underline is short, tight and tailored. Depth of chest to the elbow.

Blending Area

Scissor

Clip sanitary areas.

Rump is tight and clean showing off a well angulated rear assembly with strong thighs.

Scissor

Hocks are well let down.

Feet are tight and round.

TERRIER

Grooming Procedures & Recommendations

**See page 76 for
Bathing & Drying Instructions**

Frequency
Bathe once a week to once every
12 weeks. Trim every four to six weeks
to maintain a stylized fashion.

Pre-Work
Trim or grind nails at least every four
to six weeks to maintain a healthy foot
structure. Swab the ears clean with a
mild ear cleaning solution. Prior to
bathing, quickly go over the entire
body with a high-velocity dryer to help
lift dirt and dander away from the skin
and to loosen any shedding coat. ***Card
and hand-strip dog prior to bathing
and drying.***

Done to breed standard, the coat is
hand-stripped to promote healthy skin
tone, proper coat texture and rich color.
Many pet owners choose to clipper-cut
their pet dog. This practice destroys the
correct harsh coat texture on most dogs
and dilutes the color on salt-and-pepper
dogs. However, it is an economical way
to keep the pet looking like the breed
standard. Finding a stylist who is willing
to commit the time and energy to hand-
strip some breeds can be difficult. Plus,
many pet owners are not willing to pay
for this highly skilled service.

Hand-Stripping
Hand-stripping is a technique in which
the outer guard coat is plucked from the
dog's skin. This procedure helps retain
the proper coat texture and rich color of
the breed. During certain times of the
year, the coat is easier to pull out. When
the coat easily comes out, it is called a
"blowing coat" or "blown coat." Ideally,
hand-stripping should correspond with
the dog's natural cycle, based on the
environment and its hormonal levels.
Using your fingers, a carding tool or a
stripping knife, pull out a few hairs at
a time to shape the coat, accentuating
the natural outline of the dog. Work
methodically, pulling small amounts of
coat at a time, always working in the
direction of the coat growth. Proper
hand-stripping removes hair with a
gentle momentum and rhythm, not
brute force, which is uncomfortable
for both groomer and pet. The wrist
stays locked in a neutral position while
the rhythmic movement stems from
the shoulder, not the wrist or elbow.
In general, the main body coat is easy
to remove. Most pets do not mind the
plucking process. The cheeks, throat
and private areas may be more sensitive,
requiring thinning shears or clippers.
Leave enough coat to be between 1 to
2 inches long. The coat should always
appear very natural, never clipped or
heavily trimmed. On some coats, a light
application of chalk or powder before the
bath will allow a better grip and make
plucking and stripping much easier.

Brushing
Use a rubber curry, shedding blade,
undercoat rake, pumice stone, carding
tool, fine stripping knife, slicker brush
or natural bristled brush to remove
any remaining loose coat or tangles. Be
careful when using any tool with metal
teeth or bristles. A heavy hand or too
much repetition in an area can cause
cuts and/or brush burns. Brushing
is not finished until all loose fur is
removed, or when it becomes difficult
to remove more than a half a brush
full after repeated brushing.

Pattern Lines in General
The pattern is based on the bone and
muscle structure of the dog. After
the final trim, all pattern lines should
be invisible. At the transition points,
feather off with the clippers in a smooth
and steady fashion. If the pattern line is
still visible after clipping, use thinning
shears to blend the line.

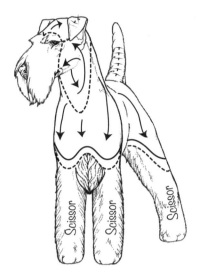

From the front and rear, the legs
drop in straight, parallel lines from
well toned shoulders and thighs.
When setting the pattern, use the
turn of the muscles to set the lines.
Chest is flat but use caution not to
bald out this area due to cowlicks
where the front legs join the chest.
Rear is short, tight and clean. Leg
furnishings are slightly longer than
the body coat.

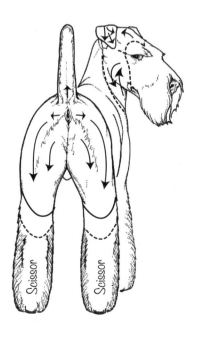

Notes From The Grooming Table ©2016

Their expression is friendly but alert and courageous. Head is brick shaped with small brows and a well blended beard and goatee. The top skull and the muzzle are equal in length with the stop area being the center point. All lines on the head are invisible.

Clip top skull with blades ranging from a #7F to a #5F, with the grain.

Use a #10 or #15 blade on the outside of the ear, a #40 blade can be used on the inside of the ear leather with a very light touch. Edge the ear with small detailing shears. The fold of the ear comes to just above the line of the top skull.

The eyebrows are very small, split at the stop area. There are no sharp lines. Shape and blend with thinning shears.

Ear Safety Tip: Remember, always keep the tips of the shears towards the tips of the ears when edging for safety.

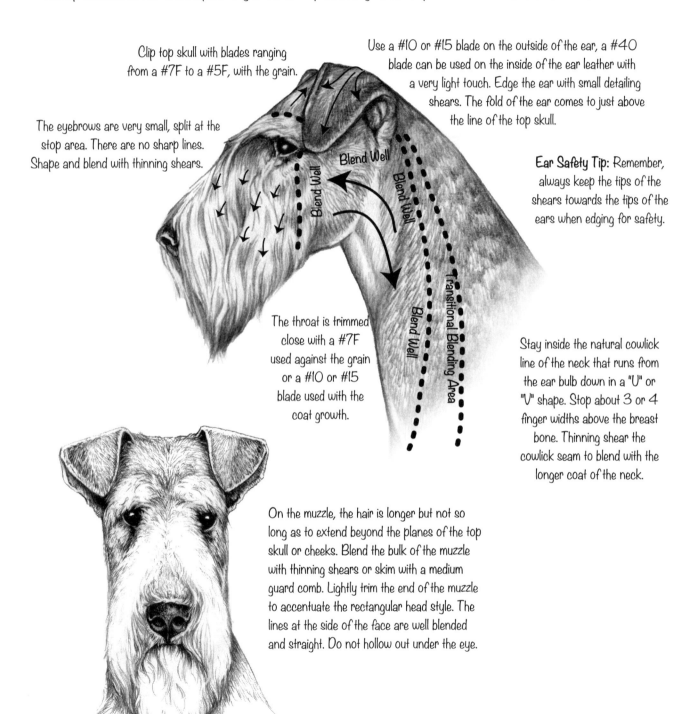

Blend Well

Blend Well

Blend Well

Transitional Blending Area

Blend Well

The throat is trimmed close with a #7F used against the grain or a #10 or #15 blade used with the coat growth.

Stay inside the natural cowlick line of the neck that runs from the ear bulb down in a "U" or "V" shape. Stop about 3 or 4 finger widths above the breast bone. Thinning shear the cowlick seam to blend with the longer coat of the neck.

On the muzzle, the hair is longer but not so long as to extend beyond the planes of the top skull or cheeks. Blend the bulk of the muzzle with thinning shears or skim with a medium guard comb. Lightly trim the end of the muzzle to accentuate the rectangular head style. The lines at the side of the face are well blended and straight. Do not hollow out under the eye.

Body

For either hand-stripped or clipper-cut dogs, the general pattern is the same. Typical blades used in pet grooming range from a #7F to a #4F or a combination of those blades for the bulk of the body work. Some stylists find reversing a slightly longer blade very effective in achieving an extremely smooth finish on the body. Reversing a blade will shorten the cutting action by about two blade lengths as the same blade used with the grain of the coat. Choose one of the methods and follow the direction of the natural coat growth of the fur. After clipping, card the coat to help promote proper coat growth while retaining some of the rich color and harsh coat texture. Carding also will assist in the removal of any minor tracking left in the coat from clipping. The pattern lines start at the turn of the shoulder and continue to just above the elbow, back to the flank on a diagonal and then drop into the thigh region.

Tail & Rear

The top side of the tail is trimmed with the same blade as the body. The underside of the tail is clipped close, with blades ranging from #15 to a #7F, used with or against the grain based on the sensitivity of the dog's skin. Continue with the same blade around the rectum and on the inner side of the cowlick lines going down the back side of the thighs.

Undercarriage

Right around the navel area, the coat will be very short and start to get longer as the line moves forward towards the brisket, creating the illusion of a deep chest. When viewed in profile, the distance from the elbow to the bottom of the foot is equal to the distance between the withers and the brisket. There is only enough fur left on the undercarriage to accentuate depth of

chest and an athletic build. The pattern line is well blended and invisible.

Hindquarters

The hindquarters should be strong and powerful. When clipping this area, expose the thigh muscle with the same blade used on the body. Start to feather off with the blade where the muscle starts to turn under on a diagonal line from the flank region to about 3 or 4 fingers above the hock. Using a short to medium guard comb can facilitate skimming in the blending line. The pattern line should be invisible when the trim is finished. Blend with thinning shears if necessary. The stifle area should have enough furnishing left to give the legs substance and angulation. The longest coat on the legs can range from 1 to 3 inches depending on the amount of bone and coat density. Shape this area by hand with shears after the clipper work is complete. When viewed from the rear, the legs should form two parallel lines to the ground. The hocks are well let down. There should be adequate coat on the hock area to accentuate the angles of the rear assembly.

Front Legs

The coat on the legs can range from ⅟₁₆ of an inch to 2½ inches in length depending on the amount of bone, the size of the dog and coat density. The front legs drop straight down from the body and have ample bone and muscle to show off a powerful and sturdy animal. The pattern line at the shoulder is about 2 or 3 fingers above the top of the elbow, at the point where the muscle begins to turn under. The coat at the transition line will be very short, and taper into the longer leg furnishings. This can be accomplished by feathering off at the blending point with the same blade used on the body. Other methods of blending off at the top of the leg

include using a short to medium attachment comb followed by hand-scissoring and blending with thinning shears. Most stylists prefer to leave the legs to shape by hand with shears. After the final trim, the legs need to form two parallel columns going down from the elbow into tight, round feet. The coat at the back of the elbow is very short and falls straight down off the back of the leg toward the ground.

Feet

The feet are small for the size of the dog. Both the front and rear feet are compact with well arched toes. To show off these traits, the feet are trimmed very close to the edge of the foot and some nail is routinely exposed. The feet should point straight ahead, toeing neither in nor out. Trim the feet round by first boxing them in the shape of a square while the dog is standing in a natural, square position. Then remove the sharp corners of the box and round the feet facing straight forward. If detailing the feet with the foot off the tabletop, always use a small pair of shears to minimize the risk of accidentally cutting the pads.

Throat & Chest

Blades ranging from #10 to #7F, with or against the grain, based on the sensitivity of the dog's skin, are common in the throat area. Follow the natural cowlick line that runs in a "V" shape from the base of the ears towards the base of the neck. The blending point begins about three or four fingers above the breast bone and drops to just below the turn of the muscle at the elbow/shoulder, creating a "W" shape when viewed straight on. When viewed in profile, the neck into the chest should be straight without a predominant forechest. When blending the chest, be aware of the heavy cowlicks in the area. Many stylists prefer to leave the chest area to blend by hand with thinning shears or shears. When finished in this area, double check your work to be sure the neck, chest and front legs drop down in a straight line when viewed in profile.

The Head Styling Top Skull

The top of the head is clipped with a #7F or #5F, used with the grain or against depending on the dog's sensitivity and density of the coat.

Ears

The ears are clipped with a close blade. It is common to see a #10 or #15 blade used on the outside of the ear leather while a #40 blade is used on the inside. When working with close blades in this delicate area, always work from the base or center of the ear out toward the edge. Gently brace the ear with your fingers to clip over it. To finish, use small finishing shears to trim around the outside edge of the ear leather, keeping the tips of the shears toward the tip of the ears.

Brows

The eyebrow on this dog is very small. Follow the eye socket rim, working with the lay of the coat. They have a slight stop between the eyes that acts as a natural split for the brows. Either lightly clip this area when clipping the top skull, leave it to do by hand with thinning shears or finger pluck the area. This area should have just enough fur removed to lend definition to the brow area, while revealing the eye. The small, triangular shape accentuates the typically keen expression found on this long legged terrier. The brow will be very short at the back corner of the eye and longer at the tip, which comes out over the stop area. When viewed in profile, the brows should barely break the line of the top skull. Use thinning shears or curved shears in reverse to set the brow.

Throat & Cheeks

The throat and cheek areas are clipped using blades ranging from a #10 to a #7F, used either with or against the grain. Use the natural cowlick line of the neck to be the guide to create the "U" or "V" shape of the throat. The lowest point will be about 3 fingers above the breast bone. The line that breaks the top skull and the cheeks is from the back corner of the eye straight back to the ear canal.

Beard & Goatee

The beard and goatee are minimal with this harsh coated type of terrier, with the goatee being a bit longer than the fur on the beard. The pattern line starts from just behind the eyes and runs on a diagonal to the back corners of the mouth. The goatee is formed by continuing the line forward on the lower jaw, 1 or 2 finger widths in from the back corner of the mouth. When viewed from the top down, no hair should fall outside the planes of the cheeks. If the dog has an overabundance of fur on the muzzle, lightly rake a medium guard comb forward over the top of the head, down the nose and along the sides. Feather the coat off to leave longer hair at the end of the muzzle. Leave all the length of coat on the goatee, leaving it to finish by hand if it needs to be shortened. Once the excessive fur is removed, refine the head with thinning shears to form the classic rectangular head. The blending line at the sides of the face should be invisible between the tight work on the cheeks and the longer coat on the beard. Blend heavily with thinning shears, but do not take out so much coat to give an hour glass shape to the head, removing the fill under the eyes. Double check your work by combing the coat up and away from the muzzle, and then lay a comb at the cheeks or top skull.

Suggested Tools & Equipment

- Nail Trimmers
- Styptic Powder
- Ear Powder
- Ear Cleaning Solution
- Cotton Balls
- Hemostat
- Clippers
- Slicker Brush
- Greyhound Comb
- Pumice Stone
- Carding Tools
- Stripping Knives
- Straight Shears
- Curved Shears
- Small Detailing Shears
- Thinning Shears
- Dematting Tools

Common Blade Options:

- #40, #15, #10
- #7F, #5F, #4F
- Variety of Guard Combs

Grooming Tip

A light setting gel, mousse or texturing shampoo can add body to the leg coat, making it easier to scissor. Try spritzing unruly eyebrows while they are still damp with a styling spray. Work the product into the damp brows. Brush or comb the brows into place or dry them into the position you want them in the final trim.

TERRIER

Notes from your Grooming Table

American Staffordshire

Breed Facts & Characteristics

Country of Origin: United States

Height at Shoulder: 17"–19"

Coat Length/Type: Short/Smooth

Color: Any color, solid, parti or patched.

Correct grooming procedure:

Bathe & Curry Brush

Common pet grooming practices:

Bathe & Curry Brush

-The Goal-
The coat should be clean and fresh smelling, with the coat laying flat against the body. No shedding hair.

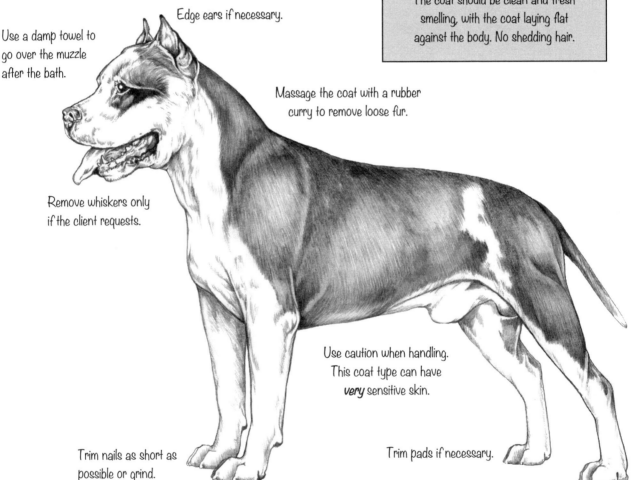

Edge ears if necessary.

Use a damp towel to go over the muzzle after the bath.

Massage the coat with a rubber curry to remove loose fur.

Remove whiskers only if the client requests.

Use caution when handling. This coat type can have *very* sensitive skin.

Trim nails as short as possible or grind.

Trim pads if necessary.

TERRIER

See page 66 for Bathing & Drying Instructions	Suggested Tools & Equipment

- Nail Trimmers
- Styptic Powder
- Ear Cleaning Solution
- Cotton Balls

- Clippers
- #40 or #15 Blade
- Rubber Curry
- Carding Tool

- Small Detailing Shears
- Thinning Shears

Notes *from your* *Grooming Table*

Australian Terrier

Breed Facts & Characteristics

Country of Origin: Australia

Height at Shoulder: 10"–11"

Coat Length/Type: Hard/Wiry

Color: Blue and tan, sandy, or red; topknot is silver or a shade lighter than head color.

Correct grooming procedure:
Brush Out/Hand-Strip

Common pet grooming practices:
Clipper-Trim/Hand-Strip

> **-The Goal-**
> This breed is small and spunky. The body coat should range from 1–2 inches, longer over back of the neck. The coat is harsh and shiny. Ears and feet are free of long hair.

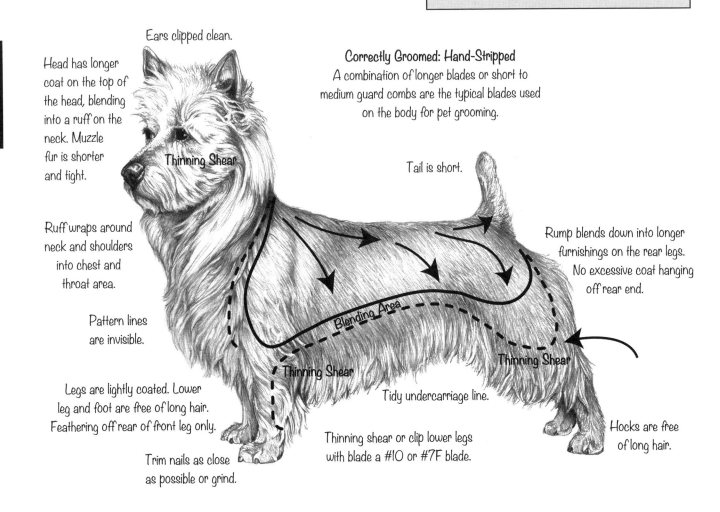

Ears clipped clean.

Head has longer coat on the top of the head, blending into a ruff on the neck. Muzzle fur is shorter and tight.

Thinning Shear

Correctly Groomed: Hand-Stripped
A combination of longer blades or short to medium guard combs are the typical blades used on the body for pet grooming.

Tail is short.

Ruff wraps around neck and shoulders into chest and throat area.

Pattern lines are invisible.

Rump blends down into longer furnishings on the rear legs. No excessive coat hanging off rear end.

Blending Area

Thinning Shear

Thinning Shear

Legs are lightly coated. Lower leg and foot are free of long hair. Feathering off rear of front leg only.

Tidy undercarriage line.

Hocks are free of long hair.

Trim nails as close as possible or grind.

Thinning shear or clip lower legs with blade a #10 or #7F blade.

Notes From The Grooming Table ©2016

Grooming Procedures & Recommendations

See page 76 for
Bathing & Drying Instructions

Frequency
Bathe once a week to once every 12 weeks.

Pre-Work
Trim or grind nails at least every four to six weeks to maintain a healthy foot structure. Swab the ears clean with a mild ear cleaning solution. Prior to bathing, quickly go over the entire body with a high-velocity dryer to help lift dirt and dander away from the skin and to loosen any shedding coat. *Card and hand-strip dog prior to bathing and drying.*

Carding
Carding is a natural technique in which the soft, downy undercoat is pulled from the dog's body. Typical tools used with this technique are: a pumice stone; an undercoat rake; a fine-toothed stripping knife, which is pulled through the coat; or a fine blade, such as a #40, held between the fingers and pulled through the coat, or used in a line carding fashion. Carding can be done before or after bathing and drying. Removal of the soft undercoat allows the topcoat to lie closer to the natural outline of the dog, accentuating the dog's structure. It also promotes a profuse harsh outer coat with a rich color and protects the skin.

Hand-Stripping the Body Pattern
Hand-stripping is a technique in which the outer guard coat is plucked from the dog's skin. This procedure helps promote the proper coat texture and rich color of the breed. During certain times of the year, the coat is easier to pull out. When the coat comes out easily, it is called a "blowing coat" or "blown coat." Ideally, hand-stripping should correspond with

the dog's natural cycle, based on its environment and hormonal levels. Using your fingers, a carding tool or a stripping knife, pull out a few hairs at a time to shape the coat and accentuate the dog's natural outline. Work methodically, pulling small amounts of coat at a time, always working in the direction of the coat growth. Proper hand-stripping employs a gentle momentum and rhythm to remove hair, not brute force, which is uncomfortable for both the groomer and the pet. Keep your wrist locked in a neutral position and allow the rhythmic movement to stem from your shoulder, not your wrist or elbow. In general, the main body coat is easily removed and most pets do not mind the plucking process. The cheeks, throat and private areas may be more sensitive, requiring the use of thinning shears or clippers. The length of coat to be left varies from under an inch to a little more than 2 inches and depends on the body section you are working. The coats should always appear very natural, never clipped or heavily trimmed. On some coats, a light application of chalk or powder before the bath allows a better grip on the coat and makes plucking and stripping much easier.

Clipper-Cutting the Body Pattern
If a client insists that their pet be clipper-cut, follow the general body pattern using blades ranging from a #7F, #5F, #4F or short to medium guard combs. The longer the trim, the more you will be able to retain the proper essence of the breed and correct coat. After clipper-cutting be sure to incorporate carding techniques which will aid in creating the proper coat texture and color.

The head is covered with harsh, somewhat longer fur than the body. The muzzle has shorter coat forming a wedge shape. There are two shorter spots of coat just behind the eyes. The coat on the neck is longer, wrapping around the neck forming a cape into the chest area. The cape blends invisibly to the shorter body coat. From the front and rear, the legs drop in straight, parallel lines from well toned shoulders and thighs. Feet are very tight and short. Under the tail is short and clean with a drape of longer fur covering the back of the thighs. Leg furnishings are hard and wiry, slightly longer than the body coat.

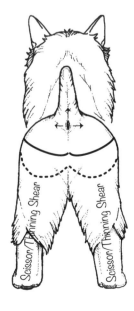

Notes From The Grooming Table ©2016

The head is covered with harsh coat, longer on the top of the skull, shorter on the muzzle and cheeks. Hand-strip or trim the muzzle and the cheeks leaving about a ½ to an inch of coat. The cheeks should be flat with a small dark spot exposed just behind the eye on the zygomatic arch. The shorter coat on the muzzle and cheeks will stop about a fingers width before the ear opening, framing in the face. On the lower jaw, the coat is shorter, transitioning into the throat and ruff right at the neck and throat junction. On the top of the head, the coat is about 2 inches in length and slightly messy in appearance. The ruff will be longer blending into the chest area.

Entire ear short—strip longer hair or use a #15 on the outside of the leather and a closer blade in the inside. Edge ears with shears.

Top skull is covered with harsh coat about 2 inches long and should look messy and wild.

Clear stop area with thinners or by hand-stripping.

Coat naturally shorter on top of muzzle.

Coat on muzzle between ½ to 1 inch long.

On the lower jaw, the coat is shorter, transitioning into the throat and ruff right at the neck and throat junction.

Sides of cheeks are flat and short.

Leave a finger's width of longer hair ahead of the ear canal.

Dark spot of shorter coat right behind eye.

Fur coming off the back and sides of neck is longer, blending into the throat and chest.

Legs & Undercarriage
The furnishings are left slightly longer on the back of the legs and the undercarriage. On the front legs, the front of the leg is covered with short, wiry hair. Longer furnishings come off the backside of the front leg from the elbow to the pastern. On the rear legs, the outer thigh is shorter. Slightly longer furnishings will be on front and back side of the rear leg. If hand-stripping the body coat, strip and finger pluck these areas. If trimming with clippers, use thinning shears to shorten and tidy the furnishings.

Head & Neck
The head is covered with harsh coat, longer on the top of the skull, shorter on the muzzle and cheeks. Hand-strip or trim the muzzle and the cheeks leaving about a ½ to an inch of coat. The cheeks should be flat with a small dark spot exposed just behind the eye on the zygomatic arch. The shorter coat on the muzzle and cheeks will stop about a fingers width before the ear open, framing in the face. On the lower jaw, the coat is shorter, transitioning into the throat and ruff right at the neck and throat junction. On the top of the head, the coat is about 2 inches in length and slightly messy in appearance. The ruff will be longer blending into the chest area.

Grooming Procedures & Recommendations

Ears
The erect ears are smooth and clean. If they are not that way naturally, clip the entire ear. Use a #15 blade on the outside and a #40 on the inside. Edge the ears with small detailing shears, keeping the tips of the shears towards the tips of the ears.

Eye Area
Clear the stop area of longer hair either by finger-plucking, or with thinning shears or a #10 blade. Use the method that will produce the best possible natural look, based on how much fur the dog has and its tolerance for work in this area. Lightly trim overly long hair that hangs over the eye, so that the topknot coat frames the eye area.

Feet & Hocks
The lower leg—from the pastern to the toes and from the hock to the toes—should be free of long hair. Hand-strip or clip the longer fur to show the natural bone structure of the dog. If clipping, use a #10 with the grain or a #7F against the grain.

Tails
The docked tail should be free of long hair. From the top, the tail should blend seamlessly from the body. On the underside, trim with a close blade, such as a #10, or use thinning shears to tidy up any long fur.

Detail Finish
For added shine, finish with a fine mist of coat polish on the body. Add a little styling gel to the topknot and ruff area. Finger work the topknot to give it a messy, lightly spiked look. Style the ruff forward over the neck towards the throat and chest. Application of bows and cologne is optional

Special Note
Clipping a wire-coated dog will result in a dramatic change in the texture and color of the coat. The correct harsh wire coat can be nurtured by plucking the blown coat when it is ready for removal. This process stimulates the hair follicles to produce new guard coat. Without hand-stripping, the guard coat usually fails to reproduce and loses its brilliant color and texture. If only undercoat grows, the guard coat color becomes that of the lighter, soft undercoat.

Suggested Tools & Equipment

- Nail Trimmers
- Styptic Powder
- Ear Powder
- Ear Cleaning Solution
- Cotton Balls
- Hemostat
- Clippers
- Slicker Brush
- Greyhound Comb
- Pumice Stone
- Carding Tools
- Stripping Knives
- Straight Shears
- Curved Shears
- Small Detailing Shears
- Thinning Shears
- Dematting Tools

Common Blade Options:
- #40, #15, #10
- #7F, #5F, #4F
- Variety of Guard Combs

Notes:

Notes From The Grooming Table ©2016

Breed Facts & Characteristics

Country of Origin: England

Height at Shoulder: 15"–17½"

Coat Length/Type: Curly/Thick

Color: Blue, sandy, liver, blue and tan, liver and tan.

Correct grooming procedure:

Hand-Scissor

Common pet grooming practices:

Clipper-Trim

General Description

The Bedlington is unique to the terrier group with its narrow, well balanced, flexible and flowing body outline. It has a silhouette more like a sighthound than most terriers. The coat consists of harsh guard hair combined with a soft, dense undercoat. The traditional Bedlington trim is highly stylized, with a distinctive head style, tasseled ears and a rat tail. This is a graceful little dog with true terrier spunk.

-The Goal-
Everything about this breed is curved and graceful. Their curly coat and unique head style makes them look similar to a small lamb.

Correctly Groomed: Hand-Scissored
Typical blades used on the body for pet grooming: #7F, #5F, #4F, and a variety of guard combs or a combination of those blades.

TERRIER

Head is narrow, without any stop. From the nose to the top of the crest is one curved line.

Scissor

Ears are tasseled.

Rump is tight and clean showing off a well angulated rear assembly with strong thighs.

Scissor

The lower jaw and throat are clipped very short.

Pattern lines are invisible on body, clearly defined on head and throat.

The chest is flat.

Blending Area

Rat Tail

The curved topline and the undercarriage line run in parallel curves.

Legs are straight and parallel.

Scissor

Scissor

Hocks are well let down.

Trim nails as close as possible or grind.

Feet are tight and round.

Grooming Procedures & Recommendations

See page 74 for
Bathing & Drying Instructions

Frequency
Bathe once a week to once every 12 weeks. Trim every four to six weeks to maintain a stylized fashion.

Pre-Work
Trim or grind nails at least every four to six weeks to maintain a healthy foot structure. Hair should be plucked from within the ear canal only as necessary for healthy ear management. Clean the ears by swabbing with a mild ear cleaning solution. Prior to bathing, quickly go over the entire body and remove any serious mats or tangles. If the tangle can be penetrated with water, leave it and remove when the dog is clean. If the pet has not been in for professional grooming for six weeks or more, remove the excessive body coat and set the pattern before bathing. Before starting the final haircut, make sure the dog's coat is throughly brushed out and tangle free.

Pattern Lines in General
The pattern is based on the bone and muscle structure. After the final trim, all pattern lines should be invisible between the body and legs. If using clippers on the main body, feather off at the transition points in a smooth and steady fashion. If the pattern line is still visible after clipping, use thinning shears or shears to blend the line. Pattern lines on the head, throat and tail should be crisp and clean.

Body
For pet dogs, the coat can be hand-scissored or clipper-cut using the same general pattern. Typical blades used in pet grooming range from a #7F for the tight work around the neck and shoulders, to blades ranging from a #4 to a longer guard combs. The pattern

lines for the front legs start at the turn of the shoulder to just above the elbow. On the rear leg, trimming continues to sweep over the upper thigh area with the same blade as on the bulk of the body, blending off into the longer coat of the lower leg. The loin is arched with longer coat left in the area to accentuate the natural rise. The topline curve will parallel the undercarriage line. At the pattern lines, the shorter fur blends seamlessly into the longer coat of the legs and undercarriage.

Neck
The head is held high by a long neck that molds into the shoulders. The throat is tight. Leave the coat on the back of the neck down to the withers. This area should be scissored later to blend with the head piece, which is unique for this breed. The sides of the neck and shoulders are clipped with a medium length blade, such as a #7F or #5F.

Undercarriage
The undercarriage line parallels the topline with its curving lines. The chest is naturally deep and the undercarriage line sweeps up towards the flank. Leave only enough fur on the undercarriage to accentuate chest depth and an athletic, racy build.

Tail
One of the unique characteristics of this breed is its "rat tail." The end two-thirds is clipped close with a #10 or #15 blade used with or against the grain. The portion closest to the body is hand-scissored short, blending from the rump and tapering into the clipped area.

Hindquarters
The rear legs will be longer than the front legs. On the rear legs, the upper thigh is trimmed to the same length as the bulk of the body. The rear of the dog is trimmed close to show off the angulation of the rear assembly. Longer

The head is unique, looking like a lamb with tasseled ears. The body is very narrow. The front and rear legs drop in parallel lines, toeing in a little bit on the front feet creating a "keyhole" front. Coat on the legs is only long enough to create the parallel lines from the body. Feet are very tight. Tail is shaved at the end to form the characteristic "rat tail."

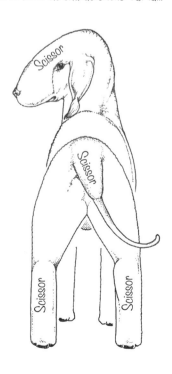

297

The head is unique with its lamb-like appearance. The skull is narrow, long and graceful. The eyes peek out from the sides of the head. The lower jaw is clipped clean and the ears are neatly tasseled. All lines on the head are clean and sharp.

The highest point of the topknot will be above the occiput and in a direct line from the front edge of the ear. This high point of the head will blend down into the scissored neck.

The eyes will be exposed from the side of the head only. The entire stop area is filled in with fur to create the lamb look of the head.

On the narrow head, the fur creates a soft arch from the nose to the peak of the occiput. Comb all the fur over to one side of the skull and cut off any hair that falls outside the planes of the skull. Trim one side all the way from the nose to above the ear, then repeat on the opposite side. Once the excessive hair is removed from the sides, trim the top line in a light, curving arch when viewed from profile.

The throat and cheeks and lower jaw are trimmed close with a #10 or #15 blade used against the grain.

Use a #10 or #15 blade on the outside of the ear. A #40 blade can be used on the inside of the ear leather with a very light touch. The tassel covers the bottom ⅓ to ¼ of the ear tip. Edge the ear with small detailing shears. The ear is low set, roughly in line with the eye.

Ear Safety Tip: Remember, always keep the tips of the shears towards the tips of the ears when edging for safety.

Stay inside the natural cowlick line of the neck that runs from the ear bulb down in a "U" or "V" shape. Stop about 2 or 3 finger widths above the breast bone. The line is very sharp and clean.

fur is left in the stifle region, lower thigh and down into the hock and foot area. When clipping this area, start to feather off where the muscle starts to turn under—on a diagonal line from the flank region to about three or four fingers above the hock. The blending should be invisible when the trim is finished. Blend with shears if necessary. The stifle area should have enough furnishing left to give the legs substance and angulation. The longest coat on the legs can range from ¹⁄₁₆ inch to 1 inch depending on the amount of bone and coat density.

Shape this area with hand shears after the clipper work is complete. When viewed from the rear, the legs should form two parallel lines to the ground. The hocks are well let down.

Front Legs
The coat on the legs can range from ¹⁄₁₆ inch to 1 inch depending on the amount of bone and coat density. The top of the front legs are wider apart than at the feet, creating a "keyhole" shape between the front legs when viewed from the front. Shape the legs so they almost touch at the pasterns

but are more open up at the top to create a keyhole shape between the front legs when viewed from the front. The pattern line at the shoulder is about 1 to 2 fingers above the top of the elbow, at the point where the muscle begins to turn under. The coat at the transition line will be very short and taper into the longer leg furnishings. This can be accomplished by skimmng off at the blending point with the same blade used on the body. Finish the legs with hand shears ranging from 8.5 inches to 10 inches in length. The legs will form two columns descending from the elbow into tight, oval feet. The pasterns have a slight bend.

Feet

Both the front and rear feet are hare-footed. To show off these traits, the feet are trimmed very close to the edge of the foot, beveling slightly into fuller leg coat. The feet should point straight ahead, or may toe in slightly. With the dog standing squarely on the table, remove the sharp edges and contour the feet to face forward. If detailing the feet with the foot lifted off the tabletop, always use a small pair of detailing shears to minimize the risk of accidentally cutting the pads. If a very close cutting blade is used to trim the pads, use a firm slicker brush to brush the longer leg coat over the outer edges of the pad and trim that hair at the same time the pads are clipped clean.

The Head in General

The head is similar to the face of a lamb. The skull is narrow, fine and rounded. The cheeks are flat and clean. The ears are tasseled. The keen, almond-shaped eyes are well set in the skull.

Throat, Lower Jaw & Cheeks

Blades ranging from #15 to #10, with or against the grain, based on the sensitivity of the dog's skin, are common for pet dogs. Clip the cheeks from the ear canal following the zygomatic arch to just behind the eye. From the back corner of the eye, create a crisp diagonal line to the back corner of the mouth. The entire lower jaw is clipped clean and continues into the throat area. Follow the natural cowlick line that runs in a "V" shape from the base of the ears toward the base of the neck. The lowest point of the pattern will be about 3 fingers above the chest bone.

Top Skull

The top skull is formed into a narrow dome with no break in the coat from the nose to the peak at the occiput. Comb the coat over to one side and trim off any hair that falls outside the line of the cheek. Repeat on the opposite side. Continue the lines from the sides of the face, over the back skull and down the sides of the neck. Once the front of the topknot has been formed, shape the neck to blend gracefully into the peak of the topknot. Fluff the coat, and, when first viewing it in profile, neaten the entire line from the nose to the occiput with long, straight shears. Re-fluff. Round the edges and trim the eyes to expose them. The line from the cheeks, over the eyes and around into the throat should be crisp and clean.

Ears

Ears are clipped to the tassel with a close blade. It is common to see a #10 or #15 blade used on the outside of the ear leather, while a #40 blade is used on the inside. When working with close blades in this delicate area, always work out from the base, or center, of the ear toward the edge. Gently brace the ear with your fingers to clip over it. Clip the ear clean, creating a sharp line where it attaches to the skull, but let the longer coat of the topknot drape over the line. Leave a tuft of fur on the lower third of the tip. The line can either be slightly curved or made with straight, diagonal lines to create a diamond shape. To finish, use small finishing shears to trim around the outside edge of the ear leather, keeping the tips of the shears toward the tip of the ears. The ear leather reaches to the corner of the mouth, and with the tassel, the ear should reach to the end of the nose. The tassel may be blunt-cut across the bottom or formed into a diamond shape.

Suggested Tools & Equipment

- Nail Trimmers
- Styptic Powder
- Ear Powder
- Ear Cleaning Solution
- Cotton Balls
- Hemostat
- Clippers
- Slicker Brush
- Greyhound Comb
- Straight Shears
- Curved Shears
- Small Detailing Shears
- Thinning Shears
- Dematting Tools
- High-Velocity Dryer

Common Blade Options:

- #40, #15, #10
- #7F, #5F, #4F
- Variety of Guard Combs

Detail Finish

Re-fluff all your work and check for stray hairs. The coat should look like smooth velvet when finished. Application of mild cologne and bows is optional.

Special Note

Grooming styles are vastly different between the United States and Europe. The American version is outlined here.

Border Terrier

Breed Facts & Characteristics

Country of Origin: Great Britain

Height at Shoulder: 11½"–15½"

Coat Length/Type: Hard/Wiry

Color: Red, grizzle and tan, blue and tan, or wheaten.

Correct grooming procedure:

Hand-Strip

Common pet grooming practices:

Clipper-Trim/Hand-Strip

-The Goal-
This breed is a small active terrier with a unique otter like head. The outer body coat is harsh and tight fitting to the body. The ears are free of long hair.

Correctly Groomed: Hand-Stripped

Typical blades used on the body for pet grooming: #7F, #5F, #4F, shorter guard comb or a combination of those blades.

The head looks like an otter head. Hand-strip or thinning shear to create the proper look.

Ears are free of long hair.

Card the body first to remove the bulk of the loose undercoat. Follow by hand-stripping the hard outer coat. Always pull in the direction of the coat growth. Legs too.

Coat on tail is the same as on the body.

There is no pattern. The harsh coat should be from ¼" to 1" all over the dog.

The harsh outer coat lays tight to the body, allowing for a clear view of the outline of the dog.

Tidy undercarriage line.

Hocks are free of long hair.

Trim nails as close as possible or grind.

Feet are tight and natural looking.

Grooming Procedures & Recommendations

See page 76 for
Bathing & Drying Instructions

Frequency
Bathe once a week to once every
12 weeks.

Pre-Work
Trim or grind nails at least every four
to six weeks to maintain a healthy foot
structure. Swab the ears clean with a
mild ear cleaning solution. Prior to
bathing, quickly go over the entire
body with a high-velocity dryer to help
lift dirt and dander away from the skin
and to loosen any shedding coat. ***Card
and hand-strip dog prior to bathing
and drying.***

Carding
Carding is a natural technique in
which the soft, downy undercoat is
pulled from the dog's body. Typical
tools used with this technique are: a
pumice stone; an undercoat rake; a
fine-toothed stripping knife, which is
pulled through the coat; or a fine blade,
such as a #40, held between the fingers
and pulled through the coat. Carding
can be done before or after bathing and
drying. Removal of the soft undercoat
allows the topcoat to lie closer to the
natural outline of the dog, accentuating
the dog's structure. It also promotes
a profuse harsh outer coat with a rich
color and protects the skin.

Hand-Stripping the Body Pattern
Hand-stripping is a technique in which
the outer guard coat is plucked from
the dog's skin. This procedure helps
promote the proper coat texture and
rich color of the breed. During certain
times of the year, the coat is easier to
pull out. When the coat comes out
easily, it is called a "blowing coat" or
"blowncoat." Ideally, hand-stripping
should correspond with the dog's
natural cycle, based on its environment
and hormonal levels. Using your fingers,
a carding tool or a stripping knife, pull
out a few hairs at a time to shape the
coat and accentuate the dog's natural
outline. Work methodically, pulling
small amounts of coat at a time, always
working in the direction of the coat
growth. Proper hand-stripping employs
a gentle momentum and rhythm to
remove hair, not brute force, which is
uncomfortable for both the groomer
and the pet. Keep your wrist locked
in a neutral position and allow the
rhythmic movement to stem from your
shoulder, not your wrist or elbow. In
general, the main body coat is easily
removed and most pets do not mind
the plucking process. The cheeks, throat
and private areas may be more sensitive,
requiring the use of thinning shears or
clippers. The length of coat to be left
varies from under an inch to a little
more than an inch and depends on the
body section you are working. The coat
should always appear very natural, never

clipped or heavily trimmed. On some
coats, a light application of chalk or
powder before the bath allows a better
grip on the coat and makes plucking
and stripping much easier.

Clipper-Cutting the Body Pattern
If a client insists that their pet be
clipper-cut, follow the general body
pattern using blades ranging from a
#7F, #5F, #4F or a #2 guard comb. The
longer the trim, the more you will be
able to retain the proper essence of the
breed and correct coat. After clipper-
cutting be sure to incorporate carding
techniques which will aid in creating the
proper coat texture and color.

Body & Legs
The entire body is covered with tight
fitting, harsh coat that is roughly
a quarter of an inch to one inch in
length, the coat is shorter on the legs.
There are no visible pattern lines
anywhere on the dog.

Head
The head of the Border Terrier closely
resembles that of an otter's. The fur
should be hard and lie tight to the
skull. The muzzle may have slightly
longer furnishings that stand off the
skin, but not enough to detract from
the overall balance of the head. The
fold of the ears should not break over
the topline of the skull.

301

Notes From The Grooming Table ©2016

Grooming Procedures & Recommendations

Ears

The folded ears are covered with very short hair. On most dogs, you will want to finger-pluck the few long strands to bring the coat down to the natural velvet length. If the ear is more substantially covered with hair, clip the entire ear. Use a #15 blade on the outside and a #40 on the inside. Edge the ears with small detailing shears, keeping the tips of the shears towards the tips of the ears.

Eye Area

Clear the stop area of long hair either by finger-plucking, or with thinning shears or a #10 blade. Use the method that will produce the best possible natural look, based on how much fur the dog has and its tolerance for work in this area. A tiny bit of fur should be left above each brow to accentuate a keen eye, but not enough to be declared an "eyebrow."

Tails

The tail should be free of any feathering. The harsh guard coat should lie tight to the skin. From the top, the tail should blend seamlessly into the body.

Feet & Hocks

Trim the pads with a close cutting blade ranging from a #15 to a #40. Use a very light touch to clean the pads of long hair. Tidy the outside edge of the foot, if needed, with small detailing shears. If the hocks have longer coat, trim lightly with thinning shears to show a neat, clean area.

Detail Finish

For added shine, finish with a fine mist of coat polish on the body. Application of bows and mild cologne is optional.

Special Note

Clipping a wire-coated dog will result in a dramatic change in the texture and color of the coat. The correct harsh wire coat can be nurtured by plucking the blown coat when it is ready for removal. This process stimulates the hair follicles to produce new guard coat. Without hand-stripping, the guard coat usually fails to reproduce and loses its brilliant color and texture. If only undercoat grows, the guard coat color becomes that of the lighter, soft undercoat.

Suggested Tools & Equipment

- Nail Trimmers
- Styptic Powder
- Ear Powder
- Ear Cleaning Solution
- Cotton Balls
- Hemostat
- Clippers
- Slicker Brush
- Greyhound Comb
- Pumice Stone
- Carding Tools
- Stripping Knives
- Straight Shears
- Curved Shears
- Small Detailing Shears
- Thinning Shears
- Dematting Tools

Common Blade Options:

- #40, #15, #10
- #7F, #5F, #4F
- Variety of Guard Combs

Notes:

Notes *from your* Grooming Table

Breed Facts & Characteristics

Country of Origin: England

Height at Shoulder: 17½"–18½"

Coat Length/Type: Fine/Short

Color: White with colored head markings or any color other than white.

Correct grooming procedure:
Bathe & Curry Brush

Common pet grooming practices:
Bathe & Curry Brush

-The Goal-
The coat should be clean and fresh smelling, with the coat laying flat against the body. No shedding hair.

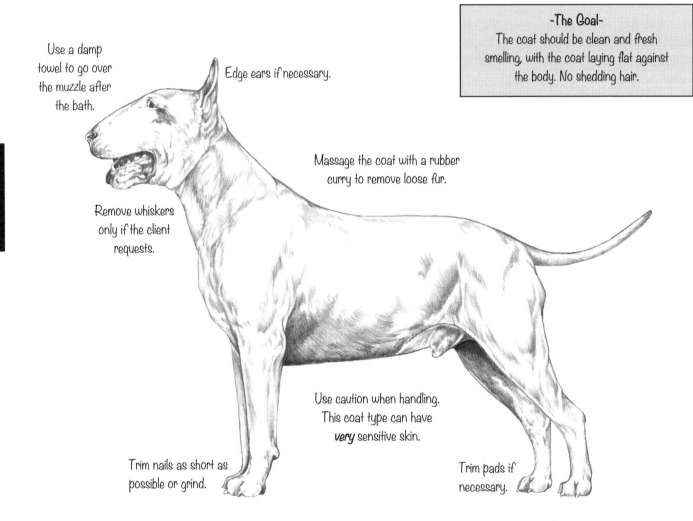

Use a damp towel to go over the muzzle after the bath.

Edge ears if necessary.

Massage the coat with a rubber curry to remove loose fur.

Remove whiskers only if the client requests.

Use caution when handling. This coat type can have **very** sensitive skin.

Trim nails as short as possible or grind.

Trim pads if necessary.

See page 66 for Bathing & Drying Instructions

Suggested Tools & Equipment

- Nail Trimmers
- Styptic Powder
- Ear Cleaning Solution
- Cotton Balls
- Clippers
- #40 or #15 Blade
- Rubber Curry
- Carding Tool
- Small Detailing Shears
- Thinning Shears

Notes from your
Grooming Table

Cairn Terrier

Breed Facts & Characteristics

Country of Origin: Scotland

Height at Shoulder: 9½"–10"

Coat Length/Type: Hard/Wiry

Color: Any color except white.

Correct grooming procedure:
Card & Hand-Strip

Common pet grooming practices:
Clipper-Trim/Hand-Strip

General Description

This is a small, spunky terrier designed to go to ground after all types of vermin. The body is covered with a harsh, moderate length coat. The head is round in shape with small, erect ears. The tail is well covered with hard hair but never feathered. The Cairn Terrier should look neat but "un-groomed."

> **-The Goal-**
> This is a small, tough terrier. They have a harsh outer coat and a thick undercoat. They have a round head style with a keen, foxy expression. Pattern lines on the body are invisible.

Correctly Groomed: Hand-Strip

Typical blades used on the body for pet grooming: #7F, #5F, #4F, short to medium guard combs, or a combination of those blades. Card coat after clipping to help maintain correct coat texture and color.

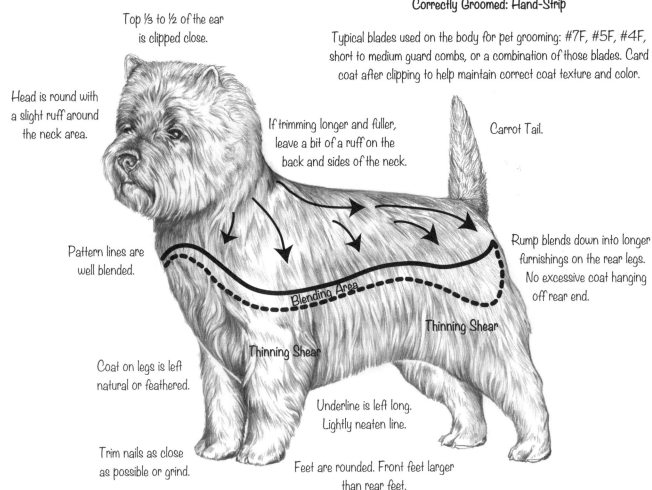

Top ⅓ to ½ of the ear is clipped close.

Head is round with a slight ruff around the neck area.

If trimming longer and fuller, leave a bit of a ruff on the back and sides of the neck.

Carrot Tail.

Rump blends down into longer furnishings on the rear legs. No excessive coat hanging off rear end.

Pattern lines are well blended.

Blending Area

Thinning Shear

Thinning Shear

Coat on legs is left natural or feathered.

Underline is left long. Lightly neaten line.

Trim nails as close as possible or grind.

Feet are rounded. Front feet larger than rear feet.

Grooming Procedures & Recommendations

See page 76 for
Bathing & Drying Instructions

Frequency
Bathe once a week to once every 12 weeks.

Pre-Work
Trim or grind nails at least every four to six weeks to maintain a healthy foot structure. Swab the ears clean with a mild ear cleaning solution. Prior to bathing, quickly go over the entire body with a high-velocity dryer to help lift dirt and dander away from the skin and to loosen any shedding coat. *Card and hand-strip dog prior to bathing and drying.*

Carding
Carding is a natural technique in which the soft, downy undercoat is pulled from the dog's body. Typical tools used with this technique are: a pumice stone; an undercoat rake; a fine-toothed stripping knife, which is pulled through the coat; or a fine blade, such as a #40, held between the fingers and pulled through the coat. Carding can be done before or after bathing and drying. Removal of the soft undercoat allows the topcoat to lie closer to the natural outline of the dog, accentuating the dog's structure. It also promotes a profuse harsh outer coat with a rich color and protects the skin.

Hand-Stripping the Body Pattern
Hand-stripping is a technique in which the outer guard coat is plucked from the dog's skin. This procedure helps promote the proper coat texture and rich color of the breed. During certain times of the year, the coat is easier to pull out. When the coat comes out easily, it is called a "blowing coat" or "blown coat." Ideally, hand-stripping should correspond with

the dog's natural cycle, based on its environment and hormonal levels. Using your fingers, a carding tool or a stripping knife, pull out a few hairs at a time to shape the coat and accentuate the dog's natural outline. Work methodically, pulling small amounts of coat at a time, always working in the direction of the coat growth. Proper hand-stripping employs a gentle momentum and rhythm to remove hair, not brute force, which is uncomfortable for both the groomer and the pet. Keep your wrist locked in a neutral position and allow the rhythmic movement to stem from your shoulder, not your wrist or elbow. In general, the main body coat is easily removed and most pets do not mind the plucking process. The cheeks, throat and private areas may be more sensitive, requiring the use of thinning shears or clippers. The length of coat to be left varies from under an inch to a little more than an inch and depends on the body section you are working. The coat should always appear very natural, never clipped or heavily trimmed. On some coats, a light application of chalk or powder before the bath allows a better grip on the coat and makes plucking and stripping much easier.

Clipper-Cutting the Body Pattern
If a client insists that their pet be clipper-cut, follow the general body pattern using blades ranging from a #7F, #5F, #4F or short to medium guard combs. The longer the trim, the more you will be able to retain the proper essence of the breed and correct coat. On longer trims, leave the back and sides of the neck slightly fuller to create a ruff in this area which is more correct for breed profile trimming. After clipper-cutting be sure to incorporate carding techniques which will aid in creating the proper coat texture and color.

The head is round and full with eyes and nose at the center. From the front and rear, the legs drop is straight, parallel lines from well-toned shoulder and thighs. When setting in the pattern, use the turn of the muscles to set the lines. Under the tail is short and clean with a drape of longer fur covering the back of the thighs. Leg furnishings are slightly longer than the body coat. Tail is a carrot shaped and very short on the back side.

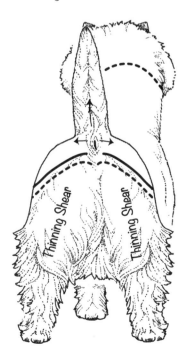

Notes From The Grooming Table ©2016

Their expression is friendly, bold and full of life. Head is full and round. The ears are small, triangular and erect. The eyes are deep set. When viewed from the front, the eyes and nose are at the center of the circle. When finished, the head is well blended and very natural looking.

Pull the hair up, trimming the coat on the top of the head, to just below the ear tips using thinning shears.

The top ⅓ to ½ of the ear tip is clipped, Use a # 10 or #15 blade on the outside of the ear, a #40 blade can be used on the inside of the ear leather with a very light touch. Edge the ear with small detailing shears.

Comb the fur forward, over the brows. With thinning shears, trim a frame around the eye area. The line is beveled with a deep set eye.

Ear Safety Tip: Remember, always keep the tips of the shears towards the tips of the ears when edging for safety.

Trim the stop area lightly with thinning shears before framing the eye area.

The line at the back of the skull is about an inch beyond the occiput, if trimming with clippers. If hand-stripping, there is a ruff of harsh coat that wraps around the neck.

The lower line of the head completes the circle that puts the eyes and nose at the center of the head piece when looking at the pet from the front. The lower line parallels the jaw bone. Comb all the coat down and trim with shears in a curved line running from the nose all the way up to behind the occiput. Soften the line with thinning shears to complete the head piece.

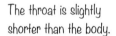

The throat is slightly shorter than the body.

Legs & Undercarriage
The furnishings are left slightly longer in these areas. If hand-stripping the body coat, strip and finger pluck these areas. If trimming with clippers, use thinning shears to shorten and tidy the furnishings.

Head
The head of the Cairn should have a "foxy expression." The coat on the top of the head should be longer than on the muzzle. It stands up and away from the skull, creating a frame for the face. When hand-stripped, the longer coat on the top of the head blends into the neck to create a ruff that covers the back of the neck, then wraps around and blends with the jowl area. If trimmed with clippers, the ruff is normally eliminated and a tidy, rounded head style is applied, especially at the junction of the back of the skull and neck. The muzzle fur is coated shorter than the tip of the head, giving it a wedge shape that enhances the fox-like expression.

Ears
The pricked, triangular ears are covered with very short hair. On most dogs, you will want to finger-pluck the few long strands of coat down to the natural velvet length. If the ear is more substantially covered

with hair, clip the top ⅓ to ½ of the ear. Use a #15 blade on the outside and a #40 on the inside. Edge the ears with small detailing shears, keeping the tips of the shears towards the tips of the ears.

Eye Area

Clear the stop area of longer hair either by finger-plucking or with thinning shears, but leave some fur. Use the method that will produce the best possible natural look, based on how much fur the dog has and its tolerance for work in this area. A tiny bit of fur should be left above each brow to accentuate a keen eye, but not enough to be declared an "eyebrow," only enough to create a deep-set eye and frame the face.

Tail

The tail is well covered and shaped like a short, thick carrot with a pointed tip. The underside is covered with short hair, but free of all feathering. From the top, the tail should blend seamlessly into the body.

Feet & Hocks

Trim the pads with a close cutting blade ranging from a #15 to a #40. Use a very light touch to clean the pads of long hair. Tidy the outside edge of the foot, if needed, with small detailing shears. If the hocks have longer coat, trim lightly with thinning shears to show a neat, clean area.

Detail Finish

For added shine, finish with a fine mist of coat polish on the body. Application of bows and mild cologne is optional.

Special Note

Clipping a wire-coated dog will result in a dramatic change in the texture and color of the coat. The correct harsh wire coat can be nurtured by plucking the blown coat when it is ready for removal. This process stimulates the hair follicles to produce new guard coat. Without hand-stripping, the guard coat usually fails to reproduce and loses its brilliant color and texture. If only undercoat grows, the guard coat color becomes that of the lighter, soft undercoat.

Suggested Tools & Equipment

- Nail Trimmers
- Styptic Powder
- Ear Powder
- Ear Cleaning Solution
- Cotton Balls
- Hemostat
- Clippers
- Slicker Brush
- Greyhound Comb
- Pumice Stone
- Carding Tools
- Stripping Knives
- Straight Shears
- Curved Shears
- Small Detailing Shears
- Thinning Shears
- Dematting Tools

Common Blade Options:

- #40, #15, #10
- #7F, #5F, #4F
- Variety of Guard Combs

Notes:

Breed Facts & Characteristics

Country of Origin: Czechoslovakia

Height at Shoulder: 10"–13"

Coat Length/Type: Long/Silky

Color: Shades of gray from charcoal to platinum.

Correct grooming procedure:
Clipper-Trim

Common pet grooming practices:
Clipper-Trim

General Description

The Cesky is short legged terrier, one and a half times longer than it is tall and has a topline that rises slightly over the loin and rump. The head is twice as long as it is wide. Everything about this breed shows off a powerful, muscular body yet the breed is lean and graceful. The clipped coat is soft and the furnishings are long and silky. The Cesky is trimmed to emphasize a slim but powerful body type. The head is well furnished with a classic terrier rectangular outline, triangular ears and a fall over the eyes. The tail is long and slender.

-The Goal-
The haircut should show off a strong, lean and well muscled terrier type dog.
Pattern lines on the body are distinct, flowing smoothly into the longer feathering.

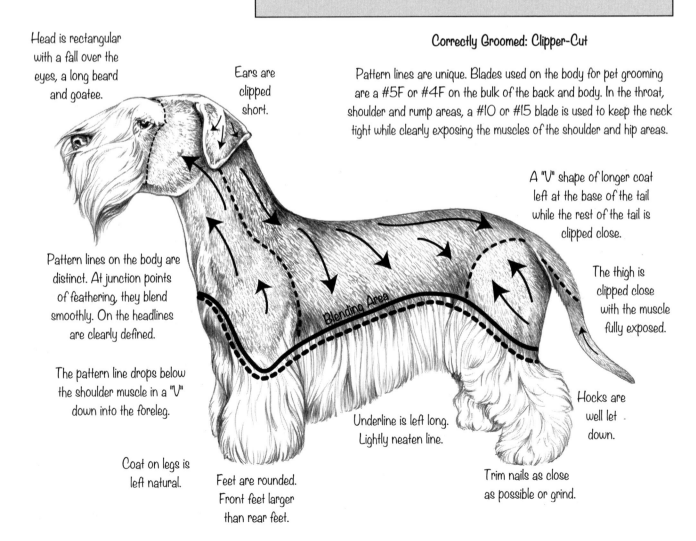

Head is rectangular with a fall over the eyes, a long beard and goatee.

Ears are clipped short.

Correctly Groomed: Clipper-Cut

Pattern lines are unique. Blades used on the body for pet grooming are a #5F or #4F on the bulk of the back and body. In the throat, shoulder and rump areas, a #10 or #15 blade is used to keep the neck tight while clearly exposing the muscles of the shoulder and hip areas.

A "V" shape of longer coat left at the base of the tail while the rest of the tail is clipped close.

The thigh is clipped close with the muscle fully exposed.

Pattern lines on the body are distinct. At junction points of feathering, they blend smoothly. On the headlines are clearly defined.

The pattern line drops below the shoulder muscle in a "V" down into the foreleg.

Blending Area

Underline is left long. Lightly neaten line.

Hocks are well let down.

Coat on legs is left natural.

Feet are rounded. Front feet larger than rear feet.

Trim nails as close as possible or grind.

Grooming Procedures & Recommendations

See page 71 for
Bathing & Drying Instructions

Frequency
Bathe once a week to once every
12 weeks. Trim every four to six weeks
to maintain a stylized fashion.

Pre-Work
Trim or grind nails every four to
six weeks to maintain a healthy foot
structure. Clean the ears by swabbing
with a mild ear cleaning solution. Hair
should be plucked from within the ear
canal only as necessary for healthy ear
management. Prior to bathing, quickly
go over the entire body and remove any
serious mats or tangles. If the tangle
can be penetrated with water, leave it
and remove when the dog is clean. If
the pet has not been in for professional
grooming for six weeks or more,
remove the excessive body coat and set
the pattern before bathing.

Pattern Lines in General
The pattern is based on the bone and
muscle structure of the dog. After the
final trim, all pattern lines on the body
should be invisible. At the transition
points, feather off with the clippers in
a smooth and steady fashion. If the
pattern line is still visible after clipping,
use thinning shears to blend the line.
On the head, the pattern lines are crisp
and clean.

Body
Typical blades used in pet grooming
range from a #10 to a #4F, or a
combination of those blades for the
bulk of the body work. Some stylists
find reversing a slightly longer blade
very effective in achieving an extremely
smooth finish on the body. Reversing
a blade will shorten the cutting action
by about two blade lengths as the same
blade used with the grain of the coat.
Choose one of the methods and follow

the direction of the natural coat growth
of the fur. The pattern is shorter on
the sides of the neck blending into the
shoulder area. The pattern lines start at
the turn of the shoulder with the shorter
length just above the elbow. The line
continues with a slightly longer blade on
the bulk of the body, back to the flank
on a diagonal. On the rear leg area, use
the same shorter blade as used on the
neck and shoulder area to expose the
upper thigh. Work in at an angle from
the flank region to a few finger widths
above the hock.

Undercarriage
The furnishings on the underside of the
dog are left in a natural state or layered
to look long and natural depending on
the extent of the feathering. The coat
on the undercarriage may be trimmed
or neatened to clear the ground or to
add a slight rise under the last rib. If
the dog is sparsely furnished, tidy the
undercarriage so it looks natural. The
pattern line is well blended and invisible.

Tail & Rear
The tail is trimmed into a "rat tail."
The end two-thirds is clipped close
with a #10 or #15 blade used with or
against the grain. The portion closest to
the body is left slightly longer, forming
a "V" using a longer blade or shorter
guard comb. The "V" comes off the
rear, accentuating a moderately slanted
croup. The "V" will be formed at the
base of the tail coming to a point about
one-third of the way down the tail
bone. Tidy the transition lines with
thinning shears. The entire underside it
clipped short.

Hindquarters
The hindquarters should be strong and
powerful. When clipping this area,
expose the thigh muscle. Use either
the same blade as used on the bulk of
the body or drop slightly to a shorter
blade in the thigh area. Start to feather

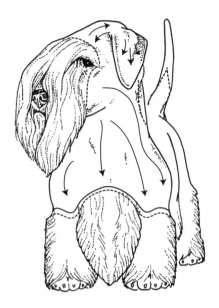

The head is long and rectangular with a fall
of hair between the eyes. From the front and
rear, the legs drop straight from muscular
shoulders and thighs. When setting the pattern,
use the turn of the muscles to set the lines.
Under the tail is short and clean with a drape
of longer fur covering the back of the thighs.
Leg furnishings are longer than the body.

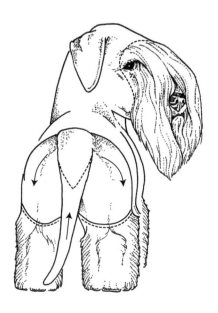

Notes From The Grooming Table ©2016

Their expression is alert and bold. Head is rectangular with a long fall of hair over the stop area with a full beard and goatee. The topskull and the muzzle are equal in length with the stop area being the center point. All lines on the head are clean and sharp.

Clip topskull with blades ranging from a #7F to a #5F, used against the grain or blades ranging from a #10 to #15 with the grain.

Use a #10 or #15 blade on the outside of the ear, a #40 blade can be used on the inside of the ear leather with a very light touch. Edge the ear with small detailing shears. The fold of the ear is level with the line of the topskull.

The line for the fall follows the eye socket rim. The back corners of the eyes are trimmed closely to expose the eye. This line arches out towards the nose. It is crisp and clean.

On the muzzle, the hair is long and natural but does not break the line of the topskull. When combing down the beard, the lines at the side of the face form a straight plane.

Just below the back corner of the eyes, the fur is short and well blended, creating fill under the eye. The clipper lines of the beard are clean and sharp.

Ear Safety Tip: Remember, always keep the tips of the shears towards the tips of the ears when edging for safety.

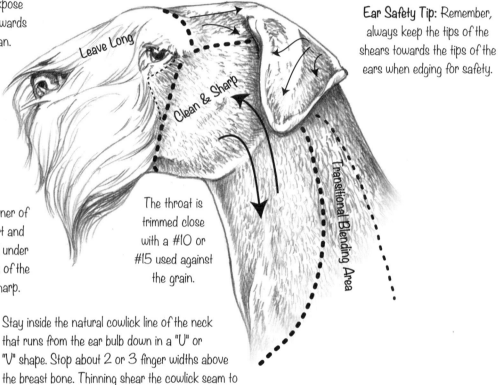

Leave Long

Clean & Sharp

Transitional Blending Area

The throat is trimmed close with a #10 or #15 used against the grain.

Stay inside the natural cowlick line of the neck that runs from the ear bulb down in a "U" or "V" shape. Stop about 2 or 3 finger widths above the breast bone. Thinning shear the cowlick seam to blend with the longer coat of the neck.

off with the blade where the muscle starts to turn under on a diagonal line from the flank region to about three or four fingers above the hock. Using a shorter to medium length guard comb, can facilitate feathering in the blending line. The pattern line should be invisible when the trim is finished. Blend with thinning shears if necessary. The stifle area should have enough furnishing left to give the legs substance and angulation. The longest coat on the legs can range from 1 to

2.5 inches depending on the amount of bone and coat density. Shape this area by hand with shears after the clipper work is complete. When viewed from the rear, the legs should form two parallel lines to the ground. The hocks are well let down. There should be adequate coat on the hock area to accentuate the angles of the rear assembly.

Front Legs
The coat on the legs can range from very short to over 1½ inches in length depending on the amount of bone, the size of the dog and coat density. The front legs drop straight down from the body and have ample bone and muscle to show off a powerful and sturdy animal. The pattern line at the shoulder is where the muscle turns under right near elbow. The coat at the transition line will be very short, and taper into the longer leg furnishings.

TERRIER

Grooming Procedures & Recommendations

This can be accomplished by feathering off at the blending point with the same blade used on the body. Other methods of blending off at the top of the leg include using an attachment comb—using a shorter to medium length guard comb—followed by hand-scissoring and blending with thinning shears. Most stylists prefer to leave the legs to shape by hand with shears. After the final trim, the legs need to form two parallel columns going down from the elbow into tight, round feet. The coat at the back of the elbow is very short and falls straight down off the back of the leg toward the ground.

Feet

The front feet are larger than the rear feet, with thick pads and strong nails which can be slightly exposed. The feet are trimmed very close. The feet should point straight ahead, but minor toeing out is acceptable on the front feet. Trim the feet round by first boxing them into the shape of a box while the dog is standing in a natural, square position. With the dog's feet firmly planted on the table, remove the sharp corners of the box and round the feet facing straight forward. Bevel the coat slightly. If detailing the feet with the foot off the tabletop, always use a small pair of shears to minimize the risk of accidentally cutting the pads.

Throat & Chest

Blades ranging from #10 to #7F, with or against the grain, based on the sensitivity of the dog's skin, are common in the throat area. Follow the natural cowlick line that runs in a "V" shape from the base of the ears towards the base of the neck. The blending point begins about 3 or 4 fingers above the breast bone and drops to just below the turn of the muscle at the elbow/shoulder, creating a "W" shape when viewed straight on. When viewed in profile, the neck into

the chest blend into a predominant fore chest. When blending the chest, be aware of the heavy cowlicks in the area. Many stylists prefer to leave the chest area to blend by hand with thinning shears or shears. When finished in this area, double check your work to be sure the neck, chest and front legs drop down in a straight line when viewed in profile. Leave longer furnishing between the front legs that blend into the undercarriage.

The Head in General

The expression is alert and bold. Head is rectangular with a long fall of hair over the stop area with a full beard and goatee. The topskull and the muzzle are equal in length with the stop being the center point. All lines on the head are clean and sharp.

Top Skull

The top of the head can be clipped as close as a #10 used with the grain; to a #7F used with the grain or against depending on the dog's sensitivity and density of the coat.

Ears

Ears are clipped with a close blade. It is common to see a #10 or #15 blade used on the outside of the ear leather while a #40 blade is used on the inside. When working with close blades in this delicate area, always work from the base or center of the ear out toward the edge. Gently brace the ear with your fingers to clip over it. To finish, use small finishing shears to trim around the outside edge of the ear leather, keeping the tips of the shears toward the tip of the ears.

Fall

The Cesky has a natural fall of hair that covers the stop area and down the bridge of the nose. As with regular eyebrows, follow the eye socket rim, working with the lay of the coat. Do

not trim any hair from between the eyes in the stop area when clipping the top skull. This section of hair makes the fall over the eyes. With curved shears in reverse or with thinners, line the tip of the shear up with a point on an outside nostril on the nose. The fur at the back corner of the eye will be very short, growing progressively longer as it arches out over the eye. Do not cut any farther than midway over the eye. By using the nose as a set point, the angle of the arch can be set identically over each eye. When you close the shears to cut the arch, bevel the blades away from the pet's skin to avoid accidentally cutting the dog at the back corner of the eye. The fall, when viewed in profile, should form a straight line from the top skull out over the bridge of the nose. If this area rises too much, top thin the coat slightly to level it or do a small amount of bulk thinning with thinning shears from beneath.

Throat & Cheeks

The throat and cheek areas are clipped using blades ranging from a #10 to a #7F, used either with or against the grain. Use the natural colic line of the neck to be the guide to create the "U" or "V" shape of the throat. The lowest point will be about 3 fingers above the breast bone. The line that breaks the top skull and the cheeks is from the back corner of the eye straight back to the ear canal.

Beard & Goatee

The fur on the muzzle is a natural length as it forms the beard. The basic transition line between the cheek and the beard runs on an imaginary line from just behind the back corner of the eyes to the whisker nodular on the cheeks. The line continues to the back corner of the mouth. The goatee is formed by continuing the line forward on the lower jaw, 1 or 2 finger widths in from the back corner of the mouth.

313

Notes From The Grooming Table ©2016

The line should be very crisp and clean. The coat under the eye area is never clipped out as this hair forms one of the critical lines of the classic rectangular head style. The line on the dog's face should be straight, from the flat cheek down into the beard area. Double check this line by laying a greyhound comb alongside the head. Any fur that sticks out beyond the comb should be removed. Any hair inside this line should remain and be blended to create the rectangular shape.

Detail Finish
Application of bows and mild cologne is optional.

Suggested Tools & Equipment

- Nail Trimmers
- Styptic Powder
- Ear Powder
- Ear Cleaning Solution
- Cotton Balls
- Hemostat
- Clippers
- Slicker Brush
- Greyhound Comb
- Straight Shears
- Curved Shears
- Small Detailing Shears
- Thinning Shears
- Dematting Tools

Common Blade Options:
- #40, #15, #10
- #7F, #5F, #4F
- Variety of Guard Combs

Notes:

Notes *from your*
Grooming Table

Breed Facts & Characteristics

Country of Origin: Scotland

Height at Shoulder: 8"–11"

Coat Length/Type: Hard/Wiry

Color: Dark bluish black to light silvery gray
or reddish brown to pale fawn.

Correct grooming procedure:

Hand-Strip

Common pet grooming practices:

Clipper-Trim/Hand-Strip

General Description

This is a long, low athletic little dog with a curvy outline. The body of the dog is toned and flexible. The topline and the undercarriage line mimic one another in their outline. The legs are furnished with moderate feathering and the tail looks like a curved saber. The head is large and round, covered with silky hair. The eyes are full and round with a soft expression. The ears are tasseled.

-The Goal-
This breed is low slung with a curvy outline. The head is large and round. The front feet are larger than the back feet, representing a digging terrier. Back coat should be harsh, furnishings much softer and lighter in color.

Correctly Groomed: Hand-Stripped
Typical blades used on the body for pet grooming: #7F, #5F, #4F or shorter guard comb or a combination of those blades. Card coat after clipping to help maintain correct coat texture and color.

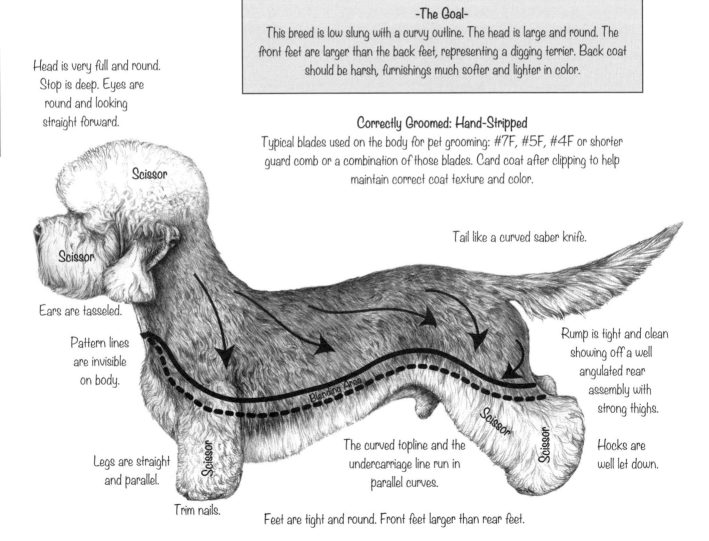

Head is very full and round. Stop is deep. Eyes are round and looking straight forward.

Ears are tasseled.

Pattern lines are invisible on body.

Legs are straight and parallel.

Trim nails.

Scissor

Scissor

Scissor

Scissor

Scissor

Blending Area

Tail like a curved saber knife.

Rump is tight and clean showing off a well angulated rear assembly with strong thighs.

Hocks are well let down.

The curved topline and the undercarriage line run in parallel curves.

Feet are tight and round. Front feet larger than rear feet.

TERRIER

See page 76 for Bathing & Drying Instructions

Frequency

Bathe once a week to once every 12 weeks.

Pre-Work

Trim or grind nails at least every four to six weeks to maintain a healthy foot structure. Swab the ears clean with a mild ear cleaning solution. Prior to bathing, quickly go over the entire body with a high-velocity dryer to help lift dirt and dander away from the skin and to loosen any shedding coat. ***Card and hand-strip dog prior to bathing and drying.***

Pattern Lines in General

The correct coat is hand-stripped. For either hand-stripped or clipper-cut pet dogs, the general pattern, based on the bone and muscle structure, is the same. After the final trim, all pattern lines should be invisible. If clipping at the transition points, feather off with the clippers in a smooth and steady fashion. If the pattern line is still visible after clipping, use thinning shears to blend the line. The head is full and round with tasseled ears.

Clipper-Cutting

Blades ranging from a #10 to a #4F are commonly used to set the pattern on the body as an alternative to hand-stripping techniques. They can be used with the grain or, with longer blades, against the grain. Keep in mind, the shorter the trim on the body pattern, the more difficult it is to blend the pattern later into the longer furnishings. A longer cut also allows you to mold the coat a bit and apply carding techniques to retain some of the proper coat texture. Carding also will remove minor tracks commonly left after clipping. Longer cutting blades are preferred.

Body Pattern

The transitional areas will be a half inch to more than an inch in width depending on the area and the conformation of the dog. At the front of the dog, the pattern starts just above the breast bone and drops on a diagonal line to almost the bottom of the shoulder muscle. The pattern line travels down the side of the dog, extending below the widest spring of rib towards the flank where it rises. As the pattern line rises over the flank, it slopes down at an angle to a point 2–3 finger widths above the hock. The entire rear section, under the tail area, is free of long hair. At the blending areas, bulk thin or top thin with thinning shears so the main body area blends invisibly with the long furnishings. After clipping, card the coat to promote proper coat growth and retain some of the rich color and harsh-coat texture.

Undercarriage

The undercarriage line of a Dandie Dinmont follows more along the lines of the long-legged terriers. The pattern line descends farther down the sides of the ribs. Leave only enough hair on the underside of the dog to accentuate the depth of chest and reflect the curves of the topline.

Tail

The tail is held like a short curved saber. There will be more coat on the underside than the top and sides of the tail. Trim off the excessive length at the tip by running your hand down the tail, thumb towards the tip, and stopping when you can feel the end of the tail bone under your thumb. With your fingers protecting the tip of the tail, trim off the long fur. Fluff the coat and shape the tail, thicker at the base, tapering to the tip. When the tail is held out behind the dog, there should be a small flag of coat on the underside to accentuate the curve of the tail. The tail is thicker at the root, tapering toward the tip.

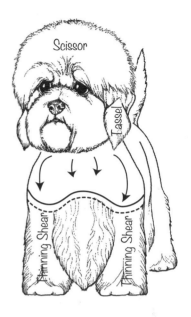

Head is large and covered with silky fur. The eyes look forward. Ears are tasseled. From the front and rear, the legs drop in straight, parallel lines from well toned shoulders and thighs. When setting the pattern, use the turn of the muscles to set the lines. Rear is short, tight and clean. Leg furnishings are slightly longer than the body coat. Tail is feathered lightly in the shape of a curved saber.

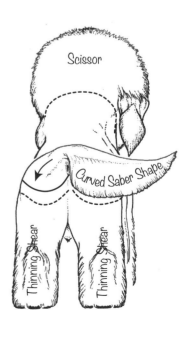

The head is unique with its full round shape and tasseled ears. The eyes are large, round and face forward under a deep set brow. The look should be soft, the expression wise and thoughtful. The topknot and muzzle are scissored large for the size but neat.

Fluff the topknot and scissor the head round and very full. The longer hair drapes over the ears and back of skull neatly.

Comb the topknot forward, over the brows. With curved shears in reverse, trim a frame around the eye area. The line is steeply beveled, creating a deep set eye. Finish by softening the line with thinning shears.

Remove long hair from the stop area and bridge of nose before trimming the topknot.

The lower line of the head completes the circle that puts the eyes and nose at the center of the head piece when looking at the pet from the front. The lower line parallels the jaw bone. Comb all the coat down and trim with shears in a curved line running from the nose all the way up to behind the occiput. Soften the line with thinning shears to complete the head piece.

Use a #10 or #15 blade on the outside of the ear, a #40 blade can be used on the inside of the ear leather with a very light touch. Remove diamonded shaped areas of fur on both the front and back edge of the ear leather. Let the longer coat of the topknot drape over the clipped area. The tassel covers the bottom 1/3 to 1/4 of the ear tip. Edge the ear with small detailing shears. The ear is low set, roughly in line with the eye.

The triangular tassel blends with the level of the line of the jaw.

The line at the back of the skull is about an inch beyond the occiput.

Ear Safety Tip: Remember, always keep the tips of the shears towards the tips of the ears when edging for safety.

The throat is clipped with a blade slightly shorter than that used on the body, in a "U" shape, about 2–3 finger widths from the breast bone.

Hindquarters

The hindquarters should be strong and powerful. When clipping this area, expose the thigh muscle with the same blade used on the body. Start to feather off with the blade where the muscle starts to turn under on a diagonal line from the flank region to about three or four fingers above the hock. Using a short to medium guard comb can facilitate feathering in the blending line. The blending should be invisible when the trim is finished. Blend with thinning shears if necessary. The stifle area should have enough furnishing left to give the legs substance and angulation. The longest coat on the legs can range from 1 to 2 inches depending on the amount of bone and coat density. Shape this area by hand with shears after the clipper work is complete. When viewed from the rear, the legs should form two parallel lines to the ground. The hocks are well let down. There should be adequate coat on the hock area to accentuate the angles of the rear assembly.

Front Legs

The pattern line at the shoulder is about 1 or 2 fingers above the top of the elbow, at the point where the muscle begins to turn under. The coat at the transition line will be very short and taper into the longer leg furnishings. This can be accomplished by feathering off at the blending point with the same blade used on the body or switching to a guard comb and blending off at the transition point. To shorten the furnishings, trim the coat with shears or thinning shears, working with the lay of the coat or by skimming the fur with a guard comb after it has been lightly fluffed. At the blending line, the transition should be invisible when the trim is finished. Blend with thinning shears by bulk thinning or top thinning if necessary.

Feet

The front feet are larger than the rear feet, with thick pads and strong nails which can be slightly exposed. The feet are trimmed very close to the edge of the foot and some nail is routinely exposed. The feet should point straight ahead, but minor toeing out is acceptable.

Throat & Chest

Blades ranging from a #10 to #7F, with or against the grain, based on skin sensitivity, are common in the throat area. Follow the natural cowlick line that runs from the base of the ears in a "V" shape toward the base of the neck. The blending point begins about 2 or 3 fingers above the breast bone and drops to just below the turn of the muscle at the elbow/shoulder, creating a "W" shape when viewed straight on. When viewed in profile, the neck into the chest should be straight without a predominant forechest. When blending the chest, be aware of the heavy cowlicks in the area. If a clipper is run over this area to create the flat chest, the result will be severe holes in the chest area. It is very easy to create two bald patches on either side of the chest, just inside the front legs. Many stylists prefer to blend the chest area by hand with thinning shears or shears. When finished in this area, double check your work to be sure the neck, chest and front legs drop down in a straight line when viewed in profile.

Head Styling

The overall shape of the head is very full and round. Clear the stop area and the top of the nose so the eyes will be clearly visible once the beveled arch is trimmed over the eyes. The eyes are large and deep set, highlighted by a tidy frame of hair over the eyes. To set this line, comb all the hair forward and use a longer pair of curved shears in reverse to form the beveled arch above the eye. The coat just above the eyelid will be very short, getting slightly longer as it moves out and away from the eye. Shape the topknot by hand to create a neat dome, letting the longer hair drape over the folds of the ear leathers and at the back of the head into the neck in a neat and natural manner. Once the topknot is nicely shaped, lightly edge the lines over the ears and at the back of the neck with thinning shears so they are still long, but tidy. The coat on the cheeks will be shorter than on the topknot or the muzzle area, about an inch in length, including under the ear leather. At the tip of the muzzle, comb the coat forward and use thinning shears to trim off the excess that hangs well beyond the end of the nose. Trimmed on a diagonal that parallels the end of the muzzle, this will leave a soft natural look. Blend the rest of the jaw line so there is a soft beard. The eyes and nose should be at the center of the head piece for balance.

Ears

It is common to use a #10 or #15 blade on the outside of the ear leather, while a #40 blade is used on the inside. When working with close blades in this delicate area, always work from the base, or center of the ear, out toward the edge. Gently brace the ear with your fingers to clip over it.

On the outside ear leather, start your clipper work at the fold near the skull. Do not clip all the way to the ear/skull junction. Let the longer coat of the topknot drape over the line. Clear the back edge of the ear starting at the fold down to a generous thumb width at the lower part of the ear tip. This tuft of hair on the ear tip will create the diamond shaped tassel. Repeat on the front edge of the ear. The front triangular clipped section is smaller than the back edge. The line for the ear tassel will be diamond shaped.

To finish, use small finishing shears to trim around the outside edges of the ear leathers, keeping the tips of the shears toward the tip of the ears for safety. The tassel is formed into a triangular shape following the line of the jaw.

Detail Finish

Application of bows and mild cologne is optional.

Special Note

Clipping a wire-coated dog will result in a dramatic change in the texture and color of the coat. The correct harsh wire coat can be nurtured by plucking the blown coat when it is ready for removal. This process stimulates the hair follicles to produce new guard coat. Without hand-stripping, the guard coat usually fails to reproduce and loses its brililant color and texture. If only undercoat grows, the guard coat color becomes that of the lighter, soft undercoat.

Suggested Tools & Equipment

- Nail Trimmers
- Styptic Powder
- Ear Powder
- Ear Cleaning Solution
- Cotton Balls
- Hemostat
- Clippers
- Slicker Brush
- Greyhound Comb
- Pumice Stone
- Carding Tools
- Stripping Knives
- Straight Shears
- Curved Shears
- Small Detailing Shears
- Thinning Shears
- Dematting Tools

Common Blade Options:

- #40, #15, #10
- #7F, #5F, #4F
- Variety of Guard Combs

Breed Facts & Characteristics

Country of Origin: Ireland

Height at Shoulder: 12½"–14½"

Coat Length/Type: Hard/Wiry

Color: Wheaten, blue or brindle.

Correct grooming procedure:
Hand-Strip

Common pet grooming practices:
Clipper-Trim /Hand-Strip

General Description

This stout short-legged terrier sports the look of terriers from years gone by. The Glen possesses great strength and should always convey the impression of incredible power for the size of the dog. The breed is slightly longer than tall. The medium length coat is a combination of harsh outer coat and soft undercoat. Characteristic to this breed are rose or half-prick ears and bowed forequarters with turned out feet are typical traits of the breed. Tails may be docked or undocked.

-The Goal-
This is a small, tough little terrier. They have a harsh outer coat and a thick undercoat. They have a natural head style with a rough and ready expression.

Correctly Groomed: Hand-Stripped

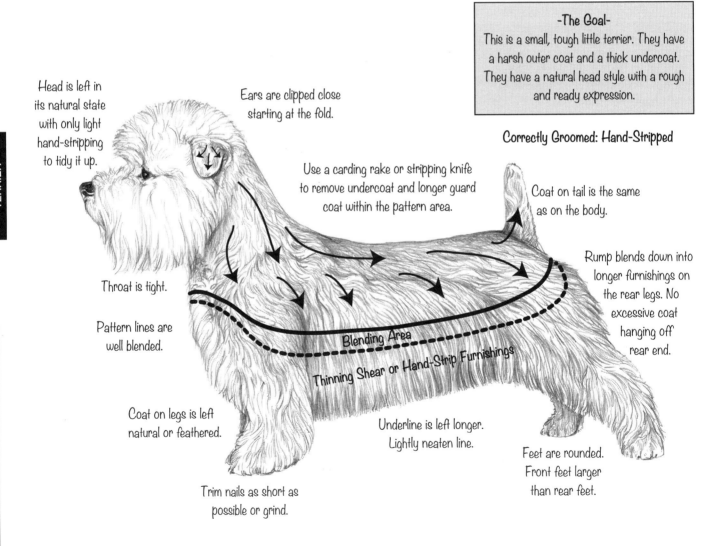

Head is left in its natural state with only light hand-stripping to tidy it up.

Ears are clipped close starting at the fold.

Use a carding rake or stripping knife to remove undercoat and longer guard coat within the pattern area.

Coat on tail is the same as on the body.

Rump blends down into longer furnishings on the rear legs. No excessive coat hanging off rear end.

Throat is tight.

Pattern lines are well blended.

Blending Area

Thinning Shear or Hand-Strip Furnishings

Coat on legs is left natural or feathered.

Underline is left longer. Lightly neaten line.

Feet are rounded. Front feet larger than rear feet.

Trim nails as short as possible or grind.

TERRIER

Grooming Procedures & Recommendations

See page 76 for
Bathing & Drying Instructions

Frequency
Bathe once a week to once every 12 weeks.

Pre-Work
Trim or grind nails at least every four to six weeks to maintain a healthy foot structure. Swab the ears clean with a mild ear cleaning solution. Prior to bathing, quickly go over the entire body with a high-velocity dryer to help lift dirt and dander away from the skin and to loosen any shedding coat. ***Card and hand-strip dog prior to bathing and drying.***

Carding
Carding is a natural technique in which the soft, downy undercoat is pulled from the dog's body. Typical tools used with this technique are: a pumice stone, undercoat rake, a fine-toothed stripping knife, which is pulled through the coat; or a fine blade, such as a #40, held between the fingers and pulled through the coat. Carding can be done before or after bathing and drying. Removal of the soft undercoat allows the topcoat to lie closer to the natural outline of the dog, accentuating the dog's structure. It also promotes a profuse harsh outer coat with a rich color and protects the skin.

Hand-Stripping the Body Pattern
Hand-stripping is a technique in which the outer guard coat is plucked from the dog's skin. This procedure helps promote the proper coat texture and rich color of the breed. During certain times of the year, the coat is easier to pull out. When the coat comes out easily, it is called a "blowing coat" or "blown coat." Ideally, hand-stripping should correspond with the dog's natural cycle, based on its environment and hormonal levels.

Using your fingers, a carding tool or a stripping knife, pull out a few hairs at a time to shape the coat and accentuate the dog's natural outline. Work methodically, pulling small amounts of coat at a time, always working in the direction of the coat growth. Proper hand-stripping employs a gentle momentum and rhythm to remove hair, not brute force, which is uncomfortable for both the groomer and the pet. Keep your wrist locked in a neutral position and allow the rhythmic movement to stem from your shoulder, not your wrist or elbow.

In general, the main body coat is easily removed and most pets do not mind the plucking process. The throat and private areas may be more sensitive, requiring the use of thinning shears or clippers. The length of coat to be left should be roughly an inch long on the upper portions of the body. The coats should always appear very natural, never clipped or heavily trimmed. On some coats, a light application of chalk or powder before the bath allows a better grip on the coat and makes plucking and stripping much easier.

Clipper-Cutting the Body Pattern
If a client insists that their pet be clipper-cut, follow the general body pattern using blades ranging from a #7F, #5F, #4F or moderate to longer guard combs. The longer the trim, the more you will be able to retain the proper essence of the breed and correct coat. After clipper-cutting be sure to incorporate carding techniques which will aid in creating the proper coat texture and color.

Legs & Undercarriage
The furnishings are left slightly longer on the legs, feet and undercarriage. If hand-stripping the body coat, strip and finger pluck these areas. If trimming with clippers, use thinning shears to shorten and tidy the furnishings. Characteristic to the breed, the front legs are bowed with toes that turn out somewhat.

Clip top ½ to ⅔ of ear or to fold.

The coat should look tidy but not sculpted. All lines are to be invisible. The ears can be rose or half-pricked. Clip the outer ½ to ⅔ tip only. Finger pluck or hand-strip the head furnishings to slighty tidy up the outline. Leave coat between the eyes in the stop area. If excessively long in the beard area, thinning shear the lower muzzle to neaten.

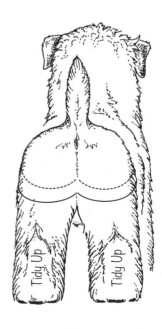

Notes From The Grooming Table ©2016

The Glen of Imaal is a hardy terrier with ancient style. The head is powerful, strong and impressive for the size of the dog. Only very minor trimming is required to tidy up the head which is left in a very natural state.

Finger pluck or thinning shear only the longest hairs on the top of the head to accentuate a broad and slightly domed skull.

If the ear is lightly coated, hand-strip the outer ear leather or clip the ear with a #10 or #15 blade on the outside, a #40 on the inside.

Remove long hair from the stop area and bridge of nose before trimming the topknot.

The line at the back of the skull is about an inch beyond the occiput.

Clear stop area with thinners or by finger plucking only the coat that is irritating the eyes.

Lightly tidy the jawline with thinning shears.

Ear Safety Tip: Remember, always keep the tips of the shears towards the tips of the ears when edging for safety.

Feet & Hocks
Trim the pads with a close cutting blade ranging from a #15 to a #40. Use a very light touch to clean the pads of long hair. Trim the feet round by first boxing them into the shape of a box while the dog is standing in a natural, square position. With the dog's feet firmly planted on the table, remove the sharp corners of the box and round the feet. Bevel the coat slightly. If detailing the feet with the foot off the tabletop, always use a small pair of shears to minimize the risk of accidentally cutting the pads.

Head
The head requires only mild shaping to maintain its natural appearance. Hand-strip or finger pluck the longer coat to retain the harsh texture and richer color. In the stop area, either finger pluck, gently hand-strip or use thinning shears, clear the excessive hair at the inside corners of the eyes. Tidy the longer fur in the stop area but do not remove all the coat. If coat is growing over the eye area, comb the coat forward over the eyes. With coarse thinners or chunkers, tidy over the eyes slightly, loosely framing them. Tidy the jawline in the same manner so it balances with the rest of the dog.

Ears
The ears are covered with very short hair. On most dogs, finger-pluck the few long strands to bring the coat down to the natural velvet length. If the ear is more substantially covered with hair, clip the ear using a #15 blade on the outside and a #40 on the inside. Edge the ears with small detailing shears, keeping the tips of the shears towards the tips of the ears.

Tails
Tails can be either docked or natural. The tail should be about the same length as the shorter coat on body. From the top, the tail

should blend seamlessly from the body. On the underside close to the body, tidy it slightly with a #10, or use thinning shears to tidy up any long fur. Undocked tails can have hint of feathering on the underside.

Detail Finish

For added shine, finish with a fine mist of coat polish on the body. Application of bows and mild cologne is optional.

Note:

Clipping a wire-coated dog will result in a dramatic change in the texture and color of the coat. The correct harsh wire coat can be nurtured by plucking the blown coat when it is ready for removal. This process stimulates the hair follicles to produce new guard coat. Without hand-stripping, the guard coat usually fails to reproduce and loses its brilliant color and texture. If only undercoat grows, the guard coat color becomes that of the lighter, soft undercoat.

Suggested Tools & Equipment

- Nail Trimmers
- Styptic Powder
- Ear Powder
- Ear Cleaning Solution
- Cotton Balls
- Hemostat
- Clippers
- Slicker Brush
- Greyhound Comb
- Pumice Stone
- Carding Tools
- Stripping Knives
- Straight Shears
- Curved Shears
- Small Detailing Shears
- Thinning Shears
- Dematting Tools

Common Blade Options:

- #40, #15, #10
- #7F, #5F, #4F
- Variety of Guard Combs

Notes:

Fox Terrier (Smooth)

TERRIER   SHORT COATED

Breed Facts & Characteristics

Country of Origin: England

Height at Shoulder: 14½"–15½"

Coat Length/Type: Hard/Wiry

Color: Predominantly white with some color.

Correct grooming procedure:
Card & Hand-Strip

Common pet grooming practices:
Bathe, Brush Out and Card

-The Goal-
The coat should be clean and fresh smelling. The harsh coat should lay tight against the body. No shedding hair.

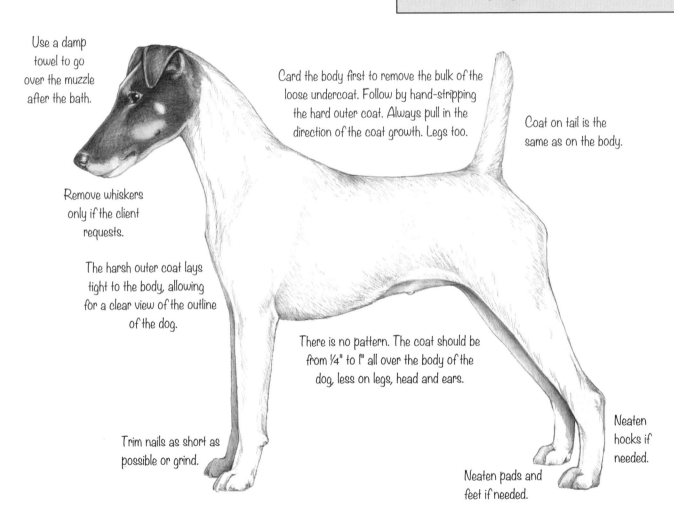

Use a damp towel to go over the muzzle after the bath.

Card the body first to remove the bulk of the loose undercoat. Follow by hand-stripping the hard outer coat. Always pull in the direction of the coat growth. Legs too.

Coat on tail is the same as on the body.

Remove whiskers only if the client requests.

The harsh outer coat lays tight to the body, allowing for a clear view of the outline of the dog.

There is no pattern. The coat should be from ¼" to 1" all over the body of the dog, less on legs, head and ears.

Trim nails as short as possible or grind.

Neaten hocks if needed.

Neaten pads and feet if needed.

See page 67 for Bathing & Drying Instructions

Suggested Tools & Equipment

- Nail Trimmers
- Styptic Powder
- Ear Cleaning Solution
- Cotton Balls
- Clippers
- #40 or #15 Blade
- Slicker Brush
- Rubber Curry
- Carding Tool
- De-Shedding Tools
- Small Detailing Shears
- Thinning Shears

Notes *from your* Grooming Table

Fox Terrier (Wire Haired)

Breed Facts & Characteristics

Country of Origin: England

Height at Shoulder: 14½"–15½"

Coat Length/Type: Hard/Wiry

Color: Predominantly white with some color.

Correct grooming procedure:

Hand-Strip

Common pet grooming practices:

Clipper-Trim

General Description

The Wire Fox is tight and tailored. They are a square, well balanced dog with a tendency to be leaner than some of the other long-legged terriers, but never racy. They have a sharp, keen expression that imparts the spirit and enthusiasm which runs in their blood. When grooming a Wire Fox Terrier, remember there is nothing soft or fluffy about the breed. In the finished groom, there is very little coat hiding the contours of its body. The leg coat is slightly longer. The head is rectangular in shape with a piercing expression, moderate muzzle coat and small brows.

> **-The Goal-**
> Everything about this breed is tight and tailored. The well-toned body is accentuated by the groom. The head is rectangular in shape. All pattern lines are invisible.

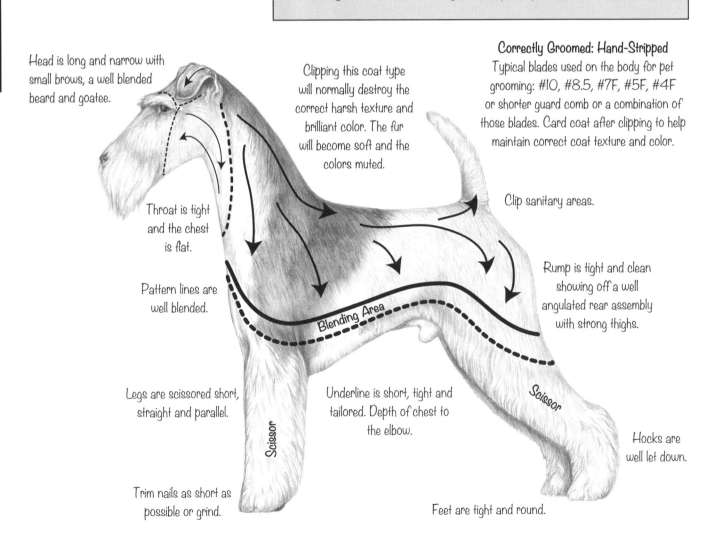

Head is long and narrow with small brows, a well blended beard and goatee.

Clipping this coat type will normally destroy the correct harsh texture and brilliant color. The fur will become soft and the colors muted.

Correctly Groomed: Hand-Stripped
Typical blades used on the body for pet grooming: #10, #8.5, #7F, #5F, #4F or shorter guard comb or a combination of those blades. Card coat after clipping to help maintain correct coat texture and color.

Throat is tight and the chest is flat.

Clip sanitary areas.

Pattern lines are well blended.

Rump is tight and clean showing off a well angulated rear assembly with strong thighs.

Blending Area

Legs are scissored short, straight and parallel.

Underline is short, tight and tailored. Depth of chest to the elbow.

Scissor

Scissor

Hocks are well let down.

Trim nails as short as possible or grind.

Feet are tight and round.

Grooming Procedures & Recommendations

See page 76 for
Bathing & Drying Instructions

Frequency
Bathe once a week to once every 12 weeks.

Pre-Work
Trim or grind nails at least every four to six weeks to maintain a healthy foot structure. Swab the ears clean with a mild ear cleaning solution. Prior to bathing, quickly go over the entire body with a high-velocity dryer to help lift dirt and dander away from the skin and to loosen any shedding coat. *Card and hand-strip dog prior to bathing and drying.*

Done to breed standard, the coat is hand-stripped to promote healthy skin tone, proper coat texture and rich color. Many pet owners choose to clipper-cut their pet dog. This practice destroys the correct harsh coat texture on most dogs and dilutes the color. However, it is an economical way to keep the pet looking like the breed standard. Finding a stylist who is willing to commit the time and energy to hand-strip the dog can be very difficult, and most pet owners are not willing to pay for this highly skilled service.

Pattern Lines in General
The pattern is based on the bone and muscle structure of the dog. After the final trim, all pattern lines should be invisible. At the transition points, feather off with the clippers in a smooth and steady fashion. If the pattern line is still visible after clipping, use thinning shears to blend the line.

Body
For either hand-stripped or clipper-cut dogs, the general pattern is the same.

Typical blades used in pet grooming range from a #7F to a #4F or a combination of those blades for the bulk of the body work. Some stylists find reversing a slightly longer blade very effective in achieving an extremely smooth finish on the body. Reversing a blade will shorten the cutting action by about two blade lengths as the same blade used with the grain of the coat. Choose one of the methods and follow the direction of the natural coat growth of the fur. After clipping, card the coat to help promote proper coat growth while retaining some of the rich color and harsh coat texture. Carding also will assist in the removal of any minor tracking left in the coat from clipping. The pattern lines start at the turn of the shoulder and continue to just above the elbow, back to the flank on a diagonal and then drop into the thigh region.

Undercarriage
Right around the navel area, the coat will be very short and start to get longer as the line moves forward towards the brisket, creating the illusion of a deep chest. When viewed in profile, the distance from the elbow to the bottom of the foot is equal to the distance between the withers and the brisket. There is only enough fur left on the undercarriage to accentuate depth of chest and an athletic build. The pattern line is well blended and invisible.

Tail & Rear
The top side of the tail is trimmed with the same blade as the body. The underside of the tail is clipped close, with blades ranging from #15 to a #7F, used with or against the grain based on the sensitivity of the dog's skin. Continue with the same blade around the rectum and on the inner side of the cowlick lines going down the back side of the thighs.

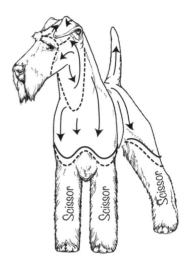

From the front and rear, the legs drop in straight, parallel lines from well toned shoulders and thighs. When setting the pattern, use the turn of the muscles to set the lines. Chest is flat but use caution not to bald out this area due to cowlicks where the front legs join the chest. Rear is short, tight and clean. Leg furnishings are slightly longer than the body coat.

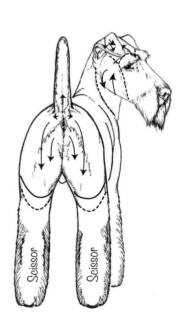

Notes From The Grooming Table ©2016

Their expression is intelligent and energetic. The head is long, narrow and rectangular with small brows and a well blended beard and goatee. The top skull and the muzzle are equal in length with the stop area being the center point. All lines on the head are invisible.

Clip top skull with blades ranging from a #7F to a #5F, with the grain.

The eyebrows are very small, split at the stop area. There are no sharp lines. Shape and blend with thinning shears.

Use a #10 or #15 blade on the outside of the ear. A #40 blade can be used on the inside of the ear leather with a very light touch. Edge the ear with small detailing shears. The fold of the ear comes to well above the line of the top skull.

On the muzzle, the hair is longer but not so long as to extend beyond the planes of the top skull or cheeks. Blend the bulk of the muzzle with thinning shears or skim with a medium guard comb. Lightly trim the end of the muzzle to accentuate the rectangular head style. The lines at the side of the face are well blended and straight. Do not hollow out under the eye.

Blend Well

Transitional Blending Area

Ear Safety Tip: Remember, always keep the tips of the shears towards the tips of the ears when edging for safety.

The throat is trimmed close with a #7F used against the grain or a #10 or #15 blade used with the coat growth.

Stay inside the natural cowlick line of the neck that runs from the ear bulb down in a "U" or "V" shape. Stop about 2 or 3 finger widths above the breast bone. Thinning shear the cowlick seam to blend with the longer coat of the neck.

Hindquarters

The hindquarters should be strong and powerful. When clipping this area, expose the thigh muscle with the same blade used on the body. Start to feather off with the blade where the muscle starts to turn under on a diagonal line from the flank region to about three or four fingers above the hock. Using a short to medium guard comb can facilitate feathering in the blending line. The pattern line should be invisible when the trim is finished. Blend with thinning shears if

necessary. The stifle area should have enough furnishing left to give the legs substance and angulation. The longest coat on the legs can range from 1 to 2 inches depending on the amount of bone and coat density. Shape this area by hand with shears after the clipper work is complete. When viewed from the rear, the legs should form two parallel lines to the ground. The hocks are well let down. There should be adequate coat on the hock area to accentuate the angles of the rear assembly.

Front Legs

The coat on the legs can range from 1/16 of an inch to 2 inches in length depending on the amount of bone, the size of the dog and coat density. The front legs drop straight down from the body and have ample bone and muscle to show off a powerful and sturdy animal. The pattern line at the shoulder is about 2 to 3 fingerss above the top of the elbow, at the point where the muscle begins to turn under. The coat at the transition line will be very short, and taper into the longer leg furnishings.

Grooming Procedures & Recommendations

This can be accomplished by feathering off at the blending point with the same blade used on the body. Other methods of blending off at the top of the leg include using a short to medium guard followed by hand-scissoring and blending with thinning shears. Most stylists prefer to leave the legs to shape by hand with shears.

After the final trim, the legs need to form two parallel columns going down from the elbow into tight, round feet. The coat at the back of the elbow is very short and falls straight down off the back of the leg toward the ground.

Feet

The feet are small for the size of the dog. Both the front and rear feet are compact with well arched toes. To show off these traits, the feet are trimmed very close to the edge of the foot and some nail is routinely exposed. The feet should point straight ahead, toeing neither in nor out. Trim the feet round by first boxing them in the shape of a square while the dog is standing in a natural, square position. Then remove the sharp corners of the box and round the feet facing straight forward. If detailing the feet with the foot off the tabletop, always use a small pair of shears to minimize the risk of accidentally cutting the pads.

Throat & Chest

Blades ranging from #10 to #7F, with or against the grain, based on the sensitivity of the dog's skin, are common in the throat area. Follow the natural cowlick line that runs in a "V" shape from the base of the ears towards the base of the neck. The blending point begins about 3 or 4 fingers above the breast bone and drops to just below the turn of the muscle at the elbow/shoulder, creating a "W" shape when viewed straight on. When viewed in profile, the neck into the chest should be straight without a predominant forechest. When blending the chest, be aware of the heavy cowlicks in the area. Many stylists prefer to leave the chest area to blend by hand with thinning shears or shears. When finished in this area, double check your work to be sure the neck, chest and front legs drop down in a straight line when viewed in profile.

The Head in General: Top Skull

The top of the head is clipped with a #7F or #5F, used with the grain or against depending on the dog's sensitivity and density of the coat.

Ears

The ears are clipped with a close blade. It is common to see a #10 or #15 blade used on the outside of the ear leather while a #40 blade is used on the inside. When working with close blades in this delicate area, always work from the base or center of the ear out toward the edge. Gently brace the ear with your fingers to clip over it. To finish, use small finishing shears to trim around the outside edge of the ear leather, keeping the tips of the shears toward the tip of the ears.

Brows

The eyebrow on this dog is very small. Follow the eye socket rim, working with the lay of the coat. They have a slight stop between the eyes that acts as a natural split for the brows. Either lightly clip this area when clipping the top skull, leave it to do by hand with thinning shears or finger pluck the area. This area should have just enough fur removed to lend definition to the brow area, while revealing the eye. The small, triangular shape accentuates the typically keen expression found on this long legged terrier. They will be very short at the back corner of the eye and longer at the tip, which comes out over the stop area. When viewed in profile, the brows should barely break the line of the top skull. Use thinning shears or curved shears in reverse to set the brow.

Suggested Tools & Equipment

- Nail Trimmers
- Styptic Powder
- Ear Powder
- Ear Cleaning Solution
- Cotton Balls
- Hemostat
- Clippers
- Slicker Brush
- Greyhound Comb
- Pumice Stone
- Carding Tools
- Stripping Knives
- Straight Shears
- Curved Shears
- Small Detailing Shears
- Thinning Shears
- Dematting Tools

Common Blade Options:

- #40, #15, #10
- #7F, #5F, #4F
- Variety of Guard Combs

Notes:

Throat & Cheeks

The throat and cheek areas are clipped using blades ranging from a #10 to a #7F, used either with or against the grain. Use the natural cowlick line of the neck to be the guide to create the "U" or "V" shape of the throat. The lowest point will be about 3 fingers above the breast bone. The line that breaks the top skull and the cheeks is from the back corner of the eye straight back to the ear canal.

Beard & Goatee

The beard and goatee are minimal with this harsh coated type of terrier, with the goatee being a bit longer than the fur on the beard. The pattern line starts from just behind the eyes and runs on a diagonal to the back corners of the mouth. The goatee is formed by continuing the line forward on the lower jaw, one or two finger widths in from the back corner of the mouth. When viewed from the top down, no hair should fall outside the planes of the cheeks. If the dog has an overabundance of fur on the muzzle, lightly rake a medium guard comb forward over the top of the head, down the nose and along the sides. Feather the coat off to leave longer hair at the end of the muzzle. Leave all the length of coat on the goatee, leaving it to finish by hand if it needs to be shortened. Once the excessive fur is removed, refine the head with thinning shears to form the classic rectangular head. The blending line at the sides of the face should be invisible between the tight work on the cheeks and the longer coat on the beard. Blend heavily with thinning shears, but do not take out so much coat to give an hour glass shape to the head, removing the fill under the eyes. Double check your work by combing the coat up and away from the muzzle, and then lay a comb on the cheeks, forming a straight line from the skull to the muzzle. Any fur that sticks out beyond the comb should be removed. Any hair inside the line should remain and be blended to create the rectangle shape.

Detail Finish

Application of bows and mild cologne is optional.

Grooming Tips

A light setting gel, mousse or texturing shampoo can add body to the leg coat, making it easier to scissor. Try spritzing unruly eyebrows while they are still damp with a styling spray. Work the product into the damp brows. Brush or comb the brows into place or dry them into the position you want them in the final trim.

Special Note

Harsh-coated terriers have a coat that will normally brush out quite easily, especially after they are clean.

Notes:

Notes *from your*
Grooming Table

Breed Facts & Characteristics

Country of Origin: Ireland

Height at Shoulder: 18"

Coat Length/Type: Hard/Wiry

Color: Bright red, golden red, red wheaten or wheaten.

Correct grooming procedure:
Hand-Strip

Common pet grooming practices:
Clipper-Trim/Hand-Strip

General Description

This breed is considered the sportsman of the long-legged terrier group. He is slightly longer than tall. The overall look is of a straightforward dog with a harsh coat that protects him from the elements. The jacket coat should be tight to the body with minimal leg furnishings. When grooming an Irish Terrier, remember there is nothing soft or fluffy about the breed. In the finished groom, *there is very little coat hiding the contours of any part of this dog.* The head is rectangular in shape with small brows, beard and a piercing expression.

> **-The Goal-**
> Everything about this breed is tight and tailored. The well-toned body is accentuated by the groom. The furnishings on this breed are very short. The head is rectangular in shape. All pattern lines are invisible.

Correctly Groomed: Hand-Stripped
Typical blades used on the body for pet grooming: #10, #8.5, #7F, #5F, #4F or short to medium guard comb or a combination of those blades. Card coat after clipping to help maintain correct coat texture and color.

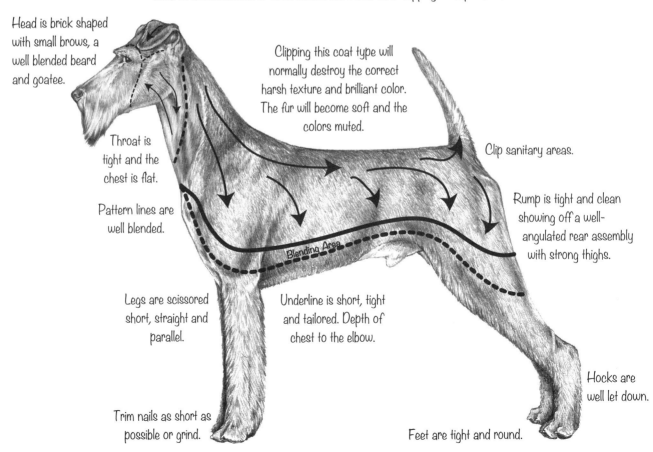

Head is brick shaped with small brows, a well blended beard and goatee.

Clipping this coat type will normally destroy the correct harsh texture and brilliant color. The fur will become soft and the colors muted.

Throat is tight and the chest is flat.

Pattern lines are well blended.

Blending Area

Clip sanitary areas.

Rump is tight and clean showing off a well-angulated rear assembly with strong thighs.

Legs are scissored short, straight and parallel.

Underline is short, tight and tailored. Depth of chest to the elbow.

Hocks are well let down.

Trim nails as short as possible or grind.

Feet are tight and round.

Grooming Procedures & Recommendations

See page 76 for
Bathing & Drying Instructions

Frequency
Bathe once a week to once every 12 weeks.

Pre-Work
Trim or grind nails at least every four to six weeks to maintain a healthy foot structure. Swab the ears clean with a mild ear cleaning solution. Prior to bathing, quickly go over the entire body with a high-velocity dryer to help lift dirt and dander away from the skin and to loosen any shedding coat. *Card and hand-strip dog prior to bathing and drying.*

Done to breed standard, the coat is hand-stripped to promote healthy skin tone, proper coat texture and rich color. Many pet owners choose to clipper-cut their pet dog. This practice destroys the correct harsh coat texture on most dogs and dilutes the color. However, it is an economical way to keep the pet looking like the breed standard. Finding a stylist who is willing to commit the time and energy to hand-strip the dog can be very difficult, and most pet owners are not willing to pay for this highly skilled service.

Pattern Lines in General
The pattern is based on the bone and muscle structure of the dog. After the final trim, all pattern lines should be invisible. At the transition points, feather off with the clippers in a smooth and steady fashion. If the pattern line is still visible after clipping, use thinning shears to blend the line.

Body
For either hand-stripped or clipper-cut dogs, the general pattern is the same.

Typical blades used in pet grooming range from a #7F to a #4F or a combination of those blades for the bulk of the body work. Some stylists find reversing a slightly longer blade very effective in achieving an extremely smooth finish on the body. Reversing a blade will shorten the cutting action by about two blade lengths as the same blade used with the grain of the coat. Choose one of the methods and follow the direction of the natural coat growth of the fur. After clipping, card the coat to help promote proper coat growth while retaining some of the rich color and harsh coat texture. Carding also will assist in the removal of any minor tracking left in the coat from clipping. The pattern lines start at the turn of the shoulder and continue to just above the elbow, back to the flank on a diagonal and then drop into the thigh region.

Undercarriage
Right around the navel area, the coat will be very short and start to get longer as the line moves forward towards the brisket, creating the illusion of a deep chest. When viewed in profile, the distance from the elbow to the bottom of the foot is equal to the distance between the withers and the brisket. There is only enough fur left on the undercarriage to accentuate depth of chest and an athletic build. The pattern line is well blended and invisible.

Tail & Rear
The top side of the tail is trimmed with the same blade as the body. The underside of the tail is clipped close, with blades ranging from #15 to a #7F, used with or against the grain based on the sensitivity of the dog's skin. Continue with the same blade around the rectum and on the inner side of the cowlick lines going down the back side of the thighs.

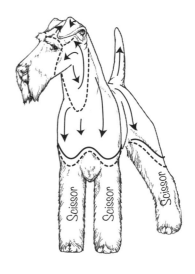

From the front and rear, the legs drop in straight, parallel lines from well toned shoulders and thighs. When setting the pattern, use the turn of the muscles to set the lines. Chest is flat but use caution not to bald out this area due to cowlicks where the front legs join the chest. Rear is short, tight and clean. Leg furnishings are slightly longer than the body coat.

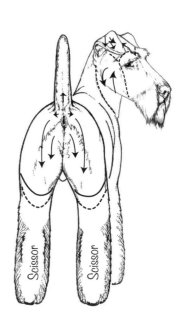

Notes From The Grooming Table ©2016

Their expression is alert, animated and friendly. Head is long and rectangular with small brows and a small, well blended beard and goatee. The top skull and the muzzle are equal in length with the stop area being the center point. All lines on the head are invisible.

Clip top skull with blades ranging from a #7F to a #5F, with the grain.

The eyebrows are very small, split at the stop area. There are no sharp lines. Shape and blend with thinning shears.

Use a #10 or #15 blade on the outside of the ear, a #40 blade can be used on the inside of the ear leather with a very light touch. Edge the ear with small detailing shears. The fold of the ear comes to just above the line of the top skull.

Ear Safety Tip: Remember, always keep the tips of the shears towards the tips of the ears when edging for safety.

On the muzzle, the hair is longer but not so long as to extend beyond the planes of the top skull or cheeks. Blend the bulk of the muzzle with thinning shears or skim with a medium guard comb. Lightly trim the end of the muzzle to accentuate the rectangular head style. The lines at the side of the face are well blended and straight. Do not hollow out under the eye.

The throat is trimmed close with a #7F used against the grain or a #10 or #15 blade used with the coat growth.

Blend Well
Blend Well
Blend Well
Blend Well
Transitional Blending Area

Stay inside the natural cowlick line of the neck that runs from the ear bulb down in a "U" or "V" shape. Stop about 2 or 3 finger widths above the breast bone. Thinning shear the cowlick seam to blend with the longer coat of the neck.

TERRIER

Hindquarters

The hindquarters should be strong and powerful. When clipping this area, expose the thigh muscle with the same blade used on the body. Start to feather off with the blade where the muscle starts to turn under on a diagonal line from the flank region to about 3 or 4 fingers above the hock. Using a short to medium guard comb can facilitate feathering in the blending line. The pattern line should be invisible when the trim is finished. Blend with thinning shears if

necessary. The stifle area should have enough furnishing left to give the legs substance and angulation. The longest coat on the legs can range from ½ to 1½ inches depending on the amount of bone and coat density. Shape this area by hand with shears after the clipper work is complete. When viewed from the rear, the legs should form two parallel lines to the ground. The hocks are well let down. There should be adequate coat on the hock area to accentuate the angles of the rear assembly.

Front Legs

The coat on the legs can range from 1/16 of an inch to 1 inch in length depending on the amount of bone, the size of the dog and coat density. The front legs drop straight down from the body and have ample bone and muscle to show off a powerful and sturdy animal. The pattern line at the shoulder is about 2 or 3 fingers above the top of the elbow, at the point where the muscle begins to turn under. The coat at the transition line will be very short, and taper into the longer leg furnishings. This can be accomplished by feathering off at the blending point with the same blade used on the body. Other methods of blending off at the top of the leg include using a short to medium guard, followed by hand-scissoring and blending with thinning shears. Most stylists prefer to leave the legs to shape by hand with shears. After the final trim, the legs need to form two parallel columns going down from the elbow into tight, round feet. The coat at the back of the elbow is very short and falls straight down off the back of the leg toward the ground.

Feet

The feet are small for the size of the dog. Both the front and rear feet are compact with well arched toes. To show off these traits, the feet are trimmed very close to the edge of the foot and some nail is routinely exposed. The feet should point straight ahead, toeing neither in nor out. Trim the feet round by first boxing them in the shape of a square while the dog is standing in a natural, square position. Then remove the sharp corners of the box and round the feet facing straight forward. If detailing the feet with the foot off the tabletop, always use a small pair of shears to minimize the risk of accidentally cutting the pads.

Throat & Chest

Blades ranging from #10 to #7F, with or against the grain, based on the sensitivity of the dog's skin, are common in the throat area. Follow the natural cowlick line that runs in a "V" shape from the base of the ears towards the base of the neck. The blending point begins about three or four fingers above the breast bone and drops to just below the turn of the muscle at the elbow/shoulder, creating a "W" shape when viewed straight on. When viewed in profile, the neck into the chest should be straight without a predominant forechest. When

blending the chest, be aware of the heavy cowlicks in the area. Many stylists prefer to leave the chest area to blend by hand with thinning shears or shears. When finished in this area, double check your work to be sure the neck, chest and front legs drop down in a straight line when viewed in profile.

The Head in General: Top Skull

The top of the head is clipped with a #7F or #5F, used with the grain or against depending on the dog's sensitivity and density of the coat.

Ears

The ears are clipped with a close blade. It is common to see a #10 or #15 blade used on the outside of the ear leather while a #40 blade is used on the inside. When working with close blades in this delicate area, always work from the base or center of the ear out toward the edge. Gently brace the ear with your fingers to clip over it. To finish, use small finishing shears to trim around the outside edge of the ear leather, keeping the tips of the shears toward the tip of the ears.

Brows

The eyebrow on this dog is very small. Follow the eye socket rim, working with the lay of the coat. They have a slight stop between the eyes that acts as a natural split for the brows. Either lightly clip this area when clipping the top skull, leave it to do by hand with thinning shears or finger pluck the area. This area should have just enough fur removed to lend definition to the brow area, while revealing the eye. The small, triangular shape accentuates the typically keen expression found on this long legged terrier. They will be very short at the back corner of the eye and longer at the tip, which comes out over the stop area. When viewed in profile, the brows should barely break the line of the top skull. Use thinning shears or curved shears in reverse to set the brow.

Suggested Tools & Equipment

- Nail Trimmers
- Styptic Powder
- Ear Powder
- Ear Cleaning Solution
- Cotton Balls
- Hemostat
- Clippers
- Slicker Brush
- Greyhound Comb
- Pumice Stone
- Carding Tools
- Stripping Knives
- Straight Shears
- Curved Shears
- Small Detailing Shears
- Thinning Shears
- Dematting Tools

Common Blade Options:

- #40, #15, #10
- #7F, #5F, #4F
- Variety of Guard Combs

Notes:

Notes From The Grooming Table ©2016

Grooming Procedures & Recommendations

Throat & Cheeks

The throat and cheek areas are clipped using blades ranging from a #10 to a #7F, used either with or against the grain. Use the natural cowlick line of the neck to be the guide to create the "U" or "V" shape of the throat. The lowest point will be about 3 fingers above the breast bone. The line that breaks the top skull and the cheeks is from the back corner of the eye straight back to the ear canal.

Beard & Goatee

The beard and goatee are minimal with this harsh coated type of terrier, with the goatee being a bit longer than the fur on the beard. The pattern line starts from just behind the eyes and runs on a diagonal to the back corners of the mouth. The goatee is formed by continuing the line forward on the lower jaw, one or two finger widths in from the back corner of the mouth. When viewed from the top down, no hair should fall outside the planes of the cheeks. If the dog has an overabundance of fur on the muzzle, lightly rake a medium guard comb forward over the top of the head, down the nose and along the sides. Feather the coat off to leave longer hair at the end of the muzzle. Leave all the length of coat on the goatee, leaving it to finish by hand if it needs to be shortened. Once the excessive fur is removed, refine the head with thinning shears to form the classic rectangular head. The blending line at the sides of the face should be invisible between the tight work on the cheeks and the longer coat on the beard. Blend heavily with thinning shears, but do not take out so much coat to give an hour glass shape to the head, removing the fill under the eyes. Double check your work by combing the coat up and away from the muzzle, and then lay a comb on the cheeks, forming a straight line from the skull to the muzzle. Any fur that sticks out beyond the comb should be removed. Any hair inside the line should remain and be blended to create the rectangle shape.

Detail Finish

Application of bows and mild cologne is optional.

Grooming Tips

A light setting gel, mousse or texturing shampoo can add body to the leg coat, making it easier to scissor. Try spritzing unruly eyebrows while they are still damp with a styling spray. Work the product into the damp brows. Brush or comb the brows into place or dry them into the position you want them in the final trim.

Special Note

Harsh-coated terriers have a coat that will normally brush out quite easily, especially after they are clean.

Notes:

Notes *from your*
Grooming Table

Kerry Blue Terrier

Breed Facts & Characteristics

Country of Origin: Ireland

Height at Shoulder: 17½"–19½"

Coat Length/Type: Curly/Thick

Color: Blue gray or gray blue.

Correct grooming procedure:
Hand-Scissor

Common pet grooming practices:
Clipper-Trim

General Description

The Kerry is a medium sized, well-balanced dog with plenty of muscle, a rectangular head, well laid back shoulders and a short back. His coat is soft, thick and wavy. The color is always a blue gray in varying shades. His use as an all-around working and utility dog in his native land, which has created a versatile dog of true terrier style and spirit.

-The Goal-
A highly stylized dog with a unique curly coat. On the finished trim, the body coat remains curly while the coat on legs and head is straight and full. The head is rectangular in shape with a fall of hair over the eyes. Mat free.

Correctly Groomed: Hand-Scissored
Typical blades used on the body for pet grooming range from #7F, #5F, and #4F blades to a variety of guard combs or a combination of those trimming tools.

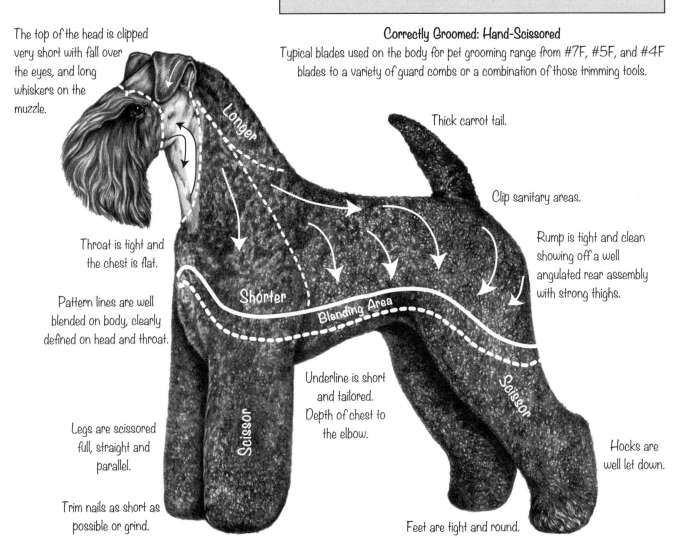

The top of the head is clipped very short with fall over the eyes, and long whiskers on the muzzle.

Throat is tight and the chest is flat.

Pattern lines are well blended on body, clearly defined on head and throat.

Legs are scissored full, straight and parallel.

Trim nails as short as possible or grind.

Longer

Shorter

Blending Area

Scissor

Underline is short and tailored. Depth of chest to the elbow.

Thick carrot tail.

Clip sanitary areas.

Rump is tight and clean showing off a well angulated rear assembly with strong thighs.

Scissor

Hocks are well let down.

Feet are tight and round.

Grooming Procedures & Recommendations

See page 74 for
Bathing & Drying Instructions

Frequency

Bathe once a week to once every 12 weeks. Trim every four to six weeks to maintain a stylized fashion.

Pre-Work

Trim or grind nails at least every four to six weeks to maintain a healthy foot structure. Clean the ears by swabbing with a mild ear cleaning solution. Pluck any long hair inside the ear canal using an ear powder and your fingers or hemostat. Prior to bathing, quickly go over the entire body and remove any serious mats or tangles. If the tangle can be penetrated with water, leave it and remove when the dog is clean. If the pet has not been in for professional grooming for six weeks or more, remove the excessive body coat and set the pattern before bathing. Before starting the final haircut, make the the dog's coat is thoroughly brushed out and free of tanlges.

Pattern Lines in General

The pattern is based on the bone and muscle structure of the dog. After the final trim, all pattern lines should be invisible on the main body. If using clippers on the main body, feather off transition points in a smooth and steady fashion. If the pattern line is still visible after clipping, use thinning shears to blend the line. On the head, the pattern lines are crisp and clean.

Body

For pet dogs, the coat can be hand-scissored or clipper-cut using the same general pattern. Typical blades used in pet grooming range from a #7F for the tight work around the neck and shoulders to blades ranging from a #4 for very short pet trims to

a longer guard comb. The pattern lines start at the turn of the shoulder and continue to just above the elbow, return to the flank on a diagonal and then drop into the thigh region. At the pattern lines, the shorter fur blends seamlessly into the longer coat of the legs and undercarriage.

Neck

The neck is moderately long and carried proudly. Leaving the coat slightly longer on the back of the neck can accentuate this characteristic. The additional coat can help create the illusion of a powerful but graceful neck as long as it tapers smoothly into the shoulders.

Undercarriage

Right around the navel area, the coat will be very short and start to get longer as the line moves forward towards the brisket, creating the illusion of a deep chest. When viewed in profile, the depth of the body and the length of the legs should be equal. There is only enough fur left on the undercarriage to accentuate depth of chest and an athletic build. The pattern line is well blended.

Tail & Rear

The top and sides of the tail are trimmed by hand, slightly thicker at the base, narrowing at the tip. The underside is clipped close, with blades ranging from #15 to a #7F, used with or against the grain based on the sensitivity of the dog's skin. On the inner side of the cowlick lines going down the back side of the thighs, use a close blade ranging between a #7F and a shorter guard comb.

Hindquarters

The hindquarters should be strong and powerful. When clipping this area, expose the thigh muscle with the same blade used on the body. Start

From the front and rear, the legs drop in straight, parallel lines from well toned shoulders and thighs. When setting the pattern, use the turn of the muscles to set the lines. Chest is flat but use caution not to bald out this area due to cowlicks where the front legs join the chest. Rear is short, tight and clean. Leg furnishings are longer than the body coat.

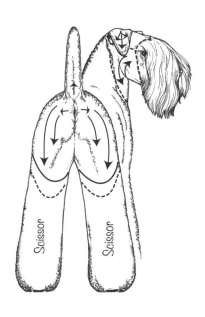

Notes From The Grooming Table ©2016

Their expression is friendly but alert and keen. Head is rectangular with a long fall of hair over the stop area with a full beard and goatee. The top skull and the muzzle are equal in length with the stop area being the center point. All lines on the head are clean and sharp.

Clip top skull with blades ranging from a #7F to a #5F, used against the grain or blades ranging from a #10 to #7F with the grain.

Use a #10 or #15 blade on the outside of the ear, a #40 blade can be used on the inside of the ear leather with a very light touch. Edge the ear with small detailing shears. The fold of the ear is level with the line of the top skull.

The line for the fall follows the eye socket rim. The back corners of the eyes are trimmed closely to expose the eye. This line arches out towards the nose. It is crisp and clean.

Ear Safety Tip: Remember, always keep the tips of the shears towards the tips of the ears when edging for safety.

On the muzzle, the hair is long and natural but does not break the line of the top skull. When combing down the beard, the lines at the side of the face form a straight plane. Just below the back corner of the eyes, the fur is short and well blended, creating fill under the eye. The clipper lines of the beard are clean and sharp.

Transitional Area

The throat and cheeks are trimmed close with a #10 or #15 blade used against the grain.

Stay inside the natural cowlick line of the neck that runs from the ear bulb down in a "U" or "V" shape. Stop about 2 or 3 finger widths above the breast bone. The line is very sharp and clean.

to feather off with the blade where the muscle starts to turn under on a diagonal line from the flank region to about three or four fingers above the hock. The blending should be invisible when the trim is finished. Blend with shears if necessary. The stifle area should have enough furnishing left to give the legs substance and angulation. The longest coat on the legs can range from 1 to 3 inches depending on the amount of bone and coat density.

Shape this area by hand with shears after the clipper work is complete. When viewed from the rear, the legs should form two parallel lines to the ground. The hocks are well let down. There should be adequate coat on the hock area to accentuate the angles of the rear assembly.

Front Legs
The longest coat on the legs can range from 1 to 3 inches depending on the amount of bone and coat

density. The pattern line at the shoulder is about 2 fingers above the top of the elbow, at the point where the muscle begins to turn under. The coat at the transition line will be very short and taper into the longer leg furnishings. This can be accomplished by feathering off at the blending point with the same blade used on the body. Most stylists prefer to leave the legs to scissor by hand.

TERRIER

Other methods of blending off at the top of the leg include using a short to medium guard comb followed by hand-scissoring and blending with thinning shears. After the final trim, the legs should form two parallel columns descending from the elbow into beveled, tight, round feet. The coat at the back of the elbow is very short and falls straight down off the back of the leg toward the ground.

Feet

Both the front and rear feet are compact with well-arched toes. To show off these traits, the feet are trimmed very close to the edge of the foot, beveling into fuller leg coat. The feet should point straight ahead, toeing neither in nor out. Begin trimming the feet by forming a square box around the foot while the dog is standing in a natural, square position. With the dog standing squarely on the table, remove the sharp edges of the box and round the feet as they face straight forward. If detailing the feet with the foot lifted off the tabletop, always use a small pair of detailing shears to minimize the risk of accidentally cutting the pads.

Throat & Chest

Blades ranging from #15 to #7F, with or against the grain, based on the sensitivity of the dog's skin, are common in the throat area. Follow the natural cowlick line that runs from the base of the ears in a "V" shape towards the base of the neck. The close work on the throat is crisp with clean lines. The blending point for the chest begins about three or four fingers above the breast bone and drops to just below the turn of the muscle at the elbow/shoulder, creating a "W" shape when viewed straight on. When viewed in profile, the neck

into the chest should be straight without a predominant forechest. When blending the chest, be aware of the heavy cowlicks in the area. Many stylists prefer to leave the chest area to blend by hand with shears.

The Head in General

The head is rectangular in shape. The length of the muzzle and the skull are about the same. The top skull is smooth and flat. The cheeks are flat and clean. There is a slight stop between the keen, sharp eyes that are accentuated by a fall of hair between them.

Ears

Ears are clipped with a close blade. It is common to see a #10 or #15 blade used on the outside of the ear leather while a #40 blade is used on the inside. When working with close blades in this delicate area, always work from the base, or center, of the ear out toward the edge. Gently brace the ear with your fingers to clip over it. To finish, use small finishing shears to trim around the outside edge of the ear leather, keeping the tips of the shears toward the tip of the ear.

Top Skull

The top of the head can be clipped as close as a #10 used with the grain, to a #7F or #5F used with the grain or against depending on the dog's sensitivity and density of the coat. To create the pattern line for the fall between the eyes, follow the eye socket rim, working with the lay of the coat. Do not clip down into the stop area. Clip the top of the head from the behind the eye bone ridges to the occiput. Use caution when clipping around the base of the ears.

Fall

The slight stop between the eyes will be filled with long fur. Shape the area over the eyes into an arch to accentuate the typically keen terrier expression. The coat will be very short at the back corner of the eye and longer as it blends out beyond the halfway point of the eye. When viewed in profile, the fall is a continuation of the top skull as it grows out over the nose. Use curved shears in reverse to set the arch line above the eyes. Line up the tip of the shear with a point on the nose. Repeat on the other eye. By using the nose as a set point, the angles of both arches are easier to match.

Beard & Goatee

The muzzle is left in a natural state as it forms the rectangular beard. The transition line for the cheek to the muzzle area runs on an imaginary line from just behind the back corner of the eye to the back corner of the mouth. The goatee is left long and natural on the lower jaw. When setting the line for the goatee, clip just ahead of the back corner of the mouth so when the dog opens its mouth, it will be free of hair. All the lines should be very crisp and clean. The coat under the eye area is never clipped as this hair forms one of the critical lines of the classic rectangular head style. Depending on the head, this line may need to be adjusted slightly. The line on the dog's face should be straight, from the flat cheek down into the muzzle area. Double check this line by laying a greyhound comb along side the head. Any fur that sticks out beyond the comb should be removed. Any hair inside this line should remain and be blended to create the rectangular shape.

Grooming Procedures & Recommendations

Detail Finish

After the body coat has been trimmed, mist the fur with water or a light coat conditioner from a spray bottle. Work the moisture into the coat with your fingers to highlight the wavy coat texture of the Kerry Blue. Work the mist only into the back and rib areas. Application of mild cologne and collar bows is optional.

Grooming Tips

A light setting gel, mousse or texturing shampoo can add body to the leg coat, making it easier to scissor. For unruly falls, try spritzing them while they are still damp with a styling spray. Work the product into the damp hair. Brush or comb the fall into place or dry it into the position you want.

Suggested Tools & Equipment

- Nail Trimmers
- Styptic Powder
- Ear Powder
- Ear Cleaning Solution
- Cotton Balls
- Hemostat
- Clippers
- Slicker Brush
- Greyhound Comb
- Straight Shears
- Curved Shears
- Small Detailing Shears
- Thinning Shears
- Dematting Tools
- High-Velocity Dryer

Common Blade Options:

- #40, #15, #10
- #7F, #5F, #4F
- Variety of Guard Combs

Notes:

TERRIER

Notes *from your* Grooming Table

Lakeland Terrier

Breed Facts & Characteristics

Country of Origin: England

Height at Shoulder: 13½"–14½"

Coat Length/Type: Hard/Wiry

Color: Black, blue, liver, red and wheaten, wheaten or golden tan with blue, black, liver or grizzle saddle.

Correct grooming procedure:

Hand-Strip

Common pet grooming practices:

Clipper-Trim/Hand-Strip

General Description

The Lakeland is the smallest of the long-legged terriers. They are a square, well balanced dog. They have a sharp, keen expression that imparts the spirit and enthusiasm which runs in their blood. When grooming a Lakeland Terrier, remember there is nothing soft or fluffy about the breed. In the finished groom, there is very little coat hiding the contours of its body. The leg coat and muzzle coat are slightly longer. The head is rectangular in shape with a piercing expression and a fall of fur between the eyes.

-The Goal-
Everything about the breed is tight and tailored. The well-toned body is accentuated by the groom. The head is rectangular in shape. All pattern lines are invisible.

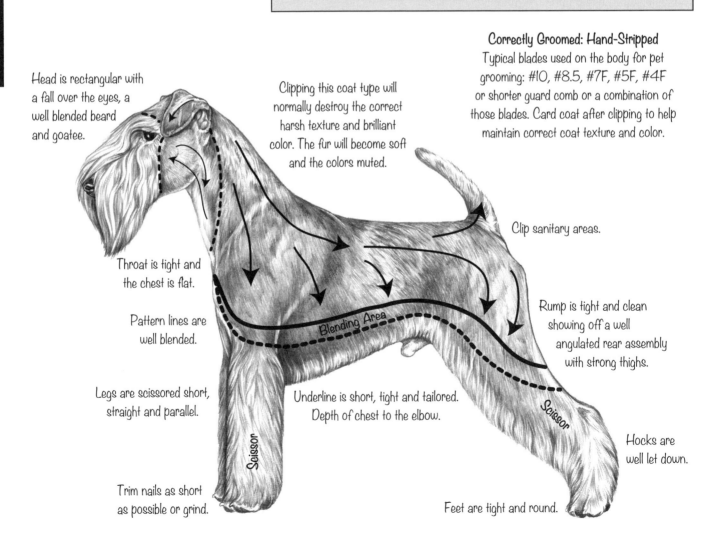

Correctly Groomed: Hand-Stripped
Typical blades used on the body for pet grooming: #10, #8.5, #7F, #5F, #4F or shorter guard comb or a combination of those blades. Card coat after clipping to help maintain correct coat texture and color.

Head is rectangular with a fall over the eyes, a well blended beard and goatee.

Clipping this coat type will normally destroy the correct harsh texture and brilliant color. The fur will become soft and the colors muted.

Clip sanitary areas.

Throat is tight and the chest is flat.

Pattern lines are well blended.

Blending Area

Rump is tight and clean showing off a well angulated rear assembly with strong thighs.

Legs are scissored short, straight and parallel.

Underline is short, tight and tailored. Depth of chest to the elbow.

Scissor

Scissor

Hocks are well let down.

Trim nails as short as possible or grind.

Feet are tight and round.

Grooming Procedures & Recommendations

See page 76 for
Bathing & Drying Instructions

Frequency
Bathe once a week to once every
12 weeks.

Pre-Work
Trim or grind nails at least every four
to six weeks to maintain a healthy foot
structure. Swab the ears clean with a
mild ear cleaning solution. Prior to
bathing, quickly go over the entire
body with a high-velocity dryer to help
lift dirt and dander away from the skin
and to loosen any shedding coat. *Card
and hand-strip dog prior to bathing
and drying.*

Done to breed standard, the coat is
hand-stripped to promote healthy
skin tone, proper coat texture and
rich color. Many pet owners choose
to clipper-cut their pet dog. This
practice destroys the correct harsh
coat texture on most dogs and
dilutes the color. However, it is
an economical way to keep the pet
looking like the breed standard.
Finding a stylist who is willing
to commit the time and energy
to hand-strip the dog can be very
difficult, and most pet owners are
not willing to pay for this highly
skilled service.

Pattern Lines In General
The pattern is based on the bone and
muscle structure of the dog. After the
final trim, all pattern lines should be
invisible on the main body. If using
clippers on the main body, feather off
transition points in a smooth and steady
fashion. If the pattern line is still visible
after clipping, use thinning shears to
blend the line. On the head, the pattern
lines are crisp and clean.

Body
For either hand-stripped or clipper-cut
dogs, the general pattern is the same.
Typical blades used in pet grooming
range from a #7F to a #4F or a
combination of those blades for the
bulk of the body work. Some stylists
find reversing a slightly longer blade
very effective in achieving an extremely
smooth finish on the body. Reversing
a blade will shorten the cutting action
by about two blade lengths as the same
blade used with the grain of the coat.
Choose one of the methods and follow
the direction of the natural coat growth
of the fur. After clipping, card the coat
to help promote proper coat growth
while retaining some of the rich color
and harsh coat texture. Carding also
will assist in the removal of any minor
tracking left in the coat from clipping.
The pattern lines start at the turn of the
shoulder and continue to just above the
elbow, back to the flank on a diagonal
and then drop into the thigh region.

Undercarriage
Right around the navel area, the coat
will be very short and start to get longer
as the line moves forward towards the
brisket, creating the illusion of a deep
chest. When viewed in profile, the
distance from the elbow to the bottom
of the foot is equal to the distance
between the withers and the brisket.
There is only enough fur left on the
undercarriage to accentuate depth of
chest and an athletic build. The pattern
line is well blended and invisible.

Tail & Rear
The top side of the tail is trimmed
with the same blade as the body. The
underside of the tail is clipped close, with
blades ranging from #15 to a #7F, used
with or against the grain based on the
sensitivity of the dog's skin. Continue
with the same blade around the rectum
and on the inner side of the cowlick lines
going down the back side of the thighs.

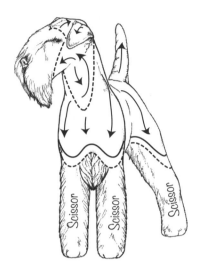

From the front and rear, the legs
drop in straight, parallel lines from
well toned shoulders and thighs. When
setting the pattern, use the turn of the
muscles to set the lines. Chest is flat
but use caution not to bald out this
area due to cowlicks where the front
legs join the chest. Rear is short, tight
and clean. Leg furnishings are slightly
longer coated than the body coat.

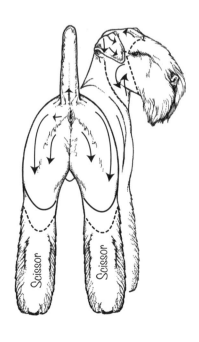

Notes From The Grooming Table ©2016

Their expression is friendly but alert and bold. Head is brick shaped with a long fall of hair over the stop area with a well blended beard and goatee. The top skull and the muzzle are equal in length with the stop area being the center point. All lines on the head are heavily blended.

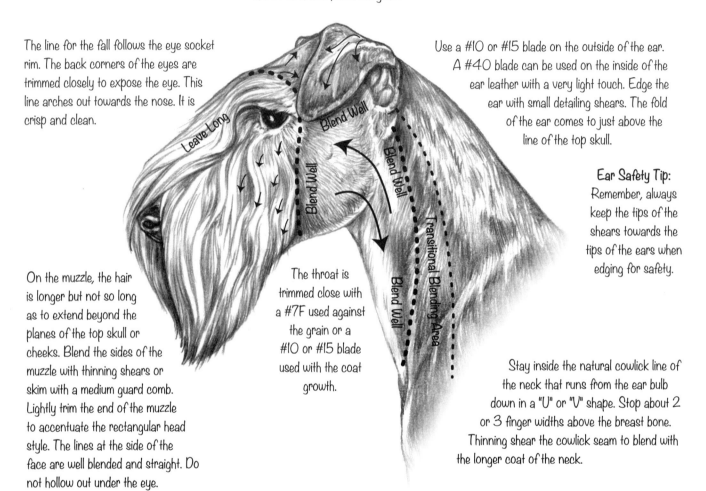

Clip top skull with blades ranging from a #7F to a #5F, with the grain.

The line for the fall follows the eye socket rim. The back corners of the eyes are trimmed closely to expose the eye. This line arches out towards the nose. It is crisp and clean.

Leave Long

Blend Well

Blend Well

Blend Well

Blend Well

Transitional Blending Area

Use a #10 or #15 blade on the outside of the ear. A #40 blade can be used on the inside of the ear leather with a very light touch. Edge the ear with small detailing shears. The fold of the ear comes to just above the line of the top skull.

Ear Safety Tip:
Remember, always keep the tips of the shears towards the tips of the ears when edging for safety.

On the muzzle, the hair is longer but not so long as to extend beyond the planes of the top skull or cheeks. Blend the sides of the muzzle with thinning shears or skim with a medium guard comb. Lightly trim the end of the muzzle to accentuate the rectangular head style. The lines at the side of the face are well blended and straight. Do not hollow out under the eye.

The throat is trimmed close with a #7F used against the grain or a #10 or #15 blade used with the coat growth.

Stay inside the natural cowlick line of the neck that runs from the ear bulb down in a "U" or "V" shape. Stop about 2 or 3 finger widths above the breast bone. Thinning shear the cowlick seam to blend with the longer coat of the neck.

Hindquarters

The hindquarters should be strong and powerful. When clipping this area, expose the thigh muscle with the same blade used on the body. After the final trim, the legs need to form two parallel columns going down from the elbow into tight, round feet. The coat at the back of the elbow is very short and falls straight down off the back of the leg toward the ground.

Feet

The feet are small for the size of the dog. Both the front and rear feet are compact with well arched toes. To show off these traits, the feet are trimmed very close to the edge of the foot and some nail is routinely exposed. The feet should point straight ahead, toeing neither in nor out. Trim the feet round by first boxing them in the shape of a square while the dog is standing in a natural, square position. Then remove the sharp corners of the box and round the feet facing straight forward. If detailing the feet with the foot off the tabletop, always use a small pair of shears to minimize the risk of accidentally cutting the pads.

TERRIER

Grooming Procedures & Recommendations

Throat & Chest

Blades ranging from #10 to #7F, with or against the grain, based on the sensitivity of the dog's skin, are common in the throat area. Follow the natural cowlick line that runs in a "V" shape from the base of the ears towards the base of the neck. The blending point begins about 3 or 4 fingers above the breast bone and drops to just below the turn of the muscle at the elbow/shoulder, creating a "W" shape when viewed straight on. When viewed in profile, the neck into the chest should be straight without a predominant forechest. When blending the chest, be aware of the heavy cowlicks in the area. Many stylists prefer to leave the chest area to blend by hand with thinning shears or shears. When finished in this area, double check your work to be sure the neck, chest and front legs drop down in a straight line when viewed in profile.

The Head in General: Top Skull

The top of the head is clipped with a #7F or #5F, used with the grain or against depending on the dog's sensitivity and density of the coat.

Ears

The ears are clipped with a close blade. It is common to see a #10 or #15 blade used on the outside of the ear leather while a #40 blade is used on the inside. When working with close blades in this delicate area, always work from the base or center of the ear out toward the edge. Gently brace the ear with your fingers to clip over it. To finish, use small finishing shears to trim around the outside edge of the ear leather, keeping the tips of the shears toward the tip of the ears.

Fall

The Lakeland has a natural fall of hair that covers the stop area and down the bridge of the nose. As with regular eyebrows, follow the eye socket rim working with the lay of the coat.

However, do not trim any hair from between the eyes. Trim only the coat from the outside edges of the eyes. Use either thinning shears or curved shears. Remove the coat from the back corner to the center of the eye, leaving the rest of the coat to create the fall. When trimming this area, follow an imaginary line from the outside edge of the eye to the outside edge of the nostril to line up the shears. The fur at the back corner of the eye will be very short, growing progressively longer as it arches out over the eye. The fall, when viewed in profile, should form a straight line from the top skull out over the bridge of the nose. If this area rises up too much, top thin the coat slightly to level it out or do a small amount of bulk thinning with thinning shears from underneath.

Start to feather off with the blade where the muscle starts to turn under on a diagonal line from the flank region to about 3 or 4 fingers above the hock. Using a short to medium guard comb can facilitate feathering in the blending line. The pattern lines should be invisible when the trim is finished. Blend with thinning shears if necessary. The stifle area should have enough furnishing left to give the legs substance and angulation. The longest coat on the legs can range from 1 to 2 inches depending on the amount of bone and coat density. Shape this area by hand with shears after the clipper work is complete. When viewed from the rear, the legs should form two parallel lines to the ground. The hocks are well let down. There should be adequate coat on the hock area to accentuate the angles of the rear assembly.

Front Legs

The coat on the legs can range from 1/16 of an inch to 1.5 inches in length depending on the amount of bone, the size of the dog and coat density. The

Suggested Tools & Equipment

- Nail Trimmers
- Styptic Powder
- Ear Powder
- Ear Cleaning Solution
- Cotton Balls
- Hemostat
- Clippers
- Slicker Brush
- Greyhound Comb
- Pumice Stone
- Carding Tools
- Stripping Knives
- Straight Shears
- Curved Shears
- Small Detailing Shears
- Thinning Shears
- Dematting Tools

Common Blade Options:

- #40, #15, #10
- #7F, #5F, #4F
- Variety of Guard Combs

Notes:

Notes From The Grooming Table ©2016

Grooming Procedures & Recommendations

front legs drop straight down from the body and have ample bone and muscle to show off a powerful and sturdy animal. The pattern line at the shoulder is about 1 or 2 fingers above the top of the elbow, at the point where the muscle begins to turn under. The coat at the transition line will be very short, and taper into the longer leg furnishings. This can be accomplished by feathering off at the blending point with the same blade used on the body. Other methods of blending off at the top of the leg include using a short to medium guard comb followed by hand-scissoring and blending with thinning shears. Most stylists prefer to leave the legs to shape by hand with shears.

Throat & Cheeks

The throat and cheek areas are clipped using blades ranging from a #10 to a #7F, used either with or against the grain. Use the natural cowlick line of the neck to be the guide to create the "U" or "V" shape of the throat. The lowest point will be about 3 fingers above the breast bone. The line that breaks the top skull and the cheeks is from the back corner of the eye straight back to the ear canal.

Beard & Goatee

The beard and goatee are minimal with this harsh coated type of terrier, with the goatee being a bit longer than the fur on the beard. The pattern line starts from just behind the eyes and runs on a diagonal to the back corners of the mouth. The goatee is formed by continuing the line forward on the lower jaw, 1 or 2 finger widths in from the back corner of the mouth. When viewed from the top down, no hair should fall outside the planes of the cheeks. If the dog has an overabundance of fur on the muzzle, lightly rake a medium guard comb forward over the top of the head, down the nose and along the sides. Feather the coat off to leave longer hair at the end of the muzzle. Leave all the length of coat on the goatee, leaving it to finish by hand if it needs to be shortened. Once the excessive fur is removed, refine the head with thinning shears to form the classic rectangular head. The blending line at the sides of the face should be invisible between the tight work on the cheeks and the longer coat on the beard. Blend heavily with thinning shears, but do not take out so much coat as to give an hour glass shape to the head,

removing the fill under the eyes. Double check your work by combing the coat up and away from the muzzle, and then lay a comb on the cheeks, forming a straight line from the skull to the muzzle. Any fur that sticks out beyond the comb should be removed. Any hair inside the line should remain and be blended to create the rectangle shape.

Detail Finish

Application of bows and mild cologne is optional.

Grooming Tips

A light setting gel, mousse or texturing shampoo can add body to the leg coat, making it easier to scissor. Try spritzing unruly eyebrows while they are still damp with a styling spray. Work the product into the damp brows. Brush or comb the brows into place or dry them into the position you want them in the final trim.

Special Note

Harsh-coated terriers have a coat that will normally brush out quite easily, especially after they are clean.

Notes:

Notes *from your* Grooming Table

Manchester Terrier (Standard)   TERRIER   SMOOTH COATED

Breed Facts & Characteristics

Country of Origin: England

Height at Shoulder: 16½"–17½"

Coat Length/Type: Fine/Short

Color: Jet black with rich mahogany.

Correct grooming procedure:

Bathe & Curry Brush

Common pet grooming practices:

Bathe & Curry Brush

-The Goal-
The coat should be clean and fresh smelling, with the coat laying flat against the body. No shedding hair.

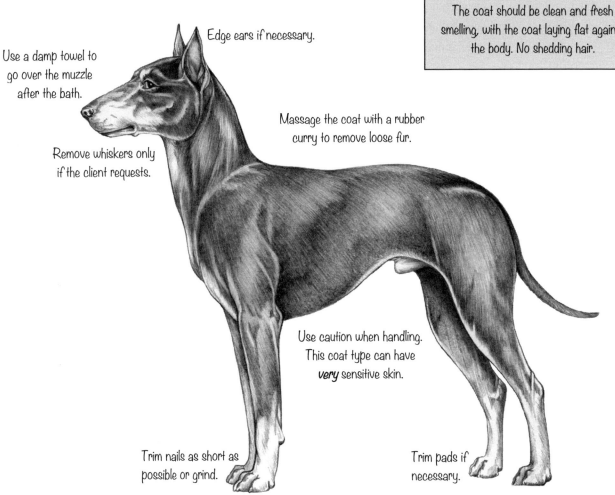

Edge ears if necessary.

Use a damp towel to go over the muzzle after the bath.

Remove whiskers only if the client requests.

Massage the coat with a rubber curry to remove loose fur.

Use caution when handling. This coat type can have *very* sensitive skin.

Trim nails as short as possible or grind.

Trim pads if necessary.

TERRIER

See page 66 for Bathing & Drying Instructions	Suggested Tools & Equipment

- Nail Trimmers
- Styptic Powder
- Ear Cleaning Solution
- Cotton Balls

- Clippers
- #40 or #15 Blade
- Rubber Curry
- Carding Tool

- Small Detailing Shears
- Thinning Shears

Miniature Bull Terrier

Breed Facts & Characteristics

Country of Origin: England

Height at Shoulder: 10"–14"

Coat Length/Type: Fine/Short

Color: Pure white, or any color to predominate.

Correct grooming procedure:
Bathe & Curry Brush

Common pet grooming practices:
Bathe & Curry Brush

-The Goal-
The coat should be clean and fresh smelling, with the coat laying flat against the body. No shedding hair.

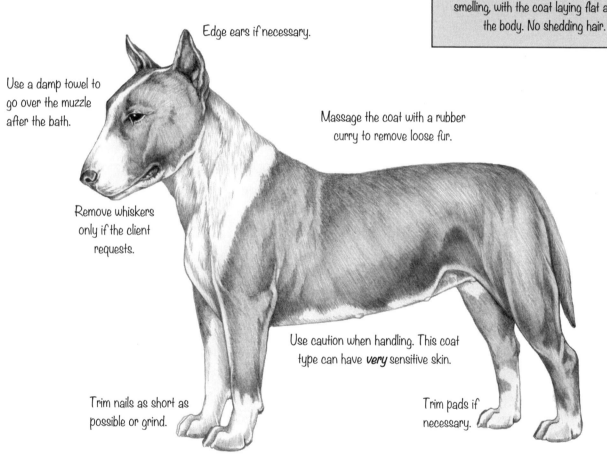

Edge ears if necessary.

Use a damp towel to go over the muzzle after the bath.

Remove whiskers only if the client requests.

Massage the coat with a rubber curry to remove loose fur.

Use caution when handling. This coat type can have *very* sensitive skin.

Trim nails as short as possible or grind.

Trim pads if necessary.

See page 66 for Bathing & Drying Instructions

Suggested Tools & Equipment

- Nail Trimmers
- Styptic Powder
- Ear Cleaning Solution
- Cotton Balls

- Clippers
- #40 or #15 Blade
- Rubber Curry
- Carding Tool

- Small Detailing Shears
- Thinning Shears

Miniature Schnauzer

Breed Facts & Characteristics

Country of Origin: Germany

Height at Shoulder: 12"–14"

Coat Length/Type: Hard/Wiry

Color: Salt and pepper, black and silver, or solid black.

Correct grooming procedure:

Hand-Strip

Common pet grooming practices:

Clipper-Trim

General Description

The Miniature Schnauzer is a powerful, muscular and squarely built dog of high energy and great intelligence. Its tail is docked short. It may have cropped or uncropped ears. When grooming a Miniature Schnauzer, remember there is nothing soft or fluffy about the breed. In the finished groom, there is very little coat hiding the contours of its body. The leg coat and muzzle coat are slightly longer. The hallmark of the breed is its rectangular head, arched eyebrows and full mustache and beard.

> **-The Goal-**
> Everything about this breed is tight and tailored. The well-toned body is accentuated by the groom. The head is rectangular in shape. All pattern lines are invisible.

Correctly Groomed: Hand-Strip
Typical blades used on the body for pet grooming: #10, #9, #8.5, #7F, #5F or a combination of those blades.

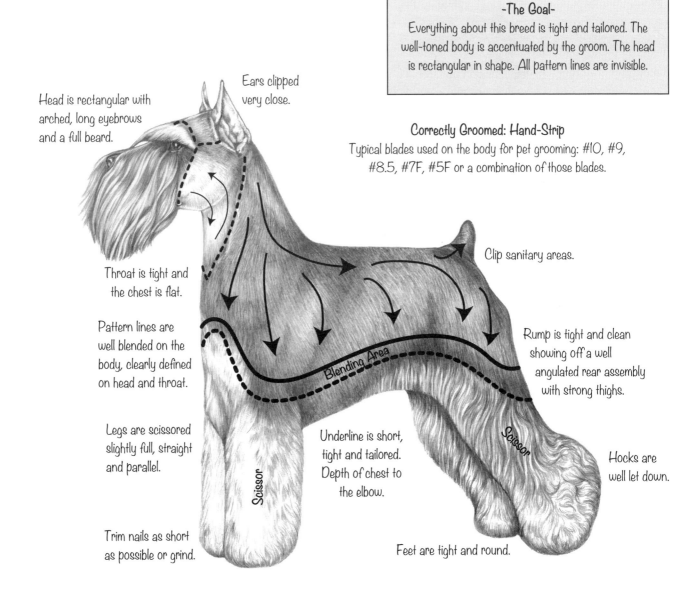

Head is rectangular with arched, long eyebrows and a full beard.

Ears clipped very close.

Clip sanitary areas.

Throat is tight and the chest is flat.

Pattern lines are well blended on the body, clearly defined on head and throat.

Blending Area

Rump is tight and clean showing off a well angulated rear assembly with strong thighs.

Legs are scissored slightly full, straight and parallel.

Scissor

Underline is short, tight and tailored. Depth of chest to the elbow.

Scissor

Hocks are well let down.

Trim nails as short as possible or grind.

Feet are tight and round.

Grooming Procedures & Recommendations

See page 76 for
Bathing & Drying Instructions

Frequency

Bathe once a week to once every 12 weeks.

Pre-Work

Trim or grind nails at least every four to six weeks to maintain a healthy foot structure. Swab the ears clean with a mild ear cleaning solution. Prior to bathing, quickly go over the entire body with a high-velocity dryer to help lift dirt and dander away from the skin and to loosen any shedding coat. ***Card and hand-strip dog prior to bathing and drying.***

Done to breed standard, the coat is hand-stripped to promote healthy skin tone, proper coat texture and rich color. Many pet owners choose to clipper-cut their pet dog. This practice destroys the correct harsh coat texture on most dogs and dilutes the color on salt-and-pepper dogs. However, it is an economical way to keep the pet looking like the breed standard. Finding a stylist who is willing to commit the time and energy to hand-strip the dog can be very difficult, and most pet owners are not willing to pay for this highly skilled service.

Pattern Lines In General

The pattern is based on the bone and muscle structure of the dog. After the final trim, all pattern lines should be invisible on the main body. If using clippers on the main body, feather off transition points in a smooth and steady fashion. If the pattern line is still visible after clipping, use thinning shears to blend the line. On the head, the pattern lines are crisp and clean.

Body

For either hand-stripped or clipper-cut dogs, the general pattern is the same. Typical blades used in pet grooming range from a #10 to a #7F, or a combination of those blades for the bulk of the body work. Some stylists find reversing a slightly longer blade very effective in achieving an extremely smooth finish on the body. Reversing a blade will shorten the cutting action by about two blade lengths as the same blade used with the grain of the coat. Choose one of the methods and follow the direction of the natural coat growth of the fur. After clipping, card the coat to help promote proper coat growth while retaining some of the rich color and harsh coat texture. Carding also will assist in the removal of any minor tracking left in the coat from clipping. The pattern lines start at the turn of the shoulder and continue to just above the elbow, back to the flank on a diagonal and then drop into the thigh region.

Undercarriage

Right around the navel area, the coat will be very short and start to get longer as the line moves forward towards the brisket, creating the illusion of a deep chest. When viewed in profile, the distance from the elbow to the bottom of the foot is equal to the distance between the withers and the brisket. There is only enough fur left on the undercarriage to accentuate depth of chest and an athletic build. The pattern line is well blended and invisible.

Tail & Rear

The top side of the tail is trimmed with the same blade as the body. The underside of the tail is clipped close, with blades ranging from #15 to a #7F, used with or against the grain based on the sensitivity of the dog's skin. Continue with the same blade around the rectum and on the inner side of the cowlick lines going down the back side of the thighs.

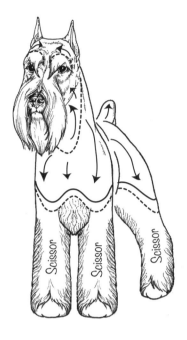

From the front and rear, the legs drop in straight, parallel lines from well toned shoulders and thighs. When setting the pattern, use the turn of the muscles to set the lines. Chest is flat but use caution not to bald out this area due to cowlicks where the front legs join the chest. Rear is short, tight and clean. Leg furnishings are longer than the body coat.

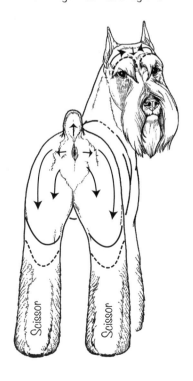

Notes From The Grooming Table ©2016

Their expression is friendly but alert and bold. Head is rectangular with long, arched eyebrows and a full beard. The top skull and the muzzle are equal in length with the stop area being the center point. All lines on the head are clean and sharp.

Clip top skull with blades ranging from a #7F to a #5F, used against the grain or blades ranging from a #10 to #7F with the grain.

The eyebrows are split, long and arched. The brows will be very short at the back corner of the eye.

The beard is long, full and natural. When combing down the beard, the lines at the side of the face form a straight plane. Just below the back corner of the eyes, the fur is short and well blended, creating fill under the eye. The clipper lines of the beard are clean and sharp.

When setting the beard, use the back corners of the eyes and the whisker nodule on the cheeks and under the jaw as basic guidelines: "Connect the dots."

The throat is trimmed close with a #7F used against the grain or a #10 or #15 blade used with the coat growth.

Use a # 10 or #15 blade on the outside of the ear, a #40 blade can be used on the inside of the ear leather with a very light touch. Edge the ear with small detailing shears.

Ear Safety Tip: Remember, always keep the tips of the shears towards the tips of the ears when edging for safety.

Stay inside the natural cowlick line of the neck that runs from the ear bulb down in a "U" or "V" shape. Stop about 2 or 3 finger widths above the breast bone. Thinning shear the cowlick seam to blend with the longer coat of the neck.

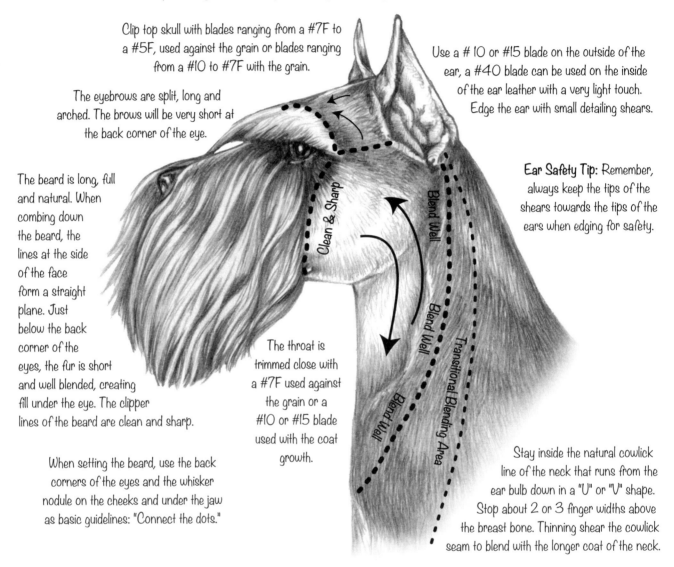

Clean & Sharp

Blend Well

Blend Well

Blend Well

Transitional Blending Area

Hindquarters

The hindquarters should be strong and powerful. When clipping this area, expose the thigh muscle with the same blade used on the body. Start to feather off with the blade where the muscle starts to turn under on a diagonal line from the flank region to about 3 or 4 fingers above the hock. Using a short to medium guard comb can facilitate feathering in the blending line. The pattern line should be invisible when the trim is finished. Blend with thinning shears if necessary. The stifle area should have enough furnishing left to give the legs substance and angulation. The longest coat on the legs can range from 1 to 2.5 inches depending on the amount of bone and coat density. Shape this area by hand with shears after the clipper work is complete. When viewed from the rear, the legs should form two parallel lines to the

ground. The hocks are well let down. There should be adequate coat on the hock area to accentuate the angles of the rear assembly.

Front Legs

The coat on the legs can range from 1/16 of an inch to 2 inches in length depending on the amount of bone, the size of the dog and coat density. The front legs drop straight down from the body and have ample bone and muscle to show off a powerful and sturdy animal. The pattern line at the shoulder is about 1 or 2 fingers above the top of the elbow, at the point where the muscle begins to turn under. The coat at the transition line will be very short, and taper into the longer leg furnishings. This can be accomplished by feathering off at the blending point with the same blade used on the body. Other methods of blending off at the top of the leg include using a short to medium comb guard followed by hand-scissoring and blending with thinning shears. Most stylists prefer to leave the legs to shape by hand with shears. After the final trim, the legs need to form two parallel columns going down from the elbow into tight, round feet. The coat at the back of the elbow is very short and falls straight down off the back of the leg toward the ground.

Feet
The feet are small for the size of the dog. Both the front and rear feet are compact with well arched toes. To show off these traits, the feet are trimmed very close to the edge of the foot and some nail is routinely exposed. The feet should point straight ahead, toeing neither in nor out. Trim the feet round by first boxing them in the shape of a square while the dog is standing in a natural, square position. Then remove the sharp corners of the box and round the feet facing straight forward. If detailing the feet with the foot off the tabletop, always use a small pair of shears to minimize the risk of accidentally cutting the pads.

Throat & Chest
Blades ranging from #10 to #7F, with or against the grain, based on the sensitivity of the dog's skin, are common in the throat area. Follow the natural cowlick line that runs in a "V" shape from the base of the

ears towards the base of the neck. The blending point begins about 3 or 4 fingers above the breast bone and drops to just below the turn of the muscle at the elbow/shoulder, creating a "W" shape when viewed straight on. When viewed in profile, the neck into the chest should be straight without a predominant forechest. When blending the chest, be aware of the heavy cowlicks in the area. Many stylists prefer to leave the chest area to blend by hand with thinning shears or shears. When finished in this area, double check your work to be sure the neck, chest and front legs drop down in a straight line when viewed in profile.

The Head in General: Top Skull
The top of the head can be clipped as close as a #10 used with the grain; to a #7F or #5F, used with the grain or against depending on the dog's sensitivity and density of the coat.

Ears
Both cropped and uncropped ears are clipped with a close blade. It is common to see a #10 or #15 blade used on the outside of the ear leather while a #40 blade is used on the inside. When working with close blades in this delicate area, always work from the base or center of the ear out toward the edge. Gently brace the ear with your fingers to clip over it. To finish, use

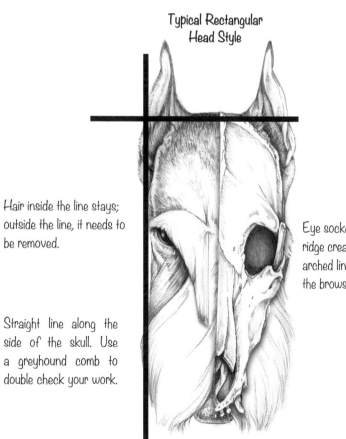

Typical Rectangular Head Style

Hair inside the line stays; outside the line, it needs to be removed.

Straight line along the side of the skull. Use a greyhound comb to double check your work.

Eye socket ridge creates the arched line for the brows.

small finishing shears to trim around the outside edge of the ear leather, keeping the tips of the shears toward the tip of the ears.

Brows

To form the arched, triangular eyebrows follow the eye socket rim, working with or against the grain of the coat. Schnauzers have a slight stop between the eyes that acts as a natural split for the brows. Either lightly clip this area when clipping the top skull or leave it to do by hand with thinning shears. Shape the brows into long arched triangles that accentuate the typically keen look. They will be very short at the back corner of the eye and longer at the tips, coming almost halfway down the bridge of the nose. When viewed in profile, the brows should barely break the line of the top skull as they arch out over the nose. Use curved shears in reverse to set the brow. Line the tip of the shear up with a point on the nose. Repeat on the other brow. By using the nose as a set point, the length and angle of both eyebrows remain the same. Bevel the blades of the shears away from the pet's skin to avoid accidentally cutting the dog at the back corner of the eye when you close the shear to cut the brow.

Throat & Cheeks

The throat and cheek areas are clipped using blades ranging from a #10 to a #7F, used either with or against the grain. Use the natural cowlick line of the neck to be the guide to create the "U" or "V" shape of the throat. The lowest point will be about 3 fingers above the breast bone. The line that breaks the top skull and the cheeks is from the back corner of the eye straight back to the ear canal.

Beard & Goatee

The fur on the muzzle is a natural length as it forms the beard. The basic transition line between the cheek and the beard runs on an imaginary line from just behind the back corner of the eyes to the whisker nodule on the cheeks. The line continues under the jaw to the single center whisker nodule. The line should be very crisp and clean, just clearing the outside corner of the mouth so when the dog pants, you can see the separation between the top and the bottom jaw. The coat under the eye area is never clipped as this hair forms one of the critical lines of the classic rectangular head style. The line on the dog's face should be straight, from the flat cheek down into the beard area. Double check this line by laying a greyhound comb along side the head. Any fur that sticks out beyond the comb should be removed. Any hair inside this line should remain and be blended to create the rectangular shape.

Detail Finish

Application of bows and mild cologne is optional.

Grooming Tips

A light setting gel, mousse or texturing shampoo can add body to the leg coat, making it easier to scissor. Try spritzing unruly eyebrows while they are still damp with a styling spray. Work the product into the damp brows. Brush or comb the brows into place or dry them into the position you want them in the final trim.

Special Note

Harsh-coated terriers have a coat that will normally brush out quite easily, especially after they are clean.

Suggested Tools & Equipment

- Nail Trimmers
- Styptic Powder
- Ear Powder
- Ear Cleaning Solution
- Cotton Balls
- Hemostat
- Clippers
- Slicker Brush
- Greyhound Comb
- Pumice Stone
- Carding Tools
- Stripping Knives
- Straight Shears
- Curved Shears
- Small Detailing Shears
- Thinning Shears
- Dematting Tools

Common Blade Options:

- #40, #15, #10
- #7F, #5F, #4F
- Variety of Guard Combs

Notes:

Notes *from your* Grooming Table

Norfolk Terrier

Breed Facts & Characteristics

Country of Origin: England

Height at Shoulder: 9"–10"

Coat Length/Type: Hard/Wiry

Color: Shades of red, wheaten, black and tan or grizzle.

Correct grooming procedure:
Hand-Strip

Common pet grooming practices:
Clipper-Trim/Hand-Strip

General Description

The Norfolk Terrier is one of the smallest working Terriers. They have dropped ears and a keen, terrier type expression. They are compact in structure. The Norfolk is robust and active. They have a very strong prey drive for small vermin. Their agreeable temperament allows them to work well with in a pack or solo. Their coat lies close to the body, ranging from about 1½ to 2 inches, and is firm to the touch.

-The Goal-
This is a small, compact, tough, terrier. They have a harsh outer coat and a thick undercoat. Hair on the body is between 1–2 inches, more about the ruff area. The natural head is accentuated by a slight brow and a small amount of whiskers on the muzzle. Pattern lines on the body are invisible.

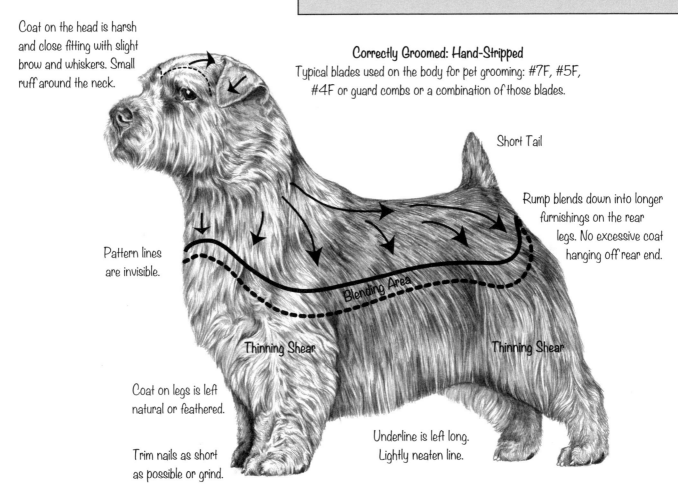

Coat on the head is harsh and close fitting with slight brow and whiskers. Small ruff around the neck.

Correctly Groomed: Hand-Stripped
Typical blades used on the body for pet grooming: #7F, #5F, #4F or guard combs or a combination of those blades.

Short Tail

Rump blends down into longer furnishings on the rear legs. No excessive coat hanging off rear end.

Pattern lines are invisible.

Blending Area

Thinning Shear

Thinning Shear

Coat on legs is left natural or feathered.

Underline is left long. Lightly neaten line.

Trim nails as short as possible or grind.

Feet are rounded. Front feet are larger than rear feet.

Grooming Procedures & Recommendations

See page 76 for
Bathing & Drying Instructions

Frequency
Bathe once a week to once every 12 weeks.

Pre-Work
Trim or grind nails at least every four to six weeks to maintain a healthy foot structure. Swab the ears clean with a mild ear cleaning solution. Prior to bathing, quickly go over the entire body with a high-velocity dryer to help lift dirt and dander away from the skin and to loosen any shedding coat. *Card and hand-strip dog prior to bathing and drying.*

Carding
Carding is a natural technique in which the soft, downy undercoat is pulled from the dog's body. Typical tools used with this technique are: a pumice stone; an undercoat rake; a fine-toothed stripping knife, which is pulled through the coat; or a fine blade, such as a #40, held between the fingers and pulled through the coat. Carding can be done before or after bathing and drying. Removal of the soft undercoat allows the topcoat to lie closer to the natural outline of the dog, accentuating the dog's structure. It also promotes a profuse harsh outer coat with a rich color and protects the skin.

Hand-Stripping the Body Pattern
Hand-stripping is a technique in which the outer guard coat is plucked from the dog's skin. This procedure helps promote the proper coat texture and rich color of the breed. During certain times of the year, the coat is easier to pull out. When the coat comes out easily, it is called a "blowing coat" or "blown coat." Ideally, hand-stripping should correspond with the dog's natural cycle, based on its environment and hormonal levels. Using your fingers, a carding tool or a stripping knife, pull out a few hairs at a time to shape the coat and accentuate the dog's natural outline. Work methodically, pulling small amounts of coat at a time, always working in the direction of the coat growth. Proper hand-stripping employs a gentle momentum and rhythm to remove hair, not brute force, which is uncomfortable for both the groomer and the pet. Keep your wrist locked in a neutral position and allow the rhythmic movement to stem from your shoulder, not your wrist or elbow. In general, the main body coat is easily removed and most pets do not mind the plucking process. The cheeks, throat and private areas may be more sensitive, requiring the use of thinning shears or clippers. The length of coat to be left varies from under an inch to a little more than an inch and depends on the body section you are working. The coats should always appear very natural, never clipped or heavily trimmed. On some coats, a light application of chalk or powder before the bath allows a better grip on the coat and makes plucking and stripping much easier.

Clipper-Cutting the Body Pattern
If a client insists that their pet be clipper-cut, follow the general body pattern using blades ranging from a #7F, #5F, #4F or short to medium guard combs. The longer the trim, the more you will be able to retain the proper essence of the breed and correct coat. After clipper-cutting be sure to incorporate carding techniques which will aid in creating the proper coat texture and color.

Legs & Undercarriage
The furnishings are left slightly longer in these areas. If hand-stripping the body coat, strip and finger pluck these areas. If trimming with clippers, use thinning shears to shorten and tidy the furnishings.

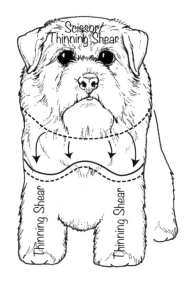

The head is covered with harsh, somewhat longer fur than the body. From the front and rear, the legs drop in straight, parallel lines from well toned shoulders and thighs. When setting the pattern, use the turn of the muscles to set the lines. Under the tail is short and clean with a drape of longer fur covering the back of the thighs. Leg furnishings are hard and wiry, slightly longer than the body coat.

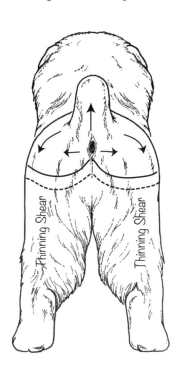

Grooming Procedures & Recommendations

Head

The head should be wedge-shaped with folded ears. The fur should be hard and lie tight to the skull. The muzzle and the brow may have slightly longer furnishings that stand off the skin, but not enough to detract from the overall balance of the head.

Ears

The folded, triangular ears are covered with very short hair and are level with the skull line. On most dogs, finger-pluck the few long strands to bring the coat down to the natural velvet length. If the ear is more substantially covered with hair, clip it. Use a #15 blade on the outside and a #40 on the inside. Edge the ears with small detailing shears, keeping the tips of the shears towards the tips of the ears.

Eye Area

Clear the stop area of longer hair either by finger-plucking, or with thinning shears or with a #10 blade, but leave some fur there. Use the method that will produce the best possible natural look, based on how much fur the dog has and its tolerance for work in this area. A tiny bit of fur should be left above each brow to accentuate a keen eye.

Tails

The docked tail should be free of long hair. From the top, the tail should blend seamlessly from the body. On the underside, trim with a close blade, such as a #10, or use thinning shears to tidy up any long fur.

Feet & Hocks

Trim the pads with a close cutting blade ranging from a #15 to a #40. Use a very light touch to clean the pads of long hair. Tidy the outside edge of the foot, if needed, with small detailing shears. If the hocks have longer coat, trim lightly with thinning shears to show a neat, clean area.

Detail Finish

For added shine, finish with a fine mist of coat polish on the body. Application of bows and mild cologne is optional.

Special Note

Clipping a wire-coated dog will result in a dramatic change in the texture and color of the coat. The correct harsh wire coat can be nurtured by plucking the blown coat when it is ready for removal. This process stimulates the hair follicles to produce new guard coat. Without hand-stripping, the guard coat usually fails to reproduce and loses its brilliant color and texture. If only undercoat grows, the guard coat color becomes that of the lighter, soft undercoat.

Suggested Tools & Equipment

- Nail Trimmers
- Styptic Powder
- Ear Powder
- Ear Cleaning Solution
- Cotton Balls
- Hemostat
- Clippers
- Slicker Brush
- Greyhound Comb
- Pumice Stone
- Carding Tools
- Stripping Knives
- Straight Shears
- Curved Shears
- Small Detailing Shears
- Thinning Shears
- Dematting Tools

Common Blade Options:

- #40, #15, #10
- #7F, #5F, #4F
- Variety of Guard Combs

Notes:

TERRIER

Notes *from your* Grooming Table

Breed Facts & Characteristics

Country of Origin: England

Height at Shoulder: 9"–10"

Coat Length/Type: Hard/Wiry

Color: Shades of red, wheaten, black and tan, or grizzle.

Correct grooming procedure:

Hand-Strip

Common pet grooming practices:

Clipper-Trim/Hand-Strip

General Description

The Norwich Terrier is one of the smallest working Terriers. They have pricked ears and a keen, fox-like expression. They are compact in structure. The Norwich is robust and active. They have a very strong prey drive for small vermin. Their agreeable temperament allows them to work well with in a pack or solo. Their coat lies close to their body and is firm to the touch.

-The Goal-

This is a small, compact, tough, terrier. They have a harsh outer coat and a thick undercoat. Hair on the body is between 1–2 inches, more about the ruff area. The natural head is accentuated by a slight brow and small a amount of whiskers on the muzzle. Pattern lines on the body are invisible.

Correctly Groomed: Hand-Stripped

Typical blades used on the body for pet grooming: #7F, #5F, #4F or guard combs or a combination of those blades.

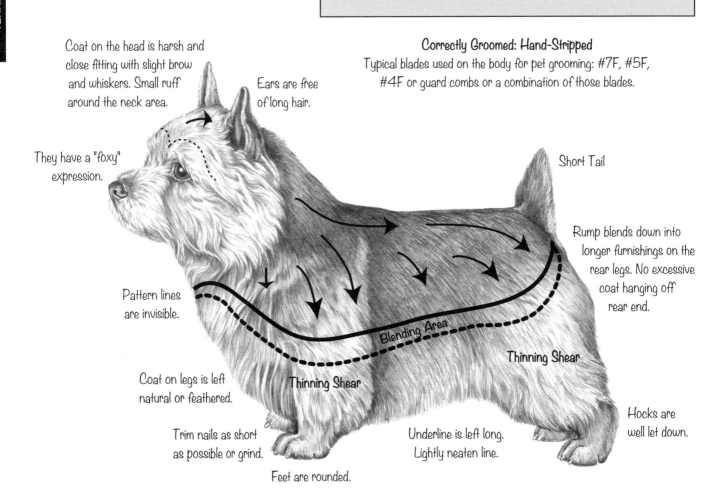

Coat on the head is harsh and close fitting with slight brow and whiskers. Small ruff around the neck area.

Ears are free of long hair.

They have a "foxy" expression.

Short Tail

Pattern lines are invisible.

Rump blends down into longer furnishings on the rear legs. No excessive coat hanging off rear end.

Blending Area

Thinning Shear

Coat on legs is left natural or feathered.

Thinning Shear

Hocks are well let down.

Trim nails as short as possible or grind.

Underline is left long. Lightly neaten line.

Feet are rounded.

TERRIER

Grooming Procedures & Recommendations

See page 76 for
Bathing & Drying Instructions

Frequency
Bathe once a week to once every
12 weeks.

Pre-Work
Trim or grind nails at least every four
to six weeks to maintain a healthy foot
structure. Swab the ears clean with a
mild ear cleaning solution. Prior to
bathing, quickly go over the entire
body with a high-velocity dryer to help
lift dirt and dander away from the skin
and to loosen any shedding coat. *Card
and hand-strip dog prior to bathing
and drying.*

Carding
Carding is a natural technique in
which the soft, downy undercoat is
pulled from the dog's body. Typical
tools used with this technique are: a
pumice stone; an undercoat rake; a
fine-toothed stripping knife, which is
pulled through the coat; or a fine blade,
such as a #40, held between the fingers
and pulled through the coat. Carding
can be done before or after bathing and
drying. Removal of the soft undercoat
allows the topcoat to lie closer to the
natural outline of the dog, accentuating
the dog's structure. It also promotes
a profuse harsh outer coat with a rich
color and protects the skin.

Hand-Stripping the Body Pattern
Hand-stripping is a technique in which
the outer guard coat is plucked from the
dog's skin. This procedure helps promote
the proper coat texture and rich color of
the breed. During certain times of the
year, the coat is easier to pull out. When
the coat comes out easily, it is called a
"blowing coat" or "blown coat." Ideally,
hand-stripping should correspond with
the dog's natural cycle, based on its
environment and hormonal levels. Using

your fingers, a carding tool or a stripping
knife, pull out a few hairs at a time to
shape the coat and accentuate the dog's
natural outline. Work methodically,
pulling small amounts of coat at a time,
always working in the direction of the
coat growth. Proper hand-stripping
employs a gentle momentum and
rhythm to remove hair, not brute force,
which is uncomfortable for both the
groomer and the pet. Keep your wrist
locked in a neutral position and allow
the rhythmic movement to stem from
your shoulder, not your wrist or elbow.
In general, the main body coat is easily
removed and most pets do not mind
the plucking process. The cheeks, throat
and private areas may be more sensitive,
requiring the use of thinning shears or
clippers. The length of coat to be left
varies from under an inch to a little
more than an inch and depends on the
body section you are working. The coats
should always appear very natural, never
clipped or heavily trimmed. On some
coats, a light application of chalk or
powder before the bath allows a better
grip on the coat and makes plucking and
stripping much easier.

Clipper-Cutting the Body Pattern
If a client insists that their pet be
clipper-cut, follow the general body
pattern using blades ranging from a
#7F, #5F, #4F or short to medium
guard combs. The longer the trim,
the more you will be able to retain the
proper essence of the breed and correct
coat. After clipper-cutting be sure to
incorporate carding techniques which
will aid in creating the proper coat
texture and color.

Legs & Undercarriage
The furnishings are left slightly longer
in these areas. If hand-stripping the
body coat, strip and finger pluck
these areas. If trimming with clippers,
use thinning shears to shorten and
tidy the furnishings.

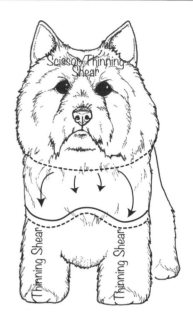

The head is covered with harsh, somewhat
longer fur than the body. From the front
and rear, the legs drop in straight, parallel
lines from well toned shoulders and thighs.
When setting the pattern, use the turn of
the muscles to set the lines. Under the tail
is short and clean with a drape of longer
fur covering the back of the thighs. Leg
furnishings are hard and wiry, slightly
longer than the body coat.

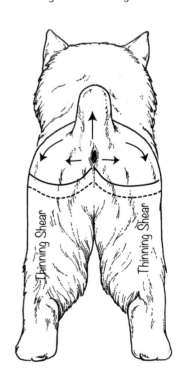

Head

The head should have a slightly fox-like expression with a wedge-shaped skull and upright, triangular ears. The fur should be hard and lie tight to the skull. The muzzle and the brow may have slightly longer furnishings that stand off the skin, but not enough to detract from the overall balance of the head.

Ears

The pricked, triangular ears are covered with very short hair. On most dogs, finger-pluck the few long strands to bring the coat down to the natural velvet length. If the ear is more substantially covered with hair, clip the top two-thirds of the ear. Use a #15 blade on the outside and a #40 on the inside. Edge the ears with small detailing shears, keeping the tips of the shears towards the tips of the ears.

Eye Area

Clear the stop area of longer hair either by finger-plucking, or with thinning shears or with a #10 blade, but leave some fur there. Use the method that will produce the best possible natural look, based on how much fur the dog has and its tolerance for work in this area. A tiny bit of fur should be left above each brow to accentuate a keen eye.

Tails

The docked tail should be free of long hair. From the top, the tail should blend seamlessly from the body. On the underside, trim with a close blade, such as a #10, or use thinning shears to tidy up any long fur.

Feet & Hocks

Trim the pads with a close cutting blade ranging from a #15 to a #40. Use a very light touch to clean the pads of long hair. Tidy the outside edge of the foot, if needed, with small detailing shears. If the hocks have longer coat, trim lightly with thinning shears to show a neat, clean area.

Detail Finish

For added shine, finish with a fine mist of coat polish on the body. Application of bows and mild cologne is optional.

Special Note

Clipping a wire-coated dog will result in a dramatic change in the texture and color of the coat. The correct harsh wire coat can be nurtured by plucking the blown coat when it is ready for removal. This process stimulates the hair follicles to produce new guard coat. Without hand-stripping, the guard coat usually fails to reproduce and loses its brililant color and texture. If only undercoat grows, the guard coat color becomes that of the lighter, soft undercoat.

Suggested Tools & Equipment

- Nail Trimmers
- Styptic Powder
- Ear Powder
- Ear Cleaning Solution
- Cotton Balls
- Hemostat
- Clippers
- Slicker Brush
- Greyhound Comb
- Pumice Stone
- Carding Tools
- Stripping Knives
- Straight Shears
- Curved Shears
- Small Detailing Shears
- Thinning Shears
- Dematting Tools

Common Blade Options:

- #40, #15, #10
- #7F, #5F, #4F
- Variety of Guard Combs

Notes:

TERRIER

Notes *from your*
Grooming Table

Breed Facts & Characteristics

Country of Origin: England

Height at Shoulder: 13"–14"

Coat Length/Type: Hard/Wiry

Color: Most of the dog is white with tan and/or black markings confined primarily to the head and the base of the tail.

Correct grooming procedure:

Hand-Strip

Common pet grooming practices:

Clipper-Trim/Hand-Strip

-The Goal-
The coat should be clean and fresh smelling. The harsh coat should lay tight against the body. The head has very small brows and a slight beard. No shedding hair.

Correctly Groomed: Hand-Stripped

Ears are free of long hair.

Coat on the head is close fitting with slight brow and whiskers.

Card the body first to remove the bulk of the loose undercoat. Follow by hand-stripping the hard outer coat. Always pull in the direction of the coat growth. Legs too.

The harsh outer coat lays tight to the body, allowing for a clear view of the outline of the dog.

There is no pattern on the body. The coat should be from ¼" to 1" all over the dog.

Neaten hocks if needed.

Trim nails as short as possible or grind.

Neaten pads and feet if needed.

TERRIER

Grooming Procedures & Recommendations

See page 76 for
Bathing & Drying Instructions

Frequency
Bathe once a week to once every
12 weeks.

Pre-Work
Trim or grind nails at least every four
to six weeks to maintain a healthy foot
structure. Swab the ears clean with a
mild ear cleaning solution. Prior to
bathing, quickly go over the entire
body with a high-velocity dryer to help
lift dirt and dander away from the skin
and to loosen any shedding coat. ***Card
and hand-strip dog prior to bathing
and drying.***

Carding
Carding is a natural technique in
which the soft, downy undercoat is
pulled from the dog's body. Typical
tools used with this technique are: a
pumice stone; an undercoat rake; a
fine-toothed stripping knife, which is
pulled through the coat; or a fine blade,
such as a #40, held between the fingers
and pulled through the coat. Carding
can be done before or after bathing and
drying. Removal of the soft undercoat
allows the topcoat to lie closer to the
natural outline of the dog, accentuating
the dog's structure. It also promotes
a profuse harsh outer coat with a rich
color and protects the skin.

Hand-Stripping the Body Pattern
Hand-stripping is a technique in which
the outer guard coat is plucked from
the dog's skin. This procedure helps
promote the proper coat texture and
rich color of the breed. During certain
times of the year, the coat is easier to
pull out. When the coat comes out
easily, it is called a "blowing coat" or
"blown coat." Ideally, hand-stripping
should correspond with the dog's
natural cycle, based on its environment

and hormonal levels. Using your fingers,
a carding tool or a stripping knife, pull
out a few hairs at a time to shape the
coat and accentuate the dog's natural
outline. Work methodically, pulling
small amounts of coat at a time, always
working in the direction of the coat
growth. Proper hand-stripping employs
a gentle momentum and rhythm to
remove hair, not brute force, which is
uncomfortable for both the groomer
and the pet. Keep your wrist locked in a
neutral position and allow the rhythmic
movement to stem from your shoulder,
not your wrist or elbow. In general, the
main body coat is easily removed and
most pets do not mind the plucking
process. The cheeks, throat and private
areas may be more sensitive, requiring
the use of thinning shears or clippers.
The length of coat to be left varies
from under an inch to a little more
than an inch and depends on the body
section you are working. The coats
should always appear very natural, never
clipped or heavily trimmed. On some
coats, a light application of chalk or
powder before the bath allows a better
grip on the coat and makes plucking
and stripping much easier.

Clipper-Cutting the Body Pattern
If a client insists that their pet be
clipper-cut, use blades ranging from
a #7F, #5F, #4F or short to medium
guard combs. The longer the trim,
the more you will be able to retain the
proper essence of the breed and correct
coat. After clipper-cutting be sure to
incorporate carding techniques which
will aid in creating the proper coat
texture and color.

Suggested Tools & Equipment

- Nail Trimmers
- Styptic Powder
- Ear Powder
- Ear Cleaning Solution
- Cotton Balls
- Hemostat
- Clippers
- Slicker Brush
- Greyhound Comb
- Pumice Stone
- Carding Tools
- Stripping Knives
- Straight Shears
- Curved Shears
- Small Detailing Shears
- Thinning Shears
- Dematting Tools

Common Blade Options:

- #40, #15, #10
- #7F, #5F, #4F
- Variety of Guard Combs

Notes:

Notes From The Grooming Table ©2016

Parson Russell Terrier (Smooth) TERRIER   SHORT COATED

Breed Facts & Characteristics

Country of Origin: England

Height at Shoulder: 13"–14"

Coat Length/Type: Short/Wiry

Color: Most of the dog is white with tan and/or black markings confined primarily to the head and the base of the tail.

Correct grooming procedure:
Card & Hand-Strip

Common pet grooming practices:
Card & Bathe & Brush Out

> -The Goal-
> The coat should be clean and fresh smelling. The harsh coat should lay tight against the body. No shedding hair.

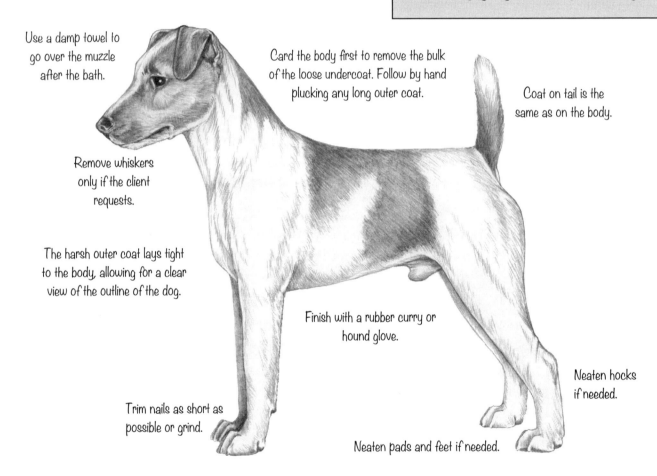

Use a damp towel to go over the muzzle after the bath.

Card the body first to remove the bulk of the loose undercoat. Follow by hand plucking any long outer coat.

Coat on tail is the same as on the body.

Remove whiskers only if the client requests.

The harsh outer coat lays tight to the body, allowing for a clear view of the outline of the dog.

Finish with a rubber curry or hound glove.

Neaten hocks if needed.

Trim nails as short as possible or grind.

Neaten pads and feet if needed.

See page 67 for Bathing & Drying Instructions

Suggested Tools & Equipment

- Nail Trimmers
- Styptic Powder
- Ear Cleaning Solution
- Cotton Balls
- Clippers
- #40 or #15 Blade
- Slicker Brush
- Rubber Curry
- Carding Tool
- De-Shedding Tools
- Small Detailing Shears
- Thinning Shears

Breed Facts & Characteristics

Country of Origin: United States

Height at Shoulder: 10"–13"

Coat Length/Type: Short/Smooth

Color: One or more large patches of color combined with white.

Correct grooming procedure:
Bathe & Curry Brush

Common pet grooming practices:
Bathe & Curry Brush

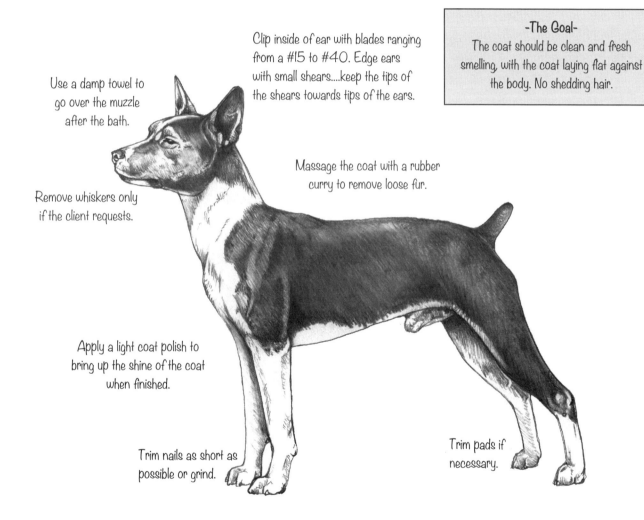

Clip inside of ear with blades ranging from a #15 to #40. Edge ears with small shears....keep the tips of the shears towards tips of the ears.

Use a damp towel to go over the muzzle after the bath.

-The Goal-
The coat should be clean and fresh smelling, with the coat laying flat against the body. No shedding hair.

Massage the coat with a rubber curry to remove loose fur.

Remove whiskers only if the client requests.

Apply a light coat polish to bring up the shine of the coat when finished.

Trim nails as short as possible or grind.

Trim pads if necessary.

See page 67 for
Bathing & Drying Instructions

Suggested Tools & Equipment

- Nail Trimmers
- Styptic Powder
- Ear Cleaning Solution
- Cotton Balls

- Clippers
- #40 or #15 Blade
- Rubber Curry
- Carding Tool

- Small Detailing Shears
- Thinning Shears

Russell Terrier (Broken and Rough)

Breed Facts & Characteristics

Country of Origin: England

Height at Shoulder: 10"–12"

Coat Length/Type: Hard/Wiry

Color: Primarily white with black and/or tan markings.

Correct grooming procedure:

Bathe & Curry Brush *or* Hand-Strip

Common pet grooming practices:

Bathe & Curry Brush *or* Hand-Strip

-The Goal-
The coat should be clean and fresh smelling. The harsh coat should lay tight against the body. The head has very small brows and a slight beard. No shedding hair.

Correctly Groomed: Hand-Stripped

Coat on the head is close fitting with slight brow and whiskers.

Ears are free of long hair.

Card the body first to remove the bulk of the loose undercoat. Follow by hand-stripping the hard outer coat. Always pull in the direction of the coat growth. Legs too.

The harsh outer coat lays tight to the body, allowing for a clear view of the outline of the dog.

Trim nails as short as possible or grind.

There is no pattern on the body. The coat should be from ¼" to 1" all over the dog.

Neaten hocks if needed.

Neaten pads and feet if needed.

See page 76 for Bathing & Drying Instructions

Frequency

Bathe once a week to once every 12 weeks.

Pre-Work

Trim or grind nails at least every four to six weeks to maintain a healthy foot structure. Swab the ears clean with a mild ear cleaning solution. Prior to bathing, quickly go over the entire body with a high-velocity dryer to help lift dirt and dander away from the skin and to loosen any shedding coat. ***Card and hand-strip dog prior to bathing and drying.***

Carding

Carding is a natural technique in which the soft, downy undercoat is pulled from the dog's body. Typical tools used with this technique are: a pumice stone; an undercoat rake; a fine-toothed stripping knife, which is pulled through the coat; or a fine blade, such as a #40, held between the fingers and pulled through the coat. Carding can be done before or after bathing and drying. Removal of the soft undercoat allows the topcoat to lie closer to the natural outline of the dog, accentuating the dog's structure. It also promotes a profuse harsh outer coat with a rich color and protects the skin.

Hand-Stripping the Body Pattern

Hand-stripping is a technique in which the outer guard coat is plucked from the dog's skin. This procedure helps promote the proper coat texture and rich color of the breed. During certain times of the year, the coat is easier to pull out. When the coat comes out easily, it is called a "blowing coat" or "blown coat." Ideally, hand-stripping should correspond with the dog's natural cycle, based on its environment and hormonal levels. Using your fingers, a carding tool or a stripping knife, pull out a few hairs at a time to shape the coat and accentuate the dog's natural outline. Work methodically, pulling small amounts of coat at a time, always working in the direction of the coat growth. Proper hand-stripping employs a gentle momentum and rhythm to remove hair, not brute force, which is uncomfortable for both the groomer and the pet. Keep your wrist locked in a neutral position and allow the rhythmic movement to stem from your shoulder, not your wrist or elbow. In general, the main body coat is easily removed and most pets do not mind the plucking process. The cheeks, throat and private areas may be more sensitive, requiring the use of thinning shears or clippers. The length of coat to be left varies from under an inch to a little more than an inch and depends on the body section you are working. The coats should always appear very natural, never clipped or heavily trimmed. On some coats, a light application of chalk or powder before the bath allows a better grip on the coat and makes plucking and stripping much easier.

Clipper-Cutting the Body Pattern

If a client insists that their pet be clipper-cut, use blades ranging from a #7F, #5F, #4F or short to medium guard combs. The longer the trim, the more you will be able to retain the proper essence of the breed and correct coat. After clipper-cutting be sure to incorporate carding techniques which will aid in creating the proper coat texture and color.

Suggested Tools & Equipment

- Nail Trimmers
- Styptic Powder
- Ear Powder
- Ear Cleaning Solution
- Cotton Balls
- Hemostat
- Clippers
- Slicker Brush
- Greyhound Comb
- Pumice Stone
- Carding Tools
- Stripping Knives
- Straight Shears
- Curved Shears
- Small Detailing Shears
- Thinning Shears
- Dematting Tools

Common Blade Options:

- #40, #15, #10
- #7F, #5F, #4F
- Variety of Guard Combs

Notes:

Notes From The Grooming Table ©2016

Russell Terrier (Smooth)
TERRIER   **SHORT COATED**

Breed Facts & Characteristics

Country of Origin: England

Height at Shoulder: 10"–12"

Coat Length/Type: Short/Smooth

Color: Primarily white with black and/or tan markings.

Correct grooming procedure:
Bathe & Curry Brush

Common pet grooming practices:
Bathe & Curry Brush

-The Goal-
The coat should be clean and fresh smelling. The harsh coat should lay tight against the body. No shedding hair.

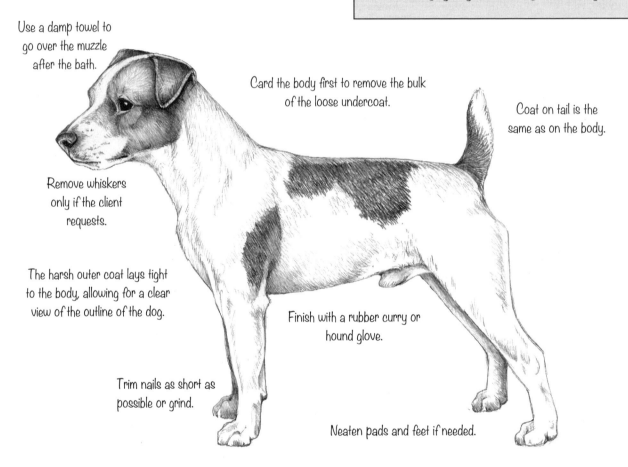

Use a damp towel to go over the muzzle after the bath.

Card the body first to remove the bulk of the loose undercoat.

Coat on tail is the same as on the body.

Remove whiskers only if the client requests.

The harsh outer coat lays tight to the body, allowing for a clear view of the outline of the dog.

Finish with a rubber curry or hound glove.

Trim nails as short as possible or grind.

Neaten pads and feet if needed.

See page 67 for Bathing & Drying Instructions

Suggested Tools & Equipment

- Nail Trimmers
- Styptic Powder
- Ear Cleaning Solution
- Cotton Balls

- Clippers
- #40 or #15 Blade
- Slicker Brush
- Rubber Curry

- Carding Tool
- De-Shedding Tools
- Small Detailing Shears
- Thinning Shears

Notes *from your*
Grooming Table

Breed Facts & Characteristics

Country of Origin: Scotland

Height at Shoulder: 9½"–10½"

Coat Length/Type: Hard/Wiry

Color: Black, wheaten or brindle, or any color.

Correct grooming procedure:

Hand-Strip

Common pet grooming practices:

Clipper-Trim

General Description

This is a compact, very powerful little dog that is very stylish and tailored. The top section shows off a broad, toned body while the lower section is feathered. The head is rectangular with accentuated long eyebrows, pricked ears with small tufts of fur at the inner base and a full beard. The expression is piercing, full of purpose and vigor.

> **-The Goal-**
> Everything about this breed is compact and tailored. The muscular body is accentuated by the groom. The head is rectangular in shape with long arched eyebrows and tufted ears. Pattern lines on the body are invisible; on the head, crisp and clean.

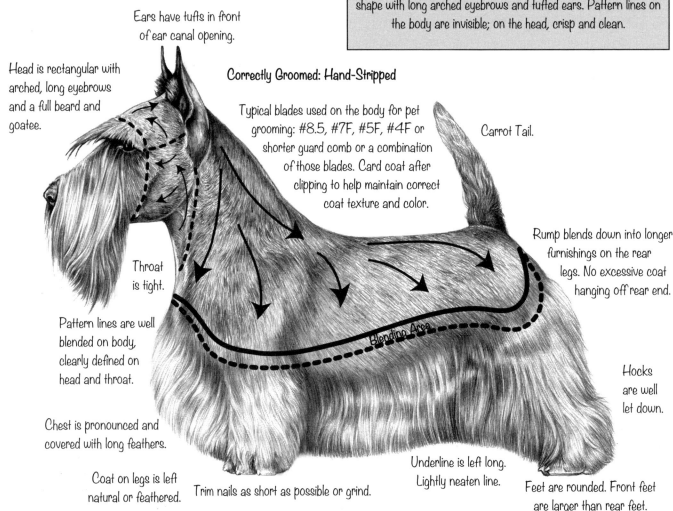

Ears have tufts in front of ear canal opening.

Head is rectangular with arched, long eyebrows and a full beard and goatee.

Correctly Groomed: Hand-Stripped

Typical blades used on the body for pet grooming: #8.5, #7F, #5F, #4F or shorter guard comb or a combination of those blades. Card coat after clipping to help maintain correct coat texture and color.

Carrot Tail.

Throat is tight.

Rump blends down into longer furnishings on the rear legs. No excessive coat hanging off rear end.

Pattern lines are well blended on body, clearly defined on head and throat.

Blending Area

Hocks are well let down.

Chest is pronounced and covered with long feathers.

Coat on legs is left natural or feathered.

Trim nails as short as possible or grind.

Underline is left long. Lightly neaten line.

Feet are rounded. Front feet are larger than rear feet.

Grooming Procedures & Recommendations

See page 76 for
Bathing & Drying Instructions

Frequency
Bathe once a week to once every
12 weeks.

Pre-Work
Trim or grind nails at least every four
to six weeks to maintain a healthy foot
structure. Swab the ears clean with a
mild ear cleaning solution. Prior to
bathing, quickly go over the entire
body with a high-velocity dryer to help
lift dirt and dander away from the skin
and to loosen any shedding coat. ***Card
and hand-strip dog prior to bathing
and drying.***

Done to breed standard, the coat is
hand-stripped to promote healthy skin
tone, proper coat texture and rich color.
Many pet owners choose to clipper-cut
their pet dog. This practice destroys the
correct harsh coat texture on most dogs
and dilutes the color on salt-and-pepper
dogs. However, it is an economical way
to keep the pet looking like the breed
standard. Finding a stylist who is willing
to commit the time and energy to hand-
strip some breeds can be difficult. Plus,
many pet owners are not willing to pay
for this highly skilled service.

Pattern Lines in General
The correct coat is hand-stripped. For
either hand-stripped or clipper-cut pet
dogs, the general pattern, based on the
bone and muscle structure, is the same.
After the final trim, all pattern lines
should be invisible. If clipping at the
transition points, feather off with the
clippers in a smooth and steady fashion.
If the pattern line is still visible after
clipping, use thinning shears to blend
the line. On the head, the pattern lines
are crisp and clean.

Clipper-Cutting
Blades ranging from a #10 to a #4F,
or shorter guard combs, are commonly
used to set the pattern on the body as an
alternative to hand-stripping techniques.
They can be used with the grain or, with
longer blades, against the grain. Keep
in mind, the shorter the trim on the
body pattern, the more difficult it is to
blend the pattern later into the longer
furnishings. A longer cut also allows you
to mold the coat a bit and apply carding
techniques to retain some of the proper
coat texture. Carding also will remove
minor tracks commonly left after clipping.
Longer cutting blades are preferred.

Body Pattern
The transitional areas will be a half
inch to more than an inch in width
depending on the area and the
conformation of the dog. At the front of
the dog, the pattern starts just above the
breast bone and drops on a diagonal line
to almost the bottom of the shoulder
muscle. The pattern line travels down
the side of the dog, at the widest arc
of the ribs towards the flank where it
may rise slightly. As the pattern line
rises over the flank, it drops into a very
shallow "U" shape to expose the upper
thigh muscle. The "U" shape rises to
just below the base of the tail, leaving
the longer furnishings at the back of the
thigh. At the blending areas, bulk thin
or top thin with thinning shears so the
main body area blends invisibly with the
long furnishings. After clipping, card the
coat to promote proper coat growth and
retain some of the rich color and harsh-
coat texture.

Undercarriage
The furnishings on the underside of the
dog are left in a natural state or layered
to look long and natural depending on
the extent of the feathering. The coat
on the undercarriage may be trimmed
or neatened to clear the ground or to
add a slight rise under the last rib. If the

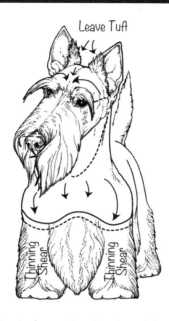

The head is long and rectangular with long,
split arched eyebrows and tufts at the base
of the ears. From the front and rear, the
legs drop in straight, parallel lines from well
toned shoulders and thighs. When setting the
pattern, use the turn of the muscles to set
the lines. Under the tail is short and clean
with a drape of longer fur covering the back
of the thighs. Leg furnishings are longer than
the body coat. Tail is carrot shaped and very
short on the back side.

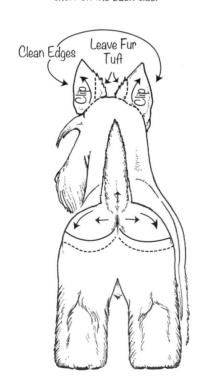

Their expression is keen, alert and bold. Head is a narrow rectangle with long, arched eyebrows and a full beard. The top skull and the muzzle are equal in length with the stop area being the center point. All lines on the head are clean and sharp.

Clip the top skull with blades ranging from a #5F to a #4F, used against the grain or blades from a #10 to #7F with the grain.

The ears have small triangular tufts at the base of the front. Almost the entire back of the ear is clipped with a #10 or #15 blade. The inside ⅓ of the ear tip is clipped clean. Detail the outer edge of the ear leather from base to tip with small detailing shears. Edge only the top ⅓ of the ear leather on the inside tip. Shape the tufts with thinning shears.

The eyebrows are split, long and arched. The brows will be very short at the back corner of the eye.

The beard is long, full and natural. When combing down the beard, the lines at the side of the face form a straight plane. Just below the back corner of the eyes, the fur is short and well blended, creating fill under the eye. The clipper lines of the beard are clean and sharp.

Ear Safety Tip: Remember, always keep the tips of the shears towards the tips of the ears when edging for safety.

Transitional Area

The line for the beard runs from the back corners of the eyes to the back corner of the mouth. To form the goatee: On the lower jaw, lift up the beard and continue to clip the lower jaw, about 1" from the back corner of the mouth.

The throat and cheeks are trimmed close with a #7F used against the grain or a #10 or #15 blade, used with the coat growth.

Stay inside the natural cowlick line of the neck that runs from the ear bulb down in a "U" or "V" shape. Stop about 2 or 3 finger widths above the breast bone. Thinning shear the cowlick seam to blend with the longer coat of the neck.

dog is sparsely furnished, tidy the undercarriage so it looks natural. The pattern line is well blended and invisible.

Tail

Shape the tail so it looks like a thick carrot. There will be more coat on the sides and top of the tail than on the underside. When trimming the

sanitary area under the tail, continue about an inch up the back side of the tail and leave the rest to do by hand. Trim off all the excessive length at the tip by running your hand down the tail, thumb towards the tip, and stopping when you can feel the end of the tail bone under your thumb. With your fingers protecting the tip of the tail, trim off the long fur. Fluff

the coat and shape the tail, thicker at the base, tapering to the tip. When the tail is held upright, there should be no dip right in front of the tail where it meets the back. The sides should blend smoothly into the rump. The back of the tail is trimmed very close, but not so close so that it is bald. Use a thinning shear or a #7F in this area.

Grooming Procedures & Recommendations

Hindquarters

The hindquarters should be strong and powerful. When clipping this area, expose the thigh muscle with the same blade used on the body. Start to feather off with the blade where the muscle bulges, creating a shallow "U" shape that rises back up to the tail area. Using a range of guard combs can facilitate feathering at the blending line. The longer feathering may be left long and natural or shortened. To shorten the furnishings, feather the coat with thinning shears working with the lay of the coat or by skimming the fur with a guard comb after it has been lightly fluffed. At the blending line, the transition should be invisible when the trim is finished. Blend with thinning shears by bulk thinning or top thinning if necessary.

Front Legs

The pattern line at the shoulder is about 1 or 2 fingers above the top of the elbow, at the point where the muscle begins to turn under. The coat at the transition line will be very short and taper into the longer leg furnishings. This can be accomplished by feathering off at the blending point with the same blade used on the body or switching to a guard comb and blending off at the transition point. As on the rear legs, the feathering on the front legs may be left long and natural or shortened. To shorten the furnishings, feather the coat with thinning shears, working with the lay of the coat or by skimming the fur with a guard comb after it has been lightly fluffed. At the blending line, the transition should be invisible when the trim is finished. Blend with thinning shears by bulk thinning or top thinning if necessary.

Feet

The front feet are larger than the rear feet, with thick pads and strong nails which can be slightly exposed. The feet are trimmed very close. The feet should point straight ahead, but minor toeing out is acceptable on the front feet. Trim the feet round by first boxing them into the shape of a box while the dog is standing in a natural, square position. With the dog's feet firmly planted on the table, remove the sharp corners of the box and round the feet facing straight forward. Bevel the coat slightly. If detailing the feet with the foot off the tabletop, always use a small pair of shears to minimize the risk of accidentally cutting the pads.

Throat & Chest

Blades ranging from a #10 to #7F, with or against the grain, based on skin sensitivity, are common in the throat and cheek areas. Follow the natural cowlick line that runs from the base of the ears in a "V" shape toward the base of the neck. The blending point begins about three or four fingers above the breast bone and drops to just below the turn of the muscle at the elbow/shoulder, creating a "W" shape when viewed straight on. When viewed in profile, the neck into the chest should be straight without a predominant forechest. When blending the chest, be aware of the heavy cowlicks in the area. If a clipper is run over this area to create the flat chest, the result will be severe holes in the chest area. It is very easy to create two bald patches on either side of the chest, just inside the front legs. Many stylists prefer to blend the chest area by hand with thinning shears or shears. When finished in this area, double check your work to be sure the neck, chest and front legs drop down in a straight line when viewed in profile.

Ears

Almost the entire backside of the ear is clipped with a #10 or #15 except for the small indentation where the ear leather meets the top skull. Leave that area unclipped as it will set up the tuft of fur that will conceal the ear canal. On the inside of the ear, clip only the excessive fur at the tips of the ears with the same blade. When working with short blades around the ear area, always work from the base or center of the ear out toward the edges. Gently brace the ear with your fingers to clip over it. The tuft is formed by leaving some long fur in front of the ear. The section starts as a small hook that begins at the indentation where the ear connects to the top skull and moves around to the outside edge of the base of the ear. To neaten the tuft, fold the ear in half lengthwise and brush the long coat out away from the ear leather. Use thinning shears to trim the long hair in a triangle, broader at the base and tapering to the ear tip. To finish the ear, use small detailing shears and keep the tip of

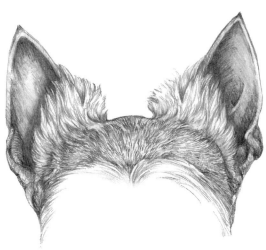

the shears towards the tip of the ears for safety. Trim the entire outside edge of the ear so no long hair falls outside the cheek and ear line. Trim all the way to the tip. On the inside edge of the ear leather, trim the top third of the leather to form a pointed ear tip. The ear tufts should not overpower the head piece. If the tuft is too full or out of balance with the head, lightly trim it with thinning shears to make it smaller and in better proportion.

Top Skull

The top of the head can be clipped with a #7F used with the grain, or a #5F or #7F used against the grain depending on the dog's sensitivity and coat density. Use caution with the Scottie not to remove the hair in front of the ear canals when trimming the top skull.

Brows

To form the arched, triangular eyebrows, follow the eye socket rim, working with or against the grain of the coat. Scotties have a slight stop between the eyes that acts as a natural split for the brows. Either lightly clip this area when clipping the top skull or do it by hand with thinning shears. Shape the brows into long arched triangles that accentuate the typically keen look. They will be very short at the back corner of the eye and longer at the tips, coming almost halfway down the bridge of the nose. When viewed in profile, the brows should barely break the line of the top skull as they arch out over the nose. Use curved shears in reverse to set the brow. Line the tip of the shear up with a point on the nose. Repeat on the other brow. By using the nose as a set point, the length and angle of both eyebrows remain the same.

When closing the shears to cut the brow, bevel the blades away from the pet's skin to avoid cutting the dog at the back corner of the eye.

Throat & Cheeks

The throat and cheek areas are clipped using blades ranging from a #10 to a #7F, used either with or against the grain. Use the natural cowlick line of the neck as a guide to create the "U" or "V" shape of the throat. The lowest point will be about 3 fingers above the breast bone. The line that breaks the top skull and the cheeks is from the back corner of the eye straight back to the ear canal.

Beard & Goatee

The fur on the muzzle is a natural length as it forms the beard. The basic transition line between the cheek and the beard runs on an imaginary line from just behind the back corner of the eyes to the whisker nodule on the cheeks. The line continues to the back corner of the mouth. The goatee is formed by continuing the line forward on the lower jaw, 1 or 2 finger widths in from the back corner of the mouth. The line should be very crisp and clean. The coat under the eye area is never clipped out as this hair forms one of the critical lines of the classic rectangular head style. The line on the dog's face should be straight, from the flat cheek down into the beard area. Double check this line by laying a greyhound comb along side the head. Any fur that sticks out beyond the comb should be removed. Any hair inside this line should remain and be blended to create the rectangular shape.

Detail Finish

Application of bows and mild cologne is optional.

Suggested Tools & Equipment

- Nail Trimmers
- Styptic Powder
- Ear Powder
- Ear Cleaning Solution
- Cotton Balls
- Hemostat
- Clippers
- Slicker Brush
- Greyhound Comb
- Pumice Stone
- Carding Tools
- Stripping Knives
- Straight Shears
- Curved Shears
- Small Detailing Shears
- Thinning Shears
- Dematting Tools

Common Blade Options:

- #40, #15, #10
- #7F, #5F, #4F
- Variety of Guard Combs

Grooming Tips

A light setting gel, mousse or texturing shampoo can add body to the leg coat, making it easier to scissor. Try spritzing unruly eyebrows with a styling spray while they are still damp. Work the product into the damp brows. Brush or comb the brows into place or dry them into the position you want them in the final trim.

Special Note

Harsh-coated terriers have a coat that will normally brush out quite easily, especially after they are clean. Shortening the leg furnishings will yield a tighter look and assist with easier maintenance.

Notes *from your* Grooming Table

Sealyham Terrier

Breed Facts & Characteristics

Country of Origin: Wales

Height at Shoulder: 10"–11"

Coat Length/Type: Hard/Wiry

Color: All white, or with lemon, tan or badger markings.

Correct grooming procedure:

Hand-Strip

Common pet grooming practices:

Clipper-Trim

General Description

This is a compact, very powerful little dog that also is very stylish and tailored. The top section shows off a toned body while the lower section is feathered. The head is rectangular, accentuated with a fall of hair over the eyes and a full beard. The expression is piercing, full of purpose and vigor.

-The Goal-

Everything about this breed is compact and tailored. The muscular body is accentuated by the groom. The head is rectangular in shape with a long fall of hair between the eyes. Pattern lines on the body are invisible, on the head, they are crisp and clean.

Correctly Groomed: Hand-Stripped

Typical blades used on the body for pet grooming: #8.5, #7F, #5F, #4F or shorter guard comb or a combination of those blades. Card coat after clipping to help maintain correct coat texture and color.

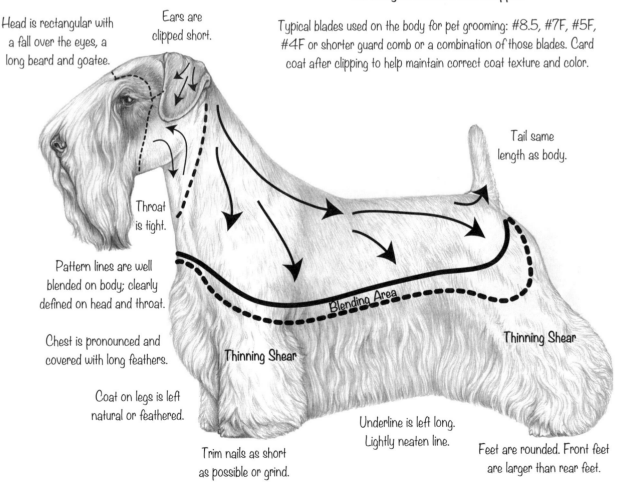

Head is rectangular with a fall over the eyes, a long beard and goatee.

Ears are clipped short.

Throat is tight.

Pattern lines are well blended on body; clearly defined on head and throat.

Chest is pronounced and covered with long feathers.

Coat on legs is left natural or feathered.

Trim nails as short as possible or grind.

Thinning Shear

Blending Area

Underline is left long. Lightly neaten line.

Tail same length as body.

Thinning Shear

Hocks are well let down.

Feet are rounded. Front feet are larger than rear feet.

See page 76 for Bathing & Drying Instructions

Frequency

Bathe once a week to once every 12 weeks.

Pre-Work

Trim or grind nails at least every four to six weeks to maintain a healthy foot structure. Swab the ears clean with a mild ear cleaning solution. Prior to bathing, quickly go over the entire body with a high-velocity dryer to help lift dirt and dander away from the skin and to loosen any shedding coat. ***Card and hand-strip dog prior to bathing and drying***.

Pattern Lines in General

The correct coat is hand-stripped. For either hand-stripped or clipper-cut pet dogs, the general pattern, based on the bone and muscle structure, is the same. After the final trim, all pattern lines should be invisible. If clipping at the transition points, feather off with the clippers in a smooth and steady fashion. If the pattern line is still visible after clipping, use thinning shears to blend the line. On the head, the pattern lines are crisp and clean.

Clipper-Cutting

Blades ranging from a #10 to a #4F, or short guard combs, are commonly used to set the pattern on the body as an alternative to hand-stripping techniques. They can be used with the grain or, with longer blades, against the grain. Keep in mind, the shorter the trim on the body pattern, the more difficult it is to blend the pattern later into the longer furnishings. A longer cut also allows you to mold the coat a bit and apply carding techniques to retain some of the proper coat texture. Carding also will remove minor tracks commonly left after clipping. Longer cutting blades are preferred.

Body Pattern

The transitional areas will be a half inch to more than an inch in width depending on the area and the conformation of the dog. At the front of the dog, the pattern starts just above the breast bone and drops on a diagonal line to almost the bottom of the shoulder muscle. The pattern line travels down the side of the dog, at the widest arc of the ribs towards the flank where it may rise slightly. As the pattern line rises over the flank, it drops into a very shallow "U" shape to expose the upper thigh muscle. The "U" shape rises to just below the base of the tail, leaving the longer furnishings at the back of the thigh. At the blending areas, bulk thin or top thin with thinning shears so the main body area blends invisibly with the long furnishings. After clipping, card the coat to promote proper coat growth and retain some of the rich color and harsh-coat texture.

Undercarriage

The furnishings on the underside of the dog are left in a natural state or layered to look long and natural depending on the extent of the feathering. The coat on the undercarriage may be trimmed or neatened to clear the ground or to add a slight rise under the last rib. If the dog is sparsely furnished, tidy the undercarriage so it looks natural. The pattern line is well blended and invisible.

Tail

Shape the tail so it looks like a short carrot. There will be more coat on the sides and top of the tail than on the underside. When trimming the sanitary area under the tail, continue about an inch up the back side of the tail and leave the rest to do by hand. Trim off all the excessive length at the tip by running your hand down the tail, thumb towards the tip, and stopping when you can feel the end of the tail bone under your thumb. With your fingers protecting the tip of the tail, trim off the long fur.

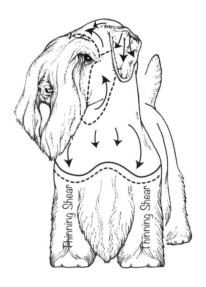

The head is long and rectangular with a fall of hair between the eyes. From the front and rear, the legs drop in straight, parallel lines from well toned shoulders and thighs. When setting the pattern, use the turn of the muscles to set the lines. Under the tail is short and clean with a drape of longer fur covering the back of the thighs. Leg furnishings are longer than the body coat.

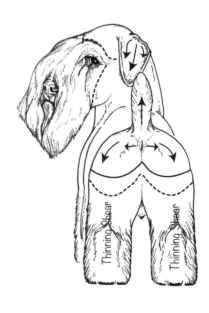

Their expression is friendly but alert and bold. Head is rectangular with a long fall of hair over the stop area with a full beard and goatee. The top skull and the muzzle are equal in length with the stop area being the center point. All lines on the head are clean and sharp.

Clip top skull with blades ranging from a #7F to a #5F, used against the grain or blades ranging from a #10 to #7F with the grain.

The line for the fall follows the eye socket rim. The back corners of the eyes are trimmed closely to expose the eye. This line arches out towards the nose. It is crisp and clean.

On the muzzle, the hair is long and natural but does not break the line of the top skull. When combing down the beard, the lines at the side of the face form a straight plane. Just below the back corner of the eyes, the fur is short and well blended, creating fill under the eye. The clipper lines of the beard are clean and sharp.

Use a #10 or #15 blade on the outside of the ear. A #40 blade can be used on the inside of the ear leather with a very light touch. Edge the ear with small detailing shears. The fold of the ear is level with the line of the top skull.

Ear Safety Tip:
Remember, always keep the tips of the shears towards the tips of the ears when edging for safety.

Leave Long

Clean & Sharp

Blend Well

Transitional Blending Area

Blend Well

The throat is trimmed close with a #7F used against the grain or a #10 or #15 blade used with the coat growth.

Stay inside the natural cowlick line of the neck that runs from the ear bulb down in a "U" or "V" shape. Stop about 2 or 3 finger widths above the breast bone. Thinning shear the cowlick seam to blend with the longer coat of the neck.

Fluff the coat and shape the tail, thicker at the base, tapering to the tip. When the tail is held upright, there should be no dip right in front of the tail where it meets the back. The sides should blend smoothly into the rump. The back of the tail is trimmed very close, but not so close that it is bald. Use a thinning shear or a #7F in this area.

Hindquarters
The hindquarters should be strong and powerful. When clipping this area, expose the thigh muscle with the same blade used on the body. Start to feather off with the blade where the muscle bulges, creating a shallow "U" shape that rises back up to the tail area. Using a range of guard combs can facilitate feathering at the blending line. The longer

feathering may be left long and natural or shortened. To shorten the furnishings, feather the coat with thinning shears working with the lay of the coat or by skimming the fur with a guard comb after it has been lightly fluffed. At the blending line, the transition should be invisible when the trim is finished. Blend with thinning shears by bulk thinning or top thinning if necessary.

TERRIER

Front Legs

The pattern line at the shoulder is about 1 or 2 fingers above the top of the elbow, at the point where the muscle begins to turn under. The coat at the transition line will be very short and taper into the longer leg furnishings.

This can be accomplished by feathering off at the blending point with the same blade used on the body or switching to a guard comb and blending off at the transition point. As on the rear legs, the feathering on the front legs may be left long and natural or shortened. To shorten the furnishings, feather the coat with thinning shears, working with the lay of the coat or by skimming the fur with a guard comb after it has been lightly fluffed. At the blending line, the transition should be invisible when the trim is finished. Blend with thinning shears by bulk thinning or top thinning if necessary.

Feet

The front feet are larger than the rear feet, with thick pads and strong nails which can be slightly exposed. The feet are trimmed very close. The feet should point straight ahead, but minor toeing out is acceptable on the front feet. Trim the feet round by first boxing them into the shape of a box while the dog is standing in a natural, square position. With the dog's feet firmly planted on the table, remove the sharp corners of the box and round the feet facing straight forward. Bevel the coat slightly. If detailing the feet with the foot off the tabletop, always use a small pair of shears to minimize the risk of accidentally cutting the pads.

Throat & Chest

Blades ranging from a #10 to #7F, with or against the grain, based on skin sensitivity, are common in the throat and cheek areas. Follow the natural cowlick line that runs from the base of the ears in a "V" shape toward the base of the neck. The blending point begins about three or four fingers above the breast bone and drops to just below the turn of the muscle at the elbow/shoulder, creating a "W" shape when viewed straight on. When viewed in profile, the neck into the chest should be straight without a predominant forechest. When blending the chest, be aware of the heavy cowlicks in the area. If a clipper is run over this area to create the flat chest, the result will be severe holes in the chest area. It is very easy to create two bald patches on either side of the chest, just inside the front legs. Many stylists prefer to blend the chest area by hand with thinning shears or shears. When finished in this area, double check your work to be sure the neck, chest and front legs drop down in a straight line when viewed in profile.

Top Skull

The top of the head can be clipped with a #7F used with the grain, or a #5F or 7F used against the grain depending on the dog's sensitivity and coat density.

Ears

The ears are clipped with a close blade. It is common to use a #10 or #15 blade on the outside of the ear leather and a #40 on the inside. When working with close blades in this delicate area, always work from the base or center of the ear out toward the edge. Gently brace the ear with your fingers to clip over it. To finish, use small finishing shears to trim around the outside edge of the ear leather, keeping the tips of the shears toward the tip of the ears for safety.

Fall

The Sealyham has a natural fall of hair that covers the stop area and down the bridge of the nose. As with regular eyebrows, follow the eye socket rim, working with the lay of the coat. Do not trim any hair from between the eyes in the stop area when clipping the top skull. This section of hair makes the fall over the eyes. Trim only the coat from the outside edges of the eyes. Use either thinning shears or curved shears. Remove the coat from the back corner to the center of the eye, leaving the rest of the coat to create the fall. When trimming this area, follow an imaginary line from the outside edge of the eye to the outside edge of the nostril to line up the shears. The fur at the back corner of the eye will be very short, growing progressively longer as it arches out over the eye. By using the nose as a set point, the angle of the arch can be set identically over each eye. When you close the shears to cut the arch, bevel the blades away from the pet's skin to avoid accidentally cutting the dog at the back corner of the eye. The fall, when viewed in profile, should form a straight line from the top skull out over the bridge of the nose. If this area rises too much, top thin the coat slightly to level it or do a small amount of bulk thinning with thinning shears from beneath.

Throat & Cheeks

The throat and cheek areas are clipped using blades ranging from a #10 to a #7F, used either with or against the grain. Use the natural cowlick line of the neck as a guide to create the "U" or "V" shape of the throat. The lowest point will be about 3 fingers above the breast bone. The line that breaks the top skull and the cheeks is from the back corner of the eye straight back to the ear canal.

Beard & Goatee

The fur on the muzzle is a natural length as it forms the beard. The basic transition line between the cheek and

Notes From The Grooming Table ©2016

the beard runs on an imaginary line from just behind the back corner of the eyes to the whisker nodule on the cheeks. The line continues to the back corner of the mouth. The goatee is formed by continuing the line forward on the lower jaw, one or two finger widths in from the back corner of the mouth. The line should be very crisp and clean. The coat under the eye area is never clipped out as this hair forms one of the critical lines of the classic rectangular head style. The line on the dog's face should be straight, from the flat cheek down into the beard area. Double check this line by laying a greyhound comb along side the head. Any fur that sticks out beyond the comb should be removed. Any hair inside this line should remain and be blended to create the rectangular shape.

Detail Finish
Application of bows and mild cologne is optional.

Grooming Tips
A light setting gel, mousse or texturing shampoo can add body to the leg coat, making it easier to scissor. Try spritzing unruly eyebrows with a styling spray while they are still damp. Work the product into the damp brows. Brush or comb the brows into place or dry them into the position you want them in the final trim.

- Harsh-coated terriers have a coat that will normally brush out quite easily, especially after they are clean.

- Shortening the leg furnishings will yield a tighter look and assist with easier maintenance.

Suggested Tools & Equipment

- Nail Trimmers
- Styptic Powder
- Ear Powder
- Ear Cleaning Solution
- Cotton Balls
- Hemostat
- Clippers
- Slicker Brush
- Greyhound Comb
- Pumice Stone
- Carding Tools
- Stripping Knives
- Straight Shears
- Curved Shears
- Small Detailing Shears
- Thinning Shears
- Dematting Tools

Common Blade Options:
- #40, #15, #10
- #7F, #5F, #4F
- Variety of Guard Combs

Notes:

Notes *from your* Grooming Table

Skye Terrier

TERRIER   **NATURAL LONG HAIRED**

Breed Facts & Characteristics

Country of Origin: Scotland

Height at Shoulder: 9½"–10"

Coat Length/Type: Long/Flowing

Color: Black, blue, dark or light gray, silver platinum, fawn or cream.

Correct grooming procedure:
Brush Out/Minor Trimming

Common pet grooming practices:
Bathe & Brush Out/Clipper-Trim

-The Goal-
Coat should be mat- and tangle-free.
The fur should be light and airy, moving
freely with the dog as it moves.

Part down center of skull.

Leave ears long.

Clear stop area with thinners or clippers.

Line comb and brush **every** inch of this dog, right down to the skin.

Lightly trim sanitary areas—both under tail and tummy.

Watch friction areas:
• Collar Area
• Arm Pits
• Behind Ears
• Legs & Thighs

Trim nails as short as possible or grind.

Shave pads and scissor feet round. Neaten undercarriage line.

🐾 Bathing and Drying Directions:
• For coats longer than 3", use Natural Long Haired
• For coats shorter than 3", use Curly and Wavy Coated.

Grooming Procedures & Recommendations

See page 72 for
Bathing & Drying Instructions

See page 602 for
Drop Coat Styling Options

Frequency
Bathe once a week to once every 12 weeks.

Pre-Work
Trim or grind nails every four to six weeks to maintain a healthy foot structure. Clean the ears by swabbing with a mild ear cleaning solution. Hair should be plucked from within the ear canal only as necessary for healthy ear management. Prior to bathing, quickly go over the entire body and remove any serious mats or tangles. If the tangle can be penetrated with water, leave it and remove when the dog is clean. If the dog is in a clipped pet trim and has not been in for professional grooming for six weeks or more, remove the excessive body coat and set the pattern before bathing if setting a pet clipper-trim.

Brushing
Systematically line brush the entire coat, right down to the skin. With a slicker brush, the motion used for line brushing is a "pat and pull." Softly pat the coat with the full pad of the brush and pull out and away from the skin with each stroke. The wrist remains in a neutral, or straight, position. The motion should be light and gentle. Start on the lower rear legs and work upwards towards the thigh. Repeat on every leg then proceed to the body, neck, head ears and tail. Work evenly over the pet, holding or pushing up the coat with one hand. It can be done with either a comb or a brush, but in most cases the comb is reserved for double checking the work of the brush. With the slicker brush, work the seam line, pulling down a small amount of fur with each stroke. Do not move to the next section until the brush stroke glides smoothly and the skin at the seam line is seen. Pay close attention to the legs, under the front legs, collar area, ears, and tail. Let your hands feel for coat density levels. If an area feels heavier or thicker, it will need special attention with a brush or a comb. If static electricity is a problem while brushing, lightly mist the coat with an anti-static product or water while brushing. When finished, each strand of hair should float freely about as the dog moves.

Head
For show, the head is left long and natural with no special treatment to the topknot area other than the hair is parted at the center. For pet dogs, it is common to hold the hair out of the eyes by banding, braiding or using barrettes. For pets, it is also common to slightly trim the stop area between the eyes.

Ears
The ears are erect and covered with long hair that drapes over them.

Feet & Hocks
Trim the pads with a close cutting action blade ranging from a #15 to a #40. Use a very light touch to clean the pads of long hair. To create a rounded foot, first block in the foot to form a square. This will help create a full circular shape with the toes pointing directly forward. Finish detailing and rounding the outline of the foot by using long, curved shears.

Detail Finish
Lightly neaten the entire outline of the dog, removing long, shaggy stray hairs that interrupt a smooth flow. The finished appearance is very natural. This can be done with thinning shears or shears as long as the look remains natural. Finish with a fine mist of coat polish on the body coat for added shine.

Suggested Tools & Equipment
- Nail Trimmers
- Styptic Powder
- Ear Powder
- Ear Cleaning Solution
- Hemostat
- Cotton Balls
- Clippers
- #40 and #15 Blades for Pads
- Slicker Brush
- Greyhound Comb
- Pin Brush
- Dematting Tools
- Straight Shears
- Curved Shears
- Small Detailing Shears
- Thinning Shears

Notes:

Notes From The Grooming Table ©2016

Breed Facts & Characteristics

Country of Origin: Ireland

Height at Shoulder: 17"–19"

Coat Length/Type: Long/Soft

Color: Always a yellow wheaten with darker gray shadowing allowed in the facial area.

Correct grooming procedure:

Hand-Scissor

Common pet grooming practices:

Clipper-Trim

General Description

The Wheaten is a medium sized, squarely built, robust dog with a great sense of humor and responsiveness to its surroundings. They have a rectangular head style and compact body with a deep chest. The silky, profuse hair falls in soft waves and is considered single coated. The color is always a yellow wheaten with darker gray shadowing allowed in the facial area.

-The Goal-
The outline of the breed is square with enough coat to float with the dog as it moves. The head is well covered with fur and rectangular in shape. All pattern lines are invisible. Mat free.

Correctly Groomed: Hand-Scissored

Typical blades used on the body for pet grooming range from a #4F blade to a variety of guard combs in a combination of lengths.

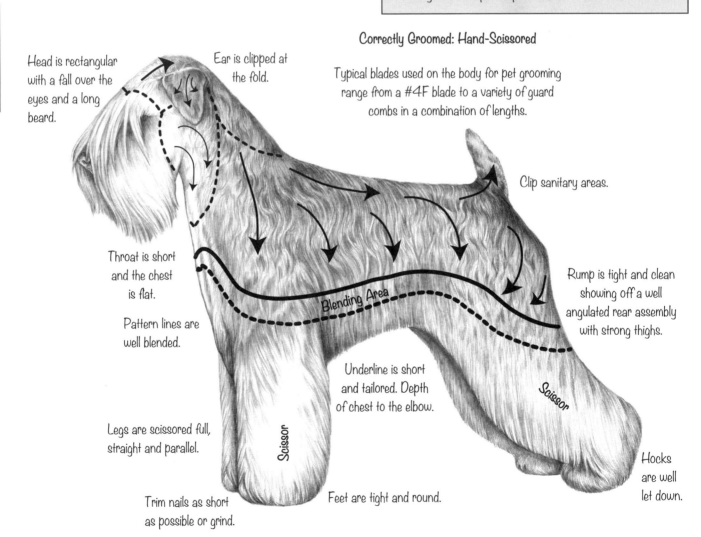

Head is rectangular with a fall over the eyes and a long beard.

Ear is clipped at the fold.

Clip sanitary areas.

Throat is short and the chest is flat.

Pattern lines are well blended.

Blending Area

Rump is tight and clean showing off a well angulated rear assembly with strong thighs.

Underline is short and tailored. Depth of chest to the elbow.

Legs are scissored full, straight and parallel.

Scissor

Scissor

Hocks are well let down.

Trim nails as short as possible or grind.

Feet are tight and round.

TERRIER

Grooming Procedures & Recommendations

See page 74 for
Bathing & Drying Instructions

Frequency

Bathe once a week to once every 12 weeks. Trim every four to six weeks to maintain a stylized fashion.

Pre-Work

Trim or grind nails at least every four to six weeks to maintain a healthy foot structure. Clean the ears by swabbing with a mild ear cleaning solution. Pluck any long hair inside the ear canal using an ear powder and your fingers or hemostat. Prior to bathing, quickly go over the entire body and remove any serious mats or tangles. If the tangle can be penetrated with water, leave it and remove when the dog is clean. If the pet has not been in for professional grooming for six weeks or more, remove the excessive body coat and set the pattern before bathing. Before starting final haircut, make sure the dog's coat is thoroughly brushed out and free of tangles.

Pattern Lines

The pattern is based on the bone and muscle structure of the dog. After the final trim, all pattern lines should be invisible on the main body. If using clippers on the main body, feather off transition points in a smooth and steady fashion. If the pattern line is still visible after clipping, use thinning shears to blend the line. On the head, the pattern lines are soft and blended.

Body

For pet dogs, the coat can be hand-scissored or clipper-cut using the same general pattern. Typical blades used in pet grooming range from a #4F for the tight work around the neck and shoulders to blades ranging from a short guard comb for very short pet trims to a longer guard combs for fuller trims. The pattern lines start at the turn of the shoulder and continue to just above the elbow, return to the flank on a diagonal and then drop into the thigh region. At the pattern lines,

the shorter fur blends seamlessly into the longer coat of the legs and undercarriage.

Neck

The neck is moderately long and carried proudly. Leaving the coat slightly longer on the back of the neck can accentuate this characteristic. The additional coat can help create the illusion of a powerful but graceful neck as long as it tapers smoothly into the shoulders.

Undercarriage

Right around the navel area, the coat will be very short and start to get longer as the line moves forward towards the brisket, creating the illusion of a deep chest. When viewed in profile, the depth of the body and the length of the legs should be equal. There is only enough fur left on the undercarriage to accentuate depth of chest and an athletic build. The pattern line is well blended and invisible.

Tail & Rear

The top of the tail is trimmed with the same blade as the body. The underside is clipped close, with blades ranging from #15 to a #7F, used with or against the grain based on the sensitivity of the dog's skin. On the inner side of the cowlick lines going down the back side of the thighs, use a close blade ranging between a #7F and a #2 guard comb.

Hindquarters

The hindquarters should be strong and powerful. When clipping this area, expose the thigh muscle with the same blade used on the body. Start to feather off with the blade where the muscle starts to turn under on a diagonal line from the flank region to about three or four fingers above the hock. The blending should be invisible when the trim is finished. Blend with thinning shears if necessary. The stifle area should have enough furnishing left to give the legs substance and angulation. The longest coat on the legs can range from 1 to 3 inches depending on the amount of bone and coat density. Shape this area by

From the front and rear, the legs drop in straight, parallel lines from well toned shoulders and thighs. When setting the pattern, use the turn of the muscles to set the lines. Chest is flat but use caution not to bald out this area due to cowlicks where the front legs join the chest. Rear is short, tight and clean. Leg furnishings are longer than the body coat.

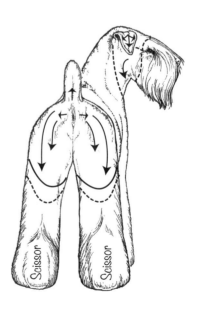

Notes From The Grooming Table ©2016

Their expression is friendly, active and self-confident. Head is rectangular with a long fall of hair over the stop area with a full beard. The top skull and the muzzle are equal in length with the stop area being the center point. All lines on the head are soft and blended.

Clip top skull with a range of medium to longer guard combs pulled forward from the occiput and feathering off at the fall area.

The line for the fall follows the eye socket rim. The back corners of the eyes are trimmed with thinning shears, slightly exposing the eye.

This ear is more coated than other terriers. Work from the center of the ear out with a #7F, #5F or a #4F blade on the outside of the ear. A #40 blade can be used on the inside of the ear leather with a very light touch. Start the clipper work at the fold, not the base of the ear. The fold of the ear is level with the line of the top skull. Edge the ear with small detailing shears.

On the muzzle, the hair is long and natural but does not break the line of the top skull. When combing down the beard, the lines at the side of the face form a straight plane. Just below the back corner of the eyes, the fur is short and well blended, creating fill under the eye. The clipper lines of the beard are soft and blended.

Ear Safety Tip:
Remember, always keep the tips of the shears towards the tips of the ears when edging for safety.

Blend Well

Transitional Blending Area

Blend Well

When setting the beard, use the back corners of the eyes and the whisker nodule on the cheeks and under the jaw as basic guidelines. "Connect the dots."

The throat is trimmed with guard combs ranging from a #4F to a #5, or short to medium guard combs, with the lay of the coat.

Stay inside the natural cowlick line of the neck that runs from the ear bulb down in a "U" or "V" shape. Stop about 3 or 4 finger widths above the breast bone. Thinning shear the cowlick seam to blend with the longer coat of the neck.

hand with shears after the clipper work is complete. When viewed from the rear, the legs should form two parallel lines to the ground. The hocks are well let down. There should be adequate coat on the hock area to accentuate the angles of the rear assembly.

Front Legs
The longest coat on the legs can range from 1 to 3 inches depending on the amount of bone and coat density. The front legs drop straight down from

the body and have ample bone and muscle to show off a powerful and sturdy animal. The pattern line at the shoulder is about 2 fingers above the top of the elbow, at the point where the muscle begins to turn under. The coat at the transition line will be very short and taper into the longer leg furnishings. This can be accomplished by feathering off at the blending point with the same blade used on the body. Most stylists prefer to leave the legs to shape by hand with shears ranging

from 8.5 to 10 inches in length. Other methods of blending off at the top of the leg include using guard combs to blend the transition line followed by hand-scissoring and blending with thinning shears. After the final trim, the legs should form two parallel columns descending from the elbow into beveled, tight, round feet. The coat at the back of the elbow is very short and falls straight down off the back of the leg toward the ground.

TERRIER

Grooming Procedures & Recommendations

Feet

Both the front and rear feet are compact with well-arched toes. To show off these traits, the feet are trimmed very close to the edge of the foot, beveling out onto fuller leg coat.

The feet should point straight ahead, toeing neither in nor out. Begin trimming the feet by forming a square box around the foot while the dog is standing in a natural, square position. With the dog standing squarely on the table, remove the sharp edges of the box and round the feet as they face straight forward. If detailing the feet with the foot lifted off the tabletop, always use a small pair of detailing shears to minimize the risk of accidentally cutting the pads.

Throat & Chest

Blades ranging from #5F to shorter guard combs, with or against the grain, based on the sensitivity of the dog's skin, are common in the throat area. Follow the natural cowlick line that runs from the base of the ears in a "V" shape towards the base of the neck. The blending point for the chest begins about three or four fingers above the breast bone and drops to just below the turn of the muscle at the elbow/shoulder, creating a "W" shape when viewed straight on. When viewed in profile, the neck into the chest should be straight without a predominant forechest. When blending the chest, be aware of the heavy cowlicks in the area. Many stylists prefer to leave the chest area to blend by hand with thinning shears or shears. When finished in this area, double check your work to be sure the neck, chest and front legs drop down in a straight line when viewed in profile.

The Head in General

The head is rectangular in shape. The length of the muzzle and the skull are about the same. The top skull is smooth and flat. The cheeks are level. There is a slight stop between the keen, sharp eyes that are accentuated by a fall of hair between them.

Ears

Ears are clipped with a medium blade and should be coated. It is common to see a #7F to a #4F blade used on the outside of the ear leather while a #40 blade is used on the inside. The clipper work starts at the ear fold, so when you look at the dog from the front, there is no break in the line from the top skull to the ear set. Gently brace the ear with your fingers to clip over it. When working with blades in this delicate area, always work from the base, or center, of the ear out toward the edge. To finish, use small finishing shears to trim around the outside edge of the ear leather.

Top Skull

Clip top skull with a range of medium to longer guard combs pulled forward from the occiput and feathering off at the fall area.

Fall

The slight stop between the eyes will be filled with long fur. Shape the area over the eyes into an arch to accentuate the typically keen terrier expression. The coat will be very short at the back corner of the eye and longer as it blends out beyond the halfway point of the eye. When viewed in profile, the fall is a continuation of the top skull as it grows out over the nose. Use curved shears in reverse to set the arch line above the eyes. Line up the tip of the shear with a point on the nose. Repeat on the other eye. By using the nose as a set point, the angles of both arches are easier to match.

Beard & Goatee

The muzzle is left in a natural state as it forms the rectangular beard. The transition line for the cheek to the muzzle area runs on an imaginary line from just behind the back corner of the eye to the cheek whisker nodule, under the jaw to the single center whisker nodule. The line should be well blended. The coat under the eye area is never clipped as this hair forms one of the critical lines of the classic rectangular head style. Depending on the

Suggested Tools & Equipment

- Nail Trimmers
- Styptic Powder
- Ear Powder
- Ear Cleaning Solution
- Cotton Balls
- Hemostat
- Clippers
- Slicker Brush
- Greyhound Comb
- Straight Shears
- Curved Shears
- Small Detailing Shears
- Thinning Shears
- Dematting Tools
- High-Velocity Dryer

Common Blade Options:
- #40, #15, #10
- #7F, #5F, #4F
- Variety of Guard Combs

head, this line may need to be adjusted slightly. The line on the dog's face should be straight, from the flat, level cheek down into the muzzle area. Double check this line by laying a greyhound comb along side the head. Any fur that sticks out beyond the comb should be removed. Any hair inside this line should remain and be blended to create the rectangular shape.

Detail Finish

Remove any scissor marks or clipper tracks with thinning shears. Application of mild cologne and collar bows is optional.

Grooming Tips

Thinning shears can be your best friends on this coat type. Soft, wavy coats mark extremely easily. Thinning shears are erasers for the professional pet stylist. They can remove most mild to moderate clipper or scissor marks left in a coat.

Breed Facts & Characteristics

Country of Origin: England

Height at Shoulder: 14"–16"

Coat Length/Type: Short/Smooth

Color: Red, fawn, white, black or blue or any of those colors with white, any shade of brindle or brindle with white.

Correct grooming procedure:
Bathe & Curry Brush

Common pet grooming practices:
Bathe & Curry Brush

-The Goal-
The coat should be clean and fresh smelling, with the coat laying flat against the body. No shedding hair.

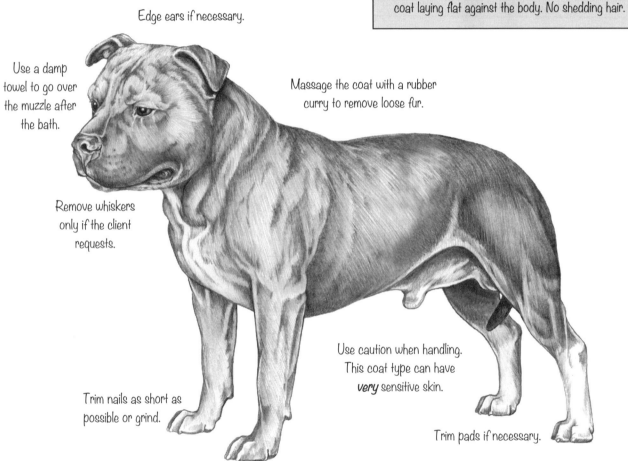

Edge ears if necessary.

Use a damp towel to go over the muzzle after the bath.

Massage the coat with a rubber curry to remove loose fur.

Remove whiskers only if the client requests.

Use caution when handling. This coat type can have **very** sensitive skin.

Trim nails as short as possible or grind.

Trim pads if necessary.

See page 66 for Bathing & Drying Instructions

Suggested Tools & Equipment

- Nail Trimmers
- Styptic Powder
- Ear Cleaning Solution
- Cotton Balls

- Clippers
- #40 or #15 Blade
- Rubber Curry
- Carding Tool

- Small Detailing Shears
- Thinning Shears

TERRIER

Notes *from your*
Grooming Table

Breed Facts & Characteristics

Country of Origin: Wales

Height at Shoulder: 14"–15½"

Coat Length/Type: Hard/Wiry

Color: Black and tan (black saddle, tan flatwork and furnishings).

Correct grooming procedure:

Hand-Strip

Common pet grooming practices:

Clipper-Trim

General Description

Everything about the Welsh Terrier is tight and tailored. This is a squarely built dog of medium size. He is hardy and sturdy, yet extremely agile. When grooming this breed, remember there is nothing soft or fluffy about it. In the finished groom, there is very little coat hiding the contours of its body. The leg coat is slightly longer. The head is rectangular in shape with a piercing expression, moderate muzzle coat and small brows.

> -The Goal-
> Everything about this breed is tight and tailored. The well-toned body is accentuated by the groom. The head is rectangular in shape. All pattern lines are invisible.

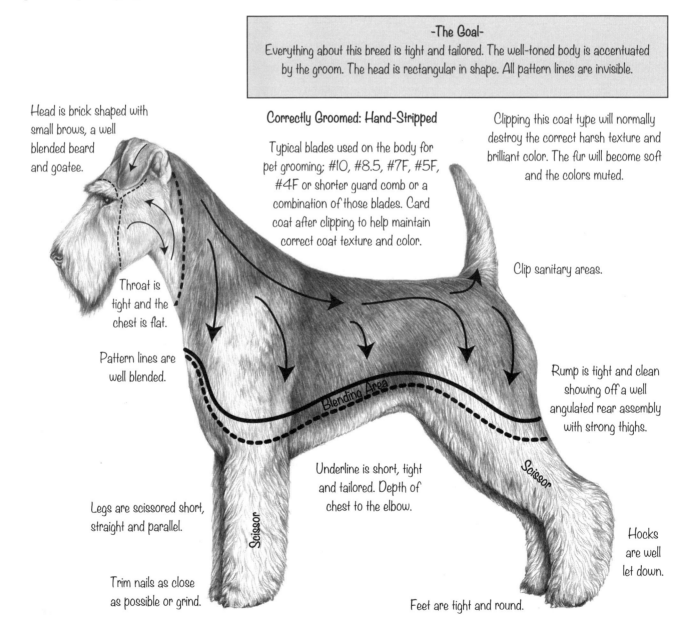

Head is brick shaped with small brows, a well blended beard and goatee.

Correctly Groomed: Hand-Stripped

Typical blades used on the body for pet grooming; #10, #8.5, #7F, #5F, #4F or shorter guard comb or a combination of those blades. Card coat after clipping to help maintain correct coat texture and color.

Clipping this coat type will normally destroy the correct harsh texture and brilliant color. The fur will become soft and the colors muted.

Throat is tight and the chest is flat.

Clip sanitary areas.

Pattern lines are well blended.

Blending Area

Rump is tight and clean showing off a well angulated rear assembly with strong thighs.

Underline is short, tight and tailored. Depth of chest to the elbow.

Legs are scissored short, straight and parallel.

Scissor

Scissor

Hocks are well let down.

Trim nails as close as possible or grind.

Feet are tight and round.

Grooming Procedures & Recommendations

See page 76 for
Bathing & Drying Instructions

Frequency
Bathe once a week to once every 12 weeks.

Pre-Work
Trim or grind nails at least every four to six weeks to maintain a healthy foot structure. Swab the ears clean with a mild ear cleaning solution. Prior to bathing, quickly go over the entire body with a high-velocity dryer to help lift dirt and dander away from the skin and to loosen any shedding coat. ***Card and hand-strip dog prior to bathing and drying.***

Done to breed standard, the coat is hand-stripped to promote healthy skin tone, proper coat texture and rich color. Many pet owners choose to clipper-cut their pet dog. This practice destroys the correct harsh coat texture on most dogs and dilutes the color on salt-and-pepper dogs. However, it is an economical way to keep the pet looking like the breed standard. Finding a stylist who is willing to commit the time and energy to hand-strip some breeds can be difficult. Plus, many pet owners are not willing to pay for this highly skilled service.

Pattern Lines in General
The pattern is based on the bone and muscle structure of the dog. After the final trim, all pattern lines should be invisible. At the transition points, feather off with the clippers in a smooth and steady fashion. If the pattern line is still visible after clipping, use thinning shears to blend the line.

Body
For either hand-stripped or clipper-cut dogs, the general pattern is the same. Typical blades used in pet grooming range from a #7F to a #4F or a combination of those blades for the bulk of the body work. Some stylists find reversing a slightly longer blade very effective in achieving an extremely smooth finish on the body. Reversing a blade will shorten the cutting action by about two blade lengths as the same blade used with the grain of the coat. Choose one of the methods and follow the direction of the natural coat growth of the fur. After clipping, card the coat to help promote proper coat growth while retaining some of the rich color and harsh coat texture. Carding also will assist in the removal of any minor tracking left in the coat from clipping. The pattern lines start at the turn of the shoulder and continue to just above the elbow, back to the flank on a diagonal and then drop into the thigh region.

Undercarriage
Right around the navel area, the coat will be very short and start to get longer as the line moves forward towards the brisket, creating the illusion of a deep chest. When viewed in profile, the distance from the elbow to the bottom of the foot is equal to the distance between the withers and the brisket. There is only enough fur left on the undercarriage to accentuate depth of chest and an athletic build. The pattern line is well blended and invisible.

Tail & Rear
The top side of the tail is trimmed with the same blade as the body. The underside of the tail is clipped close, with blades ranging from #15 to a #7F, used with or against the grain based on the sensitivity of the dog's skin. Continue with the same blade around the rectum and on the inner side of the cowlick lines going down the back side of the thighs.

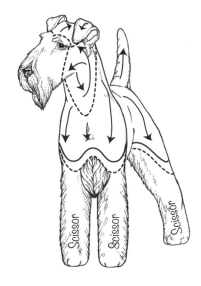

From the front and rear, the legs drop in straight, parallel lines from well toned shoulders and thighs. When setting the pattern, use the turn of the muscles to set the lines. Chest is flat but use caution not to bald out this area due to cowlicks where the front legs join the chest. Rear is short, tight and clean. Leg furnishings are slightly longer than the body coat.

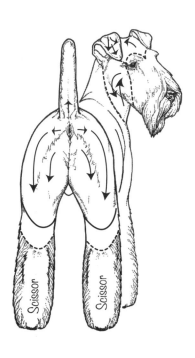

Notes From The Grooming Table ©2016

Head is brick shaped with small brows and a well blended beard and goatee. Their expression is friendly but alert and bold. The top skull and the muzzle are equal in length with the stop area being the center point. All lines on the head are invisible.

Clip top skull with blades ranging from a #7F to a #5F, with the grain.

Use a #10 or #15 blade on the outside of the ear. A #40 blade can be used on the inside of the ear leather with a very light touch. Edge the ear with small detailing shears. The fold of the ear comes to just above the line of the top skull.

The eyebrows are very small, split at the stop area. There are no sharp lines. Shape and blend with thinning shears.

Ear Safety Tip: Remember, always keep the tips of the shears towards the tips of the ears when edging for safety.

On the muzzle, the hair is longer but not so long as to extend beyond the planes of the top skull or cheeks. Blend the bulk of the muzzle with thinning shears or skim with a medium guard comb. Lightly trim the end of the muzzle to accentuate the rectangular head style. The lines at the side of the face are well blended and straight. Do not hollow out under the eye.

Blend Well

Blend Well

Blend Well

Blend Well

Transitional Blending Area

The throat is trimmed close with a #7F used against the grain or a #10 or #15 blade used with the coat growth.

Stay inside the natural cowlick line of the neck that runs from the ear bulb down in a "U" or "V" shape. Stop about 2 or 3 finger widths above the breast bone. Thinning shear the cowlick seam to blend with the longer coat of the neck.

Hindquarters

The hindquarters should be strong and powerful. When clipping this area, expose the thigh muscle with the same blade used on the body. Start to feather off with the blade where the muscle starts to turn under on a diagonal line from the flank region to about three or four fingers above the hock. Using a short to medium guard comb can facilitate feathering in the blending line. The pattern line should be invisible when the trim is finished. Blend with thinning shears

if necessary. The stifle area should have enough furnishing left to give the legs substance and angulation. The longest coat on the legs can range from 1 to 2 inches depending on the amount of bone and coat density. Shape this area by hand with shears after the clipper work is complete. When viewed from the rear, the legs should form two parallel lines to the ground. The hocks are well let down. There should be adequate coat on the hock area to accentuate the angles of the rear assembly.

Front Legs

The coat on the legs can range from 1/16 of an inch to 1.5 inches in length depending on the amount of bone, the size of the dog and coat density. The front legs drop straight down from the body and have ample bone and muscle to show off a powerful and sturdy animal. The pattern line at the shoulder is about 2 or 3 fingers above the top of the elbow, at the point where the muscle begins to turn under. The coat at the transition line will be very short and taper into the longer leg furnishings. This can be accomplished by feathering off at the blending point with the same blade used on the body. Other methods of blending off at the top of the leg include using a guard comb to blend the transition line followed by hand-scissoring and blending with thinning shears. Most stylists prefer to leave the legs to shape by hand with shears. After the final trim, the legs need to form two parallel columns going down from the elbow into tight, round feet. The coat at the back of the elbow is very short and falls straight down off the back of the leg toward the ground.

Feet
The feet are small for the size of the dog. Both the front and rear feet are compact with well arched toes. To show off these traits, the feet are trimmed very close to the edge of the foot and some nail is routinely exposed. The feet should point straight ahead, toeing neither in nor out. Trim the feet round by first boxing them in the shape of a square while the dog is standing in a natural, square position. Then remove the sharp corners of the box and round the feet facing straight forward. If detailing the feet with the foot off the tabletop, always use a small pair of shears to minimize the risk of accidentally cutting the pads.

Throat & Chest
Blades ranging from #10 to #7F, with or against the grain, based on the sensitivity of the dog's skin, are common in the throat area. Follow the natural cowlick line that runs in a "V" shape from the base of the ears towards the base of the neck. The blending point begins about three or four fingers above the breast bone and drops to just below the turn of the muscle at the elbow/shoulder, creating a "W" shape when viewed straight on. When viewed in profile, the neck into the chest should be straight without a predominant forechest. When

blending the chest, be aware of the heavy cowlicks in the area. Many stylists prefer to leave the chest area to blend by hand with thinning shears or shears. When finished in this area, double check your work to be sure the neck, chest and front legs drop down in a straight line when viewed in profile.

The Head in General: Top Skull
The top of the head is clipped with a #7F or #5F, used with the grain or against depending on the dog's sensitivity and density of the coat.

Ears
The ears are clipped with a close blade. It is common to see a #10 or #15 blade used on the outside of the ear leather while a #40 blade is used on the inside. When working with close blades in this delicate area, always work from the base or center of the ear out toward the edge. Gently brace the ear with your fingers to clip over it. To finish, use small finishing shears to trim around the outside edge of the ear leather, keeping the tips of the shears toward the tip of the ears.

Brows
The eyebrow on this dog is very small. Follow the eye socket rim, working with the lay of the coat. They have a slight stop between the eyes that acts as a natural split for the brows. Either lightly clip this area when clipping the top skull, leave it to do by hand with thinning shears or finger pluck the area. This area should have just enough fur removed to lend definition to the brow area, while revealing the eye. The small, triangular shape accentuates the typically keen expression found on this long legged terrier. They will be very short at the back corner of the eye and longer at the tip, which comes out over the stop area. When viewed in profile, the brows should barely break the line of the top skull. Use thinning shears or curved shears in reverse to set the brow.

Notes:

Notes From The Grooming Table ©2016

Throat & Cheeks

The throat and cheek areas are clipped using blades ranging from a #10 to a #7F, used either with or against the grain. Use the natural cowlick line of the neck to be the guide to create the "U" or "V" shape of the throat. The lowest point will be about 3 fingers above the breast bone. The line that breaks the top skull and the cheeks is from the back corner of the eye straight back to the ear canal.

Beard & Goatee

The beard and goatee are minimal with this harsh coated type of terrier, with the goatee being a bit longer than the fur on the beard. The pattern line starts from just behind the eyes and runs on a diagonal to the back corners of the mouth. The goatee is formed by continuing the line forward on the lower jaw, one or two finger widths in from the back corner of the mouth. When viewed from the top down, no hair should fall outside the planes of the cheeks. If the dog has an overabundance of fur on the muzzle, lightly rake a medium guard comb forward over the top of the head, down the nose and along the sides. Feather the coat off to leave longer hair at the end of the muzzle. Leave all the length of coat on the goatee, leaving it to finish by hand if it needs to be shortened. Once the excessive fur is removed, refine the head with thinning shears to form the classic rectangular head. The blending line at the sides of the face should be invisible between the tight work on the cheeks and the longer coat on the beard. Blend heavily with thinning shears, but do not take out so much coat to give an hour glass shape to the head, removing the fill under the eyes. Double check your work by combing the coat up and away from the

muzzle, and then lay a comb on the cheeks, forming a straight line from the skull to the muzzle. Any fur that sticks out beyond the comb should be removed. Any hair inside the line should remain and be blended to create the rectangle shape.

Detail Finish

Application of bows and mild cologne is optional.

Grooming Tips

A light setting gel, mousse or texturing shampoo can add body to the leg coat, making it easier to scissor. Try spritzing unruly eyebrows while they are still damp with a styling spray. Work the product into the damp brows. Brush or comb the brows into place or dry them into the position you want them in the final trim.

Special Note

Harsh-coated terriers have a coat that will normally brush out quite easily, especially after they are clean.

Suggested Tools & Equipment

- Nail Trimmers
- Styptic Powder
- Ear Powder
- Ear Cleaning Solution
- Cotton Balls
- Hemostat
- Clippers
- Slicker Brush
- Greyhound Comb
- Pumice Stone
- Carding Tools
- Stripping Knives
- Straight Shears
- Curved Shears
- Small Detailing Shears
- Thinning Shears
- Dematting Tools

Common Blade Options:

- #40, #15, #10
- #7F, #5F, #4F
- Variety of Guard Combs

Notes:

Notes *from your* Grooming Table

West Highland White Terrier   TERRIER   WIRE COATED

Breed Facts & Characteristics

Country of Origin: Scotland

Height at Shoulder: 10"–11"

Coat Length/Type: Hard/Wiry

Color: White only.

Correct grooming procedure:

Hand-Strip

Common pet grooming practices:

Clipper-Trim

General Description

This is a resilient little dog with great strength and agility. The top section shows off a toned body while the lower section is feathered. The head is round in shape, accentuated by dark, piercing eyes and small erect ears that peek out above the coat on top of the head. The expression is piercing, full of purpose and vigor.

-The Goal-
Everything about this breed is compact and tailored. The muscular body is accentuated by the groom. The head is full and round with the eyes and nose in the center of the head piece. Pattern lines on the body are invisible.

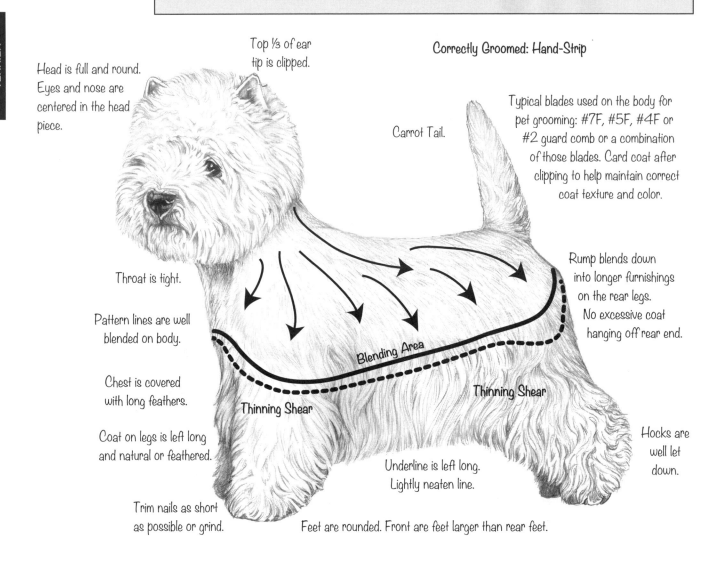

Head is full and round. Eyes and nose are centered in the head piece.

Top ⅓ of ear tip is clipped.

Correctly Groomed: Hand-Strip

Carrot Tail.

Typical blades used on the body for pet grooming: #7F, #5F, #4F or #2 guard comb or a combination of those blades. Card coat after clipping to help maintain correct coat texture and color.

Throat is tight.

Pattern lines are well blended on body.

Chest is covered with long feathers.

Coat on legs is left long and natural or feathered.

Trim nails as short as possible or grind.

Blending Area

Thinning Shear

Thinning Shear

Rump blends down into longer furnishings on the rear legs. No excessive coat hanging off rear end.

Hocks are well let down.

Underline is left long. Lightly neaten line.

Feet are rounded. Front are feet larger than rear feet.

Grooming Procedures & Recommendations

See page 76 for
Bathing & Drying Instructions

Frequency
Bathe once a week to once every 12 weeks.

Pre-Work
Trim or grind nails at least every four to six weeks to maintain a healthy foot structure. Swab the ears clean with a mild ear cleaning solution. Prior to bathing, quickly go over the entire body with a high-velocity dryer to help lift dirt and dander away from the skin and to loosen any shedding coat. *Card and hand-strip dog prior to bathing and drying.*

Done to breed standard, the coat is hand-stripped to promote healthy skin tone, proper coat texture and rich color. Many pet owners choose to clipper-cut their pet dog. This practice destroys the correct harsh coat texture on most dogs and dilutes the color on salt-and-pepper dogs. However, it is an economical way to keep the pet looking like the breed standard. Finding a stylist who is willing to commit the time and energy to hand-strip some breeds can be difficult. Plus, many pet owners are not willing to pay for this highly skilled service.

Pattern Lines in General
The correct coat is hand-stripped. For either hand-stripped or clipper-cut pet dogs, the general pattern, based on the bone and muscle structure, is the same. After the final trim, all pattern lines should be invisible. If clipping at the transition points, feather off with the clippers in a smooth and steady fashion. If the pattern line is still visible after clipping, use thinning shears to blend the line. The head is full and round.

Clipper-Cutting
Blades ranging from a #10 to a #4F are commonly used to set the pattern on the body as an alternative to hand-stripping techniques. They can be used with the grain or, with longer blades, against the grain. Keep in mind, the shorter the trim on the body pattern, the more difficult it is to blend the pattern later into the longer furnishings. A longer cut also allows you to mold the coat a bit and apply carding techniques to retain some of the proper coat texture. Carding also will remove minor tracks commonly left after clipping. Longer cutting blades are preferred.

Body Pattern
The transitional areas will be a half inch to more than an inch in width depending on the area and the conformation of the dog. At the front of the dog, the pattern starts just above the breast bone and drops on a diagonal line to almost the bottom of the shoulder muscle. The pattern line travels down the side of the dog, at the widest arc of the ribs towards the flank where it may rise slightly. As the pattern line rises over the flank, it drops into a very shallow "U" shape to expose the upper thigh muscle. The "U" shape rises to just below the base of the tail, leaving the longer furnishings at the back of the thigh. At the blending areas, bulk thin or top thin with thinning shears so the main body area blends invisibly with the long furnishings. After clipping, card the coat to promote proper coat growth and retain some of the rich color and harsh-coat texture.

Undercarriage
The furnishings on the underside of the dog are left in a natural state or layered to look long and natural depending on the extent of the feathering. The coat on the undercarriage may be trimmed or neatened to clear the ground or to

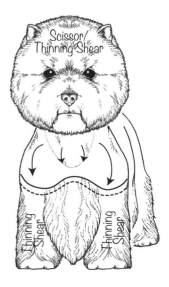

The head is round and full with eyes and nose at the center. From the front and rear, the legs drop in straight, parallel lines from well toned shoulders and thighs. When setting the pattern, use the turn of the muscles to set the lines. Under the tail is short and clean with a drape of longer fur covering the back of the thighs. Leg furnishings are longer than the body coat. Tail is carrot shaped and very short on the back side.

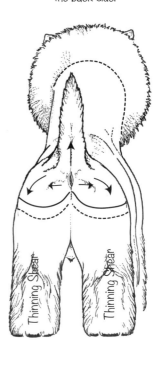

Their expression is friendly, inquisitive and bold. Head is full and round. The ears are small, triangular and erect. The eyes are deep set. When viewed from the front, the eyes and nose are at the center of a well balanced circle. When finished, the head is well blended and soft.

Pull the hair up, trimming the coat on the top of the head, to just below level with the ear tips using thinning shears.

Comb the fur forward, over the brows. With curved shears in reverse, trim a frame around the eye area. The line is beveled with a deep set eye. Finish by softening the line with thinning shears.

Trim the stop area lightly with thinning shears before framing the eye area.

The lower line of the head completes the circle that puts the eyes and nose at the center of the head piece when looking at the pet from the front. The lower line parallels the jaw bone. Comb all the coat down and trim with shears in a curved line running from the nose all the way up to behind the occiput. Soften the line with thinning shears to complete the head piece.

The top ⅓ of the ear tip is clipped. Use a # 10 or #15 blade on the outside of the ear. A #40 blade can be used on the inside of the ear leather with a very light touch. Edge the ear with small detailing shears.

Ear Safety Tip: Remember, always keep the tips of the shears towards the tips of the ears when edging for safety.

The line at the back of the skull is about an inch beyond the occiput.

The throat is clipped with a blade slightly shorter than that used on the body, in a "U" shape, about 2–3 finger widths from the breast bone.

add a slight rise under the last rib. If the dog is sparsely furnished, tidy the undercarriage so it looks natural. The pattern line is well blended and invisible.

Tail
Shape the tail so it looks like a thick carrot. There will be more coat on the sides and top of the tail than on the underside. When trimming the sanitary area under the tail, continue about an inch up the back side of the tail and leave the rest to do by hand. Trim off all the excessive length at the tip by running your hand down the tail, thumb towards the tip, and stopping when you can feel the end of the tail bone under your thumb. With your fingers protecting the tip of the tail, trim off the long fur. Fluff the coat and shape the tail, thicker at the base, tapering to the tip. When the tail is held upright, there should be no dip right in front of the tail where it meets the back. The sides should blend smoothly into the rump. The back of the tail is trimmed very close, but not so close so that it is bald. Use a thinning shear or a #7F in this area.

Hindquarters
The hindquarters should be strong and powerful. When clipping this area, expose the thigh muscle with the same blade used on the body.

Start to feather off with the blade where the muscle bulges, creating a shallow "U" shape that rises back up to the tail area. Using guard combs can facilitate blending at the transition line. The longer feathering may be left long and natural or shortened. To shorten the furnishings, feather the coat with thinning shears working with the lay of the coat or by skimming the fur with a guard comb after it has been lightly fluffed. At the blending line, the transition should be invisible when the trim is finished. Blend with thinning shears by bulk thinning or top thinning if necessary.

Front Legs
The pattern line at the shoulder is about 1 or 2 fingers above the top of the elbow, at the point where the muscle begins to turn under. The coat at the transition line will be very short and taper into the longer leg furnishings. This can be accomplished by feathering off at the blending point with the same blade used on the body or switching to a guard comb and blending off at the transition point. As on the rear legs, the feathering on the front legs may be left long and natural or shortened. To shorten the furnishings, feather the coat with thinning shears, working with the lay of the coat or by skimming the fur with a guard comb after it has been lightly fluffed. At the blending line, the transition should be invisible when the trim is finished. Blend with thinning shears by bulk thinning or top thinning if necessary.

Feet
The front feet are larger than the rear feet, with thick pads and strong nails which can be slightly exposed. The feet are trimmed very close. The feet should point straight ahead, but minor toeing out is acceptable on the front feet. Trim the feet round by first boxing them into the shape of a box while the

dog is standing in a natural, square position. With the dog's feet firmly planted on the table, remove the sharp corners of the box and round the feet facing straight forward. Bevel the coat slightly. If detailing the feet with the foot off the tabletop, always use a small pair of shears to minimize the risk of accidentally cutting the pads.

Throat & Chest
Blades ranging from a #10 to #7F, with or against the grain, based on skin sensitivity, are common in the throat area. The throat is clipped with the same blade/guard comb as on the body or slightly shorter. Clip only the throat area, leaving the clean line between the head piece and the throat. Follow the natural cowlick line that runs from the base of the ears in a "V" shape toward

the base of the neck. The blending point begins about 3 or 4 fingers above the breast bone and drops to just below the turn of the muscle at the elbow/shoulder, creating a "W" shape when viewed straight on. When viewed in profile, the neck into the chest should be straight without a predominant forechest. When blending the chest, be aware of the heavy cowlicks in the area. If a clipper is run over this area to create the flat chest, the result will be severe holes in the chest area. It is very easy to create two bald patches on either side of the chest, just inside the front legs. Many stylists prefer to blend the chest area by hand with thinning shears or shears. When finished in this area, double check your work to be sure the neck, chest and front legs drop down in a straight line when viewed in profile.

The eyes and the nose are at the center of the head piece.

Grooming Procedures & Recommendations

Head

When viewed from the front, the Westie head is full and round. The fur on a pet dog normally does not have the harsh texture required to frame the face the way a hand-stripped coat does, although the same general rules apply. The coat should look very natural, with no scissor marks. The eyes and nose are at the center of the head piece. With thinning shears, clear the excessive hair at the inside corners of the eyes, but leave the longer fur in the stop area. There is a small cowlick just above the inside corners of the eye. With thinning shears, lightly remove the coat from this cowlick, but leave all the longer hair over the brow. This will serve as a frame for the deep-set eyes. Standing to the side of the dog, rest your hand gently at the top of the head, fingers toward the eye area. Comb all the hair from the sides of the face up to the top of the skull, from the eye area to the ears, catching the long coat between your fingers. Once all the hair is combed up and held firmly between your fingers, find the median line of the skull, or the center groove. Draw the coat up directly above that line. With thinning shears, trim the coat to the length of the ear tips, trimming in a line just above your fingers. When you release the coat, the hair will feather beautifully over the top part of the head. Repeat the process with the hair from the center point of the skull and the occiput. With curved shears used in reverse, create a deep-set arch over the eyes to frame them. Buffer the line with thinning shears to soften it once the shape has been set. Comb the fur in an outward and downward fashion out over the nose. Neaten with thinning shears on a diagonal line that parallels the end of the muzzle, leaving at least an inch or two of hair. Looking from the side, comb the coat down over the muzzle and cheeks. Trim the lower jaw line to balance with the round head piece, keeping the nose and eyes at the center of the circle. Neaten the neck area with thinning shears so that the longer fur of the head piece is even but very natural looking. Edge the ear tips with small detailing shears, keeping the tips of the shears towards the tips of the ears for safety. Finish by reviewing the outline, combing all the hair up and out, allowing it to drop in a natural manner. Trim any long hair that falls outside the lines of a natural, neat head style with deep set eyes.

Ears

The top third of the ear tips are clipped with a close blade. It is common to use a #10 or #15 blade on the outside of the ear leather and a #40 on the inside. When working with close blades in this delicate area, always work from the base or center of the ear out toward the edge. Gently brace the ear with your fingers to clip over it. To finish, use small detailing shears to trim around the outside edge of the ear tip, keeping the tips of the shears toward the tip of the ears for safety.

Detail Finish

Application of bows and mild cologne is optional.

Grooming Tips

A light setting gel, mousse or texturing shampoo can add body to the head and/or leg coat, making it easier to trim and style.

Special Notes

- Harsh-coated terriers have a coat that will normally brush out quite easily, especially after they are clean.
- Shortening the leg furnishings will yield a tighter look and assist with easier maintenance.

Suggested Tools & Equipment

- Nail Trimmers
- Styptic Powder
- Ear Powder
- Ear Cleaning Solution
- Cotton Balls
- Hemostat
- Clippers
- Slicker Brush
- Greyhound Comb
- Pumice Stone
- Carding Tools
- Stripping Knives
- Straight Shears
- Curved Shears
- Small Detailing Shears
- Thinning Shears
- Dematting Tools

Common Blade Options:

- #40, #15, #10
- #7F, #5F, #4F
- Variety of Guard Combs

Notes:

Notes from your Grooming Table

Dogs in the Toy Group were developed to be human companions. All of them are small in stature, allowing them to easily share a lap or a bed with their owners. Their small size also makes them fit in well with homes of limited size, city dwellers or the elderly. Their love of attention serves them well both inside and outside their homes. They are exceptionally loyal and cuddly.

Affenpinscher

Breed Facts & Characteristics

Country of Origin: Central Europe

Height at Shoulder: 9.5"–11½"

Coat Length/Type: Moderate/Wiry

Color: Black, black and tan, all shades of gray and red.

Correct grooming procedure:

Hand-Strip

Common pet grooming practices:

Clipper-Trim

General Description

This breed, done to breed standard, has a coat that is hand-stripped. For most Toy breeds, the primary emphasis is on the head. The body is compact, sturdy and squarely built. The pattern is based on basic bone and muscle structure. For pet dogs, whether hand-stripped or clipper-cut, the pattern is the same.

-The Goal-
This is a small, squarely built dog with a harsh, rough coat that is to be left about one inch in length on most of the dog with only minor neatening to accentuate the it's form.

Correctly Groomed: Hand-Stripped

Typical blades used on the body for pet grooming: #7F, #5F, #4F, short to medium guard combs, or a combination of those blades. Card coat after clipping to help maintain correct coat texture and color.

Ears are clipped very close.

Head is full and round: "monkey like."

Clear stop area to expose eyes.

On mature dogs, the neck coat will form a cape of longer hair.

Trim back side of tail and rear legs shorter to create a well balanced, square outline.

Neaten muzzle area to create a well balanced, round head style.

Blending Area

Lightly clip sanitary areas: Under tail and tummy if needed with a #10.

Rear legs have moderate angulation.

Tidy leg coat to about 1" in length to form straight columns.

Neaten undercarriage line lightly.

Neaten hocks.

Trim nails as short as possible or grind.

Shave pads and scissor feet round.

Notes From The Grooming Table ©2016   408

TOY

Grooming Procedures & Recommendations

**See page 76 for
Bathing & Drying Instructions**

Frequency

Bathe once a week to once every 12 weeks.

Pre-Work

Trim or grind nails at least every four to six weeks to maintain a healthy foot structure. Swab the ears clean with a mild ear cleaning solution. Prior to bathing, quickly go over the entire body with a high-velocity dryer to help lift dirt and dander away from the skin and to loosen any shedding coat. ***Card and hand-strip dog prior to bathing and drying.***

Carding

Carding is a natural technique in which the soft, downy undercoat is pulled from the dog's body. Typical tools used with this technique are: a pumice stone; a fine-toothed stripping knife that is pulled through the coat; an undercoat rake; or a fine blade, such as a #40, held between the fingers and pulled through the coat. Carding can be done before or after bathing and drying. Removal of the soft undercoat allows the topcoat to lie closer to the natural outline of the dog and accentuate the dog's structure. It also promotes profuse harsh outer coat, creates a rich coat color and protects the skin.

Hand-Stripping

Hand-stripping is a technique in which the outer guard coat is plucked from the dog's skin. This procedure helps retain the proper coat texture and rich color of the breed. During certain times of the year, the coat is easier to pull out. When the coat easily comes out, it is called a "blowing coat" or "blown coat." Ideally, hand-stripping should correspond with the dog's natural cycle, based on the environment and its hormonal levels. Using your fingers, a carding tool or a stripping knife, pull out a few hairs at a time to shape the coat, accentuating

the natural outline of the dog. Work methodically, pulling small amounts of coat at a time, always working in the direction of the coat growth. Proper hand-stripping removes hair with a gentle momentum and rhythm, not brute force, which is uncomfortable for both groomer and pet. The wrist stays locked in a neutral position while the rhythmic movement stems from the shoulder, not the wrist or elbow. In general, the main body coat is easy to remove. Most pets do not mind the plucking process. The cheeks, throat and private areas may be more sensitive, requiring thinning shears or clippers. On the body, the coat is left between a half inch to one and a half inches long, the head is more sculpted and shaped. The coats always should appear very natural, never clipped or heavily trimmed. On some coats, a light application of chalk or powder before the bath will allow a better grip and make plucking and stripping much easier.

Body

If clipper-cut in a pet style, typical blades range from a #7F, #5F, #4F to short to medium guard combs, to set the bulk of the body work. Follow the direction of the natural coat growth. The Affenpinscher has longer fur left over the back of the neck, almost forming a short cape. This cape blends a full head style with the neck and then into the body. Clip down the back, over the ribs and the top of the thighs. At the transition points, feather off with the clippers in a smooth and steady fashion. If the pattern line still is visible after clipping, use thinning shears to blend the line. After clipping, card the clipped areas to promote proper coat growth and retain some of the rich color and harsh coat texture. Carding also will help remove minor clip tracks left in the coat. The topline should be level. The pattern lines start at the turn of the shoulder and continue to just above the elbow, return to the flank on a diagonal and then drop into the thigh region.

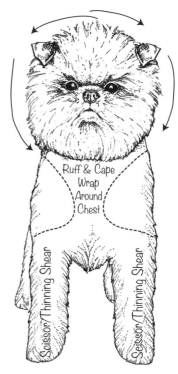

Round the head by hand-stripping or trimming with thinning shears. Expose ear tips. Clear stop area to show full, round eyes. Ruff wraps around neck to form a cape. Legs are trimmed about the same length as the body but shaped by hand to hide minor conformational faults. The tail is trimmed to the same length as body and can be either docked or undocked.

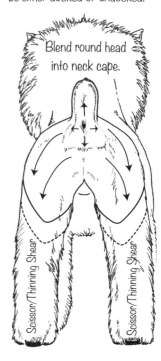

Blend round head into neck cape.

Ears are natural or cropped. In both cases, the fur on the entire ear is clipped very close, using a #10 or #15 blade on the outside of the leather and #40 on the inside. Edge ears with small detail finishing shears.

Clear the stop area with thinning shears or clippers to expose the round eye that looks straight forward.

On most dogs, the coat will be longer and fuller off the back of the skull, going down the back of the neck. Leave this fur to help create the full, round head and the "cape" that comes down the back of the neck, wrapping around the throat and blending into the chest.

Lightly shape the jaw line with thinning shears to create a neat but ragged appearance.

Coarse coat should stand off the face and head, serving as a frame to accentuate the round head and "monkey-like" expression, which is hallmark of this breed.

Brisket

The chest is deep and, when viewed in profile, the distance between the withers and chest and the length of the legs should be equal. There should be only enough fur left on the undercarriage of the dog to accentuate the chest depth and an athletic build. The pattern line is well blended and invisible.

Tail & Rear

The top of the tail is trimmed with the same blade as the body. The underside is clipped close, with blades ranging from #15 to a #7F, used with or against the grain based on the dog's skin sensitivity. This same blade work is continued around the rectum and on the inner side of the cowlick lines, down the backside of the thighs.

Front Legs

The coat on the legs will be a bit longer than on the body and stands off the leg to create straight columns. The front legs drop straight down from the body. The pattern line at the shoulder is about 1 finger width above the top of the elbow, at the point where the muscle begins to turn under. The coat at the transition line will be very short, and taper into the longer leg furnishings. This can be accomplished by feathering off at the blending point with the clipper, or by hand with thinning shears. Many stylists prefer to shape the legs by hand with shears. Other methods of blending off at the top of the leg include an attachment comb, such as a short guard comb, followed by hand-scissoring and blending with thinning shears. In the final trim, the legs should form two parallel columns descending from the elbow into tight, round feet. The coat at the back of the elbow is very short and falls straight down off the back of the leg toward the ground.

Grooming Procedures & Recommendations

Hindquarters

The hindquarters should appear sturdy. When clipping this area, expose the thigh muscle with the same blade used on the body. Start to skim off the blade work where the muscle starts to turn under on a diagonal line from the flank region to about 2 fingers above the hock. The blending should be invisible when the trim is finished. Blend with thinning shears if necessary. The stifle area should have enough furnishings left to give the legs substance and angulation. The longest coat on the legs can range from only a fraction of an inch to 1.5 inches, depending on the dog. Shape the longer fur with shears after the clipper work is complete. When viewed from the rear, the rear legs should form two parallel lines to the ground. Viewed from the side, there should be moderate angulation between the point of rump, stifle and hock area.

Feet

The feet are small for this size dog. Both the front and rear feet are compact with well-arched toes. To show off these traits, the feet are trimmed very close to the edge of the foot and some nail is routinely exposed. Pads may be trimmed with blades ranging from #10 to a #40. To detail the feet, always use a small pair of detailing shears to minimize the risk of accidentally cutting the pads. If a very close cutting blade is used to trim the pads, use a firm brush to brush the longer coat over the outer edges of the foot and trim that fur at the same time the pads are clipped.

Throat & Chest

Blending off from the head, the back of the neck has longer coat that forms the ruff. The ruff wraps around the neck into the throat and then down into the chest creating a "cape." Hand-strip this area or blend it by hand with thinning shears. All transition areas should be invisible, blending into the tighter body coat. When finished in this area, double-check your work to be sure the neck, chest and cape are in overall balance with the dog. It should look proud with all areas well blended and very natural looking.

Undercarriage

The groin is normally trimmed close with a #10 or #15 blade to a point near the navel and a short distance down the inside of the thigh. From the navel forward, the undercarriage has little coat in the finished trim. Trim lightly with shears or thinning shears depending on the amount of coat.

The Head in General

The skull is round with eyes that are large, round and look straight forward, in a "monkey-like" fashion. The jaw is slightly undershot and the nose very short with a deep stop. The coat serves as a frame about the head to accentuate these points.

Stop

The eyes are very deep-set and fully exposed. Clear the stop area of long hair, either with thinning shears or a close clipper blade such as a #10 or #15. Be very cautious of the eye while trimming this area.

Ears

Ears may be cropped or uncropped. In either case, the entire ear is clipped close, working out from the center of the ear to the edges. For the outside of the leather, a # 10 or #15 blade is common. For the inside, a surgical length, such as a #40, gets the ear really clean. Finish by edging the ear with small detailing shears, keeping the tip of the shear, towards the tip of the ear.

Muzzle

The head should be full and round in shape. Neaten the muzzle and jaw line to complete the circular frame that outlines the headpiece, keeping it in balance with the rest of the dog.

Suggested Tools & Equipment

- Nail Trimmers
- Styptic Powder
- Ear Powder
- Ear Cleaning Solution
- Cotton Balls
- Hemostat
- Clippers
- Slicker Brush
- Greyhound Comb
- Pumice Stone
- Carding Tools
- Stripping Knives
- Straight Shears
- Curved Shears
- Small Detailing Shears
- Thinning Shears
- Dematting Tools

Common Blade Options:
- #40, #15, #10
- #7F, #5F, #4F
- Variety of Guard Combs

Top of Head

The hair about the top of the head is not as coarse as on the body. It stands away from the skull and frames the monkey-like expression. The hair should be a little over an inch long. At the occiput, or back of the skull, the longer hair blends with the neck coat to create a cape of fur.

Special Note

The Affenpinscher can have either cropped or uncropped ears. They can have a docked or undocked tail.

Notes From The Grooming Table ©2016

Breed Facts & Characteristics

Country of Origin: Belgium

Height at Shoulder: 7"–9"

Coat Length/Type: Moderate/Wiry

Color: Reds, black and tan, black or a combination of red and black hairs over the body with a black mask on the face. Lighter colored dogs may have a dark mask.

Correct grooming procedure:
Hand-Strip

Common pet grooming practices:
Clipper-Trim

General Description
This breed, done to breed standard, has a coat that is hand-stripped. For most Toy breeds, the primary emphasis is on the head. The body is compact, sturdy and squarely built. The pattern is based on basic bone and muscle structure. For pet dogs, whether hand-stripped or clipper-cut, the pattern is the same.

If clipping, typical blades used on the body for pet grooming: #7F, #5F, #4F, short to medium guard combs, or a combination of those blades. Card coat after clipping to help maintain correct coat texture and color.

-The Goal-
Rough coated variety has a neat body outline. The facial expression is almost "human-like." Body coat should be short, hard and very close fitting to the body. Hand-stripping is the only way to retain this proper coat texture.

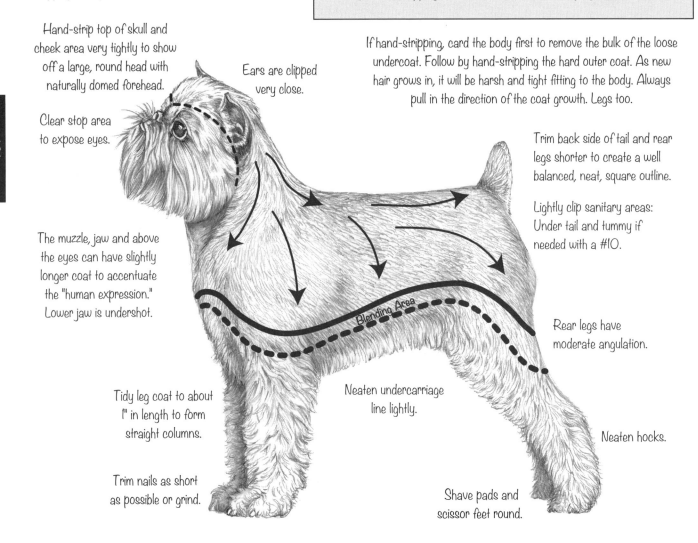

Hand-strip top of skull and cheek area very tightly to show off a large, round head with naturally domed forehead.

Ears are clipped very close.

Clear stop area to expose eyes.

If hand-stripping, card the body first to remove the bulk of the loose undercoat. Follow by hand-stripping the hard outer coat. As new hair grows in, it will be harsh and tight fitting to the body. Always pull in the direction of the coat growth. Legs too.

The muzzle, jaw and above the eyes can have slightly longer coat to accentuate the "human expression." Lower jaw is undershot.

Trim back side of tail and rear legs shorter to create a well balanced, neat, square outline.

Lightly clip sanitary areas: Under tail and tummy if needed with a #10.

Blending Area

Rear legs have moderate angulation.

Tidy leg coat to about 1" in length to form straight columns.

Neaten undercarriage line lightly.

Neaten hocks.

Trim nails as short as possible or grind.

Shave pads and scissor feet round.

Grooming Procedures & Recommendations

See page 76 for
Bathing & Drying Instructions

Frequency
Bathe once a week to once every
12 weeks.

Pre-Work
Trim or grind nails at least every four
to six weeks to maintain a healthy foot
structure. Swab the ears clean with a
mild ear cleaning solution. Prior to
bathing, quickly go over the entire
body with a high-velocity dryer to help
lift dirt and dander away from the skin
and to loosen any shedding coat. *Card
and hand-strip dog prior to bathing
and drying.*

Carding
Carding is a natural technique in which
the soft, downy undercoat is pulled
from the dog's body. Typical tools used
with this technique are: a pumice stone;
a fine-toothed stripping knife that is
pulled through the coat; an undercoat
rake; or a fine blade, such as a #40, held
between the fingers and pulled through
the coat. Carding can be done before or
after bathing and drying. Removal of the
soft undercoat allows the topcoat to lie
closer to the natural outline of the dog
and accentuate the dog's structure. It also
promotes profuse harsh outer coat, creates
a rich coat color and protects the skin.

Hand-Stripping
Hand-stripping is a technique in which
the outer guard coat is plucked from the
dog's skin. This procedure helps retain
the proper coat texture and rich color of
the breed. During certain times of the
year, the coat is easier to pull out. When
the coat easily comes out, it is called a
"blowing coat" or "blown coat." Ideally,
hand-stripping should correspond with
the dog's natural cycle, based on the
environment and its hormonal levels.
Using your fingers, a carding tool or a

stripping knife, pull out a few hairs at
a time to shape the coat, accentuating
the natural outline of the dog. Work
methodically, pulling small amounts of
coat at a time, always working in the
direction of the coat growth. Proper
hand-stripping removes hair with a gentle
momentum and rhythm, not brute
force, which is uncomfortable for both
groomer and pet. The wrist stays locked
in a neutral position while the rhythmic
movement stems from the shoulder, not
the wrist or elbow. In general, the main
body coat is easy to remove. Most pets
do not mind the plucking process. The
cheeks, throat and private areas may be
more sensitive, requiring thinning shears
or clippers. On the body, the coat is left
between a half inch to one and a half
inches long, the head is more sculpted
and shaped. The coats always should
appear very natural, never clipped or
heavily trimmed. On some coats, a light
application of chalk or powder before the
bath will allow a better grip and make
plucking and stripping much easier.

Body
If clipper-cut in a pet style, typical
blades range from a #7F, #5F, #4F to
short to medium guard combs, to set
the bulk of the body work. Follow the
direction of the natural coat growth,
starting just behind the base of the skull.
Clip down the back, around the neck,
over the ribs and the top of the thighs.
At the transition points, feather off with
the clippers in a smooth and steady
fashion. If the pattern line still is visible
after clipping, use thinning shears to
blend the line. After clipping, card the
clipped areas to promote proper coat
growth and retain some of the rich color
and harsh coat texture. Carding also
will help remove minor clip tracks left
in the coat. The topline should be level.
The pattern lines start at the turn of the
shoulder and continue to just above the
elbow, return to the flank on a diagonal
and then drop into the thigh region.

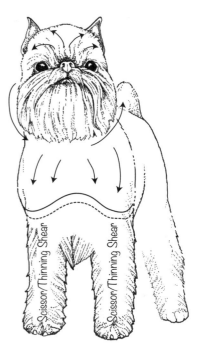

The top of the round head is trimmed close,
showing off a deep stop and domed skull.
Ears are trimmed very close. Clear stop area
to show full, round eyes. The lower jaw is
undershot. Shape the entire lower jaw into a
rounded fashion to show off this unique trait
for this breed. Legs are trimmed about the
same length as the body but shaped by hand
to hide minor conformational faults. The tail
is trimmed to the same length as body.

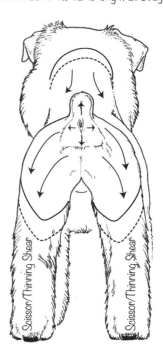

Notes From The Grooming Table ©2016

Ears are natural or cropped. In both cases, the fur on the entire ear is clipped very close, using a #10 or #15 blade on the outside of the leather and #40 on the inside. Edge ears with small detail finishing shears.

The top skull is covered with short coat conforming to the natural roundness of the skull. Use a #7F, #5F, or a 4F on the top skull or hand-strip the top of the head close. Due to the deep stop, rounded skull and forward facing eyes, only a tiny bit of added coat is needed to form the eyebrows. Use the eye socket rim to create the brows.

Clear the stop area with thinning shears or clippers to expose the large, round eyes that look straight forward.

The coat on the jaw is left longer. Lightly shape the jaw line with thinning shears into a curved shape. The jaw on this breed must be undershot.

The cheeks and throat are smooth and clean. Blades ranging from a #10 to a #15, used with or against the grain, are common in pet styling.

The natural cowlick line assists with setting the throat area. Create a soft "V" or "U" shape coming about 2 finger widths above the breast bone.

TOY

Brisket
The chest is deep and, when viewed in profile, the distance between the withers and chest and the length of the legs should be equal. There should be only enough fur left on the undercarriage of the dog to accentuate the chest depth and an athletic build. The pattern line is well blended and invisible.

Tail & Rear
The top of the tail is trimmed with the same blade as the body. The underside is clipped close, with blades ranging from #15 to a #7F, used with or against the grain based on the dog's skin sensitivity. This same blade work is continued around the rectum and on the inner side of the cowlick lines, down the backside of the thighs.

Front Legs
The coat on the legs will be a bit longer than on the body and stand off the leg to create straight columns. The front legs drop straight down from the body. The pattern line at the shoulder is about 1 finger width above the top of the elbow, at the point where the muscle begins to turn under. The coat at the transition line will be very short, and taper into the longer leg furnishings. This can be accomplished by feathering off at the blending point with the clipper, or by hand with thinning shears. Many stylists prefer to shape the legs by hand with shears. Other methods of blending off at the top of the leg include an attachment comb, such as a #2 guard comb, followed by hand-scissoring and

blending with thinning shears. In the final trim, the legs should form two parallel columns descending from the elbow into tight, round feet. The coat at the back of the elbow is very short and falls straight down off the back of the leg toward the ground.

Hindquarters
The hindquarters should appear sturdy. When clipping this area, expose the thigh muscle with the same blade used on the body. Start to feather off the blade work where the muscle starts to turn under on a diagonal line from the flank region to about 2 fingers above the hock. The blending should be invisible when the trim is finished. Blend with thinning shears if necessary.

Grooming Procedures & Recommendations

The stifle area should have enough furnishings left to give the legs substance and angulation. The longest coat on the legs can range from only a fraction of an inch to 1.5 inches, depending on the dog. Shape the longer fur with shears after the clipper work is complete. When viewed from the rear, the rear legs should form two parallel lines to the ground. Viewed from the side, there should be moderate angulation between the point of rump, stifle and hock area.

Feet
The feet are small for this size dog. Both the front and rear feet are compact with well-arched toes. To show off these traits, the feet are trimmed very close to the edge of the foot and some nail is routinely exposed. Pads may be trimmed with blades ranging from #10 to a #40. To detail the feet, always use a small pair of detailing shears to minimize the risk of accidentally cutting the pads. If a very close cutting blade is used to trim the pads, use a firm brush to brush the longer coat over the outer edges of the foot and trim that fur at the same time the pads are clipped.

Throat & Chest
Blades ranging from #10 to #7F, with or against the grain based on the sensitivity of the dog's skin, are common in the throat area. Follow the natural colic line that runs in a "V" shape from the base of the ears toward the base of the neck. The chest drops straight off from the throat and neck area. The pattern line for the chest and front legs forms an upside down "W" just below the turn of the muscle at the elbow/shoulder. When viewed in profile, the neck into the chest should be straight without a predominant forechest. When blending the chest, be aware of the natural cowlicks found in this area. It is very easy to bald a patch on either side of the chest, just inside the front legs. Many stylists prefer to blend this area by hand

with thinning shears or shears. When finished in this area, double-check your work to be sure the neck, chest and front legs drop down in a straight line when viewed in profile.

Undercarriage
The groin is normally trimmed close with a #10 or #15 blade to a point near the navel and a short distance down the inside of the thigh. From the navel forward, the undercarriage has little coat in the finished trim. Trim lightly with shears or thinning shears depending on the amount of coat.

The Head in General
The skull is round with eyes that are large, round and look straight forward, almost in a human fashion. Use a #7F, #5F, or a 4F on the top skull or hand-strip the top of the head close. The jaw is slightly undershot and the nose very short with a deep stop. The coat serves as a frame about the head to accentuate these points.

Stop
The eyes are very deep-set and fully exposed. Clear the stop area of long hair, either with thinning shears or a close clipper blade such as a #10 or #15. Be very cautious of the eye while trimming this area.

Ears
May be cropped or uncropped. In either case, the entire ear is clipped close, working out from the center of the ear to the edges. For the outside of the leather, a #10 or #15 blade is common. For the inside, a surgical length, such as a #40, gets the ear really clean. Finish by edging the ear with small detailing shears, keeping the tip of the shear, towards the tip of the ear.

Muzzle
The head should be full and round in shape. Neaten the muzzle and jaw line to complete the circular frame that

outlines the headpiece, keeping it in balance with the rest of the dog.

Top of Head
For the Brussels Griffon, the top of the head is smooth and conforms to the shape of the skull. Above the eyes, the coat is left fuller, creating a very deep-set eye and an intelligent expression, but not so much coat as to give the dog "eyebrows." The back of the head blends smoothly into the neck.

Special Notes
- The Brussels Griffon has two coat types, smooth and rough. Other than the coat type, the two dogs are the same.
- The Brussels can have either cropped or uncropped ears.

Suggested Tools & Equipment

- Nail Trimmers
- Styptic Powder
- Ear Powder
- Ear Cleaning Solution
- Cotton Balls
- Hemostat
- Clippers
- Slicker Brush
- Greyhound Comb
- Pumice Stone
- Carding Tools
- Stripping Knives
- Straight Shears
- Curved Shears
- Small Detailing Shears
- Thinning Shears
- Dematting Tools

Common Blade Options:
- #40, #15, #10
- #7F, #5F, #4F
- Variety of Guard Combs

Breed Facts & Characteristics

Country of Origin: England

Height at Shoulder: 12"–13"

Coat Length/Type: Combination/Silky

Color: Rich chestnut with white. Black and tan. Tricolor with base color of white with black patches and tan points. Solid deep rich red. Can have a small white patch on chest.

Correct grooming procedure:
Bathe & Brush Out/Card

Common pet grooming practices:
Bathe & Brush Out/Card

-The Goal-
Coat should be mat free shiny, light and airy. The coat should bounce and float with the dog as it moves.

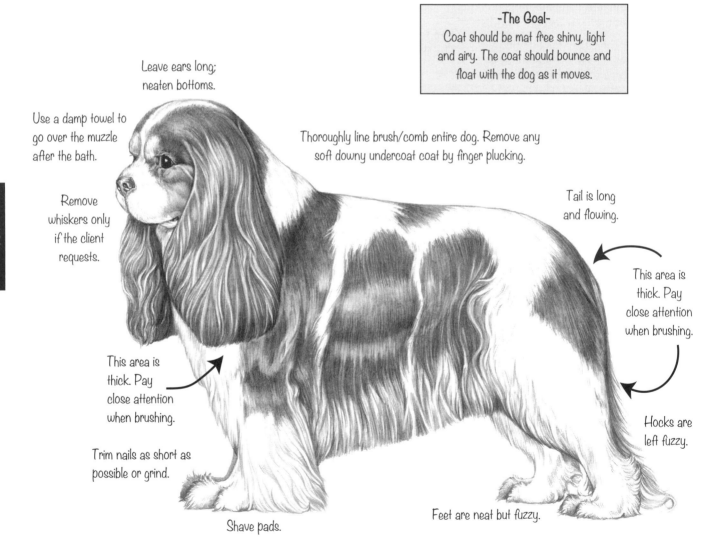

Leave ears long; neaten bottoms.

Use a damp towel to go over the muzzle after the bath.

Remove whiskers only if the client requests.

Thoroughly line brush/comb entire dog. Remove any soft downy undercoat coat by finger plucking.

Tail is long and flowing.

This area is thick. Pay close attention when brushing.

This area is thick. Pay close attention when brushing.

Hocks are left fuzzy.

Trim nails as short as possible or grind.

Shave pads.

Feet are neat but fuzzy.

TOY

Grooming Procedures & Recommendations

See page 68 for
Bathing & Drying Instructions

Frequency
Bathe once a week to once every 12 weeks.

Pre-Work
Trim or grind nails every four to six weeks to maintain a healthy foot structure. Clean the ears by swabbing with a mild ear cleaning solution. Use a rubber curry, shedding blade, undercoat rake, pumice stone, carding tool, fine stripping knife or natural bristle brush to loosen skin dander and remove loose coat. Use a high-velocity dryer over the coat to quickly and effectively lift dirt and debris away from the skin and loosen coat. Brush out or remove any matting found in the long-coated areas. If the tangles are loose enough so water can fully penetrate the area, remove them after bathing and drying. If water cannot penetrate, remove the mat or tangle prior to bathing.

Brushing
Line brush, working in sections until the dog is entirely tangle-free and all loose coat is removed. When finished, there should be little, if any, fur still being removed with a firm slicker brush. Double-check the work with a wide-toothed comb and your hands. Go over the entire body, feeling for any inconsistencies in the density levels of the coat. If an area seems moist to the touch or fuller than the rest of the coat, rework the area with the appropriate tool. Mats, tangles and excessive coat are easily trapped in the following areas: behind the ears, around the ruff, the thigh area, the undercarriage and the tail. Give extra attention to these areas before finishing the groom.

Card
If a dog has an abundance of loose undercoat, card the areas with a carding tool. Common tools can be a fine stripping knife, undercoat rake, a pumice stone, or a #40 blade held between your fingers. Any carding tool should be pulled over the body, working in the direction of the coat growth. This will remove the soft, downy undercoat, allowing the guard coat to conform more closely to the natural outline of the body. It will also aid in the removal of loose, shedding coat, a seasonal problem for many pet owners.

Feet & Hocks
Trim the pads with a close blade ranging from a #15 to a #40. Use a very light touch to clean the pads of long hair.

Detail Finish
Edge the ears lightly with thinning shears to neaten and keep a natural look. Hand pluck any long wispy, flyaway hair from around the ears. Removal of whiskers on the muzzle is optional based on client preference. Finish with a fine mist of coat polish on the body coat for added shine. Application of bows and mild cologne is optional.

Special Note
This is one of the few breeds that does not have the top of the foot heavily neatened, nor the hock neatly tidied up, as with other breeds. In the conformation ring, these two areas are left in a very natural state with only minor neatening. The hair on the top of the foot and between the toes is left longer. The outer perimeter can be lightly shaped into an oval with shears or thinning shears. The pads are clipped close.

Suggested Tools & Equipment

- Nail Trimmers
- Styptic Powder
- Ear Cleaning Solution
- Cotton Balls
- Clippers
- #40 and #15 Blades for Pads
- #4F for Feet & Hocks (optional)
- Slicker Brush
- Greyhound Comb
- Rubber Curry
- Carding Tools
- De-Shedding Tools
- Small Detailing Shears
- Thinning Shears

Notes:

Notes From The Grooming Table ©2016

Breed Facts & Characteristics

Country of Origin: Mexico

Height at Shoulder: 5"–6"

Coat Length/Type: Combination/Silky

Color: All colors.

Correct grooming procedure:
Bathe & Brush Out/Card

Common pet grooming practices:
Bathe & Brush Out/Card

-The Goal-
Coat should be mat free shiny, light and airy. The coat should bounce and float with the dog as it moves.

Edge ears lightly to neaten.

Thoroughly line brush/comb entire dog. Remove any soft downy undercoat coat by finger plucking.

Use a damp towel to go over the muzzle after the bath.

Remove whiskers only if the client requests.

This area is thick. Pay close attention when brushing.

Tail is long.

Hip area is thick. Pay close attention when brushing.

Trim nails as short as possible or grind.

Shave pads and neaten feet.

Neaten hocks.

TOY

Grooming Procedures & Recommendations

See page 68 for
Bathing & Drying Instructions

Frequency
Bathe once a week to once every 12 weeks.

Pre-Work
Trim or grind nails every four to six weeks to maintain a healthy foot structure. Clean the ears by swabbing with a mild ear cleaning solution. Use a rubber curry, shedding blade, undercoat rake, pumice stone, carding tool, fine stripping knife or natural bristle brush to loosen skin dander and remove loose coat. Use a high-velocity dryer over the coat to quickly and effectively lift dirt and debris away from the skin and loosen coat. Brush out or remove any matting found in the long-coated areas. If the tangles are loose enough so water can fully penetrate the area, remove them after bathing and drying. If water cannot penetrate, remove the mat or tangle prior to bathing.

Brushing
Line brush, working in sections until the dog is entirely tangle-free and all loose coat is removed. When finished, there should be little, if any, fur still being removed with a firm slicker brush. Double-check the work with a comb and your hands. Go over the entire body, feeling for any inconsistencies in the density levels of the coat. If an area seems moist to the touch or fuller than the rest of the coat, rework the area with the appropriate tool. Mats, tangles and excessive coat are easily trapped in the following areas: behind the ears, around the ruff, the thigh area, the undercarriage and the tail. Give extra attention to these areas before finishing the groom.

Carding
If a dog has an abundance of loose undercoat, card the areas with a carding tool. Common tools can be a fine stripping knife, undercoat rake, a pumice stone, or a #40 blade held between your fingers. Any carding tool should be pulled over the body, working in the direction of the coat growth. This will remove the soft, downy undercoat, allowing the guard coat to conform more closely to the natural outline of the body. It will also aid in the removal of loose, shedding coat, a seasonal problem for many pet owners.

Feet & Hocks
Trim the pads with a close blade ranging from a #15 to a #40. Use a very light touch to clean the pads of long hair. If there is long fur between the toes, back brush the fur so it stands up on top of and away from the foot. With thinning shears, trim the excess to create a neat and very natural looking foot. Tidy the outside edge of the foot, if needed, with small detailing shears. If the hocks have longer coat, trim lightly with thinning shears to show a neat, clean area. A #4F blade, used carefully in reverse, works well for trimming the tops of the feet and the hocks on some dogs.

Detail Finish
Edge the ears lightly with thinning shears to neaten and keep a natural look. Hand pluck any long wispy, flyaway hair from around the ears. Removal of whiskers on the muzzle is optional based on client preference. Finish with a fine mist of coat polish on the body coat for added shine. Application of bows and mild cologne is optional.

Suggested Tools & Equipment

- Nail Trimmers
- Styptic Powder
- Ear Cleaning Solution
- Cotton Balls
- Clippers
- #40 and #15 Blades for Pads
- #4F for Feet & Hocks (optional)
- Slicker Brush
- Greyhound Comb
- Rubber Curry
- Carding Tool
- De-Shedding Tools
- Small Detailing Shears
- Thinning Shears

Notes:

Notes From The Grooming Table ©2016

Chihuahua (Short Haired)

TOY   **SMOOTH COATED**

Breed Facts & Characteristics

Country of Origin: Mexico

Height at Shoulder: 5"–6"

Coat Length/Type: Short/Smooth

Color: All colors.

Correct grooming procedure:
Bathe & Curry Brush

Common pet grooming practices:
Bathe & Curry Brush

-The Goal-
The coat should be clean and fresh smelling, with the coat laying flat against the body. No shedding hair.

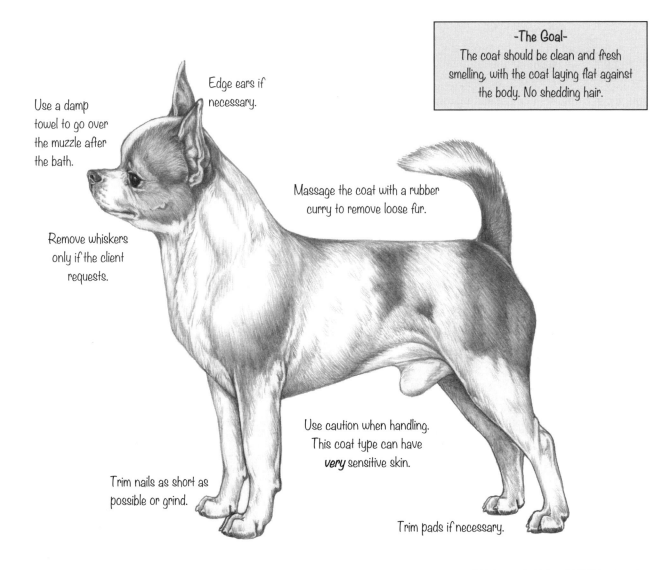

Edge ears if necessary.

Use a damp towel to go over the muzzle after the bath.

Massage the coat with a rubber curry to remove loose fur.

Remove whiskers only if the client requests.

Use caution when handling. This coat type can have **very** sensitive skin.

Trim nails as short as possible or grind.

Trim pads if necessary.

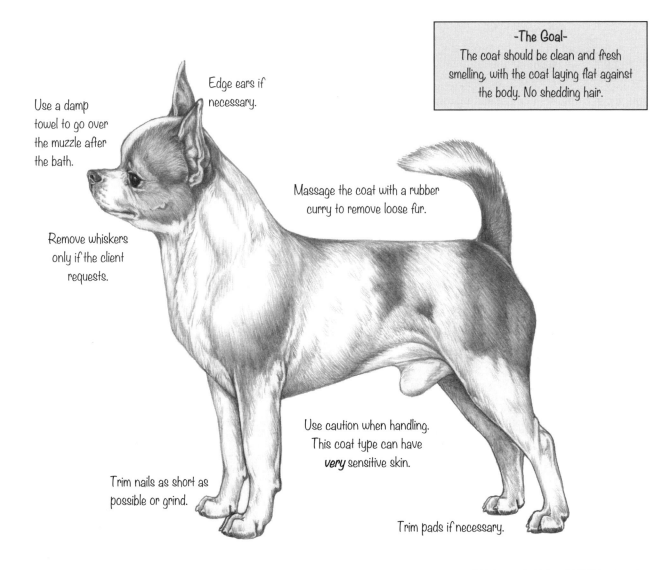

See page 66 for Bathing & Drying Instructions

Suggested Tools & Equipment

- Nail Trimmers
- Styptic Powder
- Ear Cleaning Solution
- Cotton Balls
- Clippers
- #40 or #15 Blade
- Rubber Curry
- Carding Tool
- Small Detailing Shears
- Thinning Shears

TOY

Notes *from your*
Grooming Table

Chinese Crested (Hairless)　　　TOY　　　HAIRLESS

Breed Facts & Characteristics

Country of Origin: China

Height at Shoulder: 11"–13"

Coat Length/Type: Long/Hairless

Color: All colors and combinations of color are acceptable.

Correct grooming procedure:
Brush Out/Close Trimming

Common pet grooming practices:
Clipper-Trim

General Description

The Chinese Crested has only a small amount of fur in some body areas. The hair on their heads is called the crest, the lower portions of their legs are called socks and the fur on the tail is called a plume. In some cases, the body needs some help to be totally hairless. For the show ring, a dog is usually shaved with a double-edged safety razor. The breed standard calls for the skin to be soft and smooth. For pet dogs, it is quite acceptable to clipper-cut these areas with a very close blade such as a #10 or #15, in reverse, over the pattern area.

-The Goal-
Coat should be mat- and tangle-free. The fur should be light and airy, moving freely with the dog as it moves. Bare skin should be hair free and smooth. Pattern lines clean and crisp.

Leave ears long or clipper clean with a close cutting blade.

Topknot is left loose.

Leave the mane long and natural on the back of the neck.

Clip body with a #10 or #15 blade in reverse, based on skin sensitivity.

Clip tail about ⅔ of the tail bone leaving plume on the end.

Clip muzzle, cheeks and throat close with a #10 or #15 blade in reverse based on skin sensitivity.

Clip legs down to just above hock and pastern. The socks should be equal in size and balanced, front to back. Round the feet. Shave the pads.

Trim nails as short as possible or grind.

TOY

See page 78 for Bathing & Drying Instructions

Frequency

Bathe once a week to once every 12 weeks.

Pre-Work

Trim or grind nails every four to six weeks to maintain a healthy foot structure. Clean the ears by swabbing with a mild ear cleaning solution. Hair should be plucked from within the ear canal only as necessary for healthy ear management. Prior to bathing, quickly go over the entire body and remove any serious mats or tangles. If the tangle can be penetrated with water, leave it and remove when the dog is clean. If the pet has not been in for professional grooming for six weeks or more, remove the excessive body coat and set the pattern before bathing.

Brushing

Systematically line brush the head crest right down to the skin. With a slicker brush, the motion used for line brushing is a "pat and pull." Softly pat the coat with the full pad of the brush and pull out and away from the skin with each stroke. The wrist remains in a neutral, or straight, position. The motion should be light and gentle.

Body

The entire body is free of hair. To help determine the natural pattern lines, use the natural coat pattern to create the crest, socks and plume. Leave any natural cape of fur that is over the back of the neck. If the hair in the neck area is sparse, clip it very close, like the rest of the body. Work with a #10 or #15 blade in reverse, based on skin sensitivity.

Head

Clip the muzzle, cheeks and throat clean, similar to the clean face of a poodle. Use a #10 or #15 blade in reverse. Leave the longer hair on the top of the skull to create the crest.

Ears

The ears may be clipped clean with a #15 blade on the outside and a #40 on the inside, or left natural with fur. If the ears are clipped, finish by edging the ears with small detailing shears, keeping the tips of the shears toward the tips of the ears.

Feet

The feet should be covered with silky coat that starts above the pastern joint on the front legs and above the hock joint on the rear legs. These socks should be uniform in size and shape from side-to-side and front-to-back.

Suggested Tools & Equipment

- Nail Trimmers
- Styptic Powder
- Ear Cleaning Solution
- Cotton Balls
- Clippers
- #40 and #15 and #10 Blades
- Slicker Brush
- Greyhound Comb
- Small Detailing Shears
- Thinning Shears

Shave the pads of the feet with blades ranging from a #15 to a #40 based on skin sensitivity. Neaten the feet with shears to form a rounded shape, toes pointing straight forward.

Tail

The plume on the tail is created by leaving the last two-thirds of the tail covered with long flowing coat. The base of the tail may be clipped to the same length as the body.

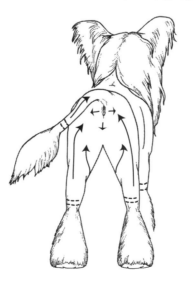

Clip the body using the shortest blade possible based on skin sensitivity. Set the "socks" just above the hock joint on the rear leg. Use this as a guide when setting the front socks. Round the feet. Clip the face clean leaving long coat on the top of the head and down the back of the neck to create the "crest." Ears may be shaved close or left natural. Leave the last ⅔ of the tail natural to form the "plume" at the end.

Breed Facts & Characteristics

Country of Origin: China

Height at Shoulder: 11"–13"

Coat Length/Type: Long/Flowing

Color: All colors and combinations of color are acceptable.

Correct grooming procedure:
Bathe & Brush Out/Close Trimming

Common pet grooming practices:
Bathe & Brush/Clipper-Trim

-The Goal-
Coat should be mat- and tangle-free.
The fur should be light and airy, moving
freely with the dog as it moves.

Topknot is left loose.

Leave ears long or clipper clean
with a close cutting blade.

Clip muzzle and cheeks
close with a #10 or #15
or leave coated, clearing
only the stop area.

Line comb and brush **every** inch of this
dog, right down to the skin.

Lightly trim sanitary
areas—both under
tail and tummy.

Watch friction areas:
• Collar Area
• Arm Pits
• Behind Ears
• Legs & Thighs

Neaten undercarriage
line lightly.

Trim nails as short as
possible or grind.

Shave pads and scissor feet round.

🐾 Bathing and Drying Directions:
• For coats longer than 3", use Natural Long Haired
• For coats shorter than 3", use Curly and Wavy Coated.

Grooming Procedures & Recommendations

See page 72 for
Bathing & Drying Instructions

See page 602 for
Drop Coat Styling Options

Frequency
Bathe once a week to once every 12 weeks.

Pre-Work
Trim or grind nails every four to six weeks to maintain a healthy foot structure. Clean the ears by swabbing with a mild ear cleaning solution. Hair should be plucked from within the ear canal only as necessary for healthy ear management. Prior to bathing, quickly go over the entire body and remove any serious mats or tangles. If the tangle can be penetrated with water, leave it and remove when the dog is clean. If the dog is in a clipped pet trim and has not been in for professional grooming for six weeks or more, remove the excessive body coat and set the pattern before bathing.

Brushing
Systematically line brush the entire coat, right down to the skin. With a slicker brush, the motion used for line brushing is a "pat and pull." Softly pat the coat with the full pad of the brush and pull out and away from the skin with each stroke. The wrist remains in a neutral, or straight, position. The motion should be light and gentle. Start on the lower rear legs and work upwards towards the thigh. Repeat on every leg then proceed to the body, neck, head ears and tail. Work evenly over the pet, holding or pushing up the coat with one hand. It can be done with either a comb or a brush, but in most cases the comb is reserved for double checking the work of the brush. With the slicker brush, work the seam line, pulling down a small amount of fur with each stroke. Do not move to the next section until the brush stroke glides smoothly and the skin at the seam line is seen. Pay close attention to the legs, under the front legs, collar area, ears, and tail. Let your hands feel for coat density levels. If an area feels heavier or thicker, it will need special attention with a brush or a comb. If static electricity is a problem while brushing, lightly mist the coat with an anti-static product or water while brushing. When finished, each strand of hair should float freely about as the dog moves.

Head
The face is clipped close, similar to the clean face of a poodle. Use a close cutting blade such as a #10 or #15, based on the sensitivity of the dog's skin. Make a straight line from the back corner of the eye to the ear canal, following the zygomatic arch ridge that divides the top skull from the cheek area. Clip under the eye and down the muzzle, creating a small, inverted "V" at the stop area between the eyes. Clip the throat area from the ear canal down into a "V" or "U" shape, 3 to 4 fingers above the breastbone. Ears may be clipped closely or left natural. In the conformation ring, this breed is shown in its natural state with very little trimming. The hair on the top skull may be left natural or braided in two braids above the eyes, one on each side of the head. Rounding the feet is permitted but all other trimming is strictly forbidden for the conformation dog.

Suggested Tools & Equipment
- Nail Trimmers
- Styptic Powder
- Ear Powder
- Ear Cleaning Solution
- Hemostat
- Cotton Balls
- Clippers
- #40 and #15 Blades for Pads
- Slicker Brush
- Greyhound Comb
- Pin Brush
- Dematting Tools
- Straight Shears
- Curved Shears
- Small Detailing Shears
- Thinning Shears

Feet & Hocks
Trim the pads with a close cutting action blade ranging from a #15 to a #40. Use a very light touch to clean the pads of long hair. To create a rounded foot, first block in the foot to form a square. This will help create a full circular shape with the toes pointing directly forward. Finish detailing and rounding the outline of the foot by using long, curved shears.

Detail Finish
Lightly neaten the entire outline of the dog, removing long, shaggy stray hairs that interrupt a smooth flow. The finished appearance is very natural. This can be done with thinning shears or shears as long as the look remains natural. Finish with a fine mist of coat polish on the body coat for added shine.

Notes From The Grooming Table ©2016

Breed Facts & Characteristics

Country of Origin: England

Height at Shoulder: 9"–10"

Coat Length/Type: Combination/Silky

Color: Rich chestnut with white. Black and tan. Tricolor with base color of white with black patches and tan points. Solid deep rich red. Can have a small white patch on chest.

Correct grooming procedure:
Bathe & Brush Out/Minor Trimming

Common pet grooming practices:
Bathe & Brush Out/Minor Trimming

-The Goal-
Coat should be mat free, shiny, light and airy. As the dog moves, the coat should bounce and float with the dog.

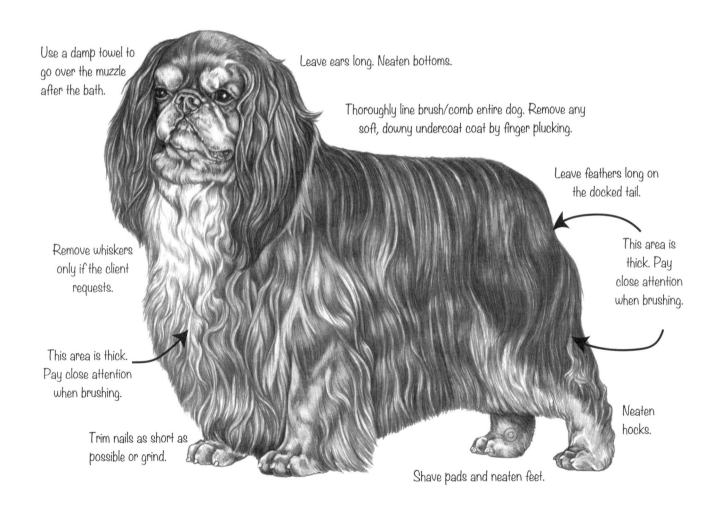

Use a damp towel to go over the muzzle after the bath.

Leave ears long. Neaten bottoms.

Thoroughly line brush/comb entire dog. Remove any soft, downy undercoat coat by finger plucking.

Leave feathers long on the docked tail.

This area is thick. Pay close attention when brushing.

Remove whiskers only if the client requests.

This area is thick. Pay close attention when brushing.

Trim nails as short as possible or grind.

Neaten hocks.

Shave pads and neaten feet.

TOY

Grooming Procedures & Recommendations

See page 68 for Bathing & Drying Instructions

Frequency
Bathe once a week to once every 12 weeks.

Pre-Work
Trim or grind nails every four to six weeks to maintain a healthy foot structure. Clean the ears by swabbing with a mild ear cleaning solution. Use a rubber curry, shedding blade, undercoat rake, pumice stone, carding tool, fine stripping knife or natural bristle brush to loosen skin dander and remove loose coat. Use a high-velocity dryer over the coat to quickly and effectively lift dirt and debris away from the skin and loosen coat. Brush out or remove any matting found in the long-coated areas. If the tangles are loose enough so water can fully penetrate the area, remove them after bathing and drying. If water cannot penetrate, remove the mat or tangle prior to bathing.

Special Note: Bathing the Face
On short, flat-muzzled pets, it is extremely important to prevent water from entering the nasal cavity. When washing the face, lower the water pressure and do not use running water near the nose. Use a moist, clean cloth to gently wipe clean the muzzle and wrinkles.

Brushing
Line brush, working in sections until the dog is entirely tangle-free and all loose coat is removed. When finished, there should be little, if any, fur still being removed with a firm slicker brush. Double-check the work with a comb and your hands. Go over the entire body, feeling for any inconsistencies in the density levels of the coat. If an area seems moist to the touch or fuller than the rest of the coat, rework the area with the appropriate tool. Mats, tangles and excessive coat are easily trapped in the following areas: behind the ears, around the ruff, the thigh area, the undercarriage and the tail. Give extra attention to these areas before finishing the groom.

Carding
If a dog has an abundance of loose undercoat, card the areas with a carding tool. Common tools can be a fine stripping knife, undercoat rake, a pumice stone, or a #40 blade held between your fingers. Any carding tool should be pulled over the body, working in the direction of the coat growth. This will remove the soft, downy undercoat, allowing the guard coat to conform more closely to the natural outline of the body. It will also aid in the removal of loose, shedding coat, a seasonal problem for many pet owners.

Feet & Hocks
Trim the pads with a close blade ranging from a #15 to a #40. Use a very light touch to clean the pads of long hair. If there is long fur between the toes, back brush the fur so it stands up on top of and away from the foot. With thinning shears, trim the excess to create a neat and very natural looking foot. Tidy the outside edge of the foot, if needed, with small detailing shears. If the hocks have longer coat, trim lightly with thinning shears to show a neat, clean area. A #4F blade, used carefully in reverse, works well for trimming the tops of the feet and the hocks on some dogs.

Detail Finish
Edge the ears lightly with thinning shears to neaten and keep a natural look. Hand pluck any long wispy, flyaway hair from around the ears. Removal of whiskers on the muzzle is optional based on client preference. Finish with a fine mist of coat polish on the body coat for added shine. Application of bows and mild cologne is optional.

Suggested Tools & Equipment

- Nail Trimmers
- Styptic Powder
- Ear Cleaning Solution
- Cotton Balls
- Clippers
- #40 and #15 Blades for Pads
- #4F for Feet & Hocks (optional)
- Slicker Brush
- Greyhound Comb
- Rubber Curry
- Carding Tool
- De-Shedding Tools
- Small Detailing Shears
- Thinning Shears

Notes:

Breed Facts & Characteristics

Country of Origin: Cuba

Height at Shoulder: 8½"–11½"

Coat Length/Type: Long/Flowing

Color: All colors and combinations of color are acceptable.

Correct grooming procedure:

Bathe & Brush Out/Corded

Common pet grooming practices:
Bathe & Brush Out/Clipper-Trim

General Description

In the conformation ring, this breed is shown in its natural state with very little trimming. The hair on the top skull may be left natural or braided in two braids above the eyes, one on each side of the head. Rounding the feet is permitted but all other trimming is strictly forbidden for the show ring.

Topknot is either left loose or braided
with two braids, one over over each eye.

Clear stop
area with
thinners or
clippers.

Leave ears long.

-The Goal-
Coat should be mat- and tangle-free.
The fur should be light and airy, moving
freely with the dog as it moves.

Line comb and brush **every** inch of
this dog, right down to the skin.

Lightly trim
sanitary area—
both under tail
and tummy.

Watch friction areas:
• Collar Area
• Arm Pits
• Behind Ears
• Legs & Thighs

Shave pads and scissor feet round.
Neaten undercarriage line lightly.

Trim nails as short as
possible or grind.

🐾 Bathing and Drying Directions:

• For coats longer than 3", use Natural Long Haired

• For coats shorter than 3", use Curly and Wavy Coated.

TOY

See page 72 for
Bathing & Drying Instructions

See page 602 for
Drop Coat Styling Options

Frequency
Bathe once a week to once every 12 weeks.

Pre-Work
Trim or grind nails every four to six weeks to maintain a healthy foot structure. Clean the ears by swabbing with a mild ear cleaning solution. Hair should be plucked from within the ear canal only as necessary for healthy ear management. Prior to bathing, quickly go over the entire body and remove any serious mats or tangles. If the tangle can be penetrated with water, leave it and remove when the dog is clean. If the dog is in a clipped pet trim and has not been in for professional grooming for six weeks or more, remove the excessive body coat and set the pattern before bathing.

Brushing
Systematically line brush the entire coat, right down to the skin. With a slicker brush, the motion used for line brushing is a "pat and pull." Softly pat the coat with the full pad of the brush and pull out and away from the skin with each stroke. The wrist remains in a neutral, or straight, position. The motion should be light and gentle. Start on the lower rear legs and work upwards towards the thigh. Repeat on every leg then proceed to the body, neck, head ears and tail. Work evenly over the pet, holding or pushing up the coat with one hand. It can be done with either a comb or a brush, but in most cases the comb is reserved for double checking the work of the brush. With the slicker brush, work the seam line, pulling down a

small amount of fur with each stroke. Do not move to the next section until the brush stroke glides smoothly and the skin at the seam line is seen. Pay close attention to the legs, under the front legs, collar area, ears, and tail. Let your hands feel for coat density levels. If an area feels heavier or thicker, it will need special attention with a brush or a comb. If static electricity is a problem while brushing, lightly mist the coat with an anti-static product or water while brushing. When finished, each strand of hair should float freely about as the dog moves.

Feet & Hocks
Trim the pads with a close cutting action blade ranging from a #15 to a #40. Use a very light touch to clean the pads of long hair. To create a rounded foot, first block in the foot to form a square. This will help create a full circular shape with the toes pointing directly forward. Finish detailing and rounding the outline of the foot by using long, curved shears.

Detail Finish
Lightly neaten the entire outline of the dog, removing long, shaggy stray hairs that interrupt a smooth flow. The finished appearance is very natural. This can be done with thinning shears or shears as long as the look remains natural. Finish with a fine mist of coat polish on the body coat for added shine.

Special Note
This coat can be corded as well. Please refer to page 77 for directions on bathing a corded coat.

Suggested
Tools & Equipment

- Nail Trimmers
- Styptic Powder
- Ear Powder
- Ear Cleaning Solution
- Hemostat
- Cotton Balls
- Clippers
- #40 and #15 Blades for Pads
- Slicker Brush
- Greyhound Comb
- Pin Brush
- Dematting Tools
- Straight Shears
- Curved Shears
- Small Detailing Shears
- Thinning Shears

Braid Option
To form the braids, gather a small amount of hair just about the eyes. Start the braid at the outside eye corner. Repeat over both eyes. Secure braids with small elastic bands.

Breed Facts & Characteristics

Country of Origin: Mediterranean

Height at Shoulder: 13"–15"

Coat Length/Type: Short/Smooth

Color: All colors except brindled and black and tan.

Correct grooming procedure:
Bathe & Curry Brush

Common pet grooming practices:
Bathe & Curry Brush

-The Goal-
The coat should be clean and fresh smelling, with the coat laying flat against the body. No shedding hair.

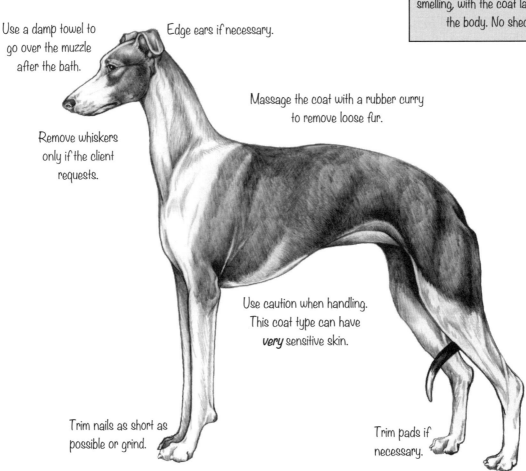

Use a damp towel to go over the muzzle after the bath.

Edge ears if necessary.

Massage the coat with a rubber curry to remove loose fur.

Remove whiskers only if the client requests.

Use caution when handling. This coat type can have *very* sensitive skin.

Trim nails as short as possible or grind.

Trim pads if necessary.

See page 66 for Bathing & Drying Instructions	Suggested Tools & Equipment

- Nail Trimmers
- Styptic Powder
- Ear Cleaning Solution
- Cotton Balls

- Clippers
- #40 or #15 Blade
- Rubber Curry
- Carding Tool

- Small Detailing Shears
- Thinning Shears

Notes *from your* Grooming Table

Breed Facts & Characteristics

Country of Origin: China

Height at Shoulder: 8"–11"

Coat Length/Type: Combination/Silky

Color: All shades of red or tan with white, black and white, or black and white with tan points.

Correct grooming procedure:
Bathe & Brush Out/Minor Trimming

Common pet grooming practices:
Bathe & Brush Out/Minor Trimming

-The Goal-
Coat should be mat free, shiny, light and airy. The coat should bounce and float with the dog as it moves.

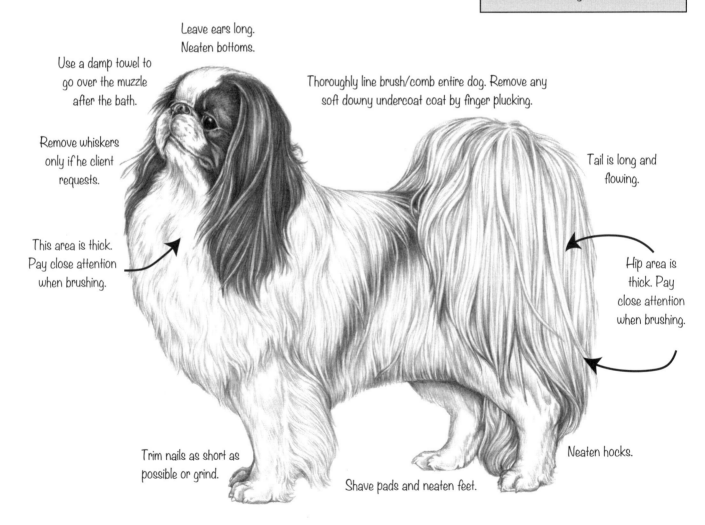

Leave ears long. Neaten bottoms.

Use a damp towel to go over the muzzle after the bath.

Thoroughly line brush/comb entire dog. Remove any soft downy undercoat coat by finger plucking.

Remove whiskers only if he client requests.

Tail is long and flowing.

This area is thick. Pay close attention when brushing.

Hip area is thick. Pay close attention when brushing.

Trim nails as short as possible or grind.

Neaten hocks.

Shave pads and neaten feet.

TOY

Grooming Procedures & Recommendations

See page 68 for Bathing & Drying Instructions

Frequency
Bathe once a week to once every 12 weeks.

Pre-Work
Trim or grind nails every four to six weeks to maintain a healthy foot structure. Clean the ears by swabbing with a mild ear cleaning solution. Use a rubber curry, shedding blade, undercoat rake, pumice stone, carding tool, fine stripping knife or natural bristle brush to loosen skin dander and remove loose coat. Use a high-velocity dryer over the coat to quickly and effectively lift dirt and debris away from the skin and loosen coat. Brush out or remove any matting found in the long-coated areas. If the tangles are loose enough so water can fully penetrate the area, remove them after bathing and drying. If water cannot penetrate, remove the mat or tangle prior to bathing.

Special Note: Bathing the Face
On short, flat-muzzled pets, it is extremely important to prevent water from entering the nasal cavity. When washing the face, lower the water pressure and do not use running water near the nose. Use a moist, clean cloth to gently wipe clean the muzzle and wrinkles.

Brushing
Line brush, working in sections until the dog is entirely tangle-free and all loose coat is removed. When finished, there should be little, if any, fur still being removed with a firm slicker brush. Double-check the work with a comb and your hands. Go over the entire body, feeling for any inconsistencies in the density levels of the coat. If an area seems moist to the touch or fuller than the rest of the coat, rework the area with the appropriate tool. Mats, tangles and excessive coat are easily trapped in the following areas: behind the ears, around the ruff, the thigh area, the undercarriage and the tail. Give extra attention to these areas before finishing the groom.

Carding
If a dog has an abundance of loose undercoat, card the areas with a carding tool. Common tools can be a fine stripping knife, undercoat rake, a pumice stone, or a #40 blade held between your fingers. Any carding tool should be pulled over the body, working in the direction of the coat growth. This will remove the soft, downy undercoat, allowing the guard coat to conform more closely to the natural outline of the body. It will also aid in the removal of loose, shedding coat, a seasonal problem for many pet owners.

Feet & Hocks
Trim the pads with a close blade ranging from a #15 to a #40. Use a very light touch to clean the pads of long hair. If there is long fur between the toes, back brush the fur so it stands up on top of and away from the foot. With thinning shears, trim the excess to create a neat and very natural looking foot. Tidy the outside edge of the foot, if needed, with small detailing shears. If the hocks have longer coat, trim lightly with thinning shears to show a neat, clean area. A #4F blade, used carefully in reverse, works well for trimming the tops of the feet and the hocks on some dogs.

Detail Finish
Edge the ears lightly with thinning shears to neaten and keep a natural look. Hand pluck any long wispy, flyaway hair from around the ears. Removal of whiskers on the muzzle is optional based on client preference. Finish with a fine mist of coat polish on the body coat for added shine. Application of bows and mild cologne is optional.

Suggested Tools & Equipment

- Nail Trimmers
- Styptic Powder
- Ear Cleaning Solution
- Cotton Balls
- Clippers
- #40 and #15 Blades for Pads
- #4F for Feet & Hocks (optional)
- Slicker Brush
- Greyhound Comb
- Rubber Curry
- Carding Tool
- De-Shedding Tools
- Small Detailing Shears
- Thinning Shears

Notes:

Breed Facts & Characteristics

Country of Origin: Mediterranean

Height at Shoulder: 5"–6½"

Coat Length/Type: Long/Flowing

Color: White

Correct grooming procedure:
Bathe & Brush Out/Minor Trimming

Common pet grooming practices:
Bathe & Brush Out/Clipper-Trim

-The Goal-
Coat should be mat- and tangle-free.
The fur should be light and airy, moving
freely with the dog as it moves

Tie up topknot in
two buttons.

Clear stop area with
thinners or clippers.

Leave ears long.

Line comb and brush **every** inch of this
dog, right down to the skin.

Lightly trim sanitary areas—
both under tail and tummy.

Watch friction areas:
• Collar Area
• Arm Pits
• Behind Ears
• Legs & Thighs

Trim nails as close as
possible or grind.

Shave pads and scissor feet round.
Neaten undercarriage line.

🐾 Bathing and Drying Directions:
• For coats longer than 3", use Natural Long Haired
• For coats shorter than 3", use Curly and Wavy Coated

Grooming Procedures & Recommendations

See page 72 for
Bathing & Drying Instructions

See page 602 for
Drop Coat Styling Options

Frequency
Bathe once a week to once every
12 weeks.

Pre-Work
Trim or grind nails every four to
six weeks to maintain a healthy foot
structure. Clean the ears by swabbing
with a mild ear cleaning solution. Hair
should be plucked from within the
ear canal only as necessary for healthy
ear management. Prior to bathing,
quickly go over the entire body and
remove any serious mats or tangles.
If the tangle can be penetrated with
water, leave it and remove when the
dog is clean. If the dog is in a clipped
pet trim and has not been in for
professional grooming for six weeks or
more, remove the excessive body coat
and set the pattern before bathing.

Brushing
Systematically line brush the entire coat,
right down to the skin. With a slicker
brush, the motion used for line brushing
is a "pat and pull." Softly pat the coat
with the full pad of the brush and pull
out and away from the skin with each
stroke. The wrist remains in a neutral,
or straight, position. The motion should
be light and gentle. Start on the lower
rear legs and work upwards towards the
thigh. Repeat on every leg then proceed
to the body, neck, head ears and tail.
Work evenly over the pet, holding or
pushing up the coat with one hand. It
can be done with either a comb or a
brush, but in most cases the comb is
reserved for double checking the work
of the brush. With the slicker brush,
work the seam line, pulling down a

small amount of fur with each stroke.
Do not move to the next section until
the brush stroke glides smoothly and
the skin at the seam line is seen. Pay
close attention to the legs, under the
front legs, collar area, ears, and tail. Let
your hands feel for coat density levels.
If an area feels heavier or thicker, it will
need special attention with a brush or
a comb. If static electricity is a problem
while brushing, lightly mist the coat
with an anti-static product or water
while brushing. When finished, each
strand of hair should float freely about
as the dog moves.

Head
The traditional way to keep the long
hair of the Maltese out of its eyes is to
tie the topknot up into a button above
each eye. The hair is pulled up into two
ponytails, folded over and caught up in
a fine rubber band to create the button
and set off the soft, very dark eyes. Tiny
bows may be attached to the buttons to
further enhance the eyes. On pet dogs it
is common to slightly trim the stop area
between the eyes.

Feet & Hocks
Trim the pads with a close cutting
action blade ranging from a #15 to a
#40. Use a very light touch to clean the
pads of long hair. To create a rounded
foot, first block in the foot to form
a square. This will help create a full
circular shape with the toes pointing
directly forward. Finish detailing and
rounding the outline of the foot by
using long, curved shears.

Detail Finish
Lightly neaten the entire outline of
the dog, removing long, shaggy stray
hairs that interrupt a smooth flow. The
finished appearance is very natural.
This can be done with thinning shears
or shears as long as the look remains
natural. Finish with a fine mist of coat
polish on the body coat for added shine.

Suggested Tools & Equipment

- Nail Trimmers
- Styptic Powder
- Ear Powder
- Ear Cleaning Solution
- Hemostat
- Cotton Balls
- Clippers
- #40 and #15 Blades for Pads
- Small Rubber Bands
- Slicker Brush
- Greyhound Comb
- Pin Brush
- Dematting Tools
- Straight Shears
- Curved Shears
- Small Detailing Shears
- Thinning Shears

Notes:

Notes From The Grooming Table ©2016

Manchester Terrier

Breed Facts & Characteristics

Country of Origin: England

Height at Shoulder: 11"–12"

Coat Length/Type: Short/Smooth

Color: Black with tan points.

Correct grooming procedure:
Bathe & Curry Brush

Common pet grooming practices:
Bathe & Curry Brush

-The Goal-
The coat should be clean fresh smelling, with the coat laying flat against the body. No shedding hair.

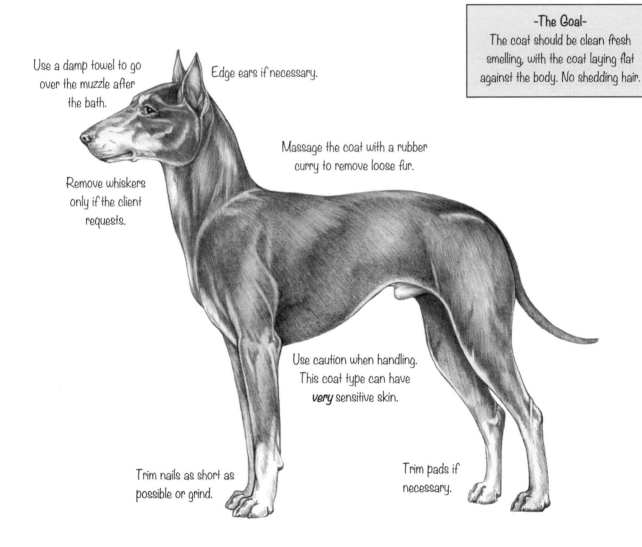

Use a damp towel to go over the muzzle after the bath.

Edge ears if necessary.

Remove whiskers only if the client requests.

Massage the coat with a rubber curry to remove loose fur.

Use caution when handling. This coat type can have **very** sensitive skin.

Trim nails as short as possible or grind.

Trim pads if necessary.

See page 66 for Bathing & Drying Instructions	Suggested Tools & Equipment

- Nail Trimmers
- Styptic Powder
- Ear Cleaning Solution
- Cotton Balls

- Clippers
- #40 or #15 Blade
- Rubber Curry
- Carding Tool

- Small Detailing Shears
- Thinning Shears

TOY

Miniature Pinscher

Breed Facts & Characteristics

Country of Origin: Germany

Height at Shoulder: 10"–12½"

Coat Length/Type: Short/Smooth

Color: Red, black with tan points or brown with tan points.

Correct grooming procedure:
Bathe & Curry Brush

Common pet grooming practices:
Bathe & Curry Brush

-The Goal-
The coat should be clean and fresh smelling, with the coat laying flat against the body. No shedding hair.

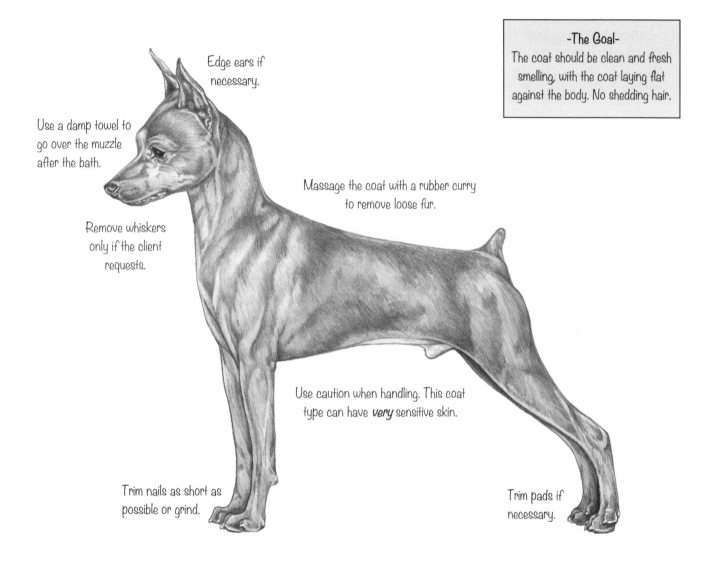

Edge ears if necessary.

Use a damp towel to go over the muzzle after the bath.

Remove whiskers only if the client requests.

Massage the coat with a rubber curry to remove loose fur.

Use caution when handling. This coat type can have **very** sensitive skin.

Trim nails as short as possible or grind.

Trim pads if necessary.

See page 66 for Bathing & Drying Instructions

Suggested Tools & Equipment

- Nail Trimmers
- Styptic Powder
- Ear Cleaning Solution
- Cotton Balls

- Clippers
- #40 or #15 Blade
- Rubber Curry
- Carding Tool

- Small Detailing Shears
- Thinning Shears

Notes From The Grooming Table ©2016

Breed Facts & Characteristics

Country of Origin: Western Europe

Height at Shoulder: 8"–11"

Coat Length/Type: Combination/Silky

Color: Base coat is white with any deeper color covering both ears and eyes. White muzzle and blaze on face highly desirable. Color on body is unimportant.

Correct grooming procedure:
Bathe & Brush Out/Minor Trimming

Common pet grooming practices:
Bathe & Brush Out/Minor Trimming

General Description

Papillon is the French word for "butterfly," and the breed gets its name from its unique butterfly ear set. The longer hair should be left to create the illusion of butterfly wings and frame the face.

-The Goal-
Coat should be mat free, shiny, light and airy. The coat should bounce and float with the dog as it moves.

Use a damp towel to go over the muzzle after the bath.

Remove whiskers only if the client requests.

Leave ears long.

Thoroughly line brush/comb entire dog.

Tail is long and flowing.

This area is thick. Pay close attention when brushing.

This area is thick. Pay close attention when brushing.

Trim nails as short as possible or grind.

Trim hocks.

Shave pads and neaten feet to look natural.

Grooming Procedures & Recommendations

See page 68 for
Bathing & Drying Instructions

Frequency

Bathe once a week to once every 12 weeks.

Pre-Work

Trim or grind nails every four to six weeks to maintain a healthy foot structure. Clean the ears by swabbing with a mild ear cleaning solution. Use a rubber curry, shedding blade, undercoat rake, pumice stone, carding tool, fine stripping knife or natural bristle brush to loosen skin dander and remove loose coat. Use a high-velocity dryer over the coat to quickly and effectively lift dirt and debris away from the skin and loosen coat. Brush out or remove any matting found in the long-coated areas. If the tangles are loose enough so water can fully penetrate the area, remove them after bathing and drying. If water cannot penetrate, remove the mat or tangle prior to bathing.

Brushing

Line brush, working in sections until the dog is entirely tangle-free and all loose coat is removed. When finished, there should be little, if any, fur still being removed with a firm slicker brush. Double-check the work with a wide-toothed comb and your hands. Go over the entire body, feeling for any inconsistencies in the density levels of the coat. If an area seems moist to the touch or fuller than the rest of the coat, rework the area with the appropriate tool. Mats, tangles and excessive coat are easily trapped in the following areas: behind the ears, around the ruff, the thigh area, the undercarriage and the tail. Give extra attention to these areas before finishing the groom.

Carding

If a dog has an abundance of loose undercoat, line card the areas with a carding tool. Common tools can be a fine stripping knife, undercoat rake, a pumice stone, or a #40 blade held between your fingers. Any carding tool should be pulled over the body, working in the direction of the coat growth. This will remove the soft, downy undercoat, allowing the guard coat to conform more closely to the natural outline of the body. It will also aid in the removal of loose, shedding coat, a seasonal problem for many pet owners.

Feet & Hocks

Trim the pads with a close blade ranging from a #15 to a #40. Use a very light touch to clean the pads of long hair. If there is long fur between the toes, back brush the fur so it stands up on top of and away from the foot. With thinning shears, trim the excess to create a neat and very natural looking foot. Tidy the outside edge of the foot, if needed, with small detailing shears. If the hocks have longer coat, trim lightly with thinning shears to show a neat, clean area. A #4F blade, used carefully in reverse, works well for trimming the tops of the feet and the hocks on some dogs.

Sanitary Area

If the dog has a sanitation problem under the tail, lightly trim this area with thinning shears. Only clear enough coat to accomplish the goal and keep it looking very natural. Trimming of the groin area is not recommended unless there is a sanitary problem. If the groin needs to be trimmed, do so very lightly and try to leave the fur long enough so that the harsh coat does not prickle the skin, causing the dog to lick at the irritation.

Suggested Tools & Equipment

- Nail Trimmers
- Styptic Powder
- Ear Cleaning Solution
- Cotton Balls
- Clippers
- #40 and #15 Blades for Pads
- #4F for Feet & Hocks (optional)
- Slicker Brush
- Greyhound Comb
- Rubber Curry
- Carding Tool
- De-Shedding Tools
- Small Detailing Shears
- Thinning Shears

Detail Finish

Edge the ears lightly with thinning shears to neaten and keep a natural look. Hand pluck any long wispy, flyaway hair from around the ears. Removal of whiskers on the muzzle is optional based on client preference. Finish with a fine mist of coat polish on the body coat for added shine. Application of bows and mild cologne is optional.

Notes:

Notes From The Grooming Table ©2016

Pekingese

Breed Facts & Characteristics

Country of Origin: China

Height at Shoulder: 7"–8"

Coat Length/Type: Soft/Thick

Color: All coat colors, patterns and markings.

Correct grooming procedure:
Bathe & Brush Out/Minor Trimming

Common pet grooming practices:
Bathe & Brush Out or Clipper-Trim

-The Goal-
Coat should be mat free, shiny, light and airy. The coat should bounce and float with the dog as it moves.

Use a high-velocity dryer both before and after the bath. Blow out loose coat, tangles and dirt. Dry and fluff.

Thoroughly line brush/comb entire dog.

Use a damp towel to go over the muzzle after the bath.

Neaten under tail and sanitary areas.

Remove whiskers only if the client requests.

This area is thick. Pay close attention when brushing.

This area is thick. Pay close attention when brushing.

Trim nails as short as possible or grind.

Neaten undercarriage.

Shave pad and neaten feet.

Grooming Procedures & Recommendations

See page 70 for
Bathing & Drying Instructions

Frequency
Bathe once a week to once every 12 weeks.

Pre-Work
Trim or grind nails at least every four to six weeks to maintain a healthy foot structure. Swab the ears clean with a mild ear cleaning solution. Quickly blow out the dog's coat with a high-velocity dryer to effectively lift dirt and debris away from the skin and loosen coat. Brush out or remove any matting found in the longer coated areas. If the tangles are loose enough so that water can fully penetrate them, remove them after bathing and drying. If water cannot penetrate, remove the mat or tangle prior to bathing.

Special Note: Bathing the Face
On short, flat-muzzled pets, it is extremely important to prevent water from entering the nasal cavity. When washing the face, lower the water pressure and do not use running water near the nose. Use a moist, clean cloth to gently wipe clean the muzzle and wrinkles.

Brushing
Line brush, working in sections, until the dog is entirely tangle-free. When finished, there should be little, if any, fur still being removed with a firm slicker brush. Double-check the work with a wide-toothed comb and your hands. Go over the entire body, feeling for any inconsistencies in the density levels of the coat. If an area seems moist to the touch or fuller than the rest of the coat, rework the area with the appropriate tool. Mats, tangles and excessive coat are easily trapped in the following areas: behind the ears, around the ruff, the thigh area, the undercarriage and the tail. Give extra attention to these areas before finishing the groom.

Feet & Hocks
Trim the pads with blades ranging from a #15 to a #40. Use a very light touch to clean the pads of long hair. If there is long fur between the toes, brush it back so the fur stands up and away from the foot. With thinning shears, trim off the excess to create a neat and very natural looking foot with well-arched toes. Tidy the outside edge of the foot, if needed, with small detailing shears. If the hocks have longer coat, trim lightly with thinning shears to show a neat, clean area. A #4F blade used in reverse works well for trimming the tops of the feet and the hocks on small to larger dogs that are light to moderately coated. With very heavy-coated or giant dogs, handle the top of the feet and hocks using hand-trimming techniques instead of a clipper.

Sanitary Area
If the dog has a sanitation problem under the tail, lightly trim this area with thinning shears. Only clear enough coat to accomplish the goal and keep it looking very natural. Trimming of the groin area is not recommended unless there is a sanitary problem. If the groin needs to be trimmed, do so very lightly and try to leave the fur long enough so that the harsh coat does not prickle the skin, causing the dog to lick at the irritation.

Detail Finish
Removal of muzzle whiskers is optional, based on client preference. For added shine, finish with a fine mist of coat polish on the body coat. Application of bows and mild cologne is optional.

Suggested Tools & Equipment

- Nail Trimmers
- Styptic Powder
- Ear Cleaning Solution
- Cotton Balls
- Clippers
- #40 and #15 Blades for Pads
- #4F for Feet & Hocks (optional)
- Slicker Brush
- Wide-Toothed Comb
- Rubber Curry
- Undercoat Rake
- Dematting Tools
- High-Velocity Dryer
- Small Detailing Shears
- Curved Shears
- Thinning Shears

Notes:

Notes From The Grooming Table ©2016

Pomeranian

Breed Facts & Characteristics

Country of Origin: Germany

Height at Shoulder: 6"–7"

Coat Length/Type: Soft/Thick

Color: All coat colors, patterns and markings.

Correct grooming procedure:
Brush Out/Minor Trimming

Common pet grooming practices:
Bathe & Brush Out or Clipper-Trim

-The Goal-
Coat should be mat free, shiny, light and airy. The coat should bounce and float with the dog as it moves.

Use a high-velocity dryer both before and after the bath. Blow out loose coat, tangles and dirt. Dry and fluff.

Edge ear tips.

Thoroughly line brush/comb entire dog.

Use a damp towel to go over the muzzle after the bath.

Remove whiskers only if the client requests.

Trim under tail to look neat and natural.

This area is thick. Pay close attention when brushing.

This area is thick. Pay close attention when brushing.

Trim nails as short as possible or grind.

Shave pad and neaten feet to look natural.

Trim hocks.

Grooming Procedures & Recommendations

See page 70 for
Bathing & Drying Instructions

Frequency
Bathe once a week to once every 12 weeks.

Pre-Work
Trim or grind nails at least every four to six weeks to maintain a healthy foot structure. Swab the ears clean with a mild ear cleaning solution. Quickly blow out the dog's coat with a high-velocity dryer to effectively lift dirt and debris away from the skin and loosen coat. Brush out or remove any matting found in the longer coated areas. If the tangles are loose enough so that water can fully penetrate them, remove them after bathing and drying. If water cannot penetrate, remove the mat or tangle prior to bathing.

Brushing
Line brush, working in sections, until the dog is entirely tangle-free. When finished, there should be little, if any, fur still being removed with a firm slicker brush. Double-check the work with a wide-toothed comb and your hands. Go over the entire body, feeling for any inconsistencies in the density levels of the coat. If an area seems moist to the touch or fuller than the rest of the coat, rework the area with the appropriate tool. Mats, tangles and excessive coat are easily trapped in the following areas: behind the ears, around the ruff, the thigh area, the undercarriage and the tail. Give extra attention to these areas before finishing the groom.

Ears
Edge the ears lightly with thinning shears to neaten, but retain a natural look. Hand-pluck any long, wispy, flyaway hair from around the ears.

Feet & Hocks
Trim the pads with blades ranging from a #15 to a #40. Use a very light touch to clean the pads of long hair. If there is long fur between the toes, brush it back so the fur stands up and away from the foot. With thinning shears, trim off the excess to create a neat and very natural looking foot with well-arched toes. Tidy the outside edge of the foot, if needed, with small detailing shears. If the hocks have longer coat, trim lightly with thinning shears to show a neat, clean area. A #4F blade used in reverse works well for trimming the tops of the feet and the hocks on small to larger dogs that are light to moderately coated. With very heavy-coated or giant dogs, handle the top of the feet and hocks using hand-trimming techniques instead of a clipper.

Sanitary Area
If the dog has a sanitation problem under the tail, lightly trim this area with thinning shears. Only clear enough coat to accomplish the goal and keep it looking very natural. Trimming of the groin area is not recommended unless there is a sanitary problem. If the groin needs to be trimmed, do so very lightly and try to leave the fur long enough so that the harsh coat does not prickle the skin, causing the dog to lick at the irritation.

Detail Finish
Removal of muzzle whiskers is optional, based on client preference. For added shine, finish with a fine mist of coat polish on the body coat. Application of bows and mild cologne is optional.

Suggested Tools & Equipment

- Nail Trimmers
- Styptic Powder
- Ear Cleaning Solution
- Cotton Balls
- Clippers
- #40 and #15 Blades for Pads
- #4F for Feet & Hocks (optional)
- Slicker Brush
- Wide-Toothed Comb
- Rubber Curry
- Undercoat Rake
- Dematting Tools
- High-Velocity Dryer
- Small Detailing Shears
- Curved Shears
- Thinning Shears

Notes:

Notes From The Grooming Table ©2016

Poodle

Breed Facts & Characteristics

Country of Origin: Germany

Height at Shoulder: 10"–25"

Coat Length/Type: Long/Curly

Color: All solid colors in shades of black, grays, browns, tans and white.

Correct grooming procedure:
Hand-Scissor

Common pet grooming practices:
Clipper-Trim

-The Goal-
The longer fur should look like a cloud, void of any clipper or scissor marks. Close clipper work is smooth and even. The coat needs to be totally mat free. The outline should be velvet smooth and neat. The breed is squarely built, well balanced and elegant.

See page 74 for
Bathing & Drying Instructions

See also pages 484–489 for
Non-Sporting Poodle

See page 590 for
Classic Pet Poodle Styles

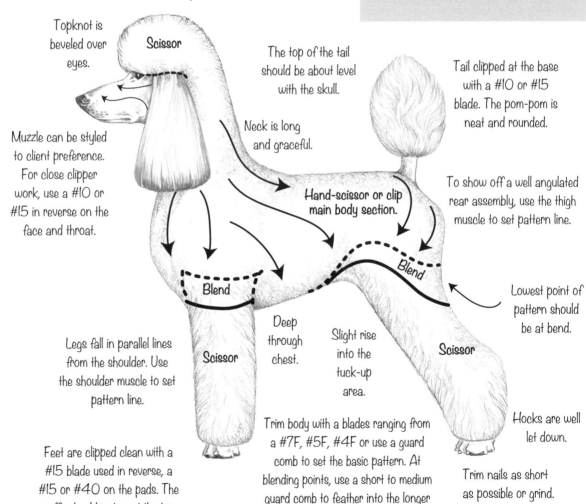

Hand-scissor topknot.

Topknot is beveled over eyes.

Scissor

The top of the tail should be about level with the skull.

Tail clipped at the base with a #10 or #15 blade. The pom-pom is neat and rounded.

Muzzle can be styled to client preference. For close clipper work, use a #10 or #15 in reverse on the face and throat.

Neck is long and graceful.

Hand-scissor or clip main body section.

To show off a well angulated rear assembly, use the thigh muscle to set pattern line.

Blend

Blend

Lowest point of pattern should be at bend.

Legs fall in parallel lines from the shoulder. Use the shoulder muscle to set pattern line.

Scissor

Deep through chest.

Slight rise into the tuck-up area.

Scissor

Hocks are well let down.

Feet are clipped clean with a #15 blade used in reverse, a #15 or #40 on the pads. The cuffs should just meet the top of the knuckle.

Trim body with a blades ranging from a #7F, #5F, #4F or use a guard comb to set the basic pattern. At blending points, use a short to medium guard comb to feather into the longer scissored areas based on the length of the general body blade length.

Trim nails as short as possible or grind.

TOY

Breed Facts & Characteristics

Country of Origin: China

Height at Shoulder: 10"–13"

Coat Length/Type: Short/Harsh

Color: Black, silver with a dark mask or shades of tan with a dark mask.

Correct grooming procedure:

Bathe & Curry Brush

Common pet grooming practices:

Bathe & Curry Brush

-The Goal-
The coat should be clean and fresh smelling, with the coat laying flat against the body. No shedding hair.

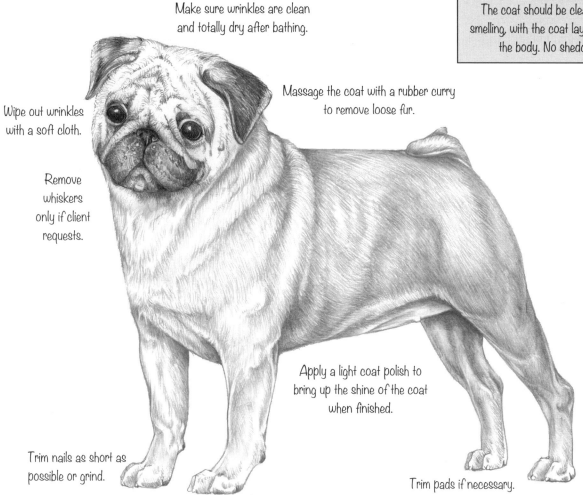

Make sure wrinkles are clean and totally dry after bathing.

Wipe out wrinkles with a soft cloth.

Remove whiskers only if client requests.

Massage the coat with a rubber curry to remove loose fur.

Apply a light coat polish to bring up the shine of the coat when finished.

Trim nails as short as possible or grind.

Trim pads if necessary.

See page 67 for Bathing & Drying Instructions

Suggested Tools & Equipment

- Nail Trimmers
- Styptic Powder
- Ear Cleaning Solution
- Cotton Balls
- Clippers
- #40 or #15 Blade
- Slicker Brush
- Rubber Curry
- Carding Tool
- De-Shedding Tools
- Small Detailing Shears
- Thinning Shears

Breed Facts & Characteristics

Country of Origin: Tibet

Height at Shoulder: 8"–11"

Coat Length/Type: Long/Flowing

Color: All coat colors, patterns and markings.

Correct grooming procedure:
Bathe & Brush Out/Minor Trimming

Common pet grooming practices:
Bathe & Brush Out/Clipper-Trim

-The Goal-
Coat should be mat- and tangle-free.
The fur should be light and airy, moving
freely with the dog as it moves.

Tie up topknot at center of head.

Line comb and brush **every** inch of this dog, right down to the skin.

Clear stop area with thinners or clippers.

Leave ears long.

Watch friction areas:
• Collar Area
• Arm Pits
• Behind Ears
• Legs & Thighs

Lightly trim sanitary areas— both under tail and tummy.

Trim nails as short as possible or grind.

Shave pads and scissor feet round. Neaten undercarriage line.

🐾 Bathing and Drying Directions:
• For coats longer than 3", use Natural Long Haired
• For coats shorter than 3", use Curly and Wavy Coated.

Grooming Procedures & Recommendations

See page 72 for
Bathing & Drying Instructions

See page 602 for
Drop Coat Styling Options

Frequency
Bathe once a week to once every 12 weeks.

Pre-Work
Trim or grind nails every four to six weeks to maintain a healthy foot structure. Clean the ears by swabbing with a mild ear cleaning solution. Hair should be plucked from within the ear canal only as necessary for healthy ear management. Prior to bathing, quickly go over the entire body and remove any serious mats or tangles. If the tangle can be penetrated with water, leave it and remove when the dog is clean. If the dog is in a clipped pet trim and has not been in for professional grooming for six weeks or more, remove the excessive body coat and set the pattern before bathing.

Brushing
Systematically line brush the entire coat, right down to the skin. With a slicker brush, the motion used for line brushing is a "pat and pull." Softly pat the coat with the full pad of the brush and pull out and away from the skin with each stroke. The wrist remains in a neutral, or straight, position. The motion should be light and gentle. Start on the lower rear legs and work upwards towards the thigh. Repeat on every leg then proceed to the body, neck, head ears and tail. Work evenly over the pet, holding or pushing up the coat with one hand. It can be done with either a comb or a brush, but in most cases the comb is reserved for double checking the work of the brush. With the slicker brush, work the seam line, pulling down a

small amount of fur with each stroke. Do not move to the next section until the brush stroke glides smoothly and the skin at the seam line is seen. Pay close attention to the legs, under the front legs, collar area, ears, and tail. Let your hands feel for coat density levels. If an area feels heavier or thicker, it will need special attention with a brush or a comb. If static electricity is a problem while brushing, lightly mist the coat with an anti-static product or water while brushing. When finished, each strand of hair should float freely about as the dog moves.

Feet & Hocks
Trim the pads with a close cutting action blade ranging from a #15 to a #40. Use a very light touch to clean the pads of long hair. To create a rounded foot, first block in the foot to form a square. This will help create a full circular shape with the toes pointing directly forward. Finish detailing and rounding the outline of the foot by using long, curved shears.

Detail Finish
Lightly neaten the entire outline of the dog, removing long, shaggy stray hairs that interrupt a smooth flow. The finished appearance is very natural. This can be done with thinning shears or shears as long as the look remains natural. Finish with a fine mist of coat polish on the body coat for added shine.

Special Note
The topknot is gathered into a single ponytail at the center of the skull. This single topknot often is made up of many smaller sections and gathered into one at the center. By dealing with more than one ponytail, the tied up topknot has a tendency to stay in place longer than a single one. On pet dogs it is common to slightly trim the stop area between the eyes.

Suggested Tools & Equipment

- Nail Trimmers
- Styptic Powder
- Ear Powder
- Ear Cleaning Solution
- Hemostat
- Cotton Balls
- Clippers
- #40 and #15 Blades for Pads
- Slicker Brush
- Greyhound Comb
- Pin Brush
- Dematting Tools
- Straight Shears
- Curved Shears
- Small Detailing Shears
- Thinning Shears

Notes:

Notes From The Grooming Table ©2016

Breed Facts & Characteristics

Country of Origin: Australia

Height at Shoulder: 9"–10"

Coat Length/Type: Long/Flowing

Color: Shades of blue and tan with the darker color creating a saddle over the back, back of neck and top of head.

Correct grooming procedure:
Bathe & Brush Out/Minor Trimming

Common pet grooming practices:
Bathe & Brush Out/Clipper-Trim

-The Goal-
Coat should be mat- and tangle-free. The fur should be light and airy, moving freely with the dog as it moves.

🐾 Bathing and Drying Directions:
• For coats longer than 3", use Natural Long Haired
• For coats shorter than 3", use Curly and Wavy Coated.

Thinning shear lightly above eyes to softly expose them.

Clip ears clean and smooth.

Clear stop area with thinners or clippers.

Line comb and brush **every** inch of this dog, right down to the skin.

Lightly trim sanitary areas—both under tail and tummy.

Watch friction areas:
• Collar Area
• Arm Pits
• Behind Ears
• Legs & Thighs

Trim nails as short as possible or grind.

Pads are shaved. The feet are clipped clean from the wrist down on the front and on the rear, from the hock down with a close blade such as a #10 or #15 used with the grain. Detail the edge of the foot by hand with small shears. Neaten undercarriage line by hand.

TOY

Grooming Procedures & Recommendations

See page 72 for
Bathing & Drying Instructions

See page 602 for
Drop Coat Styling Options

Frequency
Bathe once a week to once every 12 weeks.

Pre-Work
Trim or grind nails every four to six weeks to maintain a healthy foot structure. Clean the ears by swabbing with a mild ear cleaning solution. Hair should be plucked from within the ear canal only as necessary for healthy ear management. Prior to bathing, quickly go over the entire body and remove any serious mats or tangles. If the tangle can be penetrated with water, leave it and remove when the dog is clean. If the dog is in a clipped pet trim and has not been in for professional grooming for six weeks or more, remove the excessive body coat and set the pattern before bathing.

Brushing
Systematically line brush the entire coat, right down to the skin. With a slicker brush, the motion used for line brushing is a "pat and pull." Softly pat the coat with the full pad of the brush and pull out and away from the skin with each stroke. The wrist remains in a neutral, or straight, position. The motion should be light and gentle. Start on the lower rear legs and work upwards towards the thigh. Repeat on every leg then proceed to the body, neck, head ears and tail. Work evenly over the pet, holding or pushing up the coat with one hand. It can be done with either a comb or a brush, but in most cases the comb is reserved for double checking the work of the brush. With the slicker brush, work the seam line, pulling down a small amount of fur with each stroke. Do not move to the next section until the brush stroke glides smoothly and the skin at the seam line is seen. Pay close attention to the legs, under the front legs, collar area, ears, and tail. Let your hands feel for coat density levels. If an area feels heavier or thicker, it will need special attention with a brush or a comb. If static electricity is a problem while brushing, lightly mist the coat with an anti-static product or water while brushing. When finished, each strand of hair should float freely about as the dog moves.

Head
The head is left in a natural state with light trimming in the eye area. The Silky topknot is left free. The entire ear is clipped clean and very close to the skin. Use a #15 blade for the backside of the ears and a #40 with a light touch for the insides. Edge the ear with small detailing shears, keeping the tips of the shears towards the tips of the ears.

Tail
Slightly neaten the underside of the tail with thinning shears.

Feet & Hocks
The feet of this breed are clean, like a poodle, but not as close to the skin and a bit higher up on the leg. Clip the top of the foot with a #10 blade with the grain of the coat, or a #7F against the coat growth. Clip from the wrist to the toes on the front and from the hock to the toes on the rear. Neaten the edges with detailing shears or a #40 when the pads are clipped.

Detail Finish
Lightly neaten the entire outline of the dog, removing long, shaggy stray hairs that interrupt a smooth flow. The finished appearance is very natural. This can be done with thinning shears or shears as long as the look remains natural. Finish with a fine mist of coat polish on the body coat for added shine.

Suggested Tools & Equipment

- Nail Trimmers
- Styptic Powder
- Ear Powder
- Ear Cleaning Solution
- Hemostat
- Cotton Balls
- Clippers
- #40 and #15 Blades for Pads
- Slicker Brush
- Greyhound Comb
- Pin Brush
- Dematting Tools
- Straight Shears
- Curved Shears
- Small Detailing Shears
- Thinning Shears

Notes:

Toy Fox Terrier

Breed Facts & Characteristics

Country of Origin: United States

Height at Shoulder: 8½"–11½"

Coat Length/Type: Short/Smooth

Color: Tricolored, bicolored. Color mostly on the head. Body is predominately white with spots of clear color.

Correct grooming procedure:
Bathe & Curry Brush

Common pet grooming practices:
Bathe & Curry Brush

-The Goal-
The coat should be clean and fresh smelling, with the coat laying flat against the body. No shedding hair.

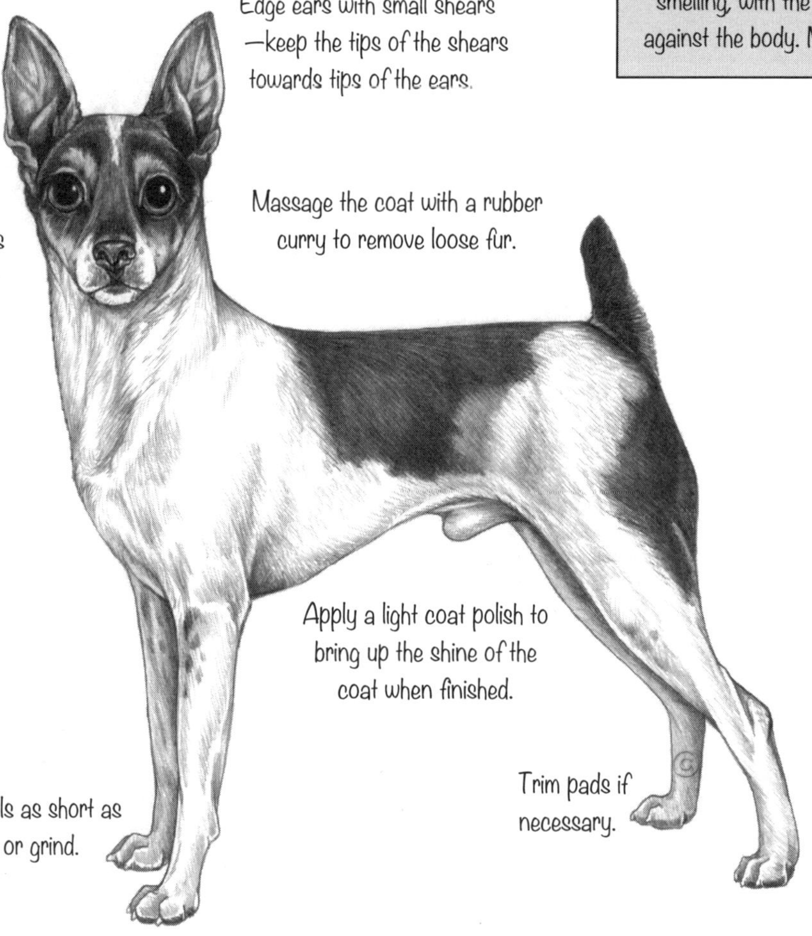

Use a damp towel to go over the muzzle after the bath.

Edge ears with small shears —keep the tips of the shears towards tips of the ears.

Remove whiskers only if the client requests.

Massage the coat with a rubber curry to remove loose fur.

Apply a light coat polish to bring up the shine of the coat when finished.

Trim nails as short as possible or grind.

Trim pads if necessary.

See page 66 for Bathing & Drying Instructions

Suggested Tools & Equipment

- Nail Trimmers
- Styptic Powder
- Ear Cleaning Solution
- Cotton Balls

- Clippers
- #40 or #15 Blade
- Rubber Curry
- Carding Tool

- Small Detailing Shears
- Thinning Shears

TOY

Notes *from your*
Grooming Table

Breed Facts & Characteristics

Country of Origin: England

Height at Shoulder: 6"–8"

Coat Length/Type: Long/Flowing

Color: Clear shades of blue and tan when mature. The blue creates a saddle over the back and the back of the neck. The tan covers the head, chest and legs.

Correct grooming procedure:
Bathe & Brush Out/Minor Trimming

Common pet grooming practices:
Bathe & Brush Out/Clipper-Trim

General Description

The Yorkshire Terrier is a small, compact and well-proportioned little dog. They are full of energy and are extremely self-confident. Their long, silky blue and tan coat is the hallmark of the breed.

Tie up topknot at center of head.

Clip the top ⅓ of the ear leather to expose the tips.

Clear stop area with thinners or clippers.

-The Goal-
Coat should be mat- and tangle-free. The fur should be light and airy, moving freely with the dog as it moves.

Line comb and brush **every** inch of this dog, right down to the skin.

Watch friction areas:
• Collar Area
• Arm Pits
• Behind Ears
• Legs & Thighs

Lightly trim sanitary areas—both under tail and tummy.

Trim nails as short as possible or grind.

Shave pads and scissor feet round. Neaten undercarriage line.

🐾 Bathing and Drying Directions:
• For coats longer than 3", use Natural Long Haired
• For coats shorter than 3", use Curly and Wavy Coated.

TOY

Grooming Procedures & Recommendations

See page 72 for
Bathing & Drying Instructions

See page 602 for
Drop Coat Styling Options

Frequency
Bathe once a week to once every 12 weeks.

Pre-Work
Trim or grind nails every four to six weeks to maintain a healthy foot structure. Clean the ears by swabbing with a mild ear cleaning solution. Hair should be plucked from within the ear canal only as necessary for healthy ear management. Prior to bathing, quickly go over the entire body and remove any serious mats or tangles. If the tangle can be penetrated with water, leave it and remove when the dog is clean. If the dog is in a clipped pet trim and has not been in for professional grooming for six weeks or more, remove the excessive body coat and set the pattern before bathing.

Brushing
Systematically line brush the entire coat, right down to the skin. With a slicker brush, the motion used for line brushing is a "pat and pull." Softly pat the coat with the full pad of the brush and pull out and away from the skin with each stroke. The wrist remains in a neutral, or straight, position. The motion should be light and gentle. Start on the lower rear legs and work upwards towards the thigh. Repeat on every leg then proceed to the body, neck, head ears and tail. Work evenly over the pet, holding or pushing up the coat with one hand. It can be done with either a comb or a brush, but in most cases the comb is reserved for double checking the work of the brush. With the slicker brush, work the seam line, pulling down a

small amount of fur with each stroke. Do not move to the next section until the brush stroke glides smoothly and the skin at the seam line is seen. Pay close attention to the legs, under the front legs, collar area, ears, and tail. Let your hands feel for coat density levels. If an area feels heavier or thicker, it will need special attention with a brush or a comb. If static electricity is a problem while brushing, lightly mist the coat with an anti-static product or water while brushing. When finished, each strand of hair should float freely about as the dog moves.

Head
The topknot can be gathered into a single ponytail at the center of the skull and folded over to create a button, or split into two buttons centered over each eye to accentuate them. A small bow may be attached to the button(s) to further enhance the eyes. The top ⅓ of the ears are shaved clean with a #15 blade on the back side of the ear and a #40 in the inside. Finish by edging with small detailing shears to present neat triangular ear tips. On pet dogs it is common to slightly trim the stop area between the eyes.

Tail
Slightly neaten the underside of the tail with thinning shears.

Feet & Hocks
Trim the pads with a close cutting action blade ranging from a #15 to a #40. Use a very light touch to clean the pads of long hair. To create a rounded foot, first block in the foot to form a square. This will help create a full circular shape with the toes pointing directly forward. Finish detailing and rounding the outline of the foot by using long, curved shears.

Suggested Tools & Equipment

- Nail Trimmers
- Styptic Powder
- Ear Powder
- Ear Cleaning Solution
- Hemostat
- Cotton Balls
- Clippers
- #40 and #15 Blades for Pads
- Slicker Brush
- Greyhound Comb
- Pin Brush
- Dematting Tools
- Straight Shears
- Curved Shears
- Small Detailing Shears
- Thinning Shears

Detail Finish
Lightly neaten the entire outline of the dog, removing long, shaggy stray hairs that interrupt a smooth flow. The finished appearance is very natural. This can be done with thinning shears or shears as long as the look remains natural. Finish with a fine mist of coat polish on the body coat for added shine.

The Non-Sporting Group is easily the most diverse of the breed groups—these dogs can be playful as well as calm and they have a great variety in size and coat type. This group includes those breeds that do not easily fit into other categories.

American Eskimo Dog NON-SPORTING   HEAVY COATED

Breed Facts & Characteristics

Country of Origin: United States

Height at Shoulder: 9"–19"

Coat Length/Type: Combination/Heavy

Color: All white with some cream or biscuit allowed.

Correct grooming procedure:
Bathe & Brush Out/Minor Trimming

Common pet grooming practices:
Bathe & Brush Out/Minor Trimming

-The Goal-
The coat should be light and stand off the dog. As the dog moves, the coat should bounce and float with it. You should be able to sink a wide-toothed comb to the skin and pull it freely out to the end of the hair shaft.

Let a powerful high-velocity dryer help in all aspects of grooming this type of coat, before and after the bath. Blow out loose coat, tangles and dirt. Dry and fluff.

~Seasonal Shedding~
In Colder Climates.

Edge ears with thinning shears to make very natural and neat.

Watch for mats.

Thoroughly line brush/comb entire dog.

Use a damp towel to go over the muzzle after the bath.

The rump can really get packed with coat. Pay close attention to this area.

Remove whiskers only if the client requests.

The neck and chest can really get packed with coat. Pay close attention to this area.

Can shed heavily here.

Can shed heavily here.

Trim hocks.

Trim nails as close as possible or grind.

Shave pads.

Neaten the back of the pastern to the stopper pad.

Neaten feet to look natural with well arched toes.

Notes From The Grooming Table ©2016   456

Grooming Procedures & Recommendations

See page 70 for
Bathing & Drying Instructions

Frequency

Bathe once a week to once every 2 weeks.

Pre-Work

Trim or grind nails at least every four to six weeks to maintain a healthy foot structure. Swab the ears clean with a mild ear cleaning solution. Quickly blow out the dog's coat with a high-velocity dryer to effectively lift dirt and debris away from the skin and loosen coat. Brush out or remove any matting found in the longer coated areas. If the tangles are loose enough so that water can fully penetrate them, remove them after bathing and drying. If water cannot penetrate, remove the mat or tangle prior to bathing.

Brushing

Line brush, working in sections, until the dog is entirely tangle-free. When finished, there should be little, if any, fur still being removed with a firm slicker brush. Double-check the work with a wide-toothed comb and your hands. Go over the entire body, feeling for any inconsistencies in the density levels of the coat. If an area seems moist to the touch or fuller than the rest of the coat, rework the area with the appropriate tool. Mats, tangles and excessive coat are easily trapped in the following areas: behind the ears, around the ruff, the thigh area, the undercarriage and the tail. Give extra attention to these areas before finishing the groom.

Feet & Hocks

Trim the pads with blades ranging from a #15 to a #40. Use a very light touch to clean the pads of long hair. If there is long fur between the toes, brush it back so the fur stands up and away from the foot. With thinning shears, trim off the excess to create a neat and very natural looking foot with well-arched toes. Tidy the outside edge of the foot, if needed, with small detailing shears. If the hocks have longer coat, trim lightly with thinning shears to show a neat, clean area. A #4F blade used in reverse works well for trimming the tops of the feet and the hocks on small to larger dogs that are light to moderately coated. With very heavy-coated or giant dogs, handle the top of the feet and hocks using hand-trimming techniques instead of a clipper.

Sanitary Area

If the dog has a sanitation problem under the tail, lightly trim this area with thinning shears. Only clear enough coat to accomplish the goal and keep it looking very natural. Trimming of the groin area is not recommended unless there is a sanitary problem. If the groin needs to be trimmed, do so very lightly and try to leave the fur long enough so that the harsh coat does not prickle the skin, causing the dog to lick at the irritation.

Detail Finish

Removal of muzzle whiskers is optional, based on client preference. For added shine, finish with a fine mist of coat polish on the body coat. Application of bows and mild cologne is optional.

Suggested Tools & Equipment

- Nail Trimmers
- Styptic Powder
- Ear Cleaning Solution
- Cotton Balls
- Clippers
- #40 and #15 Blades for Pads
- #4F for Feet & Hocks (optional)
- Slicker Brush
- Wide-Toothed Comb
- Rubber Curry
- Undercoat Rake
- Dematting Tools
- High-Velocity Dryer
- Small Detailing Shears
- Curved Shears
- Thinning Shears

Notes:

Notes From The Grooming Table ©2016

Bichon Frise

Breed Facts & Characteristics

Country of Origin: Mediterranean

Height at Shoulder: 9½"–11½"

Coat Length/Type: Curly/Thick

Color: All white but some cream or biscuit coloring is allowed.

Correct grooming procedure:

Scissor-Trim

Common pet grooming practices:

Clipper-Trim or Scissor-Trim

General Description

The Bichon Frise is an active, happy little dog with great enthusiasm for life. Everything about the look of this breed is soft and rounded, thus earning it the label of "powderpuff." Their bodies are compact, yet they are longer than they are tall. The fun loving, curious expression is set off by deep dark eyes and a dark nose. The coat is curly and dense and considered non-shedding. Their color is always white, but a small amount of cream or buff is allowed.

> **-The Goal-**
> The fur should look like a powderpuff, void of any marks or lines. The coat needs to be totally mat free. The outline should be velvet smooth and neat. The breed is to be well balanced, slightly longer than tall.

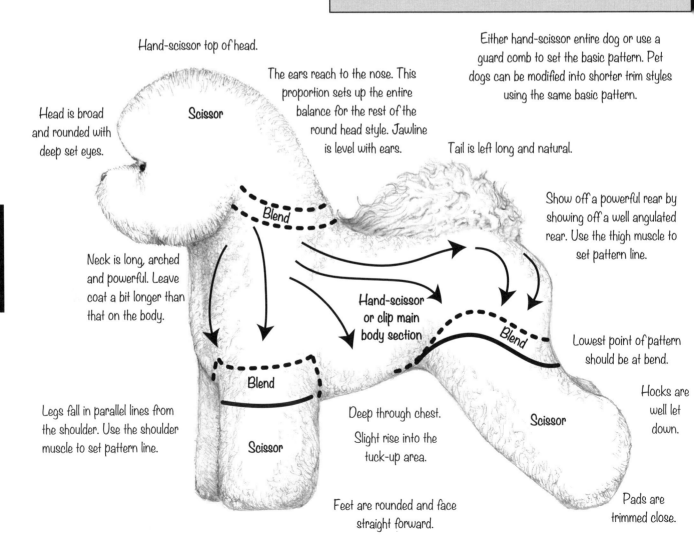

Hand-scissor top of head.

The ears reach to the nose. This proportion sets up the entire balance for the rest of the round head style. Jawline is level with ears.

Either hand-scissor entire dog or use a guard comb to set the basic pattern. Pet dogs can be modified into shorter trim styles using the same basic pattern.

Head is broad and rounded with deep set eyes.

Scissor

Tail is left long and natural.

Show off a powerful rear by showing off a well angulated rear. Use the thigh muscle to set pattern line.

Blend

Neck is long, arched and powerful. Leave coat a bit longer than that on the body.

Hand-scissor or clip main body section

Blend

Lowest point of pattern should be at bend.

Blend

Hocks are well let down.

Legs fall in parallel lines from the shoulder. Use the shoulder muscle to set pattern line.

Scissor

Deep through chest.

Slight rise into the tuck-up area.

Scissor

Pads are trimmed close.

Feet are rounded and face straight forward.

Grooming Procedures & Recommendations

See page 74 for
Bathing & Drying Instructions

Frequency

Bathe once a week to once every 12 weeks. Trim every four to six weeks to maintain a stylized fashion.

Pre-Work

Trim or grind nails at least every four to six weeks to maintain a healthy foot structure. Clean the ears by swabbing with a mild ear cleaning solution. Pluck any long hair inside the ear canal using an ear powder and your fingers or hemostat. Prior to bathing, quickly go over the entire body and remove any serious mats or tangles. If the tangle can be penetrated with water, leave it and remove when the dog is clean. If the pet has not been in for professional grooming for six weeks or more, remove the excessive body coat and set the pattern before bathing.

Brushing

Prior to the haircut, the dog must be completely tangle-free. Use a firm slicker brush or comb to methodically work over the entire body in a line brush fashion. If the pet has very fine fur or delicate skin, use a soft slicker brush instead. Pay close attention to the friction points where mats and tangles typically hide: behind the ears, around the ruff, in the armpits, the thigh area, the undercarriage and the tail. Be careful when using any tool with metal teeth or bristles. A heavy hand or too much repetition in an area can cause cuts and/or brush burns.

General Pattern Lines

This pattern calls for the coat to be about 1 inch long all over. The actual coat length may vary slightly to accentuate or lessen key conformation points of the dog. There are no broken lines anywhere, and the coat outlines the natural contour of the body.

Body

The body can be either hand-scissored or clipper-cut with a longer guard comb. Leave coat about 1 inch long over the entire body. Follow the contour of the body. The finish should be smooth and even without any scissor or clipper marks. Many pet owners opt for less than 1 inch of coat for easier home maintenance trim styling.

Crest & Neck

The crest starts from the top of the head to the withers area. The crest is left longer than the coat on the body. Hand-scissor the neck to accentuate a proud, upright head carriage. Follow the contour at the neck blending in with the body. The finish should be smooth and even without any scissor marks. For a pet trim version, shorten the length of the crest and neck coat, but leave it longer than the main body.

Tail

The tail is left in a totally long and natural state.

Front Leg

The longest coat on the legs can range from 1 to 2 inches depending on the amount of bone and coat density. The front legs drop straight down from the body. When viewed in profile, the front legs fall directly below the withers. The pattern line at the shoulder is about 2 fingers above the top of the elbow, at the point where the muscle begins to turn under. The coat at the transition line will be very short and taper into the longer leg furnishings if blade has been used. This can be accomplished by feathering off at the blending point with the same blade used on the body. To effectively feather off in this manner, you need a steady hand and a dog that stands still. Most stylists prefer to finish the legs by hand with shears ranging from 8.5 to 10 inches in length.

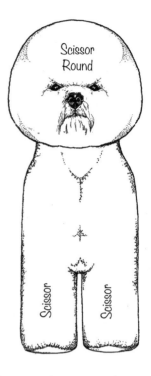

The eyes and nose are at the center of the round head piece. Ears are level with the jaw line. At transition points between the body and the legs, blend the lines so they are invisible. The legs should fall into straight columns, from the body to the rounded feet, when viewed from the front or rear. There are no breaks in the pattern anywhere on the dog.

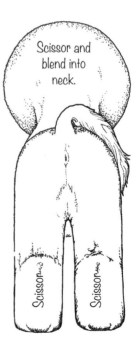

Their expression is friendly and alert. The topknot, ears and muzzle all lend themselves to a balanced, well rounded head style with no broken lines. The dark eyes and nose are at the center of the head. The eyes are deep set. The ear feathering is equal in length to the nose.

Shape the top of the head into an smooth, even extension of the skull. The coat is softly rounded with curved shears to create a well formed head style that balances with the overall trim and blends into the neck. There are no breaks over the ears.

Bevel the topknot line steeply so it is very short right above the eyes, getting longer as it moves out and away from the eyes. Bevel area does not exceed much beyond the outside corners of the eyes.

Once the ear length is trimmed to the end of the nose, the amount of fur left on the jaw will be determined. The ears and jawline should be equal. Round the jawline with large, curved shears. The coat at the end of the muzzle will be beveled to blend with the longer coat of the jaw.

The only way to get the correct look and size for the Bichon head style is to leave the neck fuller, blending the rounded topknot into the crested neck. The fuller neck will extend to the withers area based on the conformation of the pet and the length of the trim. The longer the trim, the farther the neck line will extend. The fuller coat on the neck should look very natural, enhancing a long neck and upright head style.

Softly round the ends of the ears to the length of the nose. The top of the ear should blend seamlessly into the topknot without any lines or indentations.

The throat is clipped with the same blade used on the body or it can be slightly shorter.

Other methods of blending off at the top of the leg include using a guard comb followed by hand-scissoring and blending with shears. After the final trim, the legs should form two parallel columns descending from the shoulder into tight, round feet. The coat at the back of the elbow is very short and falls straight down off the back of the leg toward the ground.

Hindquarters
The hindquarters are wide with muscular thighs. If working with medium to longer guard combs when clipping this area, clip over the thigh muscle with the same blade used on the body. For pet trims using a closer guard comb, or shorter blade, blend the transitional areas with a short to medium guard comb. Start to blend off with the clipper where the muscle starts to turn under on a diagonal line

from the flank region to about 3 or 4 fingers above the hock. The blending should be invisible when the trim is finished. Blend with shears if necessary. The stifle area should have enough furnishing left to give the legs substance and angulation. The longest coat on the legs can range from 1 to 2 inches depending on the amount of bone and coat density. Shape this area by hand with shears after the clipper work is complete. When viewed from the rear, the legs should form two parallel lines to the ground. The hocks are well let down. There should be adequate coat on the hock area to accentuate the angles of the rear assembly.

Feet

Both the front and rear feet are compact with well-arched toes. To show off these traits, the feet are trimmed very close to the edge of the foot, beveling out onto fuller leg coat. The feet should point straight ahead, toeing neither in nor out. Begin trimming the feet by forming a square box around the foot while the dog is standing in a natural, square position. With the dog's feet firmly planted on the table, remove the sharp edges of the box and round the feet as they face straight forward. If detailing the feet with the foot lifted off the tabletop, always use a small pair of detailing shears to minimize the risk of accidentally cutting the pads. If a very close cutting blade is used to trim the pads, use a firm slicker brush to brush the longer leg coat over the outer edges of the pad and trim that hair at the same time the pads are clipped clean.

Head

The head is broad with a domed skull. When looking straight at the face, the eyes and nose create a triangular shape and should look like three lumps of coal. These three features create the focal point for the rounded head style. They are the center of the head piece. The eyes are round in shape, framed with dark pigment and set off by a well-defined stop. Trim the stop area just enough to expose the eye, either with thinning shears or a moderately close blade, such as a #10. Create a deep-set eye by clearing the fur over the eye area at a steep angle, closer right above the eyelids and longer as it moves away from the eye, in a slight visor. The top of the head should be shaped by hand with shears to blend the head with the

neck and body, creating a soft, domed shape. There are no breaks in the coat, either over the ears or at the back of the head where the head joins the neck or crest. It should balance with the overall dog. Do not trim beyond the outside corners of the eyes. The top of the head should be shaped by hand with shears to blend the head with the neck and body, creating a soft, domed shape. There are no breaks in the coat, either over the ears or at the back of the head where the head joins the neck or crest. It should balance with the overall dog.

Ears

The ears blend seamlessly into the head piece without any breaks. When pulled forward, the length should be trimmed to the length of the nose. This is a key element for setting up the correct look of a Bichon head piece. Once the ear length has been established, then softly bevel the ears.

Muzzle

The ears will determine the length of coat left on the muzzle and jaw. They are equal in length. The line should be clean and neat. Around the tip of the muzzle/nose area, the coat is shorter and trimmed on an angle, getting closer to the skin as you get closer to the nose. When viewed from the front, the domed top skull and the ears blend together in one continuous line, while the lowest point of the ear does not fall below the line of the jaw. To eliminate a double-chin effect, trim out a soft "V" shape up between the jawbones (mandible) when clipping the throat area.

Grooming Tips & Trends

The current trend for grooming the Bichon Frise is to highly stylize the trim, either for pet or show. To remain current with national grooming trends, attend or watch the top winning dogs at AKC-sanctioned dog shows or talk

Suggested Tools & Equipment

- Nail Trimmers
- Styptic Powder
- Ear Powder
- Ear Cleaning Solution
- Cotton Balls
- Hemostat
- Clippers
- Slicker Brush
- Greyhound Comb
- Straight Shears
- Curved Shears
- Small Detailing Shears
- Thinning Shears
- Dematting Tools
- High-Velocity Dryer

Common Blade Options:

- #40, #15, #10
- #7F, #5F, #4F
- Medium to Long Guard Combs

with award-winning pet stylists at pet grooming shows. Many pet owners opt for much shorter trim styles to fit into a busy family environment. If trimming in a much shorter style, modify the head to balance with the body, but try to maintain the integrity of the breed by maintaining the principle of no breaks in the coat, on the body or on the head. Shape the head by using the ears as your key reference points

Boston Terrier

Breed Facts & Characteristics

Country of Origin: United States

Height at Shoulder: 10"–16"

Coat Length/Type: Short/Smooth

Color: Black or dark brindle with white markings. White muzzle, facial blaze, white chest required with white feet.

Correct grooming procedure:
Bathe & Curry Brush

Common pet grooming practices:
Bathe & Curry Brush

-The Goal-
The coat should be clean and fresh smelling, with the coat laying flat against the body. No shedding hair.

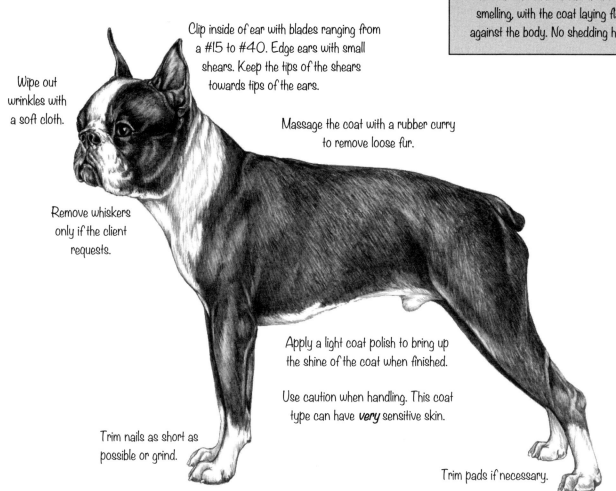

Wipe out wrinkles with a soft cloth.

Clip inside of ear with blades ranging from a #15 to #40. Edge ears with small shears. Keep the tips of the shears towards tips of the ears.

Massage the coat with a rubber curry to remove loose fur.

Remove whiskers only if the client requests.

Apply a light coat polish to bring up the shine of the coat when finished.

Use caution when handling. This coat type can have *very* sensitive skin.

Trim nails as short as possible or grind.

Trim pads if necessary.

See page 66 for Bathing & Drying Instructions

Suggested Tools & Equipment

- Nail Trimmers
- Styptic Powder
- Ear Cleaning Solution
- Cotton Balls

- Clippers
- #40 or #15 Blade
- Rubber Curry
- Carding Tool

- Small Detailing Shears
- Thinning Shears

Notes *from your* Grooming Table

Breed Facts & Characteristics

Country of Origin: British Isles

Height at Shoulder: 12"–16"

Coat Length/Type: Short/Smooth

Color: Brindles, solid white, reds, tans, and piebald with color and white clearly mixed in large patches.

Correct grooming procedure:
Bathe & Curry Brush

Common pet grooming practices:
Bathe & Curry Brush

-The Goal-
The coat should be clean and fresh smelling, with the coat laying flat against the body. No shedding hair.

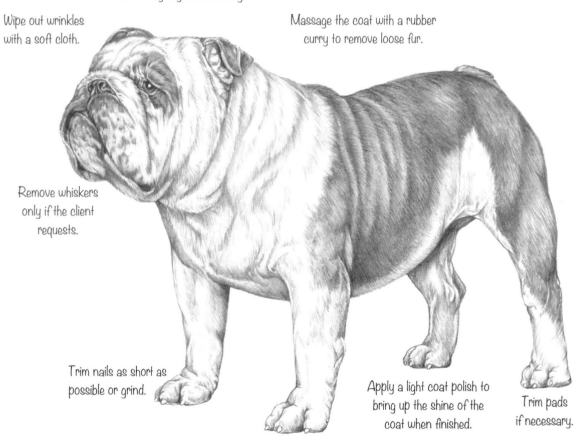

Make sure wrinkles are clean and totally dry after bathing.

Wipe out wrinkles with a soft cloth.

Massage the coat with a rubber curry to remove loose fur.

Remove whiskers only if the client requests.

Trim nails as short as possible or grind.

Apply a light coat polish to bring up the shine of the coat when finished.

Trim pads if necessary.

See page 66 for
Bathing & Drying Instructions

Suggested Tools & Equipment

- Nail Trimmers
- Styptic Powder
- Ear Cleaning Solution
- Cotton Balls
- Clippers
- #40 or #15 Blade
- Rubber Curry
- Carding Tool
- Small Detailing Shears
- Thinning Shears

Chinese Shar-Pei

NON-SPORTING   SHORT COATED

Breed Facts & Characteristics

Country of Origin: China

Height at Shoulder: 18"–20"

Coat Length/Type: Short/Harsh

Color: All solid colors and sable. Slightly darker shading on the ears and down the dorsal line acceptable.

Correct grooming procedure:
Bathe & Brush Out

Common pet grooming practices:
Bathe & Brush Out

-The Goal-
The coat should be clean and fresh smelling, with the coat laying smoothly against the body. No shedding hair.

Wipe out wrinkles with a soft cloth.

Make sure wrinkles are clean and totally dry after the bath.

Remove whiskers only if the client requests.

Massage the coat with a rubber curry to remove loose fur.

Trim nails as short as possible or grind.

Trim pads if necessary.

See page 67 for Bathing & Drying Instructions

Suggested Tools & Equipment

- Nail Trimmers
- Styptic Powder
- Ear Cleaning Solution
- Cotton Balls

- Clippers
- #40 or #15 Blade
- Slicker Brush
- Rubber Curry

- Carding Tool
- De-Shedding Tools
- Small Detailing Shears
- Thinning Shears

Notes From The Grooming Table ©2016

Chow Chow

Breed Facts & Characteristics

Country of Origin: China

Height at Shoulder: 17"–20"

Coat Length/Type: Combination/Heavy

Color: Black, blue, all shades of red and cream. Lighter shades of the base coat acceptable in the ruff, tail, and feathers of the legs.

Correct grooming procedure:
Bathe & Brush Out

Common pet grooming practices:
Bathe & Brush Out/Clipper-Trim

-The Goal-
Coat should be mat free, shiny, light and airy. The coat should bounce and float with the dog as it moves.

Edge ear tips.

Use a damp towel to go over the muzzle after the bath.

Remove whiskers only if the client requests.

This area is thick. Pay close attention when brushing.

Trim nails as close as possible or grind.

Use a high-velocity dryer both before and after the bath. Blow out loose coat, tangles and dirt. Dry and fluff.

Thoroughly line brush and comb entire dog.

This area is thick. Pay close attention when brushing.

Trim hocks.

Shave pads and neaten feet to look natural.

Grooming Procedures & Recommendations

See page 70 for
Bathing & Drying Instructions

SPECIAL NOTE
In some areas, owners commonly request a lion-styled trim on their Chow Chow. Follow the same basic pattern lines found on page 263 for the Portuguese Water Dog.

Frequency
Bathe once a week to once every 12 weeks.

Pre-Work
Trim or grind nails at least every four to six weeks to maintain a healthy foot structure. Swab the ears clean with a mild ear cleaning solution. Quickly blow out the dog's coat with a high-velocity dryer to effectively lift dirt and debris away from the skin and loosen coat. Brush out or remove any matting found in the longer coated areas. If the tangles are loose enough so that water can fully penetrate them, remove them after bathing and drying. If water cannot penetrate, remove the mat or tangle prior to bathing.

Brushing
Line brush, working in sections, until the dog is entirely tangle-free. When finished, there should be little, if any, fur still being removed with a firm slicker brush. Double-check the work with a wide-toothed comb and your hands. Go over the entire body, feeling for any inconsistencies in the density levels of the coat. If an area seems moist to the touch or fuller than the rest of the coat, rework the area with the appropriate tool. Mats, tangles and excessive coat are easily trapped in the following areas: behind the ears, around the ruff, the thigh area, the undercarriage and the tail. Give extra attention to these areas before finishing the groom.

Feet & Hocks
Trim the pads with blades ranging from a #15 to a #40. Use a very light touch to clean the pads of long hair. If there is long fur between the toes, brush it back so the fur stands up and away from the foot. With thinning shears, trim off the excess to create a neat and very natural looking foot with well-arched toes. Tidy the outside edge of the foot, if needed, with small detailing shears. If the hocks have longer coat, trim lightly with thinning shears to show a neat, clean area. A #4F blade used in reverse works well for trimming the tops of the feet and the hocks on small to larger dogs that are light to moderately coated. With very heavy-coated or giant dogs, handle the top of the feet and hocks using hand-trimming techniques instead of a clipper.

Sanitary Area
If the dog has a sanitation problem under the tail, lightly trim this area with thinning shears. Only clear enough coat to accomplish the goal and keep it looking very natural. Trimming of the groin area is not recommended unless there is a sanitary problem. If the groin needs to be trimmed, do so very lightly and try to leave the fur long enough so that the harsh coat does not prickle the skin, causing the dog to lick at the irritation.

Suggested Tools & Equipment
- Nail Trimmers
- Styptic Powder
- Ear Cleaning Solution
- Cotton Balls
- Clippers
- #40 and #15 Blades for Pads
- #4F for Feet & Hocks (optional)
- Slicker Brush
- Wide-Toothed Comb
- Rubber Curry
- Undercoat Rake
- Dematting Tools
- High-Velocity Dryer
- Small Detailing Shears
- Curved Shears
- Thinning Shears

Detail Finish
Removal of muzzle whiskers is optional, based on client preference. For added shine, finish with a fine mist of coat polish on the body coat. Application of bows and mild cologne is optional.

Notes:

Notes From The Grooming Table ©2016

Breed Facts & Characteristics

Country of Origin: Madagascar

Height at Shoulder: 8½"–12"

Coat Length/Type: Long/Flowing

Color: White

Correct grooming procedure:
Bathe & Brush Out

Common pet grooming practices:
Clipper-Trim

-The Goal-
Coat should be mat- and tangle-free.
The fur should be light and airy, moving
freely with the dog as it moves.

Lightly clear stop area with thinners or clippers.

Leave ears long.

Thoroughly line brush and comb **every inch** of this dog, right down to the skin.

Lightly trim sanitary area, under the tail, and the tummy.

Watch friction areas:
• Collar Area
• Arm Pits
• Behind Ears
• Legs and Thighs

Lightly neaten undercarriage line.

Shave pads and scissor feet round.

NON-SPORTING

See page 72 for
Bathing & Drying Instructions

See page 602 for
Drop Coat Styling Options

Frequency

Bathe once a week to once every 12 weeks.

Pre-Work

Trim or grind nails every four to six weeks to maintain a healthy foot structure. Clean the ears by swabbing with a mild ear cleaning solution. Hair should be plucked from within the ear canal only as necessary for healthy ear management. Prior to bathing, quickly go over the entire body and remove any serious mats or tangles. If the tangle can be penetrated with water, leave it and remove when the dog is clean. If the dog is staying in a clipped pet trim and has not been in for professional grooming for six weeks or more, remove the excessive body coat and set the pattern before bathing.

Brushing

Systematically line brush the entire coat, right down to the skin. With a slicker brush, the motion used for line brushing is a "pat and pull." Softly pat the coat with the full pad of the brush and pull out and away from the skin with each stroke. The wrist remains in a neutral, or straight, position. The motion should be light and gentle. Start on the lower rear legs and work upwards towards the thigh. Repeat on every leg then proceed to the body, neck, head, ears and tail. Work evenly over the pet, holding or pushing up the coat with one hand. It can be done with either a comb or a brush,

but in most cases the comb is reserved for double checking the work of the brush. With the slicker brush, work the seam line, pulling down a small amount of fur with each stroke. Do not move to the next section until the brush stroke glides smoothly and the skin at the seam line is seen. Pay close attention to the legs, under the front legs, collar area, ears, and tail. Let your hands feel for coat density levels. If an area feels heavier or thicker, it will need special attention with a brush or a comb. If static electricity is a problem while brushing, lightly mist the coat with an anti-static product or water while brushing. When finished, each strand of hair should float freely about as the dog moves.

Head

For show, the head is left long and natural with no special treatment to the topknot area other than the hair is parted at the center. For pet dogs, it is common to hold the hair out of the eyes by banding, braiding or using barrettes. For pets, it is also common to slightly trim the stop area between the eyes.

Ears

The ears are erect and covered with long hair that drapes over them.

Feet & Hocks

Trim the pads with a close cutting action blade ranging from a #15 to a #40. Use a very light touch to clean the pads of long hair. To create a rounded foot, first block in the foot to form a square. This will help create a full circular shape with the toes pointing directly forward. Finish detailing and rounding the outline of the foot by using long, curved shears.

Suggested Tools & Equipment

- Nail Trimmers
- Styptic Powder
- Ear Powder
- Ear Cleaning Solution
- Hemostat
- Cotton Balls
- Clippers
- #40 and #15 Blades for Pads
- Slicker Brush
- Greyhound Comb
- Pin Brush
- Dematting Tools
- Straight Shears
- Curved Shears
- Small Detailing Shears
- Thinning Shears

Detail Finish

Lightly neaten the entire outline of the dog, removing long, shaggy stray hairs that interrupt a smooth flow. The finished appearance is very natural. This can be done with thinning shears or shears as long as the look remains natural. Finish with a fine mist of coat polish on the body coat for added shine.

Notes:

Notes From The Grooming Table ©2016

Dalmatian

Breed Facts & Characteristics

Country of Origin: Yugoslavia

Height at Shoulder: 19"–23"

Coat Length/Type: Short/Smooth

Color: Clear, well defined spots of black or brown on a white back ground.

Correct grooming procedure:
Bathe & Curry Brush

Common pet grooming practices:
Bathe & Curry Brush

-The Goal-
The coat should be clean and fresh smelling, with the coat laying flat against the body. No shedding hair.

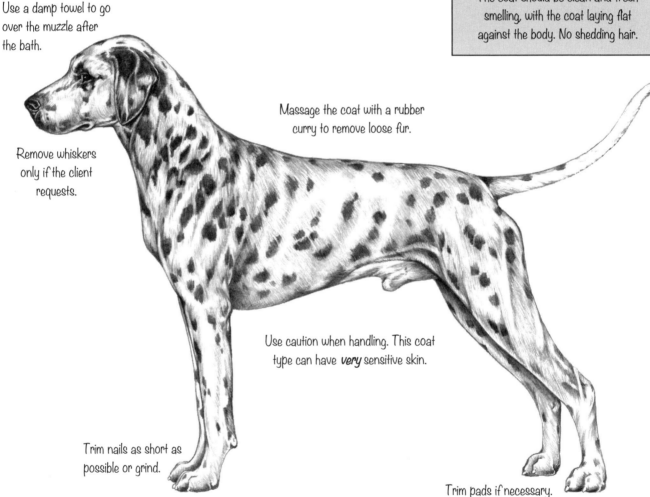

Use a damp towel to go over the muzzle after the bath.

Remove whiskers only if the client requests.

Massage the coat with a rubber curry to remove loose fur.

Use caution when handling. This coat type can have **very** sensitive skin.

Trim nails as short as possible or grind.

Trim pads if necessary.

See page 66 for Bathing & Drying Instructions

Suggested Tools & Equipment

- Nail Trimmers
- Styptic Powder
- Ear Cleaning Solution
- Cotton Balls

- Clippers
- #40 or #15 Blade
- Rubber Curry
- Carding Tool

- Small Detailing Shears
- Thinning Shears

NON-SPORTING

Notes *from your* Grooming Table

Breed Facts & Characteristics

Country of Origin: Finland

Height at Shoulder: 15½"–20"

Coat Length/Type: Double Coated/Thick

Color: All shades of reds. The undercoat is lighter and is seen through the darker outer coat.

Correct grooming procedure:
Bathe & Brush Out/Minor Trimming

Common pet grooming practices:
Bathe & Brush Out/Minor Trimming

-The Goal-
The coat should be fresh smelling, light and stand off the body. No loose hair.

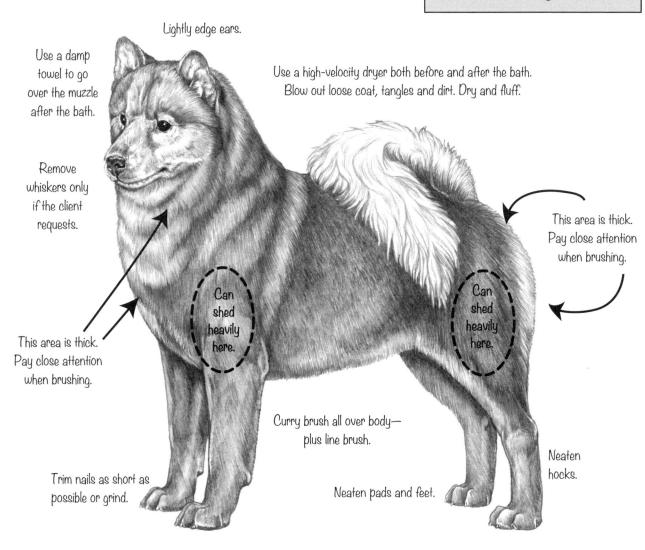

Lightly edge ears.

Use a damp towel to go over the muzzle after the bath.

Use a high-velocity dryer both before and after the bath. Blow out loose coat, tangles and dirt. Dry and fluff.

Remove whiskers only if the client requests.

This area is thick. Pay close attention when brushing.

Can shed heavily here.

Can shed heavily here.

This area is thick. Pay close attention when brushing.

This area is thick. Pay close attention when brushing.

Trim nails as short as possible or grind.

Curry brush all over body— plus line brush.

Neaten hocks.

Neaten pads and feet.

NON-SPORTING

Grooming Procedures & Recommendations

See page 69 for
Bathing & Drying Instructions

Frequency
Bathe once a week to once every 12 weeks.

Pre-Work
Trim or grind nails at least every four to six weeks to maintain a healthy foot structure. Clean the ears by swabbing with a mild ear cleaning solution. Prior to bathing, quickly go over the entire body with a high-velocity dryer to help lift dirt and dander away from the skin and loosen any shedding coat.

Brushing
Use a slicker brush, rubber curry, shedding blade, dematting tool or undercoat rake to loosen skin dander and remove loose coat. Be careful when using any tool with metal teeth or bristles. A heavy hand or too much repetition in an area can cause cuts and/or brush burns. Brushing and combing is not finished until all loose fur is removed, or it has become difficult to remove more than a half a brush full after repeated brushing.

Sanitary Area
If the dog has a sanitation problem under the tail, lightly trim this area with thinning shears. Only clear enough coat to accomplish the goal and keep it looking very natural. Trimming of the groin area is not recommended unless there is a sanitary problem. If the groin needs to be trimmed, do so very lightly and try to leave the fur long enough so that the harsh coat does not prickle the skin, causing the dog to lick at the irritation.

Feet & Hocks
Trim the pads with a close cutting action blade, ranging from a #15 to a #40. Use a very light touch to clean the pads of long hair. If there is long fur between the toes, back brush the fur so it stands up and away from the foot. With thinning shears, trim off the excess creating a neat and very natural looking foot with well arched toes. Tidy the outside edge of the foot, if needed, with small detailing shears. If the hocks have longer coat on them, trim lightly with thinning shears showing a neat, clean area. A #4F blade used in reverse works well for trimming the tops of the feet and the hocks on some dogs.

Detail Finish
Removal of whiskers on the muzzle is optional, based on client preference. Finish with a fine mist of coat polish on the body for added shine. Application of bows and mild cologne is optional.

Grooming Tip
Let your hands guide you. Learn to feel for differences in coat density levels. Areas that feel heavier or more dense than other areas need special attention when bathing, brushing and drying.

Suggested Tools & Equipment

- Nail Trimmers
- Styptic Powder
- Ear Cleaning Solution
- Cotton Balls
- Clippers
- #40 and #15 Blades for Pads
- #4F for Feet & Hocks (optional)
- Slicker Brush
- Greyhound Comb
- Rubber Curry
- Carding Tool
- De-Shedding Tools
- Small Detailing Shears
- Thinning Shears
- High-Velocity Dryer

Notes:

French Bulldog

Breed Facts & Characteristics

Country of Origin: England

Height at Shoulder: 11"–12"

Coat Length/Type: Short/Smooth

Color: Tan, white, all shades of brindle, brindle and white.

Correct grooming procedure:

Bathe & Curry Brush

Common pet grooming practices:

Bathe & Curry Brush

-The Goal-
The coat should be clean and fresh smelling laying flat against the body. No shedding hair.

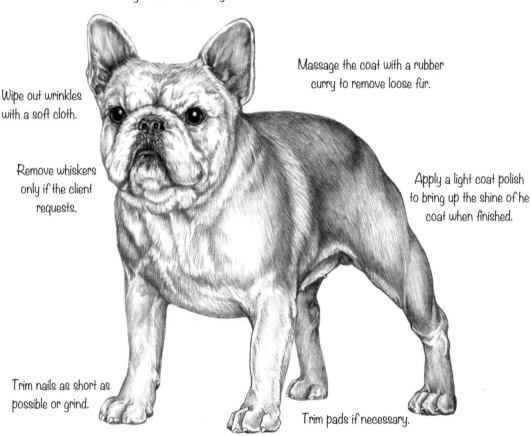

Edge ears if necessary.

Wipe out wrinkles with a soft cloth.

Remove whiskers only if the client requests.

Massage the coat with a rubber curry to remove loose fur.

Apply a light coat polish to bring up the shine of he coat when finished.

Trim nails as short as possible or grind.

Trim pads if necessary.

See page 66 for
Bathing & Drying Instructions

Suggested Tools & Equipment

- Nail Trimmers
- Styptic Powder
- Ear Cleaning Solution
- Cotton Balls
- Clippers
- #40 or #15 Blade
- Rubber Curry
- Carding Tool
- Small Detailing Shears
- Thinning Shears

Notes *from your* Grooming Table

Breed Facts & Characteristics

Country of Origin: Holland

Height at Shoulder: 17"–18"

Coat Length/Type: Combination/Thick

Color: A combination of black, gray and cream colors. The outer guard coat is tipped with the darker tones creating unique color patterns on each dog. Eye rims are always etched in black giving the dog its characteristic "spectacles."

Correct grooming procedure:
Bathe & Brush Out/Minor Trimming

Common pet grooming practices:
Bathe & Brush Out/Minor Trimming

-The Goal-
Coat should be mat free shiny, light and airy. The coat should bounce and float with the dog as it moves.

Edge ear tips.

Use a damp towel to go over the muzzle after the bath.

Remove whiskers only if the client requests.

This area is thick. Pay close attention when brushing.

Can shed heavily here.

Trim nails as short as possible or grind.

Use a high-velocity dryer both before and after the bath. Blow out loose coat, tangles and dirt. Dry and fluff.

Thoroughly line brush and comb entire dog.

This area is thick. Pay close attention when brushing.

Can shed heavily here.

Trim hocks.

Shave pads and neaten feet to look natural.

NON-SPORTING

Grooming Procedures & Recommendations

See page 70 for
Bathing & Drying Instructions

Frequency

Bathe once a week to once every 12 weeks.

Pre-Work

Trim or grind nails at least every four to six weeks to maintain a healthy foot structure. Swab the ears clean with a mild ear cleaning solution. Quickly blow out the dog's coat with a high-velocity dryer to effectively lift dirt and debris away from the skin and loosen coat. Brush out or remove any matting found in the longer coated areas. If the tangles are loose enough so that water can fully penetrate them, remove them after bathing and drying. If water cannot penetrate, remove the mat or tangle prior to bathing.

Brushing

Line brush, working in sections, until the dog is entirely tangle-free. When finished, there should be little, if any, fur still being removed with a firm slicker brush. Double-check the work with a wide-toothed comb and your hands. Go over the entire body, feeling for any inconsistencies in the density levels of the coat. If an area seems moist to the touch or fuller than the rest of the coat, rework the area with the appropriate tool. Mats, tangles and excessive coat are easily trapped in the following areas: behind the ears, around the ruff, the thigh area, the undercarriage and the tail. Give extra attention to these areas before finishing the groom.

Feet & Hocks

Trim the pads with blades ranging from a #15 to a #40. Use a very light touch to clean the pads of long hair. If there is long fur between the toes, brush it back so the fur stands up and away from the foot. With thinning shears, trim off the excess to create a neat and very natural looking foot with well-arched toes. Tidy the outside edge of the foot, if needed, with small detailing shears. If the hocks have longer coat, trim lightly with thinning shears to show a neat, clean area. A #4F blade used in reverse works well for trimming the tops of the feet and the hocks on small to larger dogs that are light to moderately coated. With very heavy-coated or giant dogs, handle the top of the feet and hocks using hand-trimming techniques instead of a clipper.

Sanitary Area

If the dog has a sanitation problem under the tail, lightly trim this area with thinning shears. Only clear enough coat to accomplish the goal and keep it looking very natural. Trimming of the groin area is not recommended unless there is a sanitary problem. If the groin needs to be trimmed, do so very lightly and try to leave the fur long enough so that the harsh coat does not prickle the skin, causing the dog to lick at the irritation.

Detail Finish

Removal of muzzle whiskers is optional, based on client preference. For added shine, finish with a fine mist of coat polish on the body coat. Application of bows and mild cologne is optional.

Suggested Tools & Equipment

- Nail Trimmers
- Styptic Powder
- Ear Cleaning Solution
- Cotton Balls
- Clippers
- #40 and #15 Blades for Pads
- #4F for Feet & Hocks (optional)
- Slicker Brush
- Wide-Toothed Comb
- Rubber Curry
- Undercoat Rake
- Dematting Tools
- High-Velocity Dryer
- Small Detailing Shears
- Curved Shears
- Thinning Shears

Notes:

Breed Facts & Characteristics

Country of Origin: Tibet

Height at Shoulder: 10"–11"

Coat Length/Type: Long/Flowing

Color: All colors and patterns acceptable.

Correct grooming procedure:
Bathe & Brush Out/Minor Trimming

Common pet grooming practices:
Bathe & Brush Out/Clipper-Trim

-The Goal-
Coat should be mat- and tangle-free. The fur should be light and airy, moving freely with the dog as it moves.

Start a part down center of skull and follow it through to the base of the tail.

Leave ears long.

Line comb and brush **every** inch of this dog, right down to the skin.

Clear stop area with thinners or clippers.

Lightly trim sanitary areas—both under tail and tummy.

Watch friction areas:
• Collar Area
• Arm Pits
• Behind Ears
• Legs & Thighs

Trim nails as short as possible or grind.

Shave pads and scissor feet round. Neaten undercarriage line.

❧ Bathing and Drying Directions:
  • For coats longer than 3", use Natural Long Haired
  • For coats shorter than 3", use Curly and Wavy Coated.

Grooming Procedures & Recommendations

See page 72 for
Bathing & Drying Instructions

See page 602 for
Drop Coat Styling Options

Frequency
Bathe once a week to once every
12 weeks.

Pre-Work
Trim or grind nails every four to
six weeks to maintain a healthy foot
structure. Clean the ears by swabbing
with a mild ear cleaning solution. Hair
should be plucked from within the ear
canal only as necessary for healthy ear
management. Prior to bathing, quickly
go over the entire body and remove any
serious mats or tangles. If the tangle can
be penetrated with water, leave it and
remove when the dog is clean. If the
dog is staying in a clippered pet trim
and has not been in for professional
grooming for six weeks or more, remove
the excessive body coat and set the
pattern before bathing.

Brushing
Systematically line brush the entire coat,
right down to the skin. With a slicker
brush, the motion used for line brushing
is a "pat and pull." Softly pat the coat
with the full pad of the brush and pull
out and away from the skin with each
stroke. The wrist remains in a neutral,
or straight, position. The motion should
be light and gentle. Start on the lower
rear legs and work upwards towards the
thigh. Repeat on every leg then proceed
to the body, neck, head ears and tail.
Work evenly over the pet, holding or
pushing up the coat with one hand. It
can be done with either a comb or a
brush, but in most cases the comb is
reserved for double checking the work
of the brush. With the slicker brush,

work the seam line, pulling down a
small amount of fur with each stroke.
Do not move to the next section until
the brush stroke glides smoothly and
the skin at the seam line is seen. Pay
close attention to the legs, under the
front legs, collar area, ears, and tail. Let
your hands feel for coat density levels.
If an area feels heavier or thicker, it will
need special attention with a brush or
a comb. If static electricity is a problem
while brushing, lightly mist the coat
with an anti-static product or water
while brushing. When finished, each
strand of hair should float freely about
as the dog moves.

Head
For show, the head is left long and
natural with no special treatment to the
topknot area other than a part down the
center. For pet dogs, it is common to
hold the hair out of the eyes by banding,
braiding or using barrettes. For pets, it
is also common to slightly trim the stop
area between the eyes.

Feet & Hocks
Trim the pads with a close cutting
action blade ranging from a #15 to a
#40. Use a very light touch to clean the
pads of long hair. To create a rounded
foot, first block in the foot to form
a square. This will help create a full
circular shape with the toes pointing
directly forward. Finish detailing and
rounding the outline of the foot by
using long, curved shears.

Detail Finish
Lightly neaten the entire outline of
the dog, removing long, shaggy stray
hairs that interrupt a smooth flow. The
finished appearance is very natural.
This can be done with thinning shears
or shears as long as the look remains
natural. Finish with a fine mist of coat
polish on the body coat for added shine.

Suggested Tools & Equipment

- Nail Trimmers
- Styptic Powder
- Ear Powder
- Ear Cleaning Solution
- Hemostat
- Cotton Balls
- Clippers
- #40 and #15 Blades for Pads
- Slicker Brush
- Greyhound Comb
- Pin Brush
- Dematting Tools
- Straight Shears
- Curved Shears
- Small Detailing Shears
- Thinning Shears

Notes:

Breed Facts & Characteristics

Country of Origin: Germany

Height at Shoulder: 12"–14"

Coat Length/Type: Long/Flowing

Color: All colors and coat patterns are allowed.

Correct grooming procedure:

Bathe & Brush Out/Clipper-Trim

Common pet grooming practices:

Bathe & Brush Out/Clipper-Trim

-The Goal-
Coat should be mat- and tangle-free. The fur should be light and airy, moving freely with the dog as it moves. Bare skin should be hair free and smooth. Pattern lines clean and crisp.

🐾 Bathing and Drying Directions:
- For coats longer than 3", use Natural Long Haired
- For coats shorter than 3", use Curly and Wavy Coated.

The head is left in a natural state.

All long fur is to be left totally natural without any trimming.

Clip tail to about the half way point of the tail bone leaving a plume on the end.

Line comb and line brush to remove any mats or tangles in the coat.

Clip the rear section of the dog with blades ranging from a #7F or #15 blade, with or against the coat growth based on skin sensitivity. Use the last rib, the top of the hock and the top of the knee to set the pattern lines. All lines should be crisp and neat.

Front legs are clipped from the elbow to just above the pastern joint.

The cuffs should be equal in size and balanced, front to back.

Trim nails as close as possible or grind.

Feet are clipped with a #10 or #15 up to the point where the dew claws have been removed. Shave the pads.

Grooming Procedures & Recommendations

See page 72 for
Bathing & Drying Instructions

See page 602 for
Drop Coat Styling Options

Frequency
Bathe once a week to once every
12 weeks.

Pre-Work
Trim or grind nails every four to six weeks
to maintain a healthy foot structure.
Clean the ears by swabbing with a mild
ear cleaning solution. Hair should be
plucked from within the ear canal only
as necessary for healthy ear management.
Prior to bathing, quickly go over the
entire body and remove any serious mats
or tangles. If the tangle can be penetrated
with water, leave it and remove when the
dog is clean. If the dog is in a clipped pet
trim and has not been in for professional
grooming for six weeks or more, remove
the excessive body coat and set the pattern
before bathing.

Brushing
Systematically line brush the entire coat,
right down to the skin. With a slicker
brush, the motion used for line brushing
is a "pat and pull." Softly pat the coat
with the full pad of the brush and pull
out and away from the skin with each
stroke. Do not move to the next section
until the brush stroke glides smoothly
and the skin at the seam line is seen. Pay
close attention to the legs, under the front
legs, collar area, ears, and tail. If static
electricity is a problem while brushing,
lightly mist the coat with an anti-static
product or water while brushing. When
finished, each strand of hair should float
freely about as the dog moves.

Lion Trim
To create the trim, the rear quarters of the
dog are shaved closely with blades ranging
from a #7F to a #15. Blade selection is
based on the sensitivity of the skin, the
climate and the owner's preference. Clip
against the grain of the coat growth to
get the smoothest trim. The head, neck,
and chest are left in full, natural coat. The
pattern line for the body starts at the last
rib. The entire rear quarters are clipped
clean to just above the hock.

Tail
Using the same blade as on the body,
continue clipping half of the tail, leaving
an untrimmed plume covering the end.

Lower Legs
The lower legs have full, untrimmed cuffs
of fur. Set the rear cuffs first, just above
the hock joint. Carry this line forward
when setting the front leg cuffs. The lower
section of the cuff is left in its natural state
with no trimming or shaping. All cuffs
should be equal in height.

Feet
The feet are clipped totally clean, letting the
longer cuff fur drape over the clipped foot.
Trim the pads with a close blade ranging
from a #15 to a #40. Use a very light touch
to clean the pads of long hair. The digits
of the foot are clipped to a point where
the bones of the feet meet the metatarsal
bones or the bones of the pasterns. There
is a slight bump on the sides of the foot
where these bones join. Use a #15 or #10
blade, in reverse with a light touch. Start
by clipping the top of the two center digits.
Start at the nail bed. Tip the blade up so
only the front edge of the blade contacts
the skin. The effective movement of the
clipper is a soft, push-push as you clear the
hair from the foot. The strokes are a very
short forward-and-back motion. Clear the
hair to the point where the bones converge
and there is a natural bend at the foot and
the wrist. Proceed to the outside digits and
repeat the process. Once the top of the
foot is cleared, place your fingers on the
underside of the foot and spread the toes.
Glide just the edge of the blade in between

the toes, using your fingers as buffers. Your
fingers will protect the webbing between
the toes from getting caught between the
teeth of the clipper blade. Again, start at
the nail bed and scoop out the long fur
between the toes. Do one side of all the
toes first, then rotate your clipper in and
repeat the procedure on all the toes on the
other side. When finished, double check
your work for long strays. Clean up around
the nail bed. There are a couple of ways to
do this. One option is to simply turn the
clipper over and touch the nail bed with
the upside down #15 or #10 blade using a
very short push motion. Another technique
is to edge the nail beds lightly with a #40
blade after the toes have been clipped.

Detail Finish
The finished appearance of the longer
hair is very natural. It is never trimmed
or shaped. Finish with a fine mist of coat
polish on the body coat for added shine.

Suggested Tools & Equipment
- Nail Trimmers
- Styptic Powder
- Ear Powder
- Ear Cleaning Solution
- Hemostat
- Cotton Balls
- Clippers
- #40 and #15 Blades for Pads
- #7 Blade
- Slicker Brush
- Greyhound Comb
- Pin Brush
- Dematting Tools
- Straight Shears
- Curved Shears
- Small Detailing Shears
- Thinning Shears

Norwegian Lundehund   NON-SPORTING   DOUBLE COATED

Breed Facts & Characteristics

Country of Origin: Norway

Height at Shoulder: 12"–15"

Coat Length/Type: Double Coated

Color: Light sable and white, or white with tan or dark markings.

Correct grooming procedure:

Bathe & Brush Out

Common pet grooming practices:

Bathe & Brush Out

General Description

The Norwegian Lundehund was developed for a specialized role; retrieving Puffin birds from extremely steep and rugged terrain in its native land of Norway. The breed has at least 6 digits on each foot, sometimes more, to aid in navigating sheer cliffs; they can close their ears so that the ear-canal is protected; the joints in their neck allow it to bend the head backwards over the shoulders, allowing the top of the skull to touch their back. Plus this breed has extremely mobile shoulder-joints, so that both front legs can stretch straight out to the sides.

-The Goal-
The coat should be light and stand off the dog. The coat should bounce and shimmer with the dog as it moves.

Edge ears with thinning shears to make very natural and neat.

Use a damp towel to go over the muzzle after the bath.

Remove whiskers only if the client requests.

The neck and chest can really get packed with coat—pay close attention to this area.

Let a powerful high velocity dryer help in all aspects of grooming this type of coat, before and after the bath— blow out loose coat, tangles, dirt—dry and fluff.

When finished you should be able to sink a wide-toothed comb to the skin and pull it freely out to the end of the hair shaft.

Can shed heavily here.

Can shed heavily here.

The rump can really get packed with coat—pay close attention to this area.

~Seasonal Shedding~
In colder climates.

When shedding—the more work you can do with a powerful high velocity dryer, the less "elbow grease" you will have to exert.

Shave pads.

Trim hocks.

Neaten feet to look natural with well arched toes.

Grooming Procedures & Recommendations

See page 69 for Bathing & Drying Instructions

Frequency
Bathe once a week to once every 12 weeks.

Pre-Work
Trim or grind nails at least every four to six weeks to maintain a healthy foot structure. Clean the ears by swabbing with a mild ear cleaning solution. Prior to bathing, quickly go over the entire body with a high-velocity dryer to help lift dirt and dander away from the skin and loosen any shedding coat.

Brushing
Use a slicker brush, rubber curry, shedding blade, dematting tool or undercoat rake to loosen skin dander and remove loose coat. Be careful when using any tool with metal teeth or bristles. A heavy hand or too much repetition in an area can cause cuts and/or brush burns. Brushing and combing is not finished until all loose fur is removed, or it has become difficult to remove more than a half a brush full after repeated brushing.

Feet & Hocks
Trim the pads with a close cutting action blade, ranging from a #15 to a #40. Use a very light touch to clean the pads of long hair. If there is long fur between the toes, back brush the fur so it stands up and away from the foot. With thinning shears, trim off the excess creating a neat and very natural looking foot with well arched toes. Tidy the outside edge of the foot, if needed, with small detailing shears. If the hocks have longer coat on them, trim lightly with thinning shears showing a neat, clean area. A #4F blade used in reverse works well for trimming the tops of the feet and the hocks on some dogs.

Detail Finish
Removal of whiskers on the muzzle is optional, based on client preference. Finish with a fine mist of coat polish on the body for added shine. Application of bows and mild cologne is optional.

Grooming Tip
Let your hands guide you. Learn to feel for differences in coat density levels. Areas that feel heavier or denser than other areas need special attention when bathing, brushing and drying.

Suggested Tools & Equipment

- Nail Trimmers
- Styptic Powder
- Ear Cleaning Solution
- Cotton Balls
- Clippers
- #40 and #15 Blades for Pads
- #4F for Feet & Hocks (optional)
- Slicker Brush
- Greyhound Comb
- Rubber Curry
- Carding Tool
- De-Shedding Tools
- Small Detailing Shears
- Thinning Shears
- High-Velocity Dryer

Notes:

Notes From The Grooming Table ©2016

Poodle

Breed Facts & Characteristics

Country of Origin: Germany

Height at Shoulder: 10"–25"

Coat Length/Type: Long/Curly

Color: All solid colors in shades of black, grays, browns, tans and white.

Correct grooming procedure:
Hand-Scissor

Common pet grooming practices:
Clipper-Cut

General Description

Poodles are stylish, squarely-built and very intelligent. They have an air of sophistication and distinction all to themselves. They are energetic, athletic and well-proportioned. Their structure allows for free, fluid and elegant movement in all their gaits. This breed's coat is considered non-shedding and hypo-allergenic.

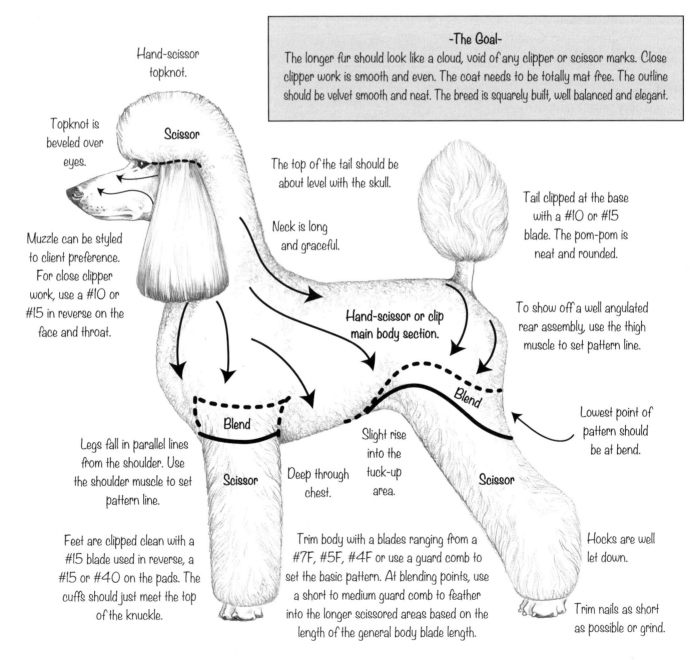

Hand-scissor topknot.

Topknot is beveled over eyes.

Scissor

-The Goal-
The longer fur should look like a cloud, void of any clipper or scissor marks. Close clipper work is smooth and even. The coat needs to be totally mat free. The outline should be velvet smooth and neat. The breed is squarely built, well balanced and elegant.

The top of the tail should be about level with the skull.

Neck is long and graceful.

Tail clipped at the base with a #10 or #15 blade. The pom-pom is neat and rounded.

Muzzle can be styled to client preference. For close clipper work, use a #10 or #15 in reverse on the face and throat.

Hand-scissor or clip main body section.

To show off a well angulated rear assembly, use the thigh muscle to set pattern line.

Blend

Blend

Lowest point of pattern should be at bend.

Legs fall in parallel lines from the shoulder. Use the shoulder muscle to set pattern line.

Scissor

Deep through chest.

Slight rise into the tuck-up area.

Scissor

Hocks are well let down.

Feet are clipped clean with a #15 blade used in reverse, a #15 or #40 on the pads. The cuffs should just meet the top of the knuckle.

Trim body with a blades ranging from a #7F, #5F, #4F or use a guard comb to set the basic pattern. At blending points, use a short to medium guard comb to feather into the longer scissored areas based on the length of the general body blade length.

Trim nails as short as possible or grind.

See page 74 for
Bathing & Drying Instructions

See page 590 for
Classic Pet Poodle Styles

Frequency
Bathe once a week to once every 12 weeks.

Pre-Work
Trim or grind nails every four to six weeks to maintain a healthy foot structure. Clean the ears by swabbing with a mild ear cleaning solution. Hair should be plucked from within the ear canal only as necessary for healthy ear management. Prior to bathing, quickly go over the entire body and remove any serious mats or tangles. If the tangle can be penetrated with water, leave it and remove when the dog is clean. If the pet has not been in for professional grooming for six weeks or more, remove the excessive body coat and set the pattern before bathing. Before starting the final haircut, make sure the dog's coat is throughly brushed out and free of tanlges.

Brushing
Systematically line brush the entire coat, right down to the skin. With a slicker brush, the motion used for line brushing is a "pat and pull." Softly pat the coat with the full pad of the brush and pull out and away from the skin with each stroke. The wrist remains in a neutral, or straight, position. The motion should be light and gentle. Start on the lower rear legs and work upwards towards the thigh. Repeat on every leg then proceed to the body, neck, head ears and tail. Work evenly over the pet, holding or pushing up the coat with one hand. It can be done with either a comb or a brush, but in most cases the comb is reserved for

double checking the work of the brush. With the slicker brush, work the seam line, pulling down a small amount of fur with each stroke. Do not move to the next section until the brush stroke glides smoothly and the skin at the seam line is seen. Pay close attention to the legs, under the front legs, collar area, ears, and tail. Let your hands feel for coat density levels. If an area feels heavier or thicker, it will need special attention with a brush or a comb. If static electricity is a problem while brushing, lightly mist the coat lightly with an anti-static product or water while brushing. When finished, each strand of hair should float freely about as the dog moves.

Sizes
The Poodle comes in three different sizes: the Toy, standing under 10 inches; the Miniature, standing between 10 and 15 inches; and the Standard, standing more than 15 inches in height at the withers. For those breeds that have close clipper work done on the face, throat, tail and feet, it is most effective to trim the shortest areas first before moving onto the main body or leg areas.

Clipping the Face
The topknot is set using landmark points on the skull as reference. The clipped line on the sides of the face that helps to establish the topknot runs from the ear canal opening to the back corner of the eye. It will parallel the zygomatic arch, which is easily felt. For efficient clipping, it's important to gently stretch the skin back toward the ear, but not up into the topknot area. Stretching the skin upward will destroy the natural, straight line from the ear canal to the back of the eye. Continue clipping forward, under the eye and down the bridge of the nose.

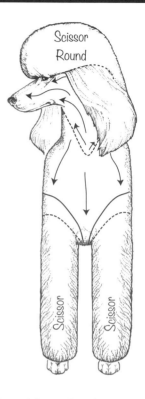

The neck line is clean, long and plunging. Cuff sits just on top of the knuckles. At transition points between the body and the legs, blend the lines so they are invisible. The legs should fall into straight columns, from the body to the cuffed feet, when viewed from the front or rear. The pom-pom on the tail is a well shaped oval.

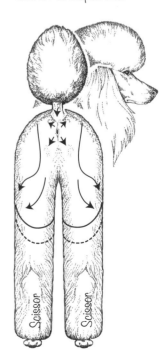

Their expression is friendly, intelligent and alert. The rounded topknot accentuates this appearance and adds balance to the overall look. The top skull and the muzzle are equal in length with the stop area being the center point. The topknot is well shaped and neat.

Shape the topknot into a smooth, even extension of the skull. The clipper lines are crisp and clean. The longer coat is softly rounded with curved shears to create a well balanced, neat topknot that balances with the overall length of the trim.

Bevel the topknot line steeply so it is very short right above the eyes, getting longer as it moves out and away from the eye.

Shape the topknot in a rounded fashion. It should appear to be an extension of the skull and be in balance with the rest of the trim. The ideal height for the topknot is the distance measured between the outside corners of the eyes.

On a clean face, the muzzle is clipped very close. Use a #10 or #15 against the grain with a light touch. Clear the entire cheek, throat and muzzle area. The line for the topknot goes from the ear canal forward following the bony ridge straight to the back corner of the eye. Clip under the eye. At the stop area, clip out an inverted triangle and continue to clip right down the bridge of the nose. Stretch the skin of the lips while clipping to ensure they are clipped clean.

Once the sides and front are trimmed, fluff the entire topknot and round it out with curved shears. Blend the topknot into the neck.

Style Options:
Ear and mustache styles may be interchanged based on client preference.

The throat is clipped clean with the same blade used on the muzzle. The line will be from the ear bulb to about 3–4 finger widths above the breast bone. The neck is elegantly clipped in a "U" or "V" shape.

Softly round the ends of the ears based on client preference.

NON-SPORTING

At the stop area, clip an inverted "V" to give definition to the eyes and to lengthen the muzzle. If you are clipping the face cleanly, work over the muzzle area and the lower jaw. To safely clip the lip area, place a finger at the back corner of the mouth and stretch the skin. Be careful not to catch the smooth skin ridges just on the inside of the lips on the lower jaw. For safety, ride that area with only the edge of the clipper blade, minimizing the chance of the ridges slipping between the cutting teeth. Hold the clipper softly, in a supple hand, as it glides over the skin.

Clipping the Throat

The pattern for the neck and throat is shaped in a "V." It accentuates a long and elegant neck. The "V" will start at the ear bulbs and plunge downward, stopping a few inches above the breastbone. Some stylists use the end of the nose as a general reference point for setting the depth of the V-shaped neckline. While the dog is standing squarely, ask the dog to tip its nose toward the chest. Where the end of the nose falls is the lowest point of the neckline. If the dog has a very short muzzle, the line may be drawn slightly farther down.

Tail

Traditionally, the Poodle tail is clipped at the base, leaving a full pom-pom on the end, although there are other trim styles as well. The tail structure should be long enough to allow you to clip a third of the base of the tail with a #10 or #15 blade in reverse. The end two-thirds is left to hand-scissor in a ball or oval shape. Continue clipping around the tail bone to the point where the tail and the body join. Clip a small inverted "V" at the top of the tail, in line with the spine. When the dog raises its tail, this indentation will eliminate the small bump of hair that is common when the clipped line is not carried up far

enough. On shorter coated trims, this line will be very minor compared with longer hand-scissored styles. This "V" shape can be extended to add style and flair to the trim. If there is not enough tail to clip in this ratio (one-third to two-thirds), make an adjustment to give the pet some form of a balanced pom-pom. On some tails, the bone may be so short or non-existent that only a puff of fur can be left, hence the "bunny tail."

Feet

The feet are clipped totally clean. Trim the pads with a close blade ranging from a #15 to a #40. Use a very light touch to clean the pads of long hair. The digits of the foot are clipped to a point where the bones of the feet meet the metatarsal bones or the bones of the pasterns. There is a slight bump on the sides of the foot where these bones join. Use a #15 or #10 blade, in reverse, with a light touch. Start by clipping the top of the two center digits. Start at the nail bed. Tip the blade up so only the front edge of the blade contacts the skin. The effective movement of the clipper is a soft, push-push as you clear the hair from the foot. The strokes are a very short forward-and-back motion. Clear the hair to the point where the bones converge and there is a natural bend at the foot and the wrist. Proceed to the outside digits and repeat the process. Once the top of the foot is cleared, place your fingers on the underside of the foot and spread the toes. Glide just the edge of the blade in between the toes, using your fingers as buffers. Your fingers will protect the webbing between the toes from getting caught between the teeth of the clipper blade. Again, start at the nail bed and scoop out the long fur between the toes. Do one side of all the toes first, then rotate your clipper in and repeat the procedure on all the toes on the other side. When finished, double check your work for long strays. Clean up around

the nail bed. There are a couple of ways to do this. One option is to simply turn the clipper over and touch the nail bed with the upside down #15 or #10 blade, using a very short, push motion. Another technique is to lightly edge the nail beds with a #40 blade after the toes have been clipped.

Main Clipper Work on Body

Start the clipper work at the base of the occiput and pull the clipper towards you. (When leaving a V-shaped or full-crested topknot, adjust your starting point accordingly.) If your clippers won't glide smoothly over the shoulder/withers area, start your clipper work at the withers instead of the occiput. (Save the neck and shoulder area until the dog is sitting down.) Work down the spine toward the tail and over the rump. Continue to clip in the direction of the arrows, as shown. Let each clipper stroke slightly overlap the previous stroke. Let the weight of the clipper do the work for you. All you need to do is let it glide smoothly along, following the natural contours of the pet. Go completely over the dog once, and then back brush if using a shorter guard comb or a #4F, #5F, or #7F blade. If using a medium to longer guard comb, combine back brushing with a body roll to get the coat to stand up off the body. A body roll is a simulation of a natural shake. Many times you can get the dog to shake by gently blowing in its ear. If this doesn't work, stand behind the dog and pinch a small amount of coat between your fingers at about the 4 and 8 o'clock positions on the dog's body. Tug quickly and gently, alternating from side to side about three or four times. Repeat the entire body clipping a second time, following the arrows. Set the coat up and check for rough or high spots. If the coat is not consistently smooth by the third pass, analyze your clipping methods and make the necessary corrections.

Notes From The Grooming Table ©2016

Grooming Procedures & Recommendations

Blending Areas

When working with a shorter guard comb, switch to a medium or longer guard for the blending areas over the rump. Swing the medium to long guard comb over the rear area, cutting in the angulation as you work. On the front legs, gently let the clipper fall off at the widest point of the shoulder, skimming and blending into the longer coat on the front legs. This technique is called "blending," "feathering" or "skimming." The goal is a smooth transition between the shorter clipped coat and the longer scissored coat. Ideally you are looking to create straight parallel lines to the ground. Clipping too quickly in these areas will create tracking, which is undesirable. Maintaining a consistent pace as you feather the blending areas allows the coat to feed efficiently into the teeth of the blade. Hold the clipper at a consistent angle for a smooth, seamless transition.

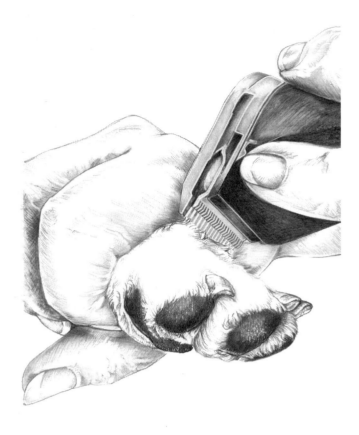

Shaping the Cuffs

Poodle cuffs are shaped two ways, either freely using long shears or by holding the coat down with your hand and using much smaller shears to trim the excess. Hand-scissor shaping is normally reserved for dogs with excellent coat texture and full, scissored legs. The second method is highly effective on pet dogs that have less than perfect coat texture. Either way, the clipped line at the cuff must be sharp and crisp.

For hand-scissoring, hold the foot off the table at a comfortable level for the pet. Comb all the fur down, then fluff it up and out. Glide a long straight shear in just below the clipper line of the foot, at a right angle to the leg. Cut cleanly, going around the entire leg. Re-fluff and continue to bevel the outer edge of the cuff with curved shears. When the dog stands naturally, the bevel of the cuff should be level and uniform in shape.

With the second method, hold the foot off the table at a comfortable level for the pet. With a firm slicker brush, brush all the hair down around the foot. Once the coat is brushed down, slide your hand down the pet's leg, thumb and forefinger closest to the foot. Stop and hold the foot with your fingers coming to rest right at the clipped cuff line. While maintaining the hold on the foot, trim at right angles around the cuff with small detailing shears. The fullness of the leg coat will determine where you place the line. For fuller legs, use the top of the crease marks on the toes. If the leg coat is shorter, move the line closer to the clipped cuff line. When you release the coat, the fur will be nicely beveled. The line should be crisp and free of all stray hairs. As with the hand-scissored cuff, check the work from profile to make sure the cuffs are level from side to

side and front to back. This second method can also be done by edging the cuff with a #40 blade.

Topknot Style Options for the Poodle

The texture of the coat on a topknot will dictate its final appearance. Poodle coat should be full of body, curly and firm in texture. With the correct coat, the fur can be sculpted into beautiful shapes that accentuate the regal, elegant and intelligent look of a poodle. Whatever the shape—flared, straight-sided or rounded—the topknot should always be a well balanced extension of the skull. It should be impeccably neat and symmetrical. The hair on poodles often is not the highest in quality. Thus, shaping a well rounded topknot can pose a challenge. Though there are a number of different ways to shape a topknot, the following formula works well on all, but exceptionally well with floppy topknots. The principle foundation is based on the structure of the skull, which leads to a pleasing balance to the head piece. The process is called the side-side-front-back formula.

Pet Poodle Topknot Styling Formula

Once the face has been clipped, the topknot can be shaped. Comb all the hair over to one side. Flip the ear over the top of the head to minimize the risk of nicking the ear leather where it joins the skull. Glide a pair of opened, straight shears under the clipped line that separates the cheek from the topknot. Rest the lower blade of the shear softly on the skin. Bevel the shear slightly away from the skin to avoid catching the skin between the blades when they close. Flip the ear over and glide the shear over the top of it, right at the junction point of the skull and the leather. Again, bevel the shear slightly and cut. Continue the line around the ear, wrapping right around the base of the ear. Join the topknot line with the neckline so it is one, flowing line. Repeat the process on the opposite side of the head.

Next, comb all the hair forward over the eyes. Glide the opened shear in at a steep bevel. The fur just above the eyes will be very short, but longer as it gently angles away. Once set, this stacked ledge holds hair away from the eyes and gives them a deep-set appearance, creating an intelligent expression for the pet. For the last line, comb all the hair to the back and blend the fur into the neck. When trimming behind the topknot, hold the dog's head in an upright natural position so the top edge of the topknot is not removed in the trimming process. Fluff the topknot with a comb. Give the ears a small tug-tug, alternating between ears to simulate a mild, natural head shake. With curved shears, round the top edge and check that all lines are well blended, neat and clean. Check the work from all angles, front, side and rear.

Special Note

This coat can be corded as well. Please refer to page 77 for directions on bathing a corded coat.

Suggested Tools & Equipment

- Nail Trimmers
- Styptic Powder
- Ear Powder
- Ear Cleaning Solution
- Cotton Balls
- Hemostat
- Clippers
- Slicker Brush
- Greyhound Comb
- Straight Shears
- Curved Shears
- Small Detailing Shears
- Thinning Shears
- Dematting Tools
- High-Velocity Dryer

Common Blade Options:

- #40, #15, #10
- #7F, #5F, #4F
- Variety of Guard Combs

 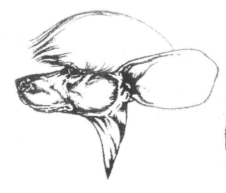 

Schipperke

Breed Facts & Characteristics

Country of Origin: Belgium

Height at Shoulder: 10"–13"

Coat Length/Type: Double Coated/Thick

Color: Black

Correct grooming procedure:
Bathe & Brush Out

Common pet grooming practices:
Bathe & Brush Out

-The Goal-
The coat should be fresh smelling, light and stand off the body. No loose hair.

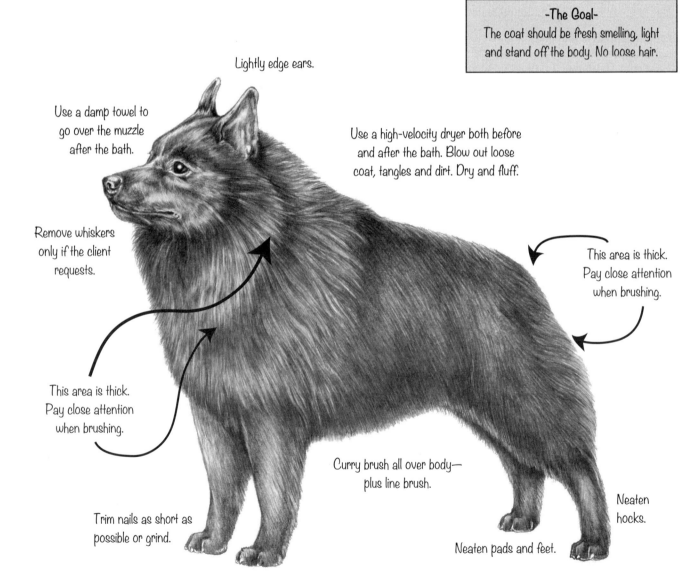

Lightly edge ears.

Use a damp towel to go over the muzzle after the bath.

Use a high-velocity dryer both before and after the bath. Blow out loose coat, tangles and dirt. Dry and fluff.

Remove whiskers only if the client requests.

This area is thick. Pay close attention when brushing.

This area is thick. Pay close attention when brushing.

Curry brush all over body— plus line brush.

Trim nails as short as possible or grind.

Neaten hocks.

Neaten pads and feet.

Grooming Procedures & Recommendations

**See page 69 for
Bathing & Drying Instructions**

Frequency
Bathe once a week to once every 12 weeks.

Pre-Work
Trim or grind nails at least every four to six weeks to maintain a healthy foot structure. Clean the ears by swabbing with a mild ear cleaning solution. Prior to bathing, quickly go over the entire body with a high-velocity dryer to help lift dirt and dander away from the skin and loosen any shedding coat.

Brushing
Use a slicker brush, rubber curry, shedding blade, dematting tool or undercoat rake to loosen skin dander and remove loose coat. Be careful when using any tool with metal teeth or bristles. A heavy hand or too much repetition in an area can cause cuts and/or brush burns. Brushing and combing is not finished until all loose fur is removed, or it has become difficult to remove more than a half a brush full after repeated brushing.

Feet & Hocks
Trim the pads with a close cutting action blade, ranging from a #15 to a #40. Use a very light touch to clean the pads of long hair. If there is long fur between the toes, back brush the fur so it stands up and away from the foot. With thinning shears, trim off the excess creating a neat and very natural looking foot with well arched toes. Tidy the outside edge of the foot, if needed, with small detailing shears. If the hocks have longer coat on them, trim lightly with thinning shears showing a neat, clean area. A #4F blade used in reverse works well for trimming the tops of the feet and the hocks on some dogs.

Sanitary Area
If the dog has a sanitation problem under the tail, lightly trim this area with thinning shears. Only clear enough coat to accomplish the goal and keep it looking very natural. Trimming of the groin area is not recommended unless there is a sanitary problem. If the groin needs to be trimmed, do so very lightly and try to leave the fur long enough so that the harsh coat does not prickle the skin, causing the dog to lick at the irritation.

Detail Finish
Removal of whiskers on the muzzle is optional, based on client preference. Finish with a fine mist of coat polish on the body for added shine. Application of bows and mild cologne is optional.

Grooming Tip
Let your hands guide you. Learn to feel for differences in coat density levels. Areas that feel heavier or more dense than other areas need special attention when bathing, brushing and drying.

Suggested Tools & Equipment

- Nail Trimmers
- Styptic Powder
- Ear Cleaning Solution
- Cotton Balls
- Clippers
- #40 and #15 Blades for Pads
- #4F for Feet & Hocks (optional)
- Slicker Brush
- Greyhound Comb
- Rubber Curry
- Carding Tool
- De-Shedding Tools
- Small Detailing Shears
- Thinning Shears
- High-Velocity Dryer

Notes:

Breed Facts & Characteristics

Country of Origin: Japan

Height at Shoulder: 13½"–16½"

Coat Length/Type: Double Coated/Thick

Color: Reds, black with tan points, and red with black-tipped hairs. The under coat is always light cream or light gray and clearly filters through the darker coat colors.

Correct grooming procedure:

Bathe & Brush Out

Common pet grooming practices:

Bathe & Brush Out

-The Goal-
The coat should be fresh smelling, light and stand off the body. No loose hair.

Lightly edge ears.

Use a high-velocity dryer both before and after the bath. Blow out loose coat, tangles and dirt. Dry and fluff.

Use a damp towel to go over the muzzle after the bath.

Remove whiskers only if the client requests.

This area is thick. Pay close attention when brushing.

This area is thick. Pay close attention when brushing.

Trim nails as short as possible or grind.

Neaten pads and feet.

Neaten hocks.

Curry brush all over body— plus line brush.

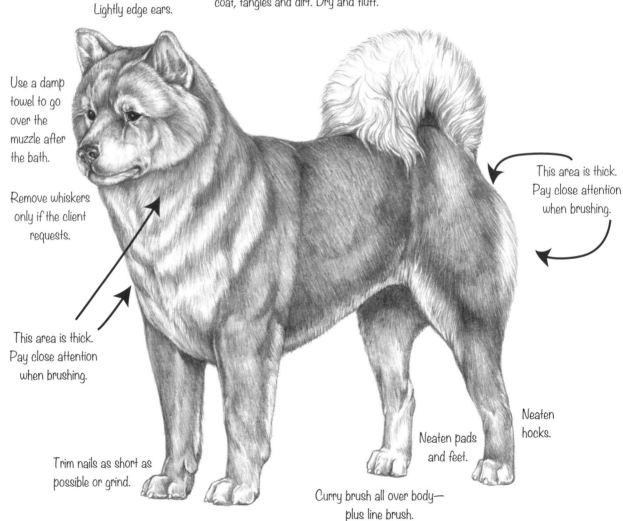

NON-SPORTING

See page 69 for Bathing & Drying Instructions

Frequency
Bathe once a week to once every 12 weeks.

Pre-Work
Trim or grind nails at least every four to six weeks to maintain a healthy foot structure. Clean the ears by swabbing with a mild ear cleaning solution. Prior to bathing, quickly go over the entire body with a high-velocity dryer to help lift dirt and dander away from the skin and loosen any shedding coat.

Brushing
Use a slicker brush, rubber curry, shedding blade, dematting tool or undercoat rake to loosen skin dander and remove loose coat. Be careful when using any tool with metal teeth or bristles. A heavy hand or too much repetition in an area can cause cuts and/or brush burns. Brushing and combing is not finished until all loose fur is removed, or it has become difficult to remove more than a half a brush full after repeated brushing.

Feet & Hocks
Trim the pads with a close cutting action blade, ranging from a #15 to a #40. Use a very light touch to clean the pads of long hair. If there is long fur between the toes, back brush the fur so it stands up and away from the foot. With thinning shears, trim off the excess creating a neat and very natural looking foot with well arched toes. Tidy the outside edge of the foot, if needed, with small detailing shears. If the hocks have longer coat on them, trim lightly with thinning shears showing a neat, clean area. A #4F blade used in reverse works well for trimming the tops of the feet and the hocks on some dogs.

Sanitary Area
If the dog has a sanitation problem under the tail, lightly trim this area with thinning shears. Only clear enough coat to accomplish the goal and keep it looking very natural. Trimming of the groin area is not recommended unless there is a sanitary problem. If the groin needs to be trimmed, do so very lightly and try to leave the fur long enough so that the harsh coat does not prickle the skin, causing the dog to lick at the irritation.

Detail Finish
Removal of whiskers on the muzzle is optional, based on client preference. Finish with a fine mist of coat polish on the body for added shine. Application of bows and mild cologne is optional.

Grooming Tip
Let your hands guide you. Learn to feel for differences in coat density levels. Areas that feel heavier or more dense than other areas need special attention when bathing, brushing and drying.

Suggested Tools & Equipment

- Nail Trimmers
- Styptic Powder
- Ear Cleaning Solution
- Cotton Balls
- Clippers
- #40 and #15 Blades for Pads
- #4F for Feet & Hocks (optional)
- Slicker Brush
- Greyhound Comb
- Rubber Curry
- Carding Tool
- De-Shedding Tools
- Small Detailing Shears
- Thinning Shears
- High-Velocity Dryer

Notes:

NON-SPORTING   COMBINATION COATED

Breed Facts & Characteristics

Country of Origin: Tibet

Height at Shoulder: 9"–11"

Coat Length/Type: Combination/Silky

Color: All colors and patterns acceptable.

Correct grooming procedure:
Bathe & Brush Out/Minor Trimming

Common pet grooming practices:
Bathe & Brush Out/Minor Trimming

-The Goal-
Coat should be mat free, shiny, light and airy. As the dog moves, the coat should bounce and float.

Use a damp towel to go over the muzzle after the bath.

Leave ears natural.

Thoroughly line brush/comb entire dog.

Remove any soft downy undercoat coat by finger plucking.

Remove whiskers only if the client requests.

This area is thick. Pay close attention when brushing.

This area is thick. Pay close attention when brushing.

Neaten hocks.

Trim nails as short as possible or grind.

Shave pads and neaten feet.

🐾 Bathing and Drying Directions:
- For coats longer than 3", use Natural Long Haired
- For coats shorter than 3", use Curly and Wavy Coated.

NON-SPORTING

Grooming Procedures & Recommendations

See page 68 for Bathing & Drying Instructions

Frequency
Bathe once a week to once every 12 weeks.

Pre-Work
Trim or grind nails every four to six weeks to maintain a healthy foot structure. Clean the ears by swabbing with a mild ear cleaning solution. Use a rubber curry, shedding blade, undercoat rake, pumice stone, carding tool, fine stripping knife or natural bristle brush to loosen skin dander and remove loose coat. Use a high-velocity dryer over the coat to quickly and effectively lift dirt and debris away from the skin and loosen coat. Brush out or remove any matting found in the long-coated areas. If the tangles are loose enough so water can fully penetrate the area, remove them after bathing and drying. If water cannot penetrate, remove the mat or tangle prior to bathing.

Brushing
Line brush, working in sections until the dog is entirely tangle-free and all loose coat is removed. When finished, there should be little, if any, fur still being removed with a firm slicker brush. Double-check the work with a comb and your hands. Go over the entire body, feeling for any inconsistencies in the density levels of the coat. If an area seems moist to the touch or fuller than the rest of the coat, rework the area with the appropriate tool. Mats, tangles and excessive coat are easily trapped in the following areas: behind the ears, around the ruff, the thigh area, the undercarriage and the tail. Give extra attention to these areas before finishing the groom.

Carding
If a dog has an abundance of loose undercoat, line card the areas with a carding tool. Common tools can be a fine stripping knife, undercoat rake, a pumice stone, or a #40 blade held between your fingers. Any carding tool should be pulled over the body, working in the direction of the coat growth. This will remove the soft, downy undercoat, allowing the guard coat to conform more closely to the natural outline of the body. It will also aid in the removal of loose, shedding coat, a seasonal problem for many pet owners.

Feet & Hocks
Trim the pads with a close blade ranging from a #15 to a #40. Use a very light touch to clean the pads of long hair. If there is long fur between the toes, back brush the fur so it stands up on top of and away from the foot. With thinning shears, trim the excess to create a neat and very natural looking foot. Tidy the outside edge of the foot, if needed, with small detailing shears. If the hocks have longer coat, trim lightly with thinning shears to show a neat, clean area. A #4F blade, used carefully in reverse, works well for trimming the tops of the feet and the hocks on some dogs.

Sanitary Area
If the dog has a sanitation problem under the tail, lightly trim this area with thinning shears. Only clear enough coat to accomplish the goal and keep it looking very natural. Trimming of the groin area is not recommended unless there is a sanitary problem. If the groin needs to be trimmed, do so very lightly and try to leave the fur long enough so that the harsh coat does not prickle the skin, causing the dog to lick at the irritation.

Suggested Tools & Equipment

- Nail Trimmers
- Styptic Powder
- Ear Cleaning Solution
- Cotton Balls
- Clippers
- #40 and #15 Blades for Pads
- #4F for Feet & Hocks (optional)
- Slicker Brush
- Greyhound Comb
- Rubber Curry
- Carding Tool
- De-Shedding Tools
- Small Detailing Shears
- Thinning Shears

Detail Finish
Edge the ears lightly with thinning shears to neaten and keep a natural look. Hand pluck any long wispy, flyaway hair from around the ears. Removal of whiskers on the muzzle is optional based on client preference. Finish with a fine mist of coat polish on the body coat for added shine. Application of bows and mild cologne is optional.

Notes:

Notes From The Grooming Table ©2016

Breed Facts & Characteristics

Country of Origin: Tibet

Height at Shoulder: 14"–16"

Coat Length/Type: Long/Flowing

Color: All colors and patterns acceptable.

Correct grooming procedure:
Bathe & Brush Out/Minor Trimming

Common pet grooming practices:
Bathe & Brush Out/Clipper-Trim

-The Goal-
Coat should be mat- and tangle-free.
The fur should be light and airy, moving
freely with the dog as it moves.

Part down center of skull.

Clear stop area
with thinners or
clippers.

Leave ears long.

Line comb and brush **every** inch of
this dog, right down to the skin.

Lightly trim sanitary
areas—both under
tail and tummy.

Watch friction areas:
• Collar Area
• Arm Pits
• Behind Ears
• Legs & Thighs

Trim nails as short as
possible or grind.

Shave pads and scissor feet
round. Neaten undercarriage line.

NON-SPORTING

Grooming Procedures & Recommendations

See page 72 for
Bathing & Drying Instructions

See page 602 for
Drop Coat Styling Options

Frequency
Bathe once a week to once every 12 weeks.

Pre-Work
Trim or grind nails every four to six weeks to maintain a healthy foot structure. Clean the ears by swabbing with a mild ear cleaning solution. Hair should be plucked from within the ear canal only as necessary for healthy ear management. Prior to bathing, quickly go over the entire body and remove any serious mats or tangles. If the tangle can be penetrated with water, leave it and remove when the dog is clean. If the dog is staying in a clippered pet trim and has not been in for professional grooming for six weeks or more, remove the excessive body coat and set the pattern before bathing.

Brushing
Systematically line brush the entire coat, right down to the skin. With a slicker brush, the motion used for line brushing is a "pat and pull." Softly pat the coat with the full pad of the brush and pull out and away from the skin with each stroke. The wrist remains in a neutral, or straight, position. The motion should be light and gentle. Start on the lower rear legs and work upwards towards the thigh. Repeat on every leg then proceed to the body, neck, head ears and tail. Work evenly over the pet, holding or pushing up the coat with one hand. It can be done with either a comb or a brush, but in most cases the comb is reserved for double checking the work of the brush. With the slicker brush, work the seam line, pulling down a

small amount of fur with each stroke. Do not move to the next section until the brush stroke glides smoothly and the skin at the seam line is seen. Pay close attention to the legs, under the front legs, collar area, ears, and tail. Let your hands feel for coat density levels. If an area feels heavier or thicker, it will need special attention with a brush or a comb. If static electricity is a problem while brushing, lightly mist the coat with an anti-static product or water while brushing. When finished, each strand of hair should float freely about as the dog moves.

Head
For show, the head is left long and natural with no special treatment to the topknot area. For pet dogs, it is common to hold the hair out of the eyes by banding, braiding or using barrettes. For pets, it is also common to slightly trim the stop area between the eyes.

Feet & Hocks
Trim the pads with a close cutting action blade ranging from a #15 to a #40. Use a very light touch to clean the pads of long hair. To create a rounded foot, first block in the foot to form a square. This will help create a full circular shape with the toes pointing directly forward. Finish detailing and rounding the outline of the foot by using long, curved shears.

Detail Finish
Lightly neaten the entire outline of the dog, removing long, shaggy stray hairs that interrupt a smooth flow. The finished appearance is very natural. This can be done with thinning shears or shears as long as the look remains natural. Finish with a fine mist of coat polish on the body coat for added shine.

Suggested Tools & Equipment
- Nail Trimmers
- Styptic Powder
- Ear Powder
- Ear Cleaning Solution
- Hemostat
- Cotton Balls
- Clippers
- #40 and #15 Blades for Pads
- Slicker Brush
- Greyhound Comb
- Pin Brush
- Dematting Tools
- Straight Shears
- Curved Shears
- Small Detailing Shears
- Thinning Shears

Notes:

Xoloitzcuintli

Breed Facts & Characteristics

Country of Origin: Mexico

Height at Shoulder: Three sizes ranging from 10"–23"

Coat Length/Type: Hairless *or* Short/Smooth

Color: Any dark, constant color. Limited white markings allowed.

Correct grooming procedure:

Bathe *or* Bathe & Curry Brush

Common pet grooming practices:

Bathe *or* Bathe & Curry Brush

-The Goal-
The coat should be clean and fresh smelling, with soft pliable skin.

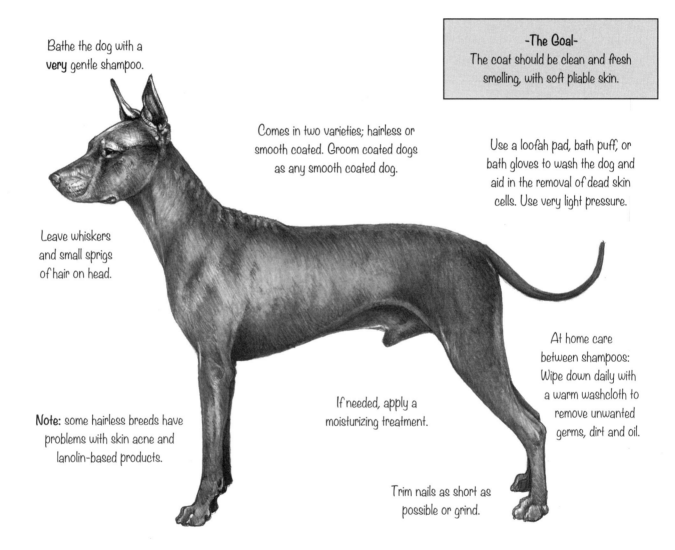

Bathe the dog with a **very** gentle shampoo.

Comes in two varieties; hairless or smooth coated. Groom coated dogs as any smooth coated dog.

Use a loofah pad, bath puff, or bath gloves to wash the dog and aid in the removal of dead skin cells. Use very light pressure.

Leave whiskers and small sprigs of hair on head.

Note: some hairless breeds have problems with skin acne and lanolin-based products.

If needed, apply a moisturizing treatment.

At home care between shampoos: Wipe down daily with a warm washcloth to remove unwanted germs, dirt and oil.

Trim nails as short as possible or grind.

See page 78 for Bathing & Drying Instructions

Suggested Tools & Equipment

- Nail Trimmers
- Styptic Powder
- Ear Cleaning Solution
- Hemostat
- Cotton Balls
- Cleansing cloth or puff
- Clippers
- #40 or #30 Blade

Notes *from your*
Grooming Table

Breeds in the Herding Group are athletic, intelligent and loyal. Their natural herding instincts have made them useful on farms gathering livestock. The instinct to herd is not limited to other animals—it extends to humans and children as well. They need plenty of room to expend their abundance of energy.

Australian Cattle Dog

Breed Facts & Characteristics

Country of Origin: Australia

Height at Shoulder: 17"–20"

Coat Length/Type: Short/Dense

Color: Blue, blue-mottled, blue speckled, red or red speckled. Evenly distributed markings are desirable.

Correct grooming procedure:
Bathe & Brush Out

Common pet grooming practices:
Bathe & Brush Out

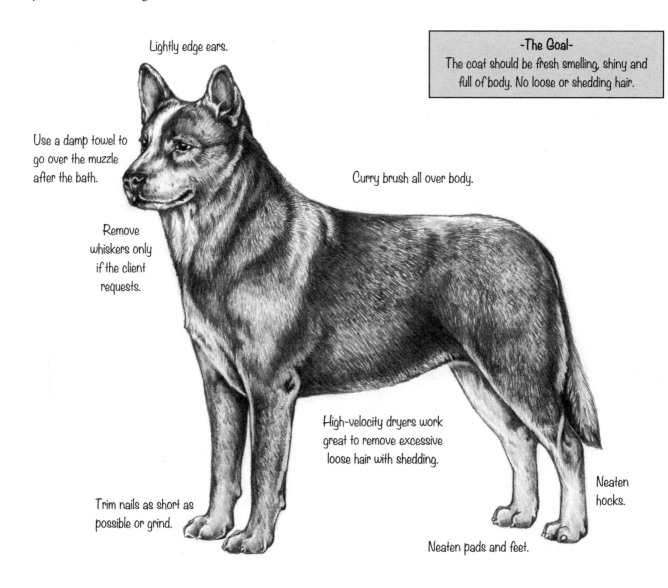

Lightly edge ears.

Use a damp towel to go over the muzzle after the bath.

Remove whiskers only if the client requests.

Curry brush all over body.

-The Goal-
The coat should be fresh smelling, shiny and full of body. No loose or shedding hair.

High-velocity dryers work great to remove excessive loose hair with shedding.

Neaten hocks.

Trim nails as short as possible or grind.

Neaten pads and feet.

See page 67 for Bathing & Drying Instructions	Suggested Tools & Equipment

- Nail Trimmers
- Styptic Powder
- Ear Cleaning Solution
- Cotton Balls

- Clippers
- #40 or #15 Blade
- Slicker Brush
- Rubber Curry

- Carding Tool
- De-Shedding Tools
- Small Detailing Shears
- Thinning Shears

HERDING

Notes *from your*
Grooming Table

Breed Facts & Characteristics

Country of Origin: United States

Height at Shoulder: 18"–23"

Coat Length/Type: Combination/Silky

Color: Black, red, black merle, red merle—all with or without white markings and tan points. A white color is acceptable but white can not splash over the body. Head should predominately be colored.

Correct grooming procedure:

Bathe & Brush Out

Common pet grooming practices:

Bathe & Brush Out

-The Goal-
Coat should be mat free, shiny, light and airy. The coat should bounce and float with the dog as it moves.

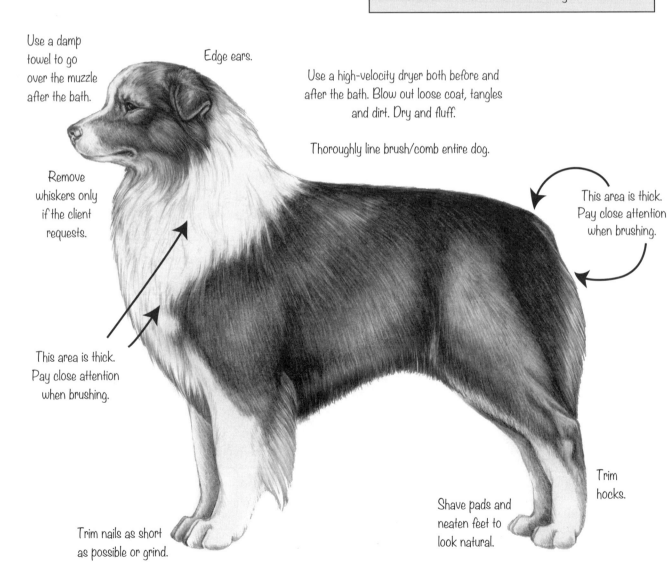

Use a damp towel to go over the muzzle after the bath.

Edge ears.

Use a high-velocity dryer both before and after the bath. Blow out loose coat, tangles and dirt. Dry and fluff.

Thoroughly line brush/comb entire dog.

Remove whiskers only if the client requests.

This area is thick. Pay close attention when brushing.

This area is thick. Pay close attention when brushing.

Trim nails as short as possible or grind.

Shave pads and neaten feet to look natural.

Trim hocks.

HERDING

Grooming Procedures & Recommendations

See page 68 for
Bathing & Drying Instructions

Frequency
Bathe once a week to once every 12 weeks.

Pre-Work
Trim or grind nails every four to six weeks to maintain a healthy foot structure. Clean the ears by swabbing with a mild ear cleaning solution. Use a rubber curry, shedding blade, undercoat rake, pumice stone, carding tool, fine stripping knife or natural bristle brush to loosen skin dander and remove loose coat. Use a high-velocity dryer over the coat to quickly and effectively lift dirt and debris away from the skin and loosen coat. Brush out or remove any matting found in the long-coated areas. If the tangles are loose enough so water can fully penetrate the area, remove them after bathing and drying. If water cannot penetrate, remove the mat or tangle prior to bathing.

Brushing
Line brush, working in sections until the dog is entirely tangle-free and all loose coat is removed. When finished, there should be little, if any, fur still being removed with a firm slicker brush. Double-check the work with a comb and your hands. Go over the entire body, feeling for any inconsistencies in the density levels of the coat. If an area seems moist to the touch or fuller than the rest of the coat, rework the area with the appropriate tool. Mats, tangles and excessive coat are easily trapped in the following areas: behind the ears, around the ruff, the thigh area, the undercarriage and the tail. Give extra attention to these areas before finishing the groom.

Carding
If a dog has an abundance of loose undercoat, card the shorter areas with a carding tool. Common tools can be a fine stripping knife, undercoat rake, a pumice stone, or a #40 blade held between your fingers. Any carding tool should be pulled over the body, working in the direction of the coat growth. This will remove the soft, downy undercoat, allowing the guard coat to conform more closely to the natural outline of the body. It will also aid in the removal of loose, shedding coat, a seasonal problem for many pet owners.

Sanitary Area
If the dog has a sanitation problem under the tail, lightly trim this area with thinning shears. Only clear enough coat to accomplish the goal and keep it looking very natural. Trimming of the groin area is not recommended unless there is a sanitary problem. If the groin needs to be trimmed, do so very lightly and try to leave the fur long enough so that the harsh coat does not prickle the skin, causing the dog to lick at the irritation.

Feet & Hocks
Trim the pads with a close blade ranging from a #15 to a #40. Use a very light touch to clean the pads of long hair. If there is long fur between the toes, back brush the fur so it stands up on top of and away from the foot. With thinning shears, trim the excess to create a neat and very natural looking foot. Tidy the outside edge of the foot, if needed, with small detailing shears. If the hocks have longer coat, trim lightly with thinning shears to show a neat, clean area. A #4F blade, used carefully in reverse, works well for trimming the tops of the feet and the hocks on some dogs.

Suggested Tools & Equipment

- Nail Trimmers
- Styptic Powder
- Ear Cleaning Solution
- Cotton Balls
- Clippers
- #40 and #15 Blades for Pads
- #4F for Feet & Hocks (optional)
- Slicker Brush
- Greyhound Comb
- Rubber Curry
- Carding Tool
- De-Shedding Tools
- Small Detailing Shears
- Thinning Shears

Detail Finish
Edge the ears lightly with thinning shears to neaten and keep a natural look. Hand pluck any long wispy, flyaway hair from around the ears. Removal of whiskers on the muzzle is optional based on client preference. Finish with a fine mist of coat polish on the body coat for added shine. Application of bows and mild cologne is optional.

Notes:

Notes From The Grooming Table ©2016

Bearded Collie

Breed Facts & Characteristics

Country of Origin: Britain

Height at Shoulder: 20"–22"

Coat Length/Type: Long/Flowing

Color: All shades of blue, gray and brown. A limited amount of white is allowed around the head, neck, chest, feet and tail.

Correct grooming procedure:

Bathe & Brush Out

Common pet grooming practices:

Bathe & Brush Out or Clipper-Trim

-The Goal-
Coat should be mat- and tangle-free.
The fur should be light and airy, moving
freely with the dog as it moves.

Part down center of skull.

Clear stop
area with
thinners or
clippers.

Leave ears long.

Line comb and brush **every** inch of
this dog, right down to the skin.

Lightly trim sanitary
areas—both under
tail and tummy.

Watch friction areas:
• Collar Area
• Arm Pits
• Behind Ear
• Legs & Thighs

Trim nails as short
as possible or grind.

Neaten undercarriage line.

Shave pads and scissor feet round.

HERDING

Grooming Procedures & Recommendations

See page 72 for
Bathing & Drying Instructions

See page 602 for
Drop Coat Styling Options

Frequency
Bathe once a week to once every 12 weeks.

Pre-Work
Trim or grind nails every four to six weeks to maintain a healthy foot structure. Clean the ears by swabbing with a mild ear cleaning solution. Hair should be plucked from within the ear canal only as necessary for healthy ear management. Prior to bathing, quickly go over the entire body and remove any serious mats or tangles. If the tangle can be penetrated with water, leave it and remove when the dog is clean. If the dog is staying in a clippered pet trim and has not been in for professional grooming for six weeks or more, remove the excessive body coat and set the pattern before bathing.

Brushing
Systematically line brush the entire coat, right down to the skin. With a slicker brush, the motion used for line brushing is a "pat and pull." Softly pat the coat with the full pad of the brush and pull out and away from the skin with each stroke. The wrist remains in a neutral, or straight, position. The motion should be light and gentle. Start on the lower rear legs and work upwards towards the thigh. Repeat on every leg then proceed to the body, neck, head ears and tail. Work evenly over the pet, holding or pushing up the coat with one hand. It can be done with either a comb or a brush, but in most cases the comb is reserved for double checking the work of the brush. With the slicker brush, work the seam line, pulling down a small amount of fur with each stroke. Do not move to the next section until the brush stroke glides smoothly and the skin at the seam line is seen. Pay close attention to the legs, under the front legs, collar area, ears, and tail. Let you hands feel for coat density levels. If an area feels heavier or thicker, it will need special attention with a brush or a comb. If static electricity is a problem while brushing, lightly mist the coat lightly with an anti-static product or water while brushing. When finished, each strand of hair should float freely about as the dog moves.

Head
For show, the head is left long and natural with no special treatment to the topknot area. For pet dogs, it is common to hold the hair out of the eyes by banding, braiding or using barrettes. For pets, it is also common to slightly trim the stop area between the eyes.

Feet & Hocks
Trim the pads with a close cutting action blade ranging from a #15 to a #40. Use a very light touch to clean the pads of long hair. To create a rounded foot, first block in the foot to form a square. This will help create a full circular shape with the toes pointing directly forward. Finish detailing and rounding the outline of the foot by using long, curved shears.

Detail Finish
Lightly neaten the entire outline of the dog, removing long, shaggy stray hairs that interrupt a smooth flow. The finished appearance is very natural. This can be done with thinning shears or shears as long as the look remains natural. Finish with a fine mist of coat polish on the body coat for added shine.

Suggested Tools & Equipment

- Nail Trimmers
- Styptic Powder
- Ear Powder
- Ear Cleaning Solution
- Hemostat
- Cotton Balls
- Clippers
- #40 and #15 Blades for Pads
- Slicker Brush
- Greyhound Comb
- Pin Brush
- Dematting Tools
- Straight Shears
- Curved Shears
- Small Detailing Shears
- Thinning Shears

Notes:

Notes From The Grooming Table ©2016

Beauceron

Breed Facts & Characteristics

Country of Origin: France

Height at Shoulder: 24"–27½"

Coat Length/Type: Short/Dense

Color: Black and tan or harlequin.

Correct grooming procedure:
Bathe & Brush Out

Common pet grooming practices:
Bathe & Brush Out

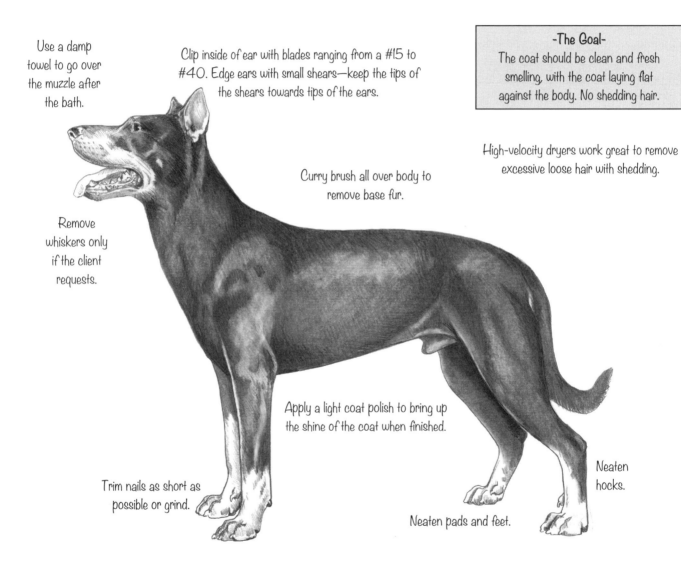

Use a damp towel to go over the muzzle after the bath.

Clip inside of ear with blades ranging from a #15 to #40. Edge ears with small shears—keep the tips of the shears towards tips of the ears.

-The Goal-
The coat should be clean and fresh smelling, with the coat laying flat against the body. No shedding hair.

High-velocity dryers work great to remove excessive loose hair with shedding.

Curry brush all over body to remove base fur.

Remove whiskers only if the client requests.

Apply a light coat polish to bring up the shine of the coat when finished.

Neaten hocks.

Trim nails as short as possible or grind.

Neaten pads and feet.

See page 67 for Bathing & Drying Instructions

Suggested Tools & Equipment

- Nail Trimmers
- Styptic Powder
- Ear Cleaning Solution
- Cotton Balls

- Clippers
- #40 or #15 Blade
- Slicker Brush
- Rubber Curry

- Carding Tool
- De-Shedding Tools
- Small Detailing Shears
- Thinning Shears

HERDING

Belgian Malinois

Breed Facts & Characteristics

Country of Origin: Belgium

Height at Shoulder: 22"–26"

Coat Length/Type: Short/Dense

Color: Sable in all shades of rich browns. A tiny amount of white is allowed on the toes and chest.

Correct grooming procedure:
Bathe & Brush Out

Common pet grooming practices:
Bathe & Brush Out

-The Goal-
The coat should be fresh smelling, shiny and full of body. No loose or shedding hair.

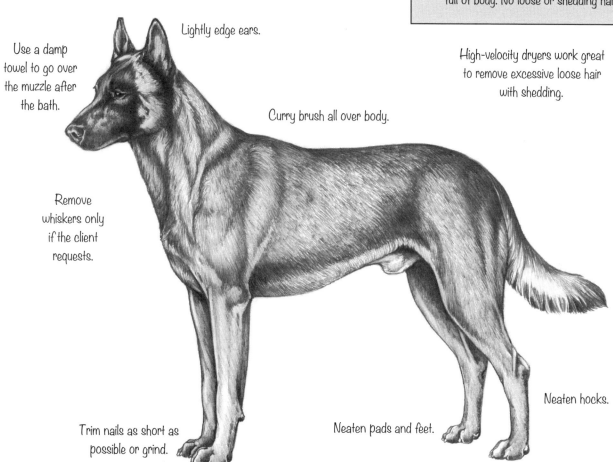

Use a damp towel to go over the muzzle after the bath.

Lightly edge ears.

High-velocity dryers work great to remove excessive loose hair with shedding.

Curry brush all over body.

Remove whiskers only if the client requests.

Trim nails as short as possible or grind.

Neaten pads and feet.

Neaten hocks.

See page 67 for Bathing & Drying Instructions	Suggested Tools & Equipment

- Nail Trimmers
- Styptic Powder
- Ear Cleaning Solution
- Cotton Balls

- Clippers
- #40 or #15 Blade
- Slicker Brush
- Rubber Curry

- Carding Tool
- De-Shedding Tools
- Small Detailing Shears
- Thinning Shears

Breed Facts & Characteristics

Country of Origin: Belgium

Height at Shoulder: 22"–26"

Coat Length/Type: Combination/Silky

Color: All black or with a very limited amount of white on the chest, feet and muzzle.

Correct grooming procedure:
Bathe & Brush Out

Common pet grooming practices:
Bathe & Brush Out

-The Goal-
The coat should be fresh smelling, light and stand off the body. No loose hair.

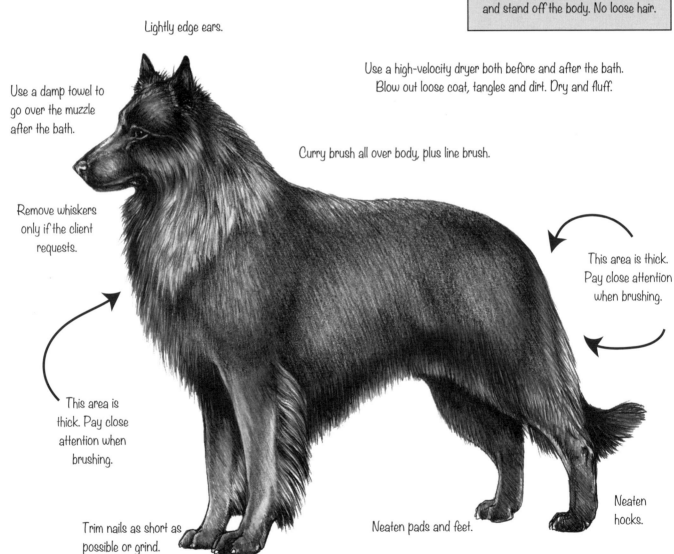

Lightly edge ears.

Use a damp towel to go over the muzzle after the bath.

Remove whiskers only if the client requests.

Use a high-velocity dryer both before and after the bath. Blow out loose coat, tangles and dirt. Dry and fluff.

Curry brush all over body, plus line brush.

This area is thick. Pay close attention when brushing.

This area is thick. Pay close attention when brushing.

Trim nails as short as possible or grind.

Neaten pads and feet.

Neaten hocks.

HERDING

Grooming Procedures & Recommendations

See page 68 for
Bathing & Drying Instructions

Frequency
Bathe once a week to once every
12 weeks.

Pre-Work
Trim or grind nails every four to
six weeks to maintain a healthy foot
structure. Clean the ears by swabbing
with a mild ear cleaning solution. Use a
rubber curry, shedding blade, undercoat
rake, pumice stone, carding tool, fine
stripping knife or natural bristle brush
to loosen skin dander and remove loose
coat. Use a high-velocity dryer over
the coat to quickly and effectively lift
dirt and debris away from the skin and
loosen coat. Brush out or remove any
matting found in the long-coated areas.
If the tangles are loose enough so water
can fully penetrate the area, remove
them after bathing and drying. If water
cannot penetrate, remove the mat or
tangle prior to bathing.

Brushing
Line brush, working in sections until
the dog is entirely tangle-free and all
loose coat is removed. When finished,
there should be little, if any, fur still
being removed with a firm slicker
brush. Double-check the work with a
wide-toothed comb and your hands.
Go over the entire body, feeling for any
inconsistencies in the density levels of
the coat. If an area seems moist to the
touch or fuller than the rest of the coat,
rework the area with the appropriate
tool. Mats, tangles and excessive coat
are easily trapped in the following areas:
behind the ears, around the ruff, the
thigh area, the undercarriage and the
tail. Give extra attention to these areas
before finishing the groom.

Carding
If a dog has an abundance of loose
undercoat, card the shorter areas with
a carding tool. Common tools can be
a fine stripping knife, undercoat rake,
a pumice stone, or a #40 blade held
between your fingers. Any carding tool
should be pulled over the body, working
in the direction of the coat growth. This
will remove the soft, downy undercoat,
allowing the guard coat to conform
more closely to the natural outline of
the body. It will also aid in the removal
of loose, shedding coat, a seasonal
problem for many pet owners.

Sanitary Area
If the dog has a sanitation problem
under the tail, lightly trim this area
with thinning shears. Only clear
enough coat to accomplish the goal
and keep it looking very natural.
Trimming of the groin area is not
recommended unless there is a sanitary
problem. If the groin needs to be
trimmed, do so very lightly and try to
leave the fur long enough so that the
harsh coat does not prickle the skin,
causing the dog to lick at the irritation.

Feet & Hocks
Trim the pads with a close blade
ranging from a #15 to a #40. Use a
very light touch to clean the pads of
long hair. If there is long fur between
the toes, back brush the fur so it
stands up on top of and away from
the foot. With thinning shears, trim
the excess to create a neat and very
natural looking foot. Tidy the outside
edge of the foot, if needed, with small
detailing shears. If the hocks have
longer coat, trim lightly with thinning
shears to show a neat, clean area. A
#4F blade, used carefully in reverse,
works well for trimming the tops of
the feet and the hocks on some dogs.

Suggested Tools & Equipment

- Nail Trimmers
- Styptic Powder
- Ear Cleaning Solution
- Cotton Balls
- Clippers
- #40 and #15 Blades for Pads
- #4F for Feet & Hocks (optional)
- Slicker Brush
- Greyhound Comb
- Rubber Curry
- Carding Tool
- De-Shedding Tools
- Small Detailing Shears
- Thinning Shears

Detail Finish
Edge the ears lightly with thinning
shears to neaten and keep a natural
look. Hand pluck any long wispy,
flyaway hair from around the ears.
Removal of whiskers on the muzzle is
optional based on client preference.
Finish with a fine mist of coat polish
on the body coat for added shine.
Application of bows and mild cologne
is optional.

Notes:

Notes From The Grooming Table ©2016

Breed Facts & Characteristics

Country of Origin: Belgium

Height at Shoulder: 22"–26"

Coat Length/Type: Combination/Silky

Color: Sable in all shades of rich browns. A tiny amount of white is allowed on the toes and chest.

Correct grooming procedure:
Bathe & Brush Out

Common pet grooming practices:
Bathe & Brush Out

-The Goal-
The coat should be fresh smelling, light and stand off the body. No loose hair.

Lightly edge ears.

Use a damp towel to go over the muzzle after the bath.

Use a high-velocity dryer both before and after the bath. Blow out loose coat, tangles and dirt. Dry and fluff.

Curry brush all over body, plus line brush.

Remove whiskers only if the client requests.

This area is thick. Pay close attention when brushing.

This area is thick. Pay close attention when brushing.

Trim nails as short as possible or grind.

Neaten pads and feet.

Neaten hocks.

HERDING

Grooming Procedures & Recommendations

See page 68 for
Bathing & Drying Instructions

Frequency
Bathe once a week to once every 12 weeks.

Pre-Work
Trim or grind nails every four to six weeks to maintain a healthy foot structure. Clean the ears by swabbing with a mild ear cleaning solution. Use a rubber curry, shedding blade, undercoat rake, pumice stone, carding tool, fine stripping knife or natural bristle brush to loosen skin dander and remove loose coat. Use a high-velocity dryer over the coat to quickly and effectively lift dirt and debris away from the skin and loosen coat. Brush out or remove any matting found in the long-coated areas. If the tangles are loose enough so water can fully penetrate the area, remove them after bathing and drying. If water cannot penetrate, remove the mat or tangle prior to bathing.

Brushing
Line brush, working in sections until the dog is entirely tangle-free and all loose coat is removed. When finished, there should be little, if any, fur still being removed with a firm slicker brush. Double-check the work with a comb and your hands. Go over the entire body, feeling for any inconsistencies in the density levels of the coat. If an area seems moist to the touch or fuller than the rest of the coat, rework the area with the appropriate tool. Mats, tangles and excessive coat are easily trapped in the following areas: behind the ears, around the ruff, the thigh area, the undercarriage and the tail. Give extra attention to these areas before finishing the groom.

Carding
If a dog has an abundance of loose undercoat, card the shorter areas with a carding tool. Common tools can be a fine stripping knife, undercoat rake, a pumice stone, or a #40 blade held between your fingers. Any carding tool should be pulled over the body, working in the direction of the coat growth. This will remove the soft, downy undercoat, allowing the guard coat to conform more closely to the natural outline of the body. It will also aid in the removal of loose, shedding coat, a seasonal problem for many pet owners.

Sanitary Area
If the dog has a sanitation problem under the tail, lightly trim this area with thinning shears. Only clear enough coat to accomplish the goal and keep it looking very natural. Trimming of the groin area is not recommended unless there is a sanitary problem. If the groin needs to be trimmed, do so very lightly and try to leave the fur long enough so that the harsh coat does not prickle the skin, causing the dog to lick at the irritation.

Feet & Hocks
Trim the pads with a close blade ranging from a #15 to a #40. Use a very light touch to clean the pads of long hair. If there is long fur between the toes, back brush the fur so it stands up on top of and away from the foot. With thinning shears, trim the excess to create a neat and very natural looking foot. Tidy the outside edge of the foot, if needed, with small detailing shears. If the hocks have longer coat, trim lightly with thinning shears to show a neat, clean area. A #4F blade, used carefully in reverse, works well for trimming the tops of the feet and the hocks on some dogs.

Suggested Tools & Equipment
- Nail Trimmers
- Styptic Powder
- Ear Cleaning Solution
- Cotton Balls
- Clippers
- #40 and #15 Blades for Pads
- #4F for Feet & Hocks (optional)
- Slicker Brush
- Greyhound Comb
- Rubber Curry
- Carding Tool
- De-Shedding Tools
- Small Detailing Shears
- Thinning Shears

Detail Finish
Edge the ears lightly with thinning shears to neaten and keep a natural look. Hand pluck any long wispy, flyaway hair from around the ears. Removal of whiskers on the muzzle is optional based on client preference. Finish with a fine mist of coat polish on the body coat for added shine. Application of bows and mild cologne is optional.

Notes:

Bergamasco

Breed Facts & Characteristics

Country of Origin: Alps Mountain Range

Height at Shoulder: 22"–23½"

Coat Length/Type: Corded/Long

Color: All shades of grey including merle and flat black. Colors can fade at the ends of the cords. Small amount of white accepted.

Correct grooming procedure:

Cording Coat

Common pet grooming practices:

Bathe & Brush/Clipper-Trim

-The Goal-
Getting the dog clean and totally dry. The flocks should be fully separated to the skin. the natural oils in this coat are important for flocking. It is not recommended to fully wash this breed more than 2–3 times a year. Spot bathing trouble areas is suggested.

This coat can take up to 24–36 hours to totally dry.

Separate flocks by gently pulling them apart down to the skin. The base of each flock should be about an 1.5 to 2.5 inches in diameter on the main body of the dog—smaller around the head region.

When shampooing, squeeze shampoo solution through the flocks. Never scrub.

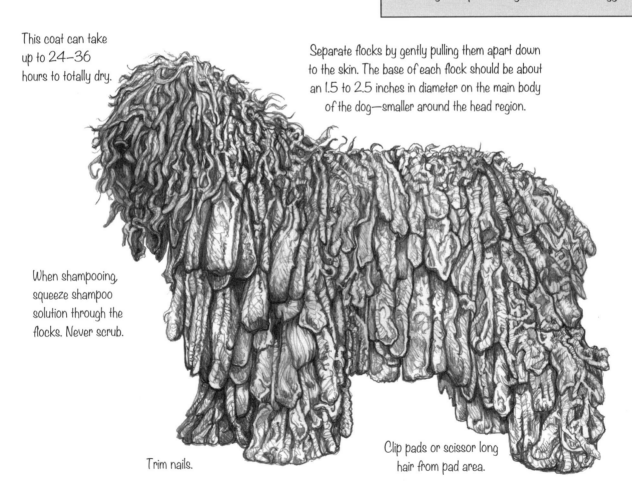

Trim nails.

Clip pads or scissor long hair from pad area.

On mature dogs, flocks will vary in width and density. Most sections on the body will be from 1.5 to 3 inches wide, getting broader and flatter at the ends. Flocks will be finer about the head, ears and throat areas.

HERDING

Grooming Procedures & Recommendations

See page 77 for Bathing & Drying Instructions

Frequency

Bathe every 12 weeks or when needed. Work the cords once a week to once every four weeks, without a full bath.

Pre-Work

Trim or grind nails at least every four to six weeks to maintain a healthy foot structure. Clean the ears every four to six weeks. If hair forms inside the ear canal, apply an ear powder and gently pluck the hair from inside the canal. Use care not to pull any coat from outside the canal opening. Clean ears by swabbing with a mild ear cleaning solution.

Cords

The base of a cord is about 1 to 2 inches square. Very often the cords or "flocks" will start to form by themselves, with little assistance. Prior to bathing, gently pull the strands away from one another to keep the cord as a separate strand. If the coat is shorter and feels "spongy" to the touch, it may not be forming natural cords. Mist the area with water or a light skin conditioner to help see the natural cord separation. Separate the area with your fingers into 1- to 2-inch sections, starting at the base of each cord. If a cord is too thick, it can be split in two by working it with your fingers or by carefully cutting the cord with shears. Try to follow the natural separation as it splits. As the cords or flocks form, they may be irregular in size and shape. Some flocks will even flatten and fan out at the end.

Feet

Trim the pads with a close cutting blade, ranging from a #15 to a #40. Use a very light touch to clean the pads of long hair. With shears, round the foot slightly to create an oval shape with toes facing forward.

Detail Finish

When the dog is dry, continue to divide and separate the cords. Pay close attention to the friction areas: ears, under the front legs, the rump and under the tail. These are the areas where the skin is the most sensitive and is prone to injury. Use extreme caution when splitting the coat in these areas. Trimming the cords to a few inches all over enables the pet dog to maintain the look of the breed yet makes care easier than for the full coat.

Pet Dogs

Some pet owners choose to keep their pets brushed out or trimmed close, not dealing with the corded coat at all.

Grooming Tip

This is coat type requires a fair amount of attention, especially in the initial cording phases. Once the cords have formed, keeping them up requires only the use of your fingers. Pet owners can do this during idle time, like watching TV. With practice, their fingers will gravitate to the areas of greatest density, and they will be able to work the area without even looking at it.

Suggested Tools & Equipment

- Nail Trimmers
- Styptic Powder
- Ear Cleaning Solution
- Cotton Balls
- Clippers
- #40 and #15 Blades for Pads
- Straight Shear
- Strong Fingers

Notes:

Berger Picard

HERDING   NATURAL LONG HAIRED

Breed Facts & Characteristics

Country of Origin: France

Height at Shoulder: 21½"–25½"

Coat Length/Type: Moderate/Harsh

Color: Fawn, tan or brindle. Lighter colored dogs can have gray mixed into their coats. Small amount of white on chest or toes is allowed.

Correct grooming procedure:
Lightly Hand-Stripped

Common pet grooming practices:
Lightly Hand-Stripped

General Description

The Berger Picard is a medium sized, energetic working farm dog. They are slightly longer than they are tall. They have a shaggy, rough, wiry coat with a beard and brows on the head. Their ears are distinct and erect. Their tail is long, forming a J-hook at the end.

-The Goal-
This is a very uncomplicated coat type in terms of grooming. Less is more. It should look very natural, rustic and non-sculpted.

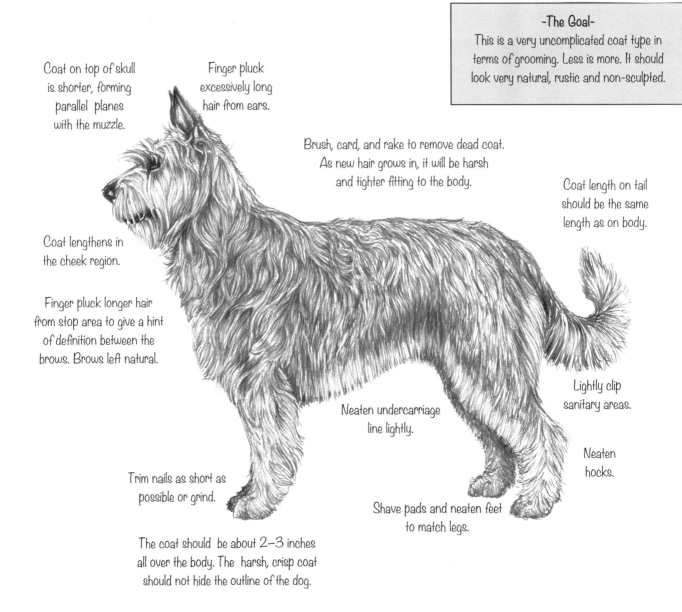

Coat on top of skull is shorter, forming parallel planes with the muzzle.

Finger pluck excessively long hair from ears.

Brush, card, and rake to remove dead coat. As new hair grows in, it will be harsh and tighter fitting to the body.

Coat length on tail should be the same length as on body.

Coat lengthens in the cheek region.

Finger pluck longer hair from stop area to give a hint of definition between the brows. Brows left natural.

Neaten undercarriage line lightly.

Lightly clip sanitary areas.

Neaten hocks.

Trim nails as short as possible or grind.

Shave pads and neaten feet to match legs.

The coat should be about 2–3 inches all over the body. The harsh, crisp coat should not hide the outline of the dog.

See page 72 for Bathing & Drying Instructions

Frequency

Bathe once a week to once every 12 weeks.

Pre-Work

Trim or grind nails at least every four to six weeks to maintain a healthy foot structure. Swab the ears clean with a mild ear cleaning solution. Prior to bathing, quickly go over the entire body with a high-velocity dryer to help lift dirt and dander away from the skin and to loosen any shedding coat. ***Card and hand-strip dog prior to bathing and drying***

Carding

Carding is a natural technique in which the soft, downy undercoat is pulled from the dog's body. Typical tools used with this technique are: a pumice stone, undercoat rake, a fine-toothed stripping knife pulled through the coat, or a fine blade, such as a #40, held between the fingers and pulled through the coat. Carding can be done before or after bathing and drying. Removal of the soft undercoat allows the topcoat to lie closer to the natural outline of the dog and accentuate the dog's structure. It also promotes profuse harsh outer coat, creates a rich coat color and protects the skin.

Hand-stripping

Hand-stripping is a technique in which the outer guard coat is plucked from the dog's skin. This procedure helps retain the proper coat texture and rich color of the breed. During certain times of the year, the coat is easier to pull out. When the coat easily comes out, it is called a "blowing coat" or "blown coat." Ideally, hand-stripping should correspond with the dog's natural cycle, based on the environment and its hormonal levels. Using your fingers pull out a few hairs at a time to shape the slightly coat, accentuating the natural outline of the dog. Work methodically, pulling small amounts of coat at a time, always working in the direction of the coat growth. Proper hand-stripping removes hair with a gentle momentum and rhythm, not brute force, which is uncomfortable for both groomer and pet. In general, the main body coat is easy to remove. Most pets do not mind the plucking process. The cheeks, throat and private areas may be more sensitive, requiring thinning shears or clippers. Leave enough coat to be between 2 to 3 inches long on the body, legs and tail. The coats always should appear very natural, never clipped or heavily trimmed.

Head

Leave the coat longer on the muzzle. The coat on the top of the head is naturally slightly shorter. Hand-strip or pluck only longest coat that detracts from the shape of the top skull. Leave triangles of coat above each eye to form the moderate eyebrows that accentuate the eye area. The top half of the ears is stripped of longer hair to show off their distinctive natural erect ear set. If the coat on the ear leather does not strip/pluck out easily, clipper with blades ranging from a #10 to a #7F on the outside and inside of the ear leather. Finish by edging the ear with detailing shears or thinning shears, keeping the tips of the shears toward the tip of the ear.

Feet & Hocks

Trim the pads with a close cutting blade ranging from a #15 to a #40. Use a very light touch to clean the pads of long hair. Tidy the outside edge of the foot, if needed, with small detailing shears. If the hocks have longer coat, trim lightly with thinning shears to show a neat, clean area.

Suggested Tools & Equipment

- Nail Trimmers
- Styptic Powder
- Ear Cleaning Solution
- Cotton Balls
- Clippers
- Slicker Brush
- Greyhound Comb
- Pumice Stone
- Carding Tools
- Undercoat Rake
- Stripping Knives
- Small Detailing Shears
- Thinning Shears
- Dematting Tools

Common Blade Options:

- #40, #15, #10

Detail Finish

Application of bows and mild cologne is optional.

Note: Clipping a wired-coated dog will result in a dramatic change in the texture and color of the coat. The correct harsh wire coat needs to be encouraged by plucking the blown coat when it is ready to be removed. This process stimulates hair follicles to produce new guard coat. Without hand-stripping, the guard coat is not stimulated and will not grow in properly. It will lose its brilliant color and texture. If only the undercoat grows, the guard coat color becomes that of the lighter, soft undercoat.

Breed Facts & Characteristics

Country of Origin: Scotland

Height at Shoulder: 18"–22"

Coat Length/Type: Combination/Silky

Color: Various combinations of patterns and markings. The most common color is black with or without a white facial blaze, collar, leg stockings and tail tip. Tan points are allowed.

Correct grooming procedure:

Bathe & Brush Out

Common pet grooming practices:

Bathe & Brush Out

-The Goal-
The coat should be fresh smelling, light and stand off the body. No loose hair.

Use a damp towel to go over the muzzle after the bath.

Lightly edge ears.

Use a high-velocity dryer both before and after the bath. Blow out loose coat, tangles and dirt. Dry and fluff.

Curry brush all over body, plus line brush.

Remove whiskers only if the client requests.

This area is thick. Pay close attention when brushing.

This area is thick. Pay close attention when brushing.

Trim nails as short as possible or grind.

Neaten pads and feet.

Neaten hocks.

See page 68 for Bathing & Drying Instructions

Frequency

Bathe once a week to once every 12 weeks.

Pre-Work

Trim or grind nails every four to six weeks to maintain a healthy foot structure. Clean the ears by swabbing with a mild ear cleaning solution. Use a rubber curry, shedding blade, undercoat rake, pumice stone, carding tool, fine stripping knife or natural bristle brush to loosen skin dander and remove loose coat. Use a high-velocity dryer over the coat to quickly and effectively lift dirt and debris away from the skin and loosen coat. Brush out or remove any matting found in the long-coated areas. If the tangles are loose enough so water can fully penetrate the area, remove them after bathing and drying. If water cannot penetrate, remove the mat or tangle prior to bathing.

Brushing

Line brush, working in sections until the dog is entirely tangle-free and all loose coat is removed. When finished, there should be little, if any, fur still being removed with a firm slicker brush. Double-check the work with a comb and your hands. Go over the entire body, feeling for any inconsistencies in the density levels of the coat. If an area seems moist to the touch or fuller than the rest of the coat, rework the area with the appropriate tool. Mats, tangles and excessive coat are easily trapped in the following areas: behind the ears, around the ruff, the thigh area, the undercarriage and the tail. Give extra attention to these areas before finishing the groom.

Carding

If a dog has an abundance of loose undercoat, card the shorter areas with a carding tool. Common tools can be a fine stripping knife, undercoat rake, a pumice stone, or a #40 blade held between your fingers. Any carding tool should be pulled over the body, working in the direction of the coat growth. This will remove the soft, downy undercoat, allowing the guard coat to conform more closely to the natural outline of the body. It will also aid in the removal of loose, shedding coat, a seasonal problem for many pet owners.

Sanitary Area

If the dog has a sanitation problem under the tail, lightly trim this area with thinning shears. Only clear enough coat to accomplish the goal and keep it looking very natural. Trimming of the groin area is not recommended unless there is a sanitary problem. If the groin needs to be trimmed, do so very lightly and try to leave the fur long enough so that the harsh coat does not prickle the skin, causing the dog to lick at the irritation.

Feet & Hocks

Trim the pads with a close blade ranging from a #15 to a #40. Use a very light touch to clean the pads of long hair. If there is long fur between the toes, back brush the fur so it stands up on top of and away from the foot. With thinning shears, trim the excess to create a neat and very natural looking foot. Tidy the outside edge of the foot, if needed, with small detailing shears. If the hocks have longer coat, trim lightly with thinning shears to show a neat, clean area. A #4F blade, used carefully in reverse, works well for trimming the tops of the feet and the hocks on some dogs.

Suggested Tools & Equipment

- Nail Trimmers
- Styptic Powder
- Ear Cleaning Solution
- Cotton Balls
- Clippers
- #40 and #15 Blades for Pads
- #4F for Feet & Hocks (optional)
- Slicker Brush
- Greyhound Comb
- Rubber Curry
- Carding Tool
- De-Shedding Tools
- Small Detailing Shears
- Thinning Shears

Detail Finish

Edge the ears lightly with thinning shears to neaten and keep a natural look. Hand pluck any long wispy, flyaway hair from around the ears. Removal of whiskers on the muzzle is optional based on client preference. Finish with a fine mist of coat polish on the body coat for added shine. Application of bows and mild cologne is optional.

Notes:

Notes From The Grooming Table ©2016

Breed Facts & Characteristics

Country of Origin: France

Height at Shoulder: 23½"–27½"

Coat Length/Type: Harsh/Long

Color: Black, gray or fawn. Typical to see salt and pepper or brindled markings in the coat.

Correct grooming procedure:

Hand-Strip

Common pet grooming practices:

Clipper-Trim

General Description

The Bouvier des Flandres is an all-purpose farm dog. The dog should look square in outline, very powerful and robust with a rough coat, massive head and strong neck. This dog has great strength but should not look heavy or coarse.

> **-The Goal-**
> This breed is a rugged, powerfully built square-bodied dog. The coat should feel harsh to the touch, yet clean and mat free. Head is full and round with a fall over the eyes. Body coat is approximately 2–2½" long.

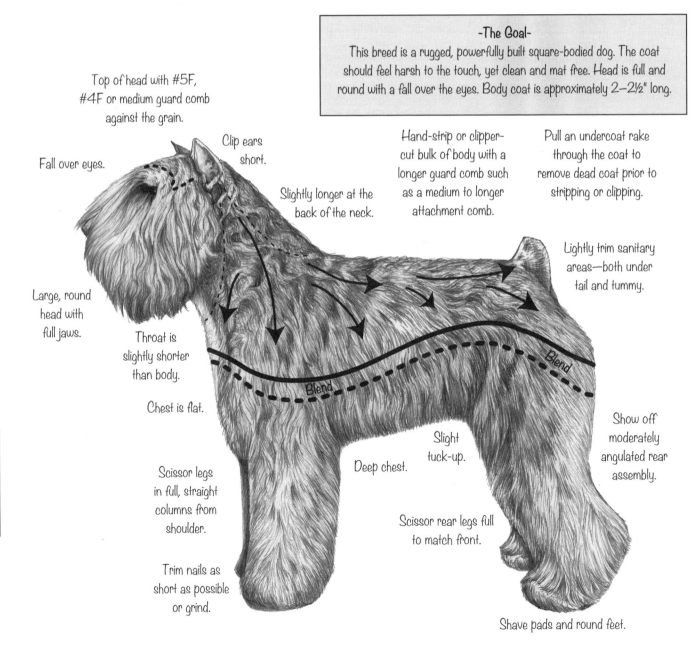

Top of head with #5F, #4F or medium guard comb against the grain.

Fall over eyes.

Clip ears short.

Slightly longer at the back of the neck.

Hand-strip or clipper-cut bulk of body with a longer guard comb such as a medium to longer attachment comb.

Pull an undercoat rake through the coat to remove dead coat prior to stripping or clipping.

Large, round head with full jaws.

Lightly trim sanitary areas—both under tail and tummy.

Throat is slightly shorter than body.

Chest is flat.

Blend

Blend

Show off moderately angulated rear assembly.

Slight tuck-up.

Deep chest.

Scissor legs in full, straight columns from shoulder.

Scissor rear legs full to match front.

Trim nails as short as possible or grind.

Shave pads and round feet.

HERDING

Grooming Procedures & Recommendations

See page 74 for
Bathing & Drying Instructions

Frequency

Bathe once a week to once every 12 weeks. Trim every four to six weeks to maintain a stylized fashion.

Pre-Work

Trim or grind nails at least every four to six weeks to maintain a healthy foot structure. Clean the ears by swabbing with a mild ear cleaning solution. Pluck any long hair inside the ear canal using an ear powder and your fingers or hemostat. Prior to bathing, quickly go over the entire body and remove any serious mats or tangles. If the tangle can be penetrated with water, leave it and remove when the dog is clean. If the pet has not been in for professional grooming for six weeks or more, remove the excessive body coat and set the pattern before bathing. Before starting the final haircut, make sure the dog's coat is thoroughly brushed out and free of tangles.

General Pattern Lines

The pattern is based on the bone and muscle structure of the dog. After the final trim, all pattern lines are to be invisible. The longer the blade choice for the body, the easier it is to blend the pattern into the longer furnishings of the legs and undercarriage. At the transition points, feather off with the clippers in a smooth, steady fashion. If the pattern line is still visible after clipping, use thinning shears to blend the line. On the head, the pattern lines are crisp and clean.

Body

The correct coat is hand-stripped. For either hand-stripped or clipper-cut dogs, the general pattern is the same. The breed standard states the body coat should be about 21/2 inches in length. Many pet owners choose a shorter trim for manageability. Typical blades used

in pet grooming range from a #4F to a long guard comb attachment blade used over a close-cutting blade, or a combination of blades that make up the bulk of the body work. The pattern lines start at the turn of the shoulder and continue to just above the elbow, back to the flank on a diagonal and then drop into the thigh region.

Throat & Chest

Blades ranging from #7F to a shorter guard comb attachment used with the grain are common in the throat area. Follow the natural cowlick line that runs in a "V" shape from the base of the ears towards the base of the neck. The chest drops straight off from the throat and neck area. The blending point begins about 3 or 4 fingers above the breast bone and drops to the turn of the muscle at the elbow/shoulder. When viewed in profile, the neck into the chest should be straight without a predominant forechest. When blending the chest, be aware of the heavy cowlicks in the area. If a clipper is run over this area to create the flat chest, the result can be severe holes in the chest area. It is very easy to create two bald patches on either side of the chest, just inside the front legs. Many stylists prefer to blend the chest area by hand with thinning shears or shears. When finished in this area, double check your work to be sure the neck, chest and front legs drop down in a straight line when viewed in profile.

Front Legs

The longest coat on the legs can range from 1 to 3 inches depending on the amount of bone and coat density. The front legs drop straight down from the body and have ample bone and muscle to show off an extremely powerful and sturdy animal. The pattern line at the shoulder is about 3 or 4 fingers above the top of the elbow, at the point where the muscle begins to turn under. The coat at the transition line will be

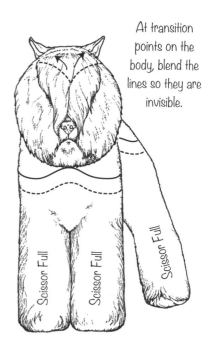

At transition points on the body, blend the lines so they are invisible.

Legs should be left fuller and fall into straight columns, from the body to the feet, on both the front and rear legs. The chest should be flat, but use caution not to bald out this area due to cowlicks found where the front legs meet the chest.

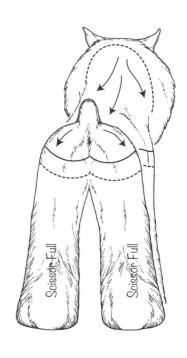

The flat top skull is accentuated by clipping it close with a #5F, or #4F with the grain, or a longer guard comb against the grain.

The fall is created by following the eye socket ridge. Leave all hair between the eyes in the stop area. The eyes are exposed by scissoring in an arch over the eye. Fur is very short at the back corner of the eye, and gets longer towards the nose. Do NOT split the brows.

Ears can be cropped or natural. Clip very close with a #10 or #15 on the outside and as close as a #40 on the inside, used with a very light touch. Edge ears with small detailing shears to finish.

The neck is arched. If a dog does not have this naturally, leave the coat on the back of the neck a bit fuller to create it.

The beard and mustache are left full and natural to highlight the impressive scale of the head piece

The jowls are left full. The line that separates the head from the neck starts at the ear bulb and follows in a semi-circle, under the throat and back up to the opposite ear bulb.

short, and taper into the longer leg furnishings. This is accomplished by feathering off at the blending point with the same blade used on the body. To do this effectively, you need a steady hand and a dog that stands still. Most stylists prefer to shape the legs by hand, with shears ranging from 8.5 inches to 10 inches in length. Other methods of blending off at the top of the leg include using one of the giant attachment combs, followed by hand-scissoring and blending with thinning shears. When the trim is complete, the legs form two parallel columns dropping from the elbow into tight, round feet. The coat at the back of the elbow is very short and falls straight down off the back of the leg toward the ground.

Hindquarters
The hindquarters should be strong and powerful. When clipping this area, use the same blade that was used on the body. Feather off at the top of the thigh muscle, blending the coat naturally into the longer leg furnishings. The pattern line starts to turn diagonally from the flank region to about the halfway point between the tail and the hock. The blending should be invisible when the trim is finished. Blend with thinning shears if necessary. The stifle area should have enough furnishing left to give the legs substance and angulation. The longest coat on the legs can range from 1 to 3 inches depending on the amount of bone and the coat density. Shape this area by hand with shears after the clipper work is complete. When viewed from the

rear, the legs should form two parallel lines to the ground. The hocks are well let down. There should be adequate coat on the hock area to accentuate the angles of the rear assembly.

Feet
Both the front and rear feet are compact with well arched toes. To emphasize this, the feet are trimmed very close to the edge of the foot and some nail is routinely exposed. The feet should point straight ahead, toeing neither in nor out. Trim the feet round by first boxing them in the shape of a square, while the dog is standing in a natural, square position. With the dog's feet firmly planted on the table, remove the square corners of the box and round the feet facing straight forward, beveling the coat into the longer leg

HERDING

Grooming Procedures & Recommendations

fur. If detailing the feet with the foot off the tabletop, always use a small pair of detailing shears to minimize the risk of accidentally cutting the pads. If a very close cutting blade is used to trim the pads, use a firm slicker brush to brush the longer leg coat over the outer edges of the pad and trim that hair at the same time the pads are clipped clean.

Undercarriage

The groin is normally trimmed close with a #10 or #15 blade to a point near the navel. From this point forward toward the brisket, the coat is longer, creating the illusion of depth of chest. There is not a lot of coat remaining in the finished trim. Most Bouviers have a well developed chest and only a small amount of coat is needed to create the proper tight and tailored look for this area. Trim lightly with shears or thinning shears depending on the amount of coat.

Tail

The top of the tail is trimmed with the same blade as the body. The underside of the tail is clipped close, with blades ranging from #15 to a #7F, used with or against the grain, based on the dog's skin sensitivity. Continue with the same blade around the rectum.

The Head in General

The head is large and impressive in scale. The keen look is accentuated by a fall of harsh brow coat that does not totally cover the eye. The beard and mustache are full and long, accentuating the sturdy head and powerful jaws. The ears can be cropped or uncropped.

Ears

Both cropped and uncropped ears are clipped with a close blade. It is common to see a #10 or #15 blade used on the outside of the ear leather while a #40 blade is used on the inside. When working with close blades in this delicate area, always work from the base or center of the ear out toward the edge.

Gently brace the ear with your fingers to clip over it. To finish, use small finishing shears to trim around the outside edge of the ear leather, keeping the tips of the shears toward the tip of the ears.

Top Skull

The top of the head can be clipped as close as a #5F or used with the grain to a #4F or moderate length guard comb, used with the grain or against, depending on the dog's sensitivity and coat density. At the eye area, follow the eye socket rim, leaving a long fall of fur covering the stop and eye areas. The pattern line that separates the top skull from the cheek and jowl area is a bony ridge, called the zygomatic arch, which runs from the back corner of the eye to the ear canal. Leave the coat in front of the ear canal opening.

Fall

The coat between the eyes is left long and full to create a fall. At the outer corners of the eyes, the hair is trimmed in an arch, allowing the dog to see clearly from the sides. It will be very short at the back corner of the eye and longer over the nose. When viewed in profile, the brows should transition smoothly between the zygomatic arch and the top skull as they arch out over the nose. Use curved shears in reverse or thinners to open up the eye area and create the arched fall that accentuates the typically keen look of a Bouvier. Remove the longer hair from the back corner of the eye to about halfway over the eye itself. Keep the tips of the shear pointed toward the outside edge on the nose. Repeat on the other brow. Using the nose as a target, aids in setting both arches the same.

Cheeks

The cheek area is left full and long. The pattern line that separates the top skull from the cheek area is a bony ridge called the zygomatic arch, running from the back corner of the eye to the ear canal. Leave the coat in front of the ear canal opening. For the jaw area,

the separation point between the neck and jaw is an imaginary line that runs from the base of each ear bulb, under the neck. To feel it, stand in front of the dog and gently place your fingers around the neck, where a collar would naturally fit, and slide them up to the throat. The point at which your hands stop, at the jaw area, is the pattern line between the neck and head.

Beard

The coat on the entire muzzle, including the jaw area, is left full and natural, giving the head a rounded appearance.

Detail Finish

Remove any scissor marks or clipper tracks with thinning shears. Application of mild cologne and collar bows is optional.

Notes From The Grooming Table ©2016

Briard

Breed Facts & Characteristics

Country of Origin: France

Height at Shoulder: 22"–27"

Coat Length/Type: Long/Flowing

Color: All colors except white are permitted so long as they are uniform. Colors are black, all shades of gray and tan. The coat can be tipped or masked with darker colors so long as the color blends gradually and is uniform in shape.

Correct grooming procedure:
Bathe & Brush Out

Common pet grooming practices:
Bathe & Brush Out or Clipper-Trim

-The Goal-
Coat should be mat- and tangle-free. The fur should be light and airy, moving freely with the dog as it moves.

Part down center of skull.

Leave ears long.

Clear stop area with thinners or clippers.

Line comb and brush *every* inch of this dog, right down to the skin.

Lightly trim sanitary areas—both under tail and tummy.

Watch friction areas:
• Collar Area
• Arm Pits
• Behind Ears
• Legs & Thighs

Neaten undercarriage line.

Trim nails as short as possible or grind.

Shave pads and scissor feet round.

HERDING

Grooming Procedures & Recommendations

See page 72 for
Bathing & Drying Instructions

See page 602 for
Drop Coat Styling Options

Frequency
Bathe once a week to once every 12 weeks.

Pre-Work
Trim or grind nails every four to six weeks to maintain a healthy foot structure. Clean the ears by swabbing with a mild ear cleaning solution. Hair should be plucked from within the ear canal only as necessary for healthy ear management. Prior to bathing, quickly go over the entire body and remove any serious mats or tangles. If the tangle can be penetrated with water, leave it and remove when the dog is clean. If the dog is staying in a clippered pet trim and has not been in for professional grooming for six weeks or more, remove the excessive body coat and set the pattern before bathing.

Brushing
Systematically line brush the entire coat, right down to the skin. With a slicker brush, the motion used for line brushing is a "pat and pull." Softly pat the coat with the full pad of the brush and pull out and away from the skin with each stroke. The wrist remains in a neutral, or straight, position. The motion should be light and gentle. Start on the lower rear legs and work upwards towards the thigh. Repeat on every leg then proceed to the body, neck, head, ears and tail. Work evenly over the pet, holding or pushing up the coat with one hand. It can be done with either a comb or a brush, but in most cases the comb is reserved for double checking the work of the brush. With the slicker brush, work the seam line, pulling down a small amount of fur with each stroke. Do not move to the next section until the brush stroke glides smoothly and the skin at the seam line is seen. Pay close attention to the legs, under the front legs, collar area, ears, and tail. Let your hands feel for coat density levels. If an area feels heavier or thicker, it will need special attention with a brush or a comb. If static electricity is a problem while brushing, lightly mist the coat with an anti-static product or water while brushing. When finished, each strand of hair should float freely about as the dog moves.

Head
For show, the head is left long and natural with no special treatment to the topknot area other than the hair is parted at the center. For pet dogs, it is common to hold the hair out of the eyes by banding, braiding or using barrettes. For pets, it is also common to slightly trim the stop area between the eyes.

Ears
The ears are erect and covered with long hair that drapes over them.

Feet & Hocks
Trim the pads with a close cutting action blade ranging from a #15 to a #40. Use a very light touch to clean the pads of long hair. To create a rounded foot, first block in the foot to form a square. This will help create a full circular shape with the toes pointing directly forward. Finish detailing and rounding the outline of the foot by using long, curved shears.

Detail Finish
Lightly neaten the entire outline of the dog, removing long, shaggy stray hairs that interrupt a smooth flow. The finished appearance is very natural. This can be done with thinning shears or shears as long as the look remains natural. Finish with a fine mist of coat polish on the body coat for added shine.

Suggested Tools & Equipment

- Nail Trimmers
- Styptic Powder
- Ear Powder
- Ear Cleaning Solution
- Hemostat
- Cotton Balls
- Clippers
- #40 and #15 Blades for Pads
- Slicker Brush
- Greyhound Comb
- Pin Brush
- Dematting Tools
- Straight Shears
- Curved Shears
- Small Detailing Shears
- Thinning Shears

Notes:

Breed Facts & Characteristics

Country of Origin: Israel

Height at Shoulder: 19"–24"

Coat Length/Type: Short/Dense

Color: There are two color patterns:
1. Mostly white with mask and with or without additional splashes of color. (Large body patches are desirable.)
2. Solid colored with or without a small amount of white.

Correct grooming procedure:

Bathe & Brush Out

Common pet grooming practices:

Bathe & Brush Out

-The Goal-
The coat should be clean and fresh smelling, laying flat against the body. No loose or shedding hair.

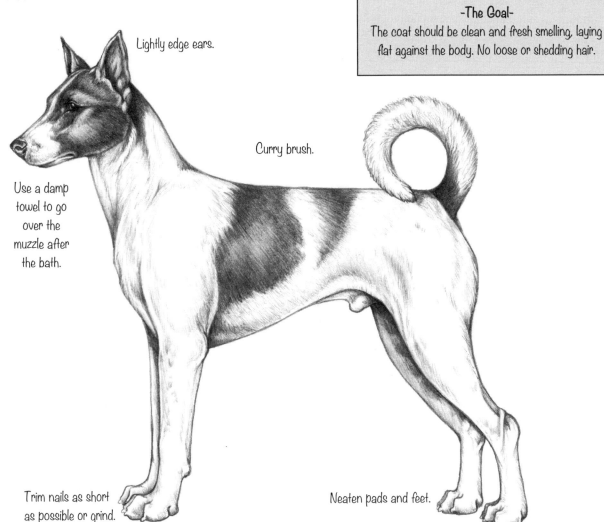

Lightly edge ears.

Curry brush.

Use a damp towel to go over the muzzle after the bath.

Trim nails as short as possible or grind.

Neaten pads and feet.

See page 67 for
Bathing & Drying Instructions

Suggested Tools & Equipment

- Nail Trimmers
- Styptic Powder
- Ear Cleaning Solution
- Cotton Balls

- Clippers
- #40 or #15 Blade
- Slicker Brush
- Rubber Curry

- Carding Tool
- De-Shedding Tools
- Small Detailing Shears
- Thinning Shears

HERDING

Notes from your Grooming Table

Collie (Rough)

Breed Facts & Characteristics

Country of Origin: Scotland

Height at Shoulder: 22"–26"

Coat Length/Type: Combination/Long

Color: Sable and white, tricolor, blue merle, or white with large patches of color desirable.

Correct grooming procedure:

Brush Out/Minor Trimming

Common pet grooming practices:

Bathe & Brush Out

> **-The Goal-**
> Coat should be mat free, shiny, light and airy. The coat should bounce and float with the dog as it moves.

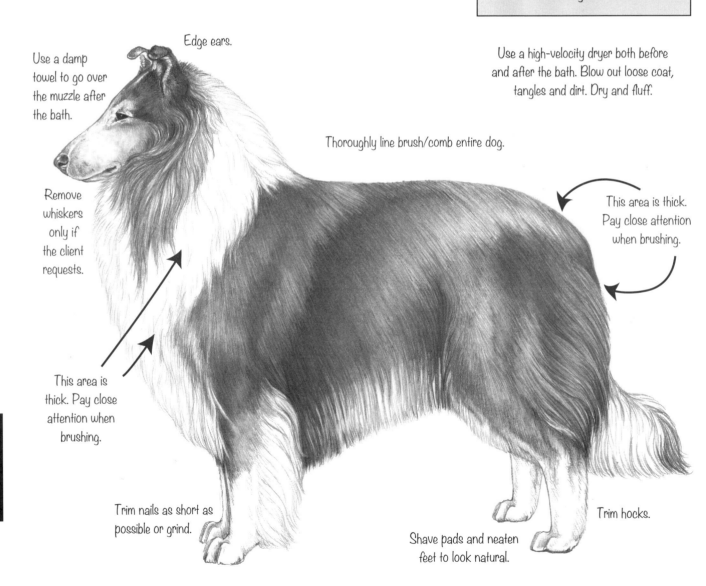

Edge ears.

Use a damp towel to go over the muzzle after the bath.

Use a high-velocity dryer both before and after the bath. Blow out loose coat, tangles and dirt. Dry and fluff.

Thoroughly line brush/comb entire dog.

Remove whiskers only if the client requests.

This area is thick. Pay close attention when brushing.

This area is thick. Pay close attention when brushing.

Trim nails as short as possible or grind.

Shave pads and neaten feet to look natural.

Trim hocks.

HERDING

Grooming Procedures & Recommendations

See page 70 for
Bathing & Drying Instructions

Frequency
Bathe once a week to once every
12 weeks.

Pre-Work
Trim or grind nails at least every four
to six weeks to maintain a healthy foot
structure. Swab the ears clean with a
mild ear cleaning solution. Quickly
blow out the dogs coat with a high-
velocity dryer to effectively lift dirt and
debris away from the skin and loosen
coat. Brush out or remove any matting
found in the longer coated areas. If
the tangles are loose enough so that
water can fully penetrate them, remove
them after bathing and drying. If water
cannot penetrate, remove the mat or
tangle prior to bathing.

Brushing
Line brush, working in sections, until
the dog is entirely tangle-free. When
finished, there should be little, if any,
fur still being removed with a firm
slicker brush. Double-check the work
with a wide-toothed comb and your
hands. Go over the entire body, feeling
for any inconsistencies in the density
levels of the coat. If an area seems
moist to the touch or fuller than the
rest of the coat, rework the area with
the appropriate tool. Mats, tangles
and excessive coat are easily trapped in
the following areas: behind the ears,
around the ruff, the thigh area, the
undercarriage and the tail. Give extra
attention to these areas before finishing
the groom.

Feet & Hocks
Trim the pads with blades ranging
from a #15 to a #40. Use a very light
touch to clean the pads of long hair.
If there is long fur between the toes,
brush it back so the fur stands up and
away from the foot. With thinning
shears, trim off the excess to create
a neat and very natural looking foot
with well-arched toes. Tidy the outside
edge of the foot, if needed, with small
detailing shears. If the hocks have
longer coat, trim lightly with thinning
shears to show a neat, clean area. A
#4F blade used in reverse works well
for trimming the tops of the feet and
the hocks on small to larger dogs
that are light to moderately coated.
With very heavy-coated or giant dogs,
handle the top of the feet and hocks
using hand-trimming techniques
instead of a clipper.

Sanitary Area
If the dog has a sanitation problem
under the tail, lightly trim this area
with thinning shears. Only clear
enough coat to accomplish the goal
and keep it looking very natural.
Trimming of the groin area is not
recommended unless there is a sanitary
problem. If the groin needs to be
trimmed, do so very lightly and try to
leave the fur long enough so that the
harsh coat does not prickle the skin,
causing the dog to lick at the irritation.

Detail Finish
Removal of muzzle whiskers is
optional, based on client preference.
For added shine, finish with a fine
mist of coat polish on the body coat.
Application of bows and mild cologne
is optional.

Suggested Tools & Equipment

- Nail Trimmers
- Styptic Powder
- Ear Cleaning Solution
- Cotton Balls
- Clippers
- #40 and #15 Blades for Pads
- #4F for Feet & Hocks (optional)
- Slicker Brush
- Wide-Toothed Comb
- Rubber Curry
- Undercoat Rake
- Dematting Tools
- High-Velocity Dryer
- Small Detailing Shears
- Curved Shears
- Thinning Shears

Notes:

Notes From The Grooming Table ©2016

Collie (Smooth)

Breed Facts & Characteristics

Country of Origin: Scotland

Height at Shoulder: 22"–26"

Coat Length/Type: Double Coated/Harsh

Color: Sable and white, tricolor, blue merle, or white with large patches of color desirable.

Correct grooming procedure:
Bathe & Brush Out

Common pet grooming practices:
Bathe & Brush Out

-The Goal-
The coat should be fresh smelling, shiny and full of body. No loose or shedding hair.

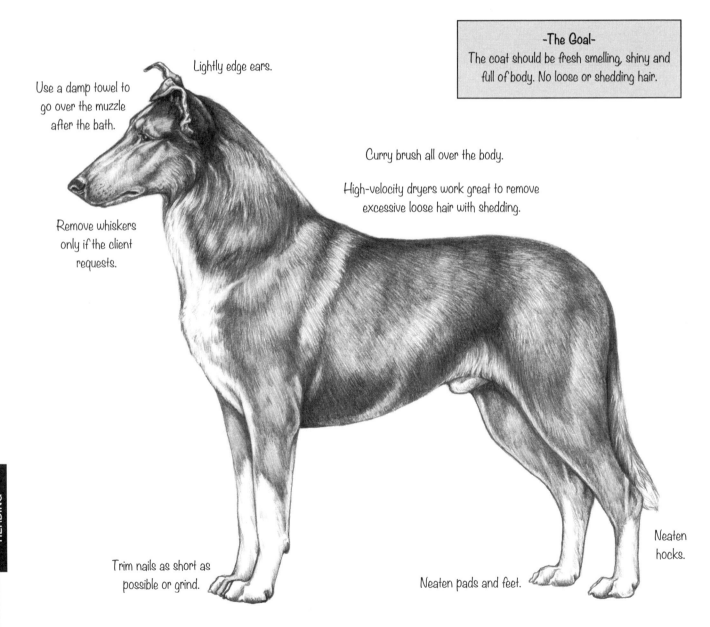

Lightly edge ears.

Use a damp towel to go over the muzzle after the bath.

Remove whiskers only if the client requests.

Curry brush all over the body.

High-velocity dryers work great to remove excessive loose hair with shedding.

Trim nails as short as possible or grind.

Neaten pads and feet.

Neaten hocks.

HERDING

Grooming Procedures & Recommendations

See page 67 for
Bathing & Drying Instructions

Frequency
Bathe once a week to once every 12 weeks.

Pre-Work
Trim or grind nails at least every four to six weeks to maintain a healthy foot structure. Clean the ears by swabbing with a mild ear cleaning solution. Prior to bathing, quickly go over the entire body with a high-velocity dryer to help lift dirt and dander away from the skin and loosen any shedding coat.

Brushing
Use a slicker brush, rubber curry, shedding blade, dematting tool or undercoat rake to loosen skin dander and remove loose coat. Be careful when using any tool with metal teeth or bristles. A heavy hand or too much repetition in an area can cause cuts and/or brush burns. Brushing and combing is not finished until all loose fur is removed, or it has become difficult to remove more than a half a brush full after repeated brushing.

Feet & Hocks
Trim the pads with a close cutting action blade, ranging from a #15 to a #40. Use a very light touch to clean the pads of long hair. If there is long fur between the toes, back brush the fur so it stands up and away from the foot. With thinning shears, trim off the excess creating a neat and very natural looking foot with well arched toes. Tidy the outside edge of the foot, if needed, with small detailing shears. If the hocks have longer coat on them, trim lightly with thinning shears showing a neat, clean area. A #4F blade used in reverse works well for trimming the tops of the feet and the hocks on some dogs.

Detail Finish
Removal of whiskers on the muzzle is optional, based on client preference. Finish with a fine mist of coat polish on the body for added shine. Application of bows and mild cologne is optional.

Grooming Tip
Let your hands guide you. Learn to feel for differences in coat density levels. Areas that feel heavier or denser than other areas need special attention when bathing, brushing and drying.

Suggested Tools & Equipment

- Nail Trimmers
- Styptic Powder
- Ear Cleaning Solution
- Cotton Balls
- Clippers
- #40 and #15 Blades for Pads
- #4F for Feet & Hocks (optional)
- Slicker Brush
- Greyhound Comb
- Rubber Curry
- Carding Tool
- De-Shedding Tools
- Small Detailing Shears
- Thinning Shears
- High-Velocity Dryer

Notes:

Notes From The Grooming Table ©2016

Entlebucher Mountain Dog   HERDING   SHORT COATED

Breed Facts & Characteristics

Country of Origin: Switzerland

Height at Shoulder: 16"–21"

Coat Length/Type: Short/Dense

Color: Deep rich tricolors of black, chestnut and white.

Correct grooming procedure:

Bathe & Brush Out

Common pet grooming practices:

Bathe & Brush Out

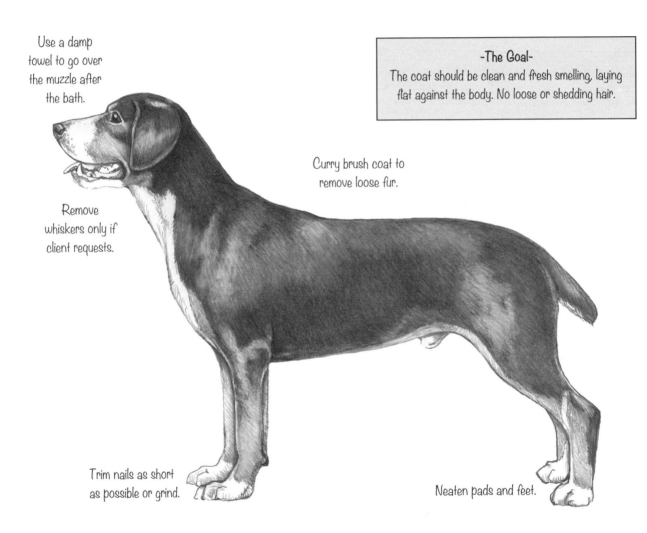

Use a damp towel to go over the muzzle after the bath.

-The Goal-
The coat should be clean and fresh smelling, laying flat against the body. No loose or shedding hair.

Curry brush coat to remove loose fur.

Remove whiskers only if client requests.

Trim nails as short as possible or grind.

Neaten pads and feet.

See page 67 for Bathing & Drying Instructions

Suggested Tools & Equipment

- Nail Trimmers
- Styptic Powder
- Ear Cleaning Solution
- Cotton Balls

- Clippers
- #40 or #15 Blade
- Slicker Brush
- Rubber Curry

- Carding Tool
- De-Shedding Tools
- Small Detailing Shears
- Thinning Shears

Notes *from your*
Grooming Table

Breed Facts & Characteristics

Country of Origin: Norway/Sweden/Finland

Height at Shoulder: 16"–21"

Coat Length/Type: Combination/Heavy

Color: Primary main color covering the bulk of the body is unlimited. It is common to see a lighter shade of the primary color present itself in a phantom color pattern in the coat.

Correct grooming procedure:
Bathe & Brush Out

Common pet grooming practices:
Bathe & Brush Out

-The Goal-
Coat should be mat free, shiny, light and airy. The coat should bounce and float with the dog as it moves. No loose coat.

Edge ear tips with thinning shears if necessary.

Use a damp towel to go over the muzzle after the bath.

Remove whiskers only if the client requests.

Thoroughly line brush/comb entire dog.

Use a high-velocity dryer both before and after the bath. Blow out loose coat, tangles and dirt. Dry and fluff.

This area is thick. Pay close attention when brushing.

This area is thick. Pay close attention when brushing.

Trim nails as short as possible or grind.

Shave pads and neaten feet to look natural.

Trim hocks.

HERDING

Grooming Procedures & Recommendations

See page 70 for
Bathing & Drying Instructions

Frequency
Bathe once a week to once every
12 weeks.

Pre-Work
Trim or grind nails at least every four
to six weeks to maintain a healthy foot
structure. Swab the ears clean with a
mild ear cleaning solution. Quickly
blow out the dog's coat with a high-
velocity dryer to effectively lift dirt and
debris away from the skin and loosen
coat. Brush out or remove any matting
found in the longer coated areas. If
the tangles are loose enough so that
water can fully penetrate them, remove
them after bathing and drying. If water
cannot penetrate, remove the mat or
tangle prior to bathing.

Brushing
Line brush, working in sections, until
the dog is entirely tangle-free. When
finished, there should be little, if any,
fur still being removed with a firm
slicker brush. Double-check the work
with a wide-toothed comb and your
hands. Go over the entire body, feeling
for any inconsistencies in the density
levels of the coat. If an area seems
moist to the touch or fuller than the
rest of the coat, rework the area with
the appropriate tool. Mats, tangles
and excessive coat are easily trapped in
the following areas: behind the ears,
around the ruff, the thigh area, the
undercarriage and the tail. Give extra
attention to these areas before finishing
the groom.

Feet & Hocks
Trim the pads with blades ranging
from a #15 to a #40. Use a very light
touch to clean the pads of long hair.
If there is long fur between the toes,
brush it back so the fur stands up and
away from the foot. With thinning
shears, trim off the excess to create
a neat and very natural looking foot
with well-arched toes. Tidy the outside
edge of the foot, if needed, with small
detailing shears. If the hocks have
longer coat, trim lightly with thinning
shears to show a neat, clean area. A
#4F blade used in reverse works well
for trimming the tops of the feet and
the hocks on small to larger dogs
that are light to moderately coated.
With very heavy-coated or giant dogs,
handle the top of the feet and hocks
using hand-trimming techniques
instead of a clipper.

Sanitary Area
If the dog has a sanitation problem
under the tail, lightly trim this area
with thinning shears. Only clear
enough coat to accomplish the goal
and keep it looking very natural.
Trimming of the groin area is not
recommended unless there is a sanitary
problem. If the groin needs to be
trimmed, do so very lightly and try to
leave the fur long enough so that the
harsh coat does not prickle the skin,
causing the dog to lick at the irritation.

Detail Finish
Removal of muzzle whiskers is
optional, based on client preference.
For added shine, finish with a fine
mist of coat polish on the body coat.
Application of bows and mild cologne
is optional.

Suggested Tools & Equipment

- Nail Trimmers
- Styptic Powder
- Ear Cleaning Solution
- Cotton Balls
- Clippers
- #40 and #15 Blades for Pads
- #4F for Feet & Hocks (optional)
- Slicker Brush
- Wide-Toothed Comb
- Rubber Curry
- Undercoat Rake
- Dematting Tools
- High-Velocity Dryer
- Small Detailing Shears
- Curved Shears
- Thinning Shears

Notes:

German Shepherd Dog

Breed Facts & Characteristics

Country of Origin: Germany

Height at Shoulder: 22"–26"

Coat Length/Type: Double Coated/Harsh

Color: One of the most common color patterns in this breed is deep, rich sable color in varying shades of browns, tans, blacks and grays.

Correct grooming procedure:
Bathe & Brush Out

Common pet grooming practices:
Bathe & Brush Out

-The Goal-
The coat should be fresh smelling, shiny and full of body. No loose or shedding hair.

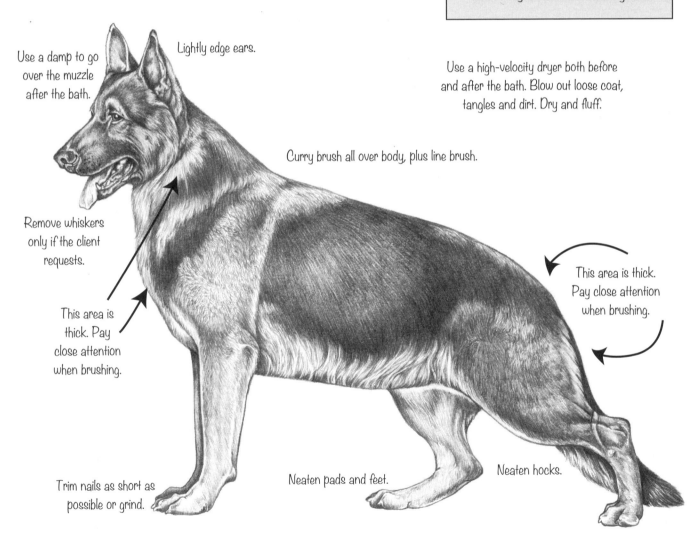

Use a damp to go over the muzzle after the bath.

Lightly edge ears.

Use a high-velocity dryer both before and after the bath. Blow out loose coat, tangles and dirt. Dry and fluff.

Curry brush all over body, plus line brush.

Remove whiskers only if the client requests.

This area is thick. Pay close attention when brushing.

This area is thick. Pay close attention when brushing.

Trim nails as short as possible or grind.

Neaten pads and feet.

Neaten hocks.

HERDING

Grooming Procedures & Recommendations

See page 69 for Bathing & Drying Instructions

Frequency

Bathe once a week to once every 12 weeks.

Pre-Work

Trim or grind nails at least every four to six weeks to maintain a healthy foot structure. Clean the ears by swabbing with a mild ear cleaning solution. Prior to bathing, quickly go over the entire body with a high-velocity dryer to help lift dirt and dander away from the skin and loosen any shedding coat.

Brushing

Use a slicker brush, rubber curry, shedding blade, dematting tool or undercoat rake to loosen skin dander and remove loose coat. Be careful when using any tool with metal teeth or bristles. A heavy hand or too much repetition in an area can cause cuts and/or brush burns. Brushing and combing is not finished until all loose fur is removed, or it has become difficult to remove more than a half a brush full after repeated brushing.

Feet & Hocks

Trim the pads with a close cutting action blade, ranging from a #15 to a #40. Use a very light touch to clean the pads of long hair. If there is long fur between the toes, back brush the fur so it stands up and away from the foot. With thinning shears, trim off the excess creating a neat and very natural looking foot with well arched toes. Tidy the outside edge of the foot, if needed, with small detailing shears. If the hocks have longer coat on them, trim lightly with thinning shears showing a neat, clean area. A #4F blade used in reverse works well for trimming the tops of the feet and the hocks on some dogs.

Detail Finish

Removal of whiskers on the muzzle is optional, based on client preference. Finish with a fine mist of coat polish on the body for added shine. Application of bows and mild cologne is optional.

Grooming Tip

Let your hands guide you. Learn to feel for differences in coat density levels. Areas that feel heavier or denser than other areas need special attention when bathing, brushing and drying.

Suggested Tools & Equipment

- Nail Trimmers
- Styptic Powder
- Ear Cleaning Solution
- Cotton Balls
- Clippers
- #40 and #15 Blades for Pads
- #4F for Feet & Hocks (optional)
- Slicker Brush
- Greyhound Comb
- Rubber Curry
- Carding Tool
- De-Shedding Tools
- Small Detailing Shears
- Thinning Shears
- High-Velocity Dryer

Notes:

Breed Facts & Characteristics

Country of Origin: Iceland

Height at Shoulder: 16½"–18"

Coat Length/Type: Double Coated *or* Long/Heavy

Color: A wide range of colors is acceptable with a single color dominating. Sections of white can accompany the primary color. Black masks and tri-color patterns are also accepted.

Correct grooming procedure:
Bathe & Brush Out

Common pet grooming practices:
Bathe & Brush Out

-The Goal-
Coat should be mat free, shiny, light and airy. The coat should bounce and float with the dog as it moves. No loose coat.

Use a damp towel to go over the muzzle after the bath.

Edge ears with thinning shears if necessary.

Use a high-velocity dryer both before and after the bath. Blow out loose coat, tangles and dirt. Dry and fluff.

Thoroughly line brush/comb entire dog.

Remove whiskers only if the client requests.

This area is thick. Pay close attention when brushing.

This area is thick. Pay close attention when brushing.

Friction Points:
• Armpits
• Inside Thighs

Trim nails as short as possible or grind.

Shave pads and neaten feet to look natural.

Trim hocks.

HERDING

Grooming Procedures & Recommendations

See page 70 for
Bathing & Drying Instructions

Frequency
Bathe once a week to once every 12 weeks.

Pre-Work
Trim or grind nails at least every four to six weeks to maintain a healthy foot structure. Swab the ears clean with a mild ear cleaning solution. Quickly blow out the dog's coat with a high-velocity dryer to effectively lift dirt and debris away from the skin and loosen coat. Brush out or remove any matting found in the longer coated areas. If the tangles are loose enough so that water can fully penetrate them, remove them after bathing and drying. If water cannot penetrate, remove the mat or tangle prior to bathing.

Brushing
Line brush, working in sections, until the dog is entirely tangle-free. When finished, there should be little, if any, fur still being removed with a firm slicker brush. Double-check the work with a wide-toothed comb and your hands. Go over the entire body, feeling for any inconsistencies in the density levels of the coat. If an area seems moist to the touch or fuller than the rest of the coat, rework the area with the appropriate tool. Mats, tangles and excessive coat are easily trapped in the following areas: behind the ears, around the ruff, the thigh area, the undercarriage and the tail. Give extra attention to these areas before finishing the groom.

Feet & Hocks
Trim the pads with blades ranging from a #15 to a #40. Use a very light touch to clean the pads of long hair. If there is long fur between the toes, brush it back so the fur stands up and away from the foot. With thinning shears, trim off the excess to create a neat and very natural looking foot with well-arched toes. Tidy the outside edge of the foot, if needed, with small detailing shears. If the hocks have longer coat, trim lightly with thinning shears to show a neat, clean area. A #4F blade used in reverse works well for trimming the tops of the feet and the hocks on small to larger dogs that are light to moderately coated. With very heavy-coated or giant dogs, handle the top of the feet and hocks using hand-trimming techniques instead of a clipper.

Sanitary Area
If the dog has a sanitation problem under the tail, lightly trim this area with thinning shears. Only clear enough coat to accomplish the goal and keep it looking very natural. Trimming of the groin area is not recommended unless there is a sanitary problem. If the groin needs to be trimmed, do so very lightly and try to leave the fur long enough so that the harsh coat does not prickle the skin, causing the dog to lick at the irritation.

Detail Finish
Removal of muzzle whiskers is optional, based on client preference. For added shine, finish with a fine mist of coat polish on the body coat. Application of bows and mild cologne is optional.

Suggested Tools & Equipment

- Nail Trimmers
- Styptic Powder
- Ear Cleaning Solution
- Cotton Balls
- Clippers
- #40 and #15 Blades for Pads
- #4F for Feet & Hocks (optional)
- Slicker Brush
- Wide-Toothed Comb
- Rubber Curry
- Undercoat Rake
- Dematting Tools
- High-Velocity Dryer
- Small Detailing Shears
- Curved Shears
- Thinning Shears

Notes:

Breed Facts & Characteristics

Country of Origin: United States

Height at Shoulder: 13"–18"

Coat Length/Type: Combination/Silky

Color: Black, red, blue merle, red merle—all with or without white marking and tan points. A white color is acceptable but white cannot dominate.

Correct grooming procedure:
Bathe & Brush Out

Common pet grooming practices:
Bathe & Brush Out

-The Goal-
Coat should be mat free, shiny, light and airy. The coat should bounce and float with the dog as it moves. No loose coat.

Use a high-velocity dryer both before and after the bath. Blow out loose coat, tangles and dirt. Dry and fluff.

Edge ears with thinners.

Use a damp towel to go over the muzzle after the bath.

Thoroughly line brush/comb entire dog..

Remove whiskers only if the client requests.

This area is thick. Pay close attention when brushing.

This area is thick. Pay close attention when brushing.

Trim nails as short as possible or grind.

Shave pads and neaten feet to look natural.

HERDING

See page 68 for Bathing & Drying Instructions

Frequency

Bathe once a week to once every 12 weeks.

Pre-Work

Trim or grind nails every four to six weeks to maintain a healthy foot structure. Clean the ears by swabbing with a mild ear cleaning solution. Use a rubber curry, shedding blade, undercoat rake, pumice stone, carding tool, fine stripping knife or natural bristle brush to loosen skin dander and remove loose coat. Use a high-velocity dryer over the coat to quickly and effectively lift dirt and debris away from the skin and loosen coat. Brush out or remove any matting found in the long-coated areas. If the tangles are loose enough so water can fully penetrate the area, remove them after bathing and drying. If water cannot penetrate, remove the mat or tangle prior to bathing.

Brushing

Line brush, working in sections until the dog is entirely tangle-free and all loose coat is removed. When finished, there should be little, if any, fur still being removed with a firm slicker brush. Double-check the work with a wide-toothed comb and your hands. Go over the entire body, feeling for any inconsistencies in the density levels of the coat. If an area seems moist to the touch or fuller than the rest of the coat, rework the area with the appropriate tool. Mats, tangles and excessive coat are easily trapped in the following areas: behind the ears, around the ruff, the thigh area, the undercarriage and the tail. Give extra attention to these areas before finishing the groom.

Carding

If a dog has an abundance of loose undercoat, line card the shorter areas with a carding tool. Common tools can be a fine stripping knife, undercoat rake, a pumice stone, or a #40 blade held between your fingers. Any carding tool should be pulled over the body, working in the direction of the coat growth. This will remove the soft, downy undercoat, allowing the guard coat to conform more closely to the natural outline of the body. It will also aid in the removal of loose, shedding coat, a seasonal problem for many pet owners.

Sanitary Area

If the dog has a sanitation problem under the tail, lightly trim this area with thinning shears. Only clear enough coat to accomplish the goal and keep it looking very natural. Trimming of the groin area is not recommended unless there is a sanitary problem. If the groin needs to be trimmed, do so very lightly and try to leave the fur long enough so that the harsh coat does not prickle the skin, causing the dog to lick at the irritation.

Feet & Hocks

Trim the pads with a close blade ranging from a #15 to a #40. Use a very light touch to clean the pads of long hair. If there is long fur between the toes, back brush the fur so it stands up on top of and away from the foot. With thinning shears, trim the excess to create a neat and very natural looking foot. Tidy the outside edge of the foot, if needed, with small detailing shears. If the hocks have longer coat, trim lightly with thinning shears to show a neat, clean area. A #4F blade, used carefully in reverse, works well for trimming the tops of the feet and the hocks on some dogs.

Suggested Tools & Equipment

- Nail Trimmers
- Styptic Powder
- Ear Cleaning Solution
- Cotton Balls
- Clippers
- #40 and #15 Blades for Pads
- #4F for Feet & Hocks (optional)
- Slicker Brush
- Greyhound Comb
- Rubber Curry
- Carding Tool
- De-Shedding Tools
- Small Detailing Shears
- Thinning Shears

Detail Finish

Edge the ears lightly with thinning shears to neaten and keep a natural look. Hand pluck any long wispy, flyaway hair from around the ears. Removal of whiskers on the muzzle is optional based on client preference. Finish with a fine mist of coat polish on the body coat for added shine. Application of bows and mild cologne is optional.

Notes:

Norwegian Buhund

Breed Facts & Characteristics

Country of Origin: Norway

Height at Shoulder: 16"–18½"

Coat Length/Type: Double Coated

Color: Wheaten or black. Wheaten colors can have a dark mask. On black dogs, a limited amount of white is acceptable; small ring around the neck, narrow blaze, small patch on chest, feet and tip of tail.

Correct grooming procedure:
Bathe & Brush Out

Common pet grooming practices:
Bathe & Brush Out

> **-The Goal-**
> The coat should be light and stand off the dog . The coat should bounce and shimmer with the dog as it moves.

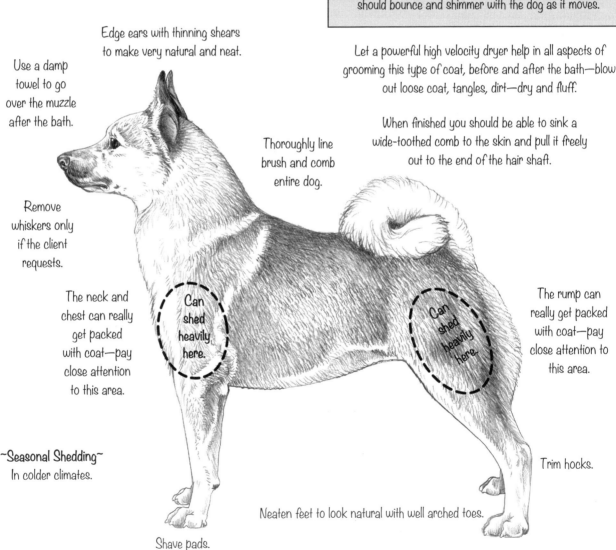

Edge ears with thinning shears to make very natural and neat.

Use a damp towel to go over the muzzle after the bath.

Remove whiskers only if the client requests.

The neck and chest can really get packed with coat—pay close attention to this area.

~Seasonal Shedding~
In colder climates.

Thoroughly line brush and comb entire dog.

Can shed heavily here.

Shave pads.

Let a powerful high velocity dryer help in all aspects of grooming this type of coat, before and after the bath—blow out loose coat, tangles, dirt—dry and fluff.

When finished you should be able to sink a wide-toothed comb to the skin and pull it freely out to the end of the hair shaft.

Can shed heavily here.

The rump can really get packed with coat—pay close attention to this area.

Trim hocks.

Neaten feet to look natural with well arched toes.

When shedding—the more work you can do with a powerful high velocity dryer, the less "elbow grease" you will have to exert.

Grooming Procedures & Recommendations

**See page 69 for
Bathing & Drying Instructions**

Frequency
Bathe once a week to once every
12 weeks.

Pre-Work
Trim or grind nails at least every four
to six weeks to maintain a healthy foot
structure. Clean the ears by swabbing
with a mild ear cleaning solution. Prior
to bathing, quickly go over the entire
body with a high-velocity dryer to help
lift dirt and dander away from the skin
and loosen any shedding coat.

Brushing
Use a slicker brush, rubber curry,
shedding blade, dematting tool or
undercoat rake to loosen skin dander
and remove loose coat. Be careful
when using any tool with metal
teeth or bristles. A heavy hand or too
much repetition in an area can cause
cuts and/or brush burns. Brushing
and combing is not finished until all
loose fur is removed, or it has become
difficult to remove more than a half a
brush full after repeated brushing.

Feet & Hocks
Trim the pads with a close cutting
action blade, ranging from a #15 to a
#40. Use a very light touch to clean
the pads of long hair. If there is long
fur between the toes, back brush the
fur so it stands up and away from the
foot. With thinning shears, trim off
the excess creating a neat and very
natural looking foot with well arched
toes. Tidy the outside edge of the
foot, if needed, with small detailing
shears. If the hocks have longer coat
on them, trim lightly with thinning
shears showing a neat, clean area. A
#4F blade used in reverse works well
for trimming the tops of the feet and
the hocks on some dogs.

Detail Finish
Removal of whiskers on the muzzle is
optional, based on client preference.
Finish with a fine mist of coat
polish on the body for added shine.
Application of bows and mild cologne
is optional.

Grooming Tip
Let your hands guide you. Learn to
feel for differences in coat density
levels. Areas that feel heavier or denser
than other areas need special attention
when bathing, brushing and drying.

Suggested Tools & Equipment

- Nail Trimmers
- Styptic Powder
- Ear Cleaning Solution
- Cotton Balls
- Clippers
- #40 and #15 Blades for Pads
- #4F for Feet & Hocks (optional)
- Slicker Brush
- Greyhound Comb
- Rubber Curry
- Carding Tool
- De-Shedding Tools
- Small Detailing Shears
- Thinning Shears
- High-Velocity Dryer

Notes:

Breed Facts & Characteristics

Country of Origin: England

Height at Shoulder: 21" and taller

Coat Length/Type: Hard/Thick

Color: All shades of blue, gray, grizzle or blue merle, with or without white and the white/gray markings.

Correct grooming procedure:

Brush Out/Minor Trim

Common pet grooming practices:

Bathe & Brush Out/Clipper-Trim

General Description

The Old English Sheep dog is a squarely built dog of good size and substance. The rump area is broader than at the shoulders. They have a profuse, harsh coat that is weather resistant. The outline of the dog is not to be changed by trimming; however, the feet and the rump are trimmed for sanitary purposes.

-The Goal-
Coat should be mat- and tangle-free.
The fur should be light and airy, moving freely with the dog as it moves.

Line comb and brush **every** inch of this dog, right down to the skin.

Scissor the coat short over rump, blending in over hips and thighs.

Clear stop area with thinners or clippers.

Lightly trim sanitary areas— both under tail and tummy.

Watch friction areas:
• Collar Area
• Arm Pits
• Behind Ears
• Legs & Thighs

Neaten undercarriage line.

Trim nails as short as possible or grind.

Shave pads and scissor feet round.

🐾 Bathing and Drying Directions:
• For coats longer than 3", use Natural Long Haired
• For coats shorter than 3", use Curly and Wavy Coated.

Grooming Procedures & Recommendations

See page 72 for
Bathing & Drying Instructions

See page 602 for
Drop Coat Styling Options

Frequency
Bathe once a week to once every 12 weeks.

Pre-Work
Trim or grind nails every four to six weeks to maintain a healthy foot structure. Clean the ears by swabbing with a mild ear cleaning solution. Hair should be plucked from within the ear canal only as necessary for healthy ear management. Prior to bathing, quickly go over the entire body and remove any serious mats or tangles. If the tangle can be penetrated with water, leave it and remove when the dog is clean. If the dog is staying in a clippered pet trim and has not been in for professional grooming for six weeks or more, remove the excessive body coat and set the pattern before bathing.

Brushing
Systematically line brush the entire coat, right down to the skin. With a slicker brush, the motion used for line brushing is a "pat and pull." Softly pat the coat with the full pad of the brush and pull out and away from the skin with each stroke. The wrist remains in a neutral, or straight, position. The motion should be light and gentle. Start on the lower rear legs and work upwards towards the thigh. Repeat on every leg then proceed to the body, neck, head ears and tail. Work evenly over the pet, holding or pushing up the coat with one hand. It can be done with either a comb or a brush, but in most cases the comb is reserved for double checking the work of the brush. With the slicker brush, work

the seam line, pulling down a small amount of fur with each stroke. Do not move to the next section until the brush stroke glides smoothly and the skin at the seam line is seen. Pay close attention to the legs, under the front legs, collar area, ears, and tail. Let your hands feel for coat density levels. If an area feels heavier or thicker, it will need special attention with a brush or a comb. If static electricity is a problem while brushing, lightly mist the coat with an anti-static product or water while brushing. When finished, each strand of hair should float freely about as the dog moves.

Head
For show, the head is left long and natural with no special treatment to the topknot area. For pet dogs, it is common to hold the hair out of the eyes by banding, braiding or using barrettes. For pets, it is also common to slightly trim the stop area between the eyes.

Hindquarters
The rear area about the tail and hips is trimmed quite close. This aids in keeping the rear of the dog clean and gives the dog a short-backed appearance. Fluff the coat with a wide-toothed comb and trim the coat level with the top line. Re-fluff the coat and scissor off the rear, near the rectal area, forming a square shape. Fluff the entire area again and blend the topline into the rear area, shaping the sides of the hips at the same time.

Feet & Hocks
Trim the pads with a close cutting action blade ranging from a #15 to a #40. Use a very light touch to clean the pads of long hair. To create a rounded foot, first block in the foot to form a square. This will help create a full circular shape with the toes pointing directly forward. Finish

Suggested Tools & Equipment

- Nail Trimmers
- Styptic Powder
- Ear Powder
- Ear Cleaning Solution
- Hemostat
- Cotton Balls
- Clippers
- #40 and #15 Blades for Pads
- Slicker Brush
- Greyhound Comb
- Pin Brush
- Dematting Tools
- Straight Shears
- Curved Shears
- Small Detailing Shears
- Thinning Shears

detailing and rounding the outline of the foot by using long, curved shears.

Detail Finish
Lightly neaten the entire outline of the dog, removing long, shaggy stray hairs that interrupt a smooth flow. The finished appearance is very natural. This can be done with thinning shears or shears as long as the look remains natural. Finish with a fine mist of coat polish on the body coat for added shine.

Notes:

Notes From The Grooming Table ©2016

Polish Lowland Sheepdog

Breed Facts & Characteristics

Country of Origin: Poland

Height at Shoulder: 17"–20"

Coat Length/Type: Long/Thick

Color: All colors are acceptable but most common is white with patches of color.

Correct grooming procedure:

Bathe & Brush Out

Common pet grooming practices:

Clipper-Trim

-The Goal-
Coat should be mat- and tangle-free. The fur should be light and airy, moving freely with the dog as it moves.

Clear stop area with thinners or clippers.

Leave ears long.

Line comb and brush **every** inch of this dog, right down to the skin.

Lightly trim sanitary areas—both under tail and tummy.

Watch friction areas:
- Collar Area
- Arm Pits
- Behind Ears
- Legs & Thighs

Neaten undercarriage line.

Trim nails as short as possible or grind.

Shave pads and scissor feet round.

HERDING

Grooming Procedures & Recommendations

See page 72 for
Bathing & Drying Instructions

See page 602 for
Drop Coat Styling Options

Frequency
Bathe once a week to once every 12 weeks.

Pre-Work
Trim or grind nails every four to six weeks to maintain a healthy foot structure. Clean the ears by swabbing with a mild ear cleaning solution. Hair should be plucked from within the ear canal only as necessary for healthy ear management. Prior to bathing, quickly go over the entire body and remove any serious mats or tangles. If the tangle can be penetrated with water, leave it and remove when the dog is clean. If the dog is staying in a clippered pet trim and has not been in for professional grooming for six weeks or more, remove the excessive body coat and set the pattern before bathing.

Brushing
Systematically line brush the entire coat, right down to the skin. With a slicker brush, the motion used for line brushing is a "pat and pull." Softly pat the coat with the full pad of the brush and pull out and away from the skin with each stroke. The wrist remains in a neutral, or straight, position. The motion should be light and gentle. Start on the lower rear legs and work upwards towards the thigh. Repeat on every leg then proceed to the body, neck, head, ears and tail. Work evenly over the pet, holding or pushing up the coat with one hand. It can be done with either a comb or a brush, but in most cases the comb is reserved for double checking the work of the brush. With the slicker brush, work the seam line, pulling down a small amount of fur with each stroke. Do not move to the next section until the brush stroke glides smoothly and the skin at the seam line is seen. Pay close attention to the legs, under the front legs, collar area, ears, and tail. Let your hands feel for coat density levels. If an area feels heavier or thicker, it will need special attention with a brush or a comb. If static electricity is a problem while brushing, lightly mist the coat with an anti-static product or water while brushing. When finished, each strand of hair should float freely about as the dog moves.

Head
For show, the head is left long and natural with no special treatment to the topknot area other than the hair is parted at the center. For pet dogs, it is common to hold the hair out of the eyes by banding, braiding or using barrettes. For pets, it is also common to slightly trim the stop area between the eyes.

Feet & Hocks
Trim the pads with a close cutting action blade ranging from a #15 to a #40. Use a very light touch to clean the pads of long hair. To create a rounded foot, first block in the foot to form a square. This will help create a full circular shape with the toes pointing directly forward. Finish detailing and rounding the outline of the foot by using long, curved shears.

Detail Finish
Lightly neaten the entire outline of the dog, removing long, shaggy stray hairs that interrupt a smooth flow. The finished appearance is very natural. This can be done with thinning shears or shears as long as the look remains natural. Finish with a fine mist of coat polish on the body coat for added shine.

Suggested Tools & Equipment

- Nail Trimmers
- Styptic Powder
- Ear Powder
- Ear Cleaning Solution
- Hemostat
- Cotton Balls
- Clippers
- #40 and #15 Blades for Pads
- Slicker Brush
- Greyhound Comb
- Pin Brush
- Dematting Tools
- Straight Shears
- Curved Shears
- Small Detailing Shears
- Thinning Shears

Notes:

Breed Facts & Characteristics

Country of Origin: Hungary

Height at Shoulder: 16"–17"

Coat Length/Type: Corded/Long

Color: Solid colors of black, gray and white are acceptable. On dark colored dogs, some white hair can be intermixed so long as the filtration is equal throughout the entire coat.

Correct grooming procedure:

Cording Coat

Common pet grooming practices:

Clipper-Trim

-The Goal-
Each cord should hang freely from the body

When shampooing, squeeze—*never* scrub a corded coat.

Gently pull and separate each cord with your fingers

Let dry naturally with little or no heat. It could take up to twelve hours to be totally dry.

The adolescent coat is the most difficult to deal with as the fur goes from puppy to adult coat.

Trim nails as short as possible or grind.

Shave pads and round feet level with the ground.

HERDING

See page 77 for
Bathing & Drying Instructions

Frequency

Bathe every 12 weeks or when needed. Work the cords once a week to once every four weeks, without a full bath.

Pre-Work

Trim or grind nails at least every four to six weeks to maintain a healthy foot structure. Clean the ears every four to six weeks. If hair forms inside the ear canal, apply an ear powder and gently pluck the hair from inside the canal. Use care not to pull any coat from outside the canal opening. Clean ears by swabbing with a mild ear cleaning solution.

Cords

The base of a cord is about ¼ to 1 inch square. Very often the cords will start to form by themselves, with little assistance. Prior to bathing, gently pull the strands away from one another to keep the cord as a separate strand. If the coat is shorter and feels "spongy" to the touch, it may not be forming natural cords. Mist the area with water or a light skin conditioner to help see the natural cord separation. Separate the area with your fingers into ¼ to 1 inch sections, starting at the base of each cord. If a cord is too thick, it can be split in two by working it with your fingers or by carefully cutting the cord with shears. Try to follow the natural separation as it splits.

Feet

Trim the pads with a close cutting blade, ranging from a #15 to a #40. Use a very light touch to clean the pads of long hair. With shears, round the foot slightly to create an oval shape with toes facing forward.

Detail Finish

When the dog is dry, continue to divide and separate the cords. Pay close attention to the friction areas: ears, under the front legs, the rump and under the tail. These are the areas where the skin is the most sensitive and is prone to injury. Use extreme caution when splitting the coat in these areas. Trimming the cords to a few inches all over enables the pet dog to maintain the look of the breed yet makes care easier than for the full coat.

Pet Dogs

Some pet owners choose to keep their pets brushed out or trimmed close, not dealing with the corded coat at all.

Grooming Tip

This is coat type requires a fair amount of attention, especially in the initial cording phases. Once the cords have formed, keeping them up requires only the use of your fingers. Pet owners can do this during idle time, like watching TV. With practice, their fingers will gravitate to the areas of greatest density, and they will be able to work the area without even looking at it.

Suggested Tools & Equipment

- Nail Trimmers
- Styptic Powder
- Ear Cleaning Solution
- Cotton Balls
- Clippers
- #40 and #15 Blades for Pads
- Straight Shear
- Strong Fingers

Notes:

Pyrenean Shepherd

Breed Facts & Characteristics

Country of Origin: France

Height at Shoulder: 15"–21"

Coat Length/Type: Multiple types ranging from Combination/Silky to Moderate/Rustic to Long/Rustic

Color: Light tan to deep copper, solid or mixed with black or gray shades, merle, brindle or black with limited white markings.

Correct grooming procedure:
Bathe & Brush Out/Cord

Common pet grooming practices:
Bathe & Brush Out/Clipper-Trim

-The Goal-
The majority of the coat should be mat- and tangle-free unless cords are present over select parts of the dog. The fur and/or cords should move freely with the dog as it moves.

Leave ears natural.

Lightly clear stop area with thinners or clippers, or finger pluck.

Line comb and brush **every** inch of this dog, right down to the skin.

Watch friction areas:
• Collar Area
• Arm Pits
• Behind Ears
• Legs & Thighs

Lightly trim sanitary areas—both under tail and tummy.

Neaten undercarriage line.

Trim nails as short as possible or grind.

Clip pads and tidy feet.

HERDING

See page 72 for
Bathing & Drying Instructions

See page 602 for
Drop Coat Styling Options

Frequency
Bathe once a week to once every 12 weeks.

Varieties
This breed comes in two varieties and three coat types. Smooth Faced varieties have coats similar to an Australian Shepherd or a Border Collie. The Rough Faced varieties come in two coat lengths—demi-long and long. The long coated dogs can have long cords form over their elbows and over their rear section but never on the head. Both the Rough Faced varieties have shorter hair on their muzzles which transition into longer hair beyond their eyes and cheeks, giving them a windblown appearance.

The directions here are for the Demi-Long Rough Faced variety. If you have another coat type variety, follow the grooming directions of another breed that best suits the individual dog you are working on.

Pre-Work
Trim or grind nails every four to six weeks to maintain a healthy foot structure. Clean the ears by swabbing with a mild ear cleaning solution. Hair should be plucked from within the ear canal only as necessary for healthy ear management. Prior to bathing, quickly go over the entire body and remove any serious mats or tangles. If the tangle can be penetrated with water, leave it and remove when the dog is clean.

Brushing
Systematically line brush the entire coat, right down to the skin. With a slicker brush, the motion used for line brushing is a "pat and pull." Softly pat the coat with the full pad of the brush and pull out and away from the skin with each stroke. The wrist remains in a neutral, or straight, position. The motion should be light and gentle. Start on the lower rear legs and work upwards towards the thigh. Repeat on every leg then proceed to the body, neck, head, ears and tail. Work evenly over the pet, holding or pushing up the coat with one hand. It can be done with either a comb or a brush, but in most cases the comb is reserved for double checking the work of the brush. With the slicker brush, work the seam line, pulling down a small amount of fur with each stroke. Do not move to the next section until the brush stroke glides smoothly and the skin at the seam line is seen.

Pay close attention to the legs, under the front legs, collar area, ears, and tail. Let your hands feel for coat density levels. If an area feels heavier or thicker, it will need special attention with a brush or a comb. If static electricity is a problem while brushing, lightly mist the coat with an anti-static product or water. When finished, each strand of hair should float freely about as the dog moves.

Head
The head is left natural. On pet dogs, if the coat is too long on the muzzle, use thinning shears or hand pluck the coat, tapering it so its shorter on the muzzle, transitioning into longer fur on the cheeks, blending into even longer coat in the neck and ruff area creating a "wind-blown" look. Use thinning shears at the inside corners of the eyes if necessary to clear the eyes slightly but leave the coat in the stop area. The hair on the top of the head is left natural.

Ears
The ears are semi pricked or cropped straight across and stand erect. They are left natural, being fully draped with longer hair or sparsely covered.

Suggested Tools & Equipment

- Nail Trimmers
- Styptic Powder
- Ear Powder
- Ear Cleaning Solution
- Hemostat
- Cotton Balls
- Clippers
- #40, #15, #10 Blades
- Slicker Brush
- Greyhound Comb
- Undercoat Rake
- Dematting Tools
- High-Velocity Dryer
- Longer Scissors
- Thinning Shears

Feet & Hocks
Trim the pads with a close cutting blade ranging from a #15 to a #40. Use a very light touch to clean the pads of long hair. To create a rounded foot, first block in the foot to form a square. This will help create a full circular shape with the toes pointing directly forward. Finish detailing and rounding the outline of the foot by using long, curved shears.

Detail Finish
If necessary, lightly tidy the outline of the dog, removing long, shaggy stray hairs that interrupt a smooth flow by finger plucking or with thinners. The finished appearance is very natural. Finish with a fine mist of coat polish on the body coat for added shine.

Shetland Sheepdog

Breed Facts & Characteristics

Country of Origin: Shetland Islands

Height at Shoulder: 13"–16"

Coat Length/Type: Combination/Long

Color: Sable, black, tricolor, or blue merle and with varying degrees of white, but never more than fifty percent white over the entire dog.

Correct grooming procedure:
Bathe & Brush Out/Minor Trimming

Common pet grooming practices:
Bathe & Brush Out/Minor Trimming

-The Goal-
Coat should be mat free, shiny, light and airy. The coat should bounce and float with the dog as it moves.

Edge ears.

Use a damp towel to go over the muzzle after the bath.

Remove whiskers only if the client requests.

Use a high-velocity dryer both before and after the bath. Blow out loose coat, tangles and dirt. Dry and fluff.

Thoroughly line brush/comb entire dog.

This area is thick. Pay close attention when brushing.

This area is thick. Pay close attention when brushing.

Trim nails as short as possible or grind.

Shave pads and neaten feet to look natural.

Trim hocks.

HERDING

Grooming Procedures & Recommendations

See page 70 for
Bathing & Drying Instructions

Frequency
Bathe once a week to once every 12 weeks.

Pre-Work
Trim or grind nails at least every four to six weeks to maintain a healthy foot structure. Swab the ears clean with a mild ear cleaning solution. Quickly blow out the dog's coat with a high-velocity dryer to effectively lift dirt and debris away from the skin and loosen coat. Brush out or remove any matting found in the longer coated areas. If the tangles are loose enough so that water can fully penetrate them, remove them after bathing and drying. If water cannot penetrate, remove the mat or tangle prior to bathing.

Brushing
Line brush, working in sections, until the dog is entirely tangle-free. When finished, there should be little, if any, fur still being removed with a firm slicker brush. Double-check the work with a wide-toothed comb and your hands. Go over the entire body, feeling for any inconsistencies in the density levels of the coat. If an area seems moist to the touch or fuller than the rest of the coat, rework the area with the appropriate tool. Mats, tangles and excessive coat are easily trapped in the following areas: behind the ears, around the ruff, the thigh area, the undercarriage and the tail. Give extra attention to these areas before finishing the groom.

Feet & Hocks
Trim the pads with blades ranging from a #15 to a #40. Use a very light touch to clean the pads of long hair. If there is long fur between the toes, brush it back so the fur stands up and away from the foot. With thinning shears, trim off the excess to create a neat and very natural looking foot with well-arched toes. Tidy the outside edge of the foot, if needed, with small detailing shears. If the hocks have longer coat, trim lightly with thinning shears to show a neat, clean area. A #4F blade used in reverse works well for trimming the tops of the feet and the hocks on small to larger dogs that are light to moderately coated. With very heavy-coated or giant dogs, handle the top of the feet and hocks using hand-trimming techniques instead of a clipper.

Sanitary Area
If the dog has a sanitation problem under the tail, lightly trim this area with thinning shears. Only clear enough coat to accomplish the goal and keep it looking very natural. Trimming of the groin area is not recommended unless there is a sanitary problem. If the groin needs to be trimmed, do so very lightly and try to leave the fur long enough so that the harsh coat does not prickle the skin, causing the dog to lick at the irritation.

Detail Finish
Removal of muzzle whiskers is optional, based on client preference. For added shine, finish with a fine mist of coat polish on the body coat. Application of bows and mild cologne is optional.

Suggested Tools & Equipment

- Nail Trimmers
- Styptic Powder
- Ear Cleaning Solution
- Cotton Balls
- Clippers
- #40 and #15 Blades for Pads
- #4F for Feet & Hocks (optional)
- Slicker Brush
- Wide-Toothed Comb
- Rubber Curry
- Undercoat Rake
- Dematting Tools
- High-Velocity Dryer
- Small Detailing Shears
- Curved Shears
- Thinning Shears

Notes:

Breed Facts & Characteristics

Country of Origin: Spain

Height at Shoulder: 15¾"–19¾"

Coat Length/Type: Rustic/Curly

Color: Any shade of a solid color or parti-colored where the secondary color is white.

Correct grooming procedure:
Rustic/Corded/Clipped

Common pet grooming practices:
Rustic/Corded/Clipped

General Description

The Spanish Water dog is an active, very smart, medium sized dog. It was originally bred as an all-purpose farm dog, herding all types of livestock. Along the coast of Spain, it assisted fishermen. It is a well-proportioned dog, slightly longer than it is tall. Traditionally this breed is never brushed or combed. It has a rustic, curly, single coat that can be curly or have cords. The breed standard states it should be totally shaved a few times a year from the tip of its nose to the tip of its tail. Rustic coated dogs **never** appear fluffy, polished or well groomed. Their coats are always air dried to maintain the springy curls characteristic of the breed.

-The Goal-
This is a rustic coated breed with hair that is one length, all over. They are clipped close a few times a year, head, ears, body, legs, and tail. For show, they are grown out to 1–5 inches long so the quality of the curl or cord can be assessed.

Clip ears same length as body.

Entire dog is clipper-cut with blades ranging from a #7F, #5F, #4F or a medium length guard comb.

Clip entire head same lengh as body.

Coat can be made up of short cords vs a 2–3 times yearly shave off.

Trim nails as short as possible or grind.

Air dry to promote a curly coat. Do not fluff dry.

Shave pads and tidy around feet.

HERDING

Grooming Procedures & Recommendations

See page 79 for
Bathing & Drying Instructions

Frequency
Bathe every 3 to 12 weeks or when needed. Rake through the coat every 1–3 weeks, with or without a bath, to keep matting under control, unless the coat is intentionally corded. To maintain the coat at a longer, clipped length, trim every 4 to 6 weeks. Lighter colored dogs with ringlets may need more frequent combing and raking as their coats tends to mat more easily than darker colored dogs. If the coat is corded, cords need to be separated on a frequent basis by the owner at home and in a professional grooming setting.

Pre-Work
To keep mats and tangles at bay, thoroughly rake out the coat prior to bathing to keep the coat from becoming a solid pelted mass. This will remove the undercoat "lint," preventing matting in the future. Trim or grind nails at least every four to six weeks to maintain a healthy foot structure. Clean the ears by swabbing with a mild ear cleaning solution. Hair should be plucked from within the ear canal only as necessary for healthy ear management. Rustic coated breeds are *never* blown or fluffed dried. They are always naturally air dried to maintain the curly, unkempt and tousled looking coat.

General Pattern Lines
The breed standard calls for no pattern whatsoever on this breed. It is one length all over. The rustic, curly or corded coat is a major part of the breed standard. Traditionally, it was shaved once a year with the sheep. No other grooming was done on the dog. If the dog is shown, they need enough coat so the quality of the coat can be evaluated, typically between 1 and 5 inches. Any aesthetic trimming

is heavily frowned upon. This breed definitely falls into the category of "less-is-more." Pet owners who typically have dogs who share their homes, groom them more frequently.

Body & Neck
The entire body is clipper-cut with blades ranging from a #7F, #5F, #4F or a medium length guard comb. Start at the withers and work back over the body towards the tail. Use caution if working with guard combs as they can get stuck in the coat. Follow the contour of the body. Do not back brush. The goal is a dog whose coat is somewhat rough and messy looking. If the coat needs to be fluffed, fluff with a coarse or wide-toothed comb. Many pet owners opt for less than 1 inch of coat for easier home maintenance trim styling.

Tail
The docked or shorter tail is clipped the same as the body.

Feet & Legs
Clip pads with blades ranging from a #40 to #15 in length. Clip the legs and feet the same length as on the body. Tidy around the feet with shears.

Head & Ears
Clip the entire head; topskull, ears and muzzle the same length as the body. If a longer guard comb has been used, tidy up between the eyes and the muzzle with thinners. Edge the ears with small detailing shears, keeping the tips of the shears towards the tip of the ears.

Detail Finish
Lightly re-fluff all your work, checking for stray hairs. The coat should not look polished and smooth. The goal is a dog that is mat- and tangle-free that looks reasonably tidy but unkempt, curly and messy at the same time. Application of mild cologne and bows is optional.

Suggested Tools & Equipment
- Nail Trimmers
- Styptic Powder
- Ear Powder
- Ear Cleaning Solution
- Cotton Balls
- Hemostat
- Clippers
- Slicker Brush
- Greyhound Comb
- Wide-Toothed Comb
- Undecoat Rake
- Small Detailing Shears
- Thinning Shears
- Dematting Tools

Common Blade Options:
- #40, #15, #10
- #7F, #5F, #4F
- Variety of Guard Combs

Corded Coats
The base of a cord is about 1 to 2 inches square. Very often the cords will start to form by themselves, with little assistance. Prior to bathing, gently pull the strands away from one another to keep the cord as a separate strand. If the coat is shorter and feels "spongy" to the touch, it may not be forming natural cords. Mist the area with water or a light skin conditioner to help see the natural cord separation. Separate the area with your fingers into 1- to 2-inch sections, starting at the base of each cord. If a cord is too thick, it can be split in two by working it with your fingers or by carefully cutting the cord with shears. Try to follow the natural separation as it splits. Cords should all be a uniform length over the entire dog, never exceeding more than 5 inches.

Grooming Procedures & Recommendations

Feet
Trim the pads with a close cutting blade, ranging from a #15 to a #40. Use a very light touch to clean the pads of long hair. With shears, round the foot slightly to create an oval shape with toes facing forward.

Detail Finish
When the dog is dry, continue to divide and separate the cords. Pay close attention to the friction areas: ears, under the front legs, the rump and under the tail. These are the areas where the skin is the most sensitive and is prone to injury. Use extreme caution when splitting the coat in these areas. Trimming the cords to a few inches all over enables the pet dog to maintain the look of the breed yet makes care easier than for the full coat.

Grooming Tip
Corded coats require a fair amount of attention, especially in the initial cording phases. Once the cords have formed, keeping them up requires only the use of your fingers. Pet owners can do this during idle time, like watching TV. With practice, their fingers will gravitate to the areas of greatest density, and they will be able to work the area without even looking at it.

Notes:

Notes *from your* Grooming Table

Breed Facts & Characteristics

Country of Origin: Sweden

Height at Shoulder: 11½"–13½"

Coat Length/Type: Double Coated

Color: Sable pattern in tones of grays to reds with lighter shades on the underside and areas of the head, as well as harness markings over the shoulder area. Dark masks are desired when offset by lighter color on the head. Some dogs have a small amount of white typically seen as a small blaze, on the throat, chest or neck area as well as white markings on the legs.

Correct grooming procedure:
Bathe & Brush Out

Common pet grooming practices:
Bathe & Brush Out

-The Goal-
The coat should be light and stand off the dog. The coat should bounce and shimmer with the dog as it moves.

Let a powerful high velocity dryer help in all aspects of grooming this type of coat, before and after the bath—blow out loose coat, tangles, dirt—dry and fluff.

When finished you should be able to sink a wide-toothed comb to the skin and pull it freely out to the end of the hair shaft.

Use a damp towel to go over the muzzle after the bath.

Edge ears with thinning shears to make very natural and neat.

Thoroughly line brush and comb entire dog.

Remove whiskers only if the client requests.

The rump can really get packed with coat—pay close attention to this area.

The neck and chest can really get packed with coat—pay close attention to this area.

Can shed heavily here.

Can shed heavily here.

Trim hocks.

~Seasonal Shedding~
In colder climates.

Shave pads.

Neaten feet to look natural with well arched toes.

When shedding—the more work you can do with a powerful high velocity dryer, the less "elbow grease" you will have to exert.

Grooming Procedures & Recommendations

See page 69 for Bathing & Drying Instructions

Frequency
Bathe once a week to once every 12 weeks.

Pre-Work
Trim or grind nails at least every four to six weeks to maintain a healthy foot structure. Clean the ears by swabbing with a mild ear cleaning solution. Prior to bathing, quickly go over the entire body with a high-velocity dryer to help lift dirt and dander away from the skin and loosen any shedding coat.

Brushing
Use a slicker brush, rubber curry, shedding blade, dematting tool or undercoat rake to loosen skin dander and remove loose coat. Be careful when using any tool with metal teeth or bristles. A heavy hand or too much repetition in an area can cause cuts and/or brush burns. Brushing and combing is not finished until all loose fur is removed, or it has become difficult to remove more than a half a brush full after repeated brushing.

Feet & Hocks
Trim the pads with a close cutting action blade, ranging from a #15 to a #40. Use a very light touch to clean the pads of long hair. If there is long fur between the toes, back brush the fur so it stands up and away from the foot. With thinning shears, trim off the excess creating a neat and very natural looking foot with well arched toes. Tidy the outside edge of the foot, if needed, with small detailing shears. If the hocks have longer coat on them, trim lightly with thinning shears showing a neat, clean area. A #4F blade used in reverse works well for trimming the tops of the feet and the hocks on some dogs.

Detail Finish
Removal of whiskers on the muzzle is optional, based on client preference. Finish with a fine mist of coat polish on the body for added shine. Application of bows and mild cologne is optional.

Grooming Tip
Let your hands guide you. Learn to feel for differences in coat density levels. Areas that feel heavier or denser than other areas need special attention when bathing, brushing and drying.

Suggested Tools & Equipment

- Nail Trimmers
- Styptic Powder
- Ear Cleaning Solution
- Cotton Balls
- Clippers
- #40 and #15 Blades for Pads
- #4F for Feet & Hocks (optional)
- Slicker Brush
- Greyhound Comb
- Rubber Curry
- Carding Tool
- De-Shedding Tools
- Small Detailing Shears
- Thinning Shears
- High-Velocity Dryer

Notes:

Welsh Corgi (Cardigan)

Breed Facts & Characteristics

Country of Origin: British Isles

Height at Shoulder: 10½"–12½"

Coat Length/Type: Double Coated/Dense

Color: Black, red, blue merle, sables and brindled. All with or without white markings and tan points. Head should predominately be colored.

Correct grooming procedure:

Bathe & Brush Out

Common pet grooming practices:

Bathe & Brush Out

-The Goal-
The coat should be fresh smelling, shiny and full of body. No loose or shedding hair.

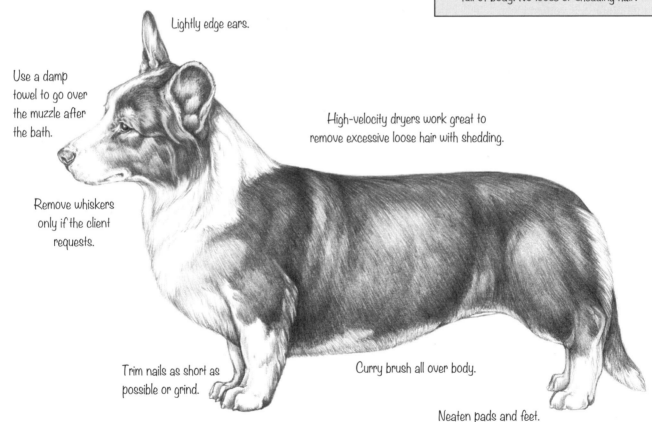

Lightly edge ears.

Use a damp towel to go over the muzzle after the bath.

High-velocity dryers work great to remove excessive loose hair with shedding.

Remove whiskers only if the client requests.

Trim nails as short as possible or grind.

Curry brush all over body.

Neaten pads and feet.

HERDING

See page 69 for
Bathing & Drying Instructions

Frequency
Bathe once a week to once every 12 weeks.

Pre-Work
Trim or grind nails at least every four to six weeks to maintain a healthy foot structure. Clean the ears by swabbing with a mild ear cleaning solution. Prior to bathing, quickly go over the entire body with a high-velocity dryer to help lift dirt and dander away from the skin and loosen any shedding coat.

Brushing
Use a slicker brush, rubber curry, shedding blade, dematting tool or undercoat rake to loosen skin dander and remove loose coat. Be careful when using any tool with metal teeth or bristles. A heavy hand or too much repetition in an area can cause cuts and/or brush burns. Brushing and combing is not finished until all loose fur is removed, or it has become difficult to remove more than a half a brush full after repeated brushing.

Feet & Hocks
Trim the pads with a close cutting action blade, ranging from a #15 to a #40. Use a very light touch to clean the pads of long hair. If there is long fur between the toes, back brush the fur so it stands up and away from the foot. With thinning shears, trim off the excess creating a neat and very natural looking foot with well arched toes. Tidy the outside edge of the foot, if needed, with small detailing shears. If the hocks have longer coat on them, trim lightly with thinning shears showing a neat, clean area. A #4F blade used in reverse works well for trimming the tops of the feet and the hocks on some dogs.

Detail Finish
Removal of whiskers on the muzzle is optional, based on client preference. Finish with a fine mist of coat polish on the body for added shine. Application of bows and mild cologne is optional.

Grooming Tip
Let your hands guide you. Learn to feel for differences in coat density levels. Areas that feel heavier or denser than other areas need special attention when bathing, brushing and drying.

Suggested Tools & Equipment

- Nail Trimmers
- Styptic Powder
- Ear Cleaning Solution
- Cotton Balls
- Clippers
- #40 and #15 Blades for Pads
- #4F for Feet & Hocks (optional)
- Slicker Brush
- Greyhound Comb
- Rubber Curry
- Carding Tool
- De-Shedding Tools
- Small Detailing Shears
- Thinning Shears
- High-Velocity Dryer

Notes:

Breed Facts & Characteristics

Country of Origin: Wales

Height at Shoulder: 10"–12"

Coat Length/Type: Double Coated/Dense

Color: Red, sables, fawns, black and tans, all with a limited amount of white about the nose; blaze on the face, neck, legs, chest and underbody.

Correct grooming procedure:
Bathe & Brush Out

Common pet grooming practices:
Bathe & Brush Out

-The Goal-
The coat should be fresh smelling, light and stand off the body. No loose hair.

Lightly edge ears.

Use a damp towel to go over the muzzle after the bath.

Remove whiskers only if the client requests.

High-velocity dryers work great to remove excessive loose hair with shedding.

Neaten hocks.

Trim nails as short as possible or grind.

Curry brush all over body.

Neaten pads and feet.

HERDING

Grooming Procedures & Recommendations

See page 69 for Bathing & Drying Instructions

Frequency
Bathe once a week to once every 12 weeks.

Pre-Work
Trim or grind nails at least every four to six weeks to maintain a healthy foot structure. Clean the ears by swabbing with a mild ear cleaning solution. Prior to bathing, quickly go over the entire body with a high-velocity dryer to help lift dirt and dander away from the skin and loosen any shedding coat.

Brushing
Use a slicker brush, rubber curry, shedding blade, dematting tool or undercoat rake to loosen skin dander and remove loose coat. Be careful when using any tool with metal teeth or bristles. A heavy hand or too much repetition in an area can cause cuts and/or brush burns. Brushing and combing is not finished until all loose fur is removed, or it has become difficult to remove more than a half a brush full after repeated brushing.

Feet & Hocks
Trim the pads with a close cutting action blade, ranging from a #15 to a #40. Use a very light touch to clean the pads of long hair. If there is long fur between the toes, back brush the fur so it stands up and away from the foot. With thinning shears, trim off the excess creating a neat and very natural looking foot with well arched toes. Tidy the outside edge of the foot, if needed, with small detailing shears. If the hocks have longer coat on them, trim lightly with thinning shears showing a neat, clean area. A #4F blade used in reverse works well for trimming the tops of the feet and the hocks on some dogs.

Detail Finish
Removal of whiskers on the muzzle is optional, based on client preference. Finish with a fine mist of coat polish on the body for added shine. Application of bows and mild cologne is optional.

Grooming Tip
Let your hands guide you. Learn to feel for differences in coat density levels. Areas that feel heavier or denser than other areas need special attention when bathing, brushing and drying.

Suggested Tools & Equipment

- Nail Trimmers
- Styptic Powder
- Ear Cleaning Solution
- Cotton Balls
- Clippers
- #40 and #15 Blades for Pads
- #4F for Feet & Hocks (optional)
- Slicker Brush
- Greyhound Comb
- Rubber Curry
- Carding Tool
- De-Shedding Tools
- Small Detailing Shears
- Thinning Shears
- High-Velocity Dryer

Notes:

Notes From The Grooming Table ©2016

564

Dogs in the Miscellaneous Group are in a transitional stage within the American Kennel Club awaiting full approval to other groups. Many of these dogs are well established in their own regions yet have not developed a wide following, limiting their numbers. Although there is no time limit set as to how long a breed stays in the miscellaneous class, typically they are in this group for one to three years before being moved into an established group that fits what the breed was developed for. Breeds within this group are constantly changing.

Breed Facts & Characteristics

Country of Origin: United States

Height at Shoulder: 12"–16"

Coat Length/Type: Hairless *or* Short/Smooth

Color: All colors or combination of colors excluding merle or albino.

Correct grooming procedure:
Bathe/Clip/Wet Shave

Common pet grooming practices:
Bathe/Clip

Comes in two varieties; hairless or smooth coated. Groom coated dogs as any smooth coated dog.

-The Goal-
The coat should be clean and fresh smelling, with soft pliable skin.

Bathe the dog with a **very** gentle shampoo.

Use a loofah pad, bath puff, or bath gloves to wash the dog and aid in the removal of dead skin cells. Use very light pressure.

If there are any sprigs of hair on the body, clip with very close blade.

Leave whiskers and small sprigs of hair on head.

Note: Some hairless breeds have problems with skin acne and lanolin based products.

If needed, apply a moisturizing treatment.

At home care between shampoos: Wipe down daily with a warm washcloth to remove unwanted germs, dirt and oil.

Trim nails as short as possible or grind.

See page 78 for Bathing & Drying Instructions

Suggested Tools & Equipment

- Nail Trimmers
- Styptic Powder
- Ear Cleaning Solution
- Hemostat
- Cotton Balls
- Cleansing cloth or puff
- Clippers
- #40 or #30 Blade

Breed Facts & Characteristics

Country of Origin: Africa

Height at Shoulder: 23"–29"

Coat Length/Type: Short/Smooth

Color: Colors and markings are unimportant.

Correct grooming procedure:
Bathe & Curry Brush

Common pet grooming practices:
Bathe & Curry Brush

-The Goal-
The coat should be clean and fresh smelling, with the coat laying flat against the body. No shedding hair.

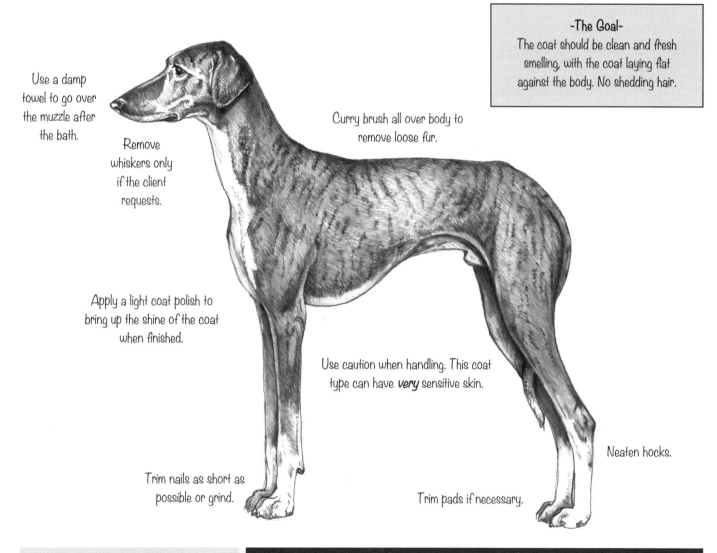

Use a damp towel to go over the muzzle after the bath.

Remove whiskers only if the client requests.

Curry brush all over body to remove loose fur.

Apply a light coat polish to bring up the shine of the coat when finished.

Use caution when handling. This coat type can have *very* sensitive skin.

Neaten hocks.

Trim nails as short as possible or grind.

Trim pads if necessary.

See page 66 for
Bathing & Drying Instructions

Suggested Tools & Equipment

- Nail Trimmers
- Styptic Powder
- Ear Cleaning Solution
- Cotton Balls

- Clippers
- #40 or #15 Blade
- Rubber Curry
- Carding Tool

- Small Detailing Shears
- Thinning Shears

Belgian Laekenois

Breed Facts & Characteristics

Country of Origin: Belgium

Height at Shoulder: 22"–26"

Coat Length/Type: Moderate/Rustic

Color: All shades of browns, tans, gray and grizzle. Limited black markings on the muzzle, head, ears and tail. Small white spots acceptable on chest, toes and frosting on muzzle.

Correct grooming procedure:
Bathe/Brush/Card/Light Hand-Strip

Common pet grooming practices:
Bathe/Brush/Card/Light Hand-Strip

General Description

The Belgian Laekenois is one of the varieties of the Belgian Sheepdog. It's a rustic coated working farm dog. They are a moderately sized, squarely built, well balanced dog. They have an unkempt looking, wiry coat unique to the breed.

-The Goal-
This is a very uncomplicated coat type in terms of grooming. Less is more. It should look very natural, rustic and non-sculpted.

Coat on top of skull is shorter, forming parallel planes with the muzzle.

Finger pluck excessively long hair from ears.

Brush, card, and rake to remove dead coat. As new hair grows in, it will have a harsh texture. The coat should look tousled and messy.

Air dry to retain the rustic look of the coat.

Coat lengthens in the cheek region.

Finger pluck longer hair from stop area to give a hint of definition between the brows. Brows left natural.

Coat length on tail should be the same length as on body.

The coat should be about 2–3 inches all over the body. The harsh, crisp coat should not hide the outline of the dog.

Neaten hocks.

Trim nails as short as possible or grind.

Shave pads and neaten feet to match legs.

See page 79 for Bathing & Drying Instructions

Frequency

Bathe once a week to once every 12 weeks.

Pre-Work

Trim or grind nails at least every four to six weeks to maintain a healthy foot structure. Swab the ears clean with a mild ear cleaning solution. Prior to bathing, quickly go over the entire body with a high-velocity dryer to help lift dirt and dander away from the skin and to loosen any shedding coat. *Rake and hand-strip dog prior to bathing and drying.*

Raking

Raking is a natural technique in which the soft, downy undercoat is pulled from the dog's body. Typical tools used with this coat type are: an undercoat rake, a course-toothed stripping knife pulled through the coat. Raking can be done before or after bathing and drying. Removal of the soft undercoat and removal of the dead, blown guard coat promotes the harsh outer coat, creates a rich coat color and protects the skin.

Hand-stripping

Hand-stripping is a technique in which the blown outer guard coat is plucked from the dog's skin. This procedure helps retain the proper coat texture and rich color of the breed. During certain times of the year, the coat is easier to pull out. When the coat easily comes out, it is called a "blowing coat" or "blown coat." Ideally, hand-stripping should correspond with the dog's natural cycle, based on the environment and its hormonal levels. Using your fingers, pull out a few hairs at a time to shape the coat, accentuating the natural outline of the dog. Work methodically, pulling small amounts of coat at a time, always working in the direction of the coat growth. Leave enough coat to be between 2 to 3 inches long over the body and shorter on the legs. The coats always should appear very natural, never clipped or trimmed. On some coats, a light application of chalk or powder before the bath will allow a better grip and make plucking and stripping much easier.

Head

The coat is shorter on the top of the head and cheeks so the head shape is not obscured. While only between ½ and 1 inch in length, it still looks rough and unkempt. They can have a hint of an eyebrow. The muzzle has slightly longer coat forming a bit of a beard. The ears are covered with shorter, hard coat. Hand-strip or pluck the top skull, throat and cheeks. Ears are stripped of excessively longer hair to show off their natural erect ear set. Finish by edging the ear lightly with thinning shears, keeping the tips of the shears toward the tip of the ear for a very natural look.

Feet & Hocks

Trim the pads with a close cutting blade ranging from a #15 to a #40. Use a very light touch to clean the pads of long hair. Tidy the outside edge of the foot and if the hocks need shaping, trim lightly with thinning shears or hand-strip those areas to tidy them up.

Detail Finish

Application of bows and mild cologne is optional.

Suggested Tools & Equipment

- Nail Trimmers
- Styptic Powder
- Ear Cleaning Solution
- Cotton Balls
- Clippers
- Slicker Brush
- Greyhound Comb
- Wide-Toothed Comb
- Undercoat Rake
- Stripping Knives
- Small Detailing Shears
- Thinning Shears
- Dematting Tools

Common Blade Options:

- #40, #15, #10

Note:

Clipping a wired-coated dog will result in a dramatic change in the texture and color of the coat. The correct harsh wire coat needs to be encouraged by plucking the blown coat when it is ready to be removed. This process stimulates hair follicles to produce new guard coat. Without hand-stripping, the guard coat is not stimulated and will not grow in properly. It will lose its brilliant color and texture. If only the undercoat grows, the guard coat color becomes that of the lighter, soft undercoat.

Notes:

Dogo Argentino

Breed Facts & Characteristics

Country of Origin: Argentina

Height at Shoulder: 23½"–27"

Coat Length/Type: Short/Smooth

Color: All white—limited dark spot covering the eye acceptable.

Correct grooming procedure:
Bathe & Curry Brush

Common pet grooming practices:
Bathe & Curry Brush

-The Goal-
The coat should be clean and fresh smelling, with the coat laying flat against the body. No shedding hair.

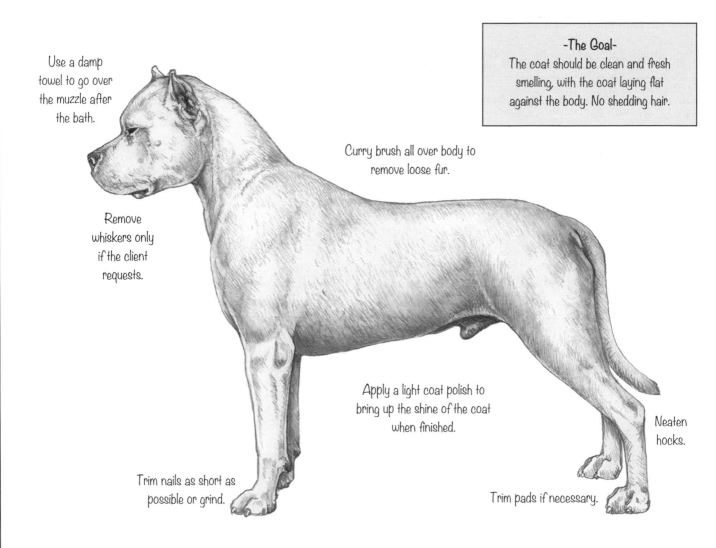

Use a damp towel to go over the muzzle after the bath.

Remove whiskers only if the client requests.

Curry brush all over body to remove loose fur.

Apply a light coat polish to bring up the shine of the coat when finished.

Neaten hocks.

Trim nails as short as possible or grind.

Trim pads if necessary.

See page 66 for
Bathing & Drying Instructions

Suggested Tools & Equipment

- Nail Trimmers
- Styptic Powder
- Ear Cleaning Solution
- Cotton Balls

- Clippers
- #40 or #15 Blade
- Rubber Curry
- Carding Tool

- Small Detailing Shears
- Thinning Shears

Notes *from your*
Grooming Table

Grand Basset Griffon Vendéen

Breed Facts & Characteristics

Country of Origin: France

Height at Shoulder: 15½"–18"

Coat Length/Type: Moderate/Wiry

Color: Tri-colored or bi-colored with white and any other color; blacks, grays or tan.

Correct grooming procedure:

Hand-Strip

Common pet grooming practices:

Card/Hand-Strip

General Description

The coat is made up of a wiry outer coat with a thick under coat. The harsh, outer guard coat is normally between 1 and 2 inches in length. The extended "eyebrows" and the typical beard give the GBGV his characteristic tousled appearance.

-The Goal-
Make this a casual looking dog with a "tousled" look. The outer coat is crisp and harsh. The undercoat is thick and short. The overall appearance of the dog is to be totally natural with only minor neatening to accentuate the dog's form.

Slight indication of triangular brows over eyes but the eye is not fully covered by the eyebrow.

Remove shedding coat by brushing with a firm slicker brush or carding. Lightly finger pluck or hand-strip exceptionally long guard coat only if it distracts from the outline.

Pluck long hairs from the tail to balance with body.

Full Beard.

Head is left natural with long ears. Pluck unruly stray hairs with fingers.

Lightly clip sanitary areas: Under tail and tummy with #10.

Trim nails as short as possible or grind.

Neaten undercarriage line lightly.

Neaten hocks.

Shave pads and scissor feet round.

MISCELLANEOUS

Grooming Procedures & Recommendations

See page 76 for
Bathing & Drying Instructions

Frequency
Bathe once a week to once every 12 weeks.

Pre-Work
Trim or grind nails at least every four to six weeks to maintain a healthy foot structure. Swab the ears clean with a mild ear cleaning solution. Prior to bathing, quickly go over the entire body with a high-velocity dryer to help lift dirt and dander away from the skin and to loosen any shedding coat. *Card and hand-strip dog prior to bathing and drying.*

Brushing
Use a rubber curry, shedding blade, undercoat rake, pumice stone, carding tool, fine stripping knife, slicker brush or natural bristled brush to remove any remaining loose coat or tangles. Be careful when using any tool with metal teeth or bristles. A heavy hand or too much repetition in an area can cause cuts and/or brush burns. Brushing is not finished until all loose fur is removed, or when it becomes difficult to remove more than a half a brush full after repeated brushing.

Carding
Carding is a natural technique in which the soft, downy undercoat is pulled from the dog's body. Typical tools used with this technique are: a pumice stone; a fine-toothed stripping knife that is pulled through the coat; an undercoat rake; or a fine blade, such as a #40, held between the fingers and pulled through the coat. Carding can be done before or after bathing and drying. Removal of the soft undercoat allows the topcoat to lie closer to the natural outline of the dog and accentuate the dog's structure. It also promotes profuse harsh outer coat, creates a rich coat color and protects the skin.

Hand-Stripping
Hand-stripping is a technique in which the outer guard coat is plucked from the dog's skin. This procedure helps retain the proper coat texture and rich color of the breed. During certain times of the year, the coat is easier to pull out. When the coat easily comes out, it is called a "blowing coat" or "blown coat." Ideally, hand-stripping should correspond with the dog's natural cycle, based on the environment and its hormonal levels. Using your fingers, a carding tool or a stripping knife, pull out a few hairs at a time to shape the coat, accentuating the natural outline of the dog. Work methodically, pulling small amounts of coat at a time, always working in the direction of the coat growth. Proper hand-stripping removes hair with a gentle momentum and rhythm, not brute force, which is uncomfortable for both groomer and pet. The wrist stays locked in a neutral position while the rhythmic movement stems from the shoulder, not the wrist or elbow. In general, the main body coat is easy to remove. Most pets do not mind the plucking process. The cheeks, throat and private areas may be more sensitive, requiring thinning shears or clippers. Leave enough coat to be between 1 to 2 inches long. The coat should always appear very natural, never clipped or heavily trimmed. On some coats, a light application of chalk or powder before the bath will allow a better grip and make plucking and stripping much easier.

Head
Leave the coat longer on the muzzle. Lightly hand-strip or pluck the top skull, throat and cheeks. Leave triangles of coat above each eye to form the moderate eyebrows that accentuate the eye area. Ears are left long and natural.

Feet & Hocks
Trim the pads with a close cutting blade ranging from a #15 to a #40. Use a very light touch to clean the pads of long hair. Tidy the outside edge of the foot,

Suggested Tools & Equipment
- Nail Trimmers
- Styptic Powder
- Ear Powder
- Ear Cleaning Solution
- Cotton Balls
- Hemostat
- Clippers
- Slicker Brush
- Greyhound Comb
- Undercoat Rake
- Pumice Stone
- Carding Tools
- Stripping Knives
- Straight Shears
- Curved Shears
- Small Detailing Shears
- Thinning Shears
- Dematting Tools

Common Blade Options:
- #40, #15, #10

if needed, with small detailing shears. If the hocks have longer coat, trim lightly with thinning shears to show a neat, clean area.

Detail Finish
Application of bows and mild cologne is optional.

Special Note
Clipping a wired-coated dog will result in a dramatic change in the texture and color of the coat. The correct harsh wire coat needs to be encouraged by plucking the blown coat when it is ready to be removed. This process stimulates hair follicles to produce new guard coat. Without hand-stripping, the guard coat is not stimulated and will not grow in properly. It will lose its brilliant color and texture. If only the undercoat grows, the guard coat color becomes that of the lighter, soft undercoat.

Notes From The Grooming Table ©2016

Breed Facts & Characteristics

Country of Origin: Sweden

Height at Shoulder: 15½"–18½"

Coat Length/Type: Double Coated

Color: Primarily white with a dark mask with color on the head and large clear patches of reds or tans on the body.

Correct grooming procedure:
Bathe & Brush

Common pet grooming practices:
Bathe & Brush

-The Goal-
The coat should be light and stand off the dog. The coat should bounce and shimmer with the dog as it moves.

Let a powerful high velocity dryer help in all aspects of grooming this type of coat, before and after the bath—blow out loose coat, tangles, dirt—dry and fluff.

When finished you should be able to sink a wide-toothed comb to the skin and pull it freely out to the end of the hair shaft.

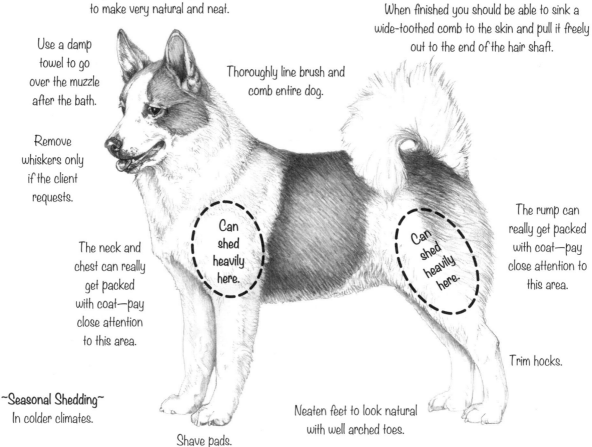

Edge ears with thinning shears to make very natural and neat.

Use a damp towel to go over the muzzle after the bath.

Remove whiskers only if the client requests.

Thoroughly line brush and comb entire dog.

The neck and chest can really get packed with coat—pay close attention to this area.

Can shed heavily here.

Can shed heavily here.

The rump can really get packed with coat—pay close attention to this area.

~Seasonal Shedding~
In colder climates.

Trim hocks.

Shave pads.

Neaten feet to look natural with well arched toes.

When shedding—the more work you can do with a powerful high velocity dryer, the less "elbow grease" you will have to exert.

MISCELLANEOUS

See page 69 for Bathing & Drying Instructions

Frequency

Bathe once a week to once every 12 weeks.

Pre-Work

Trim or grind nails at least every four to six weeks to maintain a healthy foot structure. Clean the ears by swabbing with a mild ear cleaning solution. Prior to bathing, quickly go over the entire body with a high-velocity dryer to help lift dirt and dander away from the skin and loosen any shedding coat.

Brushing

Use a slicker brush, rubber curry, shedding blade, dematting tool or undercoat rake to loosen skin dander and remove loose coat. Be careful when using any tool with metal teeth or bristles. A heavy hand or too much repetition in an area can cause cuts and/or brush burns. Brushing and combing is not finished until all loose fur is removed, or it has become difficult to remove more than a half a brush full after repeated brushing.

Feet & Hocks

Trim the pads with a close cutting action blade, ranging from a #15 to a #40. Use a very light touch to clean the pads of long hair. If there is long fur between the toes, back brush the fur so it stands up and away from the foot. With thinning shears, trim off the excess creating a neat and very natural looking foot with well arched toes. Tidy the outside edge of the foot, if needed, with small detailing shears. If the hocks have longer coat on them, trim lightly with thinning shears showing a neat, clean area. A #4F blade used in reverse works well for trimming the tops of the feet and the hocks on some dogs.

Detail Finish

Removal of whiskers on the muzzle is optional, based on client preference. Finish with a fine mist of coat polish on the body for added shine. Application of bows and mild cologne is optional.

Grooming Tip

Let your hands guide you. Learn to feel for differences in coat density levels. Areas that feel heavier or denser than other areas need special attention when bathing, brushing and drying.

Suggested Tools & Equipment

- Nail Trimmers
- Styptic Powder
- Ear Cleaning Solution
- Cotton Balls
- Clippers
- #40 and #15 Blades for Pads
- #4F for Feet & Hocks (optional)
- Slicker Brush
- Greyhound Comb
- Rubber Curry
- Carding Tool
- De-Shedding Tools
- Small Detailing Shears
- Thinning Shears
- High-Velocity Dryer

Notes:

Breed Facts & Characteristics

Country of Origin: Peru

Height at Shoulder: Three sizes, ranging from 9¾"–25¾"

Coat Length/Type: Hairless *or* Short/Smooth

Color: The coat comes in all shades of brown and liver tones to blend into the areas he is hunting.

Correct grooming procedure:
Bathe Or Bathe & Curry

Common pet grooming practices:
Bathe Or Bathe & Curry

-The Goal-
The coat should be clean and fresh smelling, with soft pliable skin.

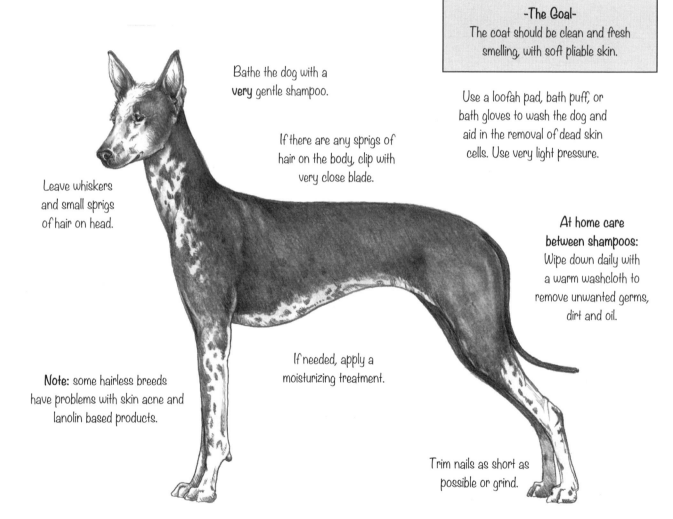

Bathe the dog with a **very** gentle shampoo.

If there are any sprigs of hair on the body, clip with very close blade.

Use a loofah pad, bath puff, or bath gloves to wash the dog and aid in the removal of dead skin cells. Use very light pressure.

Leave whiskers and small sprigs of hair on head.

At home care between shampoos: Wipe down daily with a warm washcloth to remove unwanted germs, dirt and oil.

Note: some hairless breeds have problems with skin acne and lanolin based products.

If needed, apply a moisturizing treatment.

Trim nails as short as possible or grind.

See page 78 for Bathing & Drying Instructions

Suggested Tools & Equipment

- Nail Trimmers
- Styptic Powder
- Ear Cleaning Solution

- Hemostat
- Cotton Balls
- Cleansing cloth or puff

- Clippers
- #40 or #30 Blade

MISCELLANEOUS

Notes *from your*
Grooming Table

Breed Facts & Characteristics

Country of Origin: Portugal

Height at Shoulder: Two sizes, ranging from 16"–28"

Coat Length/Type: Short/Smooth

Color: Primarily shades of yellow or fawn combined with white. Shades of black or brown combined with white are acceptable but not preferred.

Correct grooming procedure:
Bathe & Curry Brush

Common pet grooming practices:
Bathe & Curry Brush

-The Goal-
The coat should be clean and fresh smelling, with the coat laying flat against the body. No shedding hair.

Use a damp towel to go over the muzzle after the bath.

If necessary, edge ears with small shears...keep the tips of the shears toward tips of the ears.

Rubber curry brush all over body to remove loose fur.

Remove whiskers only if the client requests.

Apply a light coat polish to bring up the shine of the coat when finished.

Trim nails as short as possible or grind.

Neaten pads and feet if needed.

See page 66 for Bathing & Drying Instructions

Suggested Tools & Equipment

- Nail Trimmers
- Styptic Powder
- Ear Cleaning Solution
- Cotton Balls

- Clippers
- #40 or #15 Blade
- Rubber Curry
- Carding Tool

- Small Detailing Shears
- Thinning Shears

Notes *from your* Grooming Table

Breed Facts & Characteristics

Country of Origin: Portugal

Height at Shoulder: Two sizes, ranging from 16"–28"

Coat Length/Type: Moderate/Wiry

Color: Primarily shades of yellow or fawn combined with white. Shades of black or brown combined with white are acceptable but not preferred.

Correct grooming procedure:
Bathe & Curry or Hand-Strip

Common pet grooming practices:
Bathe & Curry or Hand-Strip

General Description

The Podengo is a hunting dog developed in a variety of sizes based on the type of quarry he is after. The smallest variety in the Hound Group; the medium and large varieties are currently in the Miscellaneous Group. The muzzle has a distinctive beard. The longer fur will be located on the back, on the back of the legs, and on the underside of the tail. Other than the coat type, the two varieties are identical in structure.

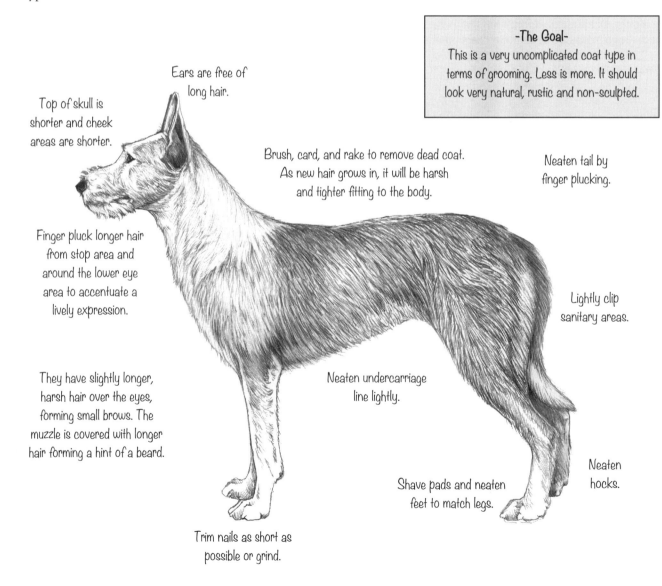

-The Goal-
This is a very uncomplicated coat type in terms of grooming. Less is more. It should look very natural, rustic and non-sculpted.

Ears are free of long hair.

Top of skull is shorter and cheek areas are shorter.

Brush, card, and rake to remove dead coat. As new hair grows in, it will be harsh and tighter fitting to the body.

Neaten tail by finger plucking.

Finger pluck longer hair from stop area and around the lower eye area to accentuate a lively expression.

Lightly clip sanitary areas.

They have slightly longer, harsh hair over the eyes, forming small brows. The muzzle is covered with longer hair forming a hint of a beard.

Neaten undercarriage line lightly.

Neaten hocks.

Shave pads and neaten feet to match legs.

Trim nails as short as possible or grind.

Grooming Procedures & Recommendations

See page 76 for
Bathing & Drying Instructions

Frequency
Bathe once a week to once every
12 weeks.

Pre-Work
Trim or grind nails at least every four
to six weeks to maintain a healthy foot
structure. Swab the ears clean with a
mild ear cleaning solution. Prior to
bathing, quickly go over the entire
body with a high-velocity dryer to help
lift dirt and dander away from the skin
and to loosen any shedding coat. *Card
and hand-strip dog prior to bathing
and drying.*

Brushing
Use a rubber curry, shedding blade,
undercoat rake, pumice stone, carding
tool, fine stripping knife, slicker brush
or natural bristled brush to remove
any remaining loose coat or tangles. Be
careful when using any tool with metal
teeth or bristles. A heavy hand or too
much repetition in an area can cause
cuts and/or brush burns. Brushing is not
finished until all loose fur is removed,
or when it becomes difficult to remove
more than a half a brush full after
repeated brushing.

Carding
Carding is a natural technique in which
the soft, downy undercoat is pulled
from the dog's body. Typical tools used
with this technique are: a pumice stone;
a fine-toothed stripping knife that is
pulled through the coat; an undercoat
rake; or a fine blade, such as a #40, held
between the fingers and pulled through
the coat. Carding can be done before or
after bathing and drying. Removal of the
soft undercoat allows the topcoat to lie
closer to the natural outline of the dog
and accentuate the dog's structure. It also
promotes profuse harsh outer coat, creates
a rich coat color and protects the skin.

Hand-Stripping
Hand-stripping is a technique in which
the outer guard coat is plucked from the
dog's skin. This procedure helps retain
the proper coat texture and rich color of
the breed. During certain times of the
year, the coat is easier to pull out. When
the coat easily comes out, it is called a
"blowing coat" or "blown coat." Ideally,
hand-stripping should correspond with
the dog's natural cycle, based on the
environment and its hormonal levels.
Using your fingers, a carding tool or a
stripping knife, pull out a few hairs at
a time to shape the coat, accentuating
the natural outline of the dog. Work
methodically, pulling small amounts of
coat at a time, always working in the
direction of the coat growth. Proper
hand-stripping removes hair with a
gentle momentum and rhythm, not
brute force, which is uncomfortable
for both groomer and pet. The wrist
stays locked in a neutral position while
the rhythmic movement stems from
the shoulder, not the wrist or elbow.
In general, the main body coat is easy
to remove. Most pets do not mind the
plucking process. The cheeks, throat
and private areas may be more sensitive,
requiring thinning shears or clippers.
Leave enough coat to be between 1 to
2 inches long. The coat should always
appear very natural, never clipped or
heavily trimmed. On some coats, a light
application of chalk or powder before the
bath will allow a better grip and make
plucking and stripping much easier.

Head
Leave the coat longer on the muzzle.
Hand-strip or pluck the top skull, throat
and cheeks. Leave triangles of coat above
each eye to form the moderate bushy
eyebrows that accentuate the eye area.
Remove any longer hair from the ears
that distract from their natural outline.

Feet & Hocks
Trim the pads with a close cutting blade
ranging from a #15 to a #40. Use a very
light touch to clean the pads of long
hair. Tidy the outside edge of the foot,

Suggested Tools & Equipment

- Nail Trimmers
- Styptic Powder
- Ear Powder
- Ear Cleaning Solution
- Cotton Balls
- Hemostat
- Clippers
- Slicker Brush
- Greyhound Comb
- Pumice Stone
- Carding Tools
- Stripping Knives
- Straight Shears
- Curved Shears
- Small Detailing Shears
- Thinning Shears
- Dematting Tools

Common Blade Options:
- #40, #15, #10

if needed, with small detailing shears. If
the hocks have longer coat, trim lightly
with thinning shears to show a neat,
clean area.

Detail Finish
For added shine, finish with a fine mist
of coat polish on the body. Application
of bows and mild cologne is optional.

Special Note
Clipping a wired-coated dog will result
in a dramatic change in the texture and
color of the coat. The correct harsh wire
coat needs to be encouraged by plucking
the blown coat when it is ready to be
removed. This process stimulates hair
follicles to produce new guard coat.
Without hand-stripping, the guard coat
is not stimulated and will not grow in
properly. It will lose its brilliant color
and texture. If only the undercoat
grows, the guard coat color becomes
that of the lighter, soft undercoat.

Notes From The Grooming Table ©2016

Breed Facts & Characteristics

Country of Origin: Hungary

Height at Shoulder: 15"–18½"

Coat Length/Type: Rustic/Curly

Color: Any solid shade of white, cream, fawn, gray or black. Tan or gray colored dogs may have limited darker shading. Small white patch acceptable on chest and toes.

Correct grooming procedure:
Rustic Hand-Scissored

Common pet grooming practices:
Rustic Hand-Scissored/Clipper-Trim

General Description

The Pumi is an active, intelligent medium sized dog with great enthusiasm for life. It is a versatile stock dog, developed to herd and drive all types of livestock. It is a relatively lean and squarely built dog. Their coats are considered rustic and double coated. It is a curly combination of soft undercoat and harsh guard hair. They have a unique wedge shaped head with a semi-pricked ear and a whimsical expression. Their long tail curls over their backs. Rustic coated dogs *never* appear fluffy, polished or well groomed. Their coats are always air dried to maintain the springy curls characteristic of the breed.

Correctly Groomed: Hand-Scissored
For pets; use a #5F, #4F or medium to longer guard combs to set the pattern on the bulk of the body.

-The Goal-
The coat is rustic. It should cover the body with well defined curls and springy ringlets. The coat looks rough and unkempt. Rake coat out prior to bathing. Air dry only.

Ears are semi-pricked with tassels at the tips.

No defined stop.

Head is a blunt wedge shape.

Throat is trimmed closer than body.

Rake through the coat to remove blown coat prior to bathing.

Legs fall in parallel lines from the shoulder. Use the shoulder muscle to set pattern line.

Feet are rounded and face straight forward.

Trim tail long enough so the coat does not part when carried over the back.

Base of tail is trimmed "a little" closer creating creating a keyhole when the tail is raised.

Use the thigh muscle to set pattern line.

Lowest point of pattern should be at the bend.

Slight rise into the tuck-up area.

Coat is curly.
~DO NOT BACKBRUSH~

Pads are trimmed close.

Hocks are parallel.

Round feet.

Either hand-scissor the entire dog or clipper-trim to set the basic pattern. Pet dogs can be modified into shorter trim styles using the same basic pattern. Blenders and thinners work great on this coat type.

MISCELLANEOUS

Grooming Procedures & Recommendations

See page 79 for Bathing & Drying Instructions

Frequency
Bathe every 3 to 12 weeks or when needed. Rake through the coat every 1–3 weeks, with or without a bath, to keep matting under control. Trim every 4 to 6 weeks. Lighter colored dogs with ringlets may need more frequent combing and raking as their coats tends to mat more easily than darker colored dogs.

Pre-Work
Thoroughly rake out the coat prior to bathing to keep the coat from becoming a solid pelted mass. This will remove the undercoat "lint," preventing matting in the future. Trim or grind nails at least every four to six weeks to maintain a healthy foot structure. Clean the ears by swabbing with a mild ear cleaning solution. Hair should be plucked from within the ear canal only as necessary for healthy ear management. Rustic coated breeds are **never** blown or fluffed dried. They are always naturally air dried to maintain the curly, unkempt and tousled looking coat.

General Pattern Lines
The breed standard calls for the wavy and curly coat to be between 1½ to 3 inches long all over. The actual coat length may vary slightly to accentuate or lessen key conformation points of the dog. There are no broken lines anywhere, and the coat outlines the natural contour of the body.

Body
The body can be either hand-scissored or clipper-cut with a longer guard comb. Start at the withers and work back over the body towards the tail. Use caution if working with guard combs as they can get stuck in the coat. Leave coat about 1 to 1½ inched long over the entire body. Follow the contour of the

body. Do not back brush. The goal is a dog whose coat is somewhat rough and messy looking. If the coat needs to be fluffed, fluff with a coarse or wide-toothed comb. Many pet owners opt for less than 1 inch of coat for easier home maintenance trim styling.

Undercarriage
The highest point of the tuck up falls just below the last rib. From that point forward, the undercarriage angles slightly down towards the elbow. The undercarriage line should not fall below the elbow between the front legs.

Tail
The bulk of the tail is trimmed with scissors or thinning shears to between 3 and 5 inches in length, from just behind the ring to the tip of the tail. When the dog carries its tail over the back, if the coat parts at the center, it's too long. Shorten the length of the tail coat to a point where it does not part when it's in its natural position. The base of the tail is trimmed shorter with thinners, creating a full ring. To place the ring, hold the tail down over the rectum. The area that is shorter is from the base to halfway between the point where the back legs converge. Trim the ring around the base of the tail the same general length as the body. When finished and the dog holds its tail over its back, you want to see a "keyhole" of light just ahead of the base of the tail.

Feet
Both the front and rear feet are compact with well-arched toes. To show off these traits, the feet are trimmed very close to the edge of the foot, beveling out into the fuller leg coat. The feet should point straight ahead, toeing neither in nor out. Begin by gently picking up the leg and with a wide-toothed comb, comb the coat over the foot. Slide your hand down the leg to the foot. Scissor off the coat

Wedge Shape

There are only slight variations in coat length over the entire dog. The head is wedge shaped. The ears are styled into overgrown tasseled Bedlington-type ears. At transition points between the body and the legs, blend the lines so they are invisible. The legs are only a little longer in length than the body. They should fall into straight columns, to the rounded feet, when viewed from the front or rear. There are no breaks in the pattern anywhere on the dog. Tail coat is slightly longer than the body and never so long that it parts when carried over the back.

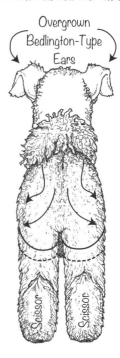

Overgrown Bedlington-Type Ears

583

Notes From The Grooming Table ©2016

The head is unique. il is shaped in a blunt wedge, narrower at the nose —widening out at the cheeks and over the topskull. There is no definition between the eyes at the stop. The ears are high-set on the head and tasseled. The expression is bright and whimsical.

Ears are semi-pricked with tassels at the tips.

Stop is level—expose eye with thinners, trimming just over each eye, beveling the shears on a diagonal to create a deep-set eye.

On the outside of the ear leather, shorten the fur with thinners leaving a generous, longer tassel on the ear tip from the fold to the tip of the leather. Slightly round the shape of the scissored tassel.

Trim longer coat from the end of the muzzle extending beyond the nose.

Trim coat short around ear base to accentuate a high-set ear.

Before scissoring in the wedged line on the sides of the head, trim cheeks between ½ and 1 inch in length to establish the shape and set a trimming target.

Remove longer hair from the inside of the ear leather with shears or thinners to remove weight.

Coat on lower jaw will be about ¾ to 1 inch in length—scissor straight back from the muzzle to the throat.

Do not straighten coat—use a wide-toothed comb sparingly to double check work.

With long, straight shears or large thinners, block in a straight line from the nose to the back-skull to start the wedge shape.

Throat is shorter starting under the base of the ears, dropping to a few fingers above the breast bone.

The Pumi has a "whimsical" expression with longer coated scissored Bedlington-type tasseled ears.

that hangs below the level of the foot pad with shears. Work around the outer perimeter of the foot with detailing shears to minimize the risk of injury—never cross over the foot pad with scissors. Set the foot on the table and neaten the foot with shears or blending shears beveled out into the longer coat on the leg. An alternative for quickly rounding the feet is to do it when the pads are trimmed. If a very close cutting blade is used to trim the pads, use a wide tooth comb to pull the longer hair over the outer edges of the pad and trim that hair at the same time the pads are clipped clean.

Front Legs

The longest coat on the legs can range from 1 to 3 inches depending on the amount of bone and coat density. The front legs drop straight down from the body. When viewed in profile, the front legs fall directly below the withers. The pattern line at the shoulder is about 2 fingers above the top of the elbow, at the point where the muscle begins to turn under. The coat at the transition line will be shorter, tapering into the longer leg furnishings. Fluff the leg lightly with a wide-toothed comb before starting the trimming process in this area. This can be accomplished

Grooming Procedures & Recommendations

by feathering off at the blending point with the same blade used on the body if the trim is very short. To effectively feather off in this manner, you need a steady hand and a dog that stands still. Most stylists prefer to leave the legs to shape by hand with thinning shears or large blenders. Other methods of blending off at the top of the leg include using a medium to longer attachment comb, followed by blending with shears. After the final trim, the legs should form two parallel columns descending from the shoulder into tight, round feet. The coat at the back of the elbow is very short and falls straight down off the back of the leg toward the ground, angling in slightly at the pasterns.

Hindquarters

The hindquarters are wide with muscular thighs. If trimming over this area with clippers, clip over the thigh muscle with the same blade used on the body when working with a medium to longer guard comb. For pet trims using shorter guard combs or blades, blend the transitional areas with a slightly longer guard comb. Start to feather off where the muscle starts to turn under on a diagonal line from the flank region to about three or four fingers above the hock. The blending should be invisible when the trim is finished. Fluff the coat with a wide tooth comb, retaining the rustic look and maintain the curls to the coat. Blend with shears or thinners if necessary. The stifle area should have enough furnishing left to give the legs substance and angulation. The longest coat on the legs can be up to 3 inches depending on the amount of bone and coat density. Shape this area by hand with shears after the clipper work is complete. When viewed from the rear, the legs should form two parallel lines to the ground. The hocks are well let down and perpendicular to the ground. There should be adequate coat on the hock area to accentuate the angles of the rear assembly.

Head

The head is a blunt wedge shaped with high set semi-pricked ears, and deep set eyes that give the dog a "whimsical" expression. Start by trimming off longer hair hanging over the end of the muzzle. To set the first line of the wedge, use a long set of straight scissors or a large pair of blending shears. Block in the angles of the wedge with shears from the nose straight back towards the top of the skull and the occiput. Trim a level, straight line. Clear a flat plane over the top of the skull. Next, set in the cheeks. Set the length from ½ to 1 inch in length. Once the length is established, then set the line from the muzzle to the cheek using the cheeks as a reference point. Make the line long and straight. The coat on the lower jaw will be between ¾ of an inch to 1 inch in length. Scissor a straight line from the chin to the throat back using a longer shear. Be careful approaching this junction to ensure you do not accidentally cut the dog. Once the wedge shape is established, then go back and round out the edges while lightly fluffing with a wide-toothed comb to check the work.

Eyes

The eyes are deep set. Use fine thinners to remove some of the length, exposing the eye slightly. Leave the coat in the stop area.

Ears

The ears are semi-pricked and set high on the head. To show this off, trim around the base of the ear with shears closely but not exposing skin. Work all the way around the ear. The ear leather itself is trimmed like a scissored tasseled ear. The upper part of the ear leather is scissored close to the leather while leaving a longer tassel on the tip of the ear leather. To encourage a pricked ear-set, clear most the underside of the ear leather of longer hair that may weigh it down. Edge both the leather and the longer tassel lightly.

Suggested Tools & Equipment

- Nail Trimmers
- Styptic Powder
- Ear Powder
- Cleaning Solution
- Cotton Balls
- Hemostat
- Clippers
- Undercoat Rake
- Greyhound Comb
- Wide-Toothed Comb
- Straight Shears
- Curved Shears
- Small Detailing Shears
- Thinning Shears
- Dematting Tools

Common Blade Options:
- #40, #15, #10
- #7F, #5F, #4F
- Medium to Long Guard Combs

Neck

The back of the neck starts from the occiput to the withers area. Leave this area to the last to trim, pulling together the head, neck and body. Fluff softly with a wide tooth comb. Scissor off long sections between the top of the head and the body. Blend the sides of the neck down to show off a moderate length, well-muscled neck with a slight arch.

Detail Finish

Lightly re-fluff all your work, checking for stray hairs. The coat should not look polished and smooth. The goal is a dog that is mat- and tangle-free that looks reasonably tidy but unkempt and messy at the same time. Application of mild cologne and bows is optional.

Notes From The Grooming Table ©2016

Breed Facts & Characteristics

Country of Origin: Africa

Height at Shoulder: 24"–29"

Coat Length/Type: Short/Smooth

Color: All shades of cream, sand, tan, red, or mahogany with or without dark mask and points and/or brindle coat pattern. Small white patch allowed on chest and toes.

Correct grooming procedure:
Bathe & Curry Brush

Common pet grooming practices:
Bathe & Curry Brush

-The Goal-
The coat should be clean and fresh smelling, with the coat laying flat against the body. No shedding hair.

Use a damp towel to go over the muzzle after the bath.

Remove whiskers only if the client requests.

Curry brush all over body to remove loose fur.

Apply a light coat polish to bring up the shine of the coat when finished.

Use caution when handling. This coat type can have *very* sensitive skin.

Trim nails as short as possible or grind.

Trim pads if necessary.

See page 66 for Bathing & Drying Instructions

Suggested Tools & Equipment

- Nail Trimmers
- Styptic Powder
- Ear Cleaning Solution
- Cotton Balls
- Clippers
- #40 or #15 Blade
- Rubber Curry
- Carding Tool
- Small Detailing Shears
- Thinning Shears

Notes *from your* Grooming Table

Classic Pet Poodles and Drop Coat Styles

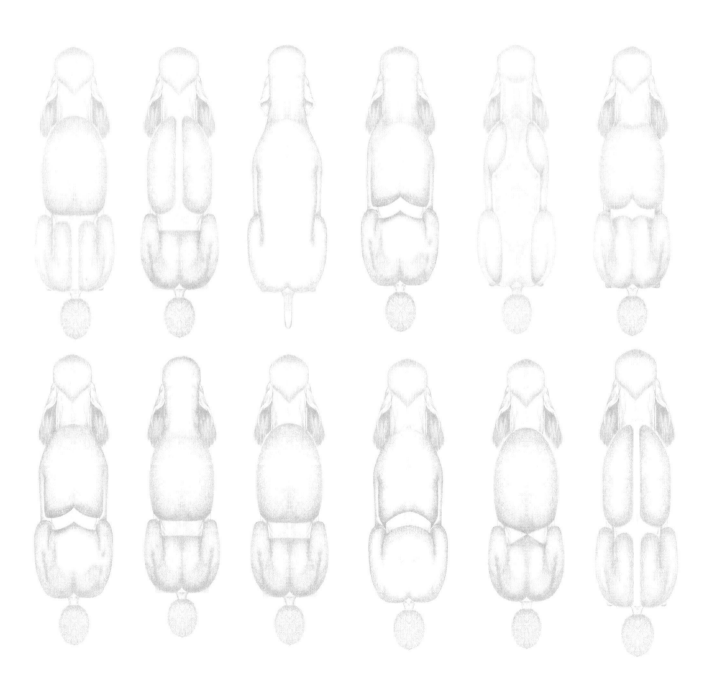

Notes From The Grooming Table ©2016

Classic Pet Poodle Styles

Pet Grooming

Pet grooming the poodle can unleash the creative spirit in many pet professionals. This seems to be one of the few purebreds where it is considered "acceptable" to have some fun with trim styles. The wide variety of sizes and colors and a coat type that lends itself to sculpture means the sky is the limit as to what may walk down the street.

For years, the poodle was No. 1 in canine popularity. Poodle trim styles seem to come and go with the same whim and fancy as fashion styles. There were the pastel-colored poodles with pom-poms of the '60s, the elaborate pattern trims of the '70s and '80s, the non-banded, classic styling of the '90s and the highly stylized chic styling common today. Will today's styles be trendy and acceptable in the pet contest ring or on the street 10 years from now? Based on recent history, probably not. However, understanding the principles behind the earlier styles helps you satisfy those clients who prefer the more traditional poodle styling of years gone by. It also allows you to appreciate where future styles may be headed. There are a few rules that aid in creating a trim that complements the breed standard, no matter how outlandish the trim. In this book, we will focus on the most common styles that are the foundation for almost all pet poodle haircuts. Minor variations can change the entire look of the haircut and often give the trim an entirely new name. Other variations to topknots, legs, ears and tails can add flair and style to pet trims. Though there are many different styles in pet poodle grooming, many of the same trims are known by different names. These may vary from salon to salon or region to region. Whenever you communicate with a client, verify that you are both talking about the same trim. An example is the "Puppy Cut." In some areas, a "Puppy Cut" refers to a very close, overall trim style such as a #5F overall. In other areas, the style may be similar, but the hair is left longer with an attach-on-comb over the clipper blade. In still other areas, a "Puppy Cut" refers to a highly stylized, much longer trim executed totally by hand-scissoring. Whatever the case may be, be sure you and the client are talking the same language when it comes to trim styles. Whenever in question, always err on the side of leaving more hair than you think the client wants. It is easier to remove more hair; it cannot be replaced once it has been trimmed. By the same token, it is only hair, and if the client doesn't care for the trim, it will grow back rather quickly.

Sizes

The poodle comes in three different sizes: the Toy, standing under 10 inches; the Miniature, standing between 10 and 15 inches; and the Standard, standing more than 15 inches in height at the withers.

Toy   Miniature   Standard

Classic Pet Poodle Styles

Common Pet Poodle Trims

These are some of the more common trims on poodles. There are several more, but most are variations of these basic trims.

- **Retriever/All/Kennel**
- **Lamb/Bladed Body: Stylized Legs**
- **Puppy Cut**
- **Euro/German**
- **Single Banded**

- **Teddy Bear**
- **New Yorker/Double Banded**
- **Dutch**
- **Town & County**
- **Miami/Clown Cut**

Retriever Trim

Also known as the "All" trim, or Kennel Cut, this low maintenance style is done with one moderate length blade used all over the body. Typical blades for this trim range from a #7F to shorter guard combs. Topknot, ear, muzzle, feet and tail styles all are left to the discretion of the owner.

Lamb Trim

This style is also known as a "Bladed Body: Stylized Leg." The main section of the body is trimmed with a moderate length blade ranging from a # 7F to a longer guard comb. The transition areas are blended into the longer leg hair. Depending on the size and length of the body blade, the legs may be cut in with a longer guard comb for smaller dogs or sculpted by hand-scissoring. Topknot, ears, muzzle, feet and tail styles all are left to the discretion of the owner, however, they should be in balance with the overall trim.

Classic Pet Poodle Styles

Puppy Cut

The Puppy Cut is a longer variation of the Lamb Trim, however, the neck is normally left fuller and sculpted by hand-scissoring to give the dog an elegant neck and crest. Based on the size of the dog, the body can be hand-scissored or cut in using a long guard comb. In order to get the full crest, the topknot style should be full and tall. Ears, muzzle, feet and tail styles all are left to the discretion of the owner, however, they should be in balance with the overall trim.

Euro or German Trim

This trim is a version of any of the Lamb or Puppy trims. The coat is left fuller over the body while the legs are styled fuller, normally by hand-scissoring. What makes this trim unique is the removal of coat from the ears and tail. Both these areas are shaved clean. Muzzle and feet styles are left to the discretion of the owner, however, they should be in balance with the overall trim.

The Single Banded Trim

This elegant trim requires only the center belly band to be trimmed clean. The rest of the trim is a variation of the Puppy Cut. The neck is left fuller and sculpted by hand-scissoring to give the dog an elegant neck and crest. The body can be hand-scissored or cut in using a long guard comb based on the size of the dog. In order to get the full crest, the topknot style should be full and tall. Ears, muzzle, feet and tail styles all are left to the discretion of the owner, however, they should be in balance with the overall trim.

Classic Pet Poodle Styles

Teddy Bear Trim

This trim is a variation of the Lamb Trim or the Puppy Cut for the body style. With the Teddy Bear Trim, the head is scissored round, the ears are feathered, the tail is normally the same length as the body and the feet are scissored round to blend with the full, stylized legs.

New Yorker Trim

This trim also is called the Double Banded Trim after the duel bands around the neck and the belly that are trimmed with a very close blade to expose the skin. For pets, a #10 or #15 blade in reverse is used for this close trimming. The longer sections of fur covering the front and rear sections are left long and full. They are hand-scissored to accentuate the correct structure of the dog. If you place your hands around the dog's neck and pull upwards, toward the head, you will find the line for the topknot at the place where your fingers come to rest at the bulb of the ears. If you slide your hands down the neck toward the shoulders, they will come to rest at the start of the pattern line. The circle made by your first finger and thumb where they join at the withers and the neck will be the lower edge of the neck band. The line will be on a diagonal that parallels the shoulder blades. The front line of the belly band will start at about the second-to-last rib. The line closer to the rear of the dog will be set in the flank area where the skin flap connects to the body of the dog. Do not clip too far into this area, or the rear section will not balance with the front of the dog. Topknot, ears, muzzle, feet and tail styles all are left to the discretion of the owner, however, they should be in balance with the overall trim.

Dutch Trim

This trim is a variation of the New Yorker. With this trim, there are duel bands around the neck and belly, plus a line down the spine, all of which are trimmed close enough to expose the skin. For pets, a #10 or #15 blade in reverse is used for this close trimming. The width of these lines will determine the trim style or the name of the trim. Whether the line down the spine splits both front and rear packs or only one section also has a bearing on the trim name. Setting the pattern is similar to the New Yorker. The longer sections of fur covering the front and rear sections are left long and full. They are hand-scissored to accentuate the correct structure of the dog. If you slide your hands down the neck toward the shoulders, they will come to rest at the start of the pattern line. The circle made by your first finger and thumb where they join at the withers and the neck will be the lower edge of the neck band. The line will be on a diagonal that parallels the shoulder blades. The front line of the belly band will start at about the second-to-last rib for a typical Dutch Trim. This line may be brought forward for other style variations. The line closer to the rear of the dog will be set in the flank area where the skin flap connects to the body of the dog. Do not clip too far into this area, or the rear section will not balance with the front of the dog. The line down the spine can be narrow or wide. The important issue with this line is that it be straight and consistent in width. Topknot, ears, muzzle, feet and tail styles all are left to the discretion of the owner, however, they should be in balance with the overall trim.

Classic Pet Poodle Styles

Town & County

This trim is a variation of the Dutch Trim, however, the short areas on the body are more expansive and can be trimmed with longer blades ranging from a #7F to a #4F, as well as the close cutting #10 or #15 blades. The fuller, hand-scissored areas cover the shoulder and hip in a semi-circular fashion. This area blends smoothly into hand-scissored legs to accentuate the structure of the dog. Topknot, ears, muzzle, feet and tail styles are all left to the discretion of the owner, however, they should be in balance with the overall trim.

Miami or Clown Cut

This is a low maintenance haircut that offers a bit of style and flair in an easy-to-care-for trim. The body is trimmed with blades ranging from a #10 to a #4F or even a longer guard comb on the larger dogs. At the lower section of all four legs are pom-poms that are left to hand-scissor into full round balls or ovals. When viewed in profile, it is important that all four pom-poms be at the same height and density. The hocks will dictate how high to set the poms, which should start just above the hock joint. When trimming the back leg, place your hand around the top of the hock to avoid accidentally trimming too far down the leg. Look at the dog in profile and repeat the procedure on the front leg, protecting the level of the pom-pom with your hand as the leg is clipped. Shape the pom-poms with rounded shears after the cuff line has been set. Shaved poodle feet are customary with this trim style. Topknot, ears, muzzle and tail styles all are left to the discretion of the owner, however, they should be in balance with the overall trim.

Classic Pet Poodle Styles

STYLING TECHNIQUES

Close Clipper Works

The face of a poodle is traditionally clipped clean. Leaving a mustache and/or a beard is a styling option left to the discretion of the owner. The typical choice for most pets is either a #10 or #15 blade used in reverse. For dogs with delicate skin, longer blades may be used, especially in the cheek area where they are the most sensitive. Keeping the blade tipped up on its cutting edge; allowing only the tips of the teeth to ride over the skin coupled with excellent, efficient clipping skills minimize possible clipper irritation for the pet.

Clipping the Face

The topknot is set using landmark points on the skull as reference. The clipped line that establishes the topknot on the sides of the face runs from the ear canal opening to the back corner of the eye. It will parallel the zygomatic arch, which is easily felt. It's important to lightly stretch the skin back towards the ear for efficient clipping, but use caution not to pull the skin up into the topknot area. Stretching the skin upward will destroy the natural, straight line from the ear canal to the back of the eye. Continue clipping forward under the eye and down the bridge of the nose. At the stop area, clip an inverted "V" to give definition to the eyes and to lengthen the muzzle. Work over the muzzle area and the lower jaw if the face is being clipped cleanly. Placing a finger at the back corner of the mouth and stretching the skin will facilitate safety while clipping over the lip area. Be careful not to catch the smooth skin ridges just on the inside of the lips on the lower jaw. Ride that area with only the edge of the clipper blade for safety, minimizing the chance of the ridges slipping between the cutting teeth. Keep the clipper very soft and supple in your hand as it glides over the skin.

Clipping the Throat

The pattern for the neck and throat is shaped in a "V." It accentuates a long and elegant neck. The "V" will start at the ear bulbs and plunge down, stopping a few inches above the breast bone. Some stylists use the end of the nose as a general reference point for setting the depth of the "V" shaped neckline. While the dog is standing squarely, ask the dog to tip their nose toward the chest. Where the end of the nose falls is the lowest point of the neckline. If the dog has a very short muzzle, the line may be drawn down slightly further.

Mustache & Beard

When setting the lines for the mustache and beard, the lines need to be clean and symmetrical. Depending on the style and the size of the dog, the pattern line for the mustache can be set on an angle between the nose and the back corner of the mouth or straight up and down. For the beard on the lower jaw, extend the clipper line a small amount ahead of the back edge line of the mouth. This will create a clean neat break when the dog opens its mouth. Mustache and beard styles will vary based on client preference. Smaller mustache and beard combinations may be set with clipper blades such as the longer "F" blades or guard combs to ensure a uniform length and shape very quickly.

On larger dogs such as Standard Poodle size, the mustache and beard would need to be set with longer guard combs to balance with the rest of the head. Mustache and beards may also be totally shaped by hand as well. With either technique, make sure to detail out the edges by working with the pet's mouth both opened and closed. Whenever working around the mouth of the pet with scissors or clippers, be highly aware of the location of the tongue. Whenever possible work on the pet with its mouth shut to avoid accidentally nicking the tongue.

Clipping the Throat

Non-Angled Mustache

Angled Mustache

More mustache styles on next page with accompanying topknot styles.

Classic Pet Poodle Styles

Topknots

Style Options for the Poodle

The texture of the coat on a topknot will dictate its final appearance. Poodle coat should be full of body, curly and firm in texture. With the correct coat, the fur can be totally sculpted into beautiful shapes that accentuate the regal, elegant and intelligent look of a poodle. What ever the shape; flared, straight sided or rounded, the topknot should always be a well balanced extension of the skull. It should be impeccably neat and symmetrical.

Pet Poodle Topknot Formula

For many poodles, the hair is not the highest in quality. Thus, shaping a well rounded topknot can pose a challenge. There are a number of different ways to shape a topknot. This formula works well on all topknots, but exceptionally well with floppy topknots. The principle foundation is based on the structure of the skull, which leads to a pleasing balance to the head piece. The process is called the side-side-front-back formula. After the face has been clipped clean, the topknot can be shaped. Comb all the hair over to one side. Flip the ear over the top of the head to minimize the risk of nicking the ear leather where it joins the skull. Glide a pair of opened, straight shears under the clipped line that separates the cheek from the topknot. The lower blade of the shear will be softly resting on the skin. Bevel the shear slightly away from the skin so as the blade closes; there is no possible risk of catching the skin between the blades. Flip the ear over, glide the shear over the top of the ear, right at the junction point of the skull and the leather. Again, bevel the shear slightly and cut. Continue the line around the ear, wrapping right around the base of the ear, joining the topknot line with the neck line so it is one, flowing line. Repeat the process on the opposite side of the head. Next comb

Setting the Topknot

Open shears and slide lower blade over the ear leather at a steep angle. Before closing blades, slightly lift the shears' tips to ensure only hair is between the blades.

Use your finger to buffer scissors on the cheek to avoid cutting the skin when trimming.

Rounded Topknot with a Clean Face

Rounded Topknot with a German Mustache

Straight-Sided Topknot with a Donut Mustache

Flared Topknot with a Small Mustache

Small Flared Topknot with a French Mustache

Classic Pet Poodle Styles

Clear all the hair in front of the ear canal.

All poodle pattern lines are crisp and clean.

Slip your finger into the back corner of the mouth to stretch the skin.

all the hair forward over the eyes. Glide the opened shear in at a steep bevel. The fur just above the eyes will be very short, as it gently angles away from the eye, the fur get longer. By creating the stacked ledge, the hair is held out of the way of the eyes and the eye becomes deep-set, creating an intelligent expression for the pet. For the last line, comb all the hair to the back and blend the fur into the neck. When trimming back of the topknot, hold the dogs head upright, in its natural position so the top edge of the topknot is not removed in the trimming process. Fluff the topknot with a comb. Give the ears a small tug-tug, alternating between ears to simulate a mild natural head shake. With curved shears, round the top edge and check all the lines so that they are well blended, neat and clean. Check the work from all angles, front, side and rear.

Feet

The feet are clipped totally clean. Trim the pads with a close blade ranging from a #15 to a #40. Use a very light touch to clean the pads of long hair. The digits of the foot are clipped to a point where the bones of the feet meet the metatarsal bones or the bones of the pasterns. There is a slight bump on the sides of the foot where these bones join. Use a #15 or #10 blade, in reverse with a light touch. Start by clipping the top of the two center digits. Start at the nail bed. Tip the blade up so only the front edge of the blade contacts the skin. The effective movement of the clipper is a soft, push-push as you clear the hair from the foot. The strokes are a very short forward-and-back motion. Clear the hair to the point where the bones converge and there is a natural bend at the foot and the wrist. Proceed to the outside digits and repeat the process. Once the top of the foot is cleared, place your fingers on the underside of the foot and spread the toes. Glide just the edge of the blade in between the toes, using your fingers as buffers. Your fingers will protect the webbing between the toes from getting caught between the teeth of the clipper blade. Again, start at the nail bed and scoop out the long fur between the toes. Do all of the toes on oneside first, then rotate your clipper

in and repeat the procedure on all of the toes on the other side. When finished, double check your work for long strays. Clean up around the nail bed. There are a couple of ways to do this. One option is to simply turn the clipper over and touch the nail bed with the upside down #15 or #10 blade using a very short push motion. Another technique is to edge the nail beds lightly with a #40 blade after the toes have been clipped.

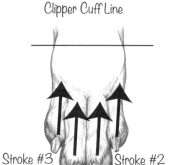

Clipper Cuff Line

Stroke #3　　Stroke #2

Stroke #1

For clipped foot styles use a close blade such as a #15 in reverse to clip the foot. Clip up the center two digits first—then clipper the outside toes. Start at the nail bed and trim up to the bulge at the side of the foot.

Classic Pet Poodle Styles

Clipping the Pattern Lines

Establish which type of trim you want to execute then use landmark points on the body for reference. If you want to visually check placement of a belly band, you can drape a piece of wide ribbon over the body, pulling it snuggly to view the line placement. Another method to get an idea of pattern placement is to lightly draw the pattern in the fluffed coat with the end of a comb. When establishing very closely clipped body pattern lines, the pet must be standing quietly and squarely on the table otherwise the pattern will end up uneven. Choose a starting point, making very small strokes with the clipper to establish the initial line. Once the clipped pattern lines are established, then go back and widen them. Work slowly and double check the work frequently to make sure the lines remain straight, clean and even from area to area or side to side.

Edging the Pattern Lines

When clipping coat extremely close to create pattern areas where the skin is fully exposed, the fur that converges at these areas needs to be crisp and clean. Upon final detailing of a haircut, double check all the pattern lines. Comb the longer coat out over the clipped area at right angles. Using a straight shear, glide the lower blade against the skin, paralleling the line. Trim off any longer strays that fall over the line, adding clear definition to the pattern line. Clean up the beveled edge of the pattern so it is uniform with other areas on the body.

Shaping the Cuffs

Poodle cuffs are shaped three ways: (1) freely using long shears, (2) holding the coat and using long shears, or (3) holding the coat down with your hand and using either detailing shears to trim away the excessive hair or clippers with a very short cutting blade. Hand-scissor shaping is normally reserved for dogs with excellent coat texture and full, scissored legs. On pet dogs that have less than perfect coat texture, the second and third methods

are highly effective. With either method, the clipped line at the cuff must be sharp and crisp. For hand-scissoring, hold the foot off the table at a comfortable level for the pet. Comb all the fur down, and then fluff it up and out. Glide a long straight shear in just below the clipper line of the foot at a right angle to the leg. Cut cleanly, going around the entire leg. Re-fluff and continue to bevel the outer edge of the cuff with curved shears. When the dog is standing naturally, the bevel of

the cuff is level and uniform in shape.

With the second method, hold the foot off the table at a comfortable level for the pet. With a firm slicker brush, brush all the hair down around the foot. Once the coat is brushed down, slide your hand down the pet's leg, thumb and first finger closest to the foot. Stop and hold the foot with your fingers coming to rest right at the clipped cuff line. While maintaining the hold on the foot, trim around the cuff at right angles with small detailing shears. Depending on how full the leg coat is, will establish where you place the line. For fuller legs, use the top of the crease marks on the toes. If the leg coat is shorter, adjust the line closer to the clipped cuff line. When you release the coat, the fur will be nicely beveled. The line is crisp and free of all stray hairs. As with the hand-scissored cuff, check the work from profile to make sure the cuffs are level from side to side and front to back. This second method can also be done by edging the cuff with a #40 blade.

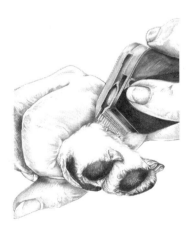

A #40 or #30 can also be used to set the cuff. It is similar to the second method listed. Simply gently touch the blade to the cuff to remove the excessive coat, creating a neat cuff line.

Ear Styles

Long, short, feathered, shaved or tasseled… ear styles can add a stylish flair or ease of care to the pet.

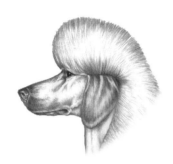

Shaved or Teddy Ear

A #10 or #15 blade used on the outside of the ear leather while a #40 blade is used on the inside. When working with close blades in this delicate area, always work from the base or center of the ear out toward the edge. Gently brace the ear with your fingers to clip over it. Longer blades may also be used but use extreme caution around the edges of the ears. They can easily slip between the teeth of the blade and get nicked or cut if the proper technique is not exercised. To finish, use small finishing shears to trim around the outside edge of the ear leather, keeping the tips of the shears toward the tip of the ears.

Tasseled Ear

It is common to see a #10 or #15 blade used on the outside of the ear leather, while a #40 blade is used on the inside. When working with close blades in this delicate area, always work out from the base, or center, of the ear toward the edge. Gently brace the ear with your fingers to clip over it. Clip the ear clean, creating a sharp line where it attaches to the skull, but let the longer coat of the topknot drape over the line. Leave a tuft of fur on the lower third of the tip. The line can either be slightly curved or made with straight, diagonal lines to create a diamond shape. To finish, use small finishing shears to trim around the outside edge of the ear leather, keeping the tips of the shears toward the tip of the ears. The ear leather reaches to the corner of the mouth. With the tassel, the ear should reach to the end of the nose. The tassel may be blunt-cut across the bottom or formed into a diamond shape.

Spaniel Ear

The tops of the ears are trimmed close to the skin using a # 10 or #15 blade. Trim the top to ⅓ of the ear leather on the outside of the ear. On the outside of the leather, the blending line will be a soft "U" shape. Keep this line above the widest section of the ear. Edge the top front section of the ear leather with detailing shears, keeping the tips of the shears towards the tips of the ears. Lightly round the long feathering at the bottom of the ears with shears for a neat look.

Feathered Ear

Use a long guard comb or thinning shears to feather the coat on the ear leather, leaving the hair between one and four inches long. If working with a guard comb, work from the center of the ear out to the edges. Make sure the outer edge of the ear does not slip between the teeth of the comb. Neaten around the edges of the ear with shears for a finished look.

Short Ear

This bobbed ear style offers a nice, low maintenance style for the pet. Trim the ear furnishing to about an inch from the bottom of the ear leather. Gently round the edge, giving it a nice curve or leave it blunt cut. If the line is too sharp, soften it with thinning shears.

Classic Pet Poodle Styles

Medium Ear
Trim the ears to the end of the nose. Gently round the edge, giving it a nice curve or leave it blunt cut. If the line is too sharp, soften it with thinning shears.

Long Ear
Long ears can be left totally natural or trimmed slightly, either with shears or thinning shears.

Tail

Traditionally the poodle tail is clipped at the base, leaving a full pom-pom on the end, although there are other styles in which to trim the tail. The tail structure should be long enough to allow you to clip one-third of the base of the tail with a #10 or #15 blade in reverse. The end two-thirds is left to hand-scissor in a ball or oval shape. Continue clipping around the tail bone to the point where the tail and the body join. Clip a small inverted "V" at the top of the tail in line with the spine. When the dog raises its tail, this indentation will eliminate the small bump of hair that is common when

the clipped line is not carried up far enough. On shorter coated trims, this line will be very minor, with longer hand-scissored styles; this "V" shape can be extended to add style and flair to the trim. If there is not enough tail to clip in this ratio, make an adjustment to give the pet some form of a balanced pom-pom. On some tails, the bone may be so short or non-existent that only a puff of fur can be left, hence the "bunny tail."

Shaping the Tail

For the traditional poodle pom-pom tail, the shape of the puff is rounded, either ball or oval in appearance based on the hair quality and the length of the tail bone. For highly stylized trims, the tip of the pom-pom should be almost in line with the top of the skull. For

pet trimming, this is normally scaled back a bit. Start by combing all the fur to the end of the tail. Twist the fur that extends beyond the bone between your fingers. While holding the firmly twisted fur, hold the tail up in a natural position. An automatically bevel will be crated by using this method to trim the end of the tail. Trim to the desired length. Once the end has been trimmed, hold the tail up and out by grasping a small section of hair, holding it between 2 fingers. Comb all the fur down towards the body and bevel the coat that falls below the clipped line on the tail bone. Re-fluff the coat and shape the center, creating either a round ball or an oval shape.

Notes From The Grooming Table ©2016

Classic Drop Coat Styles

The common denominator of a "drop coat" is fine, straight hair texture. If you comb the coat up or fluff it out, it has a natural tendency to drop back towards the ground. Typical breeds with this coat type include Shih Tzus, Lhasas, Maltese or any pets of similar coat type, purebred or mixed breed. The look, style and variety of even the most simple trims can be astounding. The style will be influenced by the physical appearance of the dog—body structure, ear and tail type, coat texture, color and the overall length of trim. Styling options for head, ears and tail are truly varied, limited only by the pet stylist's abilities, pet owner's discretion and the pet's lifestyle. A knowledgeable and talented pet stylist can impart style and flair to any trim option, creating an adorable haircut style for the pet.

General Description

This trim style is highly versatile for many coat and body types. This application provides a low maintenance trim style for drop coat breed types that leaves the pet cute and cuddly. Most drop coated breed types are fun loving with sweet, soft expressions. The coat is straight or wavy and considered non-shedding. A well executed trim on a drop coated pet should make the dog look like a charming, soft, fuzzy stuffed animal. The face is round with a soft, kind expression. The ears and tail can be of various lengths based on client preference. In the finished trim, the pet is well balanced, smooth and track free from scissor or clipper marks.

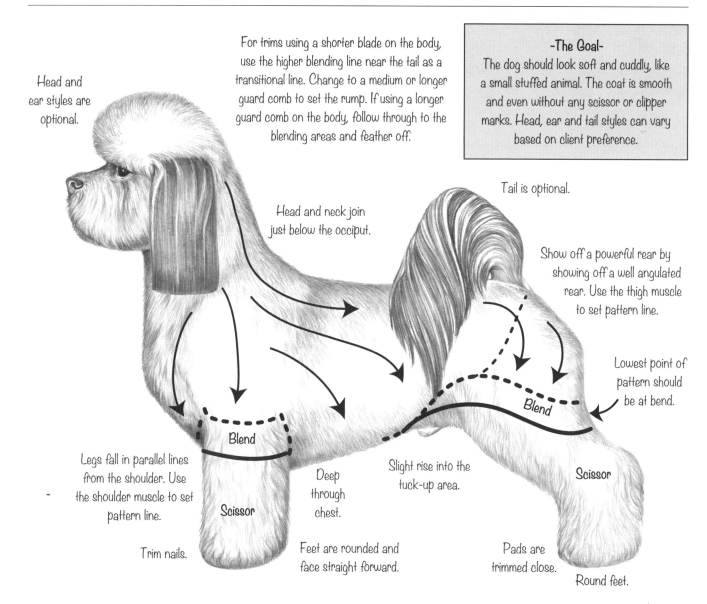

Head and ear styles are optional.

For trims using a shorter blade on the body, use the higher blending line near the tail as a transitional line. Change to a medium or longer guard comb to set the rump. If using a longer guard comb on the body, follow through to the blending areas and feather off.

-The Goal-
The dog should look soft and cuddly, like a small stuffed animal. The coat is smooth and even without any scissor or clipper marks. Head, ear and tail styles can vary based on client preference.

Head and neck join just below the occiput.

Tail is optional.

Show off a powerful rear by showing off a well angulated rear. Use the thigh muscle to set pattern line.

Lowest point of pattern should be at bend.

Blend

Legs fall in parallel lines from the shoulder. Use the shoulder muscle to set pattern line.

Blend

Deep through chest.

Slight rise into the tuck-up area.

Scissor

Scissor

Trim nails.

Feet are rounded and face straight forward.

Pads are trimmed close.

Round feet.

Classic Drop Coat Styles

Clipper Work

Start the clipper work at the base of the occiput and pull the clipper towards you. If your clippers won't glide smoothly over the shoulder/withers area, start your clipper work at that withers instead of the occiput. (Save the neck and shoulder area until the dog is sitting down.) Work down the spine towards the tail and over the rump. Continue to clip in the directions of the arrows, as shown. Let each clipper stroke slightly overlap the previous stroke. Let the weight of the clipper do the work for you, all you need to do is let it glide smoothly along, following the natural contours of the pet. Go completely over the dog once, then back brush if using a #4F, #5F or #7F blade. If using a medium to longer guard comb, do a body roll to get the coat to stand up off the body. The shorter guard is the in-between blade. A combination of back brushing and a body roll may be used to set the coat up for the second pass. Repeat the entire body clipping a second time, following the arrows. Set the coat up and check for rough or high spots. If the coat is not consistently smooth by the third pass, analyze your clipping methods and make the necessary corrections.

Blending Areas

When working with shorter guard combs, switch to a medium or longer guard for the blending areas. Swing over the rump area with a medium to long guard comb, cutting in the angulation as you work. On the front legs, gently let the clipper fall off at the widest point of the shoulder, skimming and blending into the longer coat on the front legs. The goal is a smooth transition between the shorter, clipped coat and the longer, scissored coat. Clipping too quickly in these areas will create tracking, which is undesirable. Maintaining a consistent pace as you feather off in the blending areas allows the coat to feed efficiently into the teeth of the blade. Hold the clipper at a consistent angle for a smooth, seamless transition.

Feet

Shave the pads with blades ranging from a #40 blade to a #15. Slide your hand down the dog's leg, thumb toward the table, and pick up the foot. First, gently clip out the pad. Using your hand and fingers as a brace, clip off the excess hair that hangs beyond the outside edge of the foot. Keep the blade level with the foot pad. Do not cut up into the side coat of the foot. You will need to finish off the foot with shears, while the dog is standing naturally on the table, to make them appear round and forward facing. Soften the line with thinning shears, if desired. This technique allows you to both trim the pads and roughly round the foot, all in one motion. This technique is better for dogs with small to moderate feet and should not be used on dogs that have extremely poor fronts or extremely large feet.

Front Legs

Once the clipper work is effectively blended into the legs and the pads have been trimmed, there should be a little coat left to hand-scissor. When viewed from the front, the legs should create parallel lines, dropping in a straight line from the widest part of the shoulder. Feet should face forward and be neatly rounded.

Rear Legs

When viewed in profile, the correct angulation of the rear legs is accentuated by removing the bulk of the excessive hair over the hip and thigh areas with the longer guard combs. When viewed from the rear, the legs appear straight and parallel to each other. When viewing the dog from this angle, think of a plumb line hanging straight down from the widest point of the thigh to the table. Scissor off any coat that falls over these imaginary lines. The hocks are straight with feet that are rounded and face straight forward.

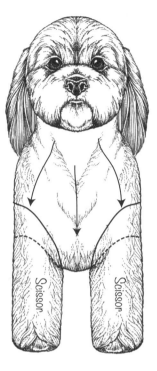

The eyes and nose are well balanced in the round head piece. At transition points between the body and the legs, blend the lines so they are invisible. The legs should fall into straight columns, from the body to the rounded feet, when viewed from the front or rear. There are no breaks in the pattern anywhere on the dog.

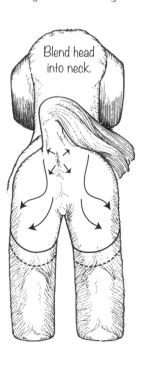

Blend head into neck.

Classic Drop Coat Styles

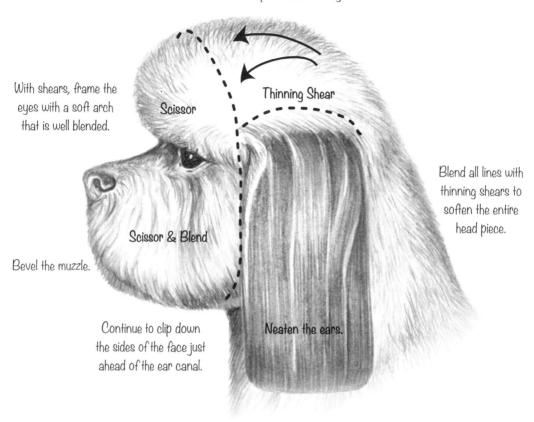

For a fuller round head style, pull a medium or longer guard comb forward from the occiput toward the eyes.

With shears, frame the eyes with a soft arch that is well blended.

Scissor

Thinning Shear

Blend all lines with thinning shears to soften the entire head piece.

Scissor & Blend

Bevel the muzzle.

Continue to clip down the sides of the face just ahead of the ear canal.

Neaten the ears.

Head

There are a number of different ways to create a round head style on a dog. The length will vary based on client preference and length of body coat. It's most important that the head be in balance with the body. With both styles outlined here, the stop area should be trimmed very close, either with thinning shears or by clipping with a close blade, such as a #10 or a #15. This will clear the eyes of long fur and accentuate a nice, deep-set eye. One style option is to take the same blade used to trim the body, and use it again for the top of the head and down the sides of the face. If a #4F, #5F, #7F or shorter guard was used on the body, follow the natural lay of the coat, working out from the center of the skull. There will be an imaginary line just behind the eyes where you can

feel the eye socket rims. The hair over the eyes in this area should be left to frame the eyes. This can be completed in the final trim by hand-scissoring. Lift the ear out of the way and come down the sides of the face, in the jowl area, blending into the clipped neck. Remember to leave just enough hair at the back corners of the eyes to complete the framework for the eyes in the finished trim. Another way to create a round head style is to use a medium to long guard comb. Due to the length of coat these combs leave, they are most effective when pulled forward from the occiput to the framed area of the eye. The sides of the face are handled the same way as outlined above. With both head styles, the framed area over the eyes should be hand-scissored. Comb the hair forward over the eyes, making

sure to get the hair in the stop area, too. Scissor off the longer hair at a 45-degree angle, starting at the stop area to create a deep-set eye. A pair of curved shears in reverse can be helpful to create the framework around the eyes. The coat immediately over each eye is very close and bevels out as it gets farther away. The beveled edge creates a ledge for the longer coat to sit on, keeps it out of the eyes and creates a soft expression. Double-check this line a number of times, as it is the most important part of the entire trim. Soften the framed area with thinning shears once the correct line is set. Double-check the line just behind the eyes where the clipper work feathers off. It should be smooth and even at the transition point.

All round heads should have the nose and eyes placed in the center of the circle.
On some drop coated breeds, elongating the muzzle is a stylish alternative.

Muzzle

With most round head styles, the muzzle area is trimmed by hand. There are multiple style options. The fur may be trimmed very short or left very long. The important thing is that the muzzle is evenly shaped and the edges are buffered into a soft, neat line.

Ears

There are many ear trims that work with this head style. Choose one that works and appeals to the owner—from shaved to very long or even tasseled. Shorter ear styles give the dog the look of a puppy. Longer ear styles could be rounded or blunt-cut to give a polished, soft look to the finished trim. The line at the skull junction should be neat and tidy. With thinning shears, create a soft line over the top of the ears to gently define them. If the ear is clipped close, edge the ear leather with small detailing shears, keeping the tips of the shears towards the tips of the ears. Trimming the ears to the length of the nose is a popular style for many pets. Trimming to the length of the nose not only balances well with the head, but also solves a sanitary issue with many dogs— ears dragging in the food or water dish. The shorter ear style eliminates that problem. Longer ear styles also are popular. Just double-check that both ears are equal in length and the bottom edge is neat. Pull the ears forward and check behind and under the ears for long or missed hairs.

Tail

The tail, like the ears, has many style options. It may be left long and natural, trimmed to any length that suits the owner or tufted with a plume. The key is that it should be in balance with the overall dog.

Detail Finish

Check all over the dog for rough spots. Soften those areas with thinning shears. Normal trouble spots include the stop area by the eyes, around the ears, under the front legs, feet, flank and under the tail. Application of bows and mild cologne is optional.

Special Note

Always discuss ear and tail options with the owner before trimming any substantial length from them. These are areas that most owners are very sensitive or passionate about. It's always easier to take more coat off; it cannot be replaced once it has been trimmed.

Classic Drop Coat Styles

Bladed All-Trim Styles

This is a popular choice by pet owners for low maintenance and warm weather. The trim is done with moderate length blades and short guard combs following the contour of the body. For a softer, slightly fuller look, use longer guard combs.

Follow the directions for the Bladed Body: Stylized-Leg Trim, but continue to clip down the legs. You will need to go over the legs repeatedly to get the coat smooth and even. The cutting blade will have very little contact with the leg surface. If you were to run the blade down the length of your finger, you would be simulating the same type of connection the blade has going down the leg bones. Make repeated passes until no hair is being removed. Remember: back brush to lift the coat back up for another pass. Smooth out any uneven spots with thinning shears on legs trimmed shorter than a #2 guard comb. If you have used anything longer than a #2 guard, then use a combination of shears and thinning shears to detail and smooth out the leg coat. Many different head, ear and tail styles will work with this type of trim. Consult with the owner to find styles that suit his or her tastes and balance well with the finished trim.

Suggested Tools & Equipment

- Nail Trimmers
- Styptic Powder
- Ear Cleaning Solution
- Cotton Balls
- Clippers
- #40 and #15 Blades for Pads
- #4F for Feet & Hocks (optional)
- Slicker Brush
- Greyhound Comb
- Rubber Curry
- Undercoat Rake
- Dematting Tools
- High-Velocity Dryer
- Straight Shears
- Small Detailing Shears
- Curved Shears
- Thinning Shears

Notes:

Classic Drop Coat Styles

Ear Options

With all ear styles, double check the length and balance from ear to ear. They should be equal in length and in balance. Double-check the line at the junction of the head and at the ear bulbs. This line should be neat and softly blended. Under the ear, just in front of the ear canal, the hair should be short and tidy. For dogs whose ears drag in their food or water dishes, trim the ears to the length of the nose to solve the problem of constantly wet, greasy and dirty ears.

Short Ear
This bobbed ear style offers a nice balance to many round head styles. Trim the ear furnishing to about an inch from the bottom of the ear leather. Gently round the edge, giving it a nice curve or leave it blunt cut. If the line is too sharp, soften it with thinning shears.

Long Ear
Long ears can be left totally natural or trimmed slightly, either with shears or thinning shears.

Shaved or Teddy Ear
Clip the outside of the ear leather with a #10 or #15 blade. Work out from the center of the ear toward the edges. Always keep the clipper blade at right angles to the outside edge of the ear leather. Otherwise, the leather could feed between the cutting teeth, resulting in a nicked ear. Hold and brace the ear with your fingers while clipping. A #40 can be used with a soft touch on the inside and around the ear canal. Edge the ear with small detailing shears, keeping the tips of the shears toward the tips of the ears. A more coated look to the ear leather can be achieved by using longer blades from a #7F to longer guard combs. These longer cutting lengths are a bit more risky to the pet because the ear leather can easily slip between the cutting teeth if the proper technique is not used. Done correctly, the result is a cute, low maintenance style that instantly makes the dog look like a puppy again.

Medium Ear
For short-muzzled dogs, this ear length will be about an inch or two beyond the length of the muzzle. On dogs with longer faces, trim the ears to the end of the nose. Gently round the edge, giving it a nice curve or leave it blunt cut. If the line is too sharp, soften it with thinning shears

Tasseled Ear
Clip the bulk of the outside of the ear leather with a #10 or #15 blade, leaving the fur on the lower third to half of the ear leather. Work out from the center of the ear toward the edges. Always keep the clipper blade at right angles to the outside edge of the ear leather as you clip. If the leather feeds between the cutting teeth, a nicked ear is likely. Hold and brace the ear with your fingers while clipping. A #40 can be used with a soft touch on the inside and around the ear canal. Edge the ear with small detailing shears, keeping the tips of the shears toward the tips of the ears. Shape the tassel or leave it natural.

Tied-Up Topknots

Single

This topknot style has a single ponytail standing upright on top the head. If the pet is light-coated, pull all the fur up into a single tail toward the center of the head. If the dog has a heavy coat, combining multiple ponytails at the center of the head piece will create a longer lasting tied-up topknot. Separating the section or sections of coat can vary from dog to dog. The outer part can start at the back corner of the eye to almost the half way point above the eye. The part should go straight back towards the ear. On some dogs, the part rides over the entire top of the ears, on other dogs, only halfway. The part line across the back of the skull can be close to the occiput or farther up on the back skull. All part lines should be straight, neat and symmetrical. Once all the hair is neatly gathered, band it snuggly at the center of the head. Slide a comb between the skin and the band and give a slight upward tug to make the topknot more comfortable for the pet. If you notice any skin being pulled in an unnatural fashion, loosen that area by inserting the comb and tugging a little bit. Also, double check that no skin is caught in the band by sliding the teeth of a comb between the skin and band. Once the single topknot is neatly pulled up and centered, apply a bow to finish off the look.

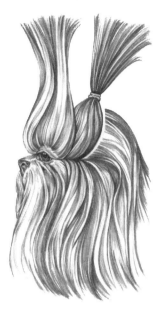
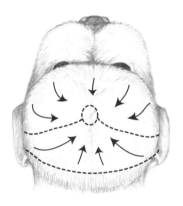

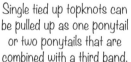

Single tied up topknots can be pulled up as one ponytail or two ponytails that are combined with a third band.

Braids

If you have a dog that will hold still long enough and you are a talented braider, this is an excellent way to hold the hair out a pet's eyes with minimal damage to the hair. From the start, keep the braid loose enough to lie down against the skull, but tight enough to stay in place. Once the braid is established, tighten the strands of hair as they cross over each other and as you move away from the skin. The braided strand can be short or long based on coat length, the dog's patience and how much time you want to spend. French braiding is another beautiful way to hold the hair out of the eyes, but it can be difficult to master the technique unless it is practiced regularly.

Classic Drop Coat Styles

Buttons

For some breeds, the custom is to pull one tail up over each eye and turn them into two small buttons. Separate the sections to be pulled up so the two ponytails will be symmetrical and balanced. The placement of the parts will vary based on the amount of coat to be pulled up and the size of the dog. Comb all the hair up and gather it in a neat bundle. Band off the section snuggly with a small elastic band, pulling the long tail repeatedly through the elastic until you can not make another pass. With that last, very snug pass, do not pull the tail all the way through, creating the button. Make sure the long tail drapes over the back of the head. The less you handle the buttons, the neater they will stay. Repeat on the other side, placing the button on the same spot on that side. If the buttons are slightly misaligned, slide a comb under them and tug them gently into position. Once the buttons are positioned and neat, apply small bows to accent them as well as the eyes of the dog. Always double check that no skin is caught up in the elastic bands by sliding a comb between the skin and the band.

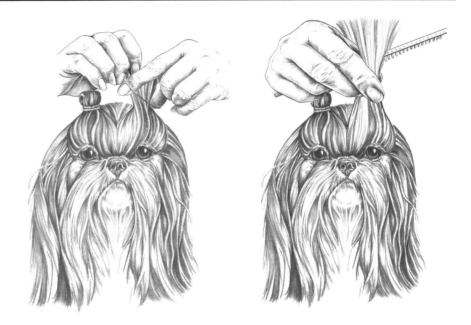

Two button topknots pulled up at the center of the head. To keep the button neat after it is formed, minimize handling the button when applying bows.

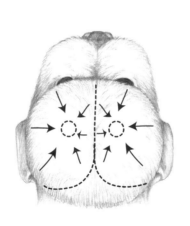

Barrettes

Children's barrettes are an excellent choice for holding long locks of hair out of a pet's eyes. They are designed to hold fine hair in place and normally stay in a pet's fur rather well. Pull the coat up in a single section or part it off into two areas. Slide the barrette into place and close it, catching enough hair to keep it firmly in place.

Notes From The Grooming Table ©2016

Tails

With all tails, make sure the area right under the tail looks neat and tidy, but natural. Many of the drop-coated breeds carry their tail in a swirled, upright fashion. It's important to double check this area before the pet leaves the grooming table.

Squirrel

This tail style leaves the coat between ½ to 2 inches in overall length. Begin by running your hand to the end of the tail and trimming off the excessive hair that extends 1 to 2 inches beyond the tailbone. Once this long fur is removed, hold the tail level with the back, letting the coat drape downward. Trim the coat to the desired length while holding the tip of the tail. Fluff and shake out the coat, holding the tail in a variety of positions. Continue to shape and mold the tail coat so it is all one length and fluffy, like a squirrel's tail.

Lion

Using the same blade that was used on the body, continue the clipper work out onto the tail. Clip to within a third to two-thirds of the base of the tailbone, leaving a natural plume on the end.

Plumed

This tail simulates a natural, long tail only in a shorter format. Run your hand down the tail, stopping where you want to establish the length. Trim off the excessive hair beyond that point. Brush out the tail and hold it over the back, mimicking the natural tail carriage, with the longer coat draping downward. With thinning shears or straight shears, nip some "V"-shaped cuts into the fur, paralleling the strands of hair as they hang. The nips can be between 1 and 3 inches deep, depending on how much length needs to be removed.

Blunt Cut

Trimming the tail straight across in a neat fashion offers a low maintenance style while retaining some length. Brush all the coat to the end of the tail. Run your hand down the tail bone and stop at the point you want to cut. While still holding the tail coat in your hand, trim off the excess in a straight line.

Docked Tails

Leave totally natural or trim to a few inches in length. If trimming, blend the edges so they blend naturally with the rest of the coat.

Natural

Brush the tail thoroughly and leave untrimmed.

Notes *from your*
Grooming Table

In Conclusion

Success is not a matter of luck. It is based on commitment and dedication to your chosen field. Education, skill enhancement and effective communication are the keys to a successful career. Never underestimate their importance. One of the greatest inspirations in any career is continued growth. Never stop learning. Look, listen and talk to as many professionals as you can. The pursuit to be the best will keep you fresh, inspired and motivated, allowing for maximum growth and the highest degree of personal success. Notes from the Grooming Table is designed to be a stepping stone to the next level of professional pet grooming and styling.

Keep pushing yourself. Be patient with yourself. Learning takes time and perseverance. Enjoy the process.

Spread your wings and fly.

Notes *from your*
Grooming Table

Notes *from your* Grooming Table

Notes *from your* Grooming Table

Notes *from your* Grooming Table

Notes *from your* Grooming Table

Notes *from your*
Grooming Table

Notes *from your*
Grooming Table

Notes *from your* Grooming Table

Notes *from your* Grooming Table

Notes *from your* Grooming Table

Notes from your Grooming Table

Notes *from your* Grooming Table

Notes *from your* Grooming Table

Notes *from your*
Grooming Table

628

"I know the next book is in here somewhere."

Megan, The White Dog Mascot

Look for more products from White Dog Enterprises.

www.whitedogenterprises.com

Index

Notes From The Grooming Table ©2016

Index

Index

Index

Index

Index

Notes From The Grooming Table ©2016

Index